ॐ श्री

LOHAN.

Ace the Technical Interview

Ace the Technical Interview

Michael Rothstein

Second Edition

McGraw-Hill

New York San Francisco Washington, D.C. Auckland Bogotá
Caracas Lisbon London Madrid Mexico City Milan
Montreal New Delhi San Juan Singapore
Sydney Tokyo Toronto

Library of Congress Cataloging-in-Publication Data
Rothstein, Michael F.
    Ace the technical interview / Michael Rothstein. —2nd ed.
      p.   cm.
    Includes index.
    ISBN 0-07-054039-X (pc)
    1. Computer science—Vocational guidance.   2. Employment
interviewing.   I. Title.
QA76.25.R68   1996
004' .023—dc20
                                        95-52517
                                               CIP

McGraw-Hill

*A Division of The **McGraw·Hill** Companies*

1 2 3 4 5 6 7 8 9 0 DOC/DOC 9 0 1 0 9 8 7 6

ISBN 0-07-054039-X

The sponsoring editor for this book was Jerry Papke, the editing supervisor was Christine H. Furry, and the production supervisor was Pamela Pelton. It was set in Palatino by North Market Street Graphics.

Printed and bound by R. R. Donnelley & Sons Company.

The following are registered trademarks of IBM Corporation in the United States and/or other countries: ACF/VTAM, IBM, MVS/ESA, NetView, PS/2, AS/400, AIX, and OS/2. CICS, DB2, System 370/390, 9672R, ES/9000, MVS, RS/6000, SAA, SNA, VM, QMF, VSAM, and VTAM are trademarks of International Business Machines Corporation. • Gupta and SQL Base are trademarks of Gupta Technologies, Inc. • Unix is a registered trademark of Unix System Laboratories, Inc. • Banyan Vines is a trademark of Banyan Systems, Inc. • MS Windows, LAN Manager, MS DOS and Visual Basic are trademarks of Microsoft Corporation. • NCA, Network File System, Java, Hot Java NFS, SunOS, SUN SPARC, Sun View, and XView are trademarks of Sun Microsystem, Inc. • Oracle, Oracle*CASE, and Oracle SQL*FORMS are trademarks of Oracle Corporation. • BASE/SAS, SAS/Stat, SAS/SFS, SAS/AF, SAS/Graph, SAS/Access, SAS/CPE, and SAS/ETS are trademarks of SAS Institute, Inc. • Delphi is a registered trademark of Borland International, Inc. • Sybase is a registered trademark of Sybase, Inc. • PowerBuilder is a trademark of the Powersoft Corporation. • Netscape is a registered trademark of Netscape Communications Corporation.

    Product names mentioned in this book are for identification purposes only and may be trademarks or registered trademarks of their respective companies. Trademarks not known as such that may have been used inadvertently in this book are the property of their respective owners.

This book is printed on acid-free paper.

*To Maya Rothstein, my granddaughter,
and her new sister, Eden Marian*

*and to my friend, Dan Rones,
who is gone . . . but not forgotten.*

Contents

Contributors

Valentin Carciu is the Unix System and Informix Data-Base administrator for Lazare Kaplan, Inc. He has been heavily involved in developing a complex software package using Informix for the company's plant in Botswana, Africa. This Unix system supports a diamond-cutting factory with more than 500 workers. Mr. Carciu currently is responsible for the analysis, design through implementation of a complex interface between the Botswana system and Lazare Kaplan's New York central office applications. (CHAPTER 6)

Daniel Robert Cohen is a senior programmer analyst with Orix Credit Alliance, Inc., Secaucus, New Jersey, which finances companies that lease or buy construction equipment. He designs ILE-based applications to run on the company's AS/400 Advanced Series system and works with the disaster (hardware failure) recovery system. Mr. Cohen works with users across the country to investigate and resolve production problems. (CHAPTER 7)

James Michael (Mike) Conners currently is a consultant with SPC Corporation. As a senior programmer/analyst at Bank of New York he worked on a team that planned and developed client/server applications using Visual Basic, Visual C++, and Microsoft Advanced SQL Server. As a developer of client/server-based systems for AT&T, he developed version 2.0 of RTB, a system using Visual Basic 3.0 and Sybase 4.92. In the Air Force Mr. Conners served as an aircraft technician and quality assurance inspector on F-16 fighter aircraft. (CHAPTER 26)

David O. Dodge is IBM's Director for SAP Consulting and Services, leading IBM's SAP consulting activities across North America. He joined IBM in 1991 as part of the headquarters team to spearhead client/server-related consulting and methodology development. Mr. Dodge previously was a senior principal with Washington, D.C.-based American Management Systems. A graduate of the U.S. Naval Academy, Mr. Dodge also holds an M.S. degree and a J.D. degree from George Washington University. He is an associate member of the Virginia Bar. (CHAPTERS 18 AND 19)

Daniel J. Donovan is an IBM advisory RS/6000 sales specialist providing consulting in planning and implementing RS/6000 SP Massively Parallel Processors, Symmetrical Multi-Processors, and uni-processor solutions. He provides consulting services for companies integrating AIX and RS/6000 client/server solutions into MVS/ESA Customer Data Center environments. His system engineering experience includes planning and implementing DOS, WINDOWS, OS2, RT, and RS/6000 hardware and software client/server solutions. (CHAPTER 10)

Patricia L. Ferdinandi is president of Strategic Business Decisions, Inc., a company specializing in project management, requirements gathering, modeling, and analysis. Her area of expertise incorporates such information technology disciplines as business reengineering, essential and event-driven analysis, facilitation, logical and physical data modeling, strategic planning, project planning, and estimating. She has managed several large-size design and implementation efforts. (CHAPTER 2)

Barry Glasgow, Ph.D. is technical manager of Intelligent Applications for a major insurance company, responsible for corporate understanding and deployment of Data Mining, CASE-Based Reasoning, and Expert Systems. He previously was VP of Technical Planning for Shearson Lehman Brothers. Since 1987 he has been concerned with aligning business needs and technology, concentrating on artificial intelligence, CASE, and electronic data interchange. Dr. Glasgow received his Ph.D. from St. Johns University in the area of Solid State Physics. (CHAPTER 3)

Peter H. Guglielmino is a consulting software architect for IBM, responsible for architecting client/server solutions, presenting client/server and object-oriented technologies to customer executives, and migrating host-based systems to RISC environment. As an instructor-developer for IBM he developed the CICS OS/2 Cooperative Processing Class and installed and maintained PS/2 LAN lab rooms. As a systems programmer he installed systems software to support applications programmers and departments using MVS/XA, JES2, ISPF/PDF Time Sharing Option, ACF/VTAM and NCP for local and remote SNA devices, CICS 1.61, and CICS 1.7. (CHAPTER 27)

Sheryl Hert Harawitz is a computer software specialist with the New York City Housing Authority, responsible for data analysis and accuracy of data and programs. She has developed and taught computer courses in both SAS and dBASE. She is the author of Psych Lab (1987), an introductory text in designing and conducting psychological experiments with computers. Her M.A. degree in Psychology is from Hunter College. (CHAPTER 28)

George W. Harrison since 1979, has been with the New York City Housing Authority. Currently he is manager of the Technical Assistance Group for Computer Operations, responsible for conversion of applications from DOS/VSE to MVS/XA, and DASD management advice and support functions. He has worked in a number of capacities, including systems programmer and assistant chief, Computer Operations. (CHAPTER 17)

Jeff Kaplan is a senior technical consultant with extensive experience in all phases of systems engineering. He has experience in the installation, maintenance, modification, and tuning of VM/XA/SP, SQL/DS, CICS/VS, VTAM, NCP/EP, and numerous other program products. He has evaluated operating environments, made hardware and software recommendations, and trained staff. He has served as a technical adviser in the application of new technologies. He is an expert on all IBM mainframe and midrange platforms, as well as IBM system and applications software for these systems. His B.S. degree in Computer Science is from Brooklyn College. (CHAPTER 9)

AnnMarie Katz has more than 20 years of experience in the development and enhancement of on-line CICS command-level applications. She is skilled in all phases of system development for both the mainframe and the PC. Her positions have included programmer, project leader/manager, and department vice president. She has used her CICS command-level experience to design, code, and implement systems for major brokerage firms and insurance companies, including Shearson Lehman Hutton and Blue Cross/Blue Shield. She received her M.B.A. in computer methodology from Baruch College. (CHAPTER 12)

James Fee Langendoen has more than 21 years of successful business experience, including more than 12 years of computer experience, the last 6 years as an independent computer consultant. He has been an instructor at Columbia University's Computer Technology and Applications Program, specializing in relational database and structured design (including CASE), using ORACLE as the relational database management system for his coursework. He is a member of the New York ORACLE User Group, the Metropolitan New York CASE User Group, IEEE Computer Society, and serves on the IEEE Technical Committee on Software Engineering. (CHAPTER 11)

Robert J. Leo is a senior consultant with Sybase, Inc. He has extensive experience with relational databases and distributed environments and his primary responsibilities have been logical database design, physical database design, performance tuning, database administration, and instruction in Sybase. Mr. Leo has used his skills working for an accounting firm, a major bank, a telecommunications company, and an emergency response agency. He holds an M.S. degree in information systems engineering from Polytechnic University in New York. (CHAPTER 16)

Jenquo (Doug) Lieu is a manager with Teleport Communications Group. His ten years of experience has focused on Unix, SunOS, Sybase, Ultrix, and MS-DOS/C, and has included network control and monitoring, facility/circuit routing, PBX billing, personnel, sales, inventory, query language development, system administration, performance management, system porting, and migration. Mr. Lieu manages a group supporting Network Monitor Center for 24×7 operation and OSS interface implementation. He works with Sun Workstation/Server, DECstation, Annex Terminal Server, AT&T 3B2, 3B15, 3B20, 6386, VAX-11, and UNIVAC 1100, using SunOS, Ultrix, Annex, Unix System V, UNIVAC/EXEC, and MS-DOS. He holds an M.S. degree in computer science from Stevens Institute of Technology, New Jersey. (CHAPTER 20)

John H. Lister is vice president of communications software at Lehman Brothers. He is responsible for the development and maintenance of a large SNA network consisting of seven mainframe hosts and approximately 20,000 devices. The SNA network has connections to approximately 20 other SNA networks. He coordinated the planning for the introduction of token-ring technology within Shearson Lehman Brothers, which now supports approximately 7000 users in the downtown Manhattan locations. He also coordinated the introduction of TCP/IP protocols to mainframes and supports a substantial amount of communications with Unix workstations and servers. He was previously with Manufacturers Hanover Trust, New York, and National Westminster Bank, London. His B.A. degree in Mathematics is from King's College, London. (CHAPTER 21)

Maria I. Martins is presently a technical analyst, DB/Technical Services, CIS at Brown University. She is responsible for implementing new large systems that run under MVS. She works with MVS/JCL, streamlines procedures for production support, performs analysis and recovery on complex abends, trains others on new procedures, and writes documentation. Since 1979 she has held a number of responsible positions dealing with applications development, production services, and technical services. She has extensive programming skills applicable to MVS and VM environments. (CHAPTER 5)

Ichi Murase has extensive experience in Internet application development, including building Web pages using the latest tools. As a consultant he has assisted NYCHA, Merril Lynch, MTV Networks, Canon USA, and American Express International. He has experience with AS/400, 38, 34, 3/15, 370/145, etc., IBM and Univac mainframes. He has worked on procedures transaction analysis and technical writing, tutorials, data dictionaries and procedural flowcharts. For eight years he ran a facilities management and software service company. (CHAPTER 29)

Robert P. Palomo is a staff consultant for Kallista, Inc., where he designs and develops commercial-grade software application programs, principally using Borland Delphi. He wrote and developed print manuals and on-line Help for Borland International's award-winning Delphi Project. He has developed on-line Help for Windows applications and MS-Multimedia Viewer titles. His programming experience is with Borland Object Pascal, MS Visual Basic, BASIC-derived database languages, and dBASE. (CHAPTER 25)

Robert Pesner is president of PC Dialogs, Inc., New York City, a firm that develops and conducts classes on various computer-related topics including OS/2, Powerbuilder, LANs, distributed processing, APPC, VM, REXX, and ISPF, in addition to custom designing applications that focus on distributed processing. He was previously manager, OS/2 curriculum with Software Education Corporation in Marlboro, New Jersey and manager of VM systems programming with Shearson Lehman Hutton, New York City. His M.A. degree is from the University of California, Irvine. (CHAPTERS 8 AND 24)

Ulka Rodgers specializes in CASE and database management systems and has written *Oracle: A Database Developer's Guide, UNIX Database Management System,* and several journal articles covering issues of interest to application designers and developers who use database management systems products. Ms. Rodgers has provided consulting services to clients on CASE, DBMS, and 4GL products such as Sybase on a DEC platform. In the capacity of database group manager, she was responsible for a Machine Translation product in four supported environments: IBM VM/CMS, MVS, Wang VS, and Unix. She earned her BTech degree in Computer Science from Brunel University. She is a chartered engineer of the British Computer Society. (CHAPTER 11)

Arthur D. Rosenberg specializes in analyzing and translating business requirements into software applications; producing accurate and readable documentation; designing and conducting training programs; developing RFPs and proposals. His positions have included project leader, analyst, trainer, and documentation specialist. For a major media corporation he hired and managed a team of eight consultants in testing, documenting, and training customized A/R installation, Mr. Rosenberg has conducted classes and training seminars in PC hardware and software, mainframe applications, and methodology to staffs at several client companies, including The Port Authority of New York and New Jersey, Viacom/MTV, Deutsche Bank, Berlitz School (Paris), University of Stockholm, and U.S. Department of Education. (CHAPTER 1)

Michael A. Senatore is a database administrator with more than 15 years of experience in data processing. His accomplishments include multiple DB2 system implementations. He is the coauthor of *Structured Analysis and Design for the CASE User,* published by McGraw-Hill. His clients have included Metropolitan Life Insurance Company, Manufacturers Hanover Trust, New York City Housing Authority, and others. His B.A. degree is from Brooklyn College, with advanced training at NYU and Columbia University. (CHAPTERS 13, 14 AND 15)

Michael Sichel, since 1978, has directed a successful technical and executive staffing and outplacement facility—RMS Computer Corporation, located in mid-Manhattan. He has more than 20 years of diversified management experience. His consulting activities in both North America and Western Europe include corporate experience with major industries such as aerospace, communications, and diversified conglomerates. His B.S. degree is from

Cornell University and he has completed additional graduate work at Columbia University's Graduate School of Business. (CHAPTER 4)

Rick Stanley is the President of RSI, a New York based software development and computer consulting firm. His company provides consulting and training in both C & C++, as well as contact software development. His clients include NYC financial firms, private trusts, and a computer based printing company. He has been working in the industry for 10 years, and for the last seven years has been on the adjunct faculty of New York University teaching the C & C++ programming languages. (CHAPTERS 22 AND 23)

Candice Zarr is responsible for assessing and identifying opportunities in software technology and methodology to improve/support the creation and maintenance of business applications. Her specialties include CASE, reengineering, object-oriented technology, project management, metrics, and methodologies. She was previously director, Systems Integration, with the New York City Transit Authority as a CASE specialist, as well as having responsibilities for introducing PC technology to the organization. (CHAPTER 22)

Preface

"What's the difference between a recession and a depression"? A recession is when you are out of work. . . . a depression is when I'm out of work.

True, this is an old joke, but it probably reflects the status of the data processing industry . . . with you and me caught somewhere in the middle.

A few years ago we could basically pick and choose the job we wanted. If we were dissatisfied we moved on. Job mobility was the order of the day. Now, in far too many cases, outsourcing and reduction in the size of the IS department workforce seems to be the order of the data processing day. Job stability often appears to be little more than words found in a dictionary.

This book has been revised and updated in order to give you even more tools to beat out the competition. Your competition is all those people trying to get the same job you're trying to get. Let's face it, as far as you are concerned there's only one person that's going to get each job. As for the job *you* want, you want it to be you, not them. If you play your cards right, try as hard as you can, prepare yourself, and never give up, *you will succeed.*

And that is what this book is all about . . . Preparing and Succeeding.

Since the first edition of this book significant technical changes have taken place that directly affect your marketability. This second edition has adjusted to these changes and is offering more relevant information, as well as more insights into the "new stuff"—client/server, Delphi, Visual Basic, and a host of other important products.

Also, chapters have been added that will help clarify your thinking and give you the added confidence you need to compete in today's job market. A chapter on Project Management will open up new areas of growth. Relational database concepts, an additional chapter on client/server systems, and a chapter on programming the Internet have also been included. Chapters have been updated and expanded to included the latest features found in many of the new versions.

All in all a lot of effort by a lot of people has been put into providing you, the technical professional whose livelihood depends on the currency of his or her technical knowledge, with as much new meaningful information as possible.

If those who have contributed to this book have been able to give you any of the information that you need to survive and succeed our effort must be considered more than worthwhile.

Michael Rothstein

Acknowledgments

Publishing a book requires the efforts of many people, often for long periods of time. I would like therefore to take the opportunity to thank many of those whose contributions were more than appreciated.

To those at McGraw-Hill, Jerry Papke, Donna Namorato, and Judy Kessler, who really made a difference, to Chris Furry, Editorial Supervisor at North Market Street Graphics, and to the reviewers and those whose ideas and recommendations shaped the book: Pat Ferdinandi, Alfreda Lewis, Kevin Kremler, Jim Greeley of IBM, and Paula Rimer—thank you. . . . And last but not least to all the authors in this book whose chapters are really what has made this book something to be proud of.

Thank you one and all.

ॐ श्री

Ace the
Technical
Interview

1

The Technical Interview: What You Need to Know and Do to Succeed

Arthur D. Rosenberg

The Competitive Edge

This chapter shows you how to gear up for—and ace—the data processing interview. Whether you are looking for a full-time position or a consulting contract, the competition is fierce. There are a lot of pros out there who are knocking on the same doors as you, and you need every advantage you can get to come in first! Interviews are a key element in winning jobs, and knowing how to present yourself will give you a leg up into the winner's circle.

We'll focus on preparation—doing your homework prior to the interview—and handling the different types of interviews you may encounter. You will discover how to market your skills and talents while avoiding the *faux pas* that can kill an otherwise successful meeting. You'll learn to exercise more control over the people who interview you, and to respond effectively to their questions and tactics. You will position yourself to better evaluate whether you want the job or not, and to receive your share of offers. From now on, you'll go to important interviews with a feeling of confidence and leave them with a smile.

Getting Interviews

Prior to preparing for an interview, you must first *get* the interview. This obvious and necessary step is generally accomplished through personal contacts, agencies, postings, and advertisements. Don't get discouraged if they don't come fast and furiously at times, and never take the brush-offs personally. Most of the reasons you don't get potential interviews have absolutely nothing to do with you, so keep your head and spirits up. Sometimes it's a numbers game: the more contacts you make, the more interviews you get, and, inevitably, the more job offers you receive.

Agencies

Placement and consulting agencies often have valuable contacts with clients who are seeking employees and/or consultants. Most are experienced at evaluating and matching skills such as yours with client needs. Bear in mind, though, that the agency traditionally receives its fees from the employer, and so its loyalties are naturally inclined in that direction.

When you negotiate a salary or rate with an agency, you have to balance two opposing facts of life: the less you agree to, the less you will have to live with; and the more you demand, the more attractive the competition may appear.

The Résumé

Your résumé is your emissary to everyone you'd like to meet. Think of it as the initial link in the job chain you wish to enter, the only voice that speaks for you until you have a chance to speak for yourself. Whether you go through an agency or contact the client directly, you need a current résumé to help you stand out among the hundreds of others who may be competing with you for the job. According to the *Résumé Handbook* (Arthur D. Rosenberg and David V. Hizer, Bob Adams, Inc., 2d edition, 1990), only one interview is granted for every 245 résumés received.

Orient your résumé specifically toward a full-time position or a consulting contract. Today, all résumés should include a summary of experience and at least two or three job-related accomplishments. The full-time position résumé should also have a chronologically organized section (filling in any significant gaps) to show growth, responsibility, and consistency. A consultant's résumé needs to display technical and related skills, experience, and clients. All résumés should be limited to two or three pages (one for recent graduates and people with limited work experience); lists of publications, patents, and other relevant credits should be attached. It doesn't hurt to maintain your résumé on a word processor to keep it up to date, and to quickly produce variations that emphasize any specific skills and applications that may be of interest to a potential client.

Your résumé must be clearly organized and detailed without being cumbersome. Particularly for consultants, it also helps to have professional business cards, an answering machine, and a fax.

Preinterview Preparations

If you are seeking a full-time position, be prepared not only for questions about the job for which you are applying, but also for more personal inquiries, such as why you left your last (or are considering leaving your current) employer, why you'd like to join company X, and more subtle queries intended to reveal your character. If you are a consultant, potential clients are more concerned with your job-related track record—specifically, the hardware, software, and applications you have mastered. Regarding the latter, it is important to be candid and objective, for it is difficult to fool people for long in a data processing environment.

Doing Your Homework

The first step in getting ready for an interview is preparing for the kinds of questions you are likely to be asked. Ask your contact or intermediary about the specific job requirements and related issues. Job requirements may include hardware, software, applications, and responsibilities such as design, installation, supervision, and management. Related issues cover location, hours, and potential future to career-minded applicants. If a technical skill is required, update your memory and knowledge by referring to the appropriate chapter of this book. Ask yourself what you would ask a candidate if you were conducting the interview, and be prepared to answer no less than that.

Try also to find out who your interviewer is likely to be—the president of the company, the MIS director, a project leader or manager, or someone from the personnel department (see "Different Types of Interviewers" in this chapter). Is the interviewer a decision maker, or merely screening for someone else? If you are going to meet a decision maker, be ready to meet some of the members of the team as well.

Objectives

Just as the objective of a résumé is to get the interview, the objective of an interview is to convince the screener to pass you on to the decision maker, or to convince the decision maker to offer you the job. When you go on an interview, always give it your best shot, with confidence and enthusiasm. Don't waste the interviewer's time—or your own—with an *I don't really want this job* attitude. And don't shoot yourself in the foot with a *you probably won't offer me the job* air because, in that case, they probably won't. Whether you are seeking a career position or a consulting assignment, the bottom line is winning the offer. You may later decide not to accept the job if you feel it isn't right for you, or if something better is available, but that decision lies in the future. At worst—if they do not offer you the job—you will have gained the experience of the interview for the investment of your time.

Psyching Up

Everyone, from the beginner to the seasoned pro, needs to be mentally ready for an interview in order to be at their impressive best. When all other things are more or less equal (i.e., when two or more candidates are of comparable competence and experience), then confidence and enthusiasm for the job may serve as the tiebreaker.

Let's face it, if you're an unusually heavyweight tech, a guru among experts, clients are very likely lined up for your services despite any apparent negatives (e.g., coffee stains on your apparel, creased clothes, or a passive attitude). They put up with you because they have to. But if you haven't yet outdistanced the competition, your appearance and attitude can work for or against you. Nobody wants to work with a negative individual, a complainer, or a sourpuss when there are more agreeable alternatives available.

Personal Appearance

While we are not supposed to judge others by *their* personal appearance, we should nevertheless make sure that ours is "correct." Reality, of course, is that personal appearance strongly influences the expectations of those who meet us for the first time.

With regard to grooming and dress, common sense dictates that the closer you conform to the norm (what you see around you), the more you look the part. Since data processing is a relatively conservative environment, men with long hair, women with flashy makeup, and anyone unusually dressed are apt to divert attention from their skills and may be taken less than seriously.

If you have reason to anticipate an extended interviewing process that could last for several hours, wear clothing that will maintain its neatness throughout the day.

References

Give references that will enhance your credibility as an employee/consultant in the job for which you are interviewing. Former employers, supervisors, and colleagues count for more than friends and casual acquaintances. By all means, use academic recommendations if you are a recent graduate, but try to avoid using any references with whom you have had no contact for a number of years. It is customary to ask permission of the person involved to use his or her name. Besides being the polite thing to do, it alerts the person to expect calls. If you are uncertain of what someone may say about you, check them out by having a friend call them as a potential employer, or just don't use them. A poor reference is worse than no reference at all.

Disabilities

If you have any handicaps that might interfere with your ability to perform activities normally associated with the job for which you wish to interview, reveal them up front. In this manner, you are more likely to overcome any doubts the interviewer may have (but may be hesitant to ask) about your ability to perform.

Different Types of Interviewers

Before getting into the potential idiosyncrasies of individual interviewers, let's take a moment to identify the two major camps by objectives: those who screen, and those who decide.

Screeners

The screening interview is usually a formal, impersonal meeting conducted by a professional interviewer in the personnel department. It is most often required for a career position, to a lesser degree for a consulting assignment. The purpose of this process is to weed out the more obviously inappropriate candidates by verifying their background, credentials, appearance, and any overt characteristics.

The screening interviewer is likely to be skilled at the kinds of techniques that encourage you to put your foot in your mouth by revealing facts you'd rather not discuss (e.g., discrepancies between what you say and what is written on your résumé, or perhaps the real reason why you left a certain company). The screener probably doesn't know a whole lot about the job for which you are interviewing, so he or she is unlikely to ask any technical questions. The screener's purpose is to gather enough relevant information about you to make a safe decision as to whether to pass you on to the decision maker or show you the door.

Since this is likely to be the only time you ever meet the screeners (even if you get the job), they are less interested in you personally than would be a potential supervisor or colleague. In a very real sense, screeners are more focused on uncovering reasons to stop you from getting any further than in your finer attributes. So it is more important that they do not find anything wrong with you than that they like you.

Your objective in a screening interview is to pass. This means providing the screener with solid facts that fit into a wholesome picture. You need only to satisfy screeners, not impress them. Avoid any hint of suspicion or controversy. Respond clearly and fully to all questions while volunteering absolutely nothing. If the screeners are not impressed with you, you won't be able to charm or fast-talk your way past them; and if they are satisfied with your credentials, the more you talk, the wider and deeper the potential pitfall.

Deciders

The decision (hiring) interview is commonly conducted by a department head, project leader, supervisor, or any combination of these. Unlike screeners, decision makers most likely know a lot more about the job and related technical details than about interviewing techniques. They are concerned with your ability to do the work, and how you will fit into the environment. They may have to deal with you on a daily basis, and so it matters, to some extent, whether or not they like you.

Since the decision-making interviewer isn't usually a professional interviewer, the decision interview tends to be a less structured affair. This is where you must be prepared for technical questions and informal conversations on a more personal level. This is where you may have to convince potential supervisors and colleagues that you are—in addition to being competent—a reasonably agreeable person. This is where you may use your interpersonal skills to direct the interview in a positive (for you) direction. And this is where you get the information and the *vibes* that help you to make up your own mind about the job.

Personalities

Whenever people with different objectives get together, potential hazards come into play. Despite the best of intentions, objectivity can give way to personal inclination when certain types of individuals confront each other. A few of the more obvious examples include status and authority, male-female, short-tall, and older-younger. Differences of national origin, accent, and style (e.g., flamboyance versus restraint) may also influence an interaction. This is especially true of job interviews.

While confidence and attention are assets in most interview situations, the following conditions call for heightened sensitivity. Since we cannot cover all of the possible personality combinations in a single chapter, we offer these examples as representative of the kinds of efforts that may be needed on both sides of the interview.

Upper management.   The president, the chairperson, and certain department heads may have large egos. When you interview with a bigwig, treat that person with the respect to which he or she is accustomed. Manifest your confidence within the confines of your arena, and tread lightly on their comfort zones.

Consultant-employee.   Interviewing with a manager or project leader who knows, and perhaps resents, the fact that you are making more money (and having a lot more fun) than they is a common occurrence. The best way to deal with this is to focus on the job to be done and your ability to do the job, and downplay any reference to your lifestyle. Your task is to convince the interviewer that you are a reliable team player who will make the interviewer look good, not to let them know about your Lamborghini or indoor swimming pool.

Male-female.   Be careful to avoid any innuendo that might be interpreted in a sexual manner. Both male and female candidates should keep their eyes up to face level and feel free to manifest their natural self confidence by sitting in a conservative manner and refraining from remarks that could possibly be "sexually" misconstrued.

Short-tall.   People whose physical dimensions are considered to be within the norm are often unaware of the sensitivities of exceptionally tall, short, overweight, and otherwise visually unusual individuals. Avoid making any references to these characteristics—your remarks may be misinterpreted.

Older-younger.   When there is a significant difference in age, the elder intervie-wee should strive to be energetic and should be careful not to condescend. The younger interviewee should be calm, respectfully confident, and an especially good listener.

One-on-One

As mentioned earlier, personal predispositions can be difficult to avoid, even dur-ing a professional interview. Focus your attention on the interviewer rather than on the impression you are trying to make. Listen carefully to what interviewers say, and try to read their reactions to you. If they appear to lose interest in what you're saying, change course by asking them a question. For example,

"Have I answered the question to your satisfaction?"

"Was there something else you wanted me to address?"

"Do you want me to go into (technical) detail?"

"How many people are there in your department?"

"When do you plan to make a decision on this position?"

Outnumbered

When you are being interviewed by two or more potential employer/clients, it may be useful to have some samples of your work, or extra copies of your résumé, to divert their attention. Try to learn, if you don't already know, who has the most authority, and be sure to address that individual at least as often as the others. Pay attention to them all by looking at them, one by one, as you talk. Get them to do most of the talking, if you can, by asking questions based on what they tell you. Answer every question as accurately and completely as you can.

If someone asks a stupid question, focus on any aspect of it that may be sensible; or divert it toward relevancy, if possible, without embarrassing the one who asked it. Example: You are interviewing for a three-to-six-month assignment, and some-one asks, "Why are you interested in working for our company?" Instead of shrug-ging it off, gaping in disbelief, or resorting to sarcasm, try to come up with a face-saver, like, "I've been hearing about your company's accomplishments/inno-vations in recent months, and this is a chance to learn more about it/them," or "I've been learning a good deal about CASE (DB, etc.), and this looks like an excellent opportunity to apply that knowledge." The point is that even if the individual who asked the silly question does not recognize or appreciate your tact, the others will.

The Interview

When you succeed in getting the interview, be punctual. Plan to arrive early enough that unforeseen delays will not make you late. Excuses for arriving late are just that—*excuses*—even if they are true. Being late is failing to arrive on time. You don't want a potential employer's initial experience with you to be tainted with any kind of failure.

If you are going to be unavoidably delayed, call the interviewer before the time of the scheduled interview to apologize for inconveniencing him or her and ask if it would be more convenient to delay the interview or reschedule it.

Credibility is the most important impression to create during an interview. This is accomplished by appearing honest, confident, enthusiastic, courteous, and inoffensive. Speak in a manner that is natural for you; if you have memorized a bunch of technical details, deliver them in a conversational manner, not as if reading from a list. Avoid slang ("like, real cool," "right on," etc.); bad English ("so he goes, 'well, yeah,' and I go, . . ."); profanity of any kind; and criticism (especially of a past employer or someone known to the interviewer). Avoid frequent use of "well," "umm," "y'know," and such.

Try to enjoy the interview; this can help you to relax and make a positive impression. Memorize the interviewer's name, and be sure to pronounce it correctly when addressing him or her. And—forgive us for adding the obvious—do not smoke, chew gum, or eat food or candy during an interview. It's OK to accept coffee, tea, or water if offered, although it may be safer to decline. Remember that the interviewer—especially the professional interviewer—is watching you and evaluating your behavior.

Body Language

Eye contact is the dominant feature in nonverbal communications. The way you meet or avoid someone's gaze can reveal volumes about your character and feelings. Consciously and unconsciously, our eyes contribute to the messages we give out. For example, looking away from the listener while speaking means *don't interrupt me even if I pause for a moment;* looking at the listener when you stop speaking is a signal that you're finished; and looking away from the person who is speaking suggests impatience or dissatisfaction with whatever that person is saying.

It has been estimated that as much as 70 percent of all face-to-face communication is nonverbal. While volumes have been written on this subject, we have summarized the function into a few action verbs:

- *Reach out* to potential employers and clients with a firm handshake on arriving and departing.
- *Smile* as pleasantly as your personality allows.
- *Look* at people when they speak, and make eye contact with each of them in turn when you are talking.
- *Relax* your body, especially your head and hands; avoid abrupt or jerky motions, fidgeting, crossing your arms, or covering your mouth with your hands.
- *Lean* slightly forward, without slouching.

- *Nod* affirmatively to show attention and agreement, and to encourage the interviewer to continue talking, but avoid nodding when they say something with which you disagree.

Evaluating

Winning teams are those that make quick adjustments to what their opponents are doing. A successful interviewee pays attention to what the interviewer says and does, and reacts accordingly. For example, if you are describing your last job or assignment, and the interviewer's eyes begin to wander around the room, it's time to change the topic or to ask a question. If the interviewer glances frequently at the clock on the wall or his or her watch, it may be wise to keep your answers brief. When you do manage to catch the interviewer's interest, hold to that subject, and to similar topics, as long as may be reasonable.

Always listen carefully to what the interviewer says, whether it is what you want to hear or not. Skilled interviewers tell you precisely what they want you to know; unskilled interviewers may reveal more than they realize. In either case, the information an interviewer provides can help you to evaluate the interviewer, the company, and the job, and to respond in an appropriate and relevant manner.

If the interviewer is terse, tense, or unpleasant, don't take it personally. He or she may be having a bad day, or perhaps that's just the personality of the interviewer. Continue to conduct yourself with professional courtesy and enthusiasm, and hope for the best. Unless you experience this sort of unpleasantness often, chances are it isn't worth a second thought.

Responding

Try to answer every question clearly, accurately, and thoroughly without overexplaining or repeating yourself. Maintain consistency between different questions. This is most easily achieved by telling the truth. Be ready for the open-ended type of question, such as, "Tell me about yourself," or "What do you consider to be your major strengths and weaknesses?" In such cases, represent yourself in a believable and work-related manner; discuss your assets in a matter-of-fact manner without overselling them. (Please refer to **Fielding Hard-to-Handle Questions** later in this chapter.)

And, above all, assume that if you are telling the truth, you are being believed. With a skilled interviewer, the way you respond to questions can be even more important than the answers; clear, decisive answers contribute to the image of intelligence and credibility.

- *Qualify.* Ask questions that help to define or clarify what is being asked of you. Example: "Are you more interested in how I designed the system, or in how I applied the methodology?" This keeps you from taking a false path, and gives you a few extra moments to prepare your answer.

- *Clarify.*   After answering a question, check the interviewers' demeanor. If they seem to be satisfied (e.g., they smile or nod), then pause to let them comment or ask another question. If they do not appear comfortable, ask if you have answered the question to their satisfaction and if there are any additional points they would like you to address.

- *Specify.*   Tell what *you* did in your last job, or in your last job related to the position/assignment for which you are applying, aside from the team on which you worked.

- *Quantify.*   Try to put your accomplishments in a meaningful context. Examples: "I wrote a hundred programs averaging half a million lines of code in two years," "We were the only group to complete our project on schedule," or "When my assignment was completed, I was assigned another task by the project leader."

- *Don't lie.*   Plausible exaggeration is the outer limit of creative expression when describing your experience and accomplishments. Employers tend to check up on their prospective employees thoroughly, and a consultant's reputation is his or her lifeline to success. Never tell a verifiable lie to a potential employer/client—even the possibility of its discovery will haunt you.

Controlling the Interview

Projecting an Image

There are three separate aspects of your behavior of which you need to be aware: how you really feel, the image you would like to project, and the interviewer's perception of your behavior.

Your personal feelings are private. You may choose to reveal a few of them, but most of us prefer to filter out at least some of our innermost views and characteristics.

Projecting an image requires an awareness of how others perceive us. Alas, many otherwise clever individuals harbor self images which are not uniformly shared by those who meet them.

To compensate for potential discrepancies, we suggest the following kind of reality check: ask three or four trusted friends and colleagues of both genders what they consider to be your two or three strongest personality characteristics, both positive and negative. Examples: nice smile, good speaking voice, nervous hand gestures, avoiding eye contact. Use these lists to make up your own list, emphasizing traits which were mentioned more than once, plus any negative traits of which you are already aware. Do not delete any negatives, no matter how strongly you may disagree, or this exercise will be worthless. Remember, you are focusing on how others perceive you, aside from what you may see in yourself. Next, ask three or four of your closest friends and family members to rearrange the list, beginning with your strongest tendencies. The combination of the rearranged lists will likely give you some idea of your public image, pro and con. Then it's up to you to work on what you want to do about it. Note that even positive qualities, when carried to excess, can be negative.

Influencing the interviewer's perception of you, as discussed earlier under "Evaluating," depends on paying careful attention to what the interviewer says and does, perceiving what he or she wants and does not want, and adjusting your approach accordingly. Always bear in mind that what the interviewer wishes to hear is more important than what the interviewee would like to say. The closer you come to emphasizing those qualities that relate specifically to what the interviewer is looking for, the more successful you will be. Just as it may be counterproductive to ramble on about your IDMS background in a DB2 environment, don't push any skills in which the interviewer appears uninterested.

Turning the Interview Around: Interviewing the Interviewer

Note: this tactic is intended primarily for the decision interview; it is rarely successful with a professional screening interviewer.

One of the most successful interviewing tactics is getting the interviewer to do most of the talking. It is a given that people who talk a lot enjoy talking. So even if you do not get to make all the points you'd like to make, avoid the temptation of interrupting a chatty interviewer. An interview dominated by the interviewer is likely to leave that interviewer with a comfortable feeling about the interviewee.

When interviewers show a tendency to talk about themselves, their company, the surf at Malibu, Bogart movies, or any other subject, let them do so with a minimum of interruption. One way to discover what makes them tick is to politely ask semipersonal questions, such as: "How long have you been working here, if you don't mind my asking?" or "Do you have a long commute?" or (in response to their question) "We have three children; how about you?" You never know what might get them going.

On the other hand, don't get too personal, avoid politics, and stay clear of references to any unusual physical characteristics. Remember, small talk can be a double-edged sword.

Fielding Hard-to-Handle Questions

Before responding to a difficult question, pause just long enough to check your body language and compose your thoughts.

If you get a technical question for which you are unprepared, tell what (if anything) you know, and admit your ignorance in a straightforward manner (e.g., "I have relatively little background in IDMS—is it essential to this position?" or "I would welcome the opportunity to sharpen my skills on the AS/400" or "I was not informed that C was a prerequisite for this assignment"). Then try to draw attention to an area in which you are more knowledgeable.

The majority of these queries break down into six major categories: *Tell me about yourself . . . , What are your strong/weak points?, How do you feel about . . . , Why did you leave your last job/do you want to leave your present job?, Why do you want to join our company?*, and *What do you want to be doing two/five/ten years from now?*

Example 1:

Q: *Tell me a little about yourself.*

Prepare a two- to five-minute mini-profile in advance for this open-ended query to avoid fumbling for words or revealing something you'd prefer not to mention. Make sure it is in no way inconsistent with your résumé. Smile, as if you welcome the opportunity. One smooth line of conversation is the progression of events in your childhood, youth, education, or earlier career that led you to your current professional level. Some of the topics you might use are your ambitions, hobbies, leisure activities, and family, but that's strictly up to you and what you're comfortable talking about.

A: In my last two jobs my responsibilities were primarily research oriented. Although I'm pretty good with numbers, I was beginning to feel isolated and would like to be more involved in customer relations.

A: I enjoy collecting stamps. My grandfather used to let me search for the right place to stick the stamps in the books when I was a kid, and he gave me his collection when I graduated from high school. By the time I finished college, I had the whole collection computerized, which is what got me interested in computers.

A: Although I have a technical background, I'm very interested in management. That's why I've been taking evening classes toward a possible MBA.

A: My husband and I are joggers, and we enjoy listening to classical music.

A: My wife and I enjoy traveling together. We like to take advantage of the chance to visit different parts of the country before starting to raise a family.

Example 2:

Q: *What are your strongest/weakest attributes?*

When you have a chance to showcase your strengths, provide two or three examples that have some relevance to your profession.

A: My manager at Gigo told me I was a very good analyst. She assigned me to establish the design standards for an important project and was very pleased with the results. I also had a reputation for picking up new programming languages quickly.

Experienced interviewers won't let you get away with stock answers and clichés these days, like "I used to get a little impatient when people held me back, but I've learned to be a team player." They know that nobody's perfect, and they want an honest answer. The best way to respond is by admitting to a (minor) human weakness within the context of how you are improving it.

> A: I missed a couple of deadlines by a week or two because I wasn't very good at delegating work to other members of my team, but I've been improving. In fact, two of my last three projects were on time, which is above average in my department.
>
> A: I was not a natural with computers in college, and so I tended to avoid them for a while. I finally wised up to the reality that computers are a fact of life and completely changed my attitude toward them. In fact, I'm signing up for an evening computer course this coming semester.

Example 3:

> Q: *How would you feel about one of your subordinates being promoted to a position above yours?*

It's O.K. (and very believable) to admit to human emotions, so long as you don't go overboard.

> A: I guess it would depend on who it was and the circumstances in which it happened. If I honestly felt that the person deserved the promotion, I might be a little jealous, but I'd also be among the first to congratulate him or her. But if I had reason to believe that it was due to backroom politics or personal favors, I'd probably be very angry.

Example 4:

> Q: *Why did you leave your last job?*

The overwhelming majority of people who aren't terminated by their employers leave their jobs for better opportunities (more money and prestige), because they're bored or dead-ended (no room to move up), or due to a conflict with a boss, colleague, or assignment. Responding to this question is tricky because you don't want to be in the position of complaining or bad-mouthing others. Having a personal problem doesn't necessarily label you a loser, but it's hard to look good when you paint yourself into a negative picture. Even if an interviewer encourages you to reveal the gory details, you're better off presenting your move, or willingness to move, in a positive light.

> A: I've been purchasing automobile parts for more than eight years, and I am ready to move ahead to the next stage of my career.
>
> A: I was typecast as a creative type and I'm looking for a managerial opportunity.
>
> A: When they merged the two divisions, it was clear that there would be heavy cuts in marketing. Frankly, I'm a lot better at promoting products than at playing politics.

However, if you were ousted because of a personality conflict that cannot be hidden, you may need to discuss it in a straightforward manner.

A: When I transferred to the central region, I found that the regional manager had a very different set of priorities than my former boss and I. He was totally production oriented, whereas I feel very strongly about quality. It was clear to both of us early on that we weren't comfortable working together.

Example 5:

Q: *Why are you interested in joining our company?*

This is the flip side to question #4, and some of the same answers may be appropriate. It's your chance to demonstrate your knowledge of the interviewer's company and their activities.

A: The innovations your company has been making in high-speed performance convinced me that this was the place to be.
A: A large organization like yours has far more opportunity for people with solid line experience.
A: A small company like yours is much more personal.
A: Your company's track record demonstrates a level playing field for women executives.

Example 6:

Q: *Where do you see yourself two/five/ten years from now?*

You are expected by your employers and potential employers to have goals. Prepare a goal description that is likely to sound reasonable: junior accountant to senior accountant (not directly to controller); upper management to vice president. Of course, you are advised to edit out your plans to leave the company for any reason. Also, it is best not to define a precise time frame that could embarrass or pressure you unreasonably. The safest ground is ambition that doesn't border upon arrogance.

A: With the courses I am taking and the experience I expect to gain in this position, I am aiming at becoming a project leader when the opportunity arises.
A: I am definitely interested in upper management, although I know I've got a long way to go. My first step is to show my manager that he or she made a good decision in adding me to the team.
A: My goal is to become a supervisor. How long has it taken other people who entered at my level to get promoted?

Managing Uncomfortable Situations

The *pressure interview* is more frequently encountered by potential employees than consultants, but every interviewee should be prepared for it. Most often, pressure interviews are devised to find out how the candidate will respond to unexpected circumstances; occasionally, they may be inadvertent, the result of internal pressure, an incompetent interviewer, etc. But generally they are intentional, premeditated ploys to see how you react to stress.

The rule of thumb when under pressure is courtesy, tact, and confidence. Don't blow your cool; never let yourself be baited into rudeness, anger, impatience, or agreeing with a point of view with which you really disagree. You can acknowledge the interviewer's point without agreeing ("I understand your point"), and you can politely disagree ("Your point is well taken, although I find that . . .").

If the interviewer stares at you strangely (e.g., in apparent disbelief), don't feel that you must justify whatever you just said. If your statement is challenged, don't back down; show confidence in your position without arguing or becoming flustered. If the interviewer lapses into a prolonged silence after you have finished talking, just sit there calmly, meeting his or her stare as pleasantly as possible, until the interviewer resumes. Don't let interviewers lure you into qualifying, overexplaining, taking back what you have told them, or fidgeting. If they haven't asked a question, you don't have to answer one. If you have been honest with interviewers, you have nothing to feel guilty about. When experienced interviewers behave strangely, their purpose is to see how you respond. Tell yourself that they are testing you, and you will very likely pass the test. If the interviewer asks you if you're nervous, there's nothing wrong with smiling and admitting to being human: "I haven't done a lot of job interviewing and I'm not very experienced at it. I guess I'm a lot better at balancing budgets than talking about my achievements," or "I was just thinking about some of the people I have interviewed in the past, and how they may have been feeling."

In the following scenarios, you are presented with stressful situations and a number of sample options. The choices are yours. There are no right or wrong answers, only a range of options. It is important to be aware of these potential courses of action, and to be ready to exercise them in time of need. The likely consequences of these options are fairly obvious; your choice is a reflection of your personality and values.

Scenario 1. You arrive for an interview and are seated by a secretary/receptionist in a typical meeting room containing a table and chairs. This person tells you that Mr./Mrs. Something-or-Other will be there shortly, and leaves. The minutes pass, and no one shows up. You recognize that you are being tested, or that the interviewer has other priorities. How long do you wait (15 minutes? 30? an hour or two or three?) before:

1. Asking the secretary to contact the interviewer

2. Telling the secretary that you have to leave at a certain time

3. Jotting a note on the back of your card and leaving

4. Just leaving

Or do you just sit back and wait, no matter how long it takes? To what extent are you influenced by how badly you want the job? How much are you willing to put up with in order to get the job? One answer is that you should wait until you begin to feel annoyed or that you are being put upon. Why? Because it is better to reschedule the interview than to have your annoyance interfere with the interview—and interfere it will, because it is difficult to hide annoyance.

Scenario 2.   After keeping you waiting for an hour or more, the interviewer arrives without apologizing, complaining that there isn't enough time to do all the things he or she needs to do (as if you are responsible for the inconvenience). Throughout the interview the interviewer takes obvious and frequent time checks and repeatedly interrupts you before you can finish what you're saying. What do you do?

1. You ignore the interruptions and continue as if everything were perfectly normal. *If interruptions really do not bother you, no problem!*

2. You ask the interviewer if it might not be preferable to reschedule the interview for a more convenient time. *This is a polite way of letting the interviewer know that you are not prepared to continue.*

3. You tell the interviewer that you do not believe you are receiving a proper opportunity to present your credentials for the job. *There are times when a degree of aggressiveness may be appropriate, as long as it suits your personality.*

4. You suggest (preferably without sarcasm) that both of you might be more comfortable if someone else continued the interview with you. *This is likely to impress the interviewer, although the impression may be negative. On the other hand, there's an outside chance that this was just what the interviewer was looking for.*

5. You refuse to put up with it and leave. *Of course, this will probably end any chance of your getting the job.*

Scenario 3.   You arrive for an interview in a conference-room-sized office. The interviewer, who is seated to one side of the room behind a desk, tells you that he or she will be with you in a minute. The only chairs in the room, aside from the interviewer's, are around the table at the opposite end of the room. What do you do?

As in the preceding scenarios, your choice should be the one with which you are most comfortable and for which you are prepared to accept the consequences.

1. You quietly wait for the interviewer to tell you what to do. *After all, the interviewer is running the show.*

2. You ask the interviewer where to sit. *This is the polite thing to do.*

3. You wander around the office, waiting for the interviewer to act. *The interviewer will get around to you when he or she is ready; meanwhile, you'll do your thing.*

4. You invite the interviewer to join you at the table. *This is a polite way of asserting yourself.*

5. You bring a chair from the table to the desk and sit down. *This is an aggressive way to assert yourself.*

6. You sit in a chair at the table, and wait. *Patience is a virtue.*

7. You sit in a chair at the table and read a newspaper (pretend to make notes in a notebook, etc.). *Two can play that game.*

8. You sit on a corner of the table and glance at your watch from time to time. *You are not intimidated, and you haven't got all day.*

9. You turn around and leave. *You don't need this.*

10. You tell the interviewer off, and then leave. *Who do they think they are, anyway?*

Postinterview Follow-Up

Communicating

If your interview was arranged by an agency, call your contact no later than the afternoon following a morning interview, or the very next morning after an afternoon interview (unless the interviewer calls you first). Avoid the temptation to call or write directly to the interviewer, unless he or she is expecting you to follow up with information.

Negotiating for a Salaried Position

Do your best to find out the company's salary range for the job you want, and how much you can reasonably expect them to pay you. Then consider the least you are willing to accept. Now you're ready to negotiate.

Never bring up the question of salary yourself; try to avoid revealing what you are currently earning, unless they insist, with a comment like, "I would rather not discuss that." If they say they need to know what you are earning in order to make you an offer, you can suggest a figure that you know to be within their range. Once you ask for a certain amount, unless you are willing to negotiate, be prepared to stick to it. If their offer is final but a little on the low side, you could ask that, if they are satisfied with your performance after six months (for example), they then give you a salary review (i.e., more money). It never hurts to try.

Negotiating for a Consulting Contract

Once your qualifications for the job have been established, try to find out what the client/agency is willing to pay. Of course, agencies are skilled negotiators, and they may have alternative resources from which to choose. Typically, they will ask you your rate. If you give them a precise number, there is little chance of their offering you more; if you give them a range, there may be room for discussion without scaring them away. If you are adamant, obviously there is no room for negotiation.

To negotiate your rate successfully, you must be aware of what the market will bear in your specialty. Your willingness to accept a lower rate than you would like, for a period of time, depends upon your need.

Managing Your Expectations

Just as you convinced the interviewer—and yourself—that you wanted the job during the interview, consider afterward the possibility that you may not get it. Try not to let any one position or contract become so important that you will be severely disappointed if it doesn't work out. Conversely, don't talk yourself into believing that you did a bad job at the interview.

Remember that—whether you get it or not—it's only a job.

Summary

The job interview is a necessary part of earning a living. Interviewing is hard work and, fortunately, a skill at which one can improve. It is definitely worth the effort. Consider it an investment not only in obtaining a job but also in keeping a job and moving on to better jobs. Keep in mind that the fundamental principles of successful interviewing (preparation and presentation) are the building blocks of nearly every aspect of your professional career.

You can improve your interviewing skills by reading up on what some of the experts say, and then practice on family members or friends. Every morning, before you pick up the phone or leave for an interview, tell yourself that *today may be the day*. Interviewing is a tough job, and getting yourself psyched up is an essential part of preparing to succeed. When you show up for an interview, present the most confident and enthusiastic candidate you're capable of being.

Bibliography

Harper, John J. Marcus, *The Complete Job Interview Handbook,* 3d ed., Perennial, 1994.
Medley, Anthony, *Sweaty Palms: The Art of Being Interviewed,* Tenspeed Press, 1993.
The National Business Employment Weekly, a weekly journal published by the *Wall Street Journal* oriented toward every aspect of seeking jobs and improving careers.

2

What You Should Know (and Do) to Succeed on an Interview for a Project Manager

Patricia L. Ferdinandi

What This Chapter Is All About

Introduction

The goal of this chapter is to prepare you for the interview. Project management provides an upward career path; the salaries are usually more than that of a programmer while utilizing the expertise you have developed in the past. Preparing for an interview for the position of project manager involves reviewing common concepts and terminology and quizzing yourself on some of the typical questions asked on an interview. It can also involve learning one or more commonly used project management planning tools. By doing so, you will be able to portray the confidence needed for the position.

Planning what you want to say and being prepared to answer a wide range of questions is the most important aspect of successful interviewing. Answers to many project management questions are subjective. Keep in mind that a technical project manager is someone responsible for seeing that people accomplish a business objective by means of a technical task. This task could be application- or support-related. Both kinds of tasks have a customer/user who must be satisfied and whose expectations and demands must be managed.

This chapter will not teach you project management. There are many excellent books, magazines, and seminars on the topic, some of which will be mentioned in this chapter. This chapter will, however, give you an idea of the type of answers to give. You can tailor them based upon your own experience, observations of other project managers, and the specific position you are interviewing for. Whatever questions are asked and whichever answers you give, remember to use what is the most valued and important trait of a project manager—*common sense.*

What Project Management Is All About

The success of a project is never due to one exceptional person. A successful project occurs through the efforts of many people extending beyond department boundaries. These people, referred to as a project team, will consist of many individuals with varying levels of skills, talents, work styles, and knowledge.

The project team, however, needs to have a common goal, a common vision, and a clear understanding of what is expected. The group of individuals, regardless of the reporting structure, must be a smoothly working, motivated *team* to achieve the business objectives.

A project manager is the leader of that team. He or she is responsible for motivating the team to achieve its objectives in a productive manner. This position requires the use of both technical and people skills, and the ability to focus every day on the:

- Business
- Company
- Project
- Team
- Individuals
- Changes in technology and methodologies

Since the skills of a project manager incorporate knowledge of technology and people, a solid technical foundation will assist you in providing technical guidance and coherence to the team, while people skills will assist in communication and problem resolution.

Managerial skills are not tied to the technology. They require skills such as issue resolution, estimating, planning, and most importantly, good people and communication skills.

You may think you are lacking in one or both of these areas. Therefore, this chapter is geared toward the individual:

- Who has never been a project manager, or
- Who has been a project manager but whose skills may be out-of-date

What Is a Project Manager?

The Role of a Project Manager

Project management is the repeated execution of estimating, planning, reorganizing, integrating, measuring, and revising until the project's business objectives are achieved. This is accomplished through people management, user involvement, and issue resolution.

What Upper Management Looks For

Every manager looks for someone he or she can depend on to handle a specific business objective. It is hard for a manager to give up control of what they know and can do in order to move up the corporate ladder. Harder yet is hiring an unknown quantity to take on the responsibility.

Therefore, you must convey the qualities of trust and dependability. This does not encompass just managing the project at hand; it includes keeping communication lines open to upper management and users. Management must be kept informed of both positive and negative situations. However, you must show management qualities by not presenting every little detail and problem without solution options. If you are involving upper management in all decisions, why are you needed? Upper management is doing your job.

People Management Skills

Understanding the psychology of people and their different work styles is an important qualification for a project manager. Everyone is different. By understanding your own work styles and those of your people, you will relieve tension and facilitate communication.

IBM's slogan for years has been "Respect for the Individual." This incorporates understanding the people you interact with on a daily basis. In order to be able to do that, however, you need to understand yourself and how your approach motivates or creates tension for others.

A good starting place is to read the Myers-Briggs book on type-indicator analysis. Katherine Briggs and her daughter Isabel Briggs-Myers developed a questionnaire (MBTI) to identify individual behavior preference and the impact it has on a group. It was built upon a philosophy developed by Carl Jung's Model of Typology (personality preference). Books on this and similar topics are available in bookstores under self-improvement and/or psychology.

Until you understand a person's work style, keep in mind these simple rules. The list needs to become second nature to you. These commonsense items are required in order for any project manager to be successful:

- Treat everyone (support groups as well as employees) with *respect.*
- *Listen* with open ears and an open mind.

- Make *well-informed* decisions.
- Be objective, *not* subjective.
- *Never* criticize in public.
- Stress strengths and what was done right *first*.
- *Sincerely* ask for advice and suggestions from your staff.
- Be *clear* on objectives and deliverables.
- Promote *cooperation* and information sharing within the information technology group.
- Understand each individual's *work style* as well as their strengths and weaknesses.
- Praise in a *sincere* manner.
- Express negatives as *opportunities for growth.*
- Provide *guidance* in a positive, non-threatening, *supportive* manner.

You Can't Manage What You Can't Control

As stated previously, project management is the carrying out of repeatable tasks to achieve a common business objective. To do this you must establish controls. Therefore, be prepared to answer questions during the interview in any of the following areas:

Metrics.   Metrics have a negative impact if not managed or used properly. It is important to use them as input in developing the plan and to achieve statistics during and at the end of the project to provide valuable insight into planning the next project or phase. An improper use of metrics would be using them to evaluate an employee's performance.

Project Plans.   Project plans provide valuable checkpoints on an assignment. They are the road maps to achieving the business objective. Keep in mind that project plans are valuable not only for new development but for any support and maintenance activity as well. Many managers develop a tailored plan but never apply actuals. In fact, they rarely follow through on the plan at all.

Budgets.   What accompanies estimating and planning is budgeting. Many project managers will be required to produce and manage their own budget. If you have been keeping your project plans complete with actuals, your job has been made simpler. Most project management tools allow the cost (at an hourly, daily, and/or yearly rate) to be associated with a resource. Many corporate accounting departments have determined the resource cost including building overhead. Some have the cost separated by title or just between users, management, employees, and consultants. (For consultants, remember to include their overtime rate.)

Included separately is the cost of equipment. Remember to include software tools and hardware along with additional software/hardware needed for the running of your application (such as color printers for sales offices). Also include any training needed for the use of the tools and methodology.

Employee Action Plans.   People are the most valuable asset to any project. An individual can make or break or seriously injure the success or progress of the project. Use action plans as a means of constructively and realistically developing an employee. Most organizations have their own format. Whatever that format is, it is important to:

- be clear and decisive about responsibilities,

- be objective when evaluating employees' strengths and weaknesses, and

- give opportunities for input from the employee both in the development and in the evaluation review.

Rewards and Stresses of Project Management

The role of a project manager is a double-edged sword. The position comes with its share of stresses and rewards. Once you accept the position, you must be prepared for both.

Everyone gains the rewards of implementing a successful system. However, the specific reward of a project manager is helping his or her employees achieve their potential. People are the most important element in any achievement of objectives. You will be proud when a well-motivated team emerges due to your management techniques.

People are also the source of the greatest stress. People are people and will always be influenced by things out of your control. Troubles at home and personality conflicts among the team members must be managed with tact and objectivity by the project manager.

The project manager is also in the first line of fire when anything related to the application or team members goes wrong. Upper management as well as the business user will hold you responsible for any delays, missed requirements, bugs in the system, or misconduct of the team.

Ways to Prepare for the Interview

Books, Magazines, Organizations, and Seminars

The bibliography for this chapter lists many places to obtain information on good management practices. Look for books both on information technology management and on business management. Look for books and articles by management gurus such as Peter Drucker, C. A. Gallagher and A. Maslow. They provide a wealth of information that is useful to a manager of any discipline. Information management gurus such as Tom De Marco, M. Page-Jones, Ed Yourdon, L. L. Constantine, and many others provide tailored, tried-and-true approaches.

As you will be working closely with users, read a book on the business subject area. Understanding the business is becoming more crucial than understanding the details of the technical environment. In fact, it is becoming increasingly popular for the business user to be one of the interviewers. To prepare further, purchase a copy of *Harvard Business Review*. It is a good management magazine that is read by business users as well as IT management.

Many IT magazines such as *CIO Magazine* and other titles listed in the bibliography have articles on project management and people management concepts. These magazines will also have articles on technical concepts, both overviews and more detailed treatments.

The American Management Association (AMA) is worth contacting for management information. A specific IT source would be the Software Engineering Institute (SEI) of Carnegie Mellon University, which gives specific insight into managing the software process in the 90s, including the latest standards (ISO 9000 and CMM).

Many technical seminars, such as the ones given by Digital Consulting and Technology Transfer Institute, have project management workshops pertaining to different philosophies as well as technology overview seminars. Another avenue to investigate would be your current organization. They may have courses on delegation, negotiation, and listening skills; all will assist you in preparation for project management.

Software Packages You Should Know

Learn a project management tool. Several exist for the PC such as Microsoft Project and Applied Business Technology/Project Workbench. Both of these tools have extensive help facilities including dictionaries of project management terms.

As a complement to the above, there is an increasingly popular tool that provides assistance in planning, estimating, and methodologies targeted toward different technological environments. This tool, LBMS/Process Engineer, also interfaces with application development, thus creating a project book.

If you have experience in these tools, make sure you list them on your résumé. However, tools alone will not help you schedule. You will need a touch of good old common sense and an understanding of project management methodologies.

A project manager must be resourceful. Communication via E-mail has superseded telephone calls and mailed memorandums. Many corporations use their own facility; however, many corporations are implementing Lotus Notes or MS/Mail for this purpose. Whatever product is used, this facility is excellent, as it:

- provides access to many people at varied locations
- provides an excellent means of keeping all groups (including support groups) notified of changes in scope and schedules
- can be used to resolve small issues quickly

Keep in mind different work styles: introverts tend to prefer communicating by E-mail. It provides them time to think about a reply vs. being put on the spot in a meeting requiring immediate answers.

As a project manager you will be called upon to give reports and presentations. Therefore, you need to know how to use common word processors as well as a graphics package. List the ones you have used on your résumé.

Look Around for Ideas

As with any profession, you have good and bad project managers. You can learn and pick up tips (what to do and what to avoid doing) from observing both types. If possible, ask a good manager what he or she believes makes a good manager. If you don't want to disclose your career plans, mention an article you've just read and ask for the project manager's opinion.

A sign of a *good manager* is one with a happy, motivated team, the trust of upper management, and the respect of the user community. Consistent action is another sign, as it provides the basis for everyone to effectively measure their leadership abilities. Good managers tend to understand each employee's strengths and weaknesses. They accept failures not as weaknesses, but as learning experiences.

Managers must set a standard of professionalism. However, management by perfect example is a sign of a bad manager. It illustrates an inability to delegate or communicate. It also burns the manager out while demotivating the very people he or she is attempting to motivate. If people doubt they can live up to your expectations, they may not bother to try. Your technical abilities should be used to coach and guide trainees. If you are spending time coding or designing, you are not developing your team and not being a project manager.

Project Plan Terminology

Below are common project planning terms and charts to study for the interview. Most project planning tools use some or all of these terms or facilities. You may wish to review the HELP facility of one or more of the project management tools to help familiarize yourself with the common terminology and functionality.

Chart types:

Gantt chart: A chart depicting the schedule in graphic form, specifically a bar chart. Each bar symbol has different meanings. For example, a critical task will probably have a different bar symbol and/or color than a noncritical task. A summary task (for activity or phase) will have a different symbol from any task.

Pert chart: A flowchart illustrating the linear dependencies of all tasks. PERT stands for Program Evaluation and Review Technique, which is represented in a network-type diagram.

Task list: Textual/column listing of the project plan. Usually includes the following minimal columns: Task Id, Task Name, Start Date, End Date, Duration, and Work Effort.

Work breakdown structure (WBS): A structure chart view of the tasks and/or activities of the project.

Critical path: The path through the project illustrating dependencies of what must be accomplished for successful completion within time constraints. Adjustment of the time period to complete a task on the critical path will impact the delivery schedule of the system. The critical path method (CPM) chart is a network diagram used in scheduling and coordinating the various activities and events of a project.

Deliverable: A tangible item to prove completion of one or more tasks. An example would be the logical data model.

Dependencies: The links between tasks indicating which tasks have an impact on the start of other tasks. For instance, you cannot code until you have identified and understood the requirements.

JAD/Facilitation: Joint Application Development (Facilitation being the 90s term). A set of results-oriented, brainstorming, information gathering/sharing meetings with a common business objective. Developed by IBM in the 1970s, this approach has strongly structured procedures and is led by an experienced facilitator. Facilitation has removed some of the structure; however, it still requires that all parties be present at all meetings and a scribe, knowledgeable about modeling techniques, be available to take notes. Attendees include the project team, management (IS and user) and the executive sponsor. In order for the meetings to be successful, everyone must understand and agree to the objectives and be quick to resolve their assignments.

Lag: Elapsed time between the end of one task and the start of the dependent one. This facility allows overlaps or long stretches of time between the end of one task and the start of the other.

Methodology: A well-defined, organized, repeatable, structured approach/technique for achieving a generic objective. These techniques or guidelines define steps, tasks, roles, objectives, and deliverables that are required for successful implementation of any system.

Metrics: A consistent and repeatable means of measuring the size and complexity of a project. Metrics is calculated using one of many methods throughout the life of the project. Popular methods used by corporations today are:

- Function Point (Allan Abrecht)
- Bang (Tom De Marco)
- Weighted Average
- Lines of Code

Milestone: A completion of an important event in the life of the project. Usually a milestone is an activity that is on the critical path. It does not necessarily need to be a tangible deliverable such as the completion of a Logical Data Model but it could be User Approval to begin the effort.

Phase/activity/summary headings: Summary group levels. Not all project management tools insist on specific phase and activity summary level formats. However, many standard development methodologies do use these terms for breakdowns.

RAD: Rapid Application Development (or Destruction, if used incorrectly). An approach to quicken the development effort through the use of application generators, modeling, and prototyping tools. The biggest enhancement is the addition of prototyping throughout the development life cycle. This provides an excellent vehicle to ascertain and clarify user requirements before and during coding efforts.

Resource constraint: A plan and schedule developed with consideration of the resources available, the level of skills of each resource, and the resource work schedule.

Scope creep: The addition of required functionality from the original design without assessing the impact on people, time, or cost. The scope creep could be initiated by a business user or a zealous programmer. Both impact delivery of the system and may not have been estimated, analyzed, or documented.

Points to Convey on the Interview (Even if the Questions Are Not Asked)

If You Don't Have Management Experience

Many people who have never officially managed a project have managed it unofficially. Identify and promote those skills you did not realize you had, while stressing the benefits of having the technological background. This can be done by mentioning how you participated on a large development team where you had a leadership role without the authority.

Stress that without a solid technical foundation, your decisions on project tasks and estimates may be oversimplified. As leader of the project, you need to provide technical coherence as well as preventing opinions being passed off as facts by your team.

If Your Technology Skills Are Out of Date or Differ from the Prospective Technical Environment

You do not need to understand the inner workings of the technical environment. You should, however, understand the general concepts and features to determine the capabilities and weaknesses of the environment.

Many project management skills cross technological boundaries. Therefore, if your technology skills are out of date, you can still stress your strengths in the technologically independent responsibilities.

Mention the size and type of applications you have managed and their business impact. Mention the effectiveness of the team in accomplishing the objectives.

Stress your management philosophy. Mention how upper management, your peers, your users, and subordinates describe your managerial strengths and areas for growth and remember to mention any business area knowledge you may have.

Put your fears of out-of-date skills aside for the duration of the interview. Once you have the job, you will be able to ask questions from the in-house experts. In every organization there is an informal matrix of knowledgeable experts on all topics. Ask around to find out who they are.

Questions to Ask the Interviewer

Even if you pass the interviewer's qualifications and are offered the position, you need information to determine if this would be a good opportunity for you. This is especially crucial if this will be the first project manager assignment. You need to understand the environment you will be working in. Therefore, you may wish to ask the following questions:

1. What are the corporate priorities?
2. What is the executive sponsorship of this project?
3. What is the company's development methodology?
4. What deadlines are imposed on this project?
5. Is there a formal measurement of project success?
6. How would your new manager prefer to be kept informed of the project?
7. What is your new manager's management philosophy and style?
8. What are the skill levels of the people on the project?
9. Is the project's scope well defined?
10. Has the technological environment already been selected?

Typical Project Management Interview Questions (and the Answers Expected)

The following is a list of commonly asked questions for a project manager position with the answers that could be given. Many questions have subjective answers: the interviewer is attempting to find out if your point of view matches theirs and the company's. The questions are organized as follows:

1. project management software tool knowledge
2. project planning techniques
3. people management skills
4. communication skills
5. methodology knowledge (standard development life cycle and project management)

Project Management Software Tool Knowledge

Q: *What is the difference between duration and work effort?*

A: Duration is Business/Calendar Elapsed Days with no correlation to the number of people or their effort involved. Work effort is person effort with no correlation to the number of calendar days. *For example:* A one-day task for someone working 50 percent of their time will have 2 duration days. Two people working full-time on a one-day task will show one duration day but a two work day effort.

Q: *How and why would you build dependencies into the project plan?*

A: Dependencies, depending on the software package, can be linked both as a precessor and successor link through the associations of the task ids involved.

   Dependencies state the need for association/coordination between tasks. As an example, the dependency could be that a task must be started and maybe completed before another task can begin: the logical data model is done before the physical data model. However, not all the programming needs to be completed before any testing can begin if the unfinished program has no impact on the specific string test.

   The value of implementing dependencies into the project plan is the ability to determine the critical path as well as identifying the impact of slippage on the entire project.

Q: *How would you incorporate a person's work pace into the plan?*

A: Depending upon the specific tool the organization is using, a resource can be adjusted to be less than a full resource/unit or you can adjust each task the individual is working on to a lower percentage of time.

Q: *How would you incorporate training, holidays, and individuals' education schedules?*

A: Each product has a corporate/global calendar where common days off can be identified. Each product also has an individual resource calendar where the person's specific time off can be incorporated. Education and training that is needed for the project should be incorporated as a task in the project plan if it is specific for the project.

Q: *How do you spread a task that occurs throughout the project requiring little time and effort, such as status meetings?*

A: Duration would be set for the entire length of the project. Work effort would be listed as a small percentage of days. Everyone assigned to the task would have an extremely low percentage of time dedicated to the task.

Q: *How are actuals supplied to the plan and what is the value of comparing the original estimates to actuals?*

A: Depending upon the specific tool the organization is using, each tool provides a separate element/field to enter in actual information. Also available are assorted reports to illustrate the change in critical path, or the adjustments in schedules for your people and support groups. These reports are valuable for post-implementation reviews as input in planning the next project or phase. Another valuable use of comparing the estimate to actuals is to document the impact that scope creep had on the project.

Project Planning Techniques

Q: *Why would you build a project plan?*

A: A project plan is a road map for implementing a successful system. It provides a vehicle to notify everyone what is expected of them as well as when it needs to be done. It assists the project manager in keeping upper management, business users, and support groups informed on project status as well as the timing of specific resources. The itemized "to do list" has dependencies built in to assist in quickly assessing any impact of slippage. Project plans, when actuals are associated to the plan, provide valuable information for the planning of future projects by clarifying over- and underestimation of tasks.

Q: *How would you go about planning the project?*

A: Scheduling is an art. It is based upon the known facts about the business objectives, the generic company standards, if available, and past experience. One can begin by defining the scope and objectives clearly. Document the risks and constraints of the project. Poor estimates stem from lack of knowledge of the business and what is involved within the project scope.

  One can then begin by dividing the project into component tasks such as phases, activities within each phase, and tasks within each activity. Identify and document milestones and deliverables.

  The project plan is a living document that needs to be developed, in its finer details, in stages, as information becomes available. Changes in schedule need to be well documented for the project manager, the team, and support groups, as well as upper management and business users.

Q: *How would you go about building a project plan?*

A: Type in the identified tasks under the appropriate activity and phase or other summary level descriptions. Associate the appropriate deliverables and milestones to the specific task. Link all tasks requiring dependency associations. Add resource roles or resource names to each task. Apply metric results to identify preliminary task work efforts, applying more time to requirements gathering, design, and testing. Apply any known holidays, training, vacations, or other resource downtime. The draft plan would be reviewed with support groups, upper management, and business users for additional input and final approval.

Q: *How do you determine staffing requirements?*

A: Develop the plan without resource constraints. Add roles such as data modeler, business analyst, and user next to the tasks. Add additional resources where tasks can be overlapped. Always plan around losing one or more resources from the project team, including support and user representatives, by adding 15 percent to each task. As the project team becomes known, supplement the roles with the names, with the appropriate skill level allocated.

Q: *What value does metrics add to the project?*

A: Metrics is a valuable tool if used properly. It provides a consistent way of measuring complexity and effort of developing a system. Metric results provide a source of input in developing a project plan as well as valuable historical information in identifying the impact of development trends. As a result, software metrics will assist in developing better software. However, three years of history is recommended.

Q: *How would you incorporate the use of a new technology into the plan?*

A: Add tasks for training as well as expanding the work effort and lowering each individual's unit of work. Add extra prototypes and checkpoints (milestones) in evaluating the impact of the new technology on the development effort.

People Management Skills

Q: *What is the first thing you would do as a project manager?*

A: Besides attending any corporate orientation and finding your way around the building, keep in mind the priorities of the project manager (business, company, project, team, individuals, and changes in technology and methodologies). Therefore, meet with the manager to identify the priorities, schedule a meeting with the users and staff, obtain status reports and appraisals of all team members. Hold meetings. The important thing is to get up to speed as soon as possible on the business, the project, and the individuals.

Q: *How would you go about complying with the corporate directive to reduce your staff by 30 percent?*

A: First identify and prioritize what projects must be accomplished over the next 18 months. Associate the absolute minimum headcount to each project. Illustrate the impact on the schedule to management *and* users. Both may be unwilling to accept any change in schedule and may give you an exception.

   Even the best of consultants is expendable over an employee. Look at each project a consultant may be assigned to and replace the consultant with an employee. Insist on a learning curve and a slow reduction of valuable consultants. Some consultants may reduce their work week to two or three days to assist with the cutback.

   If the company is offering an early retirement package, look for those employees who qualify and might apply. Keep in mind that by losing "old-timers" you may be losing valuable knowledge. Assign any possible retiree another person to act as a mentor as soon as possible.

   Of the staff remaining, prioritize those who are crucial in meeting the business objectives. Prioritize them within each project. Make sure you have an even mix of trainees and senior-level people. Both are an asset to the continued success of the project and the company.

Q: *Your team is primarily junior-level people and you are behind schedule with a drop-dead deliverable date. What would you do?*

A: Keep in mind that it is extremely rare for a project to be canceled due to a missed deadline. Projects are canceled due to lack of funds, lack of user support, or unsatisfied business objectives.

Therefore, the first thing to do is to set up training either in-house or outside via classroom or videotapes. An additional option would be to transfer qualified employees or hire consultants to act as mentors and coaches.

Hold individual meetings with review and coach sessions. Help each employee accurately assess his or her strengths and weaknesses. Use that time to describe assignments clearly, making clear any standards or guidelines that must be followed. Supply each employee with templates from other successful projects as a guide, still allowing them the opportunity to apply their own flair. If needed, work intensively with them. Give prompt feedback on any questions or tasks completed.

With each large task, ask to see their plan of attack to determine if they understand scope and objective as well as to see if they can handle the task at hand. Listen to the employees' views as they may be on the right track or have a better way of accomplishing the task at hand. However, prevent professional pride from getting the person into deeper trouble that leads to frustration and poor morale.

Q: *How will you interface with the employee who expected the position you are applying for?*

A: This is an uncomfortable situation but one that occurs often. Employees sometimes think they are ready for a position before management does. Therefore, perform the following research:

- find out management's perception of the employee
- read appraisals and status reports
- find out if any transfer options are available if the employee becomes uncooperative
- hold a meeting with the individual to discuss the situation by:
  — identifying the situation
  — discussing qualities the employee has that qualifies him or her for the promotion
  — discussing qualities that need to be improved
  — stressing the need for assistance during the early stages and how the cooperation will be viewed highly by management

Q: *How much freedom would you give your employees in decisions and work style?*

A: The amount of freedom would depend on the level of skills and professionalism of each individual. A good manager is results oriented and creates an environment of open team communication. However, weekly status reports, tied to the project plan and business objectives, need to be submitted by each employee and reviewed by the manager. This will enforce constructive structure while keeping each employee focused on the ultimate deliverables.

Q: *How would you deal with an "on-the-job-retirement" employee?*
A: On-the-job-retirement types provide a great deal of information. One must think twice before letting all that business and people network knowledge out the door. Therefore, use the person's strength:

- assign to a junior team member as a mentor for a specific skill
- identify key work interest and align with a project that incorporates the skill
- use as a facilitator to grease wheels for needed favors from the informal network (and get a job done without going through the normal bureaucratic channels)

Q: *How would you deal with a consistently late employee?*
A: Good managers evaluate employees by results vs. time at desk. However, one needs to also assess the impact the lateness has on the company policy and the team members. One person coming in whenever he or she pleases creates a sense of favoritism and low morale on the team. Also, the person may be meeting his or her deadlines but impacting others' deadlines. Professionalism includes dependability. If others depend on their work, then their work schedule matters to the team.

First determine the employee's pattern. In other words, has it just started or is this a consistent habit? Next identify the company policy on flex time, definition of lateness, and warning policy. Determine if the employee's deliverables have been met and check deliverables of coworkers as well as their reaction to lateness.

Next the employee needs to be spoken to firmly and objectively. The topics discussed would be:

- company policy
- impact on the team
- impact on appraisal
- warning schedule
- mutual compromise and agreement

Q: *How would you go about building morale in a cost cutting environment?*
A: Money is not the only motivator. People need to feel that they are making a positive contribution to the business. Therefore, stress pride of ownership and hold business meetings where users talk about the positive impact they are having. At a similar meeting, have the business user give a general overview of their function and the business.

Training is a motivator. Therefore, status meetings could be used as informal training sessions. Run an occasional in-house workshop on new approaches in technology. Rent technological videotapes if courses are too expensive. Order magazine subscriptions—many technological magazines are available free of charge.

It is important to remember that if you ignore training, morale will deteriorate, thus affecting the quality and quantity of work produced.

Q: *How would you go about hiring someone?*
A: First create a job description of skills needed. It is hard to hire someone when you do not have an understanding of your requirements. Next understand the personality of the group. Itemize any skill or work style that is currently missing from the group. Discuss all of this with the Human Resources department including the transfer of existing employees. When a candidate arrives, interview the person for the job they already have as well as for the skills needed for the new position.

Q: *How would you resolve personality conflicts among team members?*
A: Identify the personality differences. Express the values of each style to each employee, individually. Be objective when attempting to isolate the specific complaint or source of the conflict when discussing them with all parties involved.

Q: *How would you monitor/manage consultants?*
A: Consultants are people too and need to be treated with respect. They must be clear on objectives and their work assignments. Insist on weekly status reports correlating the billing hours and the work accomplished.

Q: *How would you manage outsourced team members?*
A: The same way as other consultants. However, there is probably a contact point/engagement manager representing the outsourcing corporation. Hold daily meetings at first with that manager. Insist on weekly status reports and copies of deliverables correlating to the billable hours/days.

Q: *How would you work with an employee who seems to be consistently late on deliverables?*
A: The problem cannot be addressed until one can isolate the cause. The cause may not necessarily be a capability or analysis paralysis issue. It may be a management issue.

The person may not have the proper training for the job; it may be beyond what the person is capable of performing. Another possibility is that the person may have too much on his or her plate with everything a top priority, or they may have no understanding of the deliverable date.

If that is not the case, watch for the revolving door syndrome. This person may be overwhelmed with requests for answers. Therefore, the person is dealing with many interruptions, which are preventing him or her from meeting deadlines.

Communication Skills

Q: *How would you keep the users involved and informed during each phase of the project?*

A: Prototype throughout the project obtaining user approval. Have users research tangible and intangible benefits for cost-benefit analysis. Work with users to develop test data, test scenarios, and acceptance criteria. E-mail Milestone Status Reports and updated/revised project plans. Review deliverables during project reviews by phase.

Q: *How would you raise and resolve issues both within the unit and outside the unit?*

A: Obtain the facts from all possible sources and document the situation objectively. Then try to resolve the situation yourself with the pertinent party. If this does not work, bring the matter up within the management structure along with possible solutions.

Q: *How would you arrange and keep consistent support from support groups?*

A: Though support groups are outside of management control, they tend to stay involved when they:

- are treated with respect
- understand the business objective
- are brought in before the rush
- supply input into the plan that affects them
- are part of the design

Therefore, get buy-ins from the support group's management early into the project. Make sure they understand the business objectives and benefits of the effort.

Q: *How would you deal with "if it ain't broke" syndrome?*

A: Implementing technology for the sake of technology is not enough to sell the effort to users or upper management. However, if the technology can be tied to real business benefits, the user will help support your proposal. It is important to point out where the existing system *is* broken, by citing something tangible that has happened in the past that both parties are aware of.

Q: *How would you deal with or manage a difficult business user who:*

- refuses to commit to requirements
- constantly changes his or her mind
- refuses to spend time on the project
- insists on an unrealistic deadline
- requires stroking

A: One must keep in mind that the business user, no matter how difficult, is the reason we have the assignment. He or she is the customer, and as such must be treated with the utmost respect and a high level of professionalism.

Communication is complicated by the fact that business users do not understand our jobs—just as we do not fully understand theirs. Therefore, we need to spend some time setting expectations and explaining what is involved. However, users need to feel that they are not wasting their time, that progress is being made, and that they are being understood. Prototyping is a valuable tool. It provides a picture users can understand and it illustrates flexibility.

Again, understanding work styles is important. Refusing to commit or consistently changing one's mind could be due to a lack of understanding, or fear of closing out future possibilities.

Users typically refuse to spend time with an information technology person because of overcommitment to their other assignments or because they feel it will be a waste of time. One needs to check the history of deliverables in the past. If users have been approached many times before and have seen no valuable output, they will resist spending any more time. To work around this situation, do your homework in the business area; you will need to earn respect from them.

Send a memo requesting a one-hour meeting (and adhere to that time limit) to cover *specific* questions. End the meeting informing the user of what the next step will be (and commit to that). Users also value interview notes. It shows them that they were listened to and allows them a chance to correct any misconceptions.

When a project is canceled it is usually because the business user's needs are not being met in a cost-effective way. Users who are kept informed throughout the project will see their needs being met. Projects are rarely canceled due to missed deadlines. Be careful of scope creep. Adding requirements to an earlier agreed-upon deadline makes that deadline unrealistic.

Q: *How would you work in an environment that implies that if you are not coding you are not working?*

A: Users are more willing to wait for coding to begin if they feel you truly understand their business objectives. Documenting requirements in a form that they can understand provides for open communication and a comfort level that says you know what you are doing. Progress is also conveyed through project plans, status reports, and prototypes. Keep users involved by reviewing requirements, prototypes, and status reports.

Methodology Knowledge

Q: *What is a life cycle and why do you need one?*

A: A development or maintenance life cycle describes an approach to the beginning, the middle, and the implementation of a specific project. A life cycle pulls in all the steps, tasks, and/or activities needed to achieve the required objective. Each activity may have a separate method associated with it. For example, a data modeling activity may follow James Martin's data modeling methodology. Object modeling activities may correlate to Ivan Jacobson's approach. The life cycle pulls all the methodologies together into a process to achieve the business objective.

Q: *Describe what development project life cycle phases, activities, and deliverables you would include in a project plan.*

A: The phases, not in a waterfall/linear order, that would be included in the project plan would be the following:

1. Project management:

   Sample Activities: Many people tend to forget to add this phase to incorporate time-consuming project control type activities such as the development and maintaining of the project plan; status meetings and reports; metric gathering and reporting; and presentation development and the actual presentation to upper management and business users.

   Sample Deliverables: Project plan, status reports, metric reports (such as function point counts)

2. Business requirements/analysis:

   Sample Activities: Scope definition, initial cost benefit analysis, recommendations

   Sample Deliverables: Scope document, current physical and logical/essential analysis, entity-relationship diagram, cost benefit analysis, business rules declaration, task definitions and scenarios

3. Design:

   Sample Activities: Setting up the development and test environment, logical modeling, technical system design, implementation plan

   Sample Deliverables: Physical data model, event model, object model, network model, physical design, state transition diagrams, specifications tailored to the implementation environment, conversion specifications, test plans, window navigation flows

4. Development:

   Sample Activities: Coding and unit testing and user documentation

   Sample Deliverables: Test scripts, procedure manuals, programs

5. Test:

   Sample Activities: Special hardware and software testing, string testing, system testing, integration testing, regression testing, and parallel testing

   Sample Deliverables: Test results, problem reporting and tracking log

6. Implementation and support:

   Sample Activities: Roll-out of first implementation phase; training sessions

   Sample Deliverables: Problem reporting procedures

7. Post review:

   Sample Activities: Three to six months after implementation to review the targeted cost, development effort, and tangible/intangible benefits

   Sample Deliverables: Post implementation report

Q: *Where does prototyping fit in to the project life cycle?*

A: Throughout the project—because seeing is believing. Prototyping is a good vehicle for verifying functionality, business rules, and data requirements with the users as well as for testing performance. Be careful, however, that prototypes do not become quick-and-dirty production applications. Production prototypes are notorious for requiring high maintenance. Prototypes should illustrate windows and window navigation without full process and data descriptions.

Q: *How does client/server and mainframe development differ in a project life cycle?*

A: Additional tasks are needed for client/server to determine the partitioning scheme. Review of events, data, and network location must be done to determine partitioning scheme. Partitioning must determine server/client split via user needs and performance. Formal modeling techniques are used in conjunction with prototyping with graphical user interface (GUI) windows in a client/server environment.

Q: *How would you manage and ensure quality on a maintenance project?*

A: Maintenance itself has a negative connotation. Many corporations view maintenance as a necessary evil and a second-class citizen. It is costly and a continual process of modifying an existing application. What must be understood is that maintenance has a life cycle of its own. Therefore, establishing a project plan around the maintenance activities assists in the control and quality of the effort. As with a new development plan, building in deliverables and the allowance of time for each task will assist in building quality. The project plan needs to have all change requests incorporated. This will enable the project manager and users to see impacts of new changes on existing schedule changes. The maintenance phases/activities are:

1. identification of the change (whether caused by a production problem, new feature, or a change in technological platforms)
2. formal recording of the change request
3. validation of the change and first estimate of size of the change
4. prioritization within list of existing changes
5. analysis of the change
7. programming of the change
8. system/regression testing of the change and the impact on the existing system
9. user acceptance of the change
10. production turnover
11. production

Q: *How does object-oriented development differ in project management techniques from traditional development?*

A: Object-oriented projects tend to require smaller and less aggressive teams. What is important is the skill set and the roles of the individuals. Each team member may need to perform different roles at different phases of the project. Therefore, the individual must be honest about their strengths and weaknesses. The roles, encompassing one or more individuals, are:

- architect (system's overall structure)
- abstractionist (class and class categories)
- application engineer (implement and assemble the classes and messages between them)

As with traditional development, individuals are not interchangeable parts. Software development is a human endeavor. Even a team of the best and brightest will not successfully implement the most simple of projects if they cannot work together toward the common goal.

Q: *How would you divide your time between employee relations, project management, and paperwork?*

A: People are the most valuable asset, and they take the most time. However, a project manager must focus on, in the following order:

1. the business objectives
2. the company objectives
3. the project
4. the team
5. individuals
6. changes in technology and methodology approaches

Q: *What is the P-CMM?*

A: People Management Capability Maturity Model. Both P-CMM and CMM are conceptual models developed by the Software Engineering Institute (SEI) in conjunction with Carnegie Mellon University. The P provides guidance for organizations in managing human resources. The five levels are:

1. Initial: no consistency in managing people
2. Repeatable: policies committing the organization to employee practices and procedures
3. Defined: employee practices tied to nature of business
4. Measured: quantitative objectives to people management
5. Optimizing: organizational focus on continual improvement of people management

Summary

A successful team is achieved when a well-motivated group of individuals with varying skills, talents, work styles, and knowledge accomplishes the business objective. It is the responsibility of the project manager to assemble and motivate this group into performing as a team.

This chapter provided guidance in preparing for the interview by reviewing common concepts and terminology and giving a sampling of the most common questions asked on the interview. It is up to you to tailor the answers based upon your knowledge and experience of what a good project manager is.

Whatever your answers, show your desire to have an impact on the organization, to be strong and influential in a positive manner, to be people oriented, with a good technical background. Remember to show common sense, confidence, and the ability to listen and make decisions.

Bibliography

Booch, Grady, "The Development Team," *Report on Object Analysis & Design,* March-April 1995, pp. 2–8.

Constantine, Larry L., and Lucy A. D. Lockwood, "Fitting Practices to the People," *American Programmer,* December 1994, pp. 21–27.

Curtis, Bill, William E. Hefley, Sally Miller, Michael Konrad, and Sandra Bond, "Increasing Software Talent," *American Programmer,* December 1994, pp. 13–20.

De Marco, Tom, "Standing Naked in the Snow," *American Programmer,* December 1994, pp. 28–30.

Ferdinandi, Patricia L., "Reengineering with the Right Types," *Software Development,* July 1994, pp. 45–51.

Gottesdiener, Ellen, "What's New in Client/Server Development Methods," *Application Development Trends,* November 1994, pp. 50–61.

Hayes, Ian S., "Project Management: How It Can Improve the Maintenance Process," *Application Development Trends,* October 1994, pp. 48–61.

Humphrey, Watts S., "A Personal Commitment to Software Quality," *American Programmer,* December 1994, pp. 2–12.

Keuffel, Warren, "Function Points: Pro and Con," *Software Development,* November 1994, pp. 23–27.

Keuffel, Warren, "More Bang for Your Modeling Bucks," *Software Development,* August 1994, pp. 27–33.

Keuffel, Warren, "Predicting with Function Point Metrics," *Software Development,* July 1994, pp. 27–35.

McClelland, David C., and David H. Burnham, "Power Is the Great Motivator," *Harvard Business Review,* January–February 1995, pp. 126–139.

Page-Jones, Meiler, *Practical Project Management: Restoring Quality to DP Projects and Systems,* Dorset House, 1985.

Rubin, Howard, *IT Metrics Strategies,* The Cutter Information Group, vol 1, no. 1.

Tagiuri, Renato, "Managing People: Ten Essential Behaviors," *Harvard Business Review,* January–February 1995, pp. 10–11.

"The Manager's Toolbox," Part 1–4, *The Type Reporter,* vol. 3, no. 9, February–August 1989.

Thomsett, Rob, "When the Rubber Hits the Road: A Guide to Implementing Self-Managing Teams," *American Programmer,* December 1994, pp. 37–45.

Wiegers, Karl, "Creating a Software Engineering Culture," *Software Development,* July 1994, pp. 59–66.

Whitaker, Ken, "Managing Software Maniacs," *American Programmer,* December 1994, pp. 31–36.

3

Interviewing Frameworks

Barry Glasgow, Ph.D.

Introduction

There are two categories of questions asked during the job interview—technical and general. This chapter is concerned with general issues, and does not concentrate on a particular job description (e.g., programmer analyst, communication engineer, C/UNIX programmer) or technology (e.g., information engineering, COBOL, DB2). Subsequent chapters will present detailed domain questions from these areas.

The goal of this chapter is to give some insight into what general questions employers ask and why they ask them, enabling the applicant to think about and prepare answers *prior to the interview.* Since the employer is also interested in nontechnical issues it is important that the job applicant have an understanding of how the interactions between interviewer and applicant occur. Many different types of nontechnical questions should be anticipated. Taking the time to prepare gives you more of a chance of getting the job. The more you prepare, the less chance there is that the interviewer will spring something at you that will catch you off guard. Hopefully this chapter will give the reader insight into what MIS managers are looking for when interviewing a job candidate. MIS managers want to:

1. Find out if the job applicant is suitable for the position.

2. Provide sufficient information for the applicant to realistically evaluate the position and the company.

The ultimate goal of the employment process is to hire a competent employee who can perform the current job, has potential for future growth, and is reasonably happy with the position.

It would be nice if the manager could describe the position, its responsibilities and technical requirements, and then ask the applicant to rate his or her qualifications and abilities to handle the position. Unfortunately, this naive approach does not work. The interview process should be structured to essentially achieve this result.

In most situations getting the job is a two-step process. The first step is to pass the personnel department interview. This is usually the "easier" interview. Personnel department interviews are designed to see that you have, as a minimum, the required credentials. The second, and harder part, is the interview(s) involving technical as well as nontechnical requirements. At least one of these interview sessions will probably be with your immediate manager. To facilitate hiring, many managers organize the informational aspects of the interview into frameworks or categories of informational needs in order to efficiently organize, analyze, and collect enough data so that a hire/no hire decision can be made.

This chapter discusses:

- Three frameworks for achieving this goal
- Knowledge to be collected from each phase
- Purpose and analysis of this data, and
- Interviewing techniques

Does every interviewer use these frameworks? No. Some interviewers have alternative sets of frameworks—different ways they determine the applicability of a job candidate. Although the organization of the interview may be different, there often is a large overlap of questions. Other interviewers will not have taken the time or expended the effort to organize their goals for this meeting.

Three frameworks I use during the job interview and applicant evaluation are:

- The Input-Analysis-Output (IAO) model
- Evidence-Analysis (EA) procedure
- The Job-Employee-Employer (JEE) model

The Input-Analysis-Output (IAO) Model

The IAO model addresses two concerns: the employer's and the applicant's.

The employer analyzes the information presented by the applicant to produce the required outputs for judging the individual suitability for the position requirements as documented in the JEE model.

The Inputs to This Model Include the Applicant's

- Résumé
- Physical appearance

- Answers during the interview
- Written work, including tests and previous work
- Questions
- Education, transcripts
- References

The Outputs of This Model Include

- Appraisal of job skills, including:
  Technical competency
  Business knowledge
  Communication skills, both verbal and written
- Work ethics evaluation, including:
  Ability to work with others
  Handling long hours, emergencies, pressure
  Honesty/integrity
- Job satisfaction forecast, including:
  Probability that applicant will stay at least two years
  Salary and benefit expectations
  Growth potential

  The applicant has less physical evidence to go on:

- Annual reports, recent news articles
- Information from company's human resource department
- Answers and questions during the interview

The Applicant's Goal Is to Assess

- What the position entails:
  Job description
  Technical skills required
  Hardware platform
  Software
  Maintenance versus development
  Chance to learn new technical skills
- Working environment, including:
  Project team or independent work
  Amount of client contact
  Overtime responsibility
  Work at home, emergencies, time and financial compensations

- Career path opportunity:

  Chances of advancement

  Current salary, potential for increases, bonus

  Benefits, education, training

  Stability of position, chances of a layoff

Evidence-Analysis (EA) Procedure

A special type of analysis beyond the IAO must be done to verify and validate the information presented. Verification is the process of checking individual facts about the employee (e.g., if the applicant actually worked at a particular company for the time period specified on the résumé). Validation looks at the applicant's total image for consistency (e.g., the applicant claims to have a master's degree in engineering from a foreign university; no transcript is available, but the applicant cannot answer questions about calculus).

The applicant wants to convey his or her competence and ability to do the job. Unless there is a total mismatch, the applicant never wants to reject the position during an interview. The employer wants to convey that this is a good opportunity, one that will advance the applicant's career. The manager, assuming it is not a complete mismatch, wants to hold out the promise that a reasonable applicant may be hired. The manager does not know if future applicants will be as good or whether a previous better applicant will accept the position.

Given the deviousness and cross-purposes of each party, it is the responsibility of each party to verify and validate what has been said and what conclusions have been reached.

It behooves each party to:

- Test the information for consistency and completeness

- When required, expand and ask for additional explanations

- Interpret

The applicant has less physical evidence to validate than the employer. His or her sources of information include the company's annual reports (if a publicly held company), individuals the applicant knows who have worked for the company or manager, and company policy as written in employee handbooks and literature.

The employer has references, previous work history, and educational records that can be verified. Data relating to work done, people supervised, courses taken, and salary history have to be checked.

The Job-Employee-Employer (JEE) Model

In the JEE framework the particular requirements of the position are assessed. The employer, through an accurate job description and understanding of the position responsibilities, attaches weights to these requirements and emphasizes them during the employment process. Similarly, it helps the employee to understand how his or her strengths relate to the particular position. JEE provides a weighting factor (on a scale from 1 to 10) to evaluate the importance of each requirement.

A programmer working on a particular algorithm may require technical competence above all else, whereas a business analyst will need balance between business knowledge, communication skills, and technical competence.

Interplay between IAO and JEE Frameworks

IAO determines how well (on a scale from 1 to 10) the applicant scored on each requirement. JEE attaches the weights to these requirements based on the particulars of the job description and the employer's needs. The applicant's score can be found by multiplying his or her grade on each requirement (from IAO) by the importance placed on that requirement (from JEE) and summing across all requirements.

Questions and Answers

Remember, the answer to a question is assembled from all the inputs described in the IAO model. The résumé will provide initial chronological ordering of your work history and highlight relevant skills for the job. The interviewer will want you to elaborate and expand on areas relevant to the position.

Question-asking is an iterative nonlinear process. The initial data supplied by your inputs, driven by the goals from JEE, suggest successive series of questions. The interviewer will sometimes focus a series of questions to clarify a detail, or ask open questions to get new material not previously covered or suspected.

A good question gets new information from you, something the interviewer did not already know, whether favorable or unfavorable. The best answer you can give is an honest answer that gives the interviewer the required information and also suggests other questions that will accentuate your positives and allow you to talk about your strengths.

Sample Questions and Analysis

Why an interviewer asks a question and what his or her goals are is germane to how you answer. I have indicated the framework or, in some cases, the multiple frameworks in which the information from a question will be used.

Technical questions will be found in the appropriate chapters. We will concentrate on questions that establish the applicant's work ethic, preferred style of work, and desired career path.

Q: *Why are you leaving your current position?*
A: (IAO, EA.) Interviewer is trying to find out if (1) you are leaving voluntarily or (2) you were let go. If (1), what are your motives (i.e., primarily financial,

career enhancement, dissatisfaction with your current position)? If (2), what was the reason (i.e., being a casualty of an overall downsizing, lack of technical skills, work ethics, working relations with fellow workers)?

References and your total work history will be used to collaborate and verify your answer.

Q: *Why have you left your last several positions after a short period (less than two years)?*
A: (EA, IAO.) A pattern of frequent job changes has to be explained.

Q: *How did you get along with your coworkers, superiors, clients?*
A: (IAO, JEE.) "I got along fine with everyone." Analysis: too general, a platitude. If you had a problem, it may be helpful and informative to describe how you solved it. Reality is that you can't have a perfect relationship with everyone, so explain how you handled a problem.

Q: *How did you communicate with your coworkers, superiors, clients?*
A: (IAO, JEE.) This is an alternate form of the previous question which can be used to probe for writing skills, familiarity with E-mail, and whether or not you use PCs.

Q: *Did you work as a team member (how many people on the team) or individually?*
A: (IAO, JEE.) How did the employee relate to a team? What role was assumed? Was the applicant a leader or a follower? (Both can be valuable depending upon the particular position.)

Q: *Do you want management responsibilities?*
A: (JEE, IAO.) Employee has shown technical ability in previous job, but this is the first position where applicant will be a project leader and assume supervisory responsibility.

Q: *Did you have management responsibilities?*
A: 1. Project management. (JEE.) Managing a multiperson, multiphase software project is a distinct skill. The interviewer is looking for familiarity with different project and task representations, such as PERT or Gantt charts, and with concepts such as critical path, resource loading, slack and lead time.

   2. Budgeting. (IAO, JEE.) You may have experience being a project leader, but not the responsibilities for budgeting the project.

   3. Supervisory experience. How did you deal with a difficult employee (incompetent, poor work habits)? (IAO, EA.) Dealing with a problem employee is a critical success factor in management. Poorly handled, it can result in an employee being fired or a project team being demoralized. The interviewer is trying to learn something about your style, how you approach interpersonal work relations. Also, if you have inflated your previous management experience, it may be hard for you to describe how you have dealt with a difficult employee.

Q: *Did you have to write? What type of documents? (JEE, IAO.) If the position involves heavy analysis, contact with operations (either computer and/or back office), or client contact, then the ability to communicate in written and verbal form is very important.*

A: Contrast these two answers:

1. Answer A: "I write memos when I have to."
2. Answer B: "I have prepared formal documents including graphical elements using a word processor and incorporating outputs from a spread sheet."

Q: *Have you made presentations to management and/or clients?*

A: (JEE, IAO.) An important skill for an analyst or project manager is the ability to present information.

Q: *Can you use a PC for presentations, word processing?*

A: (IAO.) You have begun to pursue new technology.

Q: *What is your salary history?*

A: (JEE, EA.) This information should already be known to the interviewer. Your answers to this question and the next allow a manager to judge how important financial considerations are in order for you to accept the job. Your answer should be factual and correct.

Q: *What are your expectations for future raises and a bonus?*

A: (IAO, EA.) The interviewer is trying to ascertain whether you will be happy, from a financial perspective, at this job. Also, if you are aggressive in your financial requirements, there is an inference that this may relate to why you are leaving your current position.

Q: *Will you be going to school, college, graduate school?*

A: (IAO, JEE.) On the positive side, going to school indicates the desire to improve your skills and motivation to stay current (assuming that your class-work relates to the required skills of the position). On the negative side, it represents time you cannot spend on the job. If the new position requires tight deadlines, overtime, and resolution of frequent production problems, then you must explain how schooling can be handled in this context. It is important to indicate whether your schooling is degree-related and to determine what the tuition reimbursement policy is.

Q: *Do you like to work independently or on teams?*

A: (JEE.) There is no right answer to this question. It gets down to your personality. Some MIS jobs are extremely technical and relatively isolated, where an asocial hacker might be acceptable. On the other hand, many MIS projects are large and require a team effort where cooperation, negotiation, and people skills are important.

Q: *Do you prefer to work directly with clients or from specifications?*

A: (JEE, IAO.) This is similar to the previous question. The nature of the position will dictate the amount of contact. An analyst's job will require heavy user interface. Hopefully, unless you are desperate, you are applying for jobs that emphasize your abilities and your likes.

Q: *What is your ideal position?*

A: (IAO.) What you say, what you don't say, and how you say it are all important. Do you emphasize personal growth, the ability to be visible, the chance to help your colleagues, financial reward?

Q: *Rate your skill level.*

A: (IAO, JEE, EA.) You know your own ability better than anyone else. The interviewer is trying to get your own evaluation. However, the interviewer has probably formed an opinion of your strengths and weaknesses already. If your evaluation basically validates the interviewer, fine; if there is a large variance, then be prepared for detailed questions to clarify the difference in opinions.

Q: *How confident are you that you can perform this job?*

A: (EA, IAO, JEE.) Employers want confident employees, especially if they believe you are being honest. If the job is a real leap for you, it may be realistic to express some of the fears you have about the position, but the employer still expects you to feel comfortable that you can handle the new position.

Q: *What do you think is the hardest part of this job? Your past jobs?*

A: (EA, JEE.) A really bad answer is, "This is an easy job. There are no problems." Whereas the employer wants you to be confident, he or she does not expect you to think of this new position as trivial.

If you have been listening, and if the interviewer has been discussing the position, you should have formed some opinion of what will be difficult for you to do in this new position. By highlighting these areas, you show that you have a good understanding of the job.

Q: *What do you know about the business domain?*

A: (JEE, IAO.) The quality of software built improves if the programmer understands the business context of the system. If you do not currently understand the business domain, are you interested in learning it?

Q: *Can you handle the pressure, deadlines, and production problems?*

A: (JEE.) If you have personal or other commitments such that you cannot handle deadlines or production problems, it is important to discuss the implications of these constraints. It may cost you a position, but getting a pressure position that you cannot manage is worse.

Q: *Can you work at home or come into the office if a problem occurs outside of your normal work hours?*

A: (JEE, IAO.) If the position involves a critical application, you will be responsible for resolving production problems.

Q: *What skills do you want to learn or improve?*

A: (IAO.) The interviewer wants to know if you have a realistic understanding of your good and bad points and a plan for improving your weak areas and capitalizing on your strengths.

Q: *Where do you want to be in two, five years?*

A: (IAO.) If your goals are too aggressive, you may not be happy with the position. If you have no aspirations for advancement, you may not be alert to the challenge of the position.

Q: *Why do you want this job?*

A: (IAO, JEE, EA.) This is an open-ended question which gives you a chance to:

Show that you understand the position

Summarize your strengths and how they dovetail with the requirements for the position

Identify any issues that have to be resolved

In summary, we have presented a model of the interaction between the interviewee and interviewer. For the employer this framework provides guidelines as to how information can be extracted from the interview process.

4
Ways an Employment Agency Can Be of Use to You

Michael Sichel

Why should you use an employment agency? The main reason should be that employment agencies have contacts. Contacts that you don't have. Contacts that have taken years to develop. In addition they are also financially motivated to place the right (best qualified to do the job) people in the right job, so that both the employer and the employee will be satisfied. What *you* have to do is show that you are the best candidate, their best chance at filling the job opening.

We all should realize that looking for a new job is serious work. The job seeker may suddenly find him or herself in the position of asking some difficult questions, such as, "What kind of work do I really want to do?" and "How much can I expect to earn?"

These questions call for realistic self-examination and appraisal, and perhaps some conversations with a few close friends and associates. Only after they have been resolved is the job seeker ready to start looking for a job and begin to initiate consultations with qualified employment agents.

Types of Employment Agencies

Private employment agents or agencies are grouped by the method in which they receive compensation. The major categories are fee-paid, retained-search, and fee paid by applicant.

Fee-paid agencies receive their compensation from the employer only after successfully placing the applicant within that company. The determination of fee is made between the company and the agent; the applicant is in no way responsible for any payment to the agent.

Fee-paid agents provide professional guidance because they are paid by hiring companies to do so. These counselors are paid for successful performance, which is measured by getting the job seeker an appropriate job (i.e., one that correctly matches the needs of the candidate and the employer). Only a fee-paid agency will provide a combination of professional evaluation, tailored job search, and interview preparation at no cost to the job seeker.

Retained-search agencies receive their compensation from the employer at the inception of the search procedure. These firms also differ from fee-paid agencies in that they rigidly search out those who possess a preestablished set of experience and credentials. A retained-search firm is not likely to be interested in a candidate who does not meet their client's criteria; they will neither counsel nor assist those job seekers whose experience deviates from predetermined requirements.

Fee paid by applicant agencies receive their compensation from the job seeker. Payment may be made in full at the beginning of the search (on the guarantee of presenting the candidate's résumé to a given number of companies), or on the installment plan after the candidate has begun work for an employer to whom they were presented by the agency. In either event, the job seeker signs a binding agreement to pay them a fee out of his or her own pocket.

Selecting Employment Agencies

Assuming you opt for a fee-paid agency, your next step is to select at least three such agents or agencies in the data processing industry for optimum coverage. One of the better selection methods is word of mouth. If, for instance, your specialty is in the mainframe area, you might do well to ask other large-systems people about the agencies that placed them in their current job. If you do not know anyone who has the kind of job you're seeking, contact local user groups to ask for referrals to quality agents. Most employment agencies specialize, so be sure to identify your level of experience to your contact—a recent graduate with a B.S. degree in computer science should seek an agency that specializes in placing beginners rather than one that focuses on placing MIS directors.

When you are given the name of an agency, try to have your source also provide you with the name of a specific counselor who specializes in placing individuals at your career level. This distinction is very important, because counselors tend to specialize in specific industry niches. You will profit most from dealing with a counselor whose interest lies in your unique market.

While you are developing your list of specialists, start updating your résumé. Be sure to list your education, job experience, and references. Before using their names, contact those people whom you would like to use as references. Always get permission. It is the polite thing to do and you can be fairly sure that they will give you a good recommendation. Three or four references are enough. Your résumé is very important. It represents you. It has to sell your skills, and sell them better than other qualified candidates'. It is a good idea to check with your local bookstore (or library) for a copy of a leading résumé book. Use a common word processing software package, if available, to create a draft of your résumé, or pay someone to input it for you. You can always make adjustments, such as those suggested by your employment counselors, later on.

With your résumé and your list of agents and agencies before you, you're now ready to phone the counselors to arrange initial evaluation meetings. Bear in mind that although a counselor may appear less formal than a prospective employer, the counselor will nevertheless evaluate your professionalism, poise, and communication skills against those of other candidates. While you should try to relax and behave in an open and friendly manner, remember that you are initiating a business relationship.

Explain briefly to the agent the reason for your call, and be prepared to give a synopsis of your experience and goals. It's best to leave the subject of salary open, but don't be too evasive about past or current compensation. Close the conversation by asking for an appointment at the agent's earliest convenience. Remember, too, that the phrase, "thank you for your time" is still one of the most underused and overappreciated phrases in business. In the event that the counselor asks you to send a fax of your résumé prior to the interview, don't forget to include a brief cover letter—a paragraph is sufficient. It is important to realize that the agent's only estimate of how you will handle yourself with their treasured clients will be based on how you interact with them.

Employment Agency Interview

Your personal interview with the employment agent will define the way your personal traits, professional history, educational background, and goals conform to job opportunities in your selected area. Prepare by bringing with you your résumé, a pad for notes, a proper (preferably dark) interview suit, and an open mind. The agent's initial impression of you is likely to set the tone for the entire business relationship, and whether you get presented to their "A" or "B" list companies. Remember to smile, offer a firm handshake, and speak up in a confident tone.

As a general rule, you and the agent will begin with a review of your history as documented in the résumé. This is where you may begin to note changes in form or emphasis. A general discussion to fill in any blanks may follow. Normally, such talks will be led with open questions that invite a free discussion (e.g., "What is your current job like?" or "What do you see yourself doing in five years?"). By contrast, a closed question is designed to produce a much shorter response by narrowing your answer to a specific area. Examples include: "How much was your gross pay in 1992?" or "What is your address?"

After determining your experience and career goals, the agent may ask you to take a standard industry test in your skill set. You are advised to take this opportunity to show the agent what you know and how you handle yourself, even if the test is presented informally. Don't be defensive or consider a test as a personal attack, and avoid behaving defensively, or you may dampen the agent's interest in promoting you to their clients.

Following this evaluation, the agent will typically begin to explore specific job opportunities. With the full range of your qualifications in mind, the agent is ready to assess your interest in current positions that meet your unique experience and skills. This process also serves to help the agent fine-tune his or her understanding of what you're looking for. Once a group of job opportunities has been uncovered, the agent may advise you how best to present your credentials on paper.

After revising the outline, content, and emphasis of your résumé, the agent may ask about your availability for interviews. Of course, agents understand that if you are currently employed, your time is not entirely your own. In fact, most counselors respect your loyalty to your current job, even though you plan to leave it for a better job. This demonstrates your conscientiousness and professionalism.

Communication procedures (when and where to call each other) are the final part of this initial meeting. Be sure to let the agent know how much notice you require for an interview, and when your revisions to the résumé will be complete.

If negotiations are confidential, i.e., your current employer is *not* to be notified or called for information—now is the time to make this fact known. You may also request that you be notified as to which companies they are going to send your résumé to—prior to it being sent. At all costs you must avoid your résumé being sent to the same company by two different employment agencies.

Preparation for the Job Interview

Following your submission of the complete résumé, you may expect a call from the agent with a time and date for your first client interview. Typically, the agent will ask you to drop by the office an hour or two before the interview for a discussion of any issues peculiar to the client and department. After a brief discussion, which may cover appropriate dress for the interview and what to bring, don't forget the little courtesies that translate into polished interpersonal skills and are likely to keep your résumé on the top of the agent's list.

At the interview strategy meeting ask the agent for information about the client, i.e., a review of the client company, position at hand, interviewer, hiring cycle, and other related information. These details may include the size of the firm, gross sales, number of employees, product line, and so on. This overview will be geared toward your job's place in the scheme of things. Try to get information related to tangible realities, such as upward mobility within your potential department, the general culture of the company, its history, and perhaps some details about one or two of your potential colleagues.

Most importantly, the agent will review with you the job description, including duties and responsibilities, a history of the last person to have held this post, technical data on the department mechanisms that may affect you, an explanation of why the job is open, the person to whom you will report, salary range, and so forth. Of course, some of these details, especially those concerning personalities, are off the record.

The interview strategy meeting continues with a review of the process through which candidates proceed at this particular company. This process is referred to as the *hiring cycle*. You will be apprised of any tests you may be expected to take, the need for any peer interviews, personnel evaluations, department-head interviews, bonding exams, etc. Thus you will know what to expect throughout the hiring procedure.

Every interview is an opportunity to learn. The best way to approach an interview is with confidence in the fact that you will learn from the experience. Adjust your expectations accordingly. Don't go to the interview with a desire to prove or disprove, or to earn points or pass out judgments. Instead, be ready to give and receive information. When you are well prepared there is no need to be nervous. Always ask the client interviewer for company literature at the close of the interview.

The rule of thumb in any client follow-up situation is to contact the agent immediately following the interview. On occasion, the client interviewer will request that certain additional documentation be brought with you to subsequent interviews. This request might be for anything from a college diploma to a writing sample. Do not send any letters or information that has not been personally reviewed by the agent to the client company.

With three professional agents dialing the phones on your behalf, discretion is your part of the bargain. If asked, let each agent know that you are working with other counselors, but keep their names to yourself. In particular, hold the names of the companies with which you are currently interviewing in the strictest of confidence. Since agents are in constant competition with each other, such information is their stock-in-trade; sharing it with another agent would constitute a serious breach of trust which may also hurt you in the long run.

The initial client interview will also help you to narrow or, in some cases, expand the focus of the job search. During your follow-up conversation with the agent, share your thoughts and feelings about the job and department; describe the place within the department which is of most interest to you. It is not uncommon to hear an applicant make a comment like, "The posting department is the front end of the business; although I am still interested in similar jobs, I couldn't help becoming curious about the research group."

As mentioned earlier, the interviewing process can be a learning experience; it may be to your advantage to keep an open mind to various job opportunities presented by the agent. The interaction between agent and job seeker is flexible by nature—there should be room for change within the parameters of career goals and compensation set up at the evaluation stage. It is the agent's duty to provide the job seeker with a variety of options, and it is the job seeker's prerogative to either accept or decline pursuit of those options.

While the initial interview is usually with someone from the Human Resources (Personnel) department, the second meeting with the client company is usually with the hiring manager (who may be your immediate boss) and one or two peers. This is followed by a collective assessment of how well you meet both the required professional skills necessary to successfully perform the job function and also the intangible qualities required to fit in with the department. To properly prepare for this step, you need a strategy meeting with the agent.

The agent will counsel you on the setup of the department. You will be clued in on the variety of power structures, skills, personalities, and peculiarities of the department's inhabitants. For example, an individual manager might look for a person who can take the ball and run with it—failure to respond to his or her questions or comments with an extemporaneous solution might damage your hopes of landing the job. An experienced and qualified counselor should prepare you to safely avoid many hidden pitfalls, and you must use this information to your advantage.

The manner in which a job is initially presented by the personnel department and the reality of the day-to-day duties performed at the functional level may differ substantially. In this area of disparity, the agent may prove to be an invaluable guide in determining more accurately what is expected of the new employee. The agent may be able to provide you with a report of the current projects in the hiring manager's department, preparing you to make some positive analogies between your past experience and some current problems with which the department is dealing.

In some cases, a third party may be perceived as less threatening and therefore more effective in a fact-finding role. The agent may be viewed by the hiring company as an extension of the human resource department, a benign helper who is part of the team. In the purest sense, the agent is all of these and, as your counselor, he or she is also your advocate. The agent will not, of course, misrepresent the skills or abilities of the candidate to the hiring company. They will, however, provide the job seeker with the necessary information required to allow his or her full abilities to be fairly evaluated. In this sense, the interests of both parties are effectively served.

After your meeting(s) with the hiring department, a follow-up call or (preferably) a meeting is scheduled to assess the potential fit of opportunity and job candidate. Here again, you should openly express both your doubts and your interest in the job opportunity.

Negotiating the Employment Offer

There is always a thrill, and a sense of pride and achievement, when the agent informs you of a positive client response. All of the work and effort have proved fruitful, and an exhilarating sense of accomplishment is well deserved. At this point, the employment agency must address the issues of compensation, benefits, and advancement. The agent has to conceive an accurate picture of the essential needs and limits of both parties in order to accurately present to each the desires of the other. The deliberateness of the coordinated effort and the appearance of natural progression are the skills of a qualified agent.

To provide you with full and accurate details of the offer, the agent provides the client with a review of the duties, compensation, and benefits acceptable to you and requests that the client draft an offer letter. There are times when there is a negotiation of the offer. To this end, it is the agent's job to use his or her negotiating skills to produce a successful conclusion.

A career move is an important turning point in your life. Be aware of the fact that you will spend the major portion of your waking hours with the people in their department, and that your success or failure may hinge on your ability to effectively interact with them. You may want to have the reporting structures spelled out. Perhaps you would feel more comfortable with a written determination of your duties.

Once an accurate adjustment of the offer has been made, the agent will inform the client company of the amendments to the offer which meet the candidate's needs. Most often, the parties are closer to agreement than may have been initially believed. Here also, the agent is an invaluable resource; having the unique view of an objective party enables the agent to suggest solutions based on the interests of both client company and job seeker.

Summary

The job of the employment agent is to find viable job openings, find suitable applicants and be a key player during all phases of the job placement process. The employment agent and the job seeker are most evenly complemented on the fee-paid level. Your value to the agent is as a respected professional, with a salable set of assets and abilities. The agent's value to you is as a qualified professional with the ability to immeasurably simplify the job-getting process and to increase the probability of successful conclusion through professional know-how.

As you use the tried and proven processes detailed in this chapter, it is my hope that you may find them to be as beneficial to your job search as they have been to the candidates who have been assisted over the years. Good hunting.

5
MVS

Maria I. Martins

Introduction

MVS dates back to the 1970s with the introduction of OS. As time passed OS became MVS, which was an expansion of OS created to address the additional data processing needs of its users. MVS continued to grow and became MVS/SP and MVS/XA. In 1990 IBM introduced the System/390, which runs under MVS/ESA. Today there is MVS/ESA Version 5, which supports sophisticated multiple image systems and runs on the 9672R and the ES/9000, working in a multiprocessing environment known as "parallel sysplex."

The main/major components of MVS are Job Management, Task Management, Data Management, Storage Management, Resource Management, Recovery Termination Management, and Systems Application Architecture. The following is a brief description of the major functions performed by these features:

1. Job Management (job entry subsystem)
   - Controls reading and scheduling of jobs
   - Controls initiation and allocation tasks for jobs
   - Controls execution and termination of jobs
   - Sends output to proper devices
   - Allows remote users to submit jobs as easily as those located near the computer

2. Task Management
   - Supervises the dispatching and service requests of work in the system

3. Data Management
   - Stores and retrieves data
   - Provides sequential, partitioned, and Virtual Storage Access Method (VSAM) dataset support

4. Storage Management (storage management subsystem)
   - Is used to manage user (disk) datasets
   - Allows datasets to be migrated to tape for long-term storage based on usage and importance
   - Consolidates fragmented disk space and moves datasets around on the disk packs to balance usage
   - Makes JCL easier for programmers because the operating system calculates an optimum block size for all datasets if the user does not supply one
   - Is available only with MVS/ESA

5. Resource Management
   - Allocates computer resources
   - Utilizes time-sharing options (such as TSO, CICS, and VTAM, which allow simultaneous use by a large number of users)
   - Supports multiprogramming, which is used to maximize the efficiency of the system

6. Recovery Termination Management
   - Ensures proper recovery from system and hardware failures

7. Systems Application Architecture (SAA)
   - Common User Access, which makes applications look alike to the user
   - Common Programming Interface, which provides the same computer languages and program services across IBM platforms
   - Common Communications Support, which allows IBM computers to talk to each other
   - Common Applications, which allows application programs to run on various IBM platforms

Virtual Storage.   Virtual storage is the component of the MVS system that allows application programs to have storage addresses independent of the addresses of the computer's central storage. When a program begins execution, the system loads it onto virtual storage and, as resources become available, it loads pages of the program into real storage to be executed. With virtual storage, a program occupies only a small amount of real storage. This gives the ability to run a program whose size exceeds the central storage available. Virtual storage also allows many programs to run on the computer simultaneously through the use of multiprogramming.

Multiprogramming.   Multiprogramming attempts to maximize the efficiency of the computer by keeping the major components (such as the CPU, I/O devices, and central storage) busy. A multiprogramming system can keep several jobs inside the computer and switch back and forth between them. It is able to do this because most jobs do not use all the storage, all the I/O devices, and the CPU at the same time.

Job Entry Subsystem (JES). Job Entry Subsystem (JES2 or JES3) interfaces with JCL. JES2 and JES3 are subsystems that provide similar functions, as if one had several computers linked together. They keep track of jobs that enter the system, determine when jobs are executed, and send output to the appropriate device—normally, a printer.

MVS Sysplex

IBM has expanded the parallel capabilities of the System/390 to include the capability, working in combination with coupled multiprocessor hardware support, to have up to 32 copies of MVS—each capable of running simultaneously with and independent of the processing taking place in any of the other copies of MVS. What is taking place internally, from an application point of view, is multiprocessing data access, i.e., data sharing across multiple systems in combination with parallel processing. For the application programmer all this should be considered transparent, i.e., non-sysplex application JCL will also run on a sysplex configuration. It is the work of the system programmer, the database administrator (DBA) and the application planner/scheduler that has become more complex. The system programmer has more options to deal with. The DBA has to determine database requirements and structure the database in a way that will support multiprocessing. The application planner/scheduler has to determine how each application can be subdivided so that sections of the application can run in parallel. Some of the new terms that apply can be found in the Terminology section of this chapter under Sysplex Terminology. The multiprocessing aspects of IBM's System/390 provide high throughput multiserver support to its users. To the application programmer this means that the mainframe has not outlived its effectiveness. Application programmers with a knowledge of MVS will continue to be in demand for years to come.

Non-Sysplex Terminology

MVS/SP: Multiple Virtual System/Systems Program.

MVS/XA: Multiple Virtual System/Extended Architecture.

MVS/ESA: Multiple Virtual System/Enterprise Systems Architecture.

Address space: A "complete" range of addresses. The maximum size of an address space is limited by the number of digits used to represent addresses.

JES: Job Entry Subsystem. Keeps track of jobs that enter the system, determines when they are executed, and sends each job's printed output to the correct printer.

SMS: Storage Management Subsystem. Manages user disk datasets.

SAA: Systems Application Architecture. A concept used to make IBM's major product lines (such as MVS and VM, AS/400, and PS/2) compatible.

Partitioned dataset: Often called PDS or library. It consists of a directory and one or more members. A PDS directory is a list of the members in a library. A member has a one-to-eight-character member name.

Master catalog: Contains catalog entries for system files and files that begin with SYS1, and user catalogs.

User catalog: Contains catalog entries for user's datasets.

Sysplex Terminology

Tightly coupled multiprocessors: Multiple computers controlled by a single copy of MVS.

Loosely coupled multiprocessors: Several computers controlled and coordinated by multiple MVS images.

MVS image: A term used to denote a copy of the MVS operating system.

Sysplex: A term combining two words—systems and complex

Basic Sysplex: Multiple computers containing multiple MVS images, all of them sharing DASD.

Enhanced Sysplex: An expansion of Basic Sysplex that is capable of supporting an even larger number of systems than Basic Sysplex.

Parallel Sysplex: An arrangement or state which permits several operations or tasks to be performed simultaneously rather than consecutively. Parallel Sysplex provides the ability to share data and balance workloads across systems, which increases throughput.

Multiprocessing: The ability of a system to simultaneously process different types of jobs, i.e., batch and online.

Parallel processing: The ability of a computer system to simultaneously process sections (parts) of a single process across more than one processor, for example, processing sections of an application concurrently, with each section being processed on a different processor. To do this the application has to be subdivided during its processing and "put together" as the last step of the processing.

Cross system coupling (XCF): A facility that allows and coordinates applications so that they can communicate with other applications in the same, or other, processor(s).

Serialization: A mechanism to guarantee data validity. It deals with access and update of data. The use of serialization allows only one application to access or update any given piece of data at a time.

Data consistency: Also known as buffer validation. Buffer validation makes sure that local copies of data across sharing systems are kept consistent and reflect the most up-to-date changes that have taken place.

Information Management System Transaction Manager (IMS TM): A facility that supports read/write data sharing across multiple MVS systems. IBM supports two categories of Transaction managers: CICS and IMS DB.

Structure: A term used to determine how to manage storage and other resources in an MVS environment as part of the coupling facility.

Coupling facility: A microprocessor with broadband fiber optic I/O links. These links provide high-speed data transfers between systems. The microprocessor is capable of dividing its storage into "structures." There are three different types of structures:

> **Cache structures:** A coupling facility that is used to manage access to shared data and cache structure resources, store and retrieve data from a cache structure, determine when shared data has changed and whether it is valid or not.

> **List structures:** A coupling facility that is used to share information organized in sets of lists or queues. Some of the operations performed in a list structure are: monitoring lists, performing serialized updates on multiple lists, and reading, creating, updating, deleting, and moving list entries in a list structure.

> **Lock structures:** A coupling facility that is used to implement customized locking protocols. The lock structure supports exclusive, shared, application-defined locks, as well as generalized and recovery locks. Some of the operations performed are: requesting a lock, changing the type of lock, releasing a lock, managing contention of a lock, and recovering a lock from a failed application.

Serialized list structure: Part of the List Structure coupling facility. It consists of a lock table that contains exclusive locks to be utilized on applications as desired. Applications can utilize the lock table to serialize on sections of the list structure, or on resources outside of the list structure.

Sysplex timer: A unit that synchronizes the time-of-day (TOD) clocks in multiple computer processors. The time stamp from the Sysplex timer can be used to monitor and sequence events within the sysplex.

Multiple Systems Coupling (MSC): Permits multiple processors to communicate with each other, regardless of their physical location.

Enterprise System Connection (ESCON): Hardware channels connecting multiple computers to I/O control units. ESCON "directors" provide a dynamic switching capability.

Questions and Answers

Abends

Q: *What is a system completion code?*

A: A system completion code is a three-position identifier controlled by MVS. Programs have no access to it. It is prefaced under MVS with literal 'S' in the form of 'Snnn'. NNN stands for a three-position hexadecimal number. The error message will print on the JCL in the format of 'Snnn-rc'. RC stands for the return code associated with the system message that further describes the error.

Q: *What is an operation exception error?*

A: An operation exception error indicates that an operation code is not assigned or the assigned operation is not available on a particular computer model. The machine did not recognize the instruction or operation used. A possible reason is a subscript error. This error could also be caused by an attempt to read a file that was not opened, a misspelled ddname, or a missing DD statement. The system completion code is 0C1.

Q: *What is a protection exception error?*

A: A protection exception error occurs when the program is attempting to access a memory address that is not within the memory area that the program is authorized to use. Some of the causes may be a subscript or index that is not initialized or has taken on a value outside the bounds of the table with which it is associated, an attempt to read an opened file, or an incorrect or missing DD statement. The system completion code is 0C4.

Q: *What is an addressing exception error?*

A: An addressing exception error occurs when a program is attempting to access a memory location that is outside the bounds of available real storage on the machine. This can be caused by a dataset not being opened at the time an I/O was directed to it, an attempt to close a dataset a second time, incorrectly called module parameters or coding, improper exit from a performed paragraph, or uninitialized subscript or index. The system completion code is 0C5.

Q: *What is a data exception error?*

A: A data exception error indicates an attempt to perform an arithmetic operation on nonnumeric data. It can also occur from incorrect input data to a program that is not performing sufficient numeric testing on it before attempting arithmetic. The system completion code is 0C7.

Q: *What return code can be issued when the operator cancels a job?*

A: There are two return codes that can be produced when the operator cancels a job. They are 122 and 222. A 122 indicates the operator canceled the job and requested a dump. A 222 indicates the operator canceled the job without a dump. It is important to ask the operator why the job was canceled. Some of the reasons this may occur are: the program needed a resource that was not available; the program appeared to be stalled in a wait state; or the program was in an apparent loop.

Q: *What return code is issued if a job or job step exceeded the time limit?*

A: The system will issue a system code of 322 when a job or job step has exceeded the time limit. If the time parameter was used on the JOB or EXEC statement, it may not have allowed enough time for the job or job step to complete. If the time parameter was not used, then it is important to check the program for possible logic loops.

Q: *When the system cannot find enough virtual storage, which system abend is issued?*

A: When the system cannot find enough virtual storage during a GETMAIN macro instruction, it generates a system abend of 804 or 80A. Check for program errors that incorrectly modify the storage request. If the REGION parameter has been used, either on the JOB or EXEC statement, it may need to be increased to satisfy the request.

Q: *Which system completion code is issued when a program module cannot be found?*

A: A system completion code of 806 will be issued when a program module cannot be found. Some of the causes may be missing the STEPLIB statement from the step or missing the JOBLIB statement from the job stream. Most likely the program name was misspelled on the EXEC statement or in a source code CALL.

Q: *What are some of the abends generated when not enough disk space is available and what do they mean?*

A: Some of the abends generated due to a lack of available disk space are:

1. B37—Disk volume out of space, cannot write output. The system gave all the primary space and as much secondary space as it could.

2. D37—Primary disk space was exceeded and either no secondary space allocation was specified or it was insufficient. One should increase the primary space as well as provide adequate secondary space allocation to eliminate this error.

3. E37—There was insufficient space on the volume. One way to solve this problem is to specify more volumes on the JCL.

Q: *Which abend is issued when the system cannot find a member on a partitioned dataset?*

A: An S013-18 abend occurs when the specified member on the JCL is not found on the indicated PDS (Partitioned Dataset). Determine if the member is spelled correctly on your JCL. If it is not, then fix member name and resubmit job. If it is correct, then determine why it is not on the PDS, take the necessary steps to place it on the PDS, and resubmit the job.

Q: *What normally causes an S013-20 abend?*

A: An S013-20 is normally caused by the block size not being a multiple of the record length or being incorrect for variable-length records. Divide your BLKSIZE by the record length to make sure it is a multiple of the BLKSIZE. If not, correct it and resubmit job. For variable-length records, it is necessary to have your BLKSIZE be at least 4 bytes greater than your record length.

Q: *What can be done to eliminate a 'NOT CATLG 2' for a particular dataset?*

A: To eliminate a 'NOT CATLG 2' message, one may take one of the following options:

1. Add a step to the beginning of the JOB which creates the dataset to first purge the dataset. One may wish to use utility IEFBR14 to perform this task.

2. Set up a job to purge the dataset and run it before the job that creates it.

3. Purge the dataset before running the job that creates it.

Q: *If a job step is in a wait state for 30 minutes or more with no activity, which abend does one receive?*

A: If a job step is in a wait state for 30 minutes or more with no activity, the job abends with an S522 indicating the time was exceeded for the wait state. This type of cancellation is unusual and is often caused by a program error or unavailable datasets/resources.

Q: *A system completion code of 813-04 is generated when a dataset name and volume serial number for a tape are not consistent with the information contained in the tape dataset label. What can be done to fix this problem?*

A: When a system completion code of 813-04 is received, one must check the spelling of the dataset name in the JCL and the volume serial number specified. If possible, dump the dataset label to see the actual dataset name on the tape. Once the problem has been identified, correct it and resubmit the job.

Q: *How does one fix a 'PROCEDURE NOT FOUND' ERROR?*

A: If one receives a 'PROCEDURE NOT FOUND' message, it indicates that it could not find the procedure on the procedure library specified on the JCL. Check the spelling of the procedure name on the EXEC statement to make sure it is correct. If it is not, fix it and resubmit the job.

   If the JCL is correct, then check to make sure the procedure has been cataloged into the procedure library. If not, have it cataloged and resubmit the job.

Generation Data Groups

Q: *What is a Generation Data Group (GDG)?*

A: A Generation Data Group is a group of chronologically or functionally related datasets. GDGs are processed periodically, often by adding a new generation, retaining previous generations, and sometimes discarding the oldest generation.

Q: *How is a GDG base created?*

A: A GDG base is created in the system catalog and keeps track of the generation numbers used for datasets in the group. IDCAMS utility is used to define the GDG base for MVS/SP, MVS/XA, and MVS/ESA. Older systems required that the IEHPROGM utility be used.

Q: *What is model dataset label (Model DSCB)?*
A: A model dataset label is a pattern for the dataset label created for any dataset named as part of the GDG group. The system needs an existing dataset to serve as a model to supply the DCB parameters for the generation data group one wishes to create. The model dataset label must be cataloged. The model DSCB name is placed on the DCB parameter on the DD statement that creates the generation data group.

Q: *What is the advantage of using generation data groups?*
A: The advantage of using generation data groups is that all datasets have the same name, and the system keeps track of adding and deleting successive generations. The JCL does not need to be changed between runs.

Q: *How are GDGs concatenated?*
A: Generation data groups are concatenated by specifying each dataset name and the generation number for all generations of the generation data group. To retrieve all generations of a generation data group, omit the generation number. The DD statement will refer to all generations. The result is the same as if all individual datasets were concatenated. If generations are not on the same volume, this will not work.

Q: *How are different generations specified?*
A: Different generations are specified by providing the dataset name and generation number for each GDG desired.

Q: *What is the status of a GDG when an abend occurs?*
A: The GDG is in a bad state because it may consist of partial information. If used in this state, it is possible to get incorrect or improper results. It is recommended to reset the current generation by deleting the bad generation before executing the job which will re-create a new generation.

Q: *How is a previous GDG coded?*
A: Previous GDGs are coded as (–1) after the dataset name. An example would be DSN=JAN.DATA(–1).

Q: *How is the current GDG coded?*
A: Current GDGs are coded as (0), (+0), or (–0) after the dataset name as follows: DSN=JAN.DATA(0). The (+0) and (–0) have the same effect as (0). Normally, it is coded as (0).

Q: *How is a new GDG coded?*
A: A new GDG is coded as (+1) after the dataset name as follows: DSN=JAN.DATA(+1). This will cause all generations to be pushed down one level at the end of the job.

DD Statements

Q: *What is the purpose of the Data Definition (DD) Statement?*

A: Data Definition statements describe each dataset (a file on a direct-access storage device, tape, or printed output) and request the allocation of I/O devices.

Q: *Describe what the DISP parameter does.*

A: The DISP parameter describes the current status of the dataset and directs the system on the disposition of the dataset either at the end of the job or when the step abnormally terminates. DISP is always required unless the dataset is created and deleted in the same step.

Q: *How many subparameters does the DISP parameter consist of and what is the meaning of each?*

A: The DISP parameter consists of three subparameters: start-status, end-status-normal and end-status-abend. Start-status indicates the status of a dataset at the beginning of the job step. End-status-normal tells MVS what needs to be done with the dataset when the job step ends. End-status-abend indicates the desired disposition of the dataset if the job step abends. It is also known as the conditional disposition.

Q: *What are the meanings of the parameters used (within) the DISP parameter at the beginning of the job step?*

A: The status NEW, MOD, OLD, or SHR is the status of the dataset at the beginning of the step. If the dataset is NEW, the system creates a dataset label; if it is OLD, the system locates the dataset and reads its label. MOD allows records to be added to an existing dataset. The system gives a program exclusive control of a dataset except when SHR is used.

Q: *What are the "normal" dispositions of the DISP parameter?*

A: The normal disposition indicates the disposition of the dataset when the dataset is closed or when the job terminates normally. Normal dispositions are: KEEP, DELETE, PASS, CATLG, UNCATLG.

Q: *What are the "abnormal" dispositions of the DISP parameter?*

A: The abnormal dispositions will be in effect only if the step abnormally terminates. They are the same as normal dispositions, except that PASS is not allowed. KEEP, CATLG, UNCATLG, and DELETE are all permitted.

Q: *When should DISP=SHR be used?*

A: DISP=SHR must be used when it is necessary to share the datasets. SHR should be used only for input datasets.

Q: *When should DISP=MOD be used?*

A: DISP=MOD is used to either extend an existing sequential dataset or to create a dataset if it does not exist. If the dataset exists, then records are appended to the dataset at the end of the existing dataset. If the dataset does not exist, the system treats MOD as if it were NEW, provided that the volume parameter has not been used. If the volume parameter is used, the system terminates the job and does not create the new dataset. MOD can be used to add to a dataset that extends onto several volumes. Always specify a disposition of CATLG with MOD for cataloged datasets, even if they are already cataloged, so that any additional volume serial numbers will be recorded in the catalog.

Q: *When should DISP=OLD be used?*
A: DISP=OLD should be used for an existing dataset. It can be used with an input dataset to read, or an output dataset to rewrite. The step that uses DISP=OLD will have exclusive control of the dataset. If an OLD dataset is cataloged, the DSN parameter is usually the only other parameter needed. If an OLD dataset is not cataloged, UNIT and VOL parameters are required.

Q: *When should DISP=NEW be used?*
A: DISP=NEW should be used when it is desired to create a new dataset. The UNIT parameter is usually required for datasets on direct access volumes.

Q: *How is a dataset passed from one step to another?*
A: A dataset is passed from one step to another based on what is coded on the DISP parameter. The dataset can only be passed to subsequent steps if PASS was used on the disposition parameter.

Q: *If a dataset is passed and the subsequent steps do not use it, what happens to the dataset at the end of the job?*
A: If a dataset is passed to subsequent steps and it is not used, at the end of the job the dataset is deleted, since DELETE is assumed for all NEW datasets, temporary or nontemporary.

Q: *What is the default for the disposition parameter if it's not coded on the DD statement for a dataset?*
A: The default disposition used on a dataset which was coded without a disposition parameter is NEW. The disposition of NEW implies exclusive control of the dataset.

Q: *How are datasets concatenated?*
A: Datasets are concatenated by writing a normal DD statement for the first dataset and then adding a DD statement without a DDNAME for each dataset to be concatenated in the order they are to be read. The following is an example of three datasets concatenated:

```
//INSMP   DD DSN=JAN.DATA,DISP=SHR
//        DD DSN=FEB.DATA,DISP=SHR
//        DD DSN=MAR.DATA,DISP=SHR
```

Q: *Can datasets of a different record length (LRECL) be concatenated?*
A: Datasets with different LRECLs can be concatenated as long as the dataset with the largest block size appears first.

Q: *Can Partitioned Datasets (PDSs) be concatenated?*
A: Partitioned Datasets can be concatenated. This is often done for program libraries so that the system can search several libraries for a member.

Q: *What is a Data Control Block (DCB)?*
A: The Data Control Block is a table of data, in storage, that describes each dataset used by the program.

Q: *What are three different places from which DCB information can be obtained and in what order?*
A: Data information can be obtained from three places in the following order:

1. The data control block, from application program, is used first.

2. Information supplied on the DD statement is used second.

3. Dataset label information for the DCB is used third.

Q: *What is the purpose of using a dataset referback?*
A: A dataset referback is used to copy a dataset name from a prior job step.

Q: *What are the disadvantages of using a dataset referback?*
A: The disadvantages of using dataset referbacks is that they tend to make JCL more difficult to maintain because close attention, scrutiny, and manual examination of preceding steps is needed to understand what a given job-stream is doing. They also complicate the restart of a job if a failure or interruption occurs.

Q: *Under which circumstances is the disposition parameter not performed?*
A: Disposition is not performed under the following circumstances:

1. The step does not start because of JCL errors.

2. The step is bypassed because of the COND parameter in the JOB or EXEC statement.

3. The step abnormally terminates because it could not find enough space to satisfy the request.

4. DUMMY or DSN=NULLFILE is coded on the DD statement.

JOB Card, EXEC Statements, and PARM Parameters

Q: *What is the purpose of the JOB statement?*
A: The purpose of the JOB statement is to inform the operating system of the start of a job, give necessary accounting information, and supply run parameters. Each job must begin with a single JOB statement.

Q: *How does one identify a job to the operating system?*
A: A job is identified to the system by the use of Jobname. Jobnames can range from one to eight alphanumeric characters. The first character must begin in column 3 and be alphabetic (A–Z). Jobs should be given unique names since

duplicate jobnames will not execute until any job having the same jobname completes execution.

Q: *What does the Accounting Information consist of?*
A: Accounting Information consists of the account number to which the job is charged and any additional information established by the installation.

Q: *What does the parameter CLASS in the JOB statement mean?*
A: Parameter CLASS specifies the job class. There are 36 possible job classes (A–Z, 0–9). Installations usually attempt to establish job classes that achieve a balance between I/O-bound and CPU-bound jobs. Job classes also determine the overall priority of a job, along with the PRTY parameter. PRTY may be coded to give special priority to a job. It may also be set by the operator.

Q: *What is parameter MSGCLASS in the JOB statement used for?*
A: The MSGCLASS parameter is used to specify the job scheduler message output class. The output class is (A–Z, 0–9). Job scheduler messages include all messages not printed by the actual job steps being executed. Some of these are: JCL statements and error messages, device allocations, dataset disposition, and accounting information.

Q: *What does parameter MSGLEVEL on the JOB statement mean and what is the advantage of using it?*
A: MSGLEVEL indicates whether or not one wishes to print the JCL statements and allocation messages. The MSGLEVEL parameter can save paper. After a job is debugged, there may be no need to print all the JCL and allocation messages each time it runs. To reduce printing to a minimum, one may wish to code MSGLEVEL=(0,0).

Q: *Which parameter allows one to run a syntax check on the JCL without executing it?*
A: TYPRUN=SCAN parameter is used to check the JCL for syntax errors and suppress the execution of the job. This checking does not include checking for duplicate datasets on volumes, insufficient space, or region size for job steps.

Q: *What does parameter TYPRUN=HOLD mean?*
A: The parameter TYPRUN=HOLD holds a job in the input queue for later execution. The job is held until the operator releases it. TYPRUN=HOLD is useful for when one job must not run until another job completes. Operator intervention is required to release the job.

Q: *What is the purpose of the EXEC statement?*
A: The purpose of the EXEC statement is to name a program or procedure to be executed. It follows the JOB statement. A job or cataloged procedure can contain several EXEC statements. A job may have up to 255 EXEC statements.

Q: *What is the stepname on the EXEC statement used for, and is it a required parameter?*

A: Stepname on the EXEC statement is used to name the job step. It is required if subsequent JCL statements refer to it or if one wishes to restart the job from the step; otherwise, it is optional. Stepnames are recommended and should have unique names. The names must begin in column 3 with an alphabetic or national character (A–Z, @ $ #).

Q: *Which parameter is used to name a program in the EXEC statement?*

A: The parameter 'PGM=' is used to name a program or utility to be executed. For example, to code a program named 'FIRST', one would code 'PGM=FIRST'. For a utility named 'IEBGENER', it would be coded as 'PGM=IEBGENER'.

Q: *What are the most commonly used parameters on the EXEC statement and what do they mean?*

A: The most commonly used parameters on the EXEC statement are: COND, PARM, REGION, and TIME. They stand for:

1. COND—Specifies conditions to execute subsequent job steps if the previous step(s) fail.
2. PARM—Passes parameters to the job step.
3. REGION—Specifies the REGION size to allocate for the job/job step.
4. TIME—Imposes a time limit on the job or job step.

Q: *What is the default for the TIME parameter if it is not coded on the EXEC statement?*

A: If the TIME parameter is omitted from the EXEC statement, the default is 30 minutes of CPU time.

Q: *What is the difference between the JOBLIB and STEPLIB statements?*

A: The JOBLIB statement is placed after the JOB statement and is effective for all job steps. It cannot be placed in a cataloged procedure. The STEPLIB statement is placed after the EXEC statement and is effective for that job step only. Unlike the JOBLIB statement, the STEPLIB can be placed in a cataloged procedure.

Q: *What can be done to resolve a JCL error that reads 'DATASET NOT FOUND'?*

A: Some of the actions one can take to resolve a JCL error of 'DATASET NOT FOUND' are:

1. One must examine the job log and the allocation/deallocation report and identify the step and DDname involved.
2. Determine whether or not the dataset name does indeed exist on the system.
3. Check the JCL to make sure the dataset name is spelled correctly.
4. If the job has more than one step and the abend is not on the first step, check to see if the dataset on the previous step was deleted.
5. Fix the problem and resubmit the job.

Q: *Does a 'DD STATEMENT MISSING' message normally abend the job?*

A: A DD statement missing message normally does not abend the job, but if not fixed it could later cause problems when least expected. It is advisable to determine why this message was generated and take action to rectify the problem.

Q: *Parameters COND, REGION, and TIME can be coded on both the JOB and the EXEC statements. What are the differences between using them on the JOB versus the EXEC statement, and in which statement are they most commonly used?*

A: Parameters COND, REGION, and TIME, when used on the JOB statement, will be in effect for the entire job. When used on the EXEC statement, they will be in effect for the job step only. The COND parameter is normally used on the EXEC statement. The REGION parameter is normally not used unless a particular program requires a lot of storage and it is necessary to override the installation's REGION default. If the REGION parameter is used on both the JOB and EXEC statements, then the parameter from the JOB statement will be in effect. The TIME parameter is most often used on the JOB statement.

Q: *Explain how virtual storage works in MVS/SP.*

A: MVS/SP stands for Multiple Virtual System/System Program. A major architectural component of MVS is virtual storage. With virtual storage, storage addresses of an application program are independent of the addresses of the computer's central storage. A hardware feature, paging supervisor, translates the user's virtual storage addresses to the computer's central addresses during execution. With virtual storage, a program needs to occupy only a relatively small amount of central storage. This allows programs to be run whose size exceeds the central storage available on the computer.

Q: *What are some of the main features of MVS/XA?*

A: MVS/XA stands for Multiple Virtual System/Extended Architecture. MVS/XA uses 32 bits for addressing. This gives an address space of approximately 2 billion bytes. The extended architecture also consists of more sophisticated input/output channels for faster I/O. Also, a separate version of the operating system is required. One of the differences is that a program for MVS/XA can go up to 2 billion bytes. Programs running under MVS/SP can go up to only 16 million bytes.

Q: *What are the "basic architecture" features of MVS/ESA?*

A: MVS/ESA stands for Multiple Virtual System/Enterprise Systems Architecture. MVS/ESA permits an application to have multiple 2-gigabyte address spaces. This allows huge applications to be segregated into functional parts. For ESA, the first address space is called *application space,* and programs can only execute in it. The other address spaces are called *dataspaces* and they contain only data. MVS/ESA also has the facility for hyperspaces, which allows temporary data to be stored or retrieved in 4-kbyte blocks under program control. Maximum address space is up to 2 trillion bytes in multiple 2-billion-byte address spaces.

Q: *What is the meaning of the "line"?*

A: The "line" indicates the maximum address space that is available for the MVS system. For MVS/SP it is 16 million bytes, for MVS/XA it is up to 2 billion bytes, and for MVS/ESA it is up to 2 trillion bytes in multiple 2-billion-byte address spaces.

Q: *When would a program run "below the line"?*

A: A program would run "below the line" if it did not exceed the maximum address space available.

Q: *When would a program run "above the line"?*

A: A program would run "above the line" if it required more than 16 megs or if it is competing with other programs that are using the same address space. Special parameters must be set for compilation and linkage editing in order for a program to run above the 16-meg line.

Procs

Q: *How are in-stream procedures (procs) built?*

A: In-stream procedures are built by coding a set of statements and placing them after the JOB statement and before the EXEC statement. In-stream procedures begin with a PROC statement and end with a PEND statement. Up to 15 in-stream procedures can be included in a single job. Each in-stream procedure may be invoked several times within the job. In-stream procedures can use symbolic parameters in the same way as cataloged procedures.

Q: *What is the difference between an in-stream procedure and a cataloged procedure?*

A: An in-stream procedure is basically the same as a cataloged procedure. The difference is that to execute an in-stream procedure one places it after the JOB statement and before the EXEC statement and must end it with the PEND statement. A cataloged procedure is cataloged on a procedure library and is called by specifying the procedure name on the EXEC statement. An in-stream procedure is useful to test the procedure before making it a cataloged procedure.

Q: *Name some of the JCL statements that are not allowed in procs.*

A: Some of the JCL statements that are not allowed in procedures are:
1. JOB, Delimiter (/*), or Null (//) statements
2. JOBLIB or JOBCAT DD statements
3. DD* or DATA statements
4. Any JES2 or JES3 control statements

Q: *What parameters are good candidates to make symbolic parameters?*

A: Any parameter, subparameter, or value in a procedure that may vary each time the procedure is called is a good candidate to be coded as a symbolic parameter.

Q: *Which type of override parameter requires that one know the parameters that can be overridden?*

A: Regular parameters require that one know the parameters that can be overridden, such as the stepnames within the procedure, the DDnames of the statements overridden, and the order of the DD statements.

Q: *How is a symbolic parameter coded?*

A: A symbolic parameter is preceded by an ampersand (&) and followed by a name (&FIRST). The first character must be alphabetic. Symbolic parameters can be coded only in the operand field of JCL statements; they cannot appear in the name or operation field. If more than one value is assigned to a symbolic parameter on a PROC or EXEC statement, only the first one is used. Symbolic parameters may be coded in any order on the PROC or EXEC statement.

Q: *How are values assigned to symbolic parameters?*

A: Values can be assigned to symbolic parameters on the PROC statement, on the EXEC statement, or on a SET command. Values containing special characters other than blank must be enclosed in apostrophes. The value assigned to a symbolic parameter can be of any length, but it cannot be continued onto another line.

Q: *Can symbolic parameters be concatenated?*

A: Symbolic parameters can be concatenated with other symbolic parameters, regular parameters, or with portions of regular parameters as follows:

Symbolic/symbolic	`PARM=&FIRST&LAST`
Symbolic/regular	`SPACE=&SPACES`
Symbolic/portion	`SPACE=(TRK,&PRIMARY)`

Q: *What are some of the rules involved in overriding parameters on the EXEC statements in a procedure?*

A: To override EXEC parameters one should follow these rules:

1. A PGM parameter cannot be overridden.
2. The parameters for each step do not need to be coded in the same order as they appear on the procedure EXEC statement.
3. To add or override a parameter on an EXEC statement, code it as follows: parameter.procstepname=value.
4. If a parameter that does not exist is coded on the EXEC statement, the parameter will be added.
5. All parameters for each step must be coded in order: the first step must be coded first, second step second, third step third, etc.

Q: *What are some of the rules involved in overriding DD statements in procs?*

A: The following rules apply when overriding a DD statement:

1. DD statement overrides precede the DDname with the procstepname.

2. The JCL parameter is replaced, unless it does not exist on the original statement, in which case it is added. For the DCB parameter, each sub-parameter can be overridden.

3. DD statement overrides should carry DDnames that already exist in the step they are to effect.

4. DD statement overrides must be coded preceding any added DD statements for the proc step.

5. DD override statements must be listed in the order in which they are shown in the proc.

6. DD override statements are only in effect for the duration of the run.

Q: *How are concatenated DD statements in procs overridden?*
A: Overriding concatenated DD statements requires the following:

1. To override only the first DD statement in a concatenation, code only one overriding DD statement.

2. To override all DD statements in a concatenation, code an overriding DD for each concatenated DD statement.

3. The overriding DD statements must be in the same order as the concatenated DD statements.

4. Code a DDname on the first overriding DD statement only. Leave the DDname blank on all following DD statements.

5. To leave a concatenated statement unchanged, code its corresponding overriding DD statement with a blank operand field.

Compiling, Link Editing, and Execution

Q: *What does a mainframe compiler output in the "object deck" and what does the linkage editor do with it?*
A: The compiler outputs the source code into the object deck in a form to be read by the linkage editor. The linkage editor combines the object dataset (object deck) from the compiler with machine language code for input/output and other tasks to create an executable "load module."

Q: *If a program executed attempts to divide a number by zero, do arithmetic on a field that does not contain numeric data, or has some other serious logic error, an abend will occur. What is the "normal" response that MVS would issue?*
A: MVS would issue a "system completion code" that would indicate the nature of the problem, dump the program's memory area, and flush the job from the system. The dump may be used for problem analysis. The dump is printed or stored in a dataset as specified in the //SYSUDUMP DD statement. If //SYSUDUMP is omitted, MVS will provide the completion code value, but not the dump.

Q: *Where must load module(s) reside?*
A: Load module(s) must reside in a Partitioned DataSet (PDS).

Q: *What are some of the common linkage editor options and what do they mean?*
A: Some of the commonly used linkage editor options are:

1. LIST—Lists the linkage editor control statements and is usually specified. Omit the parameter if no listing is desired.
2. MAP—Produces a storage map showing the length and relative locations of all control sections. Default is NOMAP.
3. XREF—Includes MAP plus a cross-reference table of the load module. (MAP and XREF are mutually exclusive.)
4. NOCALL—Cancels the automatic library call mechanism. NOCALL is used for creating subroutine libraries so that the load module contains a single subroutine. CALL is the default.
5. LET—Marks load modules as executable even if minor errors are found. NOLET is the default.
6. PRINT—Allows the messages to be written to a SYSOUT DD statement and it is the default. NOPRINT suppresses the messages.
7. AMODE—Specifies whether the program uses 24- or 31-bit addressing. AMODE ANY specifies both 24- and 31-bit addressing. AMODE 24 requires the program to run below the 16-meg line. The default is established by the compiler and is usually AMODE 24.
8. RMODE—Indicates where the program can reside in virtual storage. RMODE ANY allows the program to reside above the 16-meg line and requires AMODE 31 or AMODE ANY. RMODE 24 requires the program to reside below the 16-meg line. The default is established by the compiler and is usually RMODE 24.
9. TERM—Causes linkage editor diagnostic messages to be written to a SYSTERM DD statement. NOTERM is the default.

Q: *What causes the message 'MODULE HAS BEEN MARKED NOT EXECUTABLE'?*
A: An unresolved external reference often causes the message 'MODULE HAS BEEN MARKED NOT EXECUTABLE'. Although the module is not executable, one may be able to recover by link-editing the control section causing the problem and replacing it in the load module.

Q: *Why would the linkage editor add a member to a load library under the name 'TEMPNAME'?*
A: The linkage editor will add a member to the load library under the name of 'TEMPNAME' when a member of the same name already exists on the library and the disposition on the SYSLMOD statement was coded as DISP=MOD. This indicates a problem and needs to be resolved.

Utilities

Q: *What is an IEBGENER used for?*

A: IEBGENER is a dataset utility used to copy sequential datasets, produce a partitioned dataset or member from a sequential dataset, produce an edited sequential or partitioned dataset, and reblock/change the logical record length of a dataset.

Q: *What is an IEBCOPY used for?*

A: IEBCOPY is a dataset utility used to copy one or more partitioned datasets or to merge partitioned datasets. A partitioned dataset that is copied to a sequential dataset is said to be unloaded. When one or more datasets created by an unload operation are used to re-create a partitioned dataset, it is called a *load operation*. Specific members of a partitioned or unloaded dataset can be selected for, or excluded from, a copy, unload, or load process.

Q: *What is an IEFBR14 used for?*

A: IEFBR14 is used to delete datasets, find datasets, catalog, and uncatalog datasets.

Q: *What is an IEHLIST used for?*

A: IEHLIST is a system utility used to list entries in an OS CVOL, entries in the directory of one or more partitioned datasets, or entries in an indexed or non-indexed volume table of contents (VTOC).

Q: *What is an IEHINITT used for?*

A: IEHINITT is a system utility used to write an IBM volume label onto any number of magnetic tapes mounted on one or more tape units. Each volume label set created by this program contains a standard volume label, an 80-byte dummy header, and a tapemark.

Q: *What is an IEBPTPCH used for?*

A: IEBPTPCH is a dataset utility used to print or punch all, or selected, portions of a sequential or partitioned dataset. Records can be printed or punched to meet either standard specifications or user specifications.

Q: *What is an IEBUPDTE used for?*

A: IEBUPDTE is a dataset utility used to create and update dataset libraries, modify existing partitioned members or sequential datasets, and change the organization of a dataset from sequential to partitioned (or vice versa).

Q: *Which utility can be both used for VSAM and non-VSAM files?*

A: IDCAMS utility is used to handle VSAM as well as non-VSAM files.

Q: *Which parameter is required to copy a dataset using IEBCOPY?*

A: The parameter 'COPY' is required to initiate one or more IEBCOPY copy, unload, or load operations. Any number of operations can follow a single COPY statement, and any number of COPY statements can appear within a single job step.

Q: *What is the parameter 'GENERATE' used for on utility IEBGENER?*

A: The parameter 'GENERATE' for the utility IEBGENER is used when output is to be partitioned, editing is to be performed, or user routines are provided and/or label processing is specified.

Q: *What is the parameter 'MEMBER' used for on utility IEBGENER?*

A: The parameter 'MEMBER' for the utility IEBGENER is used when the output is to be partitioned. One MEMBER statement must be included for each member to be created by IEBGENER. All RECORD statements following a MEMBER statement pertain to the member named in that MEMBER statement.

Q: *What is the parameter 'RECORD' used for on utility IEBGENER?*

A: The parameter 'RECORD' for the utility IEBGENER is used to define a record group and to supply editing information. A record group consists of records that are to be processed identically.

Q: *Which utility uses the 'REPRO' command and what function does it perform?*

A: The utility IDCAMS uses the 'REPRO' command. The REPRO command copies sequential datasets. It performs much the same function as IEBGENER.

Q: *How does one verify that a utility has ended normally?*

A: To verify if a utility has ended normally, one must check the JCL for a return code of zero. Various utilities generate return codes of 0004, 0008, 0012, and higher, in increments of 4, when problems or unusual conditions have been encountered.

Q: *When a utility ends with a nonzero return code, what must be done to resolve the problem?*

A: When a utility ends with a nonzero return code, it is necessary to determine what caused the error. One may start by checking for error messages generated by the utility and look them up on a utility messages manual. Also, the JCL statements and/or control statements should be checked to make sure they were properly coded. Once the error has been identified, it should be fixed and the job resubmitted.

6
UNIX

Val Carciu

Introduction

The Unix system has a strange, maybe unique, history. Like many great ideas, it started as a game, a space travel game developed by Ken Thompson and Dennis Ritchie for the DEC PDP at the beginning of 1970. Following this, they created a new file system structure, similar in concept to the file system currently in use. A processing environment with scheduling was added and the rest, of what today would be considered a rudimentary operating system, followed. This original version was written in assembly language. At the same time the "C" programming language was being developed by the same group beginning in 1971. C then became the language used in the development of the Unix system. The kernel (memory resident part of the operating system) was recoded in C in 1973. Today, with very few exceptions, the entire Unix operating system is coded in the C language. C's portability is widely regarded as a major reason for the popularity of the Unix system.

The new operating system, Unix, captured the imagination of the computer scientists at AT&T Bell Laboratories. After three years there were about a dozen Unix systems running on different machines. However, by the mid-1970s Unix became a functional operating system running on the DEC PDP-11. At the same time AT&T released copies of the Unix system to universities around the world. That is how the BSD (Berkeley Software Distribution) from the University of California at Berkeley came into being. Today's BSD implementation can be found in many universities and engineering communities. AT&T also has moved to optimize the Unix system for the business community. After a period of transition and changes they came up with a standardized release—the Unix System V. Today, the Unix System V represents a majority of the Unix market.

Over the years several computer manufacturers have developed their own versions of Unix System V: SCO Unix System V, IBM AIX, HP-UX, SunOS and Solaris. The latest is UnixWare from Novell.

The Unix Job Interview

An interviewer will normally target specific areas of knowledge. The level of expertise expected is as follows:

- A "novice" Unix programer should have knowledge about how to log in and out, what a password is and how to change it, the structure of directories and files, most of the commands related to directories and files, the vi editor, and probably the most important of all, how to get help using Unix's on-line HELP facilities.

- An intermediate programmer, in addition to all of the above, should have knowledge about permissions and the related commands, pipes and redirection, processes, writing small scripts, different types of shells and environment, the structure of filesystems, print services, and related commands.

- An expert (usually the Unix system administrator) should know how to start and stop the system (including customatization), using the audit subsystem, administering user accounts, managing filesystems, and backing up filesystems. In addition he or she should know how to upgrade the hardware configuration, maintain system security, administer terminals, utilize modems, (i.e., remote logins), build a network using UUCP, "tune" system performance and, probably most important of all, how to troubleshoot the system.

Questions and Answers

Q: *Describe the steps the system goes through, at **boot** time, before the users may sign on.*

A: When the computer is turned on, the Unix system bootstrap program gets loaded and the "Boot" prompt is displayed. At this point press <Return> to load the Unix kernel or specify the name of an old kernel if you want to load an older version. The system will now display information, among which the hardware recognition is the most important (here is where, for example, you can see if your parallel port is recognized). Next it verifies if the root filesystem needs checking (is "dirty" or is "clean"). If the root filesystem needs checking, you will be prompted to allow the checking and repair (**fsck** utility) of the root filesystem. When the cleaning is complete, the system asks to choose the mode of operation: single (by entering root password) or multiuser (press <Ctrl-d>) mode. Single-user mode is chosen mostly when system maintenance is needed. Once multiuser mode is chosen, you are prompted to enter the system time or take the default. The system then executes commands found in the /etc/rc directories, generating startup messages for the various system services, such as the printer or network services. Finally the system displays the **login** prompt.

Q: *When, and depending on what, are the other filesystems checked and mounted?*

A: The other filesystems are mounted when the system enters multiuser mode. They are checked and mounted depending on the entries found by the system in /etc/default/filesys file at **boot** time.

Q: *Name two ways to bring the system down. (Do not even think about turning the power off.)*

A: The most commonly used (and the recommended way) is **shutdown.** This will warn the user that the system is coming down and unless otherwise specified, will have a one-minute grace period (may be different from one implementation to another).

   The second way is the **haltsys** (or **halt** for BSD) command. This command halts the system immediately. It should not be used unless in single-user mode. The users are logged out (their work will be lost) and network servers and other programs are terminated abnormally.

Q: *How can you find out the hardware configuration recognized at **boot** time?*

A: There are two ways: first is by issuing the **hwconfig** command (on SCO Unix) and second by simply checking in the /usr/adm/messages file.

Q: *What are the files checked or scripts executed when a user logs in?*

A: The order they are checked/executed are: /etc/passwd, /etc/profile, $HOME/.profile and in case the Korn shell is used, $HOME/.kshrc. If the C shell is used, .profile is replaced by .login and .kshrc by .cshrc.

Q: *When an account, for various reasons, is not used anymore, how can the system administrator disable it?*

A: There are two ways: (1) using **sysadmsh,** the user can be "retired"; the second one is to use **rmuser** utility to remove the user (the files and the home directory have to be manually removed by the system administrator).

Q: *How can a user ensure that certain sensitive files cannot be read by others?*

A: The **crypt** command can be used or one of the editors (**ed, edit, ex** or **vi**) with **-x** option. All of the above use a user-assigned password to encrypt or decrypt the file.

Q: *How can a user remind another user about an important meeting taking place on a certain date, at a certain hour?*

A: A very good way is to use the **at** command as it follows:

$ at 9:30am Mar 29
banner Meeting at 10 : mail frank
<Ctrl-d>

Q: *How can a user execute a long command and still have the terminal available for work?*

A: The user may execute the long command in background using the **&** command as follows:

$ wc -c hugefile > wordcount &

Q: *Once the background command has been started, can it be aborted like any other foreground command?*

A: Foreground commands can be aborted by pressing the INTERRUPT key (default is the <Delete> key). Background commands cannot be aborted this way. Instead you have to use the **kill** command.

Q: *What is a filesystem?*

A: A filesystem is a distinct division of the operating system, consisting of files, directories and the information needed to locate them. A filesystem can be thought of as a structure upon which directories and files are constructed.

Q: *What happens if you have, for example, a directory, /tmp, and you mount a filesystem, say /dev/u, on this directory?*

A: If any files existed in the directory /tmp before the filesystem was mounted, they will disappear and they will reappear when the filesystem is unmounted.

Q: *Can the system administrator enable users to mount a filesystem (on SCO Unix)?*

A: Only the super user can **mount** or **umount** filesystems. However the super user can set up parameters to define which filesystem can be mounted by users with the **mnt** command. These parameters may include an access password, if desired. The users may use the **umnt** command to unmount a filesystem.

Q: *Does it make sense for a directory to have the **execute** permission on it?*

A: Yes, it does. If a directory does not have the **execute** permission on it you cannot do a **cd** command to it.

Q: *By default, the GID (group identifier) of a newly created file is set to the GID of the creating process or user. How can this behavior be changed?*

A: This behavior can be changed by setting the SGID bit on that directory. That results in a new file having the GID of the directory.

Q: *What is a **link** between files and what is the command you would use to link files?*

A: A link is a directory entry referring to a file. The same file can have several links. Any changes made to the file are effectively independent of the name by which the file is known. The command is **ln.**

Q: *What is the most common way of locating files?*

A: The most common way is by using the **find** command, which enables you to locate all files with a specified name, permissions setting, size, type, owner, or last access or modification date.

Q: *How can you search a file for occurrences of a word or phrase?*

A: The **grep** command displays all lines in a file that contain the key word or phrase. It is a good practice to enclose the search pattern in single quotes to protect it from command substitution in the shell.

Q: *How can you list the names of all files in which there is a certain pattern?*

A: You can use a combination of two commands:

find . -exec grep -l "pattern" {} \;

Q: *Assuming you have a big file and you want to clear it (empty it) but you want to keep the file and its permissions, what could you do?*

A: You may use the following commands:

$ > filename (for Bourne or Korn shell)

or

$ **cat /dev/null** > filename (for C shell)

Q: *Assuming that a directory becomes too large (has too many entries) and you decide to make two directories out of it (one of which has the same name), how would you proceed?*

A: Since a directory, even if you remove all files it contains, never shrinks, you should make two new directories, move all files into them, remove the old directory, and then rename one of the new directories using the name of the old one.

Q: *What is used for the **lost+found** directory in a filesystem?*

A: During **fsck** (filesystem check) command, any files that are unreferenced but valid are placed in this special directory called **lost+found**. The **fsck** command does not create or extend this directory, therefore it has to contain a sufficient number of empty slots for **fsck** to use when reconnecting files.

Q: *Assuming a certain user has to print invoices on invoice paper, how would you deny other users access to that printer?*

A: To deny access use the following command:

/usr/lib/lpadmin -p printername **-u allow:**user-name

Q: *What should you do if you cannot redirect the output to a printer?*

A: Follow these steps:

1. Verify that the device file for the port exists in **/dev** directory. Make sure it is a device and not a file.
2. Test the cable connection using a cable from a working system.
3. Try to print a file from DOS.
4. Check the printer hardware configuration.

Q: *What can you do if you have a garbled printout?*

A: You can:

- Check the baud rate and parity settings for the (serial) printer and interface scripts.
- Check for **tab** and **newline** handling for the printer and the interface scripts.
- Check for proper handshaking (both the printer and the port are set for the same protocol, either **XON/XOFF** or **DTR**).

Q: *List three commands most often used for archive or data transfer.*

A: The three most common are: **tar, cpio,** and **dd.**

Q: *If you were to make a script to back up your system, how would you make it?*

A: The script would look something like:

cd /

find . -follow -print | cpio -ovaBL > /dev/rct0 2> /u/list where in the file /u/list we would obtain a list of the backed-up files. This script should have root's permissions.

Q: *Once you obtain a stable system, that is, a good kernel, what are some of the first things the system administrator should do?*

A: First he should do a backup of the entire system. Then make a bootable diskette and then a root filesystem diskette. This way, if the root filesystem gets corrupted beyond repair, you can boot the system and restore the system from tapes.

Q: *What steps should be followed when you find you have an unusable root filesystem?*

A: In case of unusable root filesystem, follow these steps:

1. Boot from the diskette.
2. Insert the root filesystem diskette, when prompted.
3. **mount /dev/hd0root /mnt**
4. **cd /mnt**
5. **./usr/bin/tar xvf ./dev/rct0**
6. **umount /dev/hd0root**
7. Reboot.

Q: *Assuming you have only one hard drive and you want to be able to run MS-DOS and Unix, how would you do it?*

A: First make a primary MS-DOS partition, format it, and install the operating system. Then start installing the Unix system, partitioning the rest of the disk as a Unix partition. At the **Boot** prompt press <Return> to boot Unix or type **dos** to boot MS-DOS. This is true when the Unix partition is the one active. If you make the DOS partition active, you will always boot MS-DOS. You can activate one partition or the other, in both operating systems, with **fdisk** command.

Q: *Can you copy DOS files on the Unix system?*

A: Yes! The command to use is **doscp.** This command permits copying in both directions. An example would be:

doscp /john/send /dev/fd0:/mary/receive

Q: *How about DOS filesystems?*

A: If the system administrator permits it, you can mount a DOS floppy disk as follows:

mount -f DOS /dev/fd0135 /mnt

Q: *What steps should be followed to connect a terminal to your COM1 serial port?*

A: The steps are as follows:

1. Connect the terminal to the serial port.
2. Set the terminal for 9600 baud, 8 data bits, 1 stop bit, no parity, full duplex and XON/XOFF handshaking.
3. As super user, check the entry for the serial port in the **/etc/inittab** file to look like **tla:2:respawn:/etc/getty ttyla m.** Also, to make the entry permanent (after a kernel relink), you have to change the file **/etc/conf/init.d/sio.**
4. Issue the command **enable /dev/ttyla.**
5. Press <Return> a few times. The "login:" prompt should appear.

Q: *How can you find out the baud rate, the parity scheme, and other information about a serial line?*

A: By using the following command:

   $ **stty < /dev/ttyla**

Q: *How do you set the terminal type?*

A: The preferable method for setting the terminal type is to assign the type to the **TERM** variable. This is usually done in **.profile** or **.login** sign-on scripts.

Q: *Can you automatically set your terminal type at login?*

A: Yes, you can. As root you have to edit **/etc/ttytype** file to contain an entry like for example: **wy50 ttyla.** Then you have to change or add the **tset** command in your **.profile** or **.login** script.

Q: *How do you remove a terminal from the system?*

A: Following these steps:

1. Turn off the power.
2. Log in as super user at another terminal (or console).
3. Issue the command **disable ttyla.**
4. Disconnect the terminal from the system.

Q: *What do you have to do if you want to use multiscreen capability?*

A: You have to configure the pseudo-ttys. Login as super user and execute the command **mkdev ptty.**

Q: *In order for **mscreen** to work with your terminal, what do you need to have?*

A: First your terminal has to have enough screen memory. Also the file **/etc/mscreencap** has to have an entry for your terminal. This entry is used by **mscreen** utility to determine how to change screen images for your particular terminal.

Q: *Which of the following serial ports have modem control:*

   /dev/ttyla

   /dev/ttyl1A

/dev/tty2a

/dev/tty2A

A: The ports with modem control are /dev/tty1A and /dev/tty2A.

Q: *Can you use both modem and nonmodem control ports?*

A: No, you cannot use them both at the same time. If you try you will get a message such as **device busy.**

Q: *Should you use a form of error correction/detection when using the modem for UUCP?*

A: No, you should not. UUCP has its own error detection scheme and this conflicts with any lower level scheme, generating poor throughput and possibly failed transfers.

Q: *How can you test a modem's ability to dial correctly?*

A: Using the port **ttyla,** you can try with the following command: **cu -lttyla dir.**

Q: *To connect a modem you need a serial port. How would you check it?*

A: First you have to make sure the port is recognized at bootup by checking **/usr/adm/messages** or using **hwconfig** command and then attach a terminal or serial printer to confirm that it is functioning.

Q: *What do you do if the modem answers the incoming calls, but there is no login prompt?*

A: Verify that the CD line is being asserted by the modem, make sure the port is enabled (the command could be **enable /dev/tty1A**), verify that the modem is using the correct **/etc/gettydefs** entry and is selecting the proper baud rate.

Q: *What commands can you use to transfer files between two Unix systems?*

A: You can use two commands: **uucp** and **uuto.**

Q: *Give an example of a **uucp** command and one of a **uuto** command.*

A: A **uucp** command can look like this:
   uucp transferfile machine2!~/transfer-file
   In this example the file will be transferred into **/usr/spool/uucppublic.**
   A **uuto** command can look like this:
   uuto /tmp/transfer file machine2!frank
   In this example the file will be transferred into the directory **/usr/spool/uucppublic/receive/frank/machine1.**

Q: *What command can you use to execute commands on remote UUCP sites? Give an example.*

A: The command you can use is **uux.** It can look like this: **uux machine2!lp machine2!/tmp/file-name.**

Q: *How can you, at a remote terminal with a modem, make the computer call you, so you can login, avoiding long distance charges?*

A: You can call the computer, login, and issue the following command: **ct -s 2400 5551212.** If a dialer is available, the computer hangs up the line and calls your terminal back.

Q: *Being signed-on on your local Unix machine, what command can you use to sign-on a remote Unix system?*

A: You can use a command similar to the following: **cu -s2400 5551212.** When the remote Unix system answers the call, **cu** notifies you that the connection has been made and then you are prompted for your login. When you are finished, logout and then enter ~. to terminate the **cu** session.

Q: *What happens if you do not specify the baud rate in the cu command?*

A: If the -s option is not specified, **cu** uses the first available dialer at the speed specified in the **Devices** file.

Q: *Can you transfer files between the two systems, while logged in during a cu session?*

A: Yes, you can, but not binary files. The command to transfer from the remote to the local computer is **take.** The command to transfer from the local to the remote computer is **put.** Both commands have to be preceded by ~%.

Q: *What performance tools can you use to diagnose system inefficiency?*

A: You may use **sar, timex,** and also **ps** commands.

Q: *What can sar command be used for?*

A: System Activity Reporter (**sar**) samples the state of the system and provides reports on various system-wide activities like buffer activity, cache activity, process throughput, CPU utilization, system tables, and swapping activity.

Q: *What can timex command be used for?*

A: This command reports both system-wide and per-process activity during the execution of a command or program.

Q: *What is swapping?*

A: As new processes request more memory in order to run, the paging daemon is responsible for freeing up memory by writing pages of memory to the disk swap area.

Q: *What should you do if the there is an intense swapping activity?*

A: This is a sign that not enough memory is available for applications. The best thing to do is to increase the memory size. A temporary solution might be to decrease the buffer cache size (although this might decrease disk performance).

Q: *What is the scatter/gather feature?*

A: **Scatter/gather** is a performance optimization that allows separate filesystem requests to be grouped together as a single request. Only requests whose destinations are physically located next to each other on the disk can be grouped.

Q: *How can you check the status of processes?*

A: You can check the status of your task using **ps** command. This command lists all the active processes that are running (both in the foreground and background).

Q: *How can you stop a runaway process?*

A: To stop a process you can use the **kill** command, followed by the process ID.

Q: *Assuming that you have to start the execution of a long command and you want to log out and go home, how do you go about it?*

A: You can start the command in background, using **nohup** command. The command would look like: **nohup command &.** You can now log out and the process continues in background.

Q: *How can you prioritize processes?*

A: Assuming you do not need the results of your command immediately, you may use the **nice** command. Something like **nice -15 latecommand.** The command will execute with the priority of 35, instead of the default of 20.

Q: *How can you make a program execute automatically?*

A: Unix systems allow you to run programs automatically at specified times by using the **cron** program. First you have to create a crontab file and then submit it to **cron** by using the **crontab** command.

Q: *What is a "shell"?*

A: A "shell" is a command interpreter. The shell gives the user a high-level language in which to communicate with the operating system. Each shell has one function: to read and execute commands from its standard input.

Q: *How does the "shell" execute the commands?*

A: For the "shell" to execute a command, it has to be executable (to have the execute permission). If the command is a compiled program, the shell, as parent, creates a child process that immediately executes that program. If the command is a shell procedure (file containing shell commands), the shell spawns another instance of itself to read the file and execute the commands inside.

Q: *How does the "shell" find the commands?*

A: The sequence of directories search is given by the shell PATH variable. Directory pathnames are separated by colons.

Q: *Which are the characters you could use to match other characters?*

A: These special characters are: the asterisk (*), which matches any string, including the null string; the question mark (?), which matches any one character; and any sequence of characters enclosed within brackets ([and]), which matches any one of the enclosed characters.

Q: *How can you redirect the output of a command?*

A: To redirect the output of a command you can use > or >> redirection arguments. When you use > argument a file will be created (or replaced if it exists) as standard output. When you use >> argument, the standard output is appended to the end of the file.

Q: *How can a command take the input from a file?*

A: You can make a file the input for a command by using < argument. For instance: **sort < infile.**

Q: *What is **command substitution**?*

A: Any command line can be placed within back quotation marks (`) so that the output of the command replaces the quoted command itself. This concept is known as **command substitution.**

Q: *What are **positional parameters**?*

A: When a shell procedure is invoked, the shell implicitly creates **positional parameters.** The name of the shell procedure itself in position zero on the command line is assigned to the positional parameter **$0.** The first command argument is called **$1,** and so on.

Q: *What is a **pipeline** for a shell script?*

A: A **pipeline** is a sequence of one or more commands separated by vertical bars (|). In a **pipeline,** the standard output of each command but the last is connected (by a **pipe**) to the standard input of the next command. Each command in a **pipeline** is run separately; the shell waits for the last command to finish.

Q: *How can you use parentheses or braces at the command line or in a shell procedure?*

A: A simple command in a pipeline can be replaced by a command list enclosed in either parentheses or braces. The output of all the commands so enclosed is combined into one stream that becomes the input to the next command in the pipeline.

Q: *What is the difference between using parentheses and using braces?*

A: When parentheses are used, the shell forks a subshell that reads and executes the enclosed commands. Unlike parentheses, no subshell is forked for braces: the enclosed commands are simply read and executed by the shell.

Q: *What are functions, from the shell's standpoint?*

A: Functions are like shell procedures except that they reside in memory and are executed by the shell process, not by a separate process.

Q: *What is a command's **environment**?*

A: All variables and their associated values that are known to a command at the beginning of its execution make up its **environment.** This environment includes variables that the command inherits from its parent process and variables specified as **keyword parameters** on the command line that invokes the command. The variables that a shell passes to its child processes are those that have been named as arguments to the **export** command.

Q: *How can you initialize new variables in a shell procedure and use them later in the sign-on shell?*

A: You can use the dot (.) command, which causes the shell to read commands from the procedure without spawning a new subshell. Changes made to variables in the procedure are in effect after the dot command finishes. The command would look like this: **. procedure**

Q: *How can you solve the following situation: You want the users, once signed on, to be put in the application program; once they quit the application, you want them signed off the system?*

A: A very efficient way is to put in their **.profile** or **.login** script, as the last command, the **exec** command, with the name of the application as an argument. In this way, once they quit the application, they are signed off the system.

Q: *How can you make sure that the work file created during the execution of a script will be removed even if the script was interrupted?*

A: Within a shell script you can still take action (in this case remove files) when an interrupt signal is received by using the **trap** command. An example of a **trap** command would be:

trap 'rm -f tempfile; exit' 0 2 3 15

Q: *Assuming you have to run backups during the night, and there is no night operator and the backup utility prompts you for answers before it starts, how would you solve this problem?*

A: Create a shell script and put it in the **crontabs** directory, to be run by the **cron** process. The script would have the interactive command (command which requires answers) followed by **<< eoi,** where **eoi** is an arbitrary string, signaling the end of input. An example would be:

command <<- eoi
0
1
2
3
eoi

Q: *How can you write the standard output and the standard error for a command to the same file?*

A: You can do this by using the file descriptors. The command would look like this:

command 1>file name 2>&1

Q: *In a **pipeline**, how can you arrange the commands, so if one of them fails, the execution of the **pipeline** stops?*

A: The **pipeline** would look something like this:
command1 && command2 && command3 && . . . && commandn

Q: *In a **pipeline**, how can you arrange the commands so that, the second one is executed only if the first one fails?*

A: The **pipeline** would look something like this:

command1 | | command2

The first command is executed, its exit status is examined and only if it has a nonzero value, the second command is executed.

Q: *What can you do to fix the problem if one of your filesystems runs out of inodes?*

A: You can back up the filesystem, unmount the filesystem, rerun **mkfs** and specify more **inodes** for the filesystem, mount the filesystem, and restore the backups.

Q: *How can you check the amount of free space on filesystems?*

A: You can use the **df** command with the options **-v** and **-i.** This utility reports sizes in 512 byte blocks.

Q: *How can you reduce filesystem fragmentation?*

A: To reduce filesystem fragmentation back up the filesystem, remove all files (including dot files), unmount the filesystem, clean the filesystem using **fsck -s** command, mount the filesystem, and restore the backups.

Q: *What does it mean if a user has write permissions on a directory but is unable to remove files from that directory?*

A: It means that the **sticky bit** has been set for that directory. The **sticky bit** is a directory protection setting that allows only the owner of the file (or super-user) to remove files from that directory.

Q: *What command can be used to compare two text files?*

A: The **diff** command can be used to find out what lines must be changed in two files to bring them into agreement. This is especially useful for finding the differences between two versions of the same source program.

Q: *How can you convert a file from Unix format to MS-DOS format?*

A: The **xtod** converts a file from Unix to MS-DOS format and the command **dtox** does the opposite.

Q: *What is **umask**?*

A: **umask** is a three-digit octal number used by the system to establish the permissions for a newly created file. The system subtracts this number from 777 and the result are the permissions for the new file.

Q: *How can you find out what variables are currently assigned?*

A: By typing the command **env,** with no arguments, you can get a list of the variables currently assigned.

Q: *How can you find out what third-party software was linked into the kernel?*

A: To display the modifications to the system software since its initialization you would use **swconfig** command.

Q: *What command can you use to archive a raw device?*

A: You can use the **dd** command, which allows you to specify the input and output block size, among other options.

Q: *What does it mean if the system hangs the "Kernel: i/o bufs" message?*

A: It means that the **/etc/init** file is missing from the system. To restore it:

1. Boot from a bootable diskette.
2. Insert the root filesystem, when prompted.

3. Mount the hard disk root filesystem:

   mount /dev/hd0root /mnt

4. Copy the **/etc/init** file from the root filesystem on the floppy to the mounted hard disk:

   cp /etc/init /mnt/etc/init

5. Unmount the hard disk.

6. With the floppy in the drive, reboot the system with **haltsys.**

7. Remove the floppy from the drive at the boot prompt and boot.

Q: *What can you do if the **mail** command hangs when a user tries to read his mail?*

A: You have to check the following:

1. Verify that the user's mailbox exists in the **/usr/spool/mail** directory.

2. Make sure that the owner and group ID of the **/usr/spool/mail** directory is **mmdf.**

3. Make sure that the mailbox is not too large (over 1000 messages).

Q: *What are device drivers?*

A: Device drivers are software routines, part of the **kernel,** which interface with the hardware. Unix represents devices as block- or character-special files located in the **/dev** directory. Each has a major and a minor device number.

Q: *Assuming you want to send mail to Eric, at "ucbvax," and your machine does not have a direct connection, but you can connect to "hplabs" machine, which has a leased line to "ucbvax", what would be the complete mail path?*

A: The complete mail path to Eric is

   hplabs!ucbvax!eric

Q: *What are Unix "daemons"?*

A: The Unix daemons (and not demons) are a collection of processes that each perform a particular system task. Two examples would be **init** and **cron** daemons.

Q: *Assuming you want to start the data-base engine every time you boot the system, how would you do it?*

A: Add the necessary commands in **/etc/rc** script, which is one of the scripts executed when the system is coming up.

Q: *How would you bring down the data-base engine when the system is coming down?*

A: Add the necessary commands in **/etc/shutdown** script, which is the pathname for the **shutdown** command.

Q: *What can you do if a scrambled terminal responds to keyboard input but the display is incorrect?*

A: First you should check the **TERM** variable by entering **env** at the command line. If the terminal type is incorrect, reset it by entering at the command line **TERM=wy60,** if the terminal is a Wyse60. After resetting the terminal type, reinitialize the terminal by entering **tset** with no arguments.

Q: *What can you do if a terminal that responds to keyboard input does not display the characters entered at the keyboard?*

A: Sometimes, when a program stops prematurely as a result of an error, or when the user presses the <Break> key, the terminal stops echoing. To restore the terminal to normal operation, enter the following: **<Ctrl>j stty sane <Ctrl>j.** The terminal should now display keyboard input.

Q: *How can you check whether the ACU (Automatic Call Unit) or modems are working correctly?*

A: By entering **uustat -q,** you can display a list of queued requests, the time of the last request attempt and the contact status. By entering **cu -x9 -l tynn phone,** you can use a specific line and print debugging information during the contact attempt.

Q: *What can you do when the **cu** command fails to connect and displays the NO DEVICES AVAILABLE message?*

A: First you should check that the **/usr/lib/uucp/Devices** file is set up correctly. For example, the entry in this file for a direct line using **ttyla** at 9600 baud should look like this:

Direct ttyla - 9600 direct

It is also possible that the remote line is busy.

Q: *What does it mean when the **cu** command fails, displaying the message SYSTEM NOT IN Systems FILE?*

A: It means that the **/usr/lib/uucp/Systems** file on your computer does not contain an entry for the system to which you are trying to connect. To display a list of all systems that your computer can connect to, enter **uuname.**

7

The AS/400 Advanced Series

Daniel Robert Cohen

Introduction

On May 3, 1994, IBM announced the new AS/400 Advanced Series. This announcement heralded many hardware and software enhancements to the AS/400 system. The AS/400 Advanced Series includes major improvements in compact design, performance, and a greatly expanded operating system. The database design was enhanced to enforce data integrity within the system. The new Integrated File System allows for fast and easy data transfer between the AS/400 and other systems. Improved language support provides programmers with additional tools that can be used to create high performance applications. Portability of software from older AS/400 models allows companies to preserve their working software while moving to the newer, more powerful AS/400.

The Advanced Series consists of two closely inter-related systems: the AS/400 Advanced System and the AS/400 Advanced Server. Both systems use OS/400, but differ in specific hardware configuration. The AS/400 Advanced System is intended for heavy on-line use and is designed for high volume cross system connectivity. The AS/400 Advanced Server is used as a file server to store and transfer data between systems. The Advanced Server is especially suited to handle I/O intensive batch processing. Older models of the AS/400 having the current release of OS/400 are compatible with the Advanced Series models. V3R1 is the release of OS/400 included in the initial announcement. The AS/400 Advanced Series is shipped with the most recent version of OS/400.

V3R1 improves upon language enhancements made in prior releases, and presents important advancements to the AS/400 database system. The database system is now called DB2/400. DB2/400 supports many new and convenient features such as enhanced SQL performance, two-step commitment control, stored procedures, triggers, and referential integrity. DB2/400 is a subset of the new Integrated File System. The Integrated File System also provides support for database structures and commands used by DOS, OS/2, POSIX (Portable Operating Systems for Computing Environments), Unix, and XPG (X/Open Portability Guide). With IFS, data storage, and retrieval between systems using different file structures, naming conventions, and operating systems are greatly simplified. A standard DOS command, for example, can be used to copy a file from the AS/400 directly to the PC.

Integrated Language Environment (ILE) provides enhanced language support for the AS/400. Prior to ILE, two language support models were used. The OPM (Original Program Model) supported RPG, COBOL, PL/I, BASIC, and CL, and the EPM (Extended Programming Model) supported Pascal and C languages. ILE unites RPG, COBOL, CL, and C under a single language support umbrella. This provides greatly improved performance for call intensive applications, and allows programs written in different languages to call one another. Older versions of AS/400 programming languages enjoy continued support in V3R1.

ILE RPG/400, otherwise known as RPGIV, is the new ILE compatible version of RPG available with V3R1. New with ILE RPG is the Definition Specification or "D spec." The E and L specs have been eliminated from ILE RPG. Functions previously done by the E spec are handled by the D spec. L spec functions are done by the F spec. Although the I spec still exists, many of the field definition functions previously relegated to the I spec can now be accomplished by the D spec. Column widths have been changed to accommodate 10 character field and file names. The C spec now allows lengthy logical expressions and mathematical operations. Most op-codes used by earlier versions of RPG are still supported, but some have been lengthened. The REDPE op-code, for example, is written READPE in ILE RPG. A utility is supplied by IBM that converts prior versions of RPG source to ILE RPG. Although V3R1, and later releases of OS/400 still provide support for older versions of RPG and COBOL, the full power of ILE can be realized only when the ILE version of these languages is utilized.

IBM has rewritten their PC-Support product for the new release with increased speed and flexibility. The new PC-Support is called CA/400 (Client Access/400). CA/400 will continue to support storage and retrieval of shared folders. New and faster techniques to access AS/400 files from the PC are made possible by IFS and the new Client Server support. DOS directories may now be stored on the AS/400 itself. IFS handles data translation when copying files between the file systems resident on the AS/400 or when copying data to the PC. Any errors encountered by the system when performing translations are immediately made known to the user. These advancements enable CA/400 to rapidly download data from any part of the AS/400 and give the user greater flexibility in how data will be stored and retrieved.

Terminology

Activation Group: An ILE based method of reducing system overhead by controlling program activation and resource usage within a job.

Binding: ILE allows programs to be created connected or "bound" to increase performance for call-intensive applications, and to provide an easy method for multi-language programs to call one another.

CA/400: Client Access/400 is the new name for PC Support/400, which has been rewritten to provide PC users with easy access to data on the AS/400.

Current Directory: IFS enables file access via directory tree structures as exists on the PC. When the system looks for a file stored in a directory, the search begins with the Current Directory.

Current Library: The library that is always at the top of the user library list, and is the first user library searched when a job is executing.

D Spec: Definition Specification. The new ILE RPG spec that replaces the E and L specs.

DB2/400: New name for the OS/400 database management system.

Dynamic Binding: The ILE method of connecting programs so that a single copy of the program exists on the system, no matter how may times it is bound to other programs.

Eval: The new RPG op-code that is used for coding lengthy logical expressions and complex mathematical operations.

FSIOP: File Server Input Output Processor is the new file server hardware added to the AS/400 that provides faster data access for PCs and Local Area Networks.

Home Directory: Specified on the user's Job Description to default as the Current Directory when the user signs on.

IFS: Integrated File System supports multiple database structures, naming conventions, and file access methods. IFS provides an environment for software developed on a variety of systems to work on the AS/400.

ILE: Integrated Language Environment is the new programming model on the AS/400.

ILE Program: An executable object that contains one or more programs or modules that are statically bound.

ILE Service Program: An executable object that contains multiple programs or modules that are dynamically bound and which can be called by any other ILE program. Modules in a Service Program may be created independently of the programs that call them.

Invocation Stack: The list of programs maintained by the system as one program calls another in a series of calls within a single task or job.

Module: A nonexecutable program object created using the Create Module command. ILE programs consist of one or more modules.

Object: Everything on the AS/400 that is referenced by a name, uses space, and is defined by specific attributes is called an object. Some examples of objects are files, libraries, programs, and user profiles.

PDM (Program Development Manager): A productivity tool for programmers providing functions such as copying, deleting, scanning, changing, or creating objects.

Referential Integrity: A new function of DB2/400 that allows creation of files with specific internal rules designed to enforce consistency of data between the related files.

Stored Procedure: A program or set of SQL or REXX statements based on the server that reduces network activity by optimizing system resource usage.

Static Binding: An ILE method of connecting programs where a copy of all bound programs is included in the final program object. Each time a program object is bound, another copy is generated, resulting in multiple copies of the program. See Dynamic Binding.

Time Slice: A finite amount of time in which a job is granted system resources while other jobs are queued. When the time-slice is over, the executing job is queued while another job is granted system resources.

Triggers: A new feature of DB2/400 that causes OS/400 to automatically invoke specified programs before and/or after a file is changed.

VRPG: Visual RPG is an IBM client/server development tool that allows easy creation of client/server applications in an OS/2 environment.

The Interview

The AS/400 Advanced Series contains many programming languages, different operating modes, and various file structures. There are a variety of ways to connect the AS/400 to other computer systems. It is therefore imperative to gain as much general knowledge as possible on the capabilities of the new system. It is also advisable to find out in advance about the AS/400 used by the company you are interviewing with. If this information is available, then your preparation should include details of the particular system configuration and programming languages used. A solid display of general knowledge always impresses interviewers.

A skilled programmer should have a thorough understanding of RPG/400, as most of that knowledge is also valid for ILE RPG/400 (otherwise known as RPGIV). It is also necessary to understand the differences between ILE RPG and prior versions of RPG. One important example of this is the D spec, which is entirely new to ILE RRG. AS/400 shops that are using ILE RPG and ILE CL will pose questions covering these topics. It is also necessary to learn how programs are bound together using the new ILE commands. There could also be questions covering Triggers, Referential Integrity, Client Access/400, SQL/400, Commitment Control, Performance Tuning, communications, VRPG, LAN, Client Server/400, IFS, various programming languages, or any subject related to the AS/400. Questions covering both old and new versions of RPG, CL, and DDS are included below. With some notable differences, most commands, keywords, op-codes, and programming techniques of the past remain valid. The COBOL language is covered in another section of this book. For those interested in further study, there are numerous books, technical journals, and IBM manuals available on the AS/400 Advanced Series.

Questions and Answers

Q: *Name the different types of files used on the AS/400.*

A: Files commonly used are physical files, source physical files, logical files, join logical files, display files, printer files, spooled files, and save files.

Q: *How does a field reference file differ from a physical file?*

A: A field reference file is a file in which field definitions and descriptions are stored, while physical files contain the data defined by the field reference file.

Q: *What does UNIQUE mean?*

A: UNIQUE is specified at file level in DDS for a keyed physical or logical file to indicate that records with duplicate keys will not be permitted.

Q: *What is the difference between FIFO and LIFO record retrieval?*

A: FIFO means first in, first out. When more than one record in a file has the same key, these records will be retrieved in the order of their addition to the file. The first added will be the first retrieved, and so on. FIFO is the default assumed for a file that allows duplicate keys.

   LIFO means last in, first out. Records with duplicate keys will be retrieved in the opposite order of their addition to the file. The last record added will be the first retrieved, and so on.

Q: *What is dynamic select?*

A: Dynamic select means: select records at execution time. This is a DDS file-level keyword (DYNSLT) that is used for logical files. When DYNSLT is specified, the system does not perform record selection (or omission) until the file is read by a program. As each record is read, it is checked using select/omit criteria specified in the file definition.

Q: *Explain how dynamic select differs from access path select.*

A: While dynamic selection always occurs when the file is read, access path selection may (but not necessarily) occur before the file is read. The reason is that access path selection is done when maintenance is performed on the files' access path. The time access path maintenance is performed depends upon what type of file maintenance is specified on the Create Logical File command (Immediate, Delay, or Rebuild).

Q: *Name two major differences between a logical file and a physical file.*

A: A physical file may have only one record format. A logical file may have multiple record formats. A physical file contains actual data. A logical file does not contain data, but provides a logical and sequenced view to the data using indexes that "point" to the records in the physical file.

Q: *Name and define the three methods used to maintain the access path of a file.*
A: 1. *Immediate.* All access paths associated with the file are updated when a change is made to the file, and it makes no difference whether the access paths are opened or closed—they are all updated immediately.
   2. *Rebuild.* With this method, only open access paths are updated when a change is made to the file. Any access paths that are closed at the time the change was made will not be updated. The next time the access path is opened, the access path will be completely rebuilt.
   3. *Delay.* When a change is made to a file, the only access paths that are updated are the ones that are open at the time the change is made. Any access paths that are closed at the time the change is made will not be updated until they are opened. The updates are accumulated and merged into the existing access path structure when it is opened. The entire access path is not rebuilt unless the accumulated changes to the access path are more than approximately 25 percent of the entire size of the access path.

Q: *Explain where each method to maintain an access path is best employed, and note a possible disadvantage to each.*
A: 1. When immediate file maintenance is used, the file can be opened quickly because the access path is kept up to date. This method is ideal for files that are used with interactive applications since they are constantly being opened and updated. The drawback to this method is the slower update (or output) operation for a file with several access paths associated since all the access paths are updated whenever a change occurs in any of them.
   2. When rebuild file maintenance is used, opening the file will take a long time because the entire access path will be rebuilt if changes occurred while the access path (that is now being opened) was closed. This method is ideal for files used with applications that are run periodically in batch.
   The advantage to this method is faster update (or output) operations for a file with several access paths associated. Since none of the closed access paths is updated when a change is made to the file, and only the particular access path now opened will be changed, the update process will occur more quickly. Rebuilding the access path of an entire file can take a long time. It is therefore generally best to avoid rebuild maintenance for a file used by programs called frequently, or where the file is very large. If the file has unique keys, this method cannot be used. If the file is being journaled, this method cannot be used.
   3. When delayed file maintenance is used, opening the file will be moderately, but not extremely, quick. The reason for this is that the access path is merged with accumulated changes, but not entirely rebuilt, when opened. This method is ideal for files used with applications run in batch. This method should be used only when there is a fairly small number of changes to be accumulated for the access paths that are closed. This method provides

a compromise between the slow update (or output) speed of immediate maintenance, and the slow open of rebuild maintenance.

The disadvantage to this method is that an extremely long open will take place if too many access path changes have accumulated since the last open operation. If the number of changes accumulated for the access path exceeds approximately 25 percent of the total size of the access path, then rebuild rather than delay maintenance should be used when the file using the access path is reopened. If the file has unique keys, this method cannot be used.

Q: *What is a join logical file? State three differences between a regular logical file and a join logical file.*

A: A join logical file is a type of logical file that contains fields from two or more physical files and combines them into a single record format.

1. A regular logical file allows for multiple record formats, and a join logical file allows for only one record format.

2. Changes to data in a physical file can be made via a logical file created over the physical. Changes to data in a physical file cannot be made via a join logical file.

3. The record format name in a logical file must be the same as that based on physical file format. The record format name in the join logical file must be different than the record format names in the "based on" files.

Q: *Name the keywords that are essential in defining a join logical file, and explain their use in the definition.*

A: JFILE—This keyword is used at the record level to specify the two or more physical files to be joined. The first physical filename specified will be the primary, and the rest will be secondary.

JOIN—This keyword is optional when only two physical files are being specified in the join, but is essential when there are more than two. It is used to identify which two physical files are being joined by the keywords and specifications that come immediately after this keyword.

JFLD—This keyword must be specified at least one time for each JOIN keyword entered. Two field names are used with this keyword. The first is taken from the primary file, and the second is taken from one of the secondary files. These are called *join fields,* and are used to control how records between the two files are combined.

JREF—This keyword is used at field-definition level to identify which physical file the specified field is from. This may be necessary since a field name included in the join logical file may exist in more than one physical file upon which the join logical is based.

Q: *What will happen if you fail to specify the JDFTVAL keyword in a join logical file?*

A: If the file-level keyword JDFTVAL is not specified, then any primary file record that does not have a matching secondary file record will be dropped from the join. If there is more than one secondary file, then a match must be found to the primary file for each secondary file.

Q: *What new method can be used to code *LIKE DEFINE in ILE RPG, and what functional advantage does it offer over the old method?*

A: The LIKE keyword specified on the D spec can be used to define a work field with the same attributes (i.e., length and decimal values, if any) as another field.

When the *LIKE DEFINE op-code is used on the C spec to define a field based on a binary or zoned numeric field, the new field is given the Packed Decimal data type. The advantage of using the LIKE keyword on the D spec is that it will carry the Binary or Zoned data type over to the newly defined field. The LIKE keyword always follows the data type of the original field.

In the following example, ZONED1 is defined on the D spec as a zoned decimal field. The LIKE keyword is used to give WRKFLD the same definition as ZONED1.

Example:

```
FMT D
.....DName++++++++++ETDsFrom+++To/L+++IDc.Functions+++++++++++++++++++
     DZONED1           S                6S 0
     DWRKFLD           S                     LIKE(ZONED1)
```

Q: *What are some of the advantages of using the D spec for field definition?*

A: 1. Confining most field definitions to the D spec simplifies coding and maintenance of programs.

2. Data Structure subfields can be indented, making them easier to read.

3. Fields can be initialized using the INZ keyword, eliminating the need to initialize them on the C spec.

4. New date data types can be defined on the D spec, which allows for easier date calculations and manipulations.

5. All fields in an externally described file can be renamed using the PREFIX keyword with a single D spec statement.

Q: *What type of data structures can be defined on the D spec?*

A: The D spec performs most of the functions formerly done by the I spec in ILE RPG, including the coding of data structures. The D spec can be used to define all data structure types including Program Described Data Structures, Data Area Data Structures, File Information Data Structures, and Program Status Data Structures.

Q: *Give an example of how a data structure might be coded on the D spec, and explain how the D spec makes it easy to code, read, and maintain.*

A: 1. Field names are up to ten positions long and contain both upper and lowercase characters. This makes them easy to read and understand.

2. Subfields are indented, and are easy to read.

3. Subfield lengths are used instead of from and to field positions. Using lengths instead of absolute positions simplifies changing, adding, or removing subfields.

4. The overlay keyword causes the subfield to occupy the same position as the other subfield name referenced by the overlay specification. In this example, FirstName takes on the same value as positions 1 through 20 of FullName. The starting position of the overlay for LastName is position 21. This causes LastName to overlay positions 21 through 40 of FullName. The OVERLAY keyword is useful for coding data structures that are easy to read and maintain.

```
FMT D
.....DName+++++++++ETDsFrom+++To/L+++IDc.Functions+++++++++++++++++++
    D Names            DS
    D FullName                     40
    D FirstName                    20      OVERLAY(FullName)
    D LastName                     20      OVERLAY(FullName:21)
```

Q: *Give an example of where a Data Area might prove useful.*

A: When an application requires a new and unique customer number to be generated whenever a new customer is added to the Customer Master File, a Data Area can be used to keep track of the last customer number added, so that the program can access the Data Area record, add 1 to it, and use the result as the new customer number (while updating the Data Area with the new number).

Q: *What is a Local Data Area?*

A: A Local Data Area (LDA) is automatically created by the system when a batch or interactive job is initiated. Every job has its own Local Data Area, which consists of a single character field of 1024 bytes. An LDA may be accessed and changed by RPG, CL, or directly (via the command entry screen).

When an interactive job initiates a batch job with the SBMJOB command, the contents of the LDA located on the interactive job are copied to the LDA created with the batch job being executed. The contents of an LDA can be passed between programs (or jobs) when placed in a regular Data Area, or placed in a program field, and passed as a parameter from one program to another. When a job ends, the LDA—along with its contents—is deleted.

Q: *How is a Data Area Data Structure defined in ILE RPG, and what data area is used by default when the data area name is not specified?*

A: UDS is specified on the D spec to define a Data Area Data Structure. The Local Data Area is used when no data area name is specified.

In the example below, the data structure is loaded from the data area "Customer." If the DTAARA keyword was not specified, the *LDA would be used.

```
FMT D
.....DName+++++++++++ETDsFrom+++To/L+++IDc.Functions+++++++++++++++++++
    DCustomer#       UDS                  DTAARA(Customer)
    D Custno                       10  0
    D CustName                     40

  update 18: QSYS38/DCLDTAARA
             QSYS38/RCVDTAARA
             QSYS38/SNDDTAARA
  delete 19.
```

Q: *Name the CL commands to create, retrieve, lock, and change a Data Area.*

A:

CRTDTAARA	Creates a Data Area
QSYS38/DCLDTAARA	Declares a Data Area, which enables a CL program to access it
CHGDTAARA	Changes the data in a Data Area
QSYS38/RCVDTAARA	Receives and copies the current value of a Data Area to a CL field with the same name as the Data Area
RTVDTAARA	Retrieves information from the Data Area, and places it in a CL variable
ALCOBJ	Can be used to lock a Data Area so that other programs cannot update it as long as it is in use by the current program
QSYS38/SNDDTAARA	Copies the data from a CL field to a Data Area

Q: *What is a figurative constant? Give some examples.*

A: A figurative constant is a type of literal that derives its definition directly from the program field with which it is associated. Figurative constants are used for field comparisons (such as FLD1 IFEQ *BLANKS), to initialize fields (i.e., MOVE *ZEROS FLD2), and to position pointers when reading a file (i.e., *LOVAL SETLL FILEX). Some examples are: *BLANKS, *ZEROS, *HIVAL, *LOVAL, *ALL'X..',*ON, and *OFF.

Q: *What is the *INZSR subroutine, and how could an ILE RPG program be coded to eliminate it?*

A: *INZSR is a special RPG subroutine coded on the C spec that automatically runs at the start of the program. The *INZSR subroutine is therefore a good place to code field initializations.

   The D spec in ILE RPG may be used to replace the *INZSR because initializations done on the D spec also take place at program start up time.

Example: Field MinimumBid is initialized to 5,000 dollars at the start of the program.

```
FMT D
.....DName+++++++++ETDsFrom+++To/L+++IDc.Functions+++++++++++++++++++
   DMinimumBid     S           12P 2 INZ(5000)
```

Q: *What is a record lock?*

A: When a file is defined with "input for update" on the F spec, and a record is read from that file, the program locks the record for update. If a second program has the same file specified as "input for update," and attempts to read the record while it is locked, the read attempt will fail.

Q: *How could the File Information Data Structure be used to check for a record lock in the ILE RPG?*

A: An entry is made on the F spec file continuation line of INFDS together with a Data Structure name. The Data Structure name specified on the F Spec is then used on the D spec to define the data structure itself. Within the data structure, RPG predefined subfields can be specified. The Data Structure subfield defined with the RPG reserved word *STATUS will contain the error code 01218 if the record is locked.

In the following example, FLD1 is defined as the File Information Data Structure, and the field name STAT1 will contain the error code 01218 if the record the program is chaining to is locked.

Example

```
FMT F
.....FFilename++IPEASFRLen+LKlen+AIDevice+.File continuation++++++++++
     FFILEX     UF  E            K DISK    INFDS(Fld1)
FMT D
.....DName++++++++++ETDsFrom+++To/L+++IDc.Functions++++++++++++++++++
     DFld1                DS
     D Stat1                    *STATUS
```

Q: *Name five ways to release a record lock in ILE RPG.*
A: 1. An UPDATE (or DELETE) operation will release a record lock.
   2. A READ (or CHAIN) operation performed on the file will unlock a record that was locked by a previous READ (or CHAIN) to the file.
   3. A SETLL (or SETGT) operation will release a record lock.
   4. The RPG operation UNLOCK will release a record lock.
   5. When an EXCEPT operation is performed to the O spec and the file name is specified by itself, without field names, the record lock is released.

Q: *Name three kinds of arrays, and explain how they are loaded.*
A: 1. A Compile Time Array is loaded into the array name specified on the E spec when the program is created (or compiled). The information used to load the array is taken from entries made by the programmer at the bottom of the RPG source code member.
   2. A Preexecution Time Array (otherwise known as a Prerun Time Array) is automatically loaded into the array name specified on the D spec when the program is called, but before the program starts processing data. The information used to load the array is taken from a Table or Array file on the system.
   3. An Execution Time Array (otherwise known as a Run-Time Array) is loaded into the array name specified on the D spec by the program after it is called, and while it operating. The data used to load the array is determined during program execution.

Q: *How do you WRITE and READ in a single RPG statement? Explain how this works.*
A: EXFMT (Execute Format) is used to first Write, then Read a Display File format. When coding an RPG program to handle a Workstation File (or Display File), EXFMT will write a Display File format to the screen, which will then wait for a response from the user. Upon user response, control returns to the program which will then READ, inputting any screen fields into the program.

Q: *Which RPG statement positions a pointer to the beginning of a group of records?*

A: When a key is used together with a SETLL operation on a keyed physical or logical file, the pointer is moved to the beginning of the group of records that are greater than or equal to the key that is specified on the SETLL operation.

Q: *Which RPG statement is used to read a group of records that all have the same key?*

A: The READE and READPE operations may be used to read a group of records with the same key.

Q: *Which single RPG op-code performs both SETLL and READE?*

A: A CHAIN op-code is the equivalent of a SETLL and READE in a single statement, since it uses a key to position the pointer and then to retrieve a specific record.

Q: *How can you add the contents of one array to another array in a single RPG statement?*

A: Use the ADD op-code to add the contents of one array to another.

Q: *What are the main differences between a primary file and a full procedural file?*

A: A primary file is read automatically and sequentially from beginning to end. The order in which the records are read cannot be changed. Only one primary file is allowed per program.

   Processing a full procedural file is controlled by op-codes in the C spec. Records may be read and processed in any order. There can be many files specified as full procedural.

Q: *Translate the following C spec from RPG/400 to ILE RPG, and explain the differences in the ILE RPG technique.*

Example 1

```
     * If this is a new order, and if more than 20 items were ordered,
     * then calculate the discount, and update the file with the
     * discount amount calculated.
FMT C
.....CLON01N02N03Factor1+++OpcdeFactor2+++ResultLenDHHiLoEqComments+++
     C           ORDTYP    IFEQ 'N'
     C           ORDQTY    ANDGT20
     C           ORDQTY    MULT ORDRT1    TOTHLD 122
     C           TOTHLD    MULT ORDRT2    DISCTO 112
     C           TOTHLD    SUB  DISCTO    ORDTOT 122
     C                     UPDATORDREC
     C                     ENDIF
```

A: Although the technique in Example 1 can be used in ILE RPG without any changes, the following new method can be used to code the ILE RPG C spec. Op-codes and field names can be written using upper- and lowercase letters. It was not necessary to define work fields to accomplish the calculation. The new C spec Eval op-code can be used with free form mathematical expressions that employ algebraic symbols and rules. Multiple C spec lines may be used for a single calculation.

Example 2

```
FMT CX
.....CLON01Factor1+++++++Opcode&ExtExtended-Factor2++++++++++++++++++
     C                      If    Ordtype = 'N' and Ordqty > 20
     C                      Eval  Ordtot = (Ordqty * Ordrt1)
     C                            - (Ordqty * Ordrt1 * Ordrt2)
     C                      UpdateOrdrec
     C                      Endif
```

Q: *Give some examples of ILE RPG op-codes that have been lengthened to six characters.*

A: CHECKR, COMMIT, DEFINE, RETURN, EXCEPT, LOOKUP, DELETE, SELECT, SETOFF, WHENxx, UPDATE, and UNLOCK.

Q: *Translate the following to ILE RPG, and explain how the new ILE technique is superior to the RPG/400 method.*

Example 1

```
FMT C
.....CLON01N02N03Factor1+++OpcdeFactor2+++ResultLenDHHiLoEqComments+++++
          * Use the cash deposit number in the cash field to load the check
          * number in the check field.
     C                      MOVE 'CASH#001'CSH       8        CASH DEPOSIT
     C                      MOVE 'CHECK  'CHK        8        CHECK FIELD
     C          3           SUBSTCSH:6    CHKHLD     3
     C                      MOVE CHKHLD   CHK                 'CHECK001'
```

A: The new ILE RPG built-in function %SUBST is used to code the string manipulation. Unlike the RPG/400 Op-code SUBST (which can still be used in ILE RPG), the ILE RPG built-in %SUBST function can use sub-strings to modify a field directly. This simplifies coding, and eliminates the need for intermediate work fields.

Example 2

```
FMT D
.....DName+++++++++++ETDsFrom+++To/L+++IDc.Functions++++++++++++++++++
     D Csh             S              8    INZ('CASH#001')
     D Chk             S              8    INZ('CHECK ')
FMT CX
.....CLON01Factor1+++++++Opcode&ExtExtended-Factor2++++++++++++++++++
     C                      Eval  %subst(Chk: 6: 3) = %subst(Csh: 6: 3)
```

Q: *Explain some approaches to creating a structured RPG program.*

A: Place all sets of logic that will be repeated into separate subroutines that can be called when required. Use proper commenting and documentation to describe each function performed by the program. Avoid GOTO statements. Try to have only one read and one update statement per file format used by the program. Use RPG structured programming op-codes.

Q: *Name some RPG op-codes used in structured programming.*

A: DOU, DOW, IF, AND, OR, ELSE, ENDxx, CASxx, ITER.

Q: *What is the difference between DOWEQ and DOUEQ RPG op-codes?*

A: DOU will execute at least one time, while a DOW may never execute because the comparison which determines whether or not to exit the loop takes place at the first statement of the loop.

Q: *An RPG program calls another program repeatedly. What ILE technique is implemented to improve performance?*

A: The ILE RPG op-code "CALLB" is used on the C spec to call the program. The programs are then made into nonexecutable objects called 'Modules' using the Create Module (CRTRPGMOD) command. Finally the Modules are 'bound' using the Create Program (CRTPGM) or the Create Service Program (CRTSRVPGM) command. After the programs are bound together, the call performance is greatly improved.

Q: *Show a new technique used in ILE RPG that allows for easy addition and subtraction of dates.*

A: ILE RPG makes it possible to add a number of days, months, or years to a date with the ADDDUR (Add Duration) op-code. It is similarly possible to subtract from a date using the SUBDUR op-code. The SUBDUR op-code also enables the difference between two dates to be easily calculated. When calculating the date, leap years and the varying length of months are taken into account to reach the correct solution.

Example 1: Modifies Begindate by adding ten months to it.

```
FMT C
.....CLON01Factor1+++++++Opcode&ExtFactor2+++++++Result++++++++Len++D+HiLoEq....
     C                   adddur 10:*months      Begindate
```

Example 2: Subtracts 45 days from Enddate, and places the result in Enddate.

```
.....CLON01Factor1+++++++Opcode&ExtFactor2+++++++Result++++++++Len++D+HiLoEq....
     C                   subdur 45:*days        Enddate
```

Example 3: Calculates the number of days between Begindate and Enddate, and places the result in Nbrdays. The modifier *D instructs RPG to perform the calculation using days as the result. If *M was specified, then the number of months between these two dates would be placed in the result field.

```
.....CLON01Factor1+++++++Opcode&ExtFactor2+++++++Result++++++++Len++D+HiLoEq....
     C     Begindate     subdur Enddate         Nbrdays:*D
```

Q: *What happens if you change a file format, re-create the file, and then run a preexisting program that uses the file?*

A: If Level Check *YES was specified for the file when it was created, the program will abend with a CPF message (CPF4131) that says there is a "File

Format Level Check." Level Check *YES is the default used by the system for file creation. If Level Check *NO was specified for the file when it was created, the program may run; however, the program may produce incorrect results.

Q: *In RPG, which statement must have preceded an UPDATE operation, and what will happen if an UPDATE is performed without that prior statement?*

A: A READ or CHAIN operation must precede an UPDATE operation. If an update is done without a Read or Chain, the program will end with the error: "Update issued without prior read or chain."

Q: *What is a subfile?*

A: A subfile is a group of records of the same type that can be written to, modified, and read from a display file. Subfiles are coded in the DDS source file member that defines the display file. A subfile is considered a "relative record" file since it may not be accessed by a key but only by a relative record number.

Q: *How many formats are needed to code a single subfile?*

A: Two record formats are required in the display file DDS to code one subfile.

Q: *What are the names of the subfile format types and the correct order of their coding in DDS?*

A: The Subfile Record Format is coded first. The Subfile Control Record format is coded second. They must be together with no other record format between them.

Q: *What is the minimum number of DDS keywords necessary to code a subfile? Name them.*

A: A minimum of five keywords are necessary to define and display a subfile. They are: (1) The SFL keyword is used on the Subfile Record Format; (2) The SFLCTL keyword with the name of the Subfile Record Format is specified on the Subfile Control Record Format; (3) The SFLDSP keyword is necessary on the Subfile Control Record Format since it causes the subfile records to be displayed; (4) The SFLSIZ is necessary to define the total size of the subfile; (5) The SFLPAG is necessary to define how many subfile records are displayed at a time.

Q: *Explain what "OS/400 control of subfile rolling" means, and the advantages to using it.*

A: When the subfile is loaded with records and then displayed, OS/400 will control rolling through pages of subfile records. When the Roll UP/DOWN keys are pressed, control does not return to the program. Control is given to OS/400, which rolls and redisplays the subfile.

The speed of rolling is fast when it is controlled by OS/400. This simplifies coding of the RPG programs that load and display subfiles, as well as DDS, which defines them. If the beginning or the end of the subfile is reached, OS/400 will automatically display a message saying it is the beginning or end of the subfile.

Q: *Why would one take control over rolling subfile records?*

A: Taking control over a rolling subfile can reduce the time it takes to display a subfile when there are a large number of records in the subfile. By taking control of rolling, it is possible to load and display the subfile a few records at a time. By defining the roll keys in DDS, control is returned to the program when the roll key is pressed. The program can then add and display more records in the subfile or display existing subfile records as necessary.

Q: *Explain how and why SFLNXTCHG is used.*

A: SFLNXTCHG is specified with an indicator on a Subfile Record Format which is defined to allow modification of subfile records by the user. When a user changes subfile records, the RPG op-code READC is used to read all records that were modified in the subfile, which will allow the program to validate them and display any errors found to the user. When this validation is performed, a record in error is updated in the subfile with the SFLNXTCHG indicator turned on. Updating a subfile record with the SFLNXTCHG indicator set on will cause the record to be considered "modified" even though no further changes are made to the record. When the subfile is read again, even though the user did not change that record, the READC op-code will pick the record up again for validation, and redisplay the same error until corrected. This will prevent the user from ignoring any errors made when changing data in a subfile.

Q: *What is a message subfile?*

A: A message subfile is a special file that may contain multiple messages taken from the Program Message Queue and placed in the message subfile for display on the screen.

Q: *Name the essential DDS keywords used to code a message subfile, and describe their function.*

A: SFLMSGRCD—A record-level keyword used on the subfile record format. This keyword identifies the subfile as being a Message Subfile and allows entry of a line number that indicates on which line of the screen the subfile will begin display of its records.

SFLMSGKEY—Field-level keyword used on the subfile record format together with a predefined field name which contains a hidden, four-position character value used as a message reference key to locate and select messages from the Program Message Queue when loading the message subfile.

SFLPGMQ—Field-level keyword used either on the Subfile Record Format or on the Subfile Control Record Format. This keyword is specified together with a predefined field name which contains a hidden, 10-position character value that holds the name of the Program Message Queue used by the system to build the message subfile. When SFLPGMQ is specified on the Subfile Record Format, the messages are added to the subfile from the Program Queue one at a time.

When SFLPGMQ is specified on the Subfile Control Record Format with SFLINZ, the entire message subfile is loaded in a single output operation as it is "initialized" with messages from the program queue name placed in the field defined with the SFLPGMQ keyword.

Q: *When coding a display (or workstation) file, what is the difference between enabling a command key such as CMD-1 using CA01 or CF01?*

A: When the prefix CA is used in defining command key CA01, any data entered on the screen is not returned to the program when the command key is pressed. When the prefix CF is used in defining command key CF01, any data entered on the screen is returned to the program when the command key is pressed.

Q: *Which DDS keyword is used to generate a plus sign in a subfile, and what is the purpose of the plus sign?*

A: The SFLEND (Subfile End) is a record-level keyword used to generate a plus sign in the lower-right-hand corner of the screen when there are more subfile records to be displayed. If *MORE is specified with the SFLEND keyword, then the screen will display the word MORE . . . on the lower right while paging through the subfile, and BOTTOM when the end of the subfile is reached.

Q: *Why use the OVERLAY keyword?*

A: When you wish to display more than one record format on the screen at the same time, you may use the OVERLAY keyword. If this keyword is not used, all existing formats on the screen will be removed whenever something new is written to any part of the screen. When OVERLAY is used with a record format written to a screen that has other record formats already on display, the only record formats cleared from the screen are the ones that partially (or fully) reside on the same line numbers as the record format now being written; all other formats will remain on the screen.

Q: *How does CLRL work? Compare it to OVERLAY.*

A: Clear Line (CLRL) is a record-level keyword that is used to clear a specific number of lines from the screen before a format is displayed. The Clear Line keyword controls the number of lines cleared. If the SLNO (Starting Line Number) keyword is specified, then the first line number to be cleared is also controlled by Clear Line. Clear Line may cause two record formats to overlap without the first format being cleared entirely. Only those lines being cleared from the first format are deleted from the screen; all other lines from the first format remain. If CLRL(*NO) is specified in a record format written to the screen, no lines in other record formats already on the screen are cleared. This includes existing lines of formats that may overlap with lines from the new format now being written, although individual characters in an overlapped line may be overlayed by characters from the new format being written with CLRL(*NO). In contrast, the OVERLAY keyword does not control the number of lines that are cleared, and does not allow two record formats to overlap. When a record format with OVERLAY specified is being written and any single line of the record format touches any line of the first format already on display, the first format is entirely deleted before the second format is sent to display.

Q: *What is an Open Query file?*

A: Open Query file is a CL command (OPNQRYF) executed that provides a variety of execution time functions on physical or logical files such as Dynamic Record Selection, Dynamic Keyed Access Path, Dynamic Join, and Group Processing. Based upon the criteria specified on the Open Query file command, a temporary access path to the file specified by the OPNQRYF command is created and shared by other programs called after OPNQRYF is initiated.

Q: *Explain how (and when) a file in an RPG program that uses the access path created by an Open Query File should be overridden.*

A: The file used in the RPG program should be overridden to the file name used in the OPNQRYF statement in the CL program with SHARE *YES specified on the override statement. The override statement must come before the OPNQRYF statement in the CL program.

Q: *Why does a file specified in an RPG program that will use the access path created by an Open Query file need to be overridden?*

A: The override with SHARE *YES done in the CL program will provide the RPG file access to the temporary Open Data Path created by the OPNQRYF command. If the override is not done, then the file opened in the RPG program will not use the logical view created by the Open Query file, and the RPG program will read the records according to specifications in the DDS of the logical file, ignoring the Open Data Path created by the Open Query file.

Q: *Why use a logical file rather than an open query?*

A: If the physical file you are working with is very large, creating and using a logical file will allow an application to perform faster than using an open query file. Since access paths created by open query files are temporary, applications that use an access path frequently will be more efficient using a logical file, since the access path will not have to be rebuilt every time the file is open.

Q: *How many files can be defined in a CL program, and what CL command is used for this?*

A: Only one file can be defined using the DCLF statement in a CL program.

Q: *Does the number of files that can be defined in a CL program cause a limit to the number of files that can be referenced by CL commands in the program?*

A: CL commands such as OPNQRYF and OVRDBF may be performed on more than one file in a CL program.

Q: *What single CL command must be used in a CL program to WRITE and READ a display file to a workstation?*

A: The CL command SNDRCVF may be used to write and read a display file record format to the workstation in a CL program.

Q: *Is it possible to set lower limits to a file in a CL program? How could this be done?*

A: There is more than one way to set lower limits in a CL program. One way is to use the POSDBF command with the parameter "File Position" set to *START. Another way is to use the OVRDBF command, which allows you to position the file by a key value, by a relative record number value, or set to *START (which positions to the beginning of the file).

Q: *How can one check for an error in a CL program to prevent the CL from abending should a command fail to execute properly?*

A: Use the CL command MONMSG with the MSGID parameter set to CPF9999. It may be specified at program level by being placed immediately after all declare statements. In that case, an error detected for any CL command in the program is caught and sent to the job log of the job where the CL program is running. A MONMSG command can be placed immediately following a CL command to monitor for a specific error condition. In that case, you need to specify the error id (or list of several error id numbers) of the error you wish to check for. Part of the MONMSG command is the ability to branch to an error routine in the CL program that can handle and possibly resolve the error, rather than merely recording the error to the job log.

Q: *How would you read a file sequentially from beginning to end in a CL program?*

A: In order to read a file from beginning to end sequentially, use the CL command RCVF followed by a GOTO statement (with the CMDLBL parameter specified in the GOTO to branch back), and execute the same command (RCVF) again until an end-of-file condition is detected by a MONMSG command, which will then branch out of the read loop. A command label must be specified prior to the RCVF statement so that the GOTO statement will branch correctly as the file is read again.

Example

```
PGM
DCLF FILE(FILEA)
READAGN:
RCVF
MONMSG MSGID(CPF0864) GOTO CMDLBL(END)
GOTO CMDLBL(READAGN)
END:
ENDPGM
```

Q: *Is it possible for a CL program submitted in batch to determine that it is, in fact, executing as part of a batch job? How would it "know"?*

A: Use the RTVJOBA command to determine whether the environment the CL program is running in is batch or interactive. Define a CL field name using the DCL statement as a single-position character. Specify that field name on the TYPE parameter in the RTVJOBA command. After the RTVJOBA command is executed by the program, check the value of the field. If the value is 0, then it is a batch job. If the value is 1, then it is an interactive job. (Note: A great deal of information concerning the executing job is available through the RTVJOBA command.)

Q: *Where in your CL program should you create a work file that you wish to be automatically deleted by the system when the job the CL is running in has concluded?*

A: Create the work file in QTEMP. When the job finishes, any contents of QTEMP are automatically deleted. The reason is that every job is created with a QTEMP library and, when the job concludes, the QTEMP library and all of its contents are deleted by the system.

Q: *If a single job takes up a large percentage of CPU, what can happen?*

A: Other users on the system will be adversely affected in the form of poor system response time and longer running time for batch programs.

Q: *What actions can be taken to prevent a single job from hogging the CPU? Give some examples.*

A: The actions taken to prevent this problem will depend upon what was found to be causing it. For example, if a program error caused a program to go into a continuous loop, the solution is to halt the program. If the problem is caused by an I/O-intensive program, it may be necessary to change the job using the CHGJOB command so that it will use fewer resources. If the problem is caused by an interactive QUERY, it may be possible to solve the problem by submitting the QUERY in batch (and provide a low priority if necessary).

Q: *What could happen if hard disk space usage approaches 100 percent?*

A: If disk space usage reaches a point where buffer and work areas needed for programs to run are not available, the system will terminate abnormally.

Q: *Name two fast ways to duplicate a file.*

A: 1. The CPYF CL command can be used to duplicate a file.

2. The CRTDUPOBJ CL command can be used to duplicate a file.

Both methods can be used interactively or by a submitted batch job.

Q: *Which CL command allows for selective record-copying from one file to another? Describe two or more ways it can be used to select records.*

A: The CPYF command can be used to selectively copy records from one file to another. There are several parameters in this command that allow selective copying:

FROMKEY/TOKEY (Copy from and to Record Key). These two parameters may be specified with key-field values that will cause records within the range of those specific key-field values to be copied.

INCCHAR (Include Records by Character Test). This parameter compares some part (or all) of a character field to a character string value entered on the command. The record will be included or excluded based upon the results of the comparison.

INCREL (Include Records by Field Test). This parameter allows entry of multiple field value tests using IF/AND/OR logic. The CPYF command will test to determine if a field satisfies the conditioning and will include or exclude based upon the results.

Q: *If you were testing a program interactively, and the Input Inhibited light stayed on longer than you thought it should, what action might you take to terminate the program?*

A: System Request, option 2. (Press the SHIFT key and the System Request key and enter the number 2 on the resulting line.)

Q: *If you have a file with a thousand fields and you are writing an RPG program that will update only one or two fields in the file, what is the most efficient manner to code the update and what pitfall is avoided by this method?*

A: When you are updating only one or two fields from a large file, it is most efficient to execute an output operation to the O spec where the file name and the field names to be updated are specified. This method causes RPG to change the contents of only the field names specified on the O spec. An update to two fields takes up far fewer system resources than an update to a thousand fields.

The possible pitfall avoided with this technique is the incorrect update of fields you never wished to change. A regular RPG UPDATE op-code changes all fields in the record regardless of whether the programmer intended them to be changed. The output operation to the O spec effects a change only to the fields explicitly specified for update on the O spec. All other fields remain as they were before the update, no matter how they were altered by the program.

Q: *If you have a 10,000-page report and you wish to print only the last 10 pages, how can you get the system to print what you want without printing the first 9,990 pages?*

A: Use the CL command CHGSPLFA (Change Spooled File Attribute) to cause a spooled file to begin printing from whatever page you specify on the command. The parameter PAGERANGE allows you to control the number of pages to be printed from the initial page specified.

Q: *There are some cases where you wish to call an RPG program without having to pass parameters, and other cases where you wish to pass parameters to the very same program when you call it. What is the difficulty with this, and how would you resolve it?*

A: If a program is coded to expect parameters, it will abend if it is called without parameters passed. If a program does not expect parameters, it will abend if parameters are passed.

If a program expects parameters to be passed and you do not wish to pass parameters, one solution is to pass the parameters with blanks and zeros, as with an initialization.

If a program expects parameters to be passed but you specifically do not wish to pass parameters in a given situation, you may specify the Program Status Data Structure which is defined on the I spec using SDS (Program Status Data Structure) with the *PARMS keyword and a field name to contain the data. The field name specified together with the *PARMS keyword will contain the number of parameters passed to the program (a three-digit, numeric amount). The code that specifies the parameter list *ENTRY PLIST on the C spec must be conditioned not to execute when the number of parameters passed to the program is zero.

Q: *The report function you are creating will require a large number of different ways to select and sort the information from a specific file. How could one CL program eliminate the need to create many logical files for this function?*

A: A CL program may be coded to receive the selection criteria specified by the user and place that criteria into a CL field that can be used with the Query Select (QRYSLT) parameter on the OPNQRYF statement. The sort sequence requested by the user can also be loaded into a CL field that will be used on the Key Field (KEYFLD) parameter of the Query Select statement. In this manner, any number of sort and select criteria can be included in the report function without having to create a separate logical for each criteria required.

Q: *The file your CL program must access may not exist on the library list of the batch job in which your CL program is running. How would you code the CL to ensure the program will find the file?*

A: Find the library the file is in, using the DSPOBJD command with *ALL specified on the LIBRARY parameter, and an OUTFILE name specified that will contain all the file information generated by this command, including the library where it is located. If more than one record is generated in the OUTFILE, the file exists in more than one library. In that case, you may wish to send an error and notify the person who called the program that there is a problem the program cannot resolve. If a list exists of legitimate libraries where the file can be found, then you can check the library names in the OUTPUT file against this list. When a library name is found that can be used, then that name will be loaded into a CL field name that will be used on the LIBRARY parameter of any CL commands in the program that use the file.

Q: *After a large report was generated and saved on the OUTQ, the files upon which the report was based were changed in the normal course of business. However, the client has decided to extract certain information contained in that report and create a second report based upon this extracted information.*

How could a program be written to extract data from the first report without using production files?

A: Find the position on the report where the required information is located. Be certain the highest possible position location has been determined. Create a nonkeyed physical file with one field defined as character. Use the high-end position of the data needed from the report as the field length. Use the CPYS-PLF (Copy Spooled File) command to copy the spooled file to the database file you have created. Every record in the file will now contain a single line of the report. Write an RPG program that uses a Data Structure to break the single field in the file into the actual fields to be used for generating the report data. It may be necessary for the RPG to convert character values in the data structure to numeric amounts.

Q: *In a CL program, the date field is divided into four separate parts, each part being an individual two-position numeric field. Without having seen the program, how do you believe the date is broken up? How would you put it together in a single date field using CL statements?*

A: The dates are broken up into century, year, month, and day. It is necessary to convert each of these two-position numeric fields into two-position character fields before they are combined into a single date field. The reason is that the CL commands used to combine fields will work only with character fields. Use the CHGVAR command to move these numeric fields into character fields. The CHGVAR command with the substring parameter (%SST) may be used to combine these fields into a single program variable. The following examples show how to accomplish a date conversion.

The following example will move the numeric date into a character field. The field name &CHARACTER will now hold the same numbers that were in &NUMERIC, but the numbers will be character values.

Example 1
```
CHGVAR VAR(&CHARACTER) VALUE(&NUMERIC)
```

Example 2 shows how CHGVAR is used with the substring function to make the date into a single field. All field names used here are defined as character. The numbers specified with the substring parameter show the starting position of the change, and how many positions will be changed.

Example 2
```
CHGVAR VAR(%SST(&FULLDATE 1 2)) VALUE(&CENTURY)
CHGVAR VAR(%SST(&FULLDATE 3 2)) VALUE(&YEAR)
CHGVAR VAR(%SST(&FULLDATE 5 2)) VALUE(&MONTH)
CHGVAR VAR(%SST(&FULLDATE 7 2)) VALUE(&DAY)
```

It is also possible to combine these four character fields using a single CHGVAR command with the *CAT (Concatenate) function.

Example 3

```
CHGVAR VAR(&FULLDATE) VALUE(&CENTURY *CAT &YEAR +
*CAT &MONTH *CAT &DAY)
```

Q: *Your interactive program has gone into a continuous loop. How would you pinpoint the problem?*

A: There are a number of actions you can take to determine the cause. While the program is looping, you can immediately use System Request 3 with Option 11 in an attempt to find out which statements are being repeated. This option shows the name of the active program, along with the statement currently being executed.

   If you know the program will loop before you call it, you can use the debug facility to pinpoint the statements in error. Use the CL command STRDBG to activate the debug function for the program name that is looping. After you have entered debug mode, you can specify which program statements are to be traced and recorded by debug using ADDTRC *ALL, which will trace and record all statements executed as the program is running. Since there is a limit to the number of statements that can be traced, the program will stop executing, no matter what statement is active, when that limit has been reached. At that point, it is possible to press Command 10 to access a command entry screen. On the command entry screen, you can display the trace data to the screen or to a list which can be printed out. Use the CL command DSPTRCDTA to display the trace data. While viewing the trace information, any statement or set of statements that execute repeatedly are probably the cause of the problem. If no statements are found that are incorrectly repeated, then you can do a CLRTRCDTA, which will clear the trace data and allow for the program to continue tracing. If you know the most likely routine to be causing the problem, then you may specify the beginning and ending statements of the routine to be traced on the ADDTRC command, which will cause the program to trace starting from and ending with those specific statements. It is possible to specify program variable names to be included in the trace information. Knowing field values at the time the loop occurred will help you to analyze why the loop happened and how to fix it.

Q: *Is it possible to view the contents of a field through debug before source statements coded by the programmer begin execution? How could this be useful?*

A: It is possible to use the command ADDBKP (Add Breakpoint) to view contents of a program variable when the program is running in debug mode. Immediately before the program executes the statement number specified on the ADDBKP command, the program stops execution and displays the contents of the program field name that was entered with the ADDBKP command. When an RPG program begins execution, there are certain compiler-generated statements that are first executed that are part of the object code and were not actually coded by the programmer. In the following example, the value in the amount field will be displayed by debug when the program is called and before source code statements are executed. If the field

AMOUNT is being passed from another program to this program, then using a breakpoint at '.ENTRY' will ensure that we are looking at the value in AMOUNT before it was changed by this program. If the value in AMOUNT is wrong, this technique can help us find which program is at fault.

Example
```
ADDBKP STMT('.ENTRY') PGMVAR(AMOUNT)
```

Q: *You are tracing a program in debug. You get a message that says, "Maximum number of traced statements reached." You decide that you want the program to continue tracing, and you do not wish to exit the program. What would you do?*

A: First press the error reset key to remove the error. Then access a command entry screen from the Debug Display Breakpoint screen you are currently on by pressing Command 10. Then enter the CL command, CHGDBG, with the number of statements you wish to trace specified on the MAXTRC parameter. For example, if the current maximum number of traced statements is 200 and you wish to increase that number to 1000, enter the following command: CHGDBG MAXTRC(1000). Exit the command entry screen using Command 3 (or Command 12) and debug will automatically continue tracing from the point where it previously stopped.

Q: *You are creating a complex application with a header file and several detail files all related to the header by a specific key. An important requirement of this application is every detail record must have a corresponding header record. A header record cannot be changed, added, or deleted unless the same action is done to all the detail files having a record with a corresponding key. Name the technique new to DB2/400 that can be used to guarantee this application requirement will be strictly adhered to, and summarize how to implement it.*

A: Use Referential Integrity to define rules to the database. These rules will control the relationships between the header and detail files, and will prevent a program from adding, deleting, or changing a record where this will violate the Referential Constraints that have been defined. Trigger programs can also be added to make file updates go more smoothly by checking on possible constraint violations, and taking corrective action before the system sends an error preventing the update.

To implement Referential Integrity, first add a primary key constraint to the header file using the ADDPFCST (Add Physical File Constraint) command. Then add referential constraints between the header file and all dependent detail files, also using the ADDPFCST command. This will cause DB2/400 to send an error message if an attempt is made to delete a header record without first having deleted all corresponding detail records, and will prevent the delete. If an attempt is made to add a detail record with no corresponding header, the add operation will fail, and an error will be sent. In this situation, a trigger program can be specified using the command

ADDPFTRG (Add Physical File Trigger). The trigger program would be invoked just before an attempt is made to add, change, or delete records from any file specified on the ADDPFTRG command. If an attempt is made to add a detail without a corresponding header, the trigger program might be designed to add a new header record with the correct key in order to allow the addition of the detail record. Since the trigger program would be executed before DB2/400 checks for referential constraints, the add operation would be successful. With no trigger program specified, the program attempting to add the detail record would receive an error, and the add operation would fail.

8
OS/2 Release 3.0

Robert Pesner

Introduction

The following topics will be covered in this chapter:

1. Using OS/2 3.0
   a. OS/2 3.0 features
   b. Installing OS/2 3.0
   c. System configuration
   d. Using the WorkPlace Shell
   e. Running DOS and Windows programs
2. Programming OS/2 3.0
   a. OS/2 Kernel Programming
   b. OS/2 Presentation Manager Programming
   c. OS/2 System Object Model Programming

Overview of OS/2 3.0

OS/2 3.0, also called Warp, is the current release of IBM's single-user, multitasking operating system for microcomputers based on chips compatible with the Intel 80386 and above. It is one of the family of IBM operating systems that support IBM's System Application Architecture (SAA). It was designed to address three major problems users face with DOS:

1. Memory constraints imposed by the 1-megabyte addressability limit of the 8086/8088 chips for which DOS was written
2. Flexibility constraints imposed by DOS's single-tasking design
3. Lack of standardization among the user interfaces of the many applications available for DOS systems.

It meets these design goals by:

1. Supporting up to 4 gigabytes of physical memory and providing 512 megabytes of virtual memory to applications in a 32-bit flat address space

2. Supporting multiple concurrent OS/2, DOS, and Windows applications using a preemptive, multithreaded, multitasking scheduler

3. Providing operating system support for a standardized, object-oriented, windows-based, mouse-oriented graphical user interface called the WorkPlace Shell, based on the most current SAA Common User Access (CUA) specifications (CUA 1991).

In the WorkPlace Shell, the screen functions as a desktop on which the user arranges icons. These icons represent objects, unlike OS/2 1.x or Windows, where icons represent minimized running applications. There are several types of objects, including program objects, printer objects, disk drive objects, data file objects, and folders, which can contain other objects, including other folders. Objects can be acted on directly, by double-clicking or dragging them with the mouse, or through a pop-up menu listing the available actions, which is accessed by clicking on the object with the right mouse button.

OS/2 provides a complete set of services to application programs, accessed by a standard subroutine call interface. These services include:

1. I/O services, including disk files and devices such as screen, keyboard, mouse, COM and LPT ports, CD-ROM, etc. Disk files can be shared by multiple applications; multiwrite access can be managed using locking services.

2. Dynamic memory management, including allocation of memory to be shared between multiple applications.

3. Event notification and resource access serialization using semaphores.

4. Interprocess communication, including queues, anonymous pipes, and local and remote-named pipes. Pipes use a programming syntax identical to the file I/O syntax except for pipe creation. Remote-named pipes allow applications to exchange data across LANs and require the support of a network operating system.

5. Process management, including starting sessions, processes and threads, and controlling execution priority. The ability of applications to spin off subroutines (threads) that execute concurrently with the application main routine is one of the most powerful features of OS/2.

6. Window management, including creating windows, displaying text and graphical output, processing mouse and keyboard events, and exchanging information with other applications.

7. Multimedia services, including support for audio, video, and movies.

8. System Object Model services, which provide object-oriented programming enhancements to standard procedural programming languages such as C.

OS/2 Warp comes in four packages. OS/2 Warp Version 3 provides support for OS/2 and DOS programs, and supports Windows programs if Windows 3.1 is installed. OS/2 Warp Version 3 with Win-OS2 supports OS/2, DOS, and Windows programs without requiring that Windows be installed. OS/2 Version 3 LAN Client includes OS/2 Warp for Win-OS2 as well as requesters for the LAN Server and Novell Netware network operating systems, the LAN Distance client (allowing remote users to dial into a LAN and become nodes) and SPM/2. OS/2 for Symmetrical Multiprocessing is designed to run on PCs with from two to 16 80486 or Pentium-compatible CPUs.

OS/2 applications that manage windows are structured as message-processing programs. All input from the keyboard, mouse, and the desktop environment is placed on a queue created by the application as part of its initialization. The main routine of the application usually creates the main application window and then enters a loop in which messages are read off the queue and passed to a subroutine for processing. The subroutine, known as a *window procedure,* is usually structured as a C-type switch block with cases for the messages the program wants to respond to. Other messages are passed back to the environment for default processing.

OS/2 provides a set of predefined window types and associated window procedures. These window types are the control window classes. They can be used in applications to include entry fields, various kinds of buttons, scroll bars, list boxes, etc., in the user interface without having to code the logic to control them. User-defined window types and associated window procedures must be registered as part of application initialization. User-defined window classes can be public, so that other applications can use them as if they were OS/2-provided control window classes.

The System Object Model provides a syntax for creating object-oriented programming objects in procedural languages. A preprocessor converts the OOP statements into native language statements for compilation. It also generates include files for use both in implementing the objects and in writing applications that use the objects. The WorkPlace Shell is written using SOM, which also allows OS/2 application developers to access the objects in the WorkPlace Shell in their own applications. WorkPlace Shell objects can be parent objects of application-defined objects, which thus can inherit complex behavior that follows the CUA 1991 standard.

OS/2 Warp comes packaged in a number of ways. For the consumer IBM offers Warp and Warp with Win-OS2. The first provides support for OS/2 and DOS programs, and supports Windows programs if Windows 3.1 is installed. The second adds support for Windows programs without requiring that Windows be installed. For the corporate desktop IBM offers OS/2 Warp Connect with and without Win-OS2. The Connect packages add requesters for the IBM LAN Server and Novell Netware network operating systems, OS/2 Peer (a peer-to-peer network operating system), TCP/IP, the LAN Distance Remote client (allowing remote users to dial into a LAN and become nodes) and Network SignOn Coordinator/2 (which manages passwords for multiple userids on LANs and mainframes). For the server market IBM offers OS/2 Warp Server. This is Warp Connect with Win-OS2 plus IBM LAN Server, LAN Distance Connection Server (which allows remote LAN Distance clients to dial into a LAN), Print Services Facility/2 (which allows printing from PCs to mainframe printers and from mainframe applications to PC printers), Personally Safe 'n' Sound (a data backup and recovery utility), and SystemView (a network management program). Finally, IBM has announced a Warp version of OS/2 for Symmetrical Multiprocessing, which is designed to run on PCs with from two to 16 80486- or Pentium-compatible CPUs.

All versions of Warp come with a Bonus Pack, a group of applications including:

- Compuserve Information Manager for OS/2
- FaxWorks for OS/2
- HyperACCESS Lite for OS/2 (a terminal emulator)
- IBM Internet Connection for OS/2 (including a World Wide Web browser, a Gopher client, E-mail, and an Internet news reader)
- IBM Works and Personal Information Manager (an integrated word processing, spreadsheet, database, and charting package)
- Multimedia Viewer (a multimedia object manager)
- Person to Person/2 (a network-based collaborative work tool)
- System Information Tool
- Video IN for OS/2 (a set of AVI utilities)

IBM provides a sophisticated tool for developing OS/2 3.0 programs called VisualAge C++. It includes a 32-bit ANSI-compatible C++ compiler; OS/2 C including files, link libraries, development tools, and sample programs; and Work-Frame/2, an integrated development environment.

Other vendors that sell C or C++ compilers that can create OS/2 applications include Borland, Zortech, Watcom, and Metaview.

OS/2 3.0 is the base operating system for a family of IBM products that provide communications, database, and networking facilities. The other products in this family include:

1. OS/2 Multi-Protocol Transport Services/2 1.0—a collection of OS/2 LAN adapter device drivers supporting Token Ring, Ethernet, and PC Network LANs. MPTS/2 is based on the Microsoft/3-COM Network Device Interface Specification (NDIS) standard. NDIS facilitates the integration of LAN adapters from multiple vendors and the sharing of LAN adapters by various protocols. MPTS/2 also provides protocol translation, allowing NetBIOS applications to use TCP/IP as a transport and TCP/IP applications to use NetBIOS as a transport.

2. Communications Manager/2 1.11—provides connectivity between OS/2 and SNA networks, LANs, X.25 networks, and time-sharing services accessed through modems. It provides 3270, 5250, and asynchronous start-stop terminal emulation and file transfer. It includes a number of application programming interfaces that can be used to develop distributed processing applications.

It also supports Advanced Peer-to-Peer Networking and can function as an APPN node server.

3. DB2/2 2.0—a 32-bit relational database engine based on the SQL database standard with a prompted query user interface (Query Manager). It also has support for transparent access of remote data in network-connected Database Manager, DB/2, and SQL/DS databases. (Mainframe access requires an additional product: SAA Distributed Database Connection Services/2.)

4. OS/2 LAN Server 4.0—a network operating system providing file, printer, and serial device sharing to OS/2, DOS, Windows, and Macintosh clients. It includes MPTS/2, User Profile Management (a security subsystem), and the LAN Support Program, a collection of LAN adapter device drivers for DOS.

5. TCP/IP for OS/2 2.0—an implementation of TCP/IP for OS/2, providing the standard set of TCP/IP applications. NFS server and X Windows client and server are add-on products to the base TCP/IP.

6. System Performance Monitor/2 2.0—collects, displays, and reports on performance, tuning, and capacity planning information, including a facility to collect data from servers to a central LAN-connected performance repository.

Terminology

Boot Manager: A facility of OS/2 that allows different operating systems, such as OS/2 and DOS, to be installed in different partitions of a hard disk. The operating system to use is chosen from a menu that appears at boot time.

Clipboard: A facility of OS/2 that allows Presentation Manager and/or Windows applications to pass data to each other. Data may be text, graphics, or in an application-dependent format. Applications must be coded to support clipboard data exchange. Clipboard data exchanges occur upon user request and under direct user control.

Command prompt: A window or full-screen session that displays a DOS-like prompt, allowing the user to issue commands. OS/2 3.0 supports multiple simultaneous OS/2 and DOS windowed or full-screen prompts.

Container: A WorkPlace Shell object that contains other objects. It can display its contents as icons, in tree format, or in table format. The most common kind of container is the folder.

Context menu: A menu providing access to the actions that can be applied to a WorkPlace Shell object, displayed by clicking on the object with the right mouse button; also known as a pop-up menu.

Device driver: A program installed in CONFIG.SYS that supports specific hardware (disk drives, printers, CD-ROM drives, etc.). Device drivers are installed with the BASEDEV and DEVICE statements.

Direct manipulation: A basic technique in the WorkPlace Shell user interface. It usually involves either double-clicking on an object to open a view or dragging an object and dropping it on another object, which then processes the dropped object.

Dynamic data exchange (DDE): A programming facility that allows Presentation Manager and/or Windows applications to exchange data. Data may be text, graphics, or in an application-dependent format. Applications must be coded to support DDE. DDE exchanges usually occur upon user request, although applications can invoke them automatically. The exchange itself occurs under application control.

Dynamic Link Library (DLL): A library of subroutines that is not incorporated into an application .EXE file at link time. Instead, a pointer is maintained to the DLL. This allows multiple applications to share one copy of the subroutines at execution time. When the application is loaded, OS/2 checks if the DLL is already loaded (due to a previous application requirement), and loads the DLL only if it is not already resident. If it is, the application's call addresses are simply fixed to point to the already-resident subroutines.

Extended attribute: The DOS file system provides four file attributes: Archive, Read-only, Hidden, and System. These are bit flags that can be either on or off. Extended attributes are an extension to this idea that allows files to have any number of attributes whose values are not limited to on or off. Extended attributes consist of a name of up to 255 characters and a value that can be virtually unlimited in length. Extended attributes on FAT disks are stored in the file 'EA DATA. SF'. Extended attributes on HPFS disks are stored as part of the file object.

File Allocation Table (FAT) file system: A method of storing files on disk partitions. The OS/2 FAT file system is compatible with but not identical to the DOS FAT file system. Disks created by either operating system can be processed by the other. The OS/2 FAT system supports extended attributes, optional disk caching for reads and writes, and optional disk error checking at boot time.

Folder: A container object that forms the basis of the WorkPlace Shell desktop organization. Folders can contain objects, including other folders, leading to a hierarchical folder structure on the desktop analogous to (and supported by) the hierarchical structure of directories and subdirectories on disks.

Hide button: A possible appearance of the "minimize" button in which the small box is made of dotted lines. This implies that when the window is "hidden," no icon indicating that it is active will appear on the desktop.

High-Performance File System (HPFS): A method of storing files on disk partitions. The OS/2 HPFS is incompatible with DOS. It supports very large partitions on very large disks, reduced file fragmentation, reduced seek time, extended attributes, optional disk caching for reads and writes, and optional disk error checking at boot time.

Launch pad: A WorkPlace Shell object that can be used to launch applications. It can be customized to include those applications the user wants immediate access to.

Message: In Presentation Manager programming, a data structure passed as a parameter to a "window procedure" to indicate that some event has occurred that requires application processing.

Minimized window viewer: An application providing a window that can be used to collect icons representing minimized applications.

Multitasking: A facility of OS/2 that allows multiple applications to share the computer's CPU and each application to execute multiple code functions "simultaneously" through CPU time-slicing.

Notebook: A window that appears like a notebook, with multiple pages and tabs separating the pages into sections. It is used most frequently to configure settings for WorkPlace Shell objects. From a Presentation Manager programming point of view, a notebook is a control window; each page is usually created as a modeless dialog box.

Object: The basic entity in the object-oriented WorkPlace Shell user interface. All objects have certain properties in common: they appear as icons somewhere in the desktop folder hierarchy; they can be looked at through views; they can be acted upon through their pop-up menu (click once with the right mouse button); they can be configured using their settings notebook; and they can be directly manipulated.

Page: A 4-kilobyte block of memory that functions as the allocation unit for all memory management. Pages are also swapped in and out of real memory from backing storage on disk to allow for memory overcommitment where total application memory needs are greater than real storage.

Pipe: A programming facility that allows OS/2 and DOS applications to exchange data. Data is passed as messages between a pipe creator (server) and a pipe user (client). Pipe partners can be running on the same machine or can be communicating across a Local Area Network (remote pipes). Except for the server actions to create the pipe and wait for a client to contact it, the data exchange can be carried out using normal programming language file read and write commands. Pipes can be either named or anonymous. Remote pipes are always named.

Process: A collection of computer resources assigned as a unit, including memory blocks, open files and devices, interprocess communications resources, system semaphores, a current disk, a current directory on each disk, and a set of environment variables. There may be more than one application active in a process and each may have more than one thread.

Queue: A programming facility that allows OS/2 applications to exchange data. Data is passed in shared memory blocks. Programming calls specific to queues are used to pass handles to the shared blocks.

Semaphore: A programming facility used for either event signaling or resource access serialization (MUTual EXclusion) between multiple applications. Applications can indicate events by posting an event semaphore, and wait for an event by waiting on an event semaphore. Applications can wait for access to a resource by requesting a mutex semaphore; when they are done using the resource, they indicate this by releasing the mutex semaphore.

Session: A virtual computer in which one or more processes execute. The session includes a virtual screen, keyboard, and mouse, which all processes in the session share.

Shadow: A copy of a WorkPlace Shell object that remains linked to its original. If a change is made to the original (for example, in its settings notebook), the change affects the shadow as well.

Shared memory: A programming facility that allows OS/2 applications to access a common memory block. Usually, OS/2 imposes a strict separation between the memory blocks allocated to applications to prevent bugs in one application from affecting others. Shared memory blocks must be managed by the sharing applications to prevent problems.

Spooling: A facility that allows multiple applications to share printers without getting interspersed output. Each application's output is held on disk in a spool file until the printer is available.

Thread: The actual executing code in an application. OS/2 applications can have more than one thread. All the threads in an application share memory blocks, open devices, and all other process resources except registers and a stack. Each thread has its own register set and its own stack.

Title bar icon: The icon at the upper-left corner of windows that can be used to access the window's object menu. This replaces the System Menu icon in OS/2 1.x and Windows.

Virtual device driver: A device driver designed for a virtual DOS machine that intercepts applications accesses to devices and passes these on to the real device driver.

Virtual DOS machine: A facility of the 80386 chip (and higher) that allows it to emulate an 8086 chip in protected mode. OS/2 3.0 uses this facility to support multiple DOS and Windows applications.

WIN-OS/2: The component of OS/2 that supports Windows applications. OS/2 2.0 supports Windows 2.0 applications in real or standard mode. OS/2 3.0 supports Windows 3.0 and 3.1 applications in standard or enhanced mode.

Window: A rectangle in which an application displays its output. Windows normally have title bars used to move the window, borders used to change its size, minimize (or hide) and maximize buttons, and a title bar icon used for accessing the window's object menu.

Window list: A WorkPlace Shell window that lists the active applications. It appears as a result of hitting Ctl-Esc on the keyboard or by clicking with both mouse buttons simultaneously at an empty spot on the desktop.

Window procedure: A subroutine in a GUI application that handles messages that indicate when events of importance to the applications window have occurred. Window procedures are usually coded as a switch structure on the message type.

Questions and Answers

Q: *What are three important problems with DOS that led to the development of OS/2?*

A: 1. DOS was written for the 8086/8088 chip, which can address only one megabyte of memory. The various mechanisms that allow DOS applications to address more memory require specific coding techniques. OS/2 3.0 can make 512 megabytes of memory available to applications in a flat address space.

2. DOS was written as a single-user, single-tasking operating system, on the assumption that the user would use one application at a time. The various mechanisms for allowing multiple applications to run simultaneously under DOS are essentially kludges. OS/2 3.0 provides a single-user, multitasking environment with a high degree of protection against application bugs affecting other running applications.

3. DOS applications use various user interfaces. OS/2 3.0 provides a consistent look and feel that application developers can adopt to make it easier for users to learn new applications.

Q: *What are the major new features of OS/2 3.0 compared to OS/2 1.x?*
A: 1. Use of the 80386 chip's 32-bit flat addressing model

2. Support for running multiple OS/2, DOS, and Windows applications simultaneously

3. The new WorkPlace Shell user interface

Q: *What is the difference between OS/2 Warp Version 3 and OS/2 Warp Version 3 with Win-OS2?*
A: OS/2 Warp Version 3 requires that Windows 3.1 be installed in order to run Windows applications. OS/2 Warp Version 3 with Win-OS2 comes with the full support necessary to run Windows applications.

Q: *Does OS/2 3.0 support Windows for WorkGroups?*
A: OS/2 Warp Version 3 can be installed on top of Windows for WorkGroups 3.1 or 3.11 and will support Windows applications. However, the networking features of Windows for WorkGroups will not be supported.

Q: *What other components are in OS/2 Warp Connect?*
A: OS/2 Version 3 LAN Client comes with requesters for the LAN Server and Novell Netware network operating systems, the LAN Distance client and NSC/2.

Q: *What is OS/2 for Symmetrical Multiprocessing?*
A: OS/2 for Symmetrical Multiprocessing is designed to make use of PCs configured with from two to 16 80486 or Pentium-compatible CPUs.

Q: *What are the major subsystems of OS/2 3.0?*
A: 1. File and I/O subsystem

2. Memory manager

3. Multitasking manager

4. Presentation manager

Q: *What are the other major members, current releases, and basic functions of IBM's OS/2 product family?*

A: 1. Multi-Protocol Transport Services/2 1.0—OS/2 device drivers for LAN adapters

 2. Communications Manager/2 1.11—communications

 3. DB2/2 2.0—database management

 4. OS/2 LAN Server 4.0—network operating system

 5. TCP/IP for OS/2 2.0—TCP/IP

 6. System Performance Manager/2 2.0—performance and tuning

Q: *What are the major advantages of OS/2 3.0 over DOS for running DOS programs?*

A: 1. The ability to run multiple DOS programs concurrently

 2. If a DOS application has a bug that would cause DOS to hang or crash, only that application will be affected; other applications would be unaffected

 3. The ability to provide more conventional memory for DOS applications than DOS can, and the ability to provide more virtual memory above 1 megabyte than is actually present on the machine

 4. The ability to run different versions and releases of DOS without rebooting

 5. Access to more sophisticated and higher-performing file systems such as OS/2's FAT and HPFS file systems

Q: *What are the major advantages of OS/2 3.0 over Windows for running Windows programs?*

A: 1. Preemptive multitasking instead of Window's cooperative multitasking

 2. The ability to run Windows applications in separate Windows sessions so that an application bug that would hang or crash Windows (and therefore all running Windows applications) would affect only that application

 3. The ability to provide more virtual memory above 1 megabyte than is actually present on the machine

 4. Access to more sophisticated and higher-performing file systems such as OS/2's FAT and HPFS file systems

Q: *What are extended attributes?*

A: Extended attributes (EAs) are file attributes beyond the traditional DOS file attributes of read-only, archive, hidden, and system. Extended attributes consist of an arbitrary name up to 255 characters and arbitrary data associated with the EA name.

Q: *Where are extended attributes stored?*

A: On FAT-formatted disks, EAs are stored in a hidden system, read-only file called 'EA DATA. SF' in the root directory of the drive containing the associated file. On HPFS-formatted disks, EAs are stored as part of the file object.

Q: *What are the documented minimum requirements for OS/2 3.0?*
A: 1. 80386SX-based PS/2 or AT-compatible computer

2. 4 megabytes of system memory

3. 18 megabytes of hard disk space

4. VGA display adapter

Q: *What is the recommended minimum for an OS/2 user workstation?*
A: 1. Fast 80386-based PS/2 or AT-compatible computer

2. 6 megabytes of system memory

3. 35 megabytes of hard disk space

4. VGA display adapter

5. Mouse

Q: *What are the possible delivery media for installing OS/2 3.0?*
A: 1. Diskettes

2. CD-ROM

3. Network server

Q: *What are the main system configuration files and their functions?*

A: CONFIG.SYS	Specifies device drivers, tuning parameters, user shells, and environment variables
STARTUP.CMD	Commands executed at system boot time
AUTOEXEC.BAT	Commands executed at creation of DOS sessions
OS2.INI	Desktop configuration and application initialization information
OS2SYS.INI	Printer and font configuration, COM and LPT port configuration, and default screen configuration

Q: *What are the tuning parameters (and their functions) for the multitasking manager?*

A: TIMESLICE	Maximum time applications can run before being interrupted
PRIORITY	Whether lower-priority applications get a dynamic boost if locked out of the CPU by higher-priority applications
MAXWAIT	How long lower-priority applications can be locked out of the CPU before getting a temporary priority boost
THREADS	Maximum number of tasks in the system

Q: *What are the tuning parameters (and their functions) for the memory manager?*

A: MEMMAN	Enables or disables system swapping
SWAPPATH	Specifies location of the system swap file

Q: *What are the tuning parameters for the I/O subsystem, and what are their functions?*

A: BUFFERS   Number of 512-byte buffers for file I/O operations

    DISKCACHE   Caching functions for FAT disks

    CACHE   Caching functions for HPFS disks

Q: *Which file systems come with OS/2 and what are the main differences between them?*

A: OS/2 comes with the File Allocation Table (FAT) system and the High-Performance File System (HPFS). FAT is compatible with the DOS FAT file system with the addition of supporting extended attributes. HPFS supports long filenames (up to 255 characters), large partitions (up to 4 gigabytes), large disks (up to 512 gigabytes), contiguous file allocation, and strategic directory placement.

Q: *What is an installable file system?*

A: OS/2 supports file systems supplied separately from the operating system. Installable file systems are installed similarly to device drivers, using an IFS=statement in CONFIG.SYS. Each IFS identifies file system devices such as disks that it owns, usually at format time. When an application uses an OS/2 system call to access a device managed by an IFS, OS/2 automatically passes the request to the IFS.

Q: *What IFSs come with OS/2? What are some other products that use IFSs?*

A: The High-Performance File System (HPFS) is an IFS that comes with OS/2, as does an IFS for CD-ROM data disks. LAN Server uses an IFS to remap local device identifiers to network server directories. TCP/IP Network File Sharing uses an IFS to remap local device identifiers to NFS server directories.

Q: *What is the difference between screen icons in OS/2 3.0 and screen icons in OS/2 1.x or Windows?*

A: Icons in OS/2 1.x or Windows represent minimized application windows; in OS/2 3.0 they represent objects that can be acted on.

Q: *What is the general method for acting on WorkPlace Shell objects?*

A: Point at the object with the mouse, click with the right mouse button, and choose the action from the resulting pop-up menu.

Q: *What happens when you double-click on a WorkPlace Shell object?*

A: You get a view of the object in a window. The information in the view will depend on the kind of object and the default view.

Q: *What are the major categories of objects in the WorkPlace Shell?*

A: 1. Program objects

   2. Data objects

   3. Printer objects

   4. Folder objects

5. Drives objects

6. Shredder objects

Q: *How are WorkPlace Shell objects configured?*

A: Each object has a settings notebook that is accessed from the "Open" sub-menu of the object's pop-up menu.

Q: *What is the difference between a copy of an object and a shadow of an object?*

A: When a change is made to a copy of an object, the original is unchanged. When a change is made to a shadow, the original is also changed.

Q: *How do you make a drag operation a copy? a move? How do you create a shadow?*

A: Hold the control key down while dragging to get a copy; hold down the Alt key to get a move. Create a shadow by dragging with both the shift and control keys down, or use the pop-up menu of the original object.

Q: *How do you configure the LaunchPad?*

A: You can drag an application object and drop it on either the LaunchPad itself or on one of the drawer handles on the LaunchPad.

Q: *What kinds of DOS programs do not run under OS/2 3.0?*

A: 1. Timing sensitive applications

2. Applications that require more than 1000 interrupts per second

3. Debuggers that attempt to access 80386 hardware

4. Applications that write to hard disks by physical sector

5. Applications that access memory above 1 megabyte using the VCPI standard or using nonstandard techniques

6. Block device drivers

Q: *What kinds of Windows programs do not run under (1) OS/2 2.0, (2) OS/2 2.1, and (3) OS/2 3.0?*

A: 1. OS/2 2.0: Applications that require Windows Enhanced mode

2. OS/2 2.1: Applications that require the WINMEM32.DLL; applications that require Windows Real mode

3. OS/2 3.0: Applications that require Windows Real mode

Q: *How are DOS applications configured?*

A: Use the DOS Settings dialog box from the Sessions page of the DOS application's Settings notebook.

Q: *What are the main DOS settings that will increase the amount of conventional memory available in a DOS session?*

A: 1. DOS_HIGH loads DOS above 640K.

2. VIDEO_MODE_RESTRICTION reclaims video buffers.

Q: *Where can DOS mode device drivers be specified and what is the effect of each choice?*

A: 1. In the OS/2 CONFIG.SYS. In this case, the device driver will be available to all DOS and Windows sessions.

   2. In the DOS settings for an icon representing a DOS command prompt, a Windows Full Screen session, or a DOS or Windows application. In this case, the device driver will be available only to programs started using the icon.

Q: *What kinds of memory above 1 megabyte can DOS and Windows applications access, and how much of each kind is available? What is the default amount of each kind assigned to a DOS session?*

A: 1. LIM EMS has 32 megabytes maximum, 2 megabytes default.

   2. LIMA XMS has 16 megabytes maximum, 2 megabytes default.

   3. DPMI has 512 megabytes maximum, 4 megabytes default.

Q: *If a DOS application fails to operate under OS/2 3.0 because it looks for a facility or version number associated with PC-DOS or MS-DOS, what steps can you take?*

A: 1. Use the DOS_VERSION setting to specify the specific version function required.

   2. Use the VM Boot facility to boot an actual DOS.

Q: *What actual versions of DOS can run in an OS/2 virtual DOS machine?*

A: All flavors of DOS, including PC-DOS and MS-DOS starting with version 1.0, and vendor-specific versions of DOS, such as Compaq DOS, and DR-DOS.

Q: *How can you use a DOS block device driver under OS/2 3.0?*

A: Create a DOS session running actual DOS and include the block device driver in the CONFIG.SYS used to boot that session.

Q: *What are the tools required to build an OS/2 3.0 application in C?*

A: 1. Include files for the OS/2 system calls

   2. A compiler that can generate 80386 32-bit code

   3. OS/2 system link libraries

   4. A 32-bit linker

Q: *What conventions are used to make OS/2 system calls? What is the VisualAge C Set ++ name for these conventions?*

A: 1. All parameters must be passed on the stack.

   2. Parameters are pushed right-to-left.

   3. Parameters are double-word aligned on the stack.

   4. The caller clears the stack.

   5. Any returned value is passed back in the EAX register.

   These are known as the "system" linkage.

Q: *What is the naming convention for OS/2 system calls?*

A: All OS/2 system calls begin with a three-character prefix that identifies the category of call:

Dos	OS/2 kernel functions
Win	Window functions
Gpi	Graphics programming interface functions
Spl	Spooler functions
Prf	Query or write user initialization file functions
Drg	Direct manipulation functions
Dev	Device query or access functions

Q: *When would you use an OS/2 system call in place of a similar language facility (i.e., DosOpen instead of a C fopen)?*

A: When the OS/2 system call provides additional functionality (i.e., the ability to open a file in various share modes).

Q: *What kinds of devices can be opened using DosOpen?*

A: Files, named pipes, and named devices such as COM and LPT ports.

Q: *What are the major options available when opening files?*

A: Access   Read, write, or read-write

   Share mode   Deny read-write, deny write, deny read, or deny none

   Caching   Prevent caching, prevent write caching

Q: *What kinds of caching are supported by the OS/2 file systems?*

A: Both the FAT and HPFS systems support both read caching and write caching ("lazywriting").

Q: *What is the unit of allocation used by the OS/2 memory manager?*

A: All memory allocation requested using OS/2 system calls is done in units of 4K.

Q: *What kinds of shared memory can applications request?*

A: Named shared memory is allocated with a name beginning with \SHARE-MEM\ and can be accessed by any other application that knows the name. Unnamed shared memory is allocated without a name. Access to unnamed shared memory is controlled by the shared memory allocator.

Q: *What is the name of the file OS/2 uses to hold memory blocks that have been swapped out of memory? Where is it located?*

A: It's called SWAPPER.DAT; its location is determined by the SWAPPATH parameter in CONFIG.SYS.

Q: *What is a dynamic link library?*

A: A library of subroutines that is not incorporated into an application .EXE file at link time. Instead, a pointer is maintained to the DLL. This allows multiple applications to share one copy of the subroutines at execution time. When the application is loaded, OS/2 checks if the DLL is already loaded (due to a previous application requirement), and loads the DLL only if it is not already resident. If it is, the application's call addresses are simply fixed to point to the already-resident subroutines.

Q: *What kinds of semaphores does OS/2 support?*

A: 1. Event notification semaphores, which are used to allow a routine to wait for or check on an event that another routine manages

   2. Mutual exclusion (mutex) semaphores, which are used to ensure that only one routine has access to a resource at a time

Q: *What kinds of interprocess communication are available to non-PM OS/2 applications?*

A: 1. Anonymous pipes

   2. Named pipes

   3. Queues

   4. Shared memory

   5. Dynamic link libraries

Q: *What kinds of named pipes are there?*

A: 1. Local named pipes, usable only between applications running on the same machine

   2. Remote named pipes, usable between applications running on different LAN-connected machines

Q: *How can a DLL be used for interprocess communication?*

A: The DLL can contain a data segment that is shared by all applications that use the DLL.

Q: *Which interprocess communication functions can be used by DOS applications?*

A: DOS applications running on LAN-connected machines can be clients on remote named pipes running on OS/2 servers. DOS applications running under OS/2 can be clients on named pipes supported by OS/2 applications running on the local machine or on LAN-connected machines.

Q: *What are the advantages of a multithreaded design?*

A: 1. Applications can conveniently manage multiple input sources without polling.

   2. Applications can divide their work into different priorities.

   3. In PM programs, applications can schedule long-running tasks, such as complex printing, while maintaining the responsiveness of the system.

Q: *How are priorities managed in OS/2?*

A: OS/2 supports 128 priorities divided into four priority classes with 32 levels in each. All applications start out with a default priority but can change to any priority without restriction. Each thread in an application can have a different priority.

Q: *How does preemptive multitasking work in OS/2?*

A: Each thread in the system is either running, runnable (i.e., has work to do), or is waiting (i.e., for user input, the completion of a disk I/O request, etc.). The running thread is allowed to execute until one of the following happens:

1. Its time-slice expires. (The default time-slice is 248 milliseconds.)

2. It requests a system service that involves a wait.

3. A higher-priority thread becomes runnable, in which case the running thread is immediately interrupted.

   If a thread's time-slice expires, other threads of equal priority get time-slices in a round-robin manner.

Q: *How can OS/2 prevent high-priority threads that are constantly runnable from locking lower-priority threads out of the CPU?*

A: If the PRIORITY statement in CONFIG.SYS contains the DYNAMIC option (the default), OS/2 will dynamically and temporarily boost the priority of low-priority threads that are locked out of the CPU for more than the number of seconds specified on the MAXWAIT parameter in CONFIG.SYS (the default is 3 seconds). This priority boost will fade out over a time period defined by the first parameter on the TIMESLICE statement in CONFIG.SYS.

Q: *What is a session?*

A: A session is a group of applications that share a virtual screen, keyboard, and mouse.

Q: *What is the technical definition of a window?*

A: A programming construct that receives messages and acts upon them. The window may or may not be visible on the screen and may or may not display output and accept input from a user. Windows are identified by window handles.

Q: *What is the technical definition of a message?*

A: A message is an element on a message queue associated with an application. It contains several fields, including a message type, the handle of the window it was sent to, two message-specific 32-bit parameters, a timestamp, and the location of the mouse when the message was generated.

Q: *What is a window procedure?*

A: A subroutine that contains the code to process messages sent to windows.

Q: *How are window procedures associated with windows?*

A: When a window is created, it is created as an instance of a window class. A window class defines the general appearance and behavior of windows created as instances of the class. When a window class is registered, its window procedure is specified. The behavior of the window is defined by the way the window procedure processes messages.

Q: *Does a window procedure have to process all possible messages?*

A: No. A window procedure can ignore messages and typically will ignore the majority of messages defined in OS/2. Any messages that are ignored must be passed back to a default window procedure defined in OS/2.

Q: *What are control windows?*

A: Control windows are instances of predefined window classes that are automatically registered in OS/2 and whose window procedures are provided by OS/2. They can be used by any application.

Q: *What are the main categories of control windows?*

A: 1. Standard window components, such as the frame window, title bar, minimize button, maximize button, and menu icon

2. User input components, such as entry fields, buttons, list boxes, and spin buttons

3. Application organization tools, such as containers and notebooks

Q: *What are the main categories of messages?*

A: 1. User input messages, including keystroke and mouse events

2. User interface messages, including messages relating to window movement, resizing, and uncovering

3. Messages from other applications

4. Messages from the system, including messages indicating changes in the environment

Q: *What facilities for screen output are provided by PM?*

A: 1. Text output

2. Font choice

3. Graphics primitives outputs, such as lines, curves, circles, ellipses, and polygons

4. Color choices for text, graphics primitives, and window components

5. Device translation, such as between the screen and a printer

Q: *What kinds of fonts are supported in OS/2?*

A: 1. OS/2 format bitmap fonts

2. OS/2 format outline fonts

3. Adobe type 1 outline fonts

Q: *What is Dynamic Data Exchange (DDE)?*

A: Dynamic Data Exchange (DDE) is an additional form of interprocess communication available to PM and Windows applications. It provides a means for applications to exchange data using messages, so that DDE events are processed in the same way as any other events.

Q: *What is window subclassing?*

A: Window subclassing can be used to add function to a control window without having to re-create all the logic provided by the control window. It involves intercepting messages before they are processed by the control window's window procedure. After taking appropriate action, the subclassing window procedure can discard the message or pass it to the original window procedure for normal processing.

Q: *What is a dialog box?*

A: Dialog boxes are complex windows built out of control windows. They are used in contexts that require specific user input, and are one major way that graphical applications dispense with command lines.

Q: *What are menus?*

A: Menus are lists of choices that applications make available to users. There are two main types of windows in PM:

1. Action bar menus, which appear as a horizontal row of choices just below a window's title bar

2. Pop-up menus, which appear as a vertical list of choices, usually when the user clicks the right mouse button over an object

Q: *What are resources?*

A: Resources are PM application components defined outside of the applications source code, in a resource file. The resource file is compiled by the resource compiler as part of the program generation process, and the resulting file is linked into the application .EXE file to create the final executable. The main types of resources are:

1. Menu definitions

2. Accelerator tables

3. Icon definitions

4. Bitmap definitions

5. Dialog box templates

Q: *What is the System Object Model?*

A: System Object Model (SOM) is a facility that adds object-oriented programming facilities to procedural languages, such as C. It provides a syntax for defining object classes—the Object Interface Definition Language (OIDL)—and a preprocessor for converting the OIDL code into procedural language components.

Q: *What are the main inputs and outputs to the SOM preprocessor?*

A: *Input*

OIDL file

Outputs

.C source template for implementing the class

.C implementation header, an include file for the program implementing the class

.C public header, an include file for programs using the class

Q: *What are the main uses of SOM in OS/2 programming?*

A: 1. As a general tool for writing object-oriented programs

2. As a tool for writing programs that use WorkPlace Shell objects

Q: *What is the relationship between SOM and the WorkPlace Shell?*

A: WorkPlace Shell objects are SOM objects. Applications that wish to extend WorkPlace Shell objects as part of the application design can use SOM to create classes that inherit the characteristics and behavior of WorkPlace Shell objects. Since WorkPlace Shell objects are varied and have complex behavior, applications can achieve levels of complexity without having to recode the behavior. Since the WorkPlace Shell closely follows CUA 1991 standards, applications can easily conform to CUA 1991 by using SOM to inherit WorkPlace Shell objects and their behavior.

9

VM—The IBM Virtual Machine Operating System

Jeff Kaplan

Introduction

IBM's Virtual Machine (VM) operating system provides for the ability to run multiple IBM operating systems simultaneously on a single, physical IBM (or compatible) processor complex. The VM operating system controls "virtual machines." A virtual (i.e., simulated) machine is the functional equivalent of a real processor complex. Each virtual machine is controlled by an operating system, with the VM operating system concurrently controlling multiple virtual machines on an actual, physical computer. Many operating systems, like the IBM MVS/ESA operating system, which normally execute on a real computer while controlling all of the resources of the computer, execute successfully within the virtual machine environment. Some operating systems—for example, the IBM Conversational Monitor System (CMS)—can execute only within a virtual machine environment, not on a real computer. CMS provides for interactive services, such as file editing and application program development, within a virtual machine. IBM has successively made available several versions of the VM operating system. The current version, known as the IBM Virtual Machine/Enterprise Systems Architecture (VM/ESA) operating system, is designed to functionally replace all of the previously released VM systems: VM/370, VM/SP, VM/SP HPO, and VM/XA SP.

The primary component of the VM operating system is known as Control Program (CP). The CP component performs the following major functions:

- Provides support for a variety of real machine operating environments such as 370, XA, or ESA processor mode, and single-image, physically partitioned, or LPAR processor operation.

- Provides support for numerous DASD, tape cartridge, communications, and unit record real input-output devices.

- Concurrent operation of multiple virtual machines, each of which is controlled by an operating system. This includes managing the demand paging for allocation of real storage in the real machine to virtual storage in the virtual machines.

- Provides support for intervirtual machine communication services such as the interuser communication vehicle (IUCV).

- Provides services to real machine operators and to executing virtual machines via CP commands and the DIAGNOSE instruction interface.

- Provides protection facilities such that a given virtual machine cannot access or interfere with the real machine CP operation or with another concurrently running virtual machine.

The CMS component of the VM operating system performs the following major functions:

- File management and maintenance such that disk files can be created, modified, copied, and erased. Files can be shared among any number of users. Access to certain types of MVS-formatted and VSE-formatted files is provided for.

- An editing facility, known as the XEDIT editor, provides for a rich set of editing capabilities.

- Program compilation and execution such that application programs written specifically for the CMS environment can be compiled and executed. Certain MVS and VSE application programs, depending on the MVS and VSE services required by those programs, can also be compiled and executed within the CMS environment.

- REXX, the REstructured eXtended eXecutor language, provides a sophisticated procedural command language environment. REXX permits access to CP commands, CMS commands, and other CMS facilities while also acting as a general-purpose programming language.

- Numerous support services, such as tape cartridge access, screen management, debugging facilities, and interuser communication are also provided for.

The Group Control System (GCS) component of the VM operating system is an operating system that is designed to execute only within a virtual machine environment, not on a real computer. GCS provides the environment that supports the facilities necessary to operate an SNA network. GCS interfaces with licensed IBM program products such as VTAM, RSCS, and NETVIEW. GCS also works with RSCS, which is the VTAM-provided component that permits SNA-connected terminals to log on to the VM Control Program.

The Dump Viewing Facility (DVF) component of the VM operating system is a set of CMS commands that aid operating systems programmers in dump analysis. The current version of the IBM VM operating system is known as IBM Virtual Machine/Enterprise Systems Architecture (VM/ESA) Version 1 Release 2. VM/ESA V1R2 is designed to functionally replace all of the previously released versions of the VM operating system.

Generally, the previous VM operating system versions can be grouped by the real processor mode supported—i.e., System/370 mode, Extended Architecture (XA) mode, or Enterprise Systems Architecture (ESA) mode.

The latest releases of the previously available VM operating system versions that are in general usage are as follows:

- VM/ESA Version 1 Release 1.1
- VM/ESA Version 1 Release 1.0
- VM/XA System Product Release 2.1
- VM/XA System Product Release 2.0
- VM/XA System Product Release 1
- VM/SP and VM/SP HPO Release 6
- VM/SP and VM/SP HPO Release 5

The Employment Interview

An interviewer will normally target specific areas of knowledge based on the general level of experience of the interviewee as follows:

- A novice user should be able to log on to VM and establish a terminal session; be comfortable with the VM environment and mode switching, including switching between the CP, CMS, and XEDIT environments; issue selected CP and CMS commands; perform simple editing of a file; access and manipulate files; access and manipulate the virtual machine's unit record devices; and know how to navigate the HELP facility.

- An intermediate user would be familiar with most of the common CP and CMS commands; write and execute simple REXX programs; be totally comfortable with manipulating files within minidisks and the Shared File System (SFS); be able to work with real and virtual tape devices and unit record devices; be able to fully utilize XEDIT and write simple XEDIT macros; and be able to compile and test application programs under the CMS environment.

- An advanced user would be able to solve technical problems within the XEDIT and REXX environments; be able to utilize selected CP services and facilities, such as the DIAGNOSE and IUCV services; be familiar with the real machine operation; have a rudimentary knowledge of the GCS environment; and be able to customize his or her own CMS working environment.

It is very important to note that certain CP and/or CMS facilities are available only in the newer releases of the VM operating system. Some of the technical questions and answers in the following section are based on knowledge of those newer services.

Questions and Answers

Novice Users

Q: *After you have logged on to VM, you receive a status message indicating "CP READ." What does this mean?*

A: The CP component of the VM operating system is waiting for you to enter a CP command. If the CMS system is not automatically IPLed when you log on, then you may IPL CMS at this time.

Q: *How do you determine which minidisks and directories you currently have accessed within CMS?*

A: The "QUERY ACCESSED" CMS command. The command response indicates the mode letter used to access a given minidisk (if a virtual device address is displayed) or a given directory (if a directory name is diplayed).

Q: *I notice that I have two different files with the same filename and filetype on two different minidisks or directories. What problems can occur because of the duplicate filenames?*

A: Some CMS commands (e.g., "EXEC") use the standard CMS search order of "A–Z" and process the first file found with the proper name. Some CMS commands (e.g., "LISTFILE") permit a specification of "*" for the filemode designation and thus will process all files with the indicated filename on all currently accessed minidisks or directories.

Q: *You would like to save a copy of the results of a sequence of CP and CMS commands that you are about to enter. How can you save a console log of your virtual machine console output on your "A" disk?*

A: You can issue the CP command "SPOOL CONSOLE START*" to start console spooling to your own virtual reader. You then can issue a "SPOOL CONSOLE STOP" command to terminate console spooling and make the console log available in your virtual reader. The log must then be stored as a CMS file using the CMS "RECEIVE" command.

Q: *Why would someone access a minidisk or directory as an extension of itself?*

A: Accessing a minidisk or directory as its own extension (i.e., "ACCESS 300 L/L") will normally cause all files in that minidisk or directory to be accessible as read-only, thus preventing accidental modification or deletion of those files.

Q: *I notice that my "A" disk is my 191 minidisk and that I do not have my top directory currently accessed. What can I do to access my directory as my "A" disk?*

A: Your system administrator has determined that you are to have access to minidisk storage, as a default, and to filepool space. You can request that your filepool space be accessed as "A," as your default, if your installation permits this option. Alternatively, the CMS "SET FILEPOOL filepoolid" command will establish the name of your default filepool. The CMS "ACCESS A" command will access your SFS top directory with a filemode of "A."

Q: *I requested "HELP" for a particular CMS command. When I look at the resultant HELP information on the screen, I notice that I received a very minimal description of the command, without any command syntax or parameter description. What can I do to receive a more detailed command description?*

A: You requested the brief HELP option. The PF1 program function key should indicate that you can enter "PF1" to select detailed or ALL HELP. You can immediately request detailed HELP by entering the CMS "HELP" command with the "DETAIL" option (e.g., "HELP CMS commandname DETAIL").

Q: *I had been editing—using XEDIT, a CMS file—for about an hour when there was a power failure and the system "crashed." I realized that I lost my file changes that I made with XEDIT because I did not have enough time to save or file my changes. What could I have done, besides periodically saving my file, that would have "automatically" prevented the loss of my changes?*

A: You should have entered the XEDIT "SET AUTOSAVE" subcommand at the beginning of the edit session or you could place this command in your "PRO-FILE XEDIT" file. The XEDIT editor will then automatically save your file at a user-requested interval.

Q: *You are in the midst of editing a CMS file when you decide to save the file. Upon saving the file you receive a message stating that the disk or filespace is full and that your file cannot be saved. What should you do?*

A: You can erase or discard a different file from your minidisk or filepool in order to make room for the saving of the file that you are currently editing. You can also, if you have other read-write minidisks available, save your file on one of those minidisks.

Q: *A programmer spooled a file to your virtual reader. When you try to receive this file you are not able to do so successfully. What could be wrong?*

A: Your virtual reader spool class probably does not match the spool class of the spool file sent to your virtual reader by the other user. You should ensure that your virtual reader will accept any reader file by using the universal reader spool class of "*" (e.g., "CP SPOOL READER CLASS*").

Q: *In the process of XEDITing a file I mistakenly entered a command that caused a pending status message to appear (e.g., " 'CC' pending"). How can I clear the pending status condition?*

A: The XEDIT "RESET" subcommand will cancel all pending status conditions.

Q: *I am editing a CMS file and I would like to insert the letter "X" in column 72 on several lines within the file. I type the desired character on those lines in the proper column, but when I depress the enter key, all of the characters disappear, leaving a blank in column 72 on those lines. What could possibly be happening?*

A: You are probably XEDITing a file that, as a default (based on filetype), has a record length and verify value (columns displayed on the screen) greater than the file's truncation value. As an example, unless changed by your installation, suppose that assembler language source files have a record length of 80, a verify value of 72, and a truncation value of 71. This means that on the screen you will be able to view 72 of the 80 columns of each source record. However, because of the truncation value of 71, you will not be permitted to enter data in columns 72 through 80.

Q: *How can a CMS user activate full-screen CMS?*

A: The CMS command "SET FULL SCREEN ON" will activate full-screen CMS.

Q: *Sometimes I have a need to move or rearrange the windows of my CMS session. What is the procedure for window manipulation?*

A: You must activate the "window management" window ("WM") via the PA1 key within full-screen CMS or the "WINDOW POP WM" command (or the older "POP WINDOW WM").

Q: *I am currently writing several execs that need to share variables among themselves. What should I do?*

A: The CMS "GLOBALV" command sets and retrieves a collection of named variables. The "GLOBALV PUT" command can be used to save the values of one or more variables. The "GLOBALV GET" command can be used to retrieve variables whose values were previously saved.

Q: *I received a certain error message while XEDITing a file. The error message description referred to an XEDIT ring. What exactly is an XEDIT ring?*

A: An XEDIT ring refers to the capability of the XEDIT editor to independently edit multiple files serially. A user can edit, for example, three files, and switch between all three files via the "XEDIT" command.

Q: *A strange problem occurred while I was XEDITing a file. I had issued the following two commands:*

```
SET PROFILE ON LEFT
SET NUM ON
```

I then issued a "delete" prefix command, "D3," on one of the file's lines. However, only one line (not three lines) was deleted. What could be the cause of this error?

A: Commands in the prefix area are decoded left to right and changes in the numbers (with "SET NUM ON") are looked for. If the prefix area contains, for example, "00034" and you type a "D3" command such that the "3" character overlays the "3" character of the prefix area ("00D34"), then your command will not be fully recognized. This problem can be avoided by always typing a blank after your prefix command.

Q: *I am trying to XEDIT a file and I have been receiving an error during execution of the XEDIT profile. How should I go about correcting the error in the XEDIT profile?*

A: It is best to edit your "PROFILE XEDIT" file by invoking the editor and requesting that a profile not be called during editor initialization:

```
XEDIT PROFILE XEDIT A (NOPROFILE
```

Q: *I have two persistent problems whenever I am editing a file. Everytime that I try to use the keyboard insert key to insert additional characters in a line, I receive an "input inhibited" message; I get around the problem by deleting some blanks from the end of the line before performing the insertion. Another problem that I seem to have is that, after typing some characters and then hitting the "enter" key, all of the characters that I had typed move to the left. I do not know what to do to correct these problems.*

A: The XEDIT commands "SET FULLREAD ON" and "SET NULLS ON" will together resolve the "left crush" problem, as it is called, and will enable character insertion at the end of a line without having to bother deleting characters or performing an "EOF" command.

Q: *I had noticed a file (that I did not recall creating) on my "A" disk. After browsing the file, I noticed that the file had been automatically deleted. What could have happened?*

A: Files with a filemode number of three (3) are automatically erased at the end of reading, whether they are on a minidisk or within the SFS system. Such temporary files are typically created as work files by some CMS commands.

Q: *The real machine operator attached a tape drive to my virtual machine at virtual address 170; the virtual address should have been 180. What can I do to correct the virtual address without detaching and reattaching the real tape drive?*

A: The CP "DEFINE" command permits redefinition of a virtual device address:

```
CP DEF 170 180
```

Q: *I am trying to XEDIT a large file and I have been receiving an XEDIT error message indicating that the file is too large. What can I do so that I can edit this particular file?*

A: The CP "DEFINE" command permits redefinition of a virtual machine's configuration, including the redefinition of the virtual machine's storage size. The following command, for example, will increase the virtual machine's storage size to 6 MB, thus permitting the editing of larger files. XEDIT retains the complete file in storage while editing.

```
CP DEF STOR 6M
```

Q: *What determines which CP commands a virtual machine user is authorized to issue?*

A: The virtual machine user's CP privilege class determines which CP commands a user is authorized to invoke. Normally, unless modified by your installation, the privilege classes range from "A", for the primary system operator, to "G", for the general user.

Q: *The system administrator has just allocated a new minidisk for my userid. After logging on, I tried to access the new minidisk, but I received an error message. What is probably wrong?*

A: The minidisk is, most likely, not formatted. All CMS minidisks must be formatted by the CMS "FORMAT" command prior to their usage by the CMS file system.

Q: *CMS module files are nonrelocatable. I do not fully understand what the term "nonrelocatable" means.*

A: When CMS modules are generated via the "LOAD" and the "GENMOD" commands, they are set up to execute at a specific location within the CMS system user-free area. The modules are said to be nonrelocatable because of their requirement of being loaded and run at a specific location within storage.

Q: *What is the distinction between guest real storage and guest virtual storage?*

A: The VM operating system handles three different types of storage:

1. The real storage of the physical machine, known as "really" real storage
2. The storage that appears to be real to a guest virtual machine (guest real storage), known as "virtually" real storage
3. The storage that a virtual operating system guest creates for its own usage (guest virtual storage), known as "virtually" virtual storage

Q: *What is the purpose of the IUCV facility?*

A: The CP IUCV facility is a CP service that enables the transfer of data among virtual machines. The IUCV service exists in conjunction with an older type of intermachine communication vehicle known as VMCF.

Q: *I had copied a file from one minidisk to another minidisk. When I issued a "FILELIST" command, the file appeared to occupy 500 blocks on one of my minidisks, but 1000 blocks on my other minidisk. Is this possible?*

A: The number of blocks that a file occupies is expressed in blocks, where the size of the block varies depending on how the minidisk was formatted. Most minidisks are formatted in either 1, 2, or 4K blocks using the CMS "FORMAT" command. A file that occupies, for example, x number of 2K blocks on a 2K-formatted minidisk may occupy about $2x$ number of 1K blocks on a 1K-formatted minidisk.

Q: *What is the distinction between the meaning of a filemode number of 0 for SFS files versus a filemode number of 0 for files stored on a minidisk?*

A: The filemode number of 0 for files stored on a minidisk indicates that the file is a private file (i.e., a user with read-only access) to that minidisk and will not be able to access the private file. A Shared File System (SFS) file, with a filemode number of 0, will be treated as if the filemode number is 1. SFS file access is controlled by granting read authority to that file.

Q: *What is one possible way to move (i.e., copy and delete) files from one SFS directory to a different SFS directory?*

A: The CMS "RELOCATE" command can be used to move files among different SFS directories. SFS file aliases and authorities remain unchanged. The command format is as follows:

```
RELOCATE myfilename myfiletype fromdir TO targetdir
```

Q: *I would like to share one of my SFS files with other users, but I update the file for an extended period of time every day. I would also like to make sure that the file is not damaged by other users. What should I do?*

A: You can use the CMS "CREATE LOCK" command to ensure serialization of access to a given SFS file. The command format is as follows:

```
CREATE LOCK myfilename EXCLUSIVE[or UPDATE]
```

Q: *I use the "PEEK" command often. One problem I have is that the command seems to let me "peek" at only a portion of the file queued in my virtual reader. What can I do to always be able to view a complete reader file?*

A: The CMS "DEFAULTS" command can be used to increase the maximum number of records that, as a default, the "PEEK" command will process.

Q: *How can I print out many CMS files and have all those files print together as one large report, without having a CP separator page between the output resulting from each print command?*

A: The CP spooling system "CONT" option can be used to "spool continuous" your virtual printer; this will batch together many little reports:

```
CP SPOOL PRT CONT      (prior to printing)
CP SPOOL PRT CLOSE     (after the "PRINT" command)
```

Q: *What is the distinction between the CP "LOGON" command and the CP "DIAL" command?*

A: The "LOGON" command permits access to the VM system as a virtual machine user. The "DIAL" command accesses a currently logged-on virtual machine as a user of that system.

Q: *I logged on to VM and then, during the IPL of CMS, I noticed that my 191 ("A") disk had been accessed with read access instead of the usual write access. What could be wrong?*

A: The minidisk is probably defined in the CP directory as "MR", meaning that a write link is established unless another user already has write access, in which case a read link is given.

Q: *I was observing a programmer entering CMS commands at a terminal. The programmer entered "AXES 301 B/B" and the result was the accessing of the 301 minidisk. I do not understand how the CMS "ACCESS" command was invoked because the programmer entered "AXES", not "ACCESS". How could this have happened since "AXES" was not the name of an exec?*

A: "AXES" is probably the name of a synonym for the "ACCESS" CMS command. Synonyms can usually be set up by the CMS user. Some installations may have a standard set of synonyms that they provide.

Q: *Certain CP commands that affect the state of the user's virtual machine (e.g., "IPL", "SYSTEM", "ATTN", and "REQUEST") are meant to simulate which capabilities of a real machine?*

A: CP commands (e.g., the "IPL" command) are meant to simulate the operation of a real machine console (i.e., the functions performed via "buttons" on a real machine). "Buttons" are not usually used on a real machine console anymore, but everyone still uses the term.

Q: *I had logged on to VM, IPLed CMS, "SET FULLSCREEN OFF", and was trying to enter a CMS command that referred to a particular CMS file when I began to have problems. This particular file contained an "@" character in the filename of the file. Every time I typed the command and the filename, the command response was "Invalid Filename". I noticed that a character in the filename next to the "@" character was missing. What could have happened?*

A: The "@" character is probably set on as the CP logical character delete symbol. The CP logical escape character (") should precede the "@" character, in order to actually code the "@" character.

Q: *What is the distinction between the "QUERY DASD" command and the "QUERY DISK" command?*

A: The CP "Q DASD" command presents information about all of the virtual DASD currently defined to a given virtual machine. The CMS "Q DISK" command presents the status of all the currently CMS-accessed minidisks or directories. There may be virtual minidisks that are CP-defined to the virtual machine, but not currently accessed in terms of the CMS operating system.

Q: *What problems could result if two or more users link to the same minidisk, "MW"?*

A: If both users are CMS users and have accessed the same minidisk in "R/W" mode, then there is the potential for permanent data loss on that minidisk. CMS does not support multiple users with write access to the same minidisk.

Q: *The response to a 'Q IMPEX' command is 'IMPEX=OFF'. What does this response imply in terms of CMS command processing?*

A: EXEC files must be preceded by the 'EXEC' command in order to be invoked correctly when your CMS session is set to 'IMPEX=OFF'.

Q: *How can a CMS file be punched without a 'READ' header control card?*

A: The CMS 'PUNCH' command with the 'NOHeader' option is used to punch a file without a header control card.

Q: *What is the purpose of the 'COPYFILE', 'FROM', and 'TO' operands?*
A: The 'COPYFILE', 'FROM', and 'TO' operands are used to copy a portion of a file.

Q: *What is the purpose of the CMS 'NAMES' command?*
A: The CMS 'NAMES' command can be used to maintain a list of other users with whom you may communicate.

Q: *How can a user unpack a CMS file?*
A: A CMS file may be unpacked by either XEDITing the file and saving the file in unpacked format or by using 'COPYFILE' with the 'UNPACK' option.

Q: *What is the purpose of CMS files that have a filemode number of '4'?*
A: CMS files with a filemode number of '4' are files that are in CMS OS simulated dataset format. These files may be accessed by OS macros in programs running under CMS control.

Q: *How are module files created?*
A: CMS module files, which are nonrelocatable executable programs, are created via the CMS 'GENMOD' command.

Q: *What is the purpose of a file with a filetype of 'AMSERV'?*
A: A CMS file with a filetype of 'AMSERV' contains VSAM Access Method Services control statements that are "performed" by the CMS 'AMSERV' command.

Q: *How can you purge a reader file from within the 'PEEK' or 'RDRLIST' screens?*
A: The CMS 'DISCARD' command is used to purge reader files from within the 'PEEK' or the 'RDRLIST' command.

Q: *What does the XEDIT 'AUTOSAVE' subcommand do?*
A: The XEDIT 'AUTOSAVE' subcommand enables the automatic saving of a file after a selected number of changes or additions to a file have been made.

Intermediate/Advanced Users

Q: *My installation has a real 4245 printer, but my virtual machine has a virtual 3211 printer defined. How can I load an 8 LPI FCB into my virtual printer?*
A: You can use the CP "LOADVFCB" command to load an FCB image into your virtual printer (e.g., "CP LOADVFCB vaddress FCB FCB8") where "FCB8" is a VM-provided 8 lines/inch, 68 lines/page FCB image.

Q: *What is the purpose of the CP "TAG" command as related to RSCS?*
A: The CP "TAG" command associates "tag information" with an output spool file. RSCS interprets this information as addressing and control data (i.e., where to transmit a file destined for a remote user).

Q: *How can a user write a program that is able to determine, when executing, that the host operating system is running within a real machine or within a virtual machine?*

A: The "STIDP" machine instruction returns an X"FF" as the version code of the CPUID, if and only if the executing operating system is running within a virtual machine.

Q: *What is the difference between the "IPL 190" and the "IPL CMS" commands?*

A: When an address such as "190" is used as the target of the CP "IPL" command, then that virtual device contains the IPL bootstrap program or the operating system nucleus program to be loaded. When the name of a system (such as "CMS") is used as the target of the CP "IPL" command, then that name represents a named saved system.

Q: *I observed the real machine system operator enter the following CP command: "ATT 120 SYSTEM volser". What is the purpose of this command?*

A: The CP "ATTACH" command can be used by the real machine operator or other authorized users to make a physical DASD volume available to the "system" for minidisk access.

Q: *What is the distinction between the "#CP" command and the "CP command" command?*

A: The "#CP" command causes the virtual machine to enter the CP environment, normally from the virtual machine environment. The "CP command" command causes a single CP command to be executed from the virtual machine environment.

Q: *How can a user acquire information about the macro members or the copy book members of a MACLIB?*

A: The CMS "MACLIST" command lists information about the members of MACLIB file.

Q: *My installation has an exec that is repeatedly called by a number of CMS users. What can be done to improve performance in regard to the use of this exec?*

A: The exec may be loaded into the CMS installation saved segment or may even be loaded into a virtual machine user's storage via the CMS "EXEC-LOAD" command.

Q: *How can certain versions of VM create a virtual machine with more virtual processors than there are real processors within the host processor complex?*

A: A given virtual machine may have more virtual processors than there are physical real processors in the host processor complex because CP dispatches one or more virtual processors on one or more real processors, as required, on a time-sliced basis.

Q: *What benefit does CP virtual reserve/release support provide?*

A: CP virtual reserve/release support enables multiple virtual machines, executing on the same real machine, to share one or more minidisks, provided that all of the virtual machine operating systems in use support real reserve/release.

Q: *If a temporary minidisk is created, after logon, for a given virtual machine, which program should be used to format or initialize the temporary mini-disk?*

A: The program that is needed to format or initialize a minidisk is dependent on the host virtual machine operating system in use. MVS, VM, VSE, and CMS either provide their own format programs or have specific initialization requirements.

Q: *What benefit does CP logical device support provide?*

A: The logical device support facility can be used to create multiple, logical 3270-type devices (i.e., a "programmable" display/printer device). The VM Pass-Through program product uses this CP facility to create multiple terminal sessions for a given user.

Q: *What are some of the benefits that a V=R or V=F virtual machine would enjoy?*

A: V=R and V=F virtual machines enjoy several benefits (e.g., nonpaged execution) such that the virtual machine's pages are kept in real storage all of the time, and no CCW translation of virtual-to-real channel program addresses for certain devices.

Q: *How can MVS application programs execute under CMS control?*

A: Certain MVS application programs can execute under CMS control because CMS can simulate the functions of many MVS operating system services, thus providing for the ability to execute MVS user-written programs.

Q: *What must be done by the CMS user to enable the execution of VSE user-written applications?*

A: The execution of user-written VSE applications is made possible by enabling the CMS/DOS environment via the CMS "SET DOS ON" command.

Q: *What service does the programmable operator facility provide?*

A: The programmable operator facility, known as "PROP," provides for the ability to intercept messages destined for a given virtual machine and to act upon those messages.

Q: *What are the primary applications that the GCS operating system supports?*

A: GCS is a virtual machine supervisor that is designed to support VTAM, NETVIEW, RSCS, and other VTAM-based applications that run natively within a virtual machine.

Q: *What kind of dumps can DVF handle?*

A: The Dump Viewing Facility (DVF) can process CP hard/soft dumps, stand-alone CP dumps, CMS, GCS, and various other program product dumps.

Q: *What is the purpose of the CP and CMS National Language Support (NLS)?*

A: The NLS feature provides for message, HELP file, and command support in various languages. Language support (other than the usual mixed-case American English support) must be installed by your installation.

Q: *What is the difference between a CP hard abend and a CP soft abend?*

A: Basically, errors that cannot be isolated to a particular virtual machine and may compromise overall system integrity result in a hard abend; otherwise, a soft abend results.

Q: *Why are some DASD volumes set up as CP-owned volumes and some DASD volumes are not set up this way?*

A: CP-owned volumes contain areas that are required for CP operation of the real machine (e.g., spooling space areas and page space areas). Volumes containing only minidisk space do not have to be marked as CP-owned.

Q: *What is the distinction, from the virtual machine's viewpoint, of dedicating a device to the virtual machine versus attaching the same device to the virtual machine?*

A: There is normally no difference, from the virtual machine's viewpoint, of attaching a device to the virtual machine versus dedicating a device to the virtual machine.

Q: *How can message traffic from a disconnected virtual machine operator's console be saved?*

A: The CP console spooling facility can be used to save the output directed to a disconnected console. Additionally, SCIF can be used to direct a disconnected console's output to another virtual machine.

Q: *What is the purpose of the CP "DEFSYS" command?*

A: The CP "DEFSYS" command creates a skeleton system data file for the purpose of saving a DCSS or NSS. The CP "SAVESEG" command saves a storage area to the defined system data file.

Q: *What are shadow page and segment tables?*

A: Shadow page and segment tables are used by CP to logically map the machine's physical storage to a virtual machine's operating system created virtual storage.

Q: *How does one "run" a VM-provided stand-alone utility (e.g., "DDR") within a virtual machine?*

A: A VM-provided stand-alone utility may be executed by punching the IPL deck to your virtual machine's virtual reader and then "IPLing" the virtual reader.

Q: *Why would a programmer use the CP DIAGNOSE interface?*

A: The CP DIAGNOSE interface, available within the assembly language or the REXX language, provides for access to selected CP services (e.g., the virtual console service that permits execution of CP commands from within a program).

Q: *What could happen if two or more DCSSs are defined, such that they have overlapping virtual storage addresses?*

A: Overlapping DCSS virtual storage addresses may be okay if a single virtual machine never requires the services of more than one of the overlapping DCSS saved segments at a time.

Q: *How can a general user check the status of the system (e.g., the current processor utilization)?*

A: The CP "INDICATE" command enables a general user to check the overall status of the "system" at a specific instant in time (e.g., the processor utilization is reported by the "INDICATE" command).

10
The RS/6000

Dan Donovan

Introduction

The IBM RISC System/6000 was introduced in February 1990. This family of computers is IBM's "Open Systems" offering, and uses IBM's Unix as its operating system—called the Advanced Interactive Executive (AIX).

At the heart of the RS/6000 processor architecture is RISC, which stands for Reduced Instruction Set Computing. RISC processors execute a set of machine instructions that is smaller and simpler than more traditional advanced processors with their large, complex instruction sets. Reduced instruction complexity allows the processor to operate at high speeds. IBM calls this architecture POWER, which stands for Performance Optimized With Enhanced RISC.

Since the last edition of this book, significant IBM RISC technology and performance enhancements have been implemented. IBM enhanced the POWER architecture with the new POWER2 architecture, and introduced the new PowerPC 601 chip technology, the first of a new generation of computer chips developed with Motorola and Apple Computer. The POWER2 technology adds another fixed and floating-point unit to the existing fixed and floating-point units and Level-2 cache. The PowerPC 601 chip is based on IBM's single-chip implementation of its POWER architecture. The PowerPC Architecture is designed for efficient implementations spanning the range from battery powered designs (laptops) to high-end processors (SMP). This chip incorporates fixed and floating-point execution units, a branch unit, and 32 KB cache, all in a chip approximately four-tenths of an inch per side. IBM, Motorola, and Apple have designed other PowerPC chips and are also designing follow-on PowerPC chips. The PowerPC 603 available today is targeted for portable personal computer systems. The 604 chip is a high performance 32-bit chip with 1.5 to 2 times the processing performance of the 601 32-bit chip. It is used for new uni-processor and multiprocessor desktop computers and workstations. The 620 is a 64-bit high performance chip for high-end workstations, servers, and multiprocessor systems. This chip will have 1.5 to 2 times the processing performance of the 604 chip.

The RS/6000 family of computers consists of uni-processors (one CPU), Symmetric Multiprocessors (multiple CPU's sharing the same memory and disk), and Massively Parallel Processors (multiple uni-processors connected via a high-speed switch acting as one system). These different types of systems come in three major lines: desktop, deskside, and rack-mounted. The primary differentiating factor between these lines is expandability in memory, disk storage, and input/output adapters. Within each RS/6000 line are machines with a variety of processor speeds and standard equipment configurations. Memory has been expanded to two gigabytes on the deskside and rack-mount systems and tape drives range from 4-mm, 8-mm, ¼-inch formats all the way to mainframe class library subsystems such as the 3494 for hundreds of gigabyte high-speed tape storage. Optical disk library subsystems have also been included for large amounts of near-online (infrequently accessed) storage and retrieval in the 188 gigabyte range. These large storage subsystems can be either ESCON channel attached or SCSI-2 Fast/Wide Differential attached for very fast data transfer rates.

Most RS/6000s are commonly configured with the components of a graphics console: keyboard, mouse, color graphics display (17"–23"), and display adapters ranging from the lower end basic 2-dimensional graphics to very high performing 3-dimensional graphical systems for CAD/CADAM applications. Available communications adapters enable connectivity to various types of local and wide area networks using TCP/IP, SNA, Netbios, and Novell network protocols to hundreds of asynchronous devices.

In 1994 IBM announced the SP2, the follow-on to the SP1. This is a Massively Parallel Processor (MPP) implementation. The SP2 enchances the SP1 with the new POWER2 processor and offers twice the processing power of the SP1 system, eight times greater memory, and four times greater bandwidth or transmission capacity. An SP2 system is basically a cluster of RS/6000s installed in a frame (rack) ranging from two RS/6000s (nodes) to 512. Each node had its own RAM memory, internal disk, and operating system. This is very unlike SMP systems, which share RAM memory, disk, and the operating system. This is why you can scale up to hundreds of systems. A high-speed switch is the key to this architecture because it keeps the latency (the time it takes for applications to communicate) between nodes the same regardless of the number of nodes. The SP2 is also popular for local area network (LAN) consolidations. You can have 2 to 16 nodes in one frame that can be administered from a single control workstation. This control workstation includes software that allows the installation, customization, and maintenance of the POWER parallel complex.

AIX

IBM's current AIX operating systems include Version 3.2 and the new 4.1 version. AIX includes TCP/IP and NFS. Version 4 includes a number of new features. These include:

- a fully threaded kernel that supports symmetric multiprocessing (SMP)
- the ability to extend file systems beyond the two-gigabyte Unix limitation
- the ability to configure file systems for disk resource savings
- high-performance capability offered by disk striping
- a graphical user interface to the installation process that reduces both the time and the complexity of installing a system

AIX Version 4 includes a number of options that provide a bridge mechanism for AIX 3.1 and 3.2 users and applications, enabling them to operate in the AIX 4.1 environment with fewer changes. Among the compatibility functions provided are file links to simulate the AIX 3.1 file structure, support for the locale and language functions provided in earlier versions, and support for the AIX 3.2 termcap functions.

The key to the AIX operating system is the ability to have applications be binary compatible across the whole product line from the laptop all the way up to the MPP systems. Another key enhancement to these operating systems is the smaller size of the AIX kernel. When new device drivers are added, the kernel is updated *dynamically* without rebuilding the kernel manually. AIX also has a JFS file system that uses database journalling techniques that perform checkpoints automatically, reducing the time to reboot the system in case of failure. The LVM (Logical Volume Manager) allows you to dynamically increase the size of the file system if you run out of space without bringing the system down. It also allows you to span your file system across multiple disk drives. SMIT (System Management Interface Tool) is integrated into the operating system so that external devices such as tape drives can be configured on the fly without bringing the system down.

Questions and Answers

These questions and answers include novice level and move into the expert level. Questions the interviewer might ask range from general background to the product's hardware and software features. Questions about product positioning (when would you use a particular configuration versus another) and configuring a system for use (system administration) have also been included.

Q: *What is POWER architecture?*
A: POWER, which stands for Performance Optimized With Enhanced RISC, is a multichip implementation that enables the CPU to perform multiple instructions within one clock cycle when optimized with the IBM XL compilers. This multi-instruction capability is often referred to as "Super Scaler" computing. The POWER2 technology enhances the POWER architecture by adding another fixed and floating-point unit to the existing fixed and floating-point units, increasing the number of instructions per clock cycle, and Level-2 cache is also added.

Q: *What is the PowerPC?*
A: The PowerPC is a single-chip implementation of the POWER architecture. It is used in the IBM entry level uni-processors (desktops) and the SMP multi-processors.

Q: *What is the difference between Unix and AIX?*
A: UNIX is an operating system first developed by AT&T's Bell Laboratories. Since then, many computer vendors have written versions of Unix to run on their systems. IBM's name for its version of Unix is AIX, which stands for Advanced Interactive Executive.

Q: *Are BSD and AT&T's commands compatible with AIX?*
A: Yes. AIX is made up of a combination of BSD and AT&T command sets. Most of the basic commands also work on AIX. The major difference comes in when you start using system kernel calls that differ from one Unix system to another.

Q: *What is the current AIX operating system?*
A: AIX has two current operating systems, 3.2 and 4.1.

The following questions and answers discuss the tools and exclusive features that come with AIX.

Q: *What "shells" does AIX support and what is the default shell?*
A: AIX supports the Korn shell, the C shell, and the Bourne shell. The Korn shell is the default shell.

Q: *What editors come with AIX?*
A: The vi and INed, a full screen IBM proprietary editor, come with AIX. However, other editors such as emac have to be purchased separately.

Q: *What does SMIT stand for and what does it do?*
A: SMIT is an acronym for System Management Interface Tool. It is an ASCII or GUI menu driven configuration tool. It is very useful for system administrators who are not familiar with the Unix syntax for commands. You can do the following with SMIT:
- Install, update, and maintain software
- Configure devices
- Make and extend file systems and paging space
- Manage users and groups
- Configure networks and communication applications
- Print jobs
- Perform problem determination
- Schedule jobs
- Manage system environments

Q: *What is the Logical Volume Manager (LVM)?*

A: The LVM partitions the disk drives into "physical partitions," the default being 4MB. The actual disk drive must be configured into a "volume group" to be recognized by the operating system. The "physical partitions" are then mapped to one or more "logical volumes." Your file systems are mounted on top of "logical volumes." The LVM is invisible to users and applications. Data on logical volumes appears to be contiguous to the user, but can be discontiguous on the physical disk(s). This allows file systems, paging space, and other logical volumes to be resized or relocated, span multiple physical disks, and have their contents replicated (mirrored) for greater flexibility and availability in the storage of data.

Q: *What is the System Resource Controller (SRC)?*

A: The SRC provides a set of commands and subroutines to make it easy to create and control subsystems (TCP/IP, SNA, etc.). It provides a mechanism to control subsystems such as communications processes using a common way to start, stop, and collect status information on processes.

Q: *What is the Object Data Manager (ODM)?*

A: The ODM is a data manager intended for the storage of system configuration data. Many system management functions use the ODM database. Many SMIT functions are stored and maintained as objects with associated characteristics. System configuration data managed by ODM are:

- Device configuration information
- Display information for SMIT (menus, selectors, and dialogs)
- Vital product data for installation and update procedures
- Communications configuration information
- System resource information

Q: *What is Software Vital Product Data (SWVPD)?*

A: Certain information about a software product and its installable options are maintained in the SWVPD database. It consists of a set of commands and the ODM object classes used for the maintenance of software product information. The SWVPD commands are provided for the user to query "lslpp" and verify "lppchk" software product information. The "installp" command uses the Object Data Manager (ODM) to maintain the following information in the SWVPD database:

- The name of the installed software product
- The version of the software product, which indicates the operating system that it operates
- The release level of the software product
- The modification level of the software product
- The fix level identification field

- The names, checksums, and sizes of the files that make up the software product or option
- The state of the software product: available, applied, committed, or broken (explained later)

Q: *What is InfoExplorer?*

A: InfoExplorer is a program that gives you access to thousands of pages of online information about using, managing, and programming the RS/6000 system. Information is stored in multiple databases so that you can install only the using and managing information or one or more of the programming information databases.

The following questions and answers have to do with how AIX 3.2 software is packaged and information on key installation terminology and procedures.

Q: *What are Optional Program Products (OPP) and License Program Products (LPP) and what is the difference?*

A: Optional Program Products (OPP) are software products that are extensions to the Base Operating System (BOS) and are shipped with the AIX Version 3.2 BOS. OPPs are *NOT* automatically installed on your system when you install the BOS. OPPs are Version 3.2 software products, such as the InfoExplorer and the INed editor, which are packaged along with the BOS. License Program Products (LPP) software are separately purchased software products, such as AIXwindows and Netware, and are not part of the BOS.

Q: *Is it necessary to install all OPPs (Optional Program Products)?*

A: No, it is not necessary to install all OPPs. Some administrators install only those OPPs that they need because of the lack of disk space. The Installation Guide lists and specifies the amount of disk space required for each OPP.

Q: *What are PTFs?*

A: PTFs (Program Temporary Fixes) are service updates. They are organized as subsystems, which are functionally related groups of software components that are part of the same OPP. They are divided into the following units:

- A "subsystem selective fix" is a group of related fixes that correct a specific problem.
- A "selective enchancement" is code that provides BOS Version 3.2 or an OPP software product with new or increased functionality.
- A "maintenance level" is an update that contains all selective enhancements and subsystems selective fixes since the last release of AIX. There is one maintenance level for each software product, including the BOS.
- The "AIX maintenance level" is an update that contains all subsystems, selective enhancements, and maintenance levels for BOS and for all of the software products installed on your system.

Q: *How are PTFs packaged?*

A: You can receive services updates in three ways:

1. Preventive Maintenance Package (PMP), which contains a maintenance level update for your system, including BOS and each optional software product that is installed on your system.

2. Release Update Package, which contains a PMP plus any new versions of OPPs and LPPs software products you have ordered. You request a release update package at the same time and in the same way that you request a new version of the Base Operating System.

3. Subsystem Selective Fix Package is shipped to customers who report specific problems to IBM support centers. These problems are corrected by the group of related fixes that comprise the subsystem selective fix package.

Q: *Do you have to install all PTFs of a PMP?*

A: You can install all of a PMP, Release Update Package, or Subsystem Selective Fix Package or only portions of the packages. Normally you would install only the PTFs required to fix your problem.

Q: *What does it mean to "apply," commit, and "reject" software products and updates?*

A: Installing an Optional Program Product and/or License Program Products or service updates involves three major actions:

1. Commit means when you install a software product to the system, you are making a commitment to that version of the software product. You would normally commit all software products with your initial install.

2. *Apply* means when you install a software product to the system, the product is installed and information is saved such that the product may be later removed from the system. The software is marked as being in the applied state. You normally would use this method when you already have an earlier version installed on the system for the reason given above. To apply over an earlier version, the early version must be first committed.

3. *Reject* means that when you "applied" a software product, the software product's files are removed from the system, and the Software Vital Product Data (SWVPD) information is changed to indicate that the product has been removed from the system. You now can use the earlier version if there was one installed.

Q: *What file system are IBM Optional Program Products and License Program Products installed in?*

A: All IBM Optional Program and License Program Products are install in the "/usr" file system.

Q: *What are the differences between a Preservation Installation, New Installation, and a Complete Overwrite Installation of AIX 3.2?*

A: A New Installation is used when your disk drives are empty. A Preservation Installation is used when a previous version of the Base Operating System

(BOS) is installed on your system and you want to preserve the root volume group and your system configuration. This method overwrites only the "/usr", "/tmp", "/var" and "/" (root) file systems of the previously installed version. A Complete Overwrite Installation completely overwrites an existing version of BOS. This procedure may impair recovery of data or destroy all existing data on your disk drives. You will also lose any system configuration information such as users, communication definitions, etc. If you do not want to lose this information use the Preservation Installation procedure.

Q: *Can you install all of the AIX 3.2 Base Operating System (BOS) or can you install just a portion of the BOS and remotely access the "/usr" file system?*

A: Yes, you can install a portion of the BOS and remotely access the "/usr" file system. This is usually how client machines with limited disk space access a remote server. The "/usr" file system contains common executable software that can be shared across AIX systems. When you install a portion of BOS, only the "/" (root) file system and the information necessary to start the system are installed. The "/usr" is not installed.

Q: *Can I install the BOS over the network?*

A: Yes, you can install the BOS, OPPs and LPPs over the network to multiple clients at the same time. The default number of simultaneous clients is nine. However, you can install more if necessary by increasing the number of system processes using SMIT. The default number of system process is 40. You will require four processes for each client.

Q: *What is the first thing you should do after you have installed a new AIX BOS, OPPs and LPPs?*

A: The first procedure a system administrator should perform after the BOS, OPPs and LPPs have been installed is to create a "mksysb." This procedure takes a snapshot of the "rootvg" and all system configurations. It is a bootable tape that can restore everything within "rootvg" and all system configurations. It can even be used to restore on a different model and size.

Q: *What does it mean when a software product is in the "broken" state when it is installed?*

A: A software product is usually in the broken state when something abnormal happens during the install process. For example, if you have an earlier version of SNA Server/6000 installed, and you do not stop the SNA subsystem before installing the new version, files can become corrupted. You can fix this problem by stopping the subsystem and reinstalling the product, indicating you want to "commit" the product.

Q: *What happens if you don't have enough room in "/usr" to install OPPs and LPPs?*

A: Fortunately, with the LVM, you can indicate YES on the "Install/Update Selectable Software Custom Install" SMIT menu to EXTEND the file systems if space is needed. SMIT will then automatically increase the space in "/usr" to accommodate the new OPPs and LPPs during the install process.

Q: *Can I have AIX pre-installed on my system at the plant?*

A: Yes, you can have the AIX BOS, OPPs and LPPs installed at the plant for a minimal cost. You can also have the system customized with your own software, another vendor's software, or just about any software that you would like installed and configured to your requirements.

The following questions and answers have to do with AIX Version 4.1 and how it is packaged, key installation terminology and procedures, and the differences between the two versions.

Q: *What are some of the new features that can be found in AIX version 4.1?*

A: Version 4 includes a flexible client and server packaging, a fully threaded kernel to support symmetric multiprocessing (SMP), the capability of extending file systems beyond the two gigabyte Unix limitation, disk striping, the ability to configure a file system's block size and a graphical user interface to the installation process that reduces both the time and the complexity of installing a system. AIX Version 4 includes a number of options that provide a bridge mechanism for AIX Version 3.1 and Version 3.2 users and applications, enabling them to operate in the AIX Version 4.1 environment with fewer changes.

Q: *What are some of the new features that can be found in the LPPs of AIX version 4.1?*

A: The following are new features that are a part of 4.1: AIXwindows 2D, Xstation Manager, and the Common Open System Environment (COSE) Desktop Snapshot.

Q: *Can I use applications written for AIX 3.2 and use them on AIX 4.1 without a recompile?*

A: Yes, you can use applications that run on AIX 3.2 on AIX 4.1 without a recompile. However, to take advantage of the fully threaded kernel that supports symmetric multiprocessing, it would be recommended that you recompile to optimize the performance of the application.

Q: *When I purchase AIX 3.2 how many users can log in to the system?*

A: That depends. The default number of users is 1 to 2. However, you can purchase additional users in "tiers" such as 3 to 8 users, 9 to 16 users, 17 to 32 users, 33 to 64 users, 65 to 128 users, 129 to 256 users, and 256 users and above.

Q: *How many users can log in to an AIX 4.1 system?*

A: The client and server versions of AIX 4.1 default to 1–2 users. The Server version is not tiered like 3.2. You can have an unlimited number of users. Each user has an incremental cost with the exception of models 2xx, 4xx, and C10, which have only two choices: 1–2 or unlimited with one cost associated to each situation.

Q: *What constitutes a licensed AIX user?*

A: Any user who either "rlogins" or "telnets" into an RS/6000 constitutes an AIX user.

The following questions and answers have to do with configuring the RS/6000.

Q: *Is it true that you can configure external I/O devices while the system is up and running?*

A: Yes, any external I/O device such as a tape drive, CD-ROM, or disk drive can be configured into the system by selecting "devices" and then selecting "configure after IPL" option with no interruption to the system. The devices will be ready for use immediately.

Q: *When you modify (add or delete) a disk drive, communication adapter, memory, tape drive, or CD-ROM, what do you have to do to have it recognized by the system?*

A: You do not have to do anything. The operating system has an Object Data Manager (ODM) that automatically configures it into the operating system. If you take an adapter, disk, tape drive, or CD-ROM out of the system, it will ask you to run the command "diag -a". When you run this command it will recognize that something has been removed, and ask you if this is correct. You then can delete it from the Object Data Manager (ODM) if it no longer is physically there or required.

Q: *Is it true that I can increase the size of a file system without bringing down the system?*

A: Yes, you can increase the size of any file system on the "fly" by allocating more space via SMIT without any interruption to the operating system or users.

Q: *When you create or change a file system using SMIT where does it put the file system on the disk drive?*

A: When you create or change a file system using SMIT it will grab available "physical partitions" including different disk drives if space is not available on the original drive on which it was created.

Q: *When using SMIT are the actions you take logged anywhere?*

A: Yes, whenever you invoke SMIT your actions are logged to "smit.log" and "smit.script". In addition, you can create script files to automate many of your SMIT tasks by editing the "smit.script" file. These files can grow quite large. You can erase them and they will automatically be created next time you use SMIT.

Q: *What is a raw device?*

A: A raw device is a logical volume without a file system mounted on it. Raw devices are usually used by databases. The database engine is then responsible for managing the data rather than the operating system.

Q: *What is the best way to ensure the "root" file system is protected?*

A: The best way to ensure that the "root" file system is protected is by "mirroring" it to another disk drive. This way, if the "root" file system is corrupted in any way, the "mirror" copy will automatically pick up without any manual intervention or interruption to the system. A more protected implementation would be to "mirror" "root" file system on a disk located on a different SCSI I/O controller. This will allow your "root" system to still be operational even if you lose the SCSI I/O controller.

Q: *Is it true that you can actually place data where you want on a disk drive?*

A: Yes, you can place data on the inner edge, inner middle, center, middle, and edge of the disk drive. You can do this by first creating a "logical volume," whereby you are prompted on where you want to place the logical volume on the disk, and then you can mount your file system on the logical volume.

The following questions and answers have to do with the more popular IBM License Program Products.

Q: *What programming languages are available for the RS/6000?*

A: In addition to the native AIX C compiler (in AIX 3.2), IBM provides a number of programming languages for the RS/6000—FORTRAN, C++, COBOL, Pascal, and Ada.

Q: *What databases are supported on AIX?*

A: DB2/6000, Oracle, Sybase, Progress, Informix, and Ingres are supported on AIX 3.2.

Q: *What does the SNA Server/6000 enable you to do?*

A: SNA Server/6000 enables you to connect between AIX and System Network Architecture (SNA) networks. Connectivity can be made over WANs using SDLC or X.25, or over LANs using Token-Ring, Ethernet, or Fiber Distributed Data Interface (FDDI). In peer-to-peer environments, SNA Server/6000 implements the Advanced Peer-to-Peer Networking (APPN) protocol to enhance the SNA architecture with dynamic routing, directory services, and network topology. It supports independent communications using APPC as well as dependent communications using LUs 0, 1, 2, 3, and 6.2.

Q: *What services does the SNA Gateway/6000 perform?*

A: With SNA Gateway/6000, a single RS/6000 platform can provide multiple downstream workstations with a single access point to one or more host systems without requiring that each workstation have a direct physical link to each host. It minimizes expensive remote links, reduces line costs, and enhances configuration flexibility.

Q: *What 3270 terminal emulators are available for AIX/6000?*
A: The tn3270 emulator is a standard component of AIX. It requires the 3270 host system to have TCP/IP.

Q: *What is AIX DCE?*
A: AIX DCE is a set of client/server foundation services that enable the development of distributed applications. These distributed applications may function over different types of computers that implement the core set of DCE services.

Q: *What is Encina for AIX/6000?*
A: Encina is an application for AIX/6000 that is supported by AIX DCE and provides a set of tools for development of transactional applications that require high levels of data integrity.

Q: *What is AIX High Availability Cluster Multi-Processing/6000 (HACMP) and what is it used for?*
A: AIX High Availability Cluster Multi-Processing/6000 (HACMP) is software that enables a backup RS/6000 application server or database server to automatically take over the clients or database in the event of one of the RS/6000s failing. You can have one system act as a standby performing no work, or you can have one system act as the primary system and the other system can perform work. In the second scenario, when the system falls over to the secondary system it will run in degraded mode. The fallover is automatic and takes between 30 seconds and 10 minutes to fallover depending on the configuration. You must have external disk subsystems connected to both RS/6000s, such as the 9333, 7135, or 7137 disk subsystems. There is a third mode of operation called concurrent access. This means that both RS/6000s can access the disk subsystem at the same time, using Oracle Parallel Server and HACMP.

Q: *What is AIX Netview/6000 and what is it used for?*
A: AIX Netview/6000 (NV/6000) is IBM's Simple Network Management Protocol (SNMP) domain network management manager software for the RS/6000. It is capable of monitoring network-attached TCP/IP and SNMP-enabled devices. The software provides a graphical user interface and an optional software called Service Point/6000, which provides for the converting and forwarding of SNMP traps to alerts and then sends them to the mainframe Netview product.

The following questions and answers have to do with graphics and graphical user interfaces.

Q: *What kind of graphical user interface is available on AIX?*
A: A version of the industry-standard X Window System, called AIX Windows Environment/6000, is supported. Included with this package is the AIX

Windows Desktop, an icon-based graphical front end to the operating system. In AIX 4.1 the Common Open System Environment (COSE) desktop comes bundled with the operating system.

Q: *Are three-dimensional graphics supported on AIX?*
A: The optional 3D feature of the AIX Windows Environment/6000 supports several 3D graphics programming interfaces, including graPHIGS, OpenGL, PEX and GL.

Q: *What size color displays are available for the RS/6000?*
A: IBM sells 17- and 20-inch color displays for the RS/6000. The entry model M20 has a built-in 17-inch color display. Models 220, 230, and 250 and Xstations 140 and 150 can use the 17V, 17P, and 21P inch displays.

Q: *What is the graphics resolution for the RS/6000?*
A: All IBM graphics adapters for the RS/6000 are capable of supporting 1280×1024 pixel resolution.

Q: *How many colors can the RS/6000 display?*
A: All color RS/6000 graphics adapters from IBM support 8-bit color and can display 256 colors. A 24-bit feature available for the GT4 and GTO adapters enables the display of 16.7 million colors.

Q: *What are the current IBM Xstations?*
A: The current IBM Xstations are the models 140 and 150. Xstation 140 includes:

- 33MHz, 32-bit CMOS Risc processor
- 4MB memory (expandable up to 68MB)
- 2MB video memory
- 2MB writable, non-volatile FLASH Memory
- Two serial ports, one parallel port, keyboard and mouse

Xstation 150 includes:

- 40MHz, 64-bit Risc Motorola 88110 processor
- 6MB memory (expandable up to 70MB)
- 2MB video memory
- 2MB writable, non-volatile FLASH Memory
- 8KB data cache
- 8KB instruction cache
- Four serial ports, one parallel port, keyboard and mouse

Q: *What graphics adapters are available for 2D graphics?*
A: The POWER GXT100, GXT150, and the GXT150L.

Q: *What graphics adapter is available for entry-level 3D graphics?*
A: The POWER Gt4e.

Q: *What graphics adapter should I use for mid-range 3D graphics?*
A: The POWER Gt4i and Gt4xi are cost-effective mid-range 3D adapters.

Q: *What graphics adapter is available for high-range 3D graphics?*

A: The GXT1000 is an external accelerator for 3D APIs, including OpenGL, PEX, PHIGS, and IBM GL 3.2 used for high-range 3D graphics.

The following questions and answers have to do with the configuring of systems that have a requirement for high availability of data. It depends on your risk assessment of how critical your data is and how long you can afford to be without it.

Q: *When would I use the IBM 9333 Serial Link drives?*

A: You use the 9333 Serial Link disk drives when your application/database require very high I/O performance and the disk requirements are in the 30GB–100GB range or more. The Serial Link adapter allows 32MB of data to flow bi-directionally, allowing for very fast I/O. Reads and writes can be processed at the same time. This solution can be highly available when used with the HACMP/6000 product with multiple paths to the disk subsystem.

Q: *How many systems can connect to a 9333 unit?*

A: Up to eight RS/6000s can be connected to the 9333 unit. Multiple paths and mirroring of the disks are used for high available configurations.

Q: *What is disk mirroring?*

A: Mirroring disks means that you can have redundant data written up to three times on different disks. When you are trying to access data, if for any reason something happens to the disk where the data resides, the operating system will automatically access the data on an alternate disk that was mirrored. This is transparent to any application. In fact, the operating system is smart enough to access the data from the mirrored disk with the actuator arm closest to the data. On the down side of mirroring, it doubles or triples the amount of disk required depending on how many mirrors you have.

Q: *When would you use the 7137 Disk Array Subsystem?*

A: The 7137 Disk Array Subsystem is similar to the 7135 RAIDiant Array. The major differences are: You can have only one Array Controller in the subsystem, only two RS/6000s can be attached to it, and you cannot have as much RAID-5 disk (33GB). The 7137 Disk Array Subsystem does have an optional dynamic "hot" spare that automatically rebuilds data. It also has a non-volatile mirrored 1MB or 4MB write cache, which allows for higher throughput when doing writes.

The following questions and answers have to do with SMPs and MPPs systems and their uses.

Q: *What is the difference between Symmetrical Multiprocessors (SMP) and Massively Parallel Processors (MPP)?*

A: The major differences between Symmetrical Multiprocessors (SMP) and Massively Parallel Processors (MPP) are: SMP systems have only one operating system that controls all CPUs. SMP boxes also share the same RAM memory and I/O bus, limiting the number of CPUs that can be added to a system. In most SMP systems, performance drops off dramatically after 8 processors. In MPP systems such as the IBM SP2 each machine or node has its own RAM memory, operating system, and I/O bus, eliminating the contention problems found in SMP systems. The SP2 also has a high-speed switch (30–40MBs bi-directional) that passes messages back and forth between the nodes, keeping the latency factor the same regardless of the number of systems. Using the switch the SP2 can scale up to 512 systems.

Q: *When would you use an SMP system versus an MPP system?*

A: SMP systems are usually used for high-end database servers ranging from 10 to 50GBs with 256 to 500 users, while the MPP system supports 300 to 500GBs with thousands of users.

Q: *What Version of AIX runs on the SP2?*

A: AIX Versions 3.2.5 and 4.1.4 currently run on the SP2 nodes.

The following questions have to do with troubleshooting RS/6000 hardware and software.

Q: *What should you do if you happen to see three flashing "888" on the LCD of an RS/6000?*

A: When you see three flashing "888" on the LCD you should: press the yellow reset button and write down the number and keep doing this until you come back to the three flashing "888". Then look up codes in the "Messages and Guide Reference" to determine if it is hardware or software.

Q: *Whom would you call if you had a hardware problem with the RS/6000?*

A: Call 1-800-IBM-SERV for hardware problems. Make sure you know what your seven-digit customer number is, the model of the RS/6000 and the Serial Number of the RS/6000, and depending on the warranty/maintenance contract, a Customer Engineer will be dispatched.

Q: *Whom would you call if you had a software problem that you were unable to solve?*

A: If you have a SupportLine Contract with IBM, you dial 1-800-225-5249, and press option "1." This provides you with access to a team of IBM specialists on RS/6000 and SP2. You can ask AIX installation questions, "how-to" type questions for AIX and IBM LPPs. If you don't have a SupportLine contract, you can mail, FAX, or E-mail over the Internet if your problem is a defect.

Q: *What should you do if the performance starts degrading on the RS/6000?*

A: First of all, to prevent this problem, it is very important that you monitor your system continually and never, never give "root" authority to any end users or application programmers unless you are working along with them. A very good tool to use to monitor your RS/6000s is the Performance

Toolbox (PTX), an IBM License Program Product. It contains tools for local and remote system-activity monitoring and tuning. The main purpose of the PTX Manager is to collect and display data from the various systems in the configuration. There is also an agent piece that monitors remote RS/6000 system activity and sends it back to the Manager. PTX does the following:

- Monitors and reports the activity of the AIX file system via a trace facility
- Monitors and displays the placement of a file's blocks within logical or physical volumes
- Monitors and displays statistics about contention for kernel locks
- Facilitates interactive placement of logical volumes within a volume group
- Reports on network I/O and network-related CPU usage
- Simulates systems with various sizes of memory for performance testing
- Captures and analyzes information about virtual-memory usage

If you do not have the luxury of having the PTX, you can use the performance monitoring tools that come with AIX such as "iostat," "netstat," "vmstat," and the "ps" command.

The following questions and answers have to do with miscellaneous subjects.

Q: *What kind of system input/output bus does the RS/6000 use?*
A: The RS/6000 uses the Micro Channel input/output bus. It is an enhanced version of the PS/2 Micro Channel bus. The latest RS/6000 models are equipped with XIO circuitry that doubles the peak Micro Channel data transfer to 40MB/second and to 80MB/second for Streaming Data Procedure transfers.

Q: *How do you shut down the RS/6000 in single user mode?*
A: First you must log in as "root," then "cd /" (root) to change into the root directory, then type "shutdown m" and press Enter. A system prompt displays and you can perform maintenance activities.

Q: *What happens when the RS/6000 boots?*
A: The first thing that happens is the On Chip Sequencer (OCS) checks to see if there are any problems with the system motherboard. Then control is passed to Read Only Storage (ROS), which performs the following:

- Checks that the machine is operational, power-on self-test (POST)
- Locates boot device
- Reads boot record and locates the kernel and boot file system images
- Loads the kernel, boot file system, base customize information into RAM
- System initialization starts
- Init executes Configuration Manager
- Paging is started

- Newroot performed to switch from boot file system to root file system
- All devices and subsystems are defined and configured

Q: *Is there an Asynchronous Transfer Mode (ATM) adapter available for the RS/6000?*

A: Yes, there is the Turboways 100 ATM Adapter, which operates at 100Mbps full-duplex between RS/6000s and other devices on the ATM network.

- Provides up to 1024 virtual connections at 100Mbps (megabits)
- Supports voice, data, video over the same network
- Provides congestion control with network
- ATM adaptation layer (AAL) 5 support

11

Oracle Release 7.3

Ulka Rodgers and James Fee Langendoen

Introduction

Oracle, a Relational Database Management System (RDBMS), is a product of Oracle Corporation. Oracle is a tightly integrated set of tools and utilities supporting the core database and was introduced to the public in 1979. Oracle provides the functionality to run on dozens of diverse systems, from large IBM mainframes through mini's and Unix systems right down to PCs. Applications that have been written for one hardware platform can be easily ported to Oracle on any of the other supported hardware platforms. In addition, Oracle has made great strides in connectivity issues, so that Oracle running on a VAX can share information with Oracle running on a SUN. In addition, Oracle uses an SQL "superset" of the ANSI standard called SQL*Plus. Since SQL*Plus is based on the ANSI standard, Oracle is able to share information with other ANSI-compliant relational database management systems.

The database kernel provides basic storage management facilities such as data storage in tables and columns, management of disk and memory space by the database, data distribution on multiple computers, and distributed access. It provides multi-user access services such as locking, security, and transaction management. It also supports server based processing such as maintaining integrity constraints like referential foreign key constraints. Procedural logic can be built into the kernel via stored procedures written in Oracle's PL/SQL language and database triggers. Triggers are procedural code that is executed when a database event such as insert, update, or delete occurs on a table regardless of which application caused the event. Optional add-ons to the kernel provide the capability of using SMP (Symmetric Multi-Processing) computers to perform a single database query in parallel. Parallel query servers make it possible to use Oracle for very large databases with hundreds of gigabytes of data. Another optional add-on allows the use of optical CD-ROM devices to store read-only data.

In addition to the RDBMS, Oracle provides a set of development tools collectively called Developer/2000, which previously was known as Cooperative Development Environment (CDE). These tools are windows-based GUI programming environments. They are available under Microsoft Windows in the IBM PC environment, and MOTIF-based Xwindows environments under operating systems such as Unix, VMS, and so on. Some of the prominent tools in CDE are interactive forms programming tool, Oracle Forms; a report generation tool, Oracle Reports; a business graphics development tool, Oracle Graphics, interface to third generation languages via the PRO* precompilers; and a graphical object-oriented development tool, Oracle Power Objects. Oracle Forms also uses a triggers concept to execute custom code when an event occurs. Forms events include starting a form, leaving a form, when cursor enters or leaves an item, before insert or update or delete, when a button is clicked, and so on. Trigger logic allows developers to use Oracle Forms to develop complex validation procedures and non-standard data manipulation.

Another set of tools, called Designer/2000, is Oracle's offering in the CASE arena. These tools support the project from early strategy and planning phases through the analysis and design phases and into development phase with code generator tools. The early phases are supported with diagrammers for business process models, entity-relationship models, function hierarchy diagrams, data flow diagrams, and matrix diagrams. Design and code generation phases are supported with data (table) diagrams, module data usage and matrix diagrams. Underlying the diagrammers is an integrated database, the Repository, which supports multi-user teamwork capabilities.

There are many other tools in Oracle's repertoire, too numerous to list and ever-changing. The prominent tools listed here are generally used for industrial-strength development projects. There are also numerous third-party offerings, such as PowerBuilder by PowerSoft, Uniface by Uniface Corp, SQLWindows by Gupta, Business Objects by Business Objects, Inc, and so on. These tools interface to the database using either proprietary protocol, Oracle SQL*Net protocol, or the de facto standard ODBC interface.

At last count, Oracle was available for about 80 hardware platforms. Rather than listing them, suffice it to say that Oracle is likely to be available for virtually all normal commercial systems.

Oracle's most current DBMS offering is Oracle 7 Version 7.3. This release includes major enhancements to support the use of Oracle for data warehouses and web servers on the World Wide Web. The optimizer in the new release is designed to efficiently process star queries, support parallel processing in loosely coupled CPU configuration (shared nothing) using data locality, and provide additional indexing methods.

SQL*Net is Oracle's proprietary networking interface that runs on top of some standard protocol such as TCP/IP, DecNet, and SPX/IPX. SQL*Net is necessary for a client/server configuration of an Oracle database, applications built using its tools, and distributed database configuration. Several third-party products are built using Oracle's PRO* languages, which allows them to use SQL*Net to communicate with an Oracle database.

Questions and Answers

Major Features

Q: *Describe Oracle.*

A: Oracle is an integrated set of tools and utilities supporting a core database. The central feature is the database product. The database provides only the back-end services. A front-end or user interface is still required to allow an end user to connect to the database and to manipulate the data. To this end, Oracle uses tools like Oracle Forms, SQL*Plus, PL/SQL, and the PRO* <language> for build applications. The choice of combinations of these tools is used to develop a user interface appropriate to the target environment.

Q: *What type of data manipulation capability does Oracle provide?*

A: Oracle provides Oracle Forms as a means to create fields and text that can be displayed so that data can then be entered or altered. The form interface is developed in Oracle Forms or may be generated from CASE tool with Generator for Forms.

Q: *What other "languages" does Oracle provide?*

A: Oracle provides the PRO* series of language programs, PRO*ADA, PRO*C, PRO*COBOL, PRO*FORTRAN, PRO*PASCAL, and PRO*PL/1.

Q: *What American National Standards Institute (ANSI) standard language does Oracle use?*

A: Oracle's SQL*Plus is based on the ANSI standard SQL language.

Q: *How "portable" are applications developed with Oracle?*

A: Portability, the ability to take an application from one hardware platform and move it to run on another hardware platform without extensive rework, has been a key feature of Oracle. Due to the consistent RDBMS structure, regardless of platform, it is possible to develop a mainframe application on one system and port it to another.

Q: *To which types of hardware platforms is Oracle limited?*

A: (This is a trick question.) The fact is that Oracle supports virtually all major platforms.

Q: *What is Oracle's optimizer?*

A: Oracle's optimizer is the part of the RDBMS kernel that "reads" a query and decides on the best manner of executing the request based on tables and indexes.

Q: *How does Oracle store information?*

A: Oracle stores information in tables. Each table has one or more columns that describe it. (These are the implementation of entities and their attributes.) The data is stored in rows. All Oracle's internal information is stored in tables (information on users, tables, columns, etc.).

Q: *How do you make a table?*

A: Creating a table in Oracle is a process of describing (in SQL*Plus) the information required by Oracle. You would log in to SQL*Plus with your Oracle username/password and issue the CREATE TABLE command followed by the table name. Then you would detail each column name, datatype, and column constraint (e.g., NOT NULL), followed by any table constraint for the column(s) (e.g., UNIQUE, PRIMARY KEY).

Example

```
CREATE TABLE [user.]tablename
      ({column_element | table_constraints}
      [,column_element | table_constraint} ] ...)
```

Q: *How do you delete a table?*

A: The command for deleting a table is DROP TABLE. This also drops all indexes and any GRANTs. Only a DBA can drop another user's table.

Q: *What is needed to make a column?*

A: Creating a column is done either when creating a table or altering a table to add a column. What is necessary (besides any table information) is the column name, the column's datatype (e.g., CHAR, INT, DATE), default (value), and any column constraint (NOT NULL, etc.).

Example

```
column_name datatype [DEFAULT expression] [column_constraint]
```

Q: *How do you delete a column?*

A: This is a trick question. There is no SQL statement to delete a column once it is created using a create table statement. However, assuming that the desired effect is a table with all other columns and corresponding data, there are a couple of ways to achieve this. The first method is to use the create table ... as select ... statement structure to create a second table that has the desired columns and data, dropping the first table, and renaming the second table to the appropriate name. The second method is to extract all data into a flat file using SQL*Plus, drop the table, create it with the desired columns, and load the extracted data using a utility like SQL*Loader.

Q: *What must the DBA do to allow a user the right to create tables?*

A: The DBA must grant the user privileges to CREATE SESSION and CREATE TABLE. The user must already have space quota on the tablespace where the table will be created. Alternatively, the DBA can grant these privileges to a role and grant that role to the user. Oracle also provides standard roles called CONNECT and RESOURCE, which includes these privileges along with other useful ones.

Example

```
GRANT CREATE SESSION to user
```

Q: *Describe NULL as used by Oracle.*

A: In Oracle a NULL value is unknown, irrelevant, or not meaningful. Any datatype can be of a null value (unless the column_constraint is NOT NULL). It is important to know that NULL in a numeric datatype is not a zero value. Because NULL represents an unknown value, two columns, each having a null value, are not equal to each other. This also means that logical and arithmetic operators do not work with NULL.

Q: *What is the purpose of an index?*

A: An index is primarily used to facilitate the access to large sets of data. By creating an index, the developer assists the RDBMS by minimizing the number of complete table scans. For example, if there is an index on a column LAST_NAME, and a query is entered for a list of last names beginning with the letter "G," the RDBMS would utilize the index's pointers to the necessary row(s) rather than scan the entire table for values that satisfied the query.

Q: *What is deadlock?*

A: A deadlock could occur in the case where two or more processes cannot complete their transaction because each process has locked the resource that the other process needed to complete its processing. Although rare, Oracle detects and resolves deadlocks by rolling back one of the processes.

Q: *What are DML statements?*

A: DML stands for Data Manipulation Language, which is one of three subsets of SQL. The others are DDL (Data Definition Language) and DCL (Data Control Language). Examples of DML commands are SELECT, INSERT, UPDATE, and DELETE.

Q: *What is the purpose of the table DUAL in Oracle?*

A: DUAL is an Oracle worktable with only one row and one column in it. The purpose for its existence is to facilitate some calculations and functions that are not dependent upon the columns in a table. So the query:

```
SELECT user from DUAL;
```

would return the current Username.

Q: *What is ROWID?*

A: ROWID is a pseudo column for a table with the logical address for each row. It is unique within the database and can be used in a SELECT statement or in a WHERE clause but cannot be changed by INSERT, UPDATE, or DELETE.

Q: *What is a synonym and how is it used?*

A: A synonym is another name given to a table or view for which you have access. It is made with the CREATE SYNONYM statement and results in an easier way of referencing the table.

The command looks like:

```
CREATE SYNONYM new_name for owner_name.table_name;
```

Q: *Give an example of an action that is prohibited in a stored procedure. Why?*

A: Any action that alters the current status of a session or transaction is prohibited. Some examples are commit and granting and revoking security roles. A commit is prohibited in a stored procedure because it may commit all components of a transaction even if they were performed prior to calling the stored procedure. Prohibiting a commit allows the calling application to rollback after completion of the stored procedure if necessary. Granting or revoking security roles from a user within a stored procedure would change the ability of the current session to perform privileged tasks. It might allow creation of security trapdoors.

Q: *Give an example of an action that is prohibited in a database trigger.*

A: Any action that alters data in the table that has the trigger is prohibited. For example, updating a row in the table from within an insert trigger defined on that table is prohibited. Tables that require such integrity maintenance processes are called mutating tables. Mutating tables are not supported by Oracle 7. Triggers can manipulate data in any other table.

Q: *How can the database get fragmented?*

A: A database can get fragmented through add/delete/update transactions that cause frequent space allocation and deallocation within tables. Through careful design of storage parameters, the likelihood of fragmentation can be reduced.

Q: *How can you reorganize a fragmented database?*

A: Each tablespace in the database needs to be reorganized. First step would be a backup, followed by initialization of the tablespace which de-fragments it, then recovery of data from the backup.

Q: *Describe Oracle's Data Dictionary.*

A: Oracle's Data Dictionary is the central source of information for the RDBMS and all the users. The information is a set of tables owned by the system (and DBAs) which is maintained by Oracle. They contain all information entered about database objects, users, privileges, events, and use. The Data Dictionary is structured to allow a DBA to query the information for system management and maintenance.

Oracle Tools

Oracle Forms

Q: *What kind of development environment is provided by Oracle?*

A: Oracle Forms is the tool used for the development of its forms-based interface. It provides the developer with an environment capable of design layout, entering or modifying trigger logic, compiling, testing, debugging, and generation of forms. This is also the tool used for modifying an existing form. By breaking down a form to its constituent parts, Oracle Forms allows you to navigate through the various parts, such as blocks, items, and triggers. In this way, logic can be attached at any or all the various levels to make the form respond to the different design needs. (For example, validation, navigation, and security can be built into the form.) The tool (also a form environment) also provides a screen painter for adding text and the positioning of fields. An item may be text, numeric, bitmap image, sound clip, and so on.

Q: *What types of files are used in forms development?*
A: The design of a form is stored in a platform independent binary form file with an extension .FMB. The form design is available in readable text format in a file with the extension .FMT. The runtime form is stored in a file with the extension .FMX. Unlike earlier versions, the readable text format file cannot be edited directly and then compiled into a runtime format. Changes must be applied using the Forms designer environment.

Q: *What is a "trigger"?*
A: A trigger is a procedure executed on the occurrence of certain events. Events are categorized into several classes, each capable of performing the procedure specified at the occurrence of the event. For example, a procedure can be executed when entering an Oracle Form; another may be specified to occur upon leaving the form. Each of these triggers is given a name and a level at which it operates. Triggers can be set for before or after executing a query, insert, update or delete, or user-defined. Triggers may also be attached to a key command or a button. An example of this is when a user hits the COMMIT key: the developer can attach logic to be performed prior to or subsequent to the commit.

Q: *At which three "levels" do triggers function?*
A: Triggers can be set to function:
   1. At the form level, which means that they are active throughout the entire form
   2. At the block level, which means that they will have meaning only within the block for which they are assigned
   3. To a specific item, in which case they will be active only in that item

   There is an order of precedence for the levels, in which the more specific trigger has precedence over the more general (i.e., a block trigger takes precedence over a form trigger and an item trigger takes precedence over either a block or form-level trigger).

Q: *What navigational features can triggers provide?*
A: Triggers can be attached to a defined key at any level (form, block, or item). It is useful to be able to add to or redefine a key's function. In this way, for example, a user hitting the KEY-NEXTFIELD key in the last field of a block can be navigated to the first field of the next block without additional keystrokes. Similarly, upon reaching the end of a form, they can be returned to the "top" of the form.

Q: *Which validation procedures can triggers be used for?*

A: A trigger may contain conditional logic so that, upon entering data (or leaving a field, or based upon data types, etc.), the form can monitor the data entry before the attempt is made to commit it. This can prevent a multirecord commit attempt from failing because the database rejects a single item. This conditional logic can enforce items not covered by the field characteristics.

Q: *What is a procedure?*

A: A procedure is a saved set of commands (SQL, PL/SQL, or both) that can be called.

Q: *Why does Oracle use a key's function as a naming convention?*

A: Since Oracle is available on many different platforms, it is far easier to express what the key does than it is to rewrite the function performed for each platform. In this way, a user on a DEC terminal using PF keys has the same abilities as a user on a PC.

Q: *What is a null canvas?*

A: A null canvas is the address Oracle uses for the nondisplayed items of a form.

Q: *What is the difference between a database trigger and an Oracle Forms trigger?*

A: A database trigger executes in the database server when a database event such as insert, update, or delete occurs on the specified table. An Oracle Forms trigger executes on occurrence of an interface event such as cursor movement in and out of items, blocks, or user actions like clicking on a button. Oracle Forms triggers execute in the client.

Oracle Forms Application Questions.   Refer to Figure 11-1. This is a simple form with seven fields visible and a series of questions as to how to modify (enhance) it. Consider this form to be a quick sketch done by the sales manager who has a basic understanding of Oracle and Oracle Forms. They want a tracking-and-query system for returns of goods sold. Block 1 represents a new table for the system. Returns_Report will need:

- A unique number for each report entered (item 1)
- The salesperson filing the report (item 2)
- The date the report was filed (item 3)
- The type of product complaint (item 4)
- A description of the complaint (item 5)

Block 2 represents the two fields needed from the Product_Information table:

- The product number (item 6)
- The product description (item 7)

Product COMPLAINT Form

Block #1—Returns__Report

Report Number   Salesperson   Date Filed

| Item #1 | | Item #2 | | Item #3 |

Product Complaint

| Item #4 |

Complaint Description

| Item #5 |

Block #2—Product__Information

Product Number involved in Complaint   Product Image

| Item #6 |

Product Description

| Item #7 |

| Item #8 |

Figure 11-1. Sample form.

Q: *How would you make item 1 an incrementing number starting at 1000?*
A: You can build the logic necessary or you can create a SEQUENCE. A SEQUENCE command would look like this:

```
CREATE SEQUENCE report_number increment by 1 start with 1000;
```

Q: *Item 2, "Salesperson," should be made to provide the defined scope of current salespeople from which the user can choose without editing. How would you provide that?*
A: The user should be able to pick from a list of values. In order to do this, a List of Values (LOV) based on a record group must be defined in Oracle Forms. This record group may obtain values from a database table (a Query record group) or from a hard-coded list (a static record group). When associating the LOV with the text item in the form, you can choose whether to use the LOV for validation, that is, to prevent the user from entering values that are not in the LOV.

Q: *Where will the cursor go when the KEY-NEXTFIELD is hit to exit item 5?*
A: The default navigation would return the cursor to the first enterable field of the current block; in this case, that would be item 1.

Q: *What types of constraints might you use in Oracle Forms for item 5, "Complaint Description"?*
A: This item is a description, so it would be of datatype CHAR. The length would be determined by the column width of the base table; however, the

display length could be altered to better tailor the form's layout—possibly resulting in a scrollable field. Input would be enabled and, quite possibly, the mandatory attribute. Query would be enabled; however, it is unclear if update should be allowed. Likewise, no mention was made as to whether the field should allow mixed-case or force uppercase entry. This would also be a good time to establish the INPUT and OUTPUT MASK for the date format desired for item 3.

Q: *What is the simplest method of having the cursor go from item 5 to item 6?*
A: The navigation between item 5 and item 6 is the same as between block 1 and block 2. To navigate without the user hitting the NEXT-BLOCK key (which is a different keystroke than KEY-NEXTFIELD), the KEY-NEXTFIELD trigger in item 5 has to be modified to perform the NEXT-BLOCK function.

Q: *Describe a way to populate item 3, "Date Filed," with the current date.*
A: The date field may be populated with the system date by giving it a DEFAULT = $$DATE$$. This would allow the field to be editable in the case that the date desired differed from the current date. The date could also be inserted through a trigger that would allow the designer to prevent a user from entering the field and editing the date.

Q: *For what would you use a default WHERE clause with this form?*
A: Since it was stated that this form would be used for both data entry and query, a WHERE clause (and possibly an ORDER BY clause) would allow the designer to specify a subset of information to be retrieved upon query. This is a practical means of tailoring the form to the end-user's needs.

Oracle Reports

Q: *Briefly describe Oracle Reports' function.*
A: Oracle Reports is the environment Oracle developed to handle report writing, formatting, and distribution. The basic program SQLREP is a menu-driven report development tool with a "fill in the blanks" style. The familiar forms type menu structure is used to enable the developer to supply standard report formats for an application. (It also facilitates the modification of existing formats.) Oracle Reports provides the means to copy, rename, drop, generate, and execute reports. The output of Oracle Reports is an executable .REP file.

Q: *What does the R20RUN program do?*
A: The R20RUN (run report) program executes an .REP file.

Q: *Describe a method other than Oracle Reports for making a report.*
A: SQL*Plus is commonly used for interactive reports and queries. It is also capable of providing formatting capabilities using the existing Oracle command structure.

SQL*Plus

Q: *Briefly describe the purpose of SQL*Plus.*

A: SQL*Plus (the program) is the command-line environment allowing a user access to Oracle through SQL or SQL*Plus (the language) commands. Ad hoc queries can be performed, databases created, modified, or dropped, files run, and a host of other functions performed outside the structure of an application. This is the primary communication medium for interfacing with the RDBMS.

Q: *How is SQL*Plus accessed?*

A: SQL*Plus is accessed by logging on to Oracle with:

```
sqlplus<username>/<password>
```

Q: *How is the special character % used?*

A: The % sign is used with logical operators as a match for any number of characters, including zero characters (i.e., a wildcard). An example would be:

```
WHERE last_name LIKE 'SMITH%'
```

This command would return 'SMITH', 'SMITHE', 'SMITHERS', etc.

Q: *What is an Oracle subquery?*

A: A subquery (also called the child query) is a query contained within a query. The child query must be executed in order to perform the parent query. The results of a subquery are not displayed, but only serve to allow the parent query to run.

Q: *How would you add a row to a table from the command line?*

A: You can use the INSERT command to insert one or more rows into a table with SQL*Plus. An example would look like this:

```
INSERT INTO table_name (a list of columns)
VALUES (a list of data values);
```

When performing this type of insert, the values must be separated with commas, CHAR and DATE values must be enclosed with apostrophes, and the values must be in the same order as the columns in the list of columns.

Q: *How would you empty all the rows in a table without affecting the structure?*

A: The DELETE command with no WHERE clause will delete all rows, that is:

```
DELETE from tablename;
```

A more efficient way, available in Oracle7, would be to use the TRUNCATE TABLE statement. Using this statement allows you to specify whether the space associated with the table and its indexes should be deallocated when data is deleted.

Q: *Describe the COMMIT and ROLLBACK commands.*

A: Insertions and other changes to tables are normally not committed until you exit from SQL*Plus (or you execute an ALTER, AUDIT, CONNECT, CREATE, DISCONNECT, DROP, GRANT, NOAUDIT, QUIT, or REVOKE). Until that time, you can see the changes if you query your tables—but other users cannot. At this point, you still have the option of performing a ROLLBACK, or undoing the changes. The COMMIT command forces the changes to the tables. Once the changes are committed, you may no longer undo them with ROLLBACK. They must be undone one at a time and any deletions must be reinserted.

Q: *What does the COUNT function do?*

A: The COUNT function counts nonnull number values, distinct number values, or the number of rows selected by a query. While COUNT does not count NULL values, it will count 0 (zero) values.

Q: *Why would you issue a CONNECT command from SQL*Plus?*

A: You would use the CONNECT command to change a user while already in SQL*Plus. This is useful when there is a difference of privileges involved. An example of this would be:

```
CONNECT username[/password] [@database]
```

CONNECT logs you off of Oracle, commits any pending changes, and then logs on the new username.

Q: *What does the NVL function do?*

A: The NVL (NULL VALUE SUBSTITUTION) function is used to substitute a true value for any NULL value found. The full command looks like this:

```
NVL(value, substitute)
```

Q: *Which function would you use to add the values in a set of data?*

A: The SUM function is used to sum all values for a group of rows. The full command would be:

```
SUM(value)
```

Languages and Commands

Q: *Describe the substring command "SUBSTR" and explain its use.*

A: The substring command is an SQL command for parsing a segment from a character string. The full command looks like this:

```
SUBSTR(string, start [,count])
```

where string is the character string, start marks the beginning of the function, and count optionally ends the function. If count is not specified, the function continues to the end of the string. An example of this would be fixed-position alphanumeric data elements (ABC1234) in which you wish to segregate the numeric value.

```
SUBSTR('ABC1234', 4) returns the string 1234
```

Q: *Describe the instring command "INSTR" and explain its use.*

A: The instring command is an SQL command for locating the position of a set of characters in a string. This function is also useful when used in conjunction with the SUBSTR function. The command format is:

```
INSTR(string, set [, start [, occurrence] ])
```

where string is the character string, set is the query string, start is the beginning of the function (optional), and occurrence is the number of times the query string appears (optional). An example of this would be finding the position of a segment in a hyphen-delimited string (breaking out a piece of an "intelligent key").

```
INSTR('ABC-1234-022-XYZ', '-', 2)
```

returns a position of 9.

Note: 2 refers to the second occurrence of the character '-'.

Q: *Describe the command DECODE and what it does.*

A: The DECODE command is used to bring IF, THEN, ELSE logic to SQL. It tests for the IF value(s) and then applies the THEN value(s) when true, the ELSE value(s) if not. The full command looks like:

```
DECODE (value, IF1, THEN1 [IF2, THEN2,]. . . , ELSE)
```

Q: *What is a pseudo column?*

A: Oracle uses pseudo columns for selecting information that is not an actual column in the table. Examples of this would be USER, UID, SYSDATE, ROWNUM, ROWID, NULL, and LEVEL.

Q: *What is the proper format for the DELETE command?*

A: The DELETE command is an SQL command used to delete all rows (optionally, that satisfy a condition) from a specified table. The full command format is:

```
DELETE FROM [user.] table [@link] [alias] [WHERE condition];
```

(As a side note, Oracle V5 does not reuse the space the deleted rows occupied unless an EXPORT and IMPORT are successfully executed. In Oracle V6 and Oracle7 this space can be reused.)

Q: *Where do you find the LOOP statement in Oracle?*

A: LOOP in Oracle is a PL/SQL statement. It gives the developer the ability to utilize a procedural construct in addition to the set manipulation available through SQL. There are four kinds of LOOPs: (1) the basic LOOP (infinite), (2) the WHILE LOOP, (3) FOR counter, and (4) FOR record IN.

Q: *What is the symbol for concatenation of values and how is it used?*

A: The concatenation symbol is the vertical double bars (||). It is used to join character values into a single string.

```
'XYZ' || 'ZZY' would result in 'XYZZZY'
```

Q: *Describe EXIT and its functions.*

A: EXIT has two functions in Oracle. In PL/SQL, it is a means of ending a LOOP, and control falls through to the statement following the LOOP. In SQL*Plus, it is the command to end a session and return the user to the operating system (or calling program, menu, etc.).

Q: *What is a BIND VARIABLE?*

A: A BIND VARIABLE is a variable in an SQL statement which must be replaced with an actual value before the statement can be executed.

Q: *What is the purpose of a CLUSTER?*
A: Oracle does not allow a user to specifically locate tables, since that is part of the function of the RDBMS. However, for the purpose of increasing performance, Oracle allows a developer to create a CLUSTER. A CLUSTER provides a means for storing data from different tables together for faster retrieval than if the table placement were left to the RDBMS.

Q: *What is a Host string?*
A: A Host string is used to specify how to connect to a remote Oracle database in client/server or distributed database environments. It contains the Oracle node name, the SQL*Net protocol type (TCP/IP, DECNET . . .), and other connection parameters. You can specify an alias (such as a meaningful name) so users do not need to understand its structure.

Q: *What is a time stamp?*
A: A time stamp is the date and time that a row is created or last modified.

Q: *What is a buffer used for in SQL*Plus?*
A: SQL*Plus uses a buffer (an area in computer memory) to allow editing of SQL and SQL*Plus commands.

Q: *Describe how Oracle interfaces with third-generation languages.*
A: Oracle, being a 4GL environment, sometimes must contend with existing 3GL systems. In order to allow this to occur with a minimum of difficulty, Oracle has provided a series of 3GL extensions which allow a precompiler to convert the PRO*<Language> code into a form which may then be compiled. This allows a developer to create user exits and other programs capable of accessing the Oracle database.

Oracle CASE Tools

CASE*Method, Designer/2000 Diagrammers and Generators

Q: *Which methodology does CASE*Method support?*
A: CASE*Method supports the Information Engineering methodology.

Q: *Which "Life Cycle" does CASE*Method support?*
A: CASE*Method is based upon the Business System Life Cycle. This is a top-down approach designed to partition the project into specific major stages. A refinement of the original SDLC (System Development Life Cycle), the Business System Life Cycle starts with the Strategy stage before moving into Analysis. The Business System Life Cycle also allows for iteration of tasks rather than the "Waterfall Model" of the original System Development Life Cycle.

Q: *What are the major stages of the Business System Life Cycle used by CASE*Method?*
A: There are seven stages. The first is Strategy, which feeds into the second, Analysis. The third is Design, which branches and supplies both Build and

User Documentation as fourth and fifth stages. They, in turn, provide the basis for the sixth stage, Transition. The seventh stage is Production.

Q: *What benefit is derived from using these stages?*

A: Any development project consists of a large number of tasks. Success of the project depends on them all being carried out. A methodical approach to breaking the project down into stages, each with clearly defined deliverables, gives greater control over the accomplishment and tracking of those tasks. The Information Engineering methodology is based upon the early stages laying the groundwork for subsequent stages.

Q: *What is the Repository?*

A: The Repository is a multiuser Oracle database designed to function as the central repository for all of the information captured through the Business System Life Cycle. This is similar to a Data Dictionary or Encyclopedia, but rather than simply recording information, it is a functioning part of an integrated toolset.

Q: *What does the Repository do?*

A: The Repository provides the focus of all the other CASE tools. It holds the information gathered during each stage, passing the information on to subsequent stages. This ability to exchange information among the tools allows for a broader range of completeness and consistency checks. Since the tools integrate with the Repository there is never a synchronization problem and any query will yield the project's most current state. The ability to query the Repository gives a developer control over the progress of a complex project.

Q: *What is the Oracle Process Modeller?*

A: The Business Process Modeller is a diagramming tool within Oracle's Designer/2000 toolset. It allows an analyst to diagrammatically represent the flow of processes in a business. These diagrams can be used as part of a strategy study feedback session, a Business Process Reengineering effort, or for prototyping new business ideas. The processes defined in this modeller can later be associated with data flows.

Q: *What is the Dataflow Diagrammer used for?*

A: The Dataflow Diagrammer is a graphic tool used to model the process side of a project. It is an analytical tool used to model the flow of information between functions. The output provides a nontechnical view of the project suitable for the basis of discussion with the end users.

Q: *What symbols are used for a dataflow diagram and what do they represent?*

A: The Dataflow Diagrammer uses a limited symbol set to model the passing of data. Data may arrive from an external source, but when it does, it is handled or processed. In Oracle's tool a PROCESS is represented by a round-cornered box. The DATAFLOW itself is represented by a directional line (an arrowhead at one end). The place where data is stored is a DATASTORE and is represented by an open-ended rectangle.

Q: *What is the Entity Relationship Diagrammer used for?*

A: The Entity Relationship Diagrammer is a graphic tool used to model the data side of a project. It is an analytical tool used to model the data required by the system. The output provides a view of the project which, when combined with end-user discussion, provides insight into how the users relate data objects to each other. This definition of relationships forms the basis of the underlying business rules of the project. This verification process ensures that the analyst has modeled the system that fulfills the needs of the users.

Q: *What symbols are used for an entity relationship diagram and what do they represent?*

A: The Entity Relationship Diagrammer also uses a limited symbol set to model the things about which information is kept (ENTITIES), which are represented by rectangles. They may be either in the system or considered external entities. Entities are related to other entities by RELATIONSHIPS, an expression of the business rules of the system being modeled. (For example, the statement "A customer must have one and only one account" reflects a one-to-one relationship between customer and account.) A relationship is represented by a line. The line is solid when defining a mandatory relationship and dotted when defining an optional relationship. A relationship line can also have an optional side and a mandatory side. A relationship also expresses the relationship degree (one-to-one, one-to-many, many-to-one, many-to-many) with a single line indicating one and a crowsfoot indicating many.

Q: *What is the Function Hierarchy Diagrammer used for?*

A: The Function Hierarchy Diagrammer is a graphic tool used to model the ordering (hierarchy) of the system's processes, enabling a developer to arrange the functions into meaningful parent/children structures. This in turn helps to lay out a project in a structure that reflects new or redefined functionality.

Q: *What is the Matrix Diagrammer used for?*

A: The Matrix Diagrammer is a general-purpose tool to aid the developer with the interrelationship of different objects in the dictionary. For example, the matrix could be of functions against entities, critical success factors against business functions, program modules to tables, or variants of these and/or other possibilities.

Q: *What is Oracle Generator?*

A: Oracle Generator is Oracle's 4GL code generator. It takes the information stored in Repository (supplied by a diagrammer, manually inputted, or a combination of both) and generates the application, module by module. The end result is a functioning product that operates in an Oracle Forms environment, complete with constraints and integrity checks. The generator is capable of also building menu structure and reports.

Q: *What benefits do Oracle's CASE tools offer over traditional development techniques?*

A: There are several benefits, starting with the basic graphic tools. Since the strategy and analysis stages are involved with user interviews, walk-throughs, and discussions, many initial requirements are subject to modification as they are more completely understood. The graphic designer tools allow these changes to be made rapidly, while capturing the underlying information in the Dictionary. The tool also provides a high degree of error checking, bringing possible problems to the analyst's attention. The tool also helps multiple analysts work on a project with a minimum of redundancy. The central dictionary makes charting progress an easier task with both packaged reports and the ability to perform ad hoc queries. The Generator function saves substantial time over hand-coding the application since it is based on elements in Dictionary.

Q: *What is the difference between an entity-relationship diagram and a data diagram?*

A: The entity-relationship diagram models business data objects and their relationships, a data diagram models database structures like tables and foreign keys. The entity-relationship diagram represents a logical view but the data diagram represents a physical implementation. While these are closely related, the physical implementation may be different due to design decisions that may be restrictive or may reflect performance-driven compromises.

Q: *How does the Oracle Forms Generator use foreign key constraints?*

A: The Forms Generator uses foreign key constraints to determine master-detail relationships in the blocks of a form. It also uses them to code a pick-list for a form field where the list is obtained from another table.

Bibliography

In addition to the Oracle documentation, the following books are recommended:

Barker, Richard, *CASE*METHOD, Entity Relationship Modelling*, Addison Wesley, 1990.

Barker, Richard, *CASE*METHOD, Tasks and Deliverables*, Addison Wesley, 1990, ISBN 0-201-41697-2.

Barker, Richard, and Cliff Longman, *CASE*METHOD, Function and Process Modelling*, Addison Wesley, 1992, ISBN 0-201-56525-0.

Koch, George, *ORACLE, the Complete Reference*, Osborne McGraw-Hill, 1991, ISBN 0-07-881635-1.

Rodgers, Ulka, *Oracle: A Database Developer's Guide*, Prentice Hall, 1991, ISBN 0-13-488925-8.

12
CICS

AnnMarie Katz

CICS is alive and well. There are more than 30,000 installations using CICS world-wide. IBM has been enhancing CICS and their mainframe support. In addition, a huge industry has grown up around CICS. Hundreds of independent software companies have successfully developed and sold CICS-related products and applications. What this means is that there are and will continue to be, for many years to come, jobs for those who know CICS.

CICS, since its first announcement in the early 1970s, has evolved into multi-platform industrial strength systems for running multiple transactions from multiple on-line terminals to update multiple databases. All on-line transaction processing (OLTP) systems have common characteristics that are sometimes referred to as the ACID properties. These common properties can be defined as follows:

AUTOMATIC   All of the processing for each transaction is considered to be a single unit and is always completed. This can be referred to as a logical unit of work. If a transaction cannot be completed then ROLLBACK will occur. This creates an ALL (all parts completed) or NOTHING (total blackout) situation.

CONSISTENT   Refers to data consistency and read/write integrity across all databases as seen by a program. For example, one transaction cannot access data that is partially committed by another transaction. This is enforced by SYNCPOINT and ROLLBACK methods.

ISOLATED   Each transaction is isolated from affecting other transactions in the system. In effect each transaction appears to be the only transaction running.

DURABLE   Once data updates have been committed by a transaction the updates are permanent and remain in that committed state when accessed by other transactions.

The CICS family of products has been developed for multiple platforms by IBM and other vendors. IBM has a distinct advantage over other OLTP systems in that 90 percent of Fortune 500 companies are currently using its software. Below is a list of CICS products developed for other platforms:

Name	Platform
CICS/MVS	ES/9000
CICS/ESA	ES/9000
CICS/VSE	ES/9000
CICS/400	AS/400
CICS/6000	RS/6000
CICS OS/2	OS/2
CICS client for Sun	Sun
CICS for HP	HP9000, HP3000
CICS for DEC	DEC Alpha
CICS for Windows NT	NT
CICS OS/2 client	Windows
CICS OS/2 client	DOS
CICS client for NetWare	NetWare LAN

Internally, CICS products are structured very differently. But from an application viewpoint they all share common API (application program interface) and ISC (intersystem communications) user interface commands. Applications developed on one platform are portable to another platform with a minimum of recoding. The details of each command differ slightly for each platform and therefore should be evaluated when converting between platforms.

Other CICS-like transaction processing systems are available from other vendors such as Micro Focus transaction system and UniKix, a UNIX based CICS-like system from BULLHN Information Systems.

CICS/MVS Interface

This chapter will explore in detail OLTP as it applies to IBM mainframe CICS. As of this writing the latest version is CICS/ESA version 4 release 1. This version (like its recent predecessors) functions like a miniature multi-user, multitasking operating system within MVS. It serves as an additional layer between the application and MVS services.

Each CICS subsystem runs as a single MVS task within its own address space (region) and as such is isolated from MVS. MVS operating system services such as terminal and file I/O are requested by CICS. There can be multiple CICS address spaces, each running a separate CICS sub-system (MRO). Since the latest release, CICS/ESA 4.1, these separate subsystems can run in separate MVS images on one machine.

Within each CICS address space there are many applications all controlled and managed by the CICS subsystem. Each CICS subsystem dispatches and schedules requests made by its applications. Any MVS service required by an application, such as terminal or file I/O, is made by the application to CICS. CICS in turn filters this request and passes it on to MVS. The actual servicing of these requests is still done by MVS.

Terminology

Conversational transaction: A process whereby a CICS transaction sends a message to the terminal user and then waits, holding all necessary resources, until the user responds. Resources are only released when the transaction has ended.

Pseudo-conversational transaction: A process whereby a CICS transaction sends a message to the terminal user and then releases all resources. When the user responds all required resources are reacquired and processing continues. From the terminal user's vantage point there is no interruption of service. From the system's vantage point another task can be executed while waiting for the user to respond. Thus there is more efficient use of the CPU, STORAGE, etc.

Re-entrant: A term that refers to MVS programs that do not modify themselves. MVS can interrupt these programs (SVCs), perform other MVS tasks, and then reenter the program and continue processing.

Quasi-re-entrant: A term that refers to programs in a CICS environment that do not modify themselves. CICS can interrupt these programs, perform other CICS tasks, and then reenter the program to continue processing. This is accomplished by separating the data (working storage) from the code. Each transaction has its own working storage area but will share its code with other transactions. MVS interrupts also occur but they will interrupt the entire region, since the entire region is one task to MVS.

Command level programming: API interface between the program and CICS. Command level commands are imbedded in source code written mostly in COBOL. C language is also widely supported. Command level commands begin with EXEC CICS and end with END-EXEC. Command level is the only API supported by CICS/ESA. IBM support for the old macro level has been dropped.

Basic Mapping Support (BMS): A CICS macro assembler language facility that enables the formatting of a native 3270 data stream. A 3270 native data stream will contain bit-level control characters, which are interpreted by the 3270 hardware, and data characters. BMS macros enable the programmer to bypass the bit-level programming details of formatting this data stream.

Application Program Interface (API): Standard commands imbedded in an application program that request services from the operating system. All CICS products use the same Command Level Interface. Some non-mainframe CICS systems can directly request operating system services without using this API.

Batch data interchange: An older CICS facility, used for the exchange of files with an external system. Often the communication was with a program in an intelligent controller. Files were exchanged by imbedding various commands (ISSUE xx) in sending/receiving programs. Newer controllers use APPC or other communication methods rather than batch interchange.

Resource Definition Online (RDO): The administrative interface used to define and modify resource definitions to CICS is accessed through the MVS/CICS transaction CEDA. Early CICS required that this information be managed with assembler language tables. Any modifications required changing the table source, reassembling the table, and restarting CICS. Today, the transaction CEDA manages a VSAM file containing most of the information in these tables (PCT, FCT, TCT, PPT, etc.). Most of the changes made through CEDA take effect immediately.

CICS transactions: Several transactions are supplied with CICS to provide utility, debugging, and administrative management functions. Some of these CICS-supplied transactions are:

CESN or CSSN	User LOGON. Used to log on to CICS.
CESF or CSSF	User LOGOFF. Used to log off of CICS.
CEDF	Execution Diagnostic Facility (EDF). An interactive debugging aid to trace and monitor the execution of an application program. The status of each CICS command can be traced and monitored as it is executed.
CEBR	Temporary storage browse transaction. Used to display the contents of a temporary storage queue. You can display the contents of a TSQ either alone (from a clear screen) or when you are using CEDF.
CECI	Command interpreter transaction. Used to verify the syntax of a CICS command and then execute it.
CEMT	Extended master terminal transaction. Used to interactively monitor and manipulate the CICS environment. Many of its functions are usually restricted to the application programmer. The user is prompted by menu-driven functions, the most common of which are INQUIRE (INQ), to inquire about a resource (i.e., transactions, files, programs, tasks); and SET, to change the attribute of a resource (i.e., to load new copy of program, enable/disable programs, etc.). Any changes made through CEMT are only for the current CICS job and are not permanent.
CEDA	Manages resource definition file access as explained above.

CICS Communications: A CICS region can communicate with other CICS and non-CICS regions running on the same or on different processors, creating a truly distributed processing environment.

Resources such as terminals, transactions, and files, can be distributed among various CICS regions and accessed using one of the following communication methods:

1. Multiple Region Option (MRO). Multiple instances of CICS regions. In releases before CICS/ESA 4.1 these regions had to reside in one MVS image. Since CICS/ESA 4.1, MRO regions can reside in multiple MVS images on one machine. It is common practice to separate all terminals into one or more terminal owning regions (TOR), all VSAM files into one or more file owning regions (FOR), and applications into several application owning regions (AOR). It still applies today that only one CICS region can have a VSAM dataset open at any one time. Separating all VSAM files into their own regions enables applications from multiple application regions to access these files. This is accomplished by using one of the dynamic inter-system communication facilities described below.

2. Intersystem Communication (ISC). Communication between CICS or non-CICS systems located on different processors. Sophisticated communication networks usually based on SNA architecture are required. The most widely used protocol is LU6.2. Links to CICS systems on other processors use ISC/LU6.2. Links to non-CICS systems or workstations use LU6.2/Advanced program-to-program communication (APPC). The concept is that two systems can communicate LU (logical unit) to LU if they both use the LU6.2 protocol.

Once the link has been established, using MRO or ISC, the multisystems are able to communicate in a standard way that is relatively transparent to the application program. Both of the above methods enable the following facilities:

- Function shipping
- Transaction routing
- Asynchronous processing
- Distributed Transaction Processing (DTP)

The region making the request is the LOCAL region, the region servicing the request is the REMOTE region. The systems programmer/administrator must set up the CICS systems tables in both the local and remote regions. For each remote resource the appropriate table must specify that the resource is remote and identify the owning region. In the region that owns the resource, the appropriate table must specify that the resource is local to that region. Once the link for a resource has been established between a local and a remote system an application can freely use it without considering who owns it.

Function shipping: A local CICS application can access resources owned by remote regions. The application does not know or care where these resources are located. These resources can be a VSAM file, a transient queue, a temporary storage queue, or an IMS database. When a request for resource access (i.e., READ VSAM file) is issued CICS will look in the FCT to see who owns this resource. If it is owned by a remote region, the request is sent to that region using either MRO (same processor) or ISC (different processor). The remote system will then start a mirror transaction to service the request. If a reply is required, the remote system will check its PCT to determine who owns the initiating transaction. If the initiating transaction is remote to itself it will route the reply back using MRO or ISC.

Transaction routing: A terminal user connected to a local CICS system can start and control a transaction owned by a remote system. The transaction executes normally and appears to be owned by the initiating terminal, even though the region it is actually executing in is not known by the user. When a transaction is initiated from a terminal the PCT is checked to see who owns this transaction and the request is routed to that region using either MRO (same processor) or ISC (different processor). This facility is often used to separate terminals into one region (terminal region) and various applications (application region) into other regions.

Asynchronous processing: A local CICS application can initiate a transaction owned by a remote system. It does not care what region owns this transaction. This is accomplished by a START command with a TRANSID = tranx. Data can be passed from the local region and be retrieved in the remote region, functioning like normal START and RETRIEVE commands. CICS will check the PCT to determine whether this transaction is owned by the local or a remote region. If it is a remote transaction the request is routed to that region using either MRO (same processor) or ISC (different processor). After issuing the START command the local application has no control over the remote application, which will start and run asynchronously.

Distributed Transaction Processing (DTP): Where two CICS systems carry on a synchronous conversation. Both systems send and receive data in an interactive manner. The basic procedure is for one system to establish a session, connect, and initiate dialogue. Both systems will then use SEND, RECEIVE, and CONVERSE commands to control conversation. Control information is passed between systems in the EIB. The details of the commands used and their sequence is different for MRO and ISC sessions. This facility is not transparent to the application program. Conversation with a non-CICS such as a PC or workstation is implemented using the LU6.2 APPC protocol. Conceptually, APPC command flow is similar to CICS command language but the command format and details are different.

Questions and Answers

Q: *How do you tell the COBOL application program that you are entering CICS command-level commands?*

A: EXEC CICS   begin

   END-EXEC   end

   All statements between EXEC CICS and END-EXEC are CICS command-level commands and related options.

Q: *What are the ways a CICS transaction can be initiated?*

A: When the transaction ID has been entered on the screen and the user hits the Enter or one of the PF or PA keys a transaction can be initiated:

- After a RETURN with TRANSID the user hits enter
- By issuing a START command from an executing application
- By ATI (automatic task initiation) Trigger level for transient data queue
- By associating the transaction with a PFKEY in the PCT

Q: *After completing the Application Source Code, what are the steps in creating a CICS command-level load module and what does each step do?*

A: 1. translator step
   converts all EXEC CICS commands into COBOL statements and calls.

   2. cobol compiler
   Normal COBOL compiler—takes COBOL code and COBOL output from translator step above and compiles creating object module(s)

   3. link editor
   Normal link editor—takes object modules from compiler step creating load module

Q: *If while creating a CICS load module there is a syntax error in an EXEC CICS SEND command where in the compile process would that error appear?*

A: Errors in CICS commands are flagged in the translator step.

Q: *In the application how can you determine which key was pressed on the keyboard?*

A: By checking either the EIBAID field or using the HANDLE AID command.

Q: *Do you need to do a RECEIVE to look at the EIBAID field or any other field in the EIB?*

A: No. The EIB (Executive interface block) is available to the application from the beginning of the program.

Q: *What type of record does a READ command invoke?*

A: A READ command reads a VSAM record into the storage buffer.

Q: *How would you READ a record with only a partial key?*

A: Use the GENERIC option on the READ command.

Q: *What does the KEYLENGTH parameter on the READ command do?*

A: For a GENERIC read the KEYLENGTH contains the length of the partial key.

Q: *Assume that you have a VSAM KSDS file containing a 6 character key, the high order 2 characters beginning with 'AA', 'BB', . . . 'ZZ'. There are currently no records with the high order 2 characters beginning with 'RR'. What would happen if you issued the following read and why?*

Move 'RR' to key-fld.

Move 2 to key-len.

```
EXEC CICS READ
     RIDFLD(key-fld)
     KEYLENGTH(key-len)
     GENERIC
     EQUAL
     . . .
     END-EXEC
```

A: The NOTFND condition will be raised as there is no record whose partial key is equal to 'RR'.

Q: *How would you prevent the NOTFND condition in the above situation?*
A: Change the EQUAL parameter to GTEQ. That will retrieve the next record 'SS'.

Q: *Why must you be careful when you issue a READ command with the UPDATE option?*
A: Exclusive control is kept over the record (actually exclusive control is kept over the entire VSAM Control Interval that contains the record) for the duration of the task.

Q: *How would you release control of the record in a READ for UPDATE?*
A: By issuing a REWRITE, DELETE, or UNLOCK command or by ending the task.

Q: *When you issue a WRITE command and a record with the same key already exists, what happens?*
A: A DUPREC condition is raised.

Q: *Can you WRITE, DELETE, and REWRITE without a prior READ for UPDATE command?*
A: You can WRITE and DELETE a record without a prior READ for UPDATE command, but you must issue a READ for UPDATE command before you can REWRITE.

Q: *If you want to delete all records with a partial key what should you do?*
A: Issue a direct DELETE with GENERIC and KEYLENGTH parameters.

Q: *What are two methods for deleting a VSAM KSDS record and which would you use when?*
A: Issue a READ for UPDATE and then DELETE. This allows you to verify the record that you want to delete.

Issue a direct DELETE (without a READ for UPDATE). GENERIC deletes are allowed using partial key. This option is used if you are absolutely certain which record(s) you want to delete.

Q: *What are some differences between a WRITE and a REWRITE command?*
A: The WRITE command writes a new record that does not exist. The REWRITE command updates a record already existing on the file (a READ for UPDATE command must have been issued previously).

Q: *What is a major difference between a READ and a STARTBR command?*

A: READ actually reads a record into the storage buffer. STARTBR sets a pointer to a starting location but does not actually read a record.

Q: *How does a STARTBR command know which record to set the pointer to?*

A: The pointer position is identified by the RIDFLD parameter.

Q: *After a STARTBR command how would you retrieve a record?*

A: By issuing a READNEXT command.

Q: *What happens if the key specified is not there?*

A: Since GTEQ is the default for browse operations, the first record after the key specified is retrieved.

Q: *After a STARTBR and a READNEXT what does a READPREV do?*

A: It will retrieve the same record as the READNEXT. The direction of the browse will be changed so that any additional READPREV commands will retrieve prior records.

Q: *How would you start a browse operation at the first record?*

A: Move LOW-VALUES to the RIDFLD parameter before issuing the STARTBR command. Since GTEQ is the default, processing will start at the first record that is GTEQ to LOW-VALUES.

Q: *What will happen if you issue a STARTBR command with an EQUAL parameter and the record is not there?*

A: A NOTFND (not found) condition is raised.

Q: *Can you update a record that you retrieved using STARTBR and READ-NEXT commands?*

A: No. STARTBR and READNEXT are only for browsing.

Q: *What happens when you issue a READNEXT command and there are no more records on the file?*

A: An ENDFILE condition is raised.

Q: *What happens when you issue a READPREV command and you are beyond the beginning of the file?*

A: An ENDFILE condition is raised.

Q: *How would you reposition your browse starting position to a new location on the file?*

A: By either of these methods:

a. RESETBR command to new location

b. ENDBR command followed by STARTBR for new location

Q: *If you have a file with a 2 char key 'AA', 'BB', . . . 'ZZ' and you do a STARTBR on key 'GG' and then 3 READNEXTS and then 1 READPREV, which record would you have in your buffer?*

A: STARTBR .. points to 'GG'

READNEXT.. reads 'GG'

READNEXT.. reads 'HH'

READNEXT.. reads 'II'

READPREV.. re-reads 'II'

You would have 'II' in your buffer.

Q: *Is it safe to do a STARTBR followed by a READPREV to retrieve a prior record?*

A: No. You need a full key in RIDFLD for READPREV. If the RIDFLD that you used with the STARTBR doesn't exist you will point to the next (GTEQ) key. You need to do a READNEXT to retrieve this record to identify the full key. Then using this full key do a READPREV to re-retrieve this record then another READPREV to retrieve the prior record.

Q: *How do allocated resources get released when "browsing"?*

A: By either of these methods:

a. ENDBR command

b. End task—which releases all resources

Q: *How can you design your application so that it knows that this is the first time it is called and that it needs to send the initial map to the terminal?*

A: If this is the first time there will be no COMMONAREA, therefore the EIB-CALEN will be zero. If it is zero send the initial map. From then on always RETURN with a COMMONAREA size of at least one.

Q: *What is the difference between a SEND and a SEND MAP command?*

A: A SEND command is used to send unformatted data to a screen or logical unit (LU). A SEND MAP sends a map that was generated by CICS's BMS facility used for formatted screen data.

Q: *What language do you use to define a BMS map?*

A: BMS maps are defined using macros written in assembler language.

Q: *What are the BMS assembler macros?*

A: DFHMSD   Mapset definition defining each mapset

DFHMDI   Defines individual maps within mapset

DFHMDF   Defines each field with individual map

Q: *When a BMS map is assembled what are the two types of BMS maps created?*

A: 1. A physical map—a load module located in the CICS loadlib used primarily by CICS contains constant default data, attribute bytes, starting positions, and length of each field.

2. A symbolic map—a source statement copybook to be copied into and used by the application. Contains field definitions, attribute bytes, etc., to be accessed by the application.

Q: *If you modify the default title by changing the INITIAL parameter of the field in your BMS map definition do you need to:*

1. Reassemble your map?

2. Recompile your application program?

A: 1. Yes, you need to reassemble your map to create a new physical map.

2. No, you do not need to recompile your application program.

Q: *What does the POS=(x,y) parameter of the DFHMDF macro do?*

A: It gives the row and column number of the attribute character for the field.

Q: *What determines the characteristics of a field on the screen (i.e., brightness, ability to enter data, etc.)?*

A: The attribute byte associated with each field.

Q: *How do you allow data input in a field?*

A: You make the field unprotected.

Q: *When a terminal user modifies data in a field on the screen what enables that data to be transmitted?*

A: When a terminal operator enters/modifies any data in a field on the screen the MDT (modified data tag) attribute bit is set for that field. This is a signal for the terminal hardware to transmit that field to the host computer when the enter or pfkey is hit.

Q: *If you define a map with CNTRL=FRSET parameter specified (on the DFHMSD or DFHMDI macros) what happens to existing MDT that were previously set on screen for:*

1. SEND MAP with DATAONLY?

2. SEND MAP with MAPONLY?

3. SEND MAP both MAP & DATA (default)?

A: The MDT bits for all input fields are set as follows:

1. For SEND MAP with DATAONLY .. retains MDT status from prior screen (except if the attribute byte is explicitly changed by application)

2. For SEND MAP with MAPONLY .. all MDT bits set/reset to off

3. For SEND MAP both MAP & DATA .. all MDT bits reset to off

Q: *What does ATTRB=FSET on the DFHMDF macro do?*

A: It initializes the MDT bit for that field to ON (data will be transmitted unless turned OFF by program).

Q: *Is data returned to the application program from a field that was unchanged by the terminal operator? If no, is there any way that the program can force unchanged data to be returned to the program?*

A: If the terminal operator does not modify a field, the MDT bit is not set ON, and data in that field is *not* returned to the program. The MDT bit for any field can be set ON/OFF by modifying its attribute byte in the application program. Any data in a field that had its MDT bit set ON by the application program, would be returned to the program even if it is unchanged.

Q: *When you receive a map into your application how can you determine if data has/has not been entered into a specific field?*
A: If no data has been entered, and the length will be zero, the input field will contain LOW-VALUES.

Q: *If you have a two-character unprotected field on the screen and you enter "A" followed by a space, what would the length and input fields contain?*
A: length = 2, input field = "A" followed by space (CICS considers space as legal data).

Q: *If you issue a SEND MAP command, what happens to the output fields that contain LOW-VALUES?*
A: They do not get transmitted to the screen.

Q: *If the length contains a × '80' what does that indicate?*
A: The field has been modified but no data was sent (field was cleared using the EOF key).

Q: *You have 5 unprotected fields defined on the screen for data entry. How would you prevent the user from typing past the end of a field and invading the gap areas?*
A: Define a stop byte or a skip byte at the end of each field. A stop byte is a one-byte field with the PROTECT attribute; this will stop the user from entering any data. A skip byte is a one-byte field with the ASKIP attribute; this will cause the cursor to skip to the next unprotected field.

Q: *How can you set the position of the cursor?*
A: The cursor can be positioned on the screen by:
   1. Defining the default screen position with attrib=(IC) when initially defining the map.
   2. Moving −1 to the length of the field where you want the cursor to be located, and using SEND MAP with CURSOR option.
   3. Using SEND MAP with absolute cursor location (i.e., CURSOR (100))

Q: *When you receive a map how can you tell the cursor position?*
A: The EIB field EIBCPOSN (halfword) contains the offset position of the cursor on the screen.

Q: *Is data always transmitted when you hit any ENTER, CLEAR, PFKEY, or PAKEY?*
A: No. CLEAR & PAKEYs do not transmit data.

Q: *What CICS facilities can you use to save data between transactions?*
A: COMMONAREA, TEMPORARY STORAGE, and TRANSIENT DATA QUEUE.

Q: *What are the two types of TEMPORARY STORAGE and how do you define each type?*

A: MAIN   located in main storage; defined dynamically

AUX   located on disk; defined in the TST

Q: *Once a Temporary queue is created are there any restrictions in accessing it from any transactions or terminals?*

A: No. Any terminal or transaction in the region can access any Temporary storage queue, multiple times, as long as it knows its name.

Q: *How would you insure that only one transaction has access to a temporary storage queue? What would prevent other transactions from also accessing this queue?*

A: You must create a unique name for the queue, known only to the accessing transaction. Since each transaction is associated with only one terminal a unique name can be derived from combining the transaction id (EIBTRNID) and terminal id (EIBTRMID) names located in the EIB. Since terminals have unique identifiers, you should associate the terminal ID with an application identifier.

Q: *If the system crashes do you lose your TEMPORARY STORAGE information?*

A: You lose any data in MAIN temporary storage. If you defined AUX Temporary storage as recoverable you will not lose your data.

Q: *How do you get rid of a TEMPORARY storage queue?*

A: You issue a DELETEQ command.

Q: *What type of reads can you issue for a TEMPORARY storage queue?*

A: Direct read using READQ with the ITEM parameter; sequential read using READQ with the NEXT parameter (sequential reads can also be accomplished by setting up a loop which increments the ITEM parameter by one and issuing a READQ with ITEM).

Q: *If a TEMPORARY storage queue has 6 items, AA, BB, CC, DD, EE, FF and transaction 1 does a READQ with ITEM = 1, followed by a READQ with NEXT.. then transaction 2 does a READQ with NEXT, which item is read by transaction 2?*

A: CC is read by transaction 2 (the NEXT option reads the next current item in the queue; it does not care which transaction is reading it).

Q: *If you are reading a TEMPORARY storage queue sequentially and you reach the end of file, what happens?*

A: An ITEMERR handle condition is raised.

Q: *How would you do a direct read of the 5th record from a TEMPORARY storage queue?*

A: You would issue a READQ with ITEM = 5. (ITEM is an identifier automatically maintained by CICS, it is set to 1 for the first record, on the queue, and incremented by 1 for each additional record.)

Q: *Which CICS facility has a trigger level and what does it do?*

A: Transient data queue has a trigger level. It will initiate a transaction when the number of records on the queue reaches the trigger level.

Q: *What are the two types of TRANSIENT data queues and how are they defined? What is the difference between the two?*

A: 1. Intrapartition TRANSIENT data queue—located within the CICS region.

   2. Extrapartition TRANSIENT data queue—located outside the CICS region.

   Both queues are defined in the DCT.

Q: *If you have an MVS batch job that creates a sequential file that you need to process via a CICS transaction, how would you accomplish this?*

A: Define an input Extrapartiton TRANSIENT data queue and issue a READQ TD from the CICS transaction.

Q: *If you read an intrapartition TRANSIENT data queue record can the same record be reread?*

A: No, once a record is read it is unavailable (a/k/a destructive read).

Q: *When you read a TRANSIENT data queue and there are no more records what happens?*

A: A QZERO handle condition is raised.

Q: *You are using a transient data queue to accumulate print lines. When print information is complete you will initiate a transaction to send this information to the printer. How would you control multiple transactions from interleaving their print lines on this queue?*

A: Each transaction can establish exclusive control over the queue by issuing an ENQ on the queue before accumulating the first line and issuing a DEQ after the print is complete. (To use ENQ, DEQ assign a unique name to the resource. Each transaction will then use this name to tell CICS/MVS that it wants exclusive control over the resource.)

Q: *What is the difference between a LINK and an XCTL?*

A: LINK passes control to a program at the next *lower* logical level. The calling program remains in storage and expects control to be returned to it.

   XCTL passes control to a program at the *same* logical level. The calling program does not remain in storage and does not expect control to be returned to it.

Q: *What does the RETURN statement do?*

A: Returns control to the next higher logical level. If there is no higher logical level control is passed to CICS.

Q: *If you have program A that LINKS to program B, program B issues a XCTL to program C, and program C issues a RETURN, what is the status of programs A, B, and C and what does the RETURN do?*

A: Program A remains in storage expecting a return.

   Program B does not remain in storage, does not expect a return.

   Program C remains in storage, returns to A.

Q: *If program A issues a RETURN with TRANID = XX, what happens?*

A: Control is passed to CICS. The TRANID parameter enables pseudo-conversational interaction with the terminal. This TRANID is stored with the terminal information and all resources associated with this transaction are released. CICS proceeds to process other tasks, awaiting a user response. When the user responds by hitting the ENTER, CLEAR, PFKEY, or PAKEY, the transaction specified in the TRANID parameter is retrieved and started.

Q: *When you issue a LINK or XCTL with the COMMONAREA option what are you passing?*

A: You are passing an address to the location of the data in the calling program to the called program.

Q: *If you use a COMMONAREA to pass data to another program where is the data defined in the calling program, in the called program, and how do you retrieve it in the called program?*

A: The calling program passes a working storage area as its COMMONAREA parameter. The called program defines the first 01 level definition in its linkage section as DFHCOMMAREA, which points to this area. DFHCOMMAREA can be accessed directly or can be moved into working storage.

Q: *If your program 'A' issues a LINK to program 'B' passing a COMMONAREA and program 'B' modifies some DFHCOMMAREA data in its linkage section, do you need to do a RETURN with the COMMONAREA option?*

A: In this case, program 'B' does not need to specify the COMMONAREA parameter on its RETURN statement. Since the address of the COMMONAREA was passed, program 'B' when modifying data in its linkage section is modifying the original fields.

Q: *Can you issue a CALL statement in CICS? If so, can you pass data to the called program? How are the caller and called programs related?*

A: Yes. In CICS you can issue a CALL to another program and pass data with the USING option. Both the calling and called programs will be linked together in the same load module. In COBOL the called program cannot contain command level statements. In COBOL II the called program can be a command level program.

Q: *What is the LOAD command used for and how do you set up addressability to it?*

A: The LOAD command is used to load but not execute a separately assembled program or table dynamically into storage. It is referenced through the linkage section definitions.

Q: *The date and time fields in the EIB (EIBDATE & EIBTIME) contain the date and time of what?*

A: These fields contain the date and time at task initiation time.

Q: *If you wanted to update EIB date/time (EIBDATE, EIBTIME) to the current date and time how would you accomplish this?*

A: Issue an ASKTIME command to update the EIB fields to the current date/time.

Q: *How could you format the EIB date/time into different formats?*

A: Issue a FORMATTIME command using one of the optional formats given.

Q: *What are the different CICS HANDLE statements?*

A: HANDLE AID   determines what key was pressed on the keyboard

   HANDLE CONDITION   traps exceptional conditions for CICS commands

   HANDLE ABEND   traps abnormal conditions that occur during execution

Q: *What is the difference between an exceptional condition and an abnormal termination, and when does each occur?*

A: An exceptional condition is analogous to a return code and is specific to each CICS command. An abnormal termination occurs when there is an execution error, not related to a CICS command, that will cause the transaction to abend.

Q: *Can a HANDLE CONDITION detect 0C7s?*

A: No. 0C7s are abend conditions not related to a CICS command.

Q: *What are two ways to trap exceptional conditions?*

A: 1) HANDLE CONDITION command, and 2) Use the RESP code option with each CICS command.

Q: *Why are RESP codes more structured than HANDLE CONDITION commands?*

A: A GOTO is generated after each CICS command for each HANDLE CONDITION routine. RESP codes are tested in-line after the CICS command is executed, keeping the logic flow sequential.

Q: *What does DFHRESP (NORMAL) mean?*

A: You test DFHRESP(XXX) in-line after each CICS command that is using RESP codes. NORMAL means no exceptional condition has occurred.

Q: *How long does the specific condition (i.e., LENGERR) that is specified in a HANDLE CONDITION command remain in effect?*

A: A specific condition remains in effect until:

- The end of the program or a transfer to another program
- Another HANDLE CONDITION command is specified overriding the first condition
- A HANDLE IGNORE CONDITION command is issued

Q: *How can one avoid confusion about which HANDLE CONDITION is in effect for which CICS command?*

A: Always pair the appropriate HANDLE CONDITION with each CICS command.

Q: *If you specify a HANDLE CONDITION command in program 'A' and then LINK or XCTL to program 'B' will the HANDLE CONDITION still be effective?*

A: No. Handle conditions are only effective in the program in which they are defined.

Q: *What could happen to the transaction if an exception condition is not trapped?*

A: The transaction could abend.

Q: *How would you trap a transaction execution time abend?*

A: Use a HANDLE ABEND command. Most installations have standardized routines to handle abends.

Q: *What is the difference between a HANDLE ABEND command and an ABEND command?*

A: A HANDLE ABEND command will trap execution errors and branch to the specified program or label for processing. An ABEND command will force the transaction to end abnormally.

Q: *How would you force an abend with a transaction dump?*

A: Issue an ABEND command with the ABCODE option to force a transaction dump. The code specified in ABCODE will identify the dump.

Q: *You have a HANDLE ABEND statement in your program to trap execution abends. In your HANDLE ABEND routine what advantages are there to terminating the program by issuing an ABEND command instead of a RETURN command?*

A: The ABEND command can give you a transaction dump and will invoke CICS's dynamic transaction backout facility. The RETURN command will just return you to the next level.

Q: *What does the concept of recovery mean?*

A: When there is a system or transaction crash, recovery is an attempt to roll-back and restore all recoverable resources, for all in-flight (incomplete) transactions, to the state they were in before the failure.

Q: *How do you specify that a resource is recoverable?*

A: You set the appropriate options in the relevant CICS table definitions.

Q: *What is a LOGICAL UNIT OF WORK (LUW)? How does this concept apply to recovery?*

A: LUW is the processing completed between two synch points. Recovery of recoverable resources is accomplished backward up to the last synch point.

Q: *What is a SYNCH POINT?*

A: A SYNCH POINT is an arbitrary point where all work is considered complete. Any further processing would be part of a new synch point.

Q: *How many synch points are there for a task that begins execution, does some processes, issues no SYNCPOINT commands, and then ends execution?*

A: There are 2 synch points, one at the beginning of the task and the second at the end of the task.

Q: *What does DYNAMIC TRANSACTION BACKOUT (DTB) mean? How do you enable it?*

A: DTB applies to a failed transaction, the rollback of all recoverable resources for that transaction up to the last synch point. CICS will automatically enable DTB if you specify the DTB option in the PCT for that transaction.

Q: *Where does DTB store its information?*

A: Each transaction uses a "dynamic log" located in main memory to store all its recoverable before-images.

Q: *Can you recover from a CICS crash using DTB?*

A: No. When CICS (or the entire MVS) system crashes you lose your main storage "dynamic log" information.

Q: *How can you recover from a CICS crash?*

A: Use a special journal referred to as a "system log" to keep a log on disk or tape of all the before-images of all CICS recoverable resources. Upon a system crash CICS will rollback and restore all recoverable resources for all in-flight tasks using this log.

Q: *When might you use a SYNCPOINT command with the ROLLBACK option in your application?*

A: If you have to ABEND the application and you want to restore all recoverable resources to the last synch point.

Q: *How would you start transaction ZZZZ from within transaction XXXX? Suppose you wanted to initiate this transaction 15 minutes later?*

A: In transaction XXXX issue the command START TRANID('ZZZZ') to initiate the new transaction. To start 15 minutes later add the option INTERVAL(001500) to the command.

Q: *Can you pass data to a started transaction? If so, how would you accomplish this in the "starting" (initiating) and started transactions?*

A: In the "starting" transaction set up the data to be passed in working storage and issue a START command with the FROM(datafld) and LENGTH(value) options. In the started transaction issue a RETRIEVE command with INTO(datafld) and LENGTH(value) options.

Q: *Can you START a task to run on a terminal other than the terminal attached to the initiating task?*

A: Yes. You issue a START command with the TERMID('termid') parameter.

Q: *What is EDF (Execution Diagnostic Facility) and when would you use it?*

A: EDF is a CICS-supplied debugging transaction. It is used to interactively monitor and debug an application and to display status at various points.

Q: *When using EDF, where can you suspend the execution of your task and display status?*

A: EDF suspends execution and displays status at the following:

- Task initiation
- Normal task termination
- The beginning of each CICS command
- The end of each CICS command
- At a task ABEND

Q: *When would using EDF not meet your debugging requirements?*

A: If you needed to stop at a specific statement or paragraph located between CICS commands. (Using EDF, you cannot suspend program execution between CICS commands.)

Q: *How will CICS handle a program abend such as a 0C4 or 0C7 from one of its COBOL application tasks?*

A: CICS will abend the task with an ASRA abend code.

Q: *What does an AICA CICS abend code mean?*

A: An AICA indicates a runaway (looping) task. When a task executes, without giving up control to CICS, for a time period that is longer than specified in the SIT system table, CICS will abend the task with an AICA code.

Q: *What is the difference between an ASSIGN and an ADDRESS command?*

A: The ASSIGN command is used to get the information from various system areas *outside* of CICS. The ADDRESS command is used to access various CICS storage areas (such as CWA, TWA, TCTUA).

Q: *What command would you use to determine which CICS system "owns" a transaction?*

A: Issue an ASSIGN command with the APPLID option.

Q: *Why would you use the POST/WAIT commands?*

A: The POST/WAIT commands can be used to synchronize two events.

Q: *How does the POST command work? How does the WAIT command work in conjunction with the POST command?*

A: The POST command specifies a "control area" and a time interval (or absolute time). The issuing of this command is a request to CICS to post this "control area" when the time interval has expired (or absolute time reached). The WAIT command will suspend execution of the task and when CICS has posted this area it will allow the task to resume.

Q: *Do you always need to issue a WAIT command to work with the POST command?*

A: No. You can periodically test the "control area" yourself to see if the time has expired (Warning: CICS needs to get control to post this area. If you are doing a lot of computation you need to issue a DELAY or SUSPEND command to allow CICS to post the area).

Q: *How can you set up an interactive session with a transaction running in another region (using either MRO or ISC)?*

A: Issue an ALLOCATE command to establish the connection. The session Id is returned in the EIB (EIBRSRCE). For an LU6.2 connection also issue a CONNECT command with the CONVID= option (CONVID= the session Id that was returned by the ALLOCATE command).

Q: *After an interactive session with another region has been established, how can you exchange information?*

A: Information with a transaction in another region can be exchanged by issuing a SEND command with the INVITE option followed by a RECEIVE command. The CONVERSE command, which combines the functions of both the SEND (with the INVITE option) and the RECEIVE commands, could also be used.

13

Understanding Important Relational Database Concepts

Michael A. Senatore

Introduction

Relational Database Management Systems (RDBMS) have become the global standard for warehousing business data and consequently should be considered important to anyone wanting to advance their career in data processing. More and more jobs require direct interaction with one or more of the currently available relational database management systems. This chapter introduces you to the concepts that sold RDBMS to corporate management worldwide. You will also learn what corporations expect from their investment in an RDBMS and some of the data processing methods that are being used to meet these expectations. We will also be discussing how RDBMSs fit into corporate information strategies and providing you with enough information so that you will feel comfortable when discussing these concepts during an interview.

Why Relational Databases?

Prior to automated data processing, information processing was limited to record-keeping applications. This was due to the limitations of the currently available technology. Most sales, inventory, marketing, and accounting functions were supported by manual and clerical procedures. Paperwork found its way to centralized offices where documents were processed. Data would be analyzed and documents and reports would be manually processed. When electronic data processing became available, it seemed natural to automate the existing procedures, converting them basically as-is to the "new automated" applications. As such, data processing and storage imitated the corporation's paper flow and the design of their business forms. The data on these forms was keypunched and processed on a schedule that was determined by the department that used the data. Scheduled deadlines for data input had to be met and some data processing even had to wait until a departmental manager gave the OK.

It was with the advent of improved, reliable, and relatively inexpensive communications and increased data processing power, that the scope and complexity of automated data processing functions expanded. The data processing user community expanded from corporate headquarters to include remote locations. Today it is not uncommon for a corporation to generate and utilize data on a 24-hour basis every day of the week. As data processing implementations evolved to support advances in user requirements, the techniques used in data and process design also changed. Today's need for corporate data processing has grown far beyond its original capabilities. It is now common for data to be generated and stored real-time from remote locations (regardless of time zone) and be immediately available to the entire user community for a host of critical functions.

Techniques for data access have also evolved to support the growing need for concurrent data inquiry and updates. What started as an access method that limited data use to one process at a time has evolved into a technology that allows multiple concurrent readers and writers. During the time when technology began to answer the need for shared data use, methods for managing the content of this data were, at best, primitive. Even when corporations grew and corporate functions were delegated to a hierarchy of departments, the use of data usually stayed within departmental boundaries. It was common for departments to have their own copies of data and much less common for departments to share data, let alone reconcile the differences among the various copies. When corporations began changing hands rapidly during the buyouts and sellouts of the last decade, corporate leadership realized that their data was a good way to evaluate the value of their business. To do this it became necessary for analysts to have an enterprisewide view of corporate data in order to be able to effectively consolidate departmental versions of data.

When the data created and stored by a variety of departmentally designed application systems were consolidated, differences of structure and content became evident and made the effort very complex. Work was done to streamline the flow of paper by reducing the number of forms used to support operations. Forms were evaluated and work flows modified as they passed from location to location, spanning departmental boundaries. These changes caused data processing efforts to become even more visible to top management. Top-level management has become increasingly aware of the need to apply an enterprisewide strategy for meeting the changing needs for information. The techniques used by top-level management to arrive at business decisions are now being applied to information management issues. Seat-of-the-pants data processing design and implementation decisions are no longer acceptable. Individual talent is no longer enough to inspire fund-flowing faith. Management requires a set of standards that have a proven track record of success.

A number of data management technologies have emerged that meet the challenge of accommodating the rapid changes that affect the corporate environment. Relational database products are available for many hardware platforms and have been successfully implemented for an extremely wide variety of applications. These products are purchased because they promise a higher standard of quality and service by virtue of their built-in services and features. These services and features can, if used properly, deliver vastly improved data integrity, availability, and flexibility.

Relational databases have the ability to enforce business rules as they apply to data entry, validation, updating, and deletions. The task of preserving a unique primary key (entity) integrity or reference key (referential) integrity or value range (domain) integrity can be built into a relational database; shifting this responsibility from an ever-changing crew of programmers to a corporate-owned asset. The use of a common data access language called Structured Query Language (SQL), which can, for example, process a multitude of "records" with a single statement, increases programmer accuracy and efficiency while providing end-users with an ad hoc query capability. This allows corporations to leverage their analysis and design investments when change occurs and make the new data available to a wider audience.

Modeling

Designing relational databases is a complex process. Existing data has to be analyzed and integrated with the new data needed to support the new requirements of the organization. The methodology that has evolved in the design of relational databases is called modeling. Modeling is the technique used to build a representation of the database as it will look once it is implemented. In order to utilize the features and services provided by an RDBMS, data must be organized to conform with the rules required by relational databases. These rules are much more rigorous and complex than those required in the design of nonrelational databases. When relational databases are properly organized all unnecessary data redundancy has been removed, reducing the volume of data used and maintained by software.

Data Organization

The process of organizing corporate data starts with a business analysis effort. There are many methodologies available that can be used to define an accurate business model. The business model will evolve to where it will contain the information about the data used and shared throughout the enterprise. Real-world objects that play a role in business are identified and then mapped to data names and descriptions that are then used in the design of a relational data model. These real-world objects are called "entities" and begin what is called Entity Relationship (E-R) analysis. During this analysis the ways that the different entities relate to each other are identified. The purpose of E-R analysis is to identify those entities that interact with each other and explain how they are involved and when they are involved. This analysis is based mostly on common sense. The real-world objects that we call entities should, if they do not already, use names with which we are familiar. For example, a teacher (a familiar entity) will be teaching one or more students (another entity) when teaching a class (another entity) in a classroom (another entity) for a department (yet another entity) of an educational institution. From this example we can observe the interaction of five entities involved in the "teaching" process. When one observes business activities as they occur, the relationships of the involved entities can be observed and recorded. If that activity is to be successfully automated or recorded by a computer application, the results of the E-R analysis will indicate the scope of information needed. There are systems available for drawing an E-R diagram that can display the interaction of entities "at work." Once the E-R diagram is accepted as an accurate model of the entities involved in a business activity, the next task is to define what each entity consists of, that is, you must create a list of attributes (fields) that will be used to describe each occurrence of an entity. For example, if the entity is an "employee," we have to make a list of employee attributes that distinguish one employee from the next. This list would probably include items like employee-id, employee-name, employee-address, employee-hire-date, etc. If all of the attribute lists started on an entity basis as in the previously mentioned employee-entity attribute list, the data organization would be well on its way to conforming to the rules guiding the development of the relational data model. Most data lists, however, are based on business forms that contain attributes of many different entities and at times, from the context of the form, it is difficult to tell what information belongs to which entity. Figure 13-1, for example, illustrates a form that might be used to record a customer's purchase. The data items (attributes) on this form include customer attributes as well as attributes that describe other business entities; namely, the order entity, the part entity, the location entity and the vendor entity (the shipping vendors shown on the form are two instances of the vendor entity).

Relationships

Prior to data modeling the contents and keys of files were specified and documented as part of the support documentation in the specification of program logic. It was during the specification of program logic that the determination was made as to which records had to be referenced in which sequence to support the requirements of the application, that is, once the order record (transaction) had been accessed the customer and part numbers in the record was used to access the cor-

CUSTOMER ORDER FORM	#2495714-130

CUST NUMBER	NAME	ADDRESS		

SHIPPING ADDRESS		CITY	STATE	ZIP

CITY	STATE	ZIP	SHIPPING METHOD
			UPS GROUND_____ AIR FREIGHT_____

PART NUMBER	PART DESCRIPTION	QUANTITY	INV LOCATION

Figure 13.1. Customer order form.

rect customer and part number records. This method of specifying which files and records to access is now treated as relationships between tables, and specified by the data modeler based upon his or her understanding of the data requirements of the organization, rather than the requirements of one or more programs.

Relationships are documented as shown in Figure 13-2. Figure 13-2 includes lines (with arrows) connecting entities. These lines and arrows specify the relationship(s) between entities. Once the attributes used to go from one table to another have been determined, when the tables are built the foreign keys become the indexes used to access other table(s).

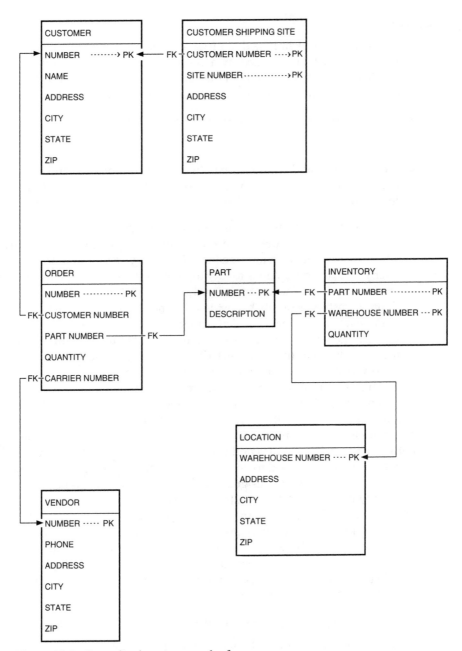

Figure 13.2. Normalized customer order form.

Normalization

Normalization is a technique that provides a clearly defined way to properly organize data that will be accessed by a vendor-supplied relational database system. Normalization was "invented" in the early '70s by Dr. E. F. Codd. The objective of normalization is the review and analysis of the format of data to be sure that:

- There are no repeating data groups in any of the entities,

and

- There is a full, valid relationship between each entity's key and all nonkey fields assigned to a given entity, in other words, that all nonkey attributes are dependent upon the whole/entire key.

The process of normalization involves several steps. The first is to identify the attributes that contain the minimum information required to identify a single occurrence of an entity (determine the primary key). Once the entity's primary key is determined, the next step is to identify the entity's attributes that are dependent on the entire key. The customer order form (Figure 13-1) has the following attributes: customer-number, customer-name, customer-address, customer-city, customer-state, customer-zip, customer-shipping-address, customer-shipping-state, customer-shipping-zip, order-number, order-customer-number, order-part-number, order-quantity, order-carrier-number, part-number, part-description, inventory-part-number, inventory-warehouse-number, inventory-quantity, location-warehouse-number, location-address, location-city, location-state, location-zip, vendor-number, vendor-phone, vendor-address, vendor-city, vendor-state, vendor-zip. By using these names, the association/relationship between the attributes and the entities is clarified. Figure 13-2 illustrates the normalized set of entities with their attributes and how these entities relate to each other. The "PK" next to an attribute is used to designate a primary key or part of a primary key. The "FK" next to an attribute designates a foreign key. A foreign key is an attribute of one entity that is, by definition, the primary key of another entity. The entity containing the foreign key is dependent on the entity with the related primary key. When the attributes of entities are normalized, it is possible to enforce the integrity of the relationships between foreign keys and primary keys. The levels of normalization (normalization has been subdivided into "levels"—called forms) are numbered starting with the first (1st) normal form and going to the fifth (5th) normal form. Normal forms are determined by the following rules:

1. first normal form (1nf): there must not be any repeating groups
2. second normal form (2nf): meets the criteria for the first normal form (no repeating groups) and all non-key attributes are fully dependent on the complete primary key
3. third normal form (3nf): meets all criteria required of the second normal form and no non-key attributes are dependent on any other non-key attributes

4. fourth normal form (4nf): meets criteria of the third normal form and entities are split into subtypes so that the range of primary key values has a business related meaning, and

5. fifth normal form (5nf): meets criteria of the fourth normal form and any dependency upon another occurrence of the same entity is placed in a structure entity. For example, if a part in the parts-table (carburetor) is made from 50 other parts in the same table, those 50 instances should be entered into a carburetor-structure table.

Although normalization appears to create redundancy by requiring duplicate attributes to form the relations that link tables (entities) together, the maintenance of this redundant data is managed entirely by vendor-supplied relational database software. If the data organization is not normalized to at least the third normal form, referential integrity cannot be maintained. Normalization causes the number of attributes per entity to decrease while causing the number of entities (tables) to increase. Whenever a report is generated from a highly normalized database, the number of tables involved in the report will be higher than for a database that is not fully normalized. When the cost of additional I/O required for linking numerous tables for a report is not acceptable, one can de-normalize the database, that is, go from the fifth to the fourth normal form, or from the fourth to the third or the third to the second. The process of de-normalization involves the selective combination of two or more normalized tables to avoid the cost of a join (the need to access two tables at the same time) process. As the efficiency of hardware increases and costs decrease, the practice of de-normalization will be less prevalent. Rather than compromise the integrity and flexibility of a database by de-normalizing the database design, it is becoming popular to create a temporary de-normalized structure for use during the report generation. This would reduce the cost of a join process to a single event. The ability to enforce entity integrity (unique key validation) or referential integrity (primary/foreign key relation validation) is dependent on the organization (normalization) of the database design.

Processing Considerations

Whenever one accesses data managed by relational database software, an RDMS, the access should be considered a request that may or may not be fulfilled depending on the circumstances that exist at the moment the request is made. Unlike other data access products, the access to data in a relational database system is not dedicated solely to a single unit of work until the task ends. The data is a shared resource that may supply on-line services while supplying numerous batch processes. For this reason, it is wise for programs to be designed to keep a "low profile." There are three main considerations involved in an I/O request for data in a relational database: 1) the volume of data involved with the request, 2) the duration the data will be involved, and 3) the number of repetitions for this request.

It is always advisable to reduce the amount of data used by a program to the least required to satisfy the design goals of the program. This is accomplished by understanding the data organization and by limiting the selection criteria of the SQL statements accordingly. Changes made to data in a relational database are not permanent until the changes are committed by an SQL Commit statement.* Until the commit is performed, however, data changed in one process will not be available to other processes. Batch processes that are intended to share data with on-line processes should be designed to keep as few uncommitted data changes as possible. While trying to accomplish this "low-profile" it is nevertheless important to remember that there is "overhead" associated with such a request. Therefore it is unwise to process data one row at a time. To arrive at the optimal processing mix, one should understand the data model, know how many concurrent processes will use the data, and know how the data is being used.

A Relational Database Management System will manage the sharing of data among processes by examining the requests and flagging the accessed data accordingly. A data locking scheme coupled with a lock escalation strategy is a part of the relational database system and prevents a process from accessing data that has been changed by another process until the changes are committed. When the RDBMS receives an "Update"[†] request, the page where data resides is locked. When the number of pages locked by a process exceeds a parameter set by the installation, the lock is escalated from the "page level" to the "table level"[‡]. If a batch process has the potential of escalating the lock level to the table level, it should not be run concurrently with on-line services. Each page lock implicitly requested by updates utilizes both storage and processor resources. It may be less costly to explicitly request a table lock at the start of the process rather than let the RDBMS escalate to this lock level after invoking many implicit page locks.

A Relational Database Management System preserves referential integrity during data insertion, deletion, and change. Since the table relationships are defined during the E-R analysis, the rules governing the integrity of these relationships can be implemented during table creation. Once data dependency is established by referential constraints, one can implement a "delete" rule that either restricts the deletion of reference data while dependent data exists in other tables or forces the deletion of dependent table entries containing foreign keys having the same value as the parent table entry that is being deleted (called a cascade delete). Where "cascade delete" rules have been implemented, it can be difficult to determine the scope of a delete statement. When evaluating the impact of an SQL process it is important to understand the network of Referential Integrity (referred to as "RI" in most technical literature) constraints affecting the tables used by the process.

---

* The results of SQL accesses against database tables are held in "temporary" workareas until a commit statement is executed.

[†] An "update" request is a "Select For Update" SQL statement. See the SQL chapter in this book for additional information.

[‡] The effect of a table level lock vs. a page level lock is to make a larger amount of data unavailable to other applications during the time the lock is in effect.

Referential Integrity can only be enforced upon the relations between primary and foreign keys of tables. If the fully normalized data model has been de-normalized for performance reasons, it may be impossible to define all of the needed RI constraints in the physical data model. Some relational database systems allow for the storage of procedures that can be used to enforce integrity between columns in the same table (column integrity). These stored procedures can be passed as parameters to refine the integrity constraint when desirable. Stored procedures can be defined to "trigger" each time an insert, update, or delete is executed. These triggers can be defined to cause a change in other tables containing triggers of their own. A chain reaction of nested triggers can be "set off" by a change to a single column in a table. As more processing power is built into the RDBMS, it becomes a necessity to fully understand the logical and physical data model. The physical data model includes the RI, triggers, and stored procedures specified to insure the integrity of corporate data. When a corporation decides to make full use of the services built into a relational database system, all programmer code that duplicates any of the built-in integrity features will prevent the corporation from achieving a full return on its investment. Hard coded integrity edits are not flexible. Changes in any business rules that are hard coded in a program would precipitate program changes that are costly and error-prone compared to changes in the physical data model.

The current trend of storing and maintaining corporate business rules in relational database management systems is maturing rapidly. As corporations try new hardware and communication platforms to manage their data, the main goal of vendor-supplied relational database software will be to provide the higher levels of concurrence and integrity. Data processing professionals who work with RDBMSs need to know and understand a corporation's business and how to make the relational database system do the required work.

14

IBM's DB2

Michael A. Senatore

Introduction

DB2 Version 4 is IBM's current relational database offering that runs under MVS. Since its first release each new release of DB2 has been accompanied by expanded functionality. This in turn has translated into an increasing need for professionals knowledgeable and familiar with the commands, procedures, and techniques used with DB2. This chapter contains questions about the way DB2 is structured, commands related to DB2 efficiency, error handling, and other related information that one is often asked at a DB2–SQL technical interview. Application developers as well as database administrators get asked questions relating to DB2. The more knowledge one has the easier it is to get a job. During most DB2 technical interviews one is asked both SQL and DB2 questions. A knowledge of DB2 would also show you as a candidate who given the chance, has the potential to move into database administration via application development. By familiarizing yourself with these questions, and those of the SQL chapter, you will perform better at your interview.

Questions and Answers

Data Definition Questions

Q: *How many ways can DB2 data storage allocation be performed?*
A: Two, user-defined VSAM and DB2 STOGROUP definition.

Q: *How many types of VSAM datasets can be defined for storing DB2 data?*
A: One, VSAM LDS (linear data set) is used from version two release one and later.

Q: *What are two reasons for defining multiple volumes in a DB2 VSAM cluster or STOGROUP?*
A: To reduce space related abend conditions and to allow for growth.

Q: *How can you determine the distribution of data on the DASD used for storage of DB2 data?*
A: Use a different volume as the first on the list while defining VSAM clusters or STOGROUPS.

Q: *What are the different types of tablespaces?*
A: Simple tablespaces, segmented tablespaces, and partitioned tablespaces.

Q: *What are some advantages segmented tablespaces have over simple tablespaces?*
A: Segmented tablespaces utilize a space allocation map to keep track of available space. Mass delete operations are more efficient because the change is recorded in this map, removing the need to read and update the tablespace data. When a table is dropped, the space is immediately made available without running the DB2 Reorg Utility.

Q: *When should partitioned tablespaces be defined?*
A: Partitioned tablespaces should be used for extremely large tables, i.e., more than one million rows.

Q: *What is the maximum number of partitions that can be defined in a partitioned tablespace?*
A: Sixty-four partitions.

Q: *How many tables can you define in a partitioned tablespace?*
A: One table.

Q: *In a partitioned tablespace, how do you direct the data to the various partitions that have been defined?*
A: In the "cluster" clause of the Create Index statement, each partition in the tablespace is correlated to a "part" subclause by a partition number. Each part subclause has a "value" clause consisting of a string of constants, one constant for each column in the clustering index, that represent the highest key value that can be placed in that particular partition.

Q: *How does one drop a clustering index of a table that is defined in a partitioned tablespace?*
A: Drop its associated partitioned tablespace. One cannot drop an index that is used for partitioning a tablespace with a "drop index" statement.

Q: *How many physical datasets are created for a partitioned tablespace?*
A: One for each partition.

Q: *When should the PCTFREE and FREEPAGE parameters be set to zero?*
A: For "read only" tablespaces.

Q: *For tablespaces with high insert activity, what is the advantage of increasing the PCTFREE parameter?*

A: By increasing the PCTFREE parameter, one allows more room on each data page for the insertion of new data without disturbing the clustering of the data. As free space on each page increases, concurrency is improved by virtue of the fact that there will be fewer rows per page, meaning less page contention. Also, the need for data reorganization is reduced since there is less unclustered data.

Q: *What are the different data types that can be used in a table definition?*

A: CHAR, DATE, DECIMAL, FLOAT, GRAPHIC, INTEGER, LONG, LONG VARCHAR, REAL, SMALLINT, TIME, TIMESTAMP, VARCHAR, VAR-GRAPHIC, LONG VARGRAPHIC.

Application Development With DB2

Q: *What is the least amount of DB2 data that can be accessed by a program?*

A: One column of one row from one table.

Q: *How much of a DB2 table can be processed by a single statement?*

A: The entire table.

Q: *Does one need a DD statement in the JCL to identify a table for program access?*

A: No. A table is identified from within the program by a "DECLARE TABLE" SQL statement.

Q: *How does one write a "DECLARE TABLE" statement?*

A: By using the DCLGEN utility that accurately creates the table declaration along with the host language file description. This declaration is usually stored in a separate library and brought into the program at preparation time by an SQL "INCLUDE" statement.

Q: *How do you separate the SQL code from the remaining host language in a program?*

A: By the use of the "EXEC SQL" and "END-EXEC" delimiters.

Q: *What structure must each DB2 application contain in order to successfully interact with DB2?*

A: Each DB2 application must "INCLUDE" the SQLCA (SQL Communication Area) in order to be informed of the status of SQL statement performed in the application.

Q: *When and how is DB2 data changed by an application made permanent?*

A: Explicitly anytime during execution time by an SQL "COMMIT" statement or Implicitly at the end of an LUW (Logical Unit of Work).

Q: *What is a host variable?*

A: It is storage allocation made by the host language and referenced in an SQL statement.

Q: *How are host variables used?*

A: Host variables are used in SQL statements as a search argument in a "WHERE" clause or as an output area for an "INTO" clause or as an input area in a "SET" clause or as a literal in a "SELECT" clause.

Q: *What is a singleton select statement?*

A: A singleton select is designed to return only one row; it must contain an "INTO" clause that will store its result. Since there is only one instance of "INTO" host variables, if more than one row is returned, only the first returned is stored and SQLCODE in the SQLCA is set to –811.

Q: *What is a cursor select statement?*

A: A cursor select is designed to return a set of rows. The cursor select statement is embedded in a "DECLARE CURSOR" SQL statement. The cursor select statement contains no "INTO" clause because the data is returned during cursor processing.

Q: *What analogy could one use to describe cursor processing?*

A: One could say that cursors are processed like one would process flat files, i.e., they (cursors or flat-files) are opened at the start of processing, individual records are read and processed until there are no more records or the design goal has been achieved, then they are closed.

Q: *Why must a cursor's declaration physically precede any of its cursor processing statements (SQL Open, Fetch, and Close)?*

A: Because the SQL statements are processed prior to the host language compiler and have no ability to interpret the host language's logical process flow. The DB2 pre-compiler (DSNHPC) can only evaluate the SQL statements in the physical order they are written.

Q: *Why is SELECT * a disadvantage in a DB2 program?*

A: Because it causes the program to become sensitive to the data model. In a changing business world, frequent data model changes are a matter of course. Select * would cause the column-name list to change automatically while the "INTO" clauses would require a development effort. All programs that access the changed tables would become inoperable.

Q: *What are the consequences of qualifying table names within a DB2 application?*

A: Since the same tables are likely to have different owner id's in different environments (development, test, and production), internal table qualification would require a program change and test for each migration. Let the tables qualification occur during the "Bind" process.

Q: *What are Dynamic SQL statements?*
A: Dynamic SQL statements are those stored in a program so that they can be changed and prepared during program execution.

Q: *When should one use Dynamic SQL in a program?*
A: Dynamic SQL should be used when information that would enable or improve the efficiency of a program's design goal is available only during run-time, i.e., not available at bind-time. For example, the nature of the SQL could be user-driven (as in an ad hoc query tool) or the DB2 optimizer may be able to choose a better path because it knows the value of a search argument at prep-time.

DB2 Program Preparation

Q: *What is the first thing that happens when one invokes the pre-compile utility (DSNHPC)?*
A: All SQL INCLUDE statements are expanded.

Q: *Where are all of the table-related SQL statements stored by DSNHPC?*
A: The SQL statements are stored in a database request module (DBRM).

Q: *Must DB2 be operational in order to run DSNHPC?*
A: No. DB2 resources are not utilized by the DSNHPC utility.

Q: *When is the DB2 Catalog updated with the contents of a DBRM?*
A: During the execution of the BIND PLAN command the DBRM identification information is placed in the SYSIBM.SYSDBRM catalog table and the contents are placed into the SYSIBM.SYSSTMT catalog table.

Q: *How is the DB2 catalog copy of DBRM information synchronized with the DBRM?*
A: A timestamp is placed in the DBRM at pre-compile time and is compared (at execution time) to the SYSIBM.SYSDBRM copy of that timestamp made at bind-time.

Q: *What program must one invoke in order to run a DB2 program in a TSO Batch environment?*
A: One must invoke the TSO Terminal Monitor Program (IKJEFT01).

Q: *What information does one need in order to run a DB2 program?*
A: One needs the name of the program load module (this should be the same as the program's DBRM) and the name of the plan in which the program was bound.

Q: *What are the steps in program preparation of a COBOL program?*
A: Program preparation steps are pre-compile, compile, link-edit, and BIND.

Q: *What are the different objects used or produced by the different program preparation steps?*

A: The source code is used by the pre-compiler to create a copy of modified source and DBRM module. The modified source is used by the host language compiler to create a load module. The Application Plan is created by the BIND statement.

Q: *What is ISOLATION LEVEL?*

A: ISOLATION LEVEL is a parameter of the bind command that affects when page locks are released. There are two valid ISOLATION levels: cursor stability (CS) and repeatable read (RR).

Q: *What is the difference between the CS and RR isolation levels?*

A: When cursor stability is specified in the BIND statement, page locks are released as soon as the cursor pointer moves off the page (if no data was changed). When repeatable read is specified, the page locks are released only when a COMMIT or a ROLLBACK is performed.

DB2 Access

Q: *What is a DB2 thread?*

A: A thread is a control structure used by DB2 to accept calls to the DB2 run-time interface module and to report status in the SQLCA.

Q: *When is a DB2 thread established?*

A: A DB2 thread is established when the first SQL statement is executed.

Q: *What happens during thread establishment?*

A: DB2 retrieves the plan cursor skeleton table and plan related Database Descriptors (DBDs) from the DB2 Directory to load into the environmental descriptor management pool (EDM pool) if not already present in the EDM pool.

Q: *How many threads can a TSO session establish for a TSO On-line Application?*

A: One.

Q: *How many threads can a TSO session establish for TSO Batch applications?*

A: As many as needed; one thread for each invocation of the Terminal Monitor Program (IKJEFT01).

Q: *What is the RCT?*

A: The RCT (the Resource Control Table) is a CICS Control Table. The RCT establishes the working environment for DB2/CICS applications by providing the connection between CICS transactions and DB2 plans.

Q: *How many different types of threads can an RCT specify?*

A: Three types of threads are used to access DB2: command threads, entry threads, and pool threads.

Q: *Which transactions use a command thread?*

A: Only the DSNC transaction uses a command thread.

Q: *What is the purpose of the DSNC transaction?*

A: The DSNC transaction is used for controlling the CICS Call Attach Facility (CAF) and for displaying CAF statistics.

Q: *Can you control what happens if no threads are available when a DB2 transaction is invoked?*

A: Yes. By specifying YES, NO, or POOL in the TWAIT parameter of the RCT. TWAIT set to YES indicates that the transaction will wait for a thread to become available. TWAIT set to NO indicates that the transaction will abort if a thread is not available. TWAIT set to POOL will cause the transaction to use a default POOL thread.

Q: *What are the different macros that are specified in the RCT?*

A: There are five different RCT macros: INIT, COMD, ENTRY, POOL, and FINAL.

Q: *What is specified in the INIT Macro of an RCT?*

A: In the INIT macro of the RCT one specifies the DB2 subsystem identifier (SUBID=XXXX), the suffix that identifies the RCT (the RCT name is DNSCRCT(@) where suffix=@), the authorization id used by the CAF when it accesses DB2 (SIGNID=XXXXXXXX), and the maximum number of threads that can be concurrently established in the CICS region (THRDMAX=NN).

Q: *Can the RCT affect the resolution of a deadlock?*

A: Yes. The ROLBE parameter of the ENTRY macro can be set to yes or no. When set to yes, a rollback is issued on a deadlock and the SQL return code is set to −911. If this ENTRY parameter is set to no, no rollback is performed and the SQL return code is set to −913.

Q: *What ENTRY macro parameter can be set to start the transaction by a terminal function key (PF key)?*

A: The TASKREQ parameter.

Q: *What is a two-phase commit?*

A: A two-phase commit is a process that synchronizes the commit and rollback of changes in two different environments (like DB2 and CICS).

Q: *What can cause the two-phase commit to fail?*

A: The two-phase commit can fail due to a connection/communication failure or an environmental crash in either environment. When such a failure happens, the commit status of the thread established for that connection is in doubt.

Q: *How are in-doubt threads resolved?*

A: One can invoke the RECOVER INDOUBT command to commit or roll back any changes associated with an in-doubt thread.

DB2 Performance Tuning

Q: *Where can the greatest opportunity for performance gains be found in an application system that interacts with DB2?*

A: The most likely place to find performance gains is in each individual program.

Q: *What is sequential prefetch?*

A: Sequential prefetch is a function that performs an asynchronous read of multiple pages ahead of the current cursor pointer position. This reduces I/O requests and has data ready for the next fetch.

Q: *How can using two columns of different data types (one from each of two different tables) for comparison in a WHERE clause hurt performance?*

A: First, data conversion will be necessary for comparison. Second, the DB2 Optimizer will not use an index to evaluate the predicate.

Q: *How can one be sure if the DB2 optimizer has chosen the use of an index?*

A: By using the EXPLAIN facility.

Q: *What information can one receive by using EXPLAIN?*

A: One can learn when and how indexes are being used, if a sort is being performed, the locking requirements, the order in which joined tables are used, and what access path has been chosen for each statement.

Q: *For a large table, what is the least efficient method for finding data?*

A: A tablespace scan.

Q: *What is a direct index lookup and when is it performed?*

A: A direct index lookup is the most direct path from the index header to the data page. This is performed when a value is provided for each column in the index (a value id, a numeric, or a character literal).

Q: *What happens when only the high order index column value is supplied for a query?*

A: A matching index scan will be performed.

DB2 Utilities

Q: *What does the CHECK Utility do?*

A: The CHECK Utility checks the Referential Integrity of table relations and checks the integrity of the indexes by matching index column values to table column values.

Q: *What types of copies can be made with the COPY Utility?*

A: The Copy Utility can make a full image copy or an incremental image copy.

Q: *Why might full image copies be faster to implement than an incremental image copy?*

A: Because an incremental image copy has to search for changed data and cannot make use of sequential prefetch. Conversely, a full image copy has no checking to do as it takes advantage of sequential prefetch.

Q: *How could one combine a set of incremental image copies into a single copy?*

A: By using the MERGECOPY Utility.

Q: *What is the purpose of the QUIESE Utility?*

A: The QUIESE Utility prevents the start of any new tablespace activity while it gives active threads a chance to finish their tasks. Once all threads are inactive, it records information to establish a point of consistency for future recovery.

Q: *What does the REORG Utility do?*

A: The REORG Utility will sort the indexspace and tablespace to conform with the primary index or clustering index specified in the DDL. It will also reclaim the space from dropped simple tablespaces.

Q: *What can the Set option of the Repair utility accomplish?*

A: The Set option of the Repair utility can reset a copy pending, check pending, and recover pending flags.

Q: *What can the Locate option of the Repair utility accomplish?*

A: The Locate option of the Repair utility can delete a row from a tablespace, repair broken tablespace pages, and replace data as specific locations in a tablespace or index.

Q: *What does the RUNSTATS Utility do?*

A: The RUNSTATS Utility collects statistical information for DB2 tablespaces, partitions, indexes, tables, and columns and stores this data in the DB2 Catalog.

Q: *Why use the RUNSTAT Utility?*

A: Because the DB2 Optimizer needs accurate data in order to formulate the most efficient access path given the state of the environment and because the information will help the DBA to monitor the condition of the object in the DB2 subsystem.

Q: *What statistic will tell the DBA how must space can be reclaimed from dropped tablespaces on the next reorg run?*

A: The DBA can see this in the PERCDROP column of the SYSIBM.SYSTABLEPART catalog table.

Q: *What DB2 catalog column tells you when an index needs to be reorganized?*

A: The FAROFFPOS column of the SYSIBM.SYSINDEXPART table.

Q: *What is the STOSPACE Utility used for?*

A: The STOSPACE Utility updates the DB2 catalog with the DASD utilization of the tablespace and indexspace datasets.

DB2 Catalog

Q: *Which DB2 catalog tables are used to produce a list of table columns by table for all tables in a database?*

A: The catalog tables to use are the SYSIBM.SYSTABLES and the SYSIBM.SYSCOLUMNS.

Q: *Which catalog tables contain authorization information?*

A: The SYSIBM tables that contain authorization information are SYSCOLAUTH, SYSDBAUTH, SYSPLANAUTH, SYSRESAUTH, SYSTABAUTH, and SYSUSERAUTH.

Q: *Which catalog table stores referential constraints?*

A: The SYSIBM.SYSRELS table.

DB2 Directory

Q: *What utility is used to migrate DB2 from one release to the next?*

A: The DUMPCAT Utility.

Q: *How would one remove old reorg information from the DB2 catalog?*

A: Run the MODIFY RECOVERY Utility.

Q: *What happens to a tablespace when its recovery information has been removed and a full recovery is no longer possible?*

A: The tablespace is put into copy pending status.

Q: *Where is the access path logic created by the DB2 Optimizer stored?*

A: The access path logic is stored as skeleton cursor tables in the SCT02 Directory table.

Q: *When is the skeleton cursor table created?*

A: During the execution of the BIND PLAN command.

Q: *How does one remove entries from the SCT02 table?*

A: Run the FREE PLAN command.

Q: *When one binds a PACKAGE (of a plan) what package information is stored and where is it stored?*

A: The access path information for the PACKAGE is stored as skeleton package tables in the SPT01 table.

Q: *Where besides the DB2 catalog is database object information stored by DB2?*

A: DB2 also stores information about DB2 objects as database descriptors (DBDs) in the DBD Directory table.

Q: *Can you access the DB2 Directory tables using SQL?*

A: No. These tables are exclusively accessed by internal DB2 processes.

Q: *When DB2 utilities are executed, where is the status of the utilities stored?*

A: DB2 stores all utility status information in the SYSUTIL Directory table.

DB2 Commands

Q: *Which DB2 command is used to retrieve environmental information?*

A: The DISPLAY command can return the following environmental data: DATABASE info, RLIMIT info, THREAD info, TRACE info, and UTILITY info.

Q: *Which command is issued to establish the Boot Strap Data Set after an I/O failure?*

A: The DBA would issue a RECOVER BSDS command.

Q: *How is the status of a utility reset after it has been stopped by DB2?*

A: The TERM UTILITY command is issued.

Q: *How can the amount of resources used by Dynamic SQL be changed?*

A: By issuing the START RLIMIT command.

Q: *How can one determine the status of a tablespace?*

A: By using the DISPLAY DATABASE command.

15
SQL

Michael A. Senatore

Introduction

Structured Query Language (SQL) provides the ability to create and define relational database objects. After these objects are defined, the language permits one to add data to these objects. Once data has been added, one can modify, retrieve, or delete that data. The language provides the capability of changing the created objects as well as removing them altogether. The language also provides the capability of defining what type of authority one might have when accessing the data.

Data Definition Language

As the name implies, there is a group of SQL statements that allows one to define the relational structures that will manage the data placed in them. The "CREATE" statement brings Relational Database Management System (RDMS) objects into existence. The types of objects one can create are Stogroup, Database, Tablespace, Table, Index, View, Synonym, and Alias. The definitions of these objects are as follows:

Stogroup: A storage group is a list of disk volume names to which one can assign a name. One defines the list of disk volumes and assigns the Stogroup name with the Create Stogroup statement.

Database: A database is a logical structure in which tables and indexes are later created. The database is defined and associated with a Stogroup with a Create Database statement.

Tablespace: A tablespace is an area on disk that is allocated and formatted by the Create Tablespace statement.

Table: A table is an organizational structure that is defined in a Create Table statement. In this statement, the data attributes are defined by column, giving each column its own unique name within the table.

Index: An index is used in conjunction with the "Primary Key" parameter of the Create Table statement. It is made with the Create Index statement and provides the duplicate record-checking necessary for a unique key.

View: A view is an alternative perspective of the data present in a database. It is made with the Create View statement and can represent a subset of the columns defined in a table. It can also represent a set of columns combined from more than one table.

Synonym: The Create Synonym statement defines an unqualified name for a table or a view.

Alias: The Create Alias statement defines an alternate qualified name for a table or a view.

After a table is created, additional columns can be added with an Alter Table statement. Any RDMS object that was made with a create statement can be removed with a drop statement.

In order to define RDMS objects, one needs various levels of authority. The following is a list of authority levels that can be granted to a user ID to operate on a designated database.

DBADM	Database administrator authority
DBCTRL	Database control authority
DBMAINT	Database maintenance authority
CREATETS	Create tablespace authority
CREATETAB	Create table authority
DROP	Drop authority on a database or subordinate objects

Data Manipulation Language

There are four SQL data manipulation statements (DML) available: Insert, Select, Update, and Delete. After tables are defined, they are ready to store data. Data is added to tables through the SQL Insert statement. Once data has been inserted into a table, it can be retrieved by the use of the Select statement. Data stored in a table can be modified by executing the SQL Update statement. Data can be deleted from a table by using the SQL Delete statement.

These SQL statements perform RDMS operations that can affect only one row at a time if desired. The same statements can, if required, affect many or all of the rows in a table. It is possible to select one row and insert it into another with one statement. It is also just as easy to select all of the rows from one table and insert all of them into another with a single statement. The same scope of operation applies to the update and delete statements. The scope of operation is controlled by the use of the WHERE clause. The operation will affect only the rows that satisfy the search condition. When no search condition is specified, the entire table is affected.

There are additional language elements available that provide the ability to process the table data while it is being retrieved. In addition, there are a variety of functions that modify the value of the data that is returned in a query. There are column functions that act on all of the values of the selected rows for a specified column and return a single answer. There also are scalar functions that return a specific answer for each row that satisfies the search condition.

As mentioned previously, SQL provides the ability to filter what data is retrieved in a select statement by including the WHERE clause. The WHERE clause specifies a variety of comparisons between two values. The values could be column values or the result of an operation involving more than one column or a constant. The comparison operators are the same as those used in COBOL, with the exception of two additional operators. The first is the IN operator that compares a single value to a set of other values. In other words, the comparison checks to see if the single value has a match in the specified list of values. The other is the LIKE operator, in which you can specify a value string that includes "wildcard" characters in such a manner that you can select rows of a table where column values are similar to the extent you require.

SQL provides four arithmetic operations: addition, subtraction, multiplication, and division. An arithmetic expression may involve any combination of column names or numbers. The arithmetic expression may itself be used as a column name or number in a Select, Insert, Update, or Delete statement.

SQL provides the ability to summarize data as it is retrieved from a table via the GROUP BY clause. In this clause, a set of column names is specified as grouping columns and the retrieved data is summarized by the changing values of those columns.

SQL provides the ability to sort the data retrieved from a table via the ORDER BY clause. In this clause, you can specify one or more sort column names as well as if each sort key is ascending or descending.

SQL also provides the ability to perform set manipulation operations. Using SQL, one can SELECT the intersection of two or more sets of data by coding a JOIN. A JOIN is any SELECT statement that has more than one DBMS object listed in its FROM clause. One can combine different sets of data by using the UNION operator. Other set manipulations can be executed by combining different operators and search conditions.

Questions and Answers

Q: *What RDMS objects are created with the SQL CREATE statement?*
A: The SQL CREATE statements are used to create the following objects:

STOGROUP	A storage group
DATABASE	A logical collection of tables

TABLESPACE	An area that stores tables
TABLE	A data structure organized by specified columns
INDEX	An alternate path to table data
VIEW	An alternate representation of one or more tables
SYNONYM	An alternate name for local table or view
ALIAS	An alternate name for a table definition which may be local or remote, existent or nonexistent

Q: *What RDMS objects are required before you can create a table?*
A: Before you create a table, you need an existing database and tablespace.

Q: *In what RDMS object does one first list column names?*
A: One first uses the column name in the CREATE TABLE statement.

Q: *What is the syntax for a Create Table statement?*
A: The syntax for a Create Table statement is:

```
CREATE TABLE table-name
        (column name list
        primary key(column name))
        in database-name.tablespace-name.
```

Q: *Can one add columns to a table after it has been defined?*
A: Yes, one can add columns to a table after it has been defined by using the SQL ALTER TABLE statement.

Q: *Where in a table are added columns located?*
A: The new columns are added to the end of the table.

Q: *After a table is defined, can columns be removed?*
A: The only way to remove columns from an existing table involves a migration program that extracts only the desired columns of data, redefining the table without the unwanted columns, then populating the new table. One would have to handle all of the old table's dependents programmatically.

Q: *Which RDMS objects can you change with the SQL ALTER statement?*
A: The SQL ALTER statement can change a table index, a table, a tablespace, or a stogroup.

Q: *What authority is required for one to create a table?*
A: In order to create tables, one needs CREATETAB privileges.

Q: *What is the minimum authority required for one to create a tablespace?*
A: In order to create tablespaces, one needs CREATETS privileges.

Q: *When is it necessary to create a table index?*
A: It is necessary to create a table index whenever you want to enforce the uniqueness of the table's primary key.

Q: *What is a synonym?*
A: A synonym is an unqualified alternative name for a table or view.

Q: *What is a view?*

A: A view is a virtual table that can represent all or part of one or more tables. A view can help simplify data access as well as provide an additional layer of access control.

Q: *Can a view involve more than one table?*

A: A view can present data that is the result of a JOIN or UNION of more than one table.

Q: *What is a foreign key?*

A: A foreign key is the key defined in one table to reference the primary key of a reference table. This foreign key must have the same structure as the reference table's primary key.

Q: *What is referential integrity?*

A: Referential integrity is the automatic enforcement of referential constraints that exist between a reference table and a referencing table. When referential integrity is enforced, the value of a foreign key exists as a primary key value in the reference table. In other words, when referential integrity is enforced, all of the foreign key values in, for example, the "department code" column in an "employee" table exist as primary key values in a "department" table.

Q: *What is the difference between cascade and restrict?*

A: Cascade and restrict are part of the delete rule when specifying the referential constraints between two tables. The "cascade on delete" specification tells the RDMS to delete all dependent rows from the dependent table, while honoring any delete rules that exist in those dependent tables. The restrict rule tells the RDMS to fail the delete request if a dependent row exists. If a table with a cascade-on-delete rule has a dependent row in a table that has its own cascade restrict rule with an existing dependent, the entire delete operation will fail. One can get around this by using the set null on delete so that its dependents can still be satisfied.

Q: *Can you cascade an update of a primary key?*

A: You can change the value of a primary key of a reference table only if it has no dependents.

Q: *What is a remote RDMS object?*

A: A remote RDMS object is one that exists in another subsystem. There may be more than one RDMS subsystem on the same platform. The only local subsystem is the one in which your application runs; all others are remote.

Q: *Can one define remote RDMS objects?*

A: No, one cannot execute an SQL CREATE, ALTER, or GRANT statement on a remote subsystem.

Q: *What can you do with an alias that you cannot do with a synonym?*

A: With an alias, one can retrieve data from remote tables and views. An alias can be used by all who have access to the source tables represented by the alias. An alias can be defined for local or remote objects before they exist. The alias definition remains intact after the object it represents has been dropped. None of this is true for a synonym.

Q: *What is a SELECT statement?*

A: A SELECT statement is an SQL statement that retrieves data from a table or view.

Q: *What is the syntax of a SELECT statement when embedded in a COBOL program?*

A:
```
EXEC SQL
    SELECT      column_name1, column_name2, column_name3
    INTO        host_variable1, host_variable2, host_variable3
    FROM        owner.tablename
    WHERE       condition
END-EXEC
```

Q: *What are column-name qualifiers?*

A: A column-name qualifier could be a table name, a view name, a synonym name, an alias name, or a correlation name.

Q: *Why are column-name qualifiers used?*

A: Column-name qualifiers are used as a table designator to avoid ambiguity when the column names referenced exist in more than one table used in the SQL statement. Column-name qualifiers are also used in correlated references.

Q: *What is a correlation name?*

A: A correlation name is a special type of column designator that connects specific columns in the various levels of a multilevel SQL query.

Q: *How do you define a correlation name?*

A: A correlation name can be defined in the FROM clause of a query and in the first clause of an UPDATE or DELETE statement.

Q: *What is a subquery?*

A: A subquery is a query that is written as part of another query's WHERE clause. For example:
```
SELECT column_name1, column_name2
FROM   table_a
WHERE  column_name3 < ( select avg(column_name3)
                        from table_a
                        where column_name4 = 'constant')
```

Q: *What is a correlated subquery?*

A: A correlated subquery is one that has a correlation name as a table or view designator in the FROM clause of the outer query and the same correlation name as a qualifier of a search condition in the WHERE clause of the subquery. For example:

```
SELECT column_name1, column_name2
FROM   table_a x1
WHERE  column_name3 <
     ( select avg(column_name3)
       from table_a
       where column_name4 = x1.column_name4)
```

Q: *How does the processing of a correlated subquery differ from a noncorrelated subquery?*

A: The subquery in a correlated subquery is reevaluated for every row of the table or view named in the outer query, while the subquery of a noncorrelated subquery is evaluated only once.

Q: *What is a results table?*

A: A results table is the product of a query against one or more tables or views (i.e., it is the place that holds the results of a query).

Q: *What is a cursor?*

A: A cursor is a named control structure used to make a set of rows available to a program.

Q: *What is the syntax required for the creation of a cursor?*

A:
```
EXEC SQL
   DECLARE cursor-name cursor for
       SELECT column1, column2...
       FROM table_name
       WHERE column1 = search-condition...
END-EXEC.
```

Q: *When is the results table for the query in a DECLARE CURSOR statement created?*

A: The results table for a query specified in a DECLARE CURSOR statement of a cursor is created during the execution of the OPEN CURSOR statement.

Q: *What is a read-only cursor?*

A: A read-only cursor is one in which the result table was created by a query containing one of the following:

- a DISTINCT keyword
- a UNION operator
- a column or scalar function
- a GROUP BY clause
- an ORDER BY clause
- a HAVING clause
- a read-only view in the FROM clause
- a FROM clause identifying more than one table or view

Q: *How do you bring data from the result table into your program?*

A: Data is brought into a program's working storage area from a results table by issuing a FETCH cursor-name statement.

Q: *What is a host variable?*

A: A host variable is a variable referenced by embedded SQL.

Q: *What is the SQL error you receive when you try to fetch data from a cursor after it has run out of data?*

A: Trying to fetch data from an empty or exhausted cursor returns an SQL error code of 100.

Q: *What is the SQLCA?*

A: The SQLCA is the SQL communication made up of a series of variables that are updated after each SQL statement is executed.

Q: *How and where is the SQLCA specified in a COBOL program?*

A: The SQLCA must be specified in the Working Storage Section of a COBOL program by an SQL INCLUDE statement.

Q: *After an SQL statement is executed, what does a positive value in the SQLCODE variable indicate?*

A: A positive value in the SQLCODE indicates a successful execution, but with an exception condition.

Q: *After an SQL statement is executed, what does a negative value in the SQLCODE variable indicate?*

A: A negative value indicates that the SQL statement did not execute due to an error condition.

Q: *What is the main difference between static SQL and dynamic SQL?*

A: The main difference between dynamic and static SQL is that in dynamic SQL, the SQL statements can be changed, prepared, and bound by the program while it is running. Static SQL statements are prepared and bound prior to execution.

Q: *When must SQLDA (SQL descriptor area) be specified in a COBOL program?*

A: An SQLDA cannot be specified in a COBOL program.

Q: *What is a JOIN?*

A: A JOIN is a relational operation in which data is retrieved from a combination of two or more tables or views based on matching values within the specified column names of each table.

Q: *How do you code a JOIN of three tables that share the same column names?*

A: The columns names in the Select clause need to be qualified by the table or view name they belong to and could be coded as follows:

```
EXEC SQL
  SELECT table1.column1, table2.column1, table3.column1,
         table1.column2, table2.column2, table3.column2
  FROM   table1, table2, table3
END-EXEC
```

Ambiguity could also be avoided by using correlation variables as follows:

```
EXEC SQL
  SELECT a.column1, b.column1, c.column1,
         a.column2, b.column2, c.column2
  FROM   table1 a, table2 b, table3 c
END-EXEC
```

In this manner, the correlation variables (A, B, and C) match the column names with their tables.

Q: *What kind of function is the SUBSTR function and what does it do?*
A: The SUBSTR function is a scalar function. It breaks up a character or graphic string according to the substr argument list as follows:

```
SUBSTR(column-name1, starting character position, length)
```

Q: *What are column functions?*
A: Column functions are features of SQL that allow you to calculate a single value derived from one or more values found in the specified column.

Q: *What column functions are available in SQL and what do they do?*
A: The column functions and descriptions are as follows:

AVG	Returns the average value of the named column
COUNT	Returns the number of rows in the result of the query
DISTINCT	Returns only one occurrence of each value from the specified column
MAX	Returns the maximum value of the specified column of the results table generated by a query
MIN	Returns the minimum value of the specified column of the results table generated by a query
SUM	Returns the sum of the values of the specified column of the results table generated by a query

Q: *What kind of averages can you calculate with the AVG function?*
A: The only type of average you can calculate with the AVG column function is the mean average, which is calculated by dividing the sum of all values by the count of values.

Q: *What is the effect of the GROUP BY clause on column functions?*
A: The column function will calculate its result based on the individual groups created by the GROUP BY specification. In other words, if 500 groups were created by a GROUP BY clause, there would be 500 individual results—one for each group.

Q: *What's wrong with the following query?*

```
EXEC SQL
  SELECT column1, column2, avg(column3), column4
  FROM   table-a
  GROUP by column1, column2, column3
END-EXEC
```

A: The grouping columns specified in the GROUP BY clause are inconsistent with the columns in the SELECT clause. All of the columns in the SELECT clause must appear as a grouping column unless they are being manipulated by a function. This example could be corrected as follows:

```
EXEC SQL
  SELECT  column1, column2, AVG(column3), column4
  FROM    table-a
  GROUP BY column1, column2, column4
END-EXEC
```

Q: *What is a predicate?*
A: A predicate is the SQL language element that specifies a condition about a value or set of values that may be true, false, or unknown.

Q: *What are the different types of predicates?*
A: In SQL, the predicate types are: Basic predicates, a Quantified predicate, the Null predicate, the In predicate, the Between predicate, the Like predicate, and the Exists predicate. These predicate types can be preceded by a "NOT" to reverse their meaning.

Q: *What are the Basic predicates?*
A: The Basic predicates are:

=	Equal
¬ =, < >	Not equal
<	Less than
>	Greater than
< =	Less than or equal
> =	Greater than or equal
¬ <	Not less than
¬ >	Not greater than

Q: *Can the table named in the From clause of a Delete statement containing a subquery be the same table referenced by the subquery?*
A: No. In a Delete statement with a subquery, the outer query and the subquery must reference different tables.

Q: *What's wrong with this query?*

```
EXEC SQL
  SELECT AVG(COUNT (employee_id))
  FROM emptable
  WHERE salary > 20000.00
  GROUP BY dept
END-EXEC
```

A: Assuming that all of the columns named exist in the EMPTABLE table, what is wrong is that you cannot nest a column function within a column function.

Q: *What are the valid possibilities for nesting functions?*

A: There are three valid ways to nest functions:

- Column functions within Scalar functions
- Scalar functions within Column functions
- Scalar functions within Scalar functions

Q: *What arithmetic operators can one apply to Date or Time data types?*

A: The only arithmetic operations one can apply to Date or Time data types are addition and subtraction.

Q: *Where and when is the HAVING clause used and what does it do?*

A: The HAVING clause is coded after the GROUP BY clause in a query that is summarizing results by one or more grouping columns. The HAVING clause behaves the same as the WHERE clause except that it is used to specify the conditions each returned group must satisfy. If one row in the group fails the conditions of the HAVING clause, the entire group is not returned as part of the result.

Q: *How can you sort the output of a query in the order of the results of an expression in the Select clause?*

A: Use the ORDER BY clause and refer to the expression by its position in the list of columns named in the SELECT clause. For example:

```
EXEC SQL
    SELECT column1, column2, column3, (column1 - column3),
            column4, column5
        FROM table-a
        ORDER BY 4
END-EXEC
```

Q: *How can you combine the results of two or more SELECT statements?*

A: One can combine the results of two or more SELECT statements by using the UNION or UNION ALL keyword. These keywords cause the results of each SELECT statement to be combined as a single result table.

Q: *Why would you use the UNION keyword instead of a Join?*

A: A Join depends on the common values of the columns named in a search condition. If there are no common values in two tables (for the specified search columns), there would be no way to combine data from two tables that did not have a common range of values. For example, if employee data was stored in separate district tables, and the districts did not share employees (have the same employee in more than one district), it would be impossible to Join the tables by employee ID. In this situation, in order to retrieve all of the employees from three districts, you would have to code a UNION of the three tables as follows:

```
EXEC SQL
    SELECT empid, empname, salary
        FROM   district1-tab
```

```
      UNION
      SELECT empid, empname, salary
        FROM   district2-tab
      UNION
      SELECT empid, empname, salary
        FROM   district3-tab
   END-EXEC
```

Q: *What is the difference between UNION and UNION ALL?*

A: During the merge of the multiple result (one for each table in the union), the UNION keyword causes the duplicate rows to be removed from the final result. The UNION ALL keyword is processed so that all of the duplicate result rows remain in the merged result table.

Q: *If you want to sort the output of a query that consists of the union of more than one table, where do you place the ORDER BY clause and how do you reference the sort columns?*

A: In a union of multiple tables, the ORDER BY clause is coded in the last SELECT statement. The sort columns are referenced by the integer that represents their position in the list of column names found in the Select clause.

Q: *Can the select statements in a union have subqueries?*

A: Yes. The results of any valid SELECT statement may be merged with the results of another.

Q: *Can a subquery have a UNION keyword?*

A: No. Only outer-level queries can use the UNION or UNION ALL keyword.

Q: *If you have four similar tables combined by the UNION keyword, how can you tell which table a result row came from?*

A: Place a different constant at the end of the column list in the SELECT clause of each SELECT statement in the union. The merged result will have this constant present to indicate which SELECT statement and therefore from which table the row came. Look at the following example:

```
   EXEC SQL
     SELECT col1, col2, col3, 'table1'
       FROM table1
     UNION
     SELECT col1, col2, col3, 'table2'
       FROM table2
   END-EXEC
```

The final result rows will have a 'TABLE1' or 'TABLE2' constant to tell you which table they came from.

Q: *When is the WHERE CURRENT OF clause used?*

A: The WHERE CURRENT OF clause is used in cursor processing in order to execute an UPDATE or DELETE statement. When a result table row is brought into the program's working storage by a FETCH statement, the cursor position remains on that row until the next FETCH statement or until the cursor is closed. During this time, the cursor position could be used to update or delete the row from the table named in the DECLARE CURSOR statement.

Q: *What clause must you code into the DECLARE CURSOR statement if you later wish to use the UPDATE WHERE CURRENT OF clause?*

A: In order to use the UPDATE WHERE CURRENT OF clause during cursor processing, you must code a FOR UPDATE OF clause listing all of the columns you wish to update. Review the following example:

```
EXEC SQL
   DECLARE cursor-name CURSOR FOR
      SELECT col1, col2, col3,
      FROM table01
      FOR UPDATE OF col1, col3
END-EXEC
```

Q: *How do you make sure that the changes made to a table become permanent?*

A: Issue an SQL COMMIT statement.

Q: *What is a Unit of Recovery?*

A: A Unit of Recovery is the amount of processing in a program that is recoverable (i.e., can be undone). A Unit of Recovery ends and a new unit begins whenever a ROLLBACK or a COMMIT is issued.

Q: *What effect does a COMMIT or ROLLBACK have on any or all of the open cursors that are being processed?*

A: As soon as a ROLLBACK or COMMIT is issued, all of the open cursors are immediately closed. When this happens, all cursor positions are lost.

Q: *If you want to continue processing the same cursor from the last position before the last COMMIT, what could you do?*

A: Construct your cursor so that it uses the unique sort key (use the ORDER BY clause) of the result table being processed as a value compared by a "greater than" predicate. Before the first DECLARE CURSOR statement is issued, set this host variable to zero so that your cursor will be positioned at the first possible row of the result table. As you fetch data from the cursor, you will automatically be keeping track of your position in the result table. After the COMMIT, simply reopen your cursor and you will be positioned as desired.

Q: *What does the "*" mean when in a SELECT statement?*

A: The asterisk allows you to select "ALL COLUMNS" from the table named in the SELECT statement without having to name the columns explicitly.

Q: *Why is it a bad practice to use the SELECT * in static SQL?*

A: The reason to avoid the SELECT * in static SQL is because database requests are validated at precompile time. If the table definitions for the tables used in a static program change (i.e., columns are added) all of the "INTO" clauses for those changed tables will become invalid, causing the programs to end abnormally. If you list all of the table column names explicitly, column additions will not affect the static programs.

Q: *What is a STOGROUP?*
A: A STOGROUP is a named object that lists the DASD volumes that are desig-nated to store DB2 data.

Q: *Where is the isolation level specified?*
A: Isolation level is specified in the BIND or REBIND statement.

Q: *What is the difference between Cursor Stability and Repeatable Read?*
A: With the isolation level set to Cursor Stability during read-only processing, a page lock is held all the while an applications cursor is positioned on it. As soon as the cursor acquires a lock on the next required page (i.e., the cursor is positioned on a different page of data), the previous page lock is released. With the isolation level set to Repeatable Read, all of the pages of data selected by the DECLARE CURSOR statement are locked until the next explicit or implicit commit.

Q: *What is the difference between a Smallint and an Integer?*
A: A Smallint data type is 2 bytes long and has a range from −32768 to +32767. An Integer is 4 bytes long and stores numeric data ranging from −2147483648 to +2147483647.

Q: *What is a solution table?*
A: A solution table is a temporary table made to store the result of an SQL query. This is another name for a results table.

Q: *What is a recursive reference?*
A: A recursive reference is the act of referring to a single table more than one time from a single SQL QUERY.

Q: *Can a UNION and a JOIN be used in the same select statement?*
A: No. The UNION keyword cannot be placed within a SELECT statement. A UNION keyword is used to combine two or more SELECT statements.

Q: *What does the LIKE search condition allow you to do?*
A: It allows you to select table rows based on a comparison of partial strings.

Q: *What is the difference between a "%" and a "_" when used with the LIKE keyword?*
A: A "_" represents a single unknown character, while a "%" represents from 0 to many characters.

Q: *How do you select the lowest value from a numeric column?*
A: Use the MIN column function.

Q: *How do you get a string representation of a signed decimal number?*
A: Use the DIGITS scalar function.

Q: *What is Authority and is it needed all of the time?*
A: Authority is the privilege level required to access data from an RDMS and is required at all times. If you have no privileges, you cannot access the data.

Q: *What SQL statement defines a foreign key?*

A: A foreign key is defined in the CREATE TABLE statement or in an ALTER TABLE statement.

Q: *Why would you want to use a synonym?*

A: A synonym is used for convenience. When a synonym is created for a table, that table can be accessed by all privileged user IDs without having to use the Authorization ID as a qualifier.

Q: *What type of table lock is used when updating a table?*

A: Before the application can change data in a table it must acquire an exclusive lock on the page on which the changing data resides.

Q: *What is the minimum lock level instituted for an inquiry?*

A: The minimum lock level is a SHARE lock.

Q: *When is the Delete command restricted?*

A: When the user does not have Delete privileges on the specified table or if there is a referential integrity constraint enforced for a dependent foreign key.

Q: *What is the difference between a searched update and a positioned update?*

A: A searched update can update one or more rows of data depending on whether the rows satisfy the search conditions written into the update statement. A positioned update updates the single row pointed to by the cursor named in the update statement.

Q: *Can you use a positioned update when the cursor is pointing to a results table made of data from more than one table?*

A: No. A positioned update cannot operate on a read-only cursor, such as one where the results table is made with a JOIN.

Q: *How can you work through a results table in reverse order?*

A: You cannot. However, you can specify the sort key as descending in the ORDER BY clause.

Q: *Can you remove a column of data from a table without dropping the table?*

A: No. You can, however, create a view and omit the column from the view.

Q: *What happens to the table data on a volume when the volume is removed from a STOGROUP with the ALTER STOGROUP statement?*

A: Nothing. The data remains available, as before. The volume, however, will not be used the next time DASD is allocated for that STOGROUP.

Q: *What happens to the table data when the primary index of that table is dropped?*

A: Nothing. Only the index space is dropped.

Q: *What is the WHENEVER SQL statement used for?*

A: The WHENEVER statement is used to specify the HOST LANGUAGE statement to execute every time the specified exception condition exists.

Q: *What exception conditions can be trapped by the WHENEVER statement?*
A: NOT FOUND, SQLERROR, and SQLWARNING.

Q: *How do you control the scope of a WHENEVER statement?*
A: The scope of a WHENEVER statement is controlled by its placement in the listing, not by its execution order.

Bibliography

1. IBM Database Version 2 Release 2 Library

   - *SQL User's Guide*, SC26-4376-0
   - *Application Programming and SQL Guide*, SC26-4377-1
   - *SQL Reference*, SC26-4380-1

2. C. J. Date, *A Guide to the SQL Standard*, Addison-Wesley, 1987.

16
Sybase

Robert J. Leo

Introduction

Sybase, Inc., is a leader in client/server technology. The entire suite of Sybase products is based on the Open Interfaces architecture. In order for you to succeed with Sybase, you must first understand some of the underlying components. It is important to have a good working knowledge of relational database concepts, the SQL language, and the fundamentals of the client/server architecture. Therefore, in addition to the material contained herein, consider testing your knowledge of the chapters:

"Understanding Important Relational Database Concepts" (Chapter 13)

"SQL" (Chapter 15)

"Clent/Server Systems Architectures" (Chapter 18)

"Client/Server Systems Design and Implementation" (Chapter 19)

Overview of Sybase Products

The following belong to the Sybase family of products:

SQL Server. The SQL Server is a powerful database engine developed around the client/server model that fully complies with the ANSI SQL89 standard. It is a high-performance relational database management system (RDBMS) for supporting mission-critical applications.

Open Server. The Open Server is the API that facilitates integration of data sources, server application, and application service. Open Server includes the programming libraries necessary to develop applications that access any data, applications, or services, and provides that data to any client or Open Client application on the network.

Open Client. A library of routines, programming services, and run-time services used to develop client applications. It enables client programs (custom programs, Sybase tools, and third-party products) to communicate with server programs (SQL Server and Open Server applications).

OmniSQL Server. A gateway that provides transparent access to distributed, heterogeneous data sources. The OmniSQL Server provides complete SQL translation, location transparency, and features like heterogeneous distributed joins and stored procedures for heterogeneous data.

Replication Server. A tool that provides data to the users for processing by replicating transactions from a primary site to a secondary site. It is a practical alternative to the two-phase commit in that it provides loose consistency of replicated data without the limitations, such as single point of failure, inherent in the two-phase commit protocol.

Enterprise SQL Server Manager. ESSM is Sybase's systems management tool for administration of large Sybase SQL Server environments. Through the graphical user interface (GUI), administrators can do server configuration and monitoring, and can administer users, schedule backups, and manage databases, devices, and segments.

Navigation Server. Enables users to exploit hardware to meet their performance needs with respect to scalability and speedup. It supports multiple machines running SQL Server to work together to provide parallel processing capabilities, including support of very large databases (VLDB).

Terminology

Data cache: Physical I/O is inversely proportional to performance. For that reason, Sybase buffers I/O requests by utilizing memory that is available to the SQL Server. The memory that is reserved for buffering data is referred to as *data cache.*

Cache/hit ratio: The cache/hit ratio is used to measure the effectiveness of the I/O buffering. If all of the data needed to fulfill a request is already resident in memory, the SQL Server will not need to perform any physical I/O to get the info from disk. In this example, the cache/hit ratio would be 100 percent.

Page swapping: When the SQL Server needs to write the pages in memory to disk to make room for other data pages we refer to this as *page swapping.* Excessive page swapping is often referred to as *thrashing* and has a serious adverse effect on performance.

Page splitting: When a data or index page is full and we need to insert a record into that page, the SQL Server performs an operation known as a page split. A page split means that the SQL Server obtains an unused page in memory and moves half of the contents of the filled page onto it to make room for the record to be inserted. The pointers are realigned to maintain the sequence of the pages. Frequent page splitting results in poor performance.

BCP: The Bulk Copy Utility (BCP) is used to import and/or export data to and from the SQL Server in a variety of formats (character, delimited, etc.). The fast version of BCP provides minimal logging, while the slow version provides transaction-level logging.

Dirty pages: Any page residing in memory that has been modified in any way.

Fill factor: The amount of free space left on each page when an index is created. This is useful for reducing lock contention and page splitting at the index levels.

Checkpoint process: The process that writes dirty pages in memory to the physical device.

Threshold: A threshold is a predefined amount of free space on a segment that invokes a user-defined stored procedure when encountered.

System stored procedure: Sybase provides a number of stored procedures that are useful for querying or performing operations on system tables.

Thread: A thread is an open connection between a client and a server.

Level of Expertise

The questions that follow cover a variety of key topics related to Sybase products. The position for which you are applying will dictate which questions you will be expected to respond to. For instance, if you are applying for a position as a programmer, you might not be expected to have in-depth knowledge of production support issues. In addition, the level of competency is also measured by the depth of your response. The answers therefore have been structured in degrees of complexity.

The beginning portion of the answer is the response that would be expected of a *novice* (6–18 months).

An *intermediate* (1.5–3 years) candidate should be able to provide a more thorough understanding of the topic by accentuating many of the key elements provided in the complete answer. Some correlations should be made based on the candidate's work experience.

An *advanced* (more than 3 years) candidate should be able to supply to the interviewer all of the key elements indicated in the answer and draw accurate correlations based on his or her work experience.

Questions and Answers

Q: *What is Transact-SQL?*

A: Transact-SQL is the Sybase extension to the standard SQL language that provides additional functionality such as flow control. It is the programming language used by stored procedures and triggers and all other data access requests.

Q: *What is a default?*

A: A default is an integrity constraint that applies to inserts that places a defined value into a column (in place of null) when no value for that column is supplied. A default is bound to a column or user-defined datatype with the sp_bindefault command.

Q: *What is a rule?*

A: A rule is an integrity constraint defined by the user that stipulates which values are not permitted in a column. A rule is bound to a column or user-defined datatype with the sp_bindrule command.

Q: *Why would we bind a rule to a user-defined datatype?*

A: We bind a rule to a user-defined datatype when we have a defined range of values that applies to multiple instances of a column or columns (sharing a common datatype). We can bind the rule once, to the datatype, instead of binding it to each column, to ensure consistency throughout the database.

Q: *We have a rule bound to a column with a user-defined datatype. If we apply a rule to the datatype at a later time, which rule takes precedence?*

A: The column level rule takes precedence, i.e., it would still apply. If we want the new rule to apply we must unbind the rule from the column.

Q: *If we define a view based on a join clause, can we update the view?*

A: The view can be updated if the columns that are affected by the update reside in a single table. For example, if we join the employees table (EMP) to the automobile table (AUTO) by employee id, we can update the color of the car because that column resides only in the AUTO table. We cannot, however, update the employee id because it resides in both EMP and AUTO. Also, we could not update the age column in the EMP table and the color column in the AUTO table with a single statement.

Q: *What effect does [ALL] have in the following query?*

```
SELECT dept, name, title, salary
FROM    employee_table
WHERE   salary > 50000
GROUP BY ALL dept
```

A: By including ALL in the GROUP BY clause, the resulting set will contain all departments whether or not there are any employees in that department making over $50,000. Without the ALL, only those departments with at least one employee making over $50,000 would be listed.

Q: *Given the following SELECT statements, explain the difference in the results that would be returned:*

```
SELECT * FROM T1 WHERE col_1 BETWEEN 10 and 20
SELECT * FROM T1 WHERE col_1 BETWEEN 20 and 10
```

A: Prior to System 10 these two statements would return the same results. However, Sybase altered the behavior to conform to the ANSI standard behavior whereby BETWEEN means greater than or equal to the first value and less than or equal to the second value. Therefore, the BETWEEN 20 and 10 would never return any rows.

Q: *What are the two trigger test tables that are commonly referenced by an update trigger?*

A: The two trigger test tables are the DELETED and the INSERTED tables. They contain the before and after image of the updated row before the data page is actually written.

Q: *How do you select all unique values for col_1 in table_A?*

A: `SELECT DISTINCT col_1 FROM table_A`

Q: *What is the difference between an inner join and an outer join?*

A: An inner join, also known as an equijoin, returns only those rows where there is an exact match as described in the where clause. An outer join returns all qualifying rows from one table and all matching rows from the associated table. Consider the following example:

```
table_A           table_B

A   B   C         D   E   F
1   4   4         1   3   2
2   3   1         3   3   1
3   2   7         4   8   3

(inner join)               (outer join)
SELECT A,B,C,E,F           SELECT A,B,C,E,F
FROM table_A, table_B      FROM table_A, table_B
WHERE A = D                WHERE A *= D

A   B   C   E   F          A   B   C   E     F
1   4   4   3   2          1   4   4   3     2
3   2   7   3   1          2   3   1   NULL  NULL
                           3   2   7   3     1
```

Q: *Where is the text stored for system-stored procedures located?*

A: The text for system-stored procedures is stored in the SYSCOMMENTS table in the SYBSYSTEMPROCS database. Prior to System 10, the system-stored procedures were stored in the MASTER database.

Q: *What are the two possible outcomes of any transaction?*

A: Commit or rollback.

Q: *What is a cursor?*

A: A cursor is a mechanism that enables the user to access (view and/or update) the cursor result set one row at a time. When the user fetches a row the cursor position points to the next row in the cursor result set.

Q: *What is a transaction?*

A: A transaction is a logical unit of work as defined by the business rules. Its behavior is such that all actions performed in the transaction must succeed or none of them succeed. It is recommended that transactions be kept as small as possible.

Q: *What is a deadlock?*

A: A deadlock occurs when two or more users have locks on resources and are waiting for each other to free up their locks so that the process can complete. Since neither process can complete while the other remains active, the SQL Server kills one of the processes. This frees up the lock and allows the other process to complete successfully. The process that was killed is the one with the least amount of CPU time and all work performed by that process is rolled back.

Q: *What is index coverage?*

A: Index coverage is when all of the columns that are needed to perform a query exist in a nonclustered index; the SQL Server will retrieve the information from the leaf level of the index without having to read any of the data pages. Index coverage, when used properly, can greatly improve query performance. However, it is typically not a good idea to create very large composite indexes for this reason, especially if the table is frequently used for transactions, as it will need to propagate the data changes to all affected indexes.

Q: *What is the major difference between the datatypes "Float" and "Numeric"?*

A: Float is not an exact datatype and is subject to rounding errors due to the placement of the mantissa. Numeric is an exact datatype and the precision is defined, as needed, when created.

Q: *A user is granted execute permission on a stored procedure that updates a table. The creator of the stored procedure has update permission on that table. However, the user has not explicitly been granted update permission on the table. What will happen when the user tries to update the table using the stored procedure?*

A: The update will work as long as it is performed via the stored procedure. If the user tries to update the table directly, an error message will indicate a permissions problem. This is an important security feature in Sybase.

Q: *What information do we get by setting showplan on?*

A: When we "set showplan on" the SQL Server displays the steps that were performed during execution. It contains the index used for each search, the type of update performed, and other useful information that can be used when troubleshooting performance problems.

Q: *What command allows us to see the time required by each step in a procedure?*

A: SET STATISTICS TIME ON

Q: *What useful information do we get by using the SET STATISTICS IO ON command?*

A: This information, which is the key to identifying performance problems in queries and stored procedures, contains the number of scans and the number of I/O (both logical and physical) required by each step in the process. A large number of physical I/O means that our cache/hit ratio is poor. This can be improved somewhat by increasing the amount of available cache. However, we need to focus on the logical I/O. A large value in logical I/O indicates that the server is scanning large amounts of data to find the appropriate records (often a table scan). This usually can be improved by creating an appropriate index and/or breaking the statement into smaller, easier-to-interpret statements.

Q: *Which command enables the user to view the text of a stored procedure?*

A: `sp_helptext PROC_NAME`

Q: *What is a remote procedure call?*

A: A remote procedure call (rpc) executes a stored procedure that resides on another SQL Server. The syntax is "exec remote_srv.db_name.owner. proc_name".

Q: *When is the execution plan for a stored procedure created?*

A: The execution plan is created the first time that a stored procedure is run. The plan is then stored in a system table and used for subsequent executions.

Q: *When a user table is modified in a way that may impact existing stored procedures that reference the table, what command should be used to find all stored procedures that reference the table?*

A: sp_depends table_name will return the names of all stored procedures that reference the specified table. If we replace the table name with the procedure name, we will get the names of all tables that are used by the stored procedure.

Q: *Which actions, when applied to a table with triggers, cause the triggers to fire?*

A: `INSERT`
   `UPDATE`
   `DELETE`

Q: *Why does Sybase use page level locking instead of record level locking?*

A: The overhead associated with record level locking has an adverse effect on performance. Generally, page locking is considered the optimal locking strategy with respect to performance.

Q: *In an effort to reduce locking overhead, SQL Server escalates from page level locks to a table lock after a predefined number of locks is reached. How many page locks cause this to happen?*

A: 200.

Q: *When are dirty data pages physically written to disk?*

A: Dirty data pages are written to disk every time a checkpoint occurs. Checkpoint is the process that writes dirty (changed) pages from memory to disk. The process is implicitly invoked when the recovery interval is met or any time that the SQL Server needs to swap the pages out to free up cache. It may also be invoked explicitly via the "checkpoint" command.

Q: *When are dirty log pages written to disk?*

A: Dirty log pages are written to disk every time a commit occurs. A commit marks the successful completion of a transaction in the transaction log and writes the log to disk. This is important in that it enables the recovery process to roll forward (or back if necessary) any completed transactions that occurred prior to a system or device failure.

Q: *Why does Sybase recommend the use of raw partitions over files for defining data and log devices?*

A: Sybase recommends the use of raw partitions for defining data and log devices for the following reason. When files are used as devices, the operating system will buffer the writes to improve performance. Sybase assumes that the physical device was written but has no control over an operating system failure. Therefore, database consistency cannot be guaranteed using a buffered file. When a raw partition is used, the operating system buffering is bypassed and writes are guaranteed.

Q: *It is sometimes desirable to place indexes on a separate physical disk than the table that they reference. How do we accomplish this with Sybase SQL Server?*

A: By using segments. A segment is a subset of the existing devices defined for a given database. We can define segments and then place the index on a specific segment with the CREATE INDEX statement.

Q: *What is the maximum record length that Sybase currently supports?*

A: 1962. A single record cannot span multiple pages and Sybase uses 2K pages. Therefore, 2024 – (header information) = 1962. When the table contains a column of type TEXT or OBJECT that holds a large amount of data (usually far exceeding 2K), the column specified contains a pointer to the page where the TEXT or OBJECT resides. Although the actual data row does not exceed a single 2K page, the associated TEXT or OBJECT is stored as a linked list spanning many data pages.

Q: *What is the minimum size that an object such as a table or index can be in Sybase?*

A: 16K. The smallest size that an object can be is one extent. Since Sybase assigns extents in 16K (8 × 2K page size) blocks, 16K is the smallest object size. In addition, as additional space is needed it will be assigned in 16K blocks.

Q: *When a record is deleted, what happens to the remaining records on that page?*

A: No physical movement of data occurs at the time a record is deleted. The record is tagged for future physical deletion. For performance reasons, Sybase does not physically move the remaining data each time a record is deleted.

Q: *When does Sybase reduce the amount of space allocated to an object when a large number of records have been deleted?*

A: When no more records reside on an extent, the extent is returned to the pool for use by other objects. There are several ways of accomplishing this. One way is to drop and recreate the clustered index, thereby placing the remaining records on contiguous pages and releasing the unused portions. Another way is to bulk copy the data out, truncate the table (deallocate the extents), and then bulk copy the data back in (allocating only enough extents to hold the data).

Q: *What are some common areas where bottlenecks can occur in a client/server environment?*

A: Physical I/O   Bottleneck at disk caused by insufficient memory or poor cache/hit ratio

CPU   Commands are waiting to be processed

Network   Packets are colliding because of excessive network activity, thereby decreasing overall throughput

Excessive page locking   Transaction is waiting to obtain the necessary locks

Q: *Explain what happens when a clustered index is created.*

A: When a clustered index is created all of the data is physically sorted. The leaf level of the index is the actual data. When creating a clustered index Sybase requires that there is a sufficient amount of unused space (approximately 1.2 times the current table size) available for the sorting process to occur. Only one clustered index can be defined per table. Sybase indexes are based on the B-Tree data structure.

Q: *What happens when a nonclustered index is created?*

A: When a nonclustered index is created no sorting of actual data takes place. A leaf level is created by copying the specified index columns. The leaf level is sorted and uses pointers to the associated data pages. Sybase indexes are based on the B-Tree data structure. Sybase allows a maximum of 16 columns and 256 total bytes for an index. Sybase allows up to 249 nonclustered indexes per table.

Q: *When you install SQL Server, what other server needs to be installed?*

A: The Backup Server.

Q: *Why would we define a fillfactor when creating an index?*

A: A fillfactor should be defined if we have an OLTP application and we are experiencing performance problems caused by page splitting or excessive locking of index pages.

Q: *How do we increase the size of a database?*
A: We increase the size of a database by using the "alter database" command.

Q: *What utility does Sybase use to import large volumes of data?*
A: Bulk Copy (BCP) utility. In the latest release of Sybase (System 11) this utility has been modified to support parallel bulk copy. This change has resulted in significant performance improvements.

Q: *When a fast bulk copy is used to load data, what effect does it have on the transaction log?*
A: When fast BCP is used to load data, Sybase does not log the actual transactions. Instead, it writes the data directly to disk and logs the pages that are written in case of a failure. Whenever a minimally logged transaction is completed the database should be dumped to ensure recovery.

Q: *What is stored in the SYSLOGS table?*
A: The transaction log.

Q: *Would frequent transaction log dumps be used for an application classified as decision support (DSS) or for on-line transaction processing (OLTP)?*
A: For on-line transaction processing.

Q: *What happens when we try to create a unique index on a column that contains duplicate values?*
A: An abend takes place when a unique index contains duplicate values. A unique index cannot contain any duplicate values. When we try to create the index, the SQL Server will check the existing data to verify that no duplicates exist. If a duplicate value is encountered the command is aborted and an error message is returned.

Q: *Does Sybase allow null values in a column with a unique index?*
A: Yes, it allows one null value. For this reason it is important to remember that if the unique index is being used to enforce a primary key rule, all columns that make up the primary key should be defined as NOT NULL. However, if the primary key constraint is used to generate the unique index then the columns will not allow nulls.

Q: *When creating a nonunique clustered index, why would we use the "ignore_dup_row" option?*
A: We would use this option when we want the SQL Server to bypass inserts that contain duplicate values rather than return an error message. This is useful when inserting a large number of records with a single insert statement.

Q: *What does the UPDATE STATISTICS command do?*
A: The UPDATE STATISTICS command updates the distribution information for the indexes. This information is used by the cost-based optimizer to determine which index will be selected in an effort to provide the best performance.

Q: *Describe some scenarios that would cause the transaction log to fill up.*

A: The transaction log could fill up:

- When the transaction log is not dumped often enough
- When a single insert, update, or delete affects a very large number of rows
- When a transaction remains open for a long period of time

Q: *What are some common DBCC commands that you include in your backup procedures?*

A: `dbcc checkdb`
`dbcc checkalloc`
`dbcc checkcatalog`

Q: *What is the command "dbcc dbrepair" used for?*

A: This command is used to drop a damaged database when the drop database command does not work. It cannot be invoked from within the damaged database.

Q: *Why should we separate the transaction log and the database onto separate physical devices?*

A: If the database and log reside on the same physical device and the device fails, all changes since the last dump will be lost. If it resides on a separate physical device and the device fails we can still dump the log and provide up-to-the-minute recoverability.

Q: *When would you use "dump tran with no_log"?*

A: The "dump tran with no_log" should be used when the transaction log is completely full and "dump tran with truncate only" fails. It removes the inactive part of the log (everything prior to the oldest open transaction). You should always dump the database immediately after performing a dump tran with no_log.

Q: *If an old transaction remains open and is causing the log to fill up, what should you do?*

A: If the log is filled up it could become necessary to kill the process that opened the transaction. When this happens the transaction will fail and roll back. Assuming there is still some space left on the log device, the transaction log can now be dumped.

Q: *What should be done if the transaction log fills up and it is unacceptable to dump tran with no_log?*

A: Increase the space allocated to the transaction log by adding another device fragment and using the alter database command. The log can then extend to the new fragment.

Q: *What is the role of sysusages in the master database?*

A: Sysusages is used to associate the device fragments to the databases. It is an associative table that resolves the many-to-many relationship between sys-devices and sysdatabases. Every time a new fragment is allocated to a database via create database or alter database, a new record is added to the sysusages table.

Q: *What is the system procedure created by the user that monitors the space usage on the segment and dumps the log when the last-chance threshold is reached?*

A: sp_thresholdaction

Q: *What is the last-chance threshold?*

A: The last-chance threshold is an estimate of the number of pages necessary to back up the transaction log. When the number of available log pages reaches this threshold, a user-defined stored procedure called sp_thresholdaction is executed. This stored procedure is usually used to dump the transaction log before it's too late.

Q: *What is the recovery interval?*

A: The recovery interval is an estimate of the time required by SQL Server to recover in case of a system failure. When this interval is reached the checkpoint process will write the dirty pages to disk. The amount of time between checkpoints is determined by the amount of activity that is going on and the speed at which the transaction log is growing.

Q: *What does truncate log on checkpoint do?*

A: When this database option is turned on, the inactive portion of the transaction log is truncated every time a checkpoint is encountered.

Q: *What is the impact on performance of increasing the packet size?*

A: The packet size determines how much data can be placed in a single network packet. There is a tradeoff between large and small packet sizes. When there are few requests being made over the network and the process that is being run is sending (bcp) or receiving large amounts of data, a larger packet size will usually improve performance. However, if there are many users sending or requesting data frequently, the large packet size may cause more collisions, which will decrease network throughput and ultimately decrease performance. In addition, specifying a large packet size requires additional memory resources.

Q: *What happens (internally) when you try to insert a row into a table with clustered index and the data page is full?*

A: Whenever a row needs to be inserted into a page that is full then a page split occurs. A page split is when the SQL Server acquires an empty page, redirects the pointers, moves half of the records from the full page to the newly acquired page, and inserts the new record in the appropriate spot. Frequent page splitting will degrade performance.

Q: *How are rows added to a table that does not have a clustered index?*

A: The newly added rows are appended to the bottom (last data page) of the table. This can cause lock contention if the application is insert-intensive. To resolve this contention, consider a clustered index (to be used as a hashing key), which would distribute the inserts in a more even manner.

Q: *What does it mean to stripe a database dump?*
A: Striping a database dump distributes the writes across multiple devices simultaneously to improve dump performance.

Q: *What is the advantage and disadvantage of performing remote backups?*
A: The advantage of using a remote backup is that a single operator has access to all of the dump devices and can centralize the process. The disadvantage is that the information needs to be transported via the network, which will cause significant network traffic.

Q: *Certain system tables contain important information that is useful in recovering the MASTER database and should be backed up (text file and/or hard copy) on a regular basis. Name some tables that would fit this description.*
A: SYSDATABASES

SYSDEVICES

SYSUSAGES

SYSLOGINROLES

SYSLOGINS

Q: *How do we recover the MASTER database after the database becomes corrupt?*
A: 1. Replace with generic master database "– buildmaster –m".

2. Start SQL Server in single-user mode "– startserver –m".

3. Load the most recent dump of master.

4. Restart the SQL Server in single-user mode.

5. Check sysusages, sysdevices, and sysdatabases against a recent backup copy.

6. Run dbcc checkalloc and dbcc checkdb on all databases.

7. Restart the server in multiuser mode.

8. Dump the master database.

Q: *Describe what the following command is used for:*
```
"SELECT data_pgs (8, doampg) FROM sysindexes WHERE id = 8"
```
A: This command is used to quickly estimate the number of pages that the transaction log is currently occupying. Assuming the transaction log is on a separate device, we can subtract the number of pages returned by this command from the total number of pages allocated to the log device to find the number of pages remaining before the log fills up. This can be incorporated in a script and used to monitor the growth over time.

Q: *Can you describe what Open Server is?*
A: The Open Server is a utility that provides additional functionality to an SQL Server. It contains libraries, tools, and interfaces that enable us to create a cus-

tom server. A gateway open server enables applications to access foreign data sources as if they were SQL Servers.

Q: *What is stored in the network libraries?*
A: The network libraries provide a standard interface to various transport protocols, including TDS, providing both protocol and operating system independence.

Q: *What is TDS?*
A: TDS, Tabular Data Stream, is the proprietary Sybase protocol format for data representation and communication between clients and servers.

Q: *What are the different API libraries available for application development in Sybase?*
A: DB-Lib, CT-Lib, Srv-Lib, CS-Lib.

Q: *What does client/server programming mean?*
A: Client/server programming is a form of distributed processing whereby one unit sends a request (client) to another unit (server). The unit that receives the request processes it and if necessary returns the results to the originator.

Q: *Give some examples of well-known client/server applications.*
A: World Wide Web, X-Windows, Gopher.

Q: *How is network and platform independence assured by Sybase libraries?*
A: Through the use of platform-specific network libraries (netlibs) provided by Sybase.

Q: *With regard to an Open Client or Open Server application, what is a context?*
A: A context is a data structure that contains information about the operating environment of a client or server application, e.g., USEnglish or German environment, etc.

Q: *What is the meaning of "passthrough mode"?*
A: The passthrough option, when utilized in a gateway application, disables translation of the clients' requests by the Open Server and the results from the remote server.

Q: *Name some of the events that can occur in an Open Server application.*
A: Attention, Connect, Disconnect, Language, RPC, Start, Stop, Bulk, Cursor, Dynamic, Client message, Option.

Q: *What are the three modes in which an Open Server application can be utilized?*
A: Stand Alone mode

    Gateway mode

    Auxiliary mode

Q: *What is the maximum number of server threads that are instantiated when a client connection is made?*
A: One.

Q: *What are the different types of threads that can be generated in an open server application?*

A: Event-driven threads

Service threads (persistent threads)

Site-handler threads (instantiated when an SQL server connects to an open server for executing an RPC, etc.)

Q: *What is a message queue?*

A: A message queue is a structure that enables threads to communicate with each other. A thread can place a message in a message queue that can be retrieved by other threads.

Q: *What is a "state transition" and how can it be detected?*

A: A state transition occurs when a thread completes its current task. For example, a state transition occurs when the thread receives a language command. State transitions can be detected by installing a callback handler using the srv_callback routine.

Q: *What is "ct_bind" used for?*

A: ct_bind is used to associate columns in the result set to variables in the program.

Q: *What is multithreading?*

A: Multithreading is the switching of threads (connections between a client and a server) that occurs within a single process.

17
VSAM

George W. Harrison

Introduction

VSAM (Virtual Storage Access Method) was produced by IBM as a replacement for ISAM. VSAM supports functions similar to those of ISAM, but provides better performance. While other access methods were device-dependent, each requiring a separate utility, VSAM supports four dataset operations—key-sequenced, entry-sequenced, relative-record, and linear—and requires only one utility. VSAM is a component of both IBM's VSE and MVS operating systems, thus allowing dataset portability between operating systems.

Questions and Answers

Terminology and Concepts

Q: *Name some of the differences between CA and CI.*

A: CI, Control Interval, is a fixed length of information and is the minimum amount of data transferred between virtual storage and DASD. The size of a control interval must be a multiple of 512 when less than or equal to 8192. If the size is larger than 8192, it must be a multiple of 2048.

   CA, Control Area, is auxiliary storage that is reserved by VSAM to hold or receive control intervals. The minimum size of a control area is two control intervals. The maximum size is one cylinder.

Q: *How do you specify the amount of CI to be used?*

A: The amount of control interval space available to a file is specified in the FREESPACE (FSPC) parameter of the DEFINE command.

Q: *How do you specify the amount of CA available to a file?*

A: The amount of control interval space available to a file is also specified in the FREESPACE (FSPC) parameter of the DEFINE command. The amount of FREESPACE specified must be large enough for at least one control interval.

Note: The FREESPACE parameter is specified as FSPC (X Y)—where X is the percentage of the control interval to be left empty, and Y is the percentage of the control area to be left empty after a key-sequenced file is initially loaded.

Q: *If, for example, FSPC (100 100) were specified, does that mean that both the control intervals and control areas would be left empty because 100 percent of both the control interval and the control areas are specified to be empty?*

A: No, they would not be left empty. One record would be written for each control interval, and one control interval would be written for each control area.

Q: *Can you run out of CA?*

A: Yes. When you run out of freespace, there will be no space available to add a new record.

Q: *If you can run out of CA, how do you know it has happened?*

A: When you try to add a new record, a message will inform you that this has happened.

Q: *If you do run out of CA, what should you do about it?*

A: You have to reorganize the file. Reorganizing a file involves copying the file (building a backup) onto another area or media (tape), deleting the file you want to reorganize, redefining the file (allocating more space, freespace, etc.), and reloading the file.

Q: *When reorganizing a file, do you have to sort the backup copy of the file prior to reloading it?*

A: If you are using IDCAMS, you do not have to sort the records.

Q: *What types of datasets are supported by VSAM?*

A: The types of datasets supported by VSAM are KSDS (key-sequenced), ESDS (entry-sequenced), RRDS (relative-record), and LDS (linear).

Q: *What is the difference in the way an application would access a relative-record dataset and a linear dataset?*

A: Records in a relative-record dataset are accessed by relative-record number, a sequential position of the record in relation to the first record in the dataset. Linear dataset records are accessed sequentially, in the same way as an entry-sequenced dataset.

Q: *How are records stored in each type of data file supported by VSAM?*

A: A key-sequenced dataset is ordered by key and is accessed by an index.

An entry-sequenced dataset has to have its data stored sequentially. Records can be added only at the end of the dataset.

Data stored in relative-record datasets are stored in "slots." Data is accessed by record number.

Data stored in linear datasets are stored sequentially, similar to the way records are stored in an entry-sequenced dataset, except that control fields used by the other access methods are not present.

Q: *Can you access variable-length blocked records using VSAM?*
A: Yes.

Q: *What is Record Level Sharing?*
A: Record Level Sharing (RLS) is a way of defining VSAM files as remote resources so that they can be accessible in a sysplex processing environment. Record Level Sharing permits multiple CICS applications in different CICS regions using different MVS images to share data.

Q: *What is a cluster?*
A: A cluster is a VSAM-defined structure and consists of data and, if the access requires a key, index components.

Q: *Where would you use the UPGRADE parameter and what function does it perform?*
A: UPGRADE is an option that can be specified when defining an alternate index. Whenever you update the base cluster, if you have specified UPGRADE, the alternate indexes dataset will also be (automatically) updated.

Q: *What is the function performed by a VSAM "ALTER"?*
A: A VSAM "ALTER" allows modification of the characteristics of a dataset.

Q: *Name the different kinds of catalogs that are accessible to a VSAM user.*
A: A VSAM user can access a VSAM master catalog as well as user catalogs.

Q: *What is the CRA?*
A: The CRA is the Catalog Recovery Area.

Q: *How do you define a CRA?*
A: A CRA is automatically created if "RECOVERABLE" parameter is specified when the VSAM master or user catalog is defined.

Q: *What is a VSAM model?*
A: A VSAM model provides different default values than the system defaults provided by the DEFINE command.

Q: *Is it advisable to use a VSAM model?*
A: It is not recommended to use VSAM models. Once created, they tend to be used by programmers without thought being given to individual dataset requirements.

Q: *Where, why, and when do you use the ERASE option when deleting a dataset?*
A: The ERASE option fills the data component of a cluster or an alternate index with binary zeros, thus erasing all previously written data. It is not recom-

mended to use this option because it is not needed for security. In addition, it is time consuming.

Alternate Indexes

Q: *What is an alternate index?*
A: An alternate index is an additional way of accessing a key-sequenced data record stored in a base cluster.

Q: *What is a path?*
A: A path is a set of linkages that connect alternate indexes to a base cluster.

Q: *What is a path used for?*
A: A path is used by VSAM to access a record in a base cluster by means of an alternate index.

Q: *When would you use an alternate index?*
A: An alternate index would be used whenever it is necessary to access data by more than one means.

Q: *Do alternate indexes have to be unique?*
A: No, alternate indexes do not have to be unique.

Q: *Can you build an alternate index for an ESDS?*
A: Yes, they can be built for KSDS as well as for ESDS.

Q: *How would you specify an alternate index (i.e., what steps do you have to execute)?*
A: To allocate an alternate index you have to:
   1. Define the alternate index and relate it to its base cluster.
   2. Define the path that will allow access to the base cluster via the alternate index.
   3. Build the alternate index.

Q: *How do you determine the record size of an alternate index?*
A: This question is best answered by using an example.
   A key-sequenced employee dataset (file) with a key of social security number needs to be accessed by department number. To access this dataset by department, department number has to be specified as an alternate index. Since each department contains more than one employee, the alternate index is nonunique. The minimum record size must account for 5 bytes of control information plus the length of the base cluster key. The maximum record must account for the control information plus the length of the alternate key plus the length of the base cluster key for each allowable prime key.
   In this example, the record key length of the base cluster is 9 bytes, the department number is 4 bytes, and each department has a maximum of 200 employees.

```
RECORD SIZE = 5 + KEY LENGTH OF THE ALTERNATE INDEX + (KEY LENGTH
  OF THE PRIME KEY * THE NUMBER OF NONUNIQUE PRIME KEYS)

MINIMUM RECORD SIZE = 5 + 4 + (9 * 1) = 9 + 9 = 18
MAXIMUM RECORD SIZE = 5 + 4 + (9 * 200) = 9 + 1800 = 1809
```

The record length of this alternate index would then be specified in the define of the alternate index as:

```
RECORDSIZE (18 1809)
```

VSAM Spaces

Q: *What is the difference between a user catalog and a master catalog?*

A: There can be only one master catalog per system, but there can be an unlimited number of user catalogs. Each user catalog has an entry in the master catalog with a connecting pointer.

Q: *What is the difference between a unique dataset and a suballocated dataset?*

A: VSAM uses two types of dataspaces: suballocatable and unique. A suballocatable dataspace can contain one or more datasets, while a unique dataspace can contain only one dataset. A dataset in a suballocated dataspace is a suballocated dataset, while a dataset in a unique dataspace is a unique dataset.

Q: *Under what conditions would you want to define a dataset as being a suballocated dataset?*

A: Under most cases, a dataset would be defined as suballocated. A dataset must be suballocated if the REUSE option is used.

Q: *How can you check how much freespace (unused space) is available for future additions in an ESDS?*

A: The freespace available for future additions to an ESDS can be obtained by checking the FREESPC-BYTES entry in the data component portion of a LISTCAT listing.

Q: *How can you check how much freespace is available for future additions in a KSDS?*

A: The technique used for determining the amount of freespace for an ESDS can also be used for a KSDS.

Q: *What are some of the more important types of information that can be obtained from a LISTCAT?*

A: Some of the information that can be obtained from a LISTCAT:

- The names of the associated entries: data component, index component, and/or alternate index clusters
- KEYLEN—the length of the primary key
- RKP—the relative key position in the record (starting with byte 0)

- AVGLRECL—the minimum record length
- MAXLRECL—the maximum record length

Q: *Where can you find LASTCC and MAXCC entries?*
A: The LASTCC and MAXCC entries can be found on the output produced by the execution of the IDCAMS program.

Q: *What does LASTCC contain?*
A: The LASTCC contains the condition code that resulted from the immediately preceding/executed function command.

Q: *What does MAXCC contain?*
A: MAXCC contains the highest condition code that resulted from the previous functional command stream.

Q: *What is the meaning of condition code "8"?*
A: Condition code "8" means that major functions were bypassed even though the function to be executed was completed. For example, an entry specified to be deleted could not be found.

AMS—Access Method Services

Q: *What is AMS?*
A: AMS stands for Access Method Services. It is an IBM-provided service program that is used to create and maintain datasets.

Q: *How are the services supplied (by AMS) invoked?*
A: Access Method Services are invoked by execution of the IDCAMS program.

Q: *Name five AMS commands and tell what each is used for.*
A: ALTER   Changes the attributes of a previously defined VSAM object
     DEFINE   Defines a VSAM object (catalogs and clusters)
     DELETE   Deletes a VSAM object
     LISTCAT   Lists information contained in a VSAM catalog
     REPRO   Copies, converts, merges, and reorganizes catalogs and datasets

Q: *Can you use AMS to build a generation dataset?*
A: Yes, you can.

Q: *Which command could you use to build a generation dataset (in AMS)?*
A: A GDG can be built by using the DEFINE GDG command.

Q: *What function does the SHAREOPTIONS perform?*
A: SHAREOPTIONS provides data integrity. SHAREOPTIONS is specified in the DEFINE command.

Q: *What is the format of the SHAREOPTIONS command?*
A: The format is

```
SHAREOPTIONS (CROSS-REGION | CROSS-SYSTEM)
```

Q: *What parameters are valid with SHAREOPTIONS?*

A: CROSS-REGION can have values 1 through 4. CROSS-SYSTEM options can have a value of only 3 or 4.

Q: *When would you use each of the SHAREOPTIONS options?*

A: CROSS-REGION: You would use the CROSS-REGION options as follows:

1. When the dataset can be opened by only one user for writing and many users for reading. Read and write integrity (VSAM) will ensure that these rules are adhered to and that someone with read access cannot update records.

2. This option is the same as option 1 except that only write integrity is provided. Read integrity must be provided by the user, as no controls are provided to prevent a user from reading a record that is being updated (by another user).

3. The dataset can be opened by multiple users for updating and reading. Read and write integrity must be provided by the user.

4. This option provides the same level of read-write integrity as option 3. The difference is that VSAM will not allow a control area (CA) split. Instead, VSAM provides a new buffer for each direct-access request (for space).

   CROSS-SYSTEM: CROSS-SYSTEM option 3 is the same as CROSS-REGION option 3, and CROSS-SYSTEM option 4 is the same as CROSS-REGION option 4.

Q: *What function does the UPGRADE option do?*

A: UPGRADE allows an alternate index to be updated at the same time as the base cluster is being updated.

Q: *What is a reusable dataset?*

A: A reusable dataset is one that can be reloaded without using the Access Method Services command DELETE/DEFINE before reloading the dataset. In addition, the REUSE option must be specified when the dataset is defined and also when reloading with the REPRO command.

Q: *What is the sequence set?*

A: The sequence set is the lowest-level index that is built (and updated) by AMS.

Q: *What function is performed by the IMBED parameter?*

A: The IMBED option places the sequence set with the data component. The sequence set for each control area is written on the first track of the control area as many times as will fit. This reduces rotational delay and increases the amount of disk storage needed for the dataset.

Q: *What function is performed by the REPLICATE parameter?*

A: The REPLICATE option writes the sequence set for each CA as many times as will fit on the first track of the CA area. If the IMBED option has been specified, the sequence set is replicated whether or not REPLICATE has been specified.

Q: *Can you build a PDS using AMS facilities?*
A: A PDS cannot be built using AMS.

Q: *What utility is used to load a VSAM dataset?*
A: REPRO is used to load a VSAM dataset.

Q: *Does data have to be sorted prior to loading a VSAM file?*
A: REPRO, while loading a dataset, does a current (record ready to be loaded) record key compare to the key of the last record that has just been loaded. As out-of-sequence conditions are treated as errors, the dataset being loaded has to be in sequence.

Q: *What utilities can be used to back up a KSDS file?*
A: EXPORT or REPRO can be used.

Miscellaneous VSAM

Q: *What can happen if you have an error condition in the master catalog?*
A: If there is an error condition in, or involving, the master catalog, access can be denied to datasets and user catalogs.

Q: *What can happen if you have an error condition in a user catalog?*
A: An error condition in the user catalog can deny access to datasets.

Q: *How can you check the status of the master catalog?*
A: Run a LISTCAT.

Q: *How can you check the status of a user catalog?*
A: Run a LISTCAT.

Q: *Name two different procedures for fixing a problem in the master or user catalog.*
A: 1. A backup copy of a nonrecoverable catalog can be reloaded using REPRO.
   2. The EXPORTCRA command can be used to retrieve catalog information from the Catalog Recovery Area (CRA).

Q: *What is a feedback code?*
A: A feedback code is the return code passed from VSAM to the processing program.

Q: *What is the meaning of a feedback code of 08?*
A: A feedback code of 08 indicates a logical error.

Q: *What is AMP and when would you use it?*
A: AMP is a JCL Access Method Services parameter and is used to override VSAM default parameters. AMP is usually invoked when an improvement in performance is desired.

Q: *What is the AMP parameter BUFNI used for?*
A: BUFNI is used to specify the number of index buffers.

Q: *In AMP, what is BUFND used for?*
A: BUFND is used to specify the number of data buffers.

Q: *What is the AMP parameter BUFSP used for?*
A: BUFSP is used to specify the amount of virtual storage. Virtual storage is used to open a VSAM dataset.

Q: *Where do you specify your BUFNI and your BUFND options?*
A: In the DD statement (MVS).

Q: *What kind of password protection (if any) is available in VSAM?*
A: Password protection can be defined for clusters as well as for data and index components.

Q: *Name and describe the various levels of password protection.*
A: There are four levels of password protection.
   1. MASTER PASSWORD—Master password protection allows all operations—read, add, update, and delete—for the dataset, its index(es), and its catalog entry.
   2. CONTROL INTERVAL PASSWORD—Control interval password protection allows users to read and write entire control intervals. This is usually not made available for general use.
   3. UPDATE PASSWORD—Update password protection allows records to be retrieved, updated, deleted, and added.
   4. READ PASSWORD—Read password protection allows read access only.

Q: *What is the purpose of the VERIFY command?*
A: The VERIFY command is used to compare the end-of-file information (high-used RBA) in the VSAM catalog with the actual end of file. If these indicators are not in agreement, the end-of-file information in the catalog is corrected.

Q: *Where and when would you use the VERIFY command?*
A: Files are verified at the OPEN, so it is rare that a VERIFY will actually be executed. Error messages will indicate when a VERIFY should be performed.

18

Client/Server Systems Architectures

David Dodge

Introduction

Like many relatively new terms in the computer industry, *client/server* means different things to different people. Generally, however, client/server is understood to mean a computer system that consists of the following elements:

- One or more intelligent workstations, personal computers, or portable devices that function as "clients" by requesting services from another system or system component

- One or more platforms (e.g., personal computers, minicomputers, or mainframe hosts) that function as a "server" by providing processing, database, and communication services to clients

- The networking infrastructure and software that links them all

From an end-user viewpoint, client/server computing usually means being able to access a range of data, applications, computing power, printing, and other services from a single workstation—without having to know which machine or component of the system is actually providing the requested service. This capability or characteristic is referred to as *transparency* of location.

The Client/Server Environment: An Overview

The catalysts for the change to client/server computing have included market forces, increased competitiveness in many dimensions of business, an emphasis on business process reengineering, and new corporate attitudes about the value of information. No one can deny, however, the role of new technologies in producing the shift. Over the past few years, a vast array of enabling products and tools has been introduced at what continues to be a blistering pace. Different languages and development techniques have followed. In fact, it is the technologies, tools, and techniques that make client/server computing something new; not simply the architectural configuration or the role of any particular piece of hardware or software. Nonetheless, most people would agree that "client/server" represents the computer architecture model of the 1990s and beyond.

The most widely used operating systems today include the various forms of Unix offered by vendors, Microsoft's Windows and Windows NT, and IBM's OS/2 and OS/2 Warp.

Networking Operating Systems

A network operating system (NOS) is the software program that makes it possible for computers to communicate with one another or with a network and to share resources. The NOS enables a user to access a database, use a printer, or use another computer's applications as if they resided on his or her workstation. The most robust LAN operating systems, such as Banyan's VINES, Novell's NetWare, and Microsoft's LAN Manager were structured more like minicomputer or Unix operating systems from the outset. Since their server software mediates simultaneous requests for network resources and runs multiple programs at one time, they are considered to be multiuser, multitasking systems. Although a server can also function as an individual workstation with some LAN operating systems or special versions, larger networks are usually not configured this way. Novell, NetWare, and Banyan VINES actually require a dedicated server.

Another advantage of the most robust, multitasking LAN operating systems is that they usually offer additional features and tools for managing the network. System administrators also normally want software that provides enhanced security, print spooling, network administration capabilities, diagnostic support, improved memory management, and greater fault tolerance when purchasing these systems. The selection of a LAN operating system is normally made based on these characteristics and on whether the organization wants to dedicate a workstation to the server role.

Database Management Systems

A database management system (DBMS) is a software program that is designed to collect, organize, store, and control data. In conjunction with a database application, it also permits the data to be updated, retrieved, and viewed. The services or capabilities typically provided by a DBMS include the following:

- *Data integrity.* Ensures that data is accurate or valid and does not become inadvertently corrupted

- *Data manipulation.* Enables an end user to create, update, modify, delete, and sort the data
- *Data definition.* Allows the data to be defined, structured, and indexed
- *Data access.* Controls and optimizes access to the data
- *Data presentation.* Displays the data
- *Data storage.* Provides the fields, records, or tables that hold the data

Most client/server databases use a relational database model. This model does not employ a parent/child concept to show the relationship between different data items. Instead, the data is organized into tables with columns and rows. Column names and indexing numbers or keys allow multiple relationships to be created among the data items. As a result, each table can be changed without changing the entire database structure. This gives the relational database model tremendous flexibility, and it provides the data through searches that do not rely on the position of the data in the database. These capabilities make relational DBMSs particularly suited for client/server architectures because of the ease with which they handle queries and the high degree of data integrity they provide.

Parallel Processing

Another evolving improvement in client/server architectures involves the use of parallel processing capabilities. Parallel processing refers to the way that some newer computer hardware and databases can simultaneously perform a set of computing tasks rather than doing each task consecutively. These technical improvements often rely on shared memory features, a redesign of the way transactions or queries are handled by the application software, and a strong linkage between the underlying hardware architecture and the relational database operations.

Parallel processing can permit increased transaction speed, better access to more data at one time, and a greater ability to add more processing power to an architecture. These improvements are generally characterized as better performance and scalability. Most computer professionals expect parallel processing to begin to heavily influence client/server architectures in large companies over the next decade.

Terminology

A partial mastery of some of the terminology and buzzwords associated with client/server computing will improve any technical interview as long as such terms aren't used to hide a lack of knowledge. A handful of the most frequently encountered terms and phrases that haven't as yet been introduced in this chapter are defined as follows:

Cooperative processing: Cooperative processing describes how a computer processing job is shared among two or more computing platforms. It implies that the processing workload is divided up in the most efficient fashion. This term and the term *distributed processing* are frequently used as synonyms for client/server computing.

Distributed processing: Distributed processing refers to computer processing carried out in different locations (i.e., geographically dispersed) on independent computer platforms connected by a network. The aim here is also the most efficient use of computing resources by dedicating each central processing unit (CPU) to the task for which it is best suited.

Downsizing: Downsizing can imply full replacement of a mainframe host environment with networks and workstations. It definitely means off-loading significant processing workload or applications from the host, and deferring or avoiding altogether the purchase of additional host-based MIPS.

Interoperability: Interoperability refers to the cooperative operation of software programs that reside on dissimilar computer systems. It implies the ready exchange of data and functionality.

Open system: Open system describes a computer system or major component that has its interface services and formats designed to enable application software built for it to interoperate with other applications on local or remote systems, and to be ported or moved to a range of other systems with minimal changes.

Topology: A topology is the layout or blueprint of a network. A logical topology describes how data and signals travel over the network to its stations—i.e., sequentially or in a broadcast. A physical topology describes how the cables or wires are laid out to connect the nodes, e.g., a star or daisy chain.

Benefits of Client/Server Architectures

Properly architected and implemented client/server systems can yield tremendous benefits and advantages. One of their key advantages is the capability they provide to distribute data and processing to the places around the system and around the organization that make the most sense. Data, for example, can be managed centrally, but distributed in servers among user departments or regional branches. This distribution scheme can put the data closer to users and improve system performance. Similarly, if processing tasks are properly shared among system components (e.g., some on the server, some on a host, and some on the personal computer), the computing strength of each central processing unit (CPU) is likely to be the best utilized. Moreover, processing can be done at the place that will minimize data transfer requirements. If 50 customer records are to be retrieved, for example, it makes more sense for the sorting to be done at the site of the database rather than transferring a quarter of a million customer records over a network to do the sorting elsewhere.

Another key advantage of client/server computing is improved access to data. Not only can data be positioned for better access, client/server technologies can improve the retrieval process and integration of the data. When data from several systems or databases must be pulled to provide a required input, or when data from multiple sources must be viewed simultaneously, client/server system interfaces and server-based extracts can meet the need.

Well-designed client/server applications are also generally easier to use than are their conventional counterparts. The graphical user interfaces that typify new client/server applications employ point-and-click symbols, pull-down menus, and other graphical features that make them easier for users to understand. These applications can be structured to reflect a more natural, intuitive workflow, as well. As a result, less training and experience are usually required for end users to be competent with the system. These are significant benefits for organizations that contend with high employee turnover or small training budgets.

More efficient use of computer resources and the capability to add computing power incrementally are further benefits of client/server technology. Clearly, the opportunity to shift processing workload from mainframe computers to microcomputers is a cost-effective strategy when the smaller machine can support the business requirements. The substantially lower costs of microcomputer processing as measured in millions of instructions per second (MIPs) is well documented. Likewise, when requirements grow or additional capabilities are needed, the modular nature of client/server systems permits additional components to be linked to the network rather than pursuing a more expensive mainframe upgrade. The fact that client/server systems can be constructed in a modular fashion also contributes to system reliability and survivability. When one part of the system malfunctions, it can usually be isolated and not impact operation of the rest of the network. Alternatively, another network CPU might be called on to perform all or part of the processing a failed CPU was handling.

Client/server technologies can increase the probability that different information systems can interoperate, as well. Common interfaces, adoption of standards, and the use of operating systems and common query languages, such as Unix and SQL, have fostered more data exchange and application sharing. The opportunity to develop highly "portable" application software is raised significantly by the same technology elements. This means that applications developed to run on one type of computer platform can also run on other platforms with little or no modification. The application development languages, tools, and techniques that are part of client/server approaches, further enhance creation of this transferable or portable quality.

Implementation of client/server computing also provides opportunities for instituting standards and controls. With the proliferation of personal computers over the past few years, some organizations believe they have lost meaningful control of these resources. Many companies are plagued by a lack of data standards, redundancies among variant database products, and multiple suites of contending personal productivity software. Organizations that successfully pursue client/server application development tend to use this activity to reassert centralized authority over key shared resources, and, at the same time, increase end user autonomy with respect to unique needs and resources. In other words, end users in each functional department can be freed to address their unique requirements, but common needs and shared client/server resources are returned to the control of the Information Systems Department.

Client/server computing additionally represents the means by which many newer and emerging information technologies can be readily integrated with business applications. Multimedia, desktop imaging, pen-based computing, wireless local area networks, and speech recognition are just a few of the technologies that client/server is positioned to accept and leverage.

The technology benefits alone, however, are usually insufficient reasons to incur the costs of moving toward client/server. Any benefit or advantage of client/server computing should really be expressed in business terms and shown to be directly applicable to a company's business requirements. Improved data access, for example, should mean improved customer service, more rapid response to market conditions, or increased competitiveness. The predicted impact on the corporate bottom line, market share, and customer loyalty are other good yardsticks for determining if implementing client/server is justified for most companies.

Questions and Answers

The questions and answers in this chapter have been broken into major headings designed to classify subject material for easy access by the reader.

Architectural Requirements and Strategies

Q: *How do you provide business justification for transitioning to client/server computing?*

A: The best business justification can differ from organization to organization. Normally, though, the expense and effort associated with the transition to client/server computing is expressed in terms of:

- Achieving better price/performance from computer platforms
- Reducing the costs of procuring computer hardware; reducing training or maintenance costs over time
- Achieving greater interoperability and portability among applications
- Improving a company's competitive posture through productivity, reduced cycle time, faster responses to market changes, etc.

Q: *Explain the relationship between business process reengineering and a client/server architecture.*

A: Business process reengineering examines how an organization operates today versus how it could operate in the future. Business processes, work flows, task integration, and decision-making levels can all be redesigned for greater efficiency and speed. A client/server architecture often provides the enabling technology set to implement reengineered processes. Shared databases, networks, teleconferencing, and horizontally integrated application software that can be remotely accessed are just some of the architecture characteristics that can be important in achieving process reengineering.

Q: *Identify some of the ways an application can be placed or distributed between a client workstation and a server.*

A: An application ordinarily has several components, including the user interface, its presentation management services, its business logic, and database logic. Any of these software components can reside on the client workstation, including a subset of the database management system services itself. The server would generally provide the DBMS services, and could house any of the other software components if required to improve processing efficiency.

Q: *What are some of the rules of thumb that can be used to decide where to place the data in a client/server-based system?*

A: Data should normally be placed as close to the primary users as possible, while still protecting data security and data integrity. If important data is likely to be lost on individual workstations because of problems such as LAN instability or lack of user training, then it is better to keep the data on a server. Typically, data should be stored at the lowest point in the architecture that satisfies sharing requirements, timeliness/performance needs, capacity as well as update and access requirements, and issues of ownership/security. The requirements of the business rather than the needs of individual users should predominate if conflict occurs.

Q: *Name some of the areas in which technical alternatives should be considered when designing a client/server architecture.*

A: Alternative technologies, standards, methodologies, and techniques should be reviewed when building a client/server system to ensure the optimum is selected. Other areas in which technical alternatives need to be considered would include data and processing placement, user interface, component configuration, transport/communications media requirements, and conversion approaches.

Q: *How should you approach identifying the end users of a system and what do you need to know from them?*

A: You need to look for both the primary user of a system, such as a customer service representative or a salesperson, and any secondary users, such as a supervisor or an executive. An executive, of course, can be a primary user. Check an organization chart, understand where the information flows, and look outside the boundaries of the organization to identify potential users, such as suppliers or customers. Each user will have his or her own expectations and needs. Ask about the types of data they want, formatting and reporting requirements, how they want to interact with the system (e.g., keyboard, mouse, light pen, touch screen), whom they communicate with, and the system speed and capacity they must have. These are only a few examples of what you need to know from each type of end user.

Q: *If an organization says it wishes to use "groupware" to improve communications, is there a need for a client/server architecture?*

A: Probably. The term "groupware" refers to a set of applications intended to provide electronic support to groups of people that usually work together. It can be loosely applied to applications such as electronic mail, and more accurately applied to structured workflow software and robust, multi-user software such as Lotus Notes. These types of software typically require significant group interaction and a client/server architecture that facilitates such electronic communication and coordination.

Q: *How is the term "peer-to-peer" applied to client/server computing?*

A: Peer-to-peer usually refers to a communication link whose two sides use the same protocol to carry on a networked exchange of data. In client/server computing, the term describes communications between equal parts of the system. Normally, every computing platform can share information with every other platform on the network without having to be reliant on a server.

Q: *When migrating from a host-based environment to a client/server architecture, what are some of the issues that must be anticipated?*

A: Migration from a mainframe host environment to client/server computing can mean a big change in technology and in other areas. Some of these other issues or areas that need to be anticipated would include the political shifts that might take place as more people have access to data, changes in training requirements, and changes in relationships with external organizations or customers. Workflow management, business processes, and internal organizational relationships could also be altered as client/server technology provides additional analytic capabilities, faster computing, and greater opportunity for productivity improvements.

Q: *How do technology and training requirements change when an organization adopts a client/server strategy?*

A: Client/server computing will demand new skills and different types of training for an organization's end users, system developers, and the information systems maintenance staff because of new design and development techniques such as data and process modeling, prototyping, windows design flow, human engineering factors, and distributed design considerations. New technology skills must also be cultivated in areas such as the use of application development tools, local area network management, system and application integration, and coding skills in languages like C and SQL.

Q: *Why is it important to understand whether you are building either an on-line transaction processing system or a decision support system (DSS)?*

A: Many of the characteristics of an OLTP system and a decision support system are different. For example, an OLTP system typically requires high performance and greater availability. A DSS usually requires greater flexibility, has fewer users, and its database values are more static. Their respective response time requirements are often different. An OLTP usually processes individual records and transactions, while a DSS more frequently looks at groups of records.

Q: *What are some key changes that take place in the roles and responsibilities of a company's Information System (I/S) department when the company adopts client/server computing?*

A: Ordinarily the Information Systems department will have to become more a source of standards and system support than purely a development and maintenance organization. Users will look to the I/S department to provide policies, technology recommendations, management of the network infrastructure, data management, and other aspects of systems management. The I/S department often will need to shift more toward responsibilities like system and software procurement, electronic software distribution and update, help desk-type operations, software licensing, and data archiving.

Q: *What are some of the key models or types of client/server architectures that companies frequently use?*

A: There are at least five commonly encountered architecture models. They are:

- *Distributed Presentation*—where part of the presentation handling executes on the client and the rest executes on the server
- *Remote Presentation*—where the presentation handling resides solely on the client workstation, while servers execute the business functions and data management
- *Distributed Function*—where the presentation resides on the client, and the application or business functions execute on both the client and the server
- *Remote Data Management*—where the presentation and business functions execute on the client, while data management resides remotely on the server
- *Distributed Database*—where the data management functions and data reside on more than one client or server, and can be accessed or updated from any system in the architecture

Q: *What is meant when someone refers to a two-tier client/server architecture or one that is described as a three-tier architecture?*

A: A two-tier client/server architecture generally has the user presentation, business logic, and enabling software on the client workstation, while the data resides on the server. A three-tier architecture usually has the user presentation on the client, the business logic and other enabling software on the server device, and the data is kept on yet another server.

Q: *Define the term "middleware" when it is used in the context of a client/ server architecture.*

A: Middleware is the collective term for the enabling software that manages all communications between clients and servers by structuring the method of communications and the protocols. Middleware brokers or conveys requests for data (queries), updates (transactions), or requests for services to the server(s). This software also tells the requesting client the outcome of its query.

Client/Server Architecture Components

Q: *Name some of the types of uses or special functions that servers support in a client/server system.*

A: Clients and servers communicate with each other over a network. Servers can perform general functions or they can be dedicated to special functions such as a database server, applications server, print server, facsimile/communications server, or image server.

Q: *Specify some types of applications or systems that can use a client/server architecture.*

A: These applications can include:

- Spreadsheets and word processing application packages
- Decision support systems or executive information systems such as those used for sales and marketing trend analysis
- On-line transaction processing systems such as those employed in order entry and fulfillment
- Data access/data integration systems such as those used in customer service support

Q: *What are some of the network architecture issues you must address in the transition to client/server computing?*

A: The first issue is whether there is any existing network architecture. If so, is it sufficient to support the number of anticipated users and the amount of traffic or transactions that users will need to send over the network? Additionally, it is important to determine if there are any corporate network protocols or standards that must be adopted or adhered to in the move to client/server.

Q: *Describe the key advantages provided by a client/server database.*

A: A key advantage of a client/server database is the ability to locate the data in the most advantageous place for large numbers of users. Most of the important advantages of a client/server system result from splitting the computer processing between the client platform and the database server. One such advantage is that the workstation needs only the power and speed to be able to run the front-end software, thereby extending the life of less capable PCs that don't have the memory and processing horsepower required to operate a complex DBMS. Client/server databases also help reduce the amount of data transferred over the network, sending only the results sets rather than an entire file.

Q: *Explain some of the pluses and minuses of using a Unix-server DBMS.*

A: A high-end Unix system can support several times the number of database users that most PC client/server DBMSs can handle. Greater speed on a Unix RISC platform is another advantage. A Unix-server DBMS also supports various forms of advanced multiprocessing and has better security features than PC-based DBMSs. On the minus side, Unix-based DBMSs are usually harder to learn and more difficult to use. There are fewer experts around, and Unix-based DBMSs are more expensive than PC DBMSs. Finally, Unix-based DBMSs need a more powerful, robust, and expensive platform on which to run.

Q: *How does a "repository" fit into a client/server architecture?*

A: A repository is simply an automated facility for storing descriptions of data, objects, processes, policies, and related information that support software development or management of a system. A repository can sit within a client/server architecture on any mode so that it is accessible to those users who need it.

Q: *What is the starting point for determining whether you should use either a client/server database management system or a stand-alone PC DBMS?*

A: The most significant question to be asked at the outset is whether you require simultaneous multi-user access. If you don't, then select a stand-alone PC DBMS. If you do, then you're likely to need a server-based DBMS.

Q: *What is IBM's DRDA?*

A: The Distributed Relational Database Architecture (DRDA) is IBM's standard for promoting multivendor database interoperability. DRDA handles SQL interoperability across heterogeneous database servers (i.e., similar operating systems, networks, and hardware platforms).

Q: *What is a remote procedure call?*

A: A remote procedure call is an element of an application program that transfers control and data to another part of the program. A Remote Procedure Call (RPC) is used to transfer control and data across a network. When an RPC is executed, the calling program is temporarily suspended while a set of parameters is transferred to another network node. It is there that the procedure is carried out. When the procedure is complete, the results are sent back to the original station where the calling program continues its operation. Remote procedure calls are important mechanisms in distributed transaction processing.

Q: *Explain what is meant by the term "two-phase commit."*

A: Two-phase commit refers to the two message-passing phases of a transaction processing event. The first phase occurs when a coordinating node sends a message to subordinate nodes on a network to determine if all required work has been completed. If so, the transactional updates are temporarily recorded in nonvolatile storage. The second phase message is sent when the coordinating node determines whether to abort the transaction or permanently commit the update to stable storage.

Q: *What is the definition of DCE (Distributed Computing Environment)?*

A: The Distributed Computing Environment (DCE) is an open systems standard published by the Open Software Foundation. It describes an integrated set of technologies that are intended to promote interoperability (i.e., make it easier to develop, use, and maintain applications in a heterogeneous distributed environment). DCE identifies specific technologies to support remote procedures calls, distributed naming services, distributed file services, time-stamping and synchronization, network security, and thread APIs.

Q: *How does disk mirroring provide database integrity?*

A: Disk mirroring provides database integrity by ensuring that data is automatically written to (recorded on) two or more storage devices so that it can be recovered even if you suffer media failure in one copy or device. Sometimes disk mirroring is accomplished by writing to a duplicate database on another platform; sometimes it is done on another portion of the same hard disk.

Local Area Networks

Q: *What are the advantages offered by each of the two basic physical LAN topologies?*

A: Under the daisy chain topology, the cable is run along the shortest path between each network node. The result is that this topology uses far less cable. This topology also does not require special power or space for a wiring hub. The star topology has each node connected via a central wiring hub, usually located in a wiring closet. This topology's primary advantage is survivability. Even if the cable between the hub and any one station is lost, the rest of the network will remain operating. With the star topology, it is easier to install, maintain, and change node locations.

Q: *What is the purpose of a network interface card (sometimes called an adapter card)?*

A: A network interface card is a printed circuit board required by each computer on the LAN. These cards take the serial signals off the network cables and move them into a parallel data stream inside the PCs. The cards also change the data from parallel back to serial and amplify the signals so they can travel the required distance over the network. Network interface cards also perform the media access control function.

Q: *Name the three standard protocols for LAN cabling and media access control.*

A: The three standard protocols for LAN cabling and media access control are Ethernet, ARC net, and Token-Ring.

Q: *When deciding which LAN cabling to use, how would you differentiate shielded twisted-pair, coaxial, and fiber-optic cable?*

A: Shielded twisted-pair cables provide protection against most electromagnetic interference, but they are relatively expensive. This type of cabling is also bulky and often requires custom installation. Coaxial cable costs less, is easier to install, and has similar resistance to electromagnetic noise. A caution with coaxial cable, though, is that you must be careful to select high-quality cable with the right impedance for the right protocol. Fiber-optic cable is more expensive than coaxial or shielded twisted-pair, but it permits signals to travel greater distances without repeaters. Fiber-optic cable is more secure and is much more reliable because it does not pick up electrical signals and impulses.

Q: *Describe the OSI model and its relevance to client/server computing.*

A: The Open Systems Interconnection (OSI) model has seven layers that describe standards by which computers can communicate with one another. These standards, ranging from physical cabling to presentation environments and application programs, provide the basis for integrating many of the client/server products available today. The OSI model also provides a reference framework for developing and evaluating communications protocols used in networks.

Q: *What is TCP/IP?*

A: Protocols are essentially rules for exchanging and interpreting data transferred over a network. The elements of a protocol typically specify the format in which data is to be sent, the signal strength to be used, an information structure for handling the data, the sequence in which the data should be sent, and the proper speed for transmitting it. The Transmission Control Protocol (TCP) and the Internet Protocol (IP) are two U.S. Department of Defense–specified protocols that have been adopted by many companies worldwide. The TCP/IP software protocols provide a standard set of communication parameters that help facilitate data exchange among dissimilar computer platforms.

Q: *What is the NetBIOS interface?*

A: NetBIOS (Network Basis Input/Output System) is a software program or protocol originally developed by IBM and Sytek to link a network operating system with a particular type of network interface card. This software program, now modified and used by many companies, operates at the OSI session and transport layers. It provides the interface between a computer and other resources on the network. In this regard, it functions much like the TCP/IP protocols. In fact, the Internet Protocol portion of TCP/IP encompasses the NetBIOS interface.

Q: *Explain how "polling" works in LAN environment.*

A: Polling involves the sequential, but extremely rapid, inquiry of each device on a network to see if it wants to transmit a signal.

Q: *What is Carrier Sense Multiple Access (CSMA)?*

A: A network interface card helps control access to network communications media. One method of executing this function is the listen-before-transmitting technique, commonly designated CSMA (Carrier Sense Multiple Access). This technique actually has the system operate like a two-way CB radio or walkie-talkie. Any station on the network must listen before it transmits a signal. If the station does not sense the carrier or transmission of another station on the network, then it is free to send its own signal. The CSMA technique is often combined with an additional method of dealing with transmission conflicts—i.e., the situation where two stations listen and detect no signal, then simultaneously transmit their own message. This additional method is referred to as Collision Detection (CD). Collision detection avoids two signals being sent at the same time, or if they are, it mediates between them.

Q: *What is the function of a bridge?*

A: A bridge is a hardware and software device that is used to link local area networks. It extends the network and helps to segment the message traffic that passes over the media. Hardware bridges forward traffic from one network to another only if the messages are properly addressed to devices or nodes on the other LAN.

Q: *How would you differentiate among the major LAN operating systems from Banyan, Novell, and Microsoft?*

A: New releases of network operating systems continue to deliver more advanced functions and features to users. Thus, any function/feature differentiation among major NOS products will be valid for only a limited time. Selecting among major operating systems should be based on specific criteria reflecting the needs of the organization. Criteria commonly of significance should include: performance, throughput, capacity, number of simultaneous users supported, server RAM usage as well as survivability and fault tolerance, and support of distributed processing.

Q: *Why is IEEE 802 important to a LAN design specialist?*

A: The Institute of Electrical and Electronics Engineers (IEEE) established a general committee to develop standards for network physical topology and cabling. These standards address the various protocols that are used in the physical and data-link layers of the OSI model. The two PC LAN standards of particular importance are 802.3 and 802.5. Standard 802.3 represents many Ethernet characteristics, while 802.5 describes the Token-Ring architecture.

Q: *How does a multitasking network operating system environment often differ from a peer-to-peer network?*

A: A peer-to-peer network allows any PC on the network to share resources such as printers and files. A peer-to-peer network server often acts as both a server and a PC workstation. In a multitasking network operating system environment, on the other hand, the server would not generally support both server software and normal PC applications. The requirements of multitasking typically demand a dedicated server.

Q: *What is the purpose of a gateway?*

A: A gateway is a device that typically links PC networks to host machines, such as a minicomputer or mainframe, or larger packet-switching networks. A gateway provides linkage at the OSI session layer and permits different protocols to communicate with each other.

Q: *Identify some of the key functions or areas that network management addresses.*

A: Most commentators agree that network management includes:

Fault management	Detecting and isolating system problems
Configuration management	Monitoring and changing network connections, equipment, and software
Asset management	Tracking the inventory of network components (i.e., cable, hardware, and software)
Security management	Safeguarding against unauthorized access to network resources or components
Performance management	Monitoring and controlling access to and/or use of network resources to maintain adequate levels of responsiveness.

Q: *What is the advantage of monitoring and controlling a network from the wiring hub?*

A: Since all LAN traffic goes through the wiring hub, it is easier to monitor and report on network activity from this point. The hub has a central view of every network node that allows better data collection and more effective control of the devices at each node.

Q: *What is the Simple Network Management Protocol (SNMP)?*

A: The Simple Network Management Protocol (SNMP) is a Department of Defense–originated network reporting and control framework that provides a structure for formatting, transmitting, and collecting information about devices operating on a network. SNMP works well and is used in many large networks today. The network management products that incorporate the SNMP structure are inexpensive and do not require a lot of CPU power or computer memory. However, variant configurations of the basic structure and lack of good security features are considered SNMP weaknesses.

Q: *Why is it important to monitor LAN performance and analyze operating statistics?*

A: Performance measurements and LAN operating statistics can help managers and administrators detect early indicators of problems, plan for network growth, justify staff and budgets, and build a base of data for comparing LAN efficiency and performance.

Q: *Describe several objectives of good security management.*

A: Good security management objectives include the following:

- Verifying and authenticating user identification
- Controlling access to network resources so that only authorized individuals can use them
- Providing secure communications
- Protecting data from unauthorized changes

Bibliography

Derfler, Frank J. Jr., *Guide to Connectivity,* Ziff-Davis Press, Emeryville, Calif., 1991.

Guengerich, Steve, *Downsizing Information Systems*, Sams Publishing, Prentice-Hall, Englewood Cliffs, N.J., 1992.

Hopple, Gerald, *State of the Art in Decision Support Systems*, QED, Wellesley, Mass., 1989.

Salemi, Joe, *Guide to Client/Server Databases*, Ziff-Davis Press, Emeryville, Calif., 1993.

Schatt, Stan, *Understanding Local Area Networks,* 2d ed., Howard W. Sams & Co., Carmel, Ind., 1990.

19

Client/Server Application Design and Implementation

David Dodge

Introduction

Designing and implementing client/server software applications requires both discipline and tools. The discipline is typically provided by methodologies and techniques that capture the business requirements the system must support. Next, these methodologies and techniques help translate the requirements into system functions and features; then they help direct how the system is to be developed and made operational.

The tools used by today's client/server professionals are many and varied. They range from programming languages to graphical development aids and to enterprise-wide software packages. Change and improvement are the watchwords for this facet of client/server implementation. This area is where an individual can be very valuable by keeping pace with the latest software innovations.

Methodologies and Design Techniques

Application design and development methodologies, including those for client/ server applications, are most often described in terms of two basic approaches, the traditional waterfall approach and an interactive, spiral (or cyclone-like) approach.

The waterfall approach essentially entails a sequential set of phases, each one producing elements of the system design or function. One phase cascades into another phase. This approach generally has strong controls, but tacks flexibility and often doesn't allow sufficient interaction with prospective application users. The spiral or interactive approach is more dependent on prototyping and piloting techniques that call for active user involvement and build on previous steps.

Both the traditional waterfall and the spiral-type approaches used by professionals today have roughly the same phases (e.g., requirements definition/refinement, analysis and design, application development/refinement, integration and testing, implementation and deployment). However, they tend to emphasize different phases and techniques.

The use of Computer-Aided Software Engineering (CASE) tools and data modeling techniques is frequently advocated today by both types of development approaches. CASE tools serve as analytic aids and as storage sites for application design characteristics and standards. Data modeling support is usually a key function of such tools. Data modeling is itself a set of procedures, graphic conventions, and techniques used to represent and organize data usage. When designing client/server applications, data modeling is a particularly valuable technique. Since client/server computing so often requires extensive data sharing and the distribution of data across multiple locations or servers, it becomes fundamentally important to understand how data needs to be organized and accessed for most efficient and accurate usage. Data modeling, with its depiction of data entities, their relationships, attributes, or characteristics, and its various levels or obstructions of the data, help application designers and developers cope with the complexity of client/server system data. Better data structures that take advantage of relational database technology are the result.

The newer object-oriented approaches to client/server application design and development involve techniques similar to data modeling and the spiral approach's emphasis on prototyping. Object-oriented approaches, however, take a somewhat different conceptual view of application software and the way we use it. In these approaches, an object is really a software "packet" that contains a set of characteristics and upon which a set of operations or access methods may be executed. The object is said to have a "state" (of value), and it exhibits a "behavior." By designing software applications around objects, professionals expect to achieve greater flexibility and responsiveness to changes in user requirements, as well as obtaining greater reuse of the application code.

Graphical Development and Data Access Tools

To many people it is the front-end application software and graphical user interface environments that have made client/server computing so alluring. To discuss the topic with greater clarity, these tools can be divided into three major groups based on their primary uses and limitations. These groups are: (1) desktop extension software, (2) application development tools, and (3) data access and query tools.

Desktop extension software products are essentially programs that add functionality to existing commercial database or application products such as Lotus

1-2-3 and dBase. The extension products make PC DBMSs and applications easier to use by providing access to servers and other databases, creating forms and reports, supporting development of ad hoc queries and data extracts, and populating spreadsheet packages with server-based data. The shortcomings of these tools include the fact that they are often tied to specific applications or DBMS products, and that they can impose a performance penalty on the workstation because of the data translations they must make. These tools can also require additional workstation processing power and memory.

Application development tools are software products used to build customized, workstation-based, client/server applications. Some of these tools simply put a graphical front end on existing mainframe host applications without changing the "back-end logic," an activity referred to as *facelifting*. Facelifting is usually a measure that yields only a small subset of the benefits of true client/server computing.

Other development tools are intended to support construction of complete client/server applications. These products use proprietary procedural or object-oriented 4GL programming languages to develop applications that have a graphical user interface and that support SQL queries to multiple back-end DBMSs. Professional developers with programming experience are the target users for most of these tools, although generally only a few days of training are needed before an individual can become competent with such a product. Most of the tools are designed to work in a Windows environment, and they enable the injection of multimedia, image, and other technologies into new applications.

Data access and query tools are most often intended for use by people who are not professional programmers. These tools support creation of database queries and the development of customized reports and forms. Some tools also support integration of data from multiple, disparate sources and are often characterized as Executive Information System (EIS) shells. Such tools are very good for users who need to retrieve data but do not need to change it.

In summary, it is worth pointing out that many of the application development and data access tools available today actually overlap the groups into which they were put for this discussion. The overlaps are increasing because vendors continue to add features and functions with each new version or release of their products. As a result, it is becoming harder to categorize them. The key, therefore, to selecting the right tool is to establish a set of criteria that helps you evaluate various products in an objective fashion, rather than simply following someone else's grouping scheme.

Application Programming Languages

Over the last few years, various database access tools and user-query products have emerged. These tools tend to simplify aspects of using a DBMS, and they generally preclude the need to develop custom programs to retrieve limited sets of data from the database. Most complex information systems requirements, however, still mandate the development of custom applications or the use of the off-the-shelf software packages. These programs are written in one or more programming languages. These languages can be grouped into three general classes: procedural languages, SQL-based languages, and object-oriented languages.

Most programming languages are considered to be procedural languages. This means the code is written as a series of procedures, with each procedure performing some task that contributes to the use of the application. Procedures to update data and to re-sort the data would be examples. The common third-generation languages (3GLs) such as COBOL, FORTRAN, Pascal, C, and BASIC are all procedural programming languages. In his guide to client/server databases, Joe Salemi also states that programming languages that are unique to particular products or DBMSs, are often called fourth-generation languages (4GLs). Examples include Microsoft's Visual BASIC language and the Paradox Application Language (PAL) used with Paradox. These procedural languages can be extended and linked to databases and other systems using Application Program Interfaces (APIs). An API is a set of precoded functions or procedural calls usually provided with a product or made available in a software library that can be coupled to an application or database.

SQL-based languages use the Structural Query Language (SQL) as their foundation. SQL was designed as a language intended to provide access to relational DBMSs. However, there is no mandatory requirement that a relational database must understand SQL, and SQL can be used to access a nonrelational DBMS. While SQL is generally considered an important standard that helped foster the transition to client/server, no one should assume that all SQL-based languages are compatible with one another. There are a variety of SQL-based languages in use today, each providing extensions or additional capabilities to the basic SQL specifications. Developers should therefore be cautious when selecting the languages and products they will use to build applications.

Object-Oriented Programming (OOP) languages are relatively new, and they require a very different approach to building application software. Rather than performing a series of procedures, OOP languages call for events or actions to be taken on objects such as a "customer," or a photographic image, or an "employee." Examples of such languages include C++ and SmallTalk. Several of the application development tools on the market today employ object-oriented languages and approaches. Other tools that up to now have used procedural or SQL-based languages have recently incorporated many of the object-oriented programming techniques and features. This blending can be expected to continue as vendors seek to optimize the strengths of the various languages and techniques.

Enterprise Client/Server Software Packages

As the move to client/server systems has accelerated, a relatively small number of vendors have produced enterprise software package solutions designed to operate in a client/server architecture. These software packages generally support major functions performed by most businesses, such as accounting and finance, human resource management, materials management, and production planning. Well-known examples are packages such as those offered by SAP, PeopleSoft, and Oracle. These software packages are important tools in facilitating the redesign of business processes and in fostering the transition to client/server computing.

Selecting and implementing a client/server software package can be a challenging endeavor. The analytic effort to pick a software package typically involves a comparison of functions and features versus a set of documented requirements. The performance and the technical environment in which the application operates can be important considerations, as well. Once a package has been selected, there is usually a phase of the implementation devoted to determining exactly what business processes the package will support completely, and how much the package might require customization. The next phase of package implementation often focuses on piloting the application and building interfaces to legacy systems with which the package must interface. Finally, package implementation calls for the software to be integrated, tested, and "rolled out" to other business locations.

Questions and Answers

The questions and answers in this chapter have been broken into major headings designed to classify subject material for easy access by the reader.

Client/Server Application Design

Q: *What is a JAD session and how does it apply to client/server?*

A: A Joint Application Design (JAD) session is a set of activities carried out jointly by systems analysts and designers and the end users of an application. These activities are focused on defining or refining the requirements for an application, how it will be used, the data needs of the users, and how the system should function. JAD sessions are but one way to gather requirements for client/server applications. The sessions are normally held with small groups of end users and led by a facilitator or systems analyst.

Q: *Explain why you would prototype an application or employ rapid application development techniques.*

A: Prototyping is a technique of interactively defining and refining end user application requirements by building portions of a proposed application system. In parallel, the developers demonstrate their work to the users to determine if their needs and vision are being satisfied by the somewhat superficial elements of the system they are seeing take shape. Rapid application development involves segmenting an application into smaller units or parts so that each one can be developed and put into operation much more quickly than conventional development techniques permit.

Q: *What is meant by business process reengineering and what is its relationship to client/server computing?*

A: Business process reengineering describes the effort associated with examining current business activities and processes used within an organization to determine if better working methods can be adopted to meet the organization's objectives. It involves a review of the rationale behind the work, the logic of information flows, the logic of who participates and in what sequence, and the consideration of alternatives for improvement. Business process reengineering often should precede or parallel development of a client/server application because of the opportunities for improvement that are inherent in the architecture, the technology, and the integration capabilities client/server computing provides.

Q: *How does object-oriented design differ from more conventional techniques?*

A: Object-oriented design focuses on identifying discrete entities called objects that have a data structure and a behavior that permits or involves operations of various types. In other words, software procedures are designed and built around objects. In more conventional structured analysis and design, the emphasis is placed on identifying and decomposing the functions a system should perform and the data it should provide to a user. Object-oriented design is more complex, but the software built using this technique is considered to be more robust and less fragile. It is argued that if functions and requirements change, objects are easier to revise than is software and a data design built around those functions. Current evidence tends to support this view, but too few object-oriented systems have been built and tested to convince everyone.

Q: *What are the characteristics of a good application design methodology?*

A: A good application development methodology is one that:

- Encompasses the entire development life cycle, from requirements definition through system maintenance
- Is modular so that it allows entry and exit at various points
- Allows the developers to select structured analysis, object-oriented, information engineering, prototyping, or any other technique that is best for the task
- Addresses the unique challenges of building client/server systems that have both distributed data and applications
- Includes iterative planning and strategy refinement to deal with issues such as systems management, documentation and training requirements, cultural and organizational implications, configuration management, software changes and upgrades, as well as operations and support.

Q: *What is the role of data modeling in client/server application design?*

A: Data modeling is a technique for depicting business information needs and the rules associated with data usage. When employing structured analysis or information engineering design techniques, data modeling is a critical step in defining the scope of an application, defining the views of data that users can obtain, determining how the data from multiple sources can be integrated, and developing the structure of the database itself. When designing a client/server application, a data model will also be important as you determine whether to distribute or centralize data and where to locate the data on the network.

Q: *What is third normal form?*

A: Normalization of data refers to a process of organizing and structuring data so that you have no redundancies or inconsistencies. Normalization is a modeling and refinement technique achieved in steps. First normal form, the first step, involves eliminating groups of "repeating" data elements. Second normal form involves aligning each portion of the data with its associated key or unique identifier. Third normal form involves removing data attributes or elements that depend on attributes other than the key. Some people like to say that in the third normal form, attributes must depend on "the key, the whole key, and nothing but the key."

Q: *What is a context diagram, as used in application design and process modeling?*

A: A context diagram is a single bubblelike drawing used in process modeling (data-flow diagramming) techniques. It depicts the scope of the system (also called its *domain*) and shows the data flows that move in and out of the system at their most abstract level.

Q: *When designing a decision support system application, what should be modeled first: the process or the data?*

A: Ordinarily, it is better to model the data first when designing a Decision Support System (DSS). The data will be more stable and predictable than decision support processes. DSS processes can often depend on what questions are being asked and the analytic processing that will be required to answer them. Ad hoc queries and processes, for example, can depend on who the questioner is. If the data is modeled and the database contains all the basic data types useful to analysts, then nearly all queries will be satisfied even though never modeled or anticipated. This is a generalization and not an ironclad rule.

Q: *What is the difference between "Upper CASE" and "Lower CASE" tools?*

A: Upper CASE tools are those that provide support for the "upper half" (planning, analysis, and high-level design) portions of a system development life cycle. Lower CASE tools support the "lower half" of the development life cycle—i.e., detailed design and construction (code generation).

Q: *What is the purpose of a dictionary or repository when designing a client/server application?*

A: A data dictionary or a repository is used to store and access information about data, programs, and objects. These tools can be helpful in designing complex client/server applications and databases by supporting data modeling, data definition, access path definition, software configuration and change management, use of software standards, and project management. Several of the most recent releases or versions of application development tools have incorporated dictionary and repository functions.

Q: *What are BLOBs?*

A: Binary Large Objects (BLOBs) are large binary files of data ranging up to two gigabytes or so in size. A BLOB can be an image, a video, a voice track, a graphic, a document, or a database snapshot that is treated as a single object by the system or application.

Client/Server Application Development and Implementation

Q: *What are some of the criteria you would use to evaluate and compare various application development tools?*

A: Because of differences in features, support, technical environments, and price, it is important to develop a set of criteria with which you can compare and evaluate application development tools to select the best one for a project. The criteria you use might include the following:

- Quality of SQL support
- Data import/export capabilities
- Quality of technical support
- Quality of documentation
- Capabilities to import images/multimedia
- Cost to run-time modules
- Operating systems supported
- DBMSs supported
- Network operating systems supported
- Object-oriented features
- Adaptability to prototyping
- Total price per developer/per end user

Q: *What is meant by an Application Development Environment (ADE)?*

A: An Application Development Environment (ADE) refers to a set of software capabilities that effectively merge upper CASE, project management, application development tool, and repository functions into an integrated suite of tools. The more advanced ADEs that are now emerging will provide a consistent user interface for all tools, along with on-line methodology and project management assistance, testing and debugging capabilities, object-oriented development tools, and repository functions that also support an index of reusable objects.

Q: *What are some of the strengths or advantages of products that "extend" the capabilities of familiar desktop applications such as Lotus 1-2-3?*

A: Desktop extension software products can help end users integrate existing PC databases into graphical client/server applications. These products may also be easier to learn and cost less than more complete application development tools. Additionally, desktop extension products tend to be extremely versatile, have good documentation, and require less workstation RAM than other development tools.

Q: *Why do "windows" applications and graphical user interfaces represent a new way of thinking for programmers?*

A: More conventional mainframe and midrange system applications are oriented toward predetermined usage patterns. Programmers know that end users will have to access the main menu, go through a series of well-laid-out steps "screen by screen," and complete one transaction or analysis before another is begun. On the other hand, with "windows" applications and graphical user interfaces, end users are no longer so restricted. A user can begin one application in the middle of another, or take any of a dozen or more routes to build and execute a query. An end user can also retrieve or input data from multiple sources on a network. Today's programmers must anticipate virtually anything an end user might want to do or might accidentally do. This means a new way of thinking about programming, and it means more complex challenges for programmers to build in safeguards, online help, and branching dialog logic.

Q: *What is referential integrity?*

A: Referential integrity refers to an operating principle of the Relational Database Model. It is an aspect of data integrity that predetermines how the database management system should react when an end user attempts to delete a database record on which other records depend. Good referential integrity features will not permit a user to inadvertently orphan data records this way.

Q: *What is a "multithreaded" application?*

A: The term *thread* describes a process within an application that performs a specific step or task. A single-threaded application does one thing at a time, while a multi-threaded application performs multiple tasks simultaneously. Multithreaded applications, for example, can update a database, display a series of graphics, and print a report all at the same time.

Q: *In graphical user interface terminology, what is a* combo box *and what is a* radio button?

A: A *combo box* is a combined data field and scrollable list box. The item that is currently selected in the list box automatically appears in the data field. The rest of the list box is displayed only upon demand by the user. This way it takes up less screen space. A *radio button* is a boolean switch used to provide settings where only one of a group of options can be selected at one time.

Q: *What is meant by the term or acronym CUA?*

A: The Common User Access (CUA) interface standard is a derivative of IBM's Systems Application Architecture. It is intended to provide users with a consistent view of the applications they employ. The standard addresses how window layouts should appear on the user's screen, how action bars and pull-down menus operate, how push buttons work, how information is displayed within a window, how fields are formatted, how items are selected from the screen, how the cursor operates, and many other presentation techniques that users often take for granted.

Q: *How does the term* animate *relate to client/server application development?*

A: Animate generally refers to the feature of an application development tool that allows you to follow along in an outline and see each line of application code highlighted as it runs. This feature is useful to see if everything is working the way the developer intended.

Q: *Explain how a DLL is used.*

A: A Dynamic Link Library (DLL) is a group (or library) of software functions/procedures that are compiled and stored outside the main body of an application program. The DLL is accessed and executed at certain points in the application, either automatically or by user choice. A DLL is typically used to add special functions to software, such as providing imaging capabilities, performing special statistical procedures, or exporting data to graphics packages. Some application development tools are sold with DLLs to make it unnecessary to develop such code.

Q: *What is a simple definition of the term data domain?*

A: A data domain is an allowable set of values for a specific data element in a particular field or table column.

Q: *What are some of the data management and control issues you encounter when building a client/server system?*

A: The management and control of data is only one aspect of client/server systems management, but a critical one. Some of the issues encountered in this area include:

- Data security and copy control
- "Ownership" of data
- Read versus update rights
- Data definitions and key standardization
- Data archiving strategy and media
- Data distribution and synchronization
- Refreshment or update strategy
- Time-stamping techniques

Q: *What is an API and how is it used?*

A: An Application Program Interface (API) is a set of program functions or a specification for them that provides the capability for applications to interact with network operating systems, DBMSs, or other application software. In other words, the API is used to link applications to other software components or database management system services.

Q: *Explain the difference between dynamic SQL and embedded SQL.*

A: Stand-alone SQL used for interactive queries of a database is commonly called *dynamic* SQL. If the SQL is contained inside an application written in a procedural programming language, it is usually referred to as *embedded* SQL.

Q: *Describe the OSI model and its relevance to client/server computing.*

A: The Open Systems Interconnection (OSI) mode has seven layers that describe standards by which computers can communicate with one another. These standards, ranging from physical cabling to presentation environments and application programs, provide the basis for integrating many of the client/server products available today. The OSI model also provides a reference framework for developing and evaluating communications protocols used in networks.

20
Performance Management for Unix-Based Systems

Douglas Lieu

Introduction

Your new system (equipment and application software) has just gone live. It's well balanced, i.e., no component of the system is overutilized. The users are getting close to the maximum performance the system is able to deliver. The users are happy. Your boss is happy. So much so that everyone wants to use the system and requests for additional functions have been approved. The additions and changes are added to the new system and what happens—the system's performance starts to degrade: response time increases and throughput decreases. Where praises were previously received, now complaints are the order of the day. What happened was that the system evolved and one or more resources became overloaded.

Performance management can help to identify and reduce resource bottlenecks before performance becomes a problem that will cost an organization time, money, and lost productivity. The reactive approach to performance management leaves little time to work on the proactive, strategic aspects. Understanding performance trends is more important than ever to ensure optimal cost-performance when demands increase. The key to sound performance management is reliable information and the knowledge to interpret and use it productively. Performance evaluation, analysis, and monitoring are required at every stage in the life cycle of system design, implementation, configuration, installation, and upgrade. Measuring performance may seem like an art, but what is really involved is a basic understanding of computer architecture, networking, and software languages.

Job Requirements

To qualify for a job in performance management you have to have an understanding of the types of problems that can occur and how to develop meaningful processing and throughput statistics. Problem determination and the implementation (or recommendation) of correct solutions is your goal. What and how to accomplish this for Unix-based systems is the basis for the questions that follow. The questions and answers cover nine major areas of concern in the performance management of Unix based systems:

1. Basic concepts and strategy
2. CPU utilization
3. Memory utilization
4. Disk I/O and capacity
5. Network layout and traffic
6. Application processing
7. NFS servers
8. Database servers
9. Performance analysis and customer expectation management

Questions and Answers

Q: *What areas need to be investigated when the end user complains about performance?*

A: CPU, memory, disk I/O, network and applications, and the state of the processes.

Q: *What information would you need so that you could quickly identify a performance problem based on the areas mentioned above?*

A: ▪ Check for CPU hog processes at all system sites.
   ▪ Check if there is heavy paging or swapping.
   ▪ Check if the client has I/O-intensive process.
   ▪ Check the network traffic and collision rate.

Q: *List commands to use in a Unix client workstation to collect the performance information for those areas mentioned above.*

A: ▪ CPU: *vmstat* or *ps*
   ▪ Memory: *vmstat, pstat,* or *ps*
   ▪ Disk I/O: *iostat*
   ▪ Network: *netstat* or *nfsstat*
   ▪ Application software: *ps*

Q: *List the common client/server models.*
A: ▪ File server
  ▪ Database server
  ▪ X server

Q: *What are the most common performance problems?*
A: ▪ Bad soft design or software bugs
  ▪ Runaway processes
  ▪ Not enough memory
  ▪ Not enough swap space
  ▪ Database or file locking
  ▪ Heavy network traffic
  ▪ Network routing errors or high collision rates

Q: *What commands could you use to collect information on the CPU performance of a Unix system?*
A: *uptime, vmstat, pstat, iostat, sar/sa,* or *perfmeter.*

Q: *What is SMP and what are its performance projections?*
A: Symmetric Multiple Processors run transactions in multiple threads evenly among the CPUs. A good design of SMP usually has less than 10 percent of overhead per CPU.

Q: *What is the first thing to check on a workstation when there is a performance problem?*
A: Always check if there are any runaway processes that may be using up the CPU time slice.

Q: *How do you find a process that hogs the CPU?*
A: Compare multiple *'ps'* command outputs for the increase of CPU usage of the processes.

Q: *What information does 'ps' report?*
A: User name/id, process id, parent process id, CPU utilization, memory utilization, process size, process stat, process priority, controlling terminal, total CPU time consumed, and command executed.

Q: *What commands in Unix could you use to collect information about memory?*
A: *ps, vmstat, sar, swap, pstat, sar,* and *size.*

Q: *What is paging and demand paging?*
A: Paging refers to the pages of the running process that are released from the physical memory for other new processes to use. Demand paging refers only to the pages that are brought into the physical memory to run the program.

Q: *How do you know if the system is paging or swapping?*
A: Use *vmstat* and compare the page-ins, page-outs, swap-ins or swap-outs section of the output.

Q: *What is a shared library and what advantage(s) can be obtained from its use?*

A: Library routines are always mapped into a system's virtual memory. When a program references a library routine, the linker generates a jump into shared library. As a result the executable file itself is usually smaller because the library code is not a part of the executable.

The program still needs the same amount of virtual memory, although the system as a whole requires less memory because all programs that reference the same function share the same copy of the function. Unless a program uses only one or two functions from the shared library, most of the programs will benefit from using shared library.

Q: *How do you reduce paging?*

A: ▪ Increase the memory.

▪ Tune the kernel buffer cache.

▪ Set the process memory limits.

▪ Use shared libraries instead of static compiled program.

Q: *How can you prevent swapping?*

A: Raise the point to start paging earlier to allow more time for the paging algorithm to find memory before a memory shortage becomes critical.

Q: *How do you tune the performance of swap area?*

A: Paging and swapping activity should be evenly distributed across the system. Place swap partitions/files on as many different disks as possible using high-speed disks, and use the fastest drive available for the root disk. Avoid configurations in which the controller, rather than the disk, limits performance.

Q: *How do you diagnose memory leakage?*

A: ▪ Compare the result of '*ps*' output per process.

▪ Utilize software (like Purify) to detect memory leaks.

Q: *How do you look for the long run queue and why?*

A: *vmstat procs r*

If the run queue or load average is more than four times the number of CPUs, processes end up waiting too long for a slice of CPU time.

Q: *What are the factors involved in I/O performance?*

A: Disk performance is the single most important aspect of I/O performance. It is usually the bottleneck of transaction throughput that affects many other aspects of system performance. You can optimize the disk performance based on the following:

▪ Per-process disk throughput

▪ Aggregate total system disk throughput, and

▪ Disk storage efficiency

Isolate performance-critical files in the same group of file systems, suffer the storage inefficiencies there, and optimize the rest of the file systems for storage efficiency.

Q: *What Unix commands can be used to collect the information about disk I/O performance?*

A: *iostat, nfsstat, sar,* and *sadp.*

Q: *What do you look for at disk bottleneck?*

A: Look for the disks that are more than 30 percent busy and where the service times are more than 50 ms.

Q: *What is the service time of 'iostat'?*

A: It is the time between a process issuing a disk read and the completion of the read. It is often the critical path for the response time.

Q: *What are the components in the disk subsystem?*

A: ■ Operation system
- Device driver
- Host adapter
- Peripheral I/O bus
- Intelligent controller
- Channel
- Disk units

Q: *What disk specifications are important in performance management?*

A: ■ *Seek times,* the time required to move the disk drive's head from one track of data to another
- *Rotational speed,* the time for the drive's head to wait until data is moved underneath the head, measured by Rotation Per Minute (RPM)
- *Raw transfer rate,* the speed at which it moves data
- *Disk capacity,* formatted and unformatted

Q: *What is SCSI?*

A: SCSI, Small Computer System Interface, is an interface standard that was developed for small computers.

Q: *What is RAID? Describe it.*

A: RAID, Redundant Arrays of Inexpensive Disks, is a technique that was developed to achieve better performance by distributing data across many smaller, inexpensive disk drives rather that storing the data on a single large expensive disk drive using proprietary controllers. Because a large number of drives are needed in RAID systems, a mechanism was needed to guard against data loss caused by failure of any single drive. The RAID approach to data storage, introduced in December 1987, can be summarized as follows:

1. It is a set of physical disk drive viewed by the user as a single device.
2. The user's data is distributed across the physical set of drives in a pre-defined manner.
3. Redundant disk capacity is added so that the user's data can be recovered even if a drive fails.

Q: *What are the basic features of RAID?*
A: ▪ Data striping to improve performance.
   ▪ Disk mirroring or parity for redundancy.

Q: *What are the RAID levels and their special features?*
A: RAID 0   Striping
   RAID 1   Mirroring
   RAID 2   Striping plus error detection and correction
   RAID 3   Striping with dedicated parity
   RAID 4   Modified striping with dedicated parity
   RAID 5   Modified striping with interleaved parity
   RAID 0+1   Striping plus mirroring
   RAID 7   Striping with dedicated parity via real time OS

Q: *What are the mandatory features for today's RAID system?*
A: ▪ High Availability
   ▪ Hot swap
   ▪ Hot standby
   ▪ Multiple fans
   ▪ N+1 power supply
   ▪ Battery backup if there is no UPS
   ▪ High performance
   ▪ Low cost

Q: *What are some of the important considerations in selecting RAID?*
A: ▪ Capacity requirements
   ▪ Required transfer rate and IOPS performance
   ▪ Transaction distribution read, write
   ▪ Capacity growth plan and upgrade cost
   ▪ Serviceability
   ▪ Disaster recovery requirements

Q: *In a Unix system what command would you use to look for processes blocked waiting for I/O, and why?*
A: *vmstat procs b*
   It is a sign of disk bottleneck when the number of processes blocked approaches or exceeds the number in the run queue.

Q: *What is* iostat *output?*
A: ▪ Number of characters waiting in the input and output terminal buffers
   ▪ Block per second
   ▪ Transaction per second
   ▪ Percent time on user stat
   ▪ Percent time for nice process

- Percent time on system stat
- Percent time on CPU idle

Q: *What is the difference between buffered and unbuffered I/O?*

A: Buffered I/O is a layer buffer between the Unix file system and the OS kernel, e.g., fopen and fgets. Unbuffered I/O is usually in the raw file system without additional buffers, e.g., *open and read.*

Q: *What strategy should you use to choose between disk performance and memory performance?*

A: Optimize disk performance or memory performance for I/O or CPU-intensive processes. If file or database is much larger than the cache, the caching will not help performance, and it's better to optimize memory performance using a smaller cache. For a CPU-bound system, it is better to use a smaller kernel buffer cache. In general, it is better to resolve the conflict between memory performance and disk performance in favor of memory.

Q: *What strategies should you employ when monitoring the performance of your network?*

A: 1. Establish and maintain the baseline, layout, and traffic history of the networks.

2. Utilize applicable monitoring tools to the critical areas, keeping in mind that there is no single product that does it all.

3. Avoid proprietary network management protocols. Stick with the standard(s).

4. Map and track the application's execution schedule, route, and traffic volume.

5. Work with vendors to create customized solutions.

6. Plan capacity upgrade(s) proactively, before the network traffic exceeds its capacity.

7. Set realistic objectives and evaluate the cost(s) of network upgrades.

Q: *How do you detect network performance problems?*

A: Network capacity may be the cause of slow performance when using network related commands or utilities. What you should do is to check if the number of collisions is higher than normal. A comparatively large number of input errors would indicate problems somewhere on the network; a large number of output errors suggests problems with the local system and its interface to the network. If there are a large number of dropped packets, the remote system most likely cannot respond to incoming data fast enough (this may be caused by I/O or CPU slowness). You should also check client RPC data to see if the NFS server is overloaded, if the network is faulty, or if one of the servers has crashed.

Q: *How do you reduce network workload?*

A: Prevent users from using it, or schedule users running I/O-intensive programs across the network. You should also:

- Partition and bridge the network.
- Minimize the number of diskless workstations.
- Re-architecture the applications to perform more computing on the workstations.

Q: *What Unix commands or utilities can be used to collect the network traffic information?*
A: *netstat, nfsstat, ping* and *sar.*

Q: *What is the function of a bridge and router?*
A: A bridge is a device that connects two or more physical networks and forwards packets between them. A router is a system responsible for making decisions on which of several paths network traffic will follow by using a routing protocol to gain information about the network, and algorithms to choose the best route based on several criteria known as *routing metrics.*

Q: *What are the Ethernet mediums?*
A: 1. 10Base-T—unshielded twisted pair (UTP) Ethernet, similar to telephone cable. It uses a star topology, point-to-point connections, and is limited to 100 meters.

2. 10Base-2—coax using BNC connector and allows daisy chaining for quick network setup with low cost. It is limited to 30 nodes with at least 0.5 m apart and max to 185 m.

3. 10Base-5—uses thick wire to create large "backbones." Supports many nodes in a bus topology up to 500 meters and maximum 100 nodes. You have to drill into the media to connect the new node via a device known as *vampire tap.*

4. 10Base-FL—a specification for point-to-point fiber optic links running at distances of up to 2 km.

Q: *What is RFC?*
A: Request For Comments. This document series, begun in 1969, describes the Internet suite of protocols and related experiments. Not all RFCs describe Internet standards, but all Internet standards are written up as RFCs.

Q: *What is the basic difference between TCP and UDP?*
A: TCP is connection-oriented protocol; UDP is connectionless and does not guarantee successful delivery of a packet.

Q: *At what level of collision rate (Ethernet) will the network begin to slow performance?*
A: When the collision rate is higher than 4 to 6 percent.

Q: *What is the speed of Ethernet, FDDI, and Faster Ethernet?*
A: - Ethernet—10 Mbits per second
   - FDDI—100 Mbits per second
   - Faster Ethernet—100 Mbits per second

Q: *What is* netstat *output?*

A: *netstat* reports information concerning:

- Sockets stat and routing table entries
- Address control
- Multicast group memberships for all interfaces
- The address resolution tables
- State of the interface protocol, and
- Network data structure

Q: *What are the basic principles used to optimize network performance?*

A: First, the network must be able to transfer data correctly. It must provide enough bandwidth to satisfy the network users. Each system on the network must be fast enough to handle the network traffic addressed to it.

Q: *What is RPC?*

A: RPC is a Remote Procedure Call, which allows a client to execute procedures on other networked computers or servers. It uses a request-and-reply communication model. The client and server processes communicate by means of two *stubs*. A stub is a communications interface that implements the RPC protocol and specifies how messages are constructed and exchanged. The stubs contain functions that map the local procedure calls into a series of network RPC functions calls.

Q: *What is route daemon (*routed*)?*

A: The daemon routes network packets destined for other networks.

Q: *When is it advisable to use an X terminal?*

A: X terminals work well when most users spend a small portion of their time actually working on the X terminal. They do not work well when most of the users are active most of the time.

Q: *How do you track the process fork (or process) when using an X terminal?*

A: Turn on the system process accounting.

Q: *List the information/service servers and their differences.*

A: ■ inetd: single master daemon, serve multiple request simultaneous

- ypbind: single master daemon, serve one request at a time
- rpcgen: multiple threaded daemon

Q: *What are the configuration factors for performance tracking?*

A: They are:

- User account profile
- Time of event
- Main application software and application revision
- File system type
- User count

- Database server
- OS version
- OS kernel configuration
- Memory size
- Disk type and configuration
- CPU type & speed
- CPU count
- Network type and protocol

Q: *What is NFS?*

A: The Network File System is a distributed file system developed by Sun Microsystems that allows a set of computers to cooperatively access each other's files in a transparent manner using RPC.

Q: *Which command is used to check the NFS state?*

A: *nfsstat*

Q: *What should you do when NFS has poor response times?*

A: Use *'nfsstat'* to look at the NFS operation mix for both the client and server of their disk I/O. Also check the network traffic and the collision rate.

Q: *What is the rule of disk configurations for NFS?*

A: An NFS read can involve two trips over the network from the client as well as a disk I/O. Perceived performance from the server requires a low latency disk system within an average service time below 40 ms.

Q: *What is the disadvantage to mixing the NFS server and database server on the same host?*

A: The NFS will use more CPU time and slow down the database when it receives a large number of NFS requests.

Q: *What are the throughput limitations of NFS version 2?*

A: Version 2 NFS protocol limits throughput to about 3 Mbytes per second per active client-site process because it has limited pre-fetch and small block sizes.

Q: *How do you determine the number of NFS threads?*

A: Two NFS threads per active client process; 16 NFS threads per Ethernet and 160 per FDDI or Faster Ethernet

Q: *What is* nfsstat *output on a server?*

A: calls   Number of RPCs received

    badcalls   Number of RPCs rejected

    nullrec   Number of RPC calls not ready to receive

    badlen   Number of calls with shorter minimum RPC len

    xdrcall   Number of bad XDR

    writes   Number of writes

Q: *What is* nfsstat *output on a client?*

A: calls   Number of requests sent

     badcalls   Number of requests rejected

     retrans   Number of retransmissions

Q: *What is* biod?

A: Block I/O daemon for NFS.

Q: *What is* nfsd?

A: NFS daemon to serve request from remote systems.

Q: *What is a* nice *number?*

A: A nice number is a number that is used to compute the priority of a process. Low nice numbers yield high priorities.

Q: *What is* rwhod?

A: Rwhod is a daemon process that provides information about users on other systems. It is required for rwho and ruptime.

Q: *How do you collect the information on resource utilization per process?*

A: System accounting will provide the details of CPU, disk, and other information. System accounting usually impacts the system performance between 5 and 10 percent.

Q: *Why does the database sometimes perform faster on the Unix file system than the raw file system?*

A: Because the Unix file system has one additional layer of buffering and aggressive prefetching for small size I/O. However, on the Unix file system, the data is not guaranteed to be written on the disk when it returns 'ok'.

Q: *What is the most commonly sought information about database performance?*

A: ▪ Database application distribution of on-line and batch

    ▪ System utilization

    ▪ Average response time per query

    ▪ Number of queries completed during the observation interval

    ▪ Average number of jobs in the system

    ▪ Average run time per transaction

Q: *What is the difference between B tree and B+ tree?*

A: B tree stores the data in the node. B+ tree stores the data at the leaf level only.

Q: *What is the advantage of using the database server of client/server architecture?*

A: The database server of client/server architecture can archive optimized performance by using dedicated hardware. Since it is independent of where and what the client software runs on, it also provides open architecture to migrate to other vendors' hardware to further improve the performance without affecting the clients.

Q: *How do you increase query performance?*
A: 1. Use index with index covering.

    2. Split the subquery into multiple smaller queries.

    3. Split large joins into smaller joins.

    4. Avoid the *sort* statement when index is covered.

    5. Avoid the use of *or* in where clause.

Q: *What affects database performance?*
A: ■ CPU, disk throughput, network traffic, and the use of the transaction log

    ■ Application design, logical design, physical design, and user's query

    ■ Database configuration, query optimizer, locking and data distribution

    ■ The number of concurrent users and the amount of table indexing

Q: *What performance impacts are involved in data normalization?*
A: Reduced data redundancy, smaller databases, and faster I/O. Normalization results in smaller tables and rows, which in turn allow more rows to fit on one page and more rows processed per I/O. The disadvantage of full normalization is that it will require more joins per query.

Q: *What are the benefits of denormalization?*
A: Denormalization minimizes the need for joins, reduces the number of foreign keys, and reduces the number of indexes.

Q: *Why use an index?*
A: An index provides a faster path of access to data, reduces the need for sorting, reduces the size of data to be processed, and enforces uniqueness of data.

Q: *What is 'index covering'?*
A: When the index contains the columns referenced by the query, the server needs to read only index pages, not data pages.

Q: *What are 'deadlocks'?*
A: Deadlocks occur when two or more processes each hold locks on data that are being requested by one of the other processes.

Q: *What can reduce lock contention?*
A: Lock contention can be reduced by:

    ■ Adjusting the index fill factor to reduce index page overflow or merge

    ■ Avoiding writing transactions that include user interaction

    ■ Keeping transactions short

    ■ Scattering the data among as many pages as possible

Q: *How can you reduce disk contention?*
A: ■ Split randomly accessed tables across multiple disks.

    ■ Separate data and nonclustered indexes and logs by using separate devices.

    ■ Be sure the recovery interval is not too long nor too frequent.

    ■ Dump database in off-hours whenever possible.

Q: *What steps can be taken to avoid having performance become a problem?*

A: ■ Make performance agreements with the users, and check regularly to make sure that the system performance meets the objective.

   ■ Identify and document both the CPU-intensive processes and I/O-intensive processes.

   ■ Keep track of CPU, memory and I/O performance regularly.

   ■ Keep track of new transactions added to the system.

Q: *How do users typically perceive performance?*

A: ■ How much time it takes to run a job

   ■ The response time to keyboard entry

   ■ The response time of form/screen updates

   ■ Takes longer to run a job than before, regardless of how fast it runs

Q: *How do you categorize the "heavy user"?*

A: ■ Users who run a large number of relatively small jobs

   ■ Users who run a small number of relatively large jobs

   ■ Users who run a small number of CPU-intensive jobs that require a lot of memory

Q: *What are the major performance measurements?*

A: Throughput, response time, and utilization.

Q: *List some throughput measurements.*

A: MIPS   Millions of Instructions Per Second

    MFLOPS   Millions of Floating-Point Operations Per Second

    TPS   Transactions Per Second

    PPS   Packet Per Second

    BPS   Bit Per Second

Q: *Define MTTR, MTTF, Reliability, Availability.*

A: MTTR   Mean Time to Repair

    MTTF   Mean Time to Fail

    Reliability   Measurement of the time from an initial instant to the next failure event or MTTF

    Availability   Measurement of the ratio of service accomplishment to elapsed time or

$$\frac{MTTF}{(MTTF + MTTR)}$$

Q: *Do you know which professional organizations and journals deal with performance issues?*

A: ■ ACM SIGMENTRICS: *Performance Evaluation Review*

   ■ IEEE Computer Society

   ■ ACM SIGSIM: *Simulation Digest*

- Computer Measurement Group (CMG): *C.G. Transaction*
- The Society for Computer Simulation
- The Society for Industrial and Applied Mathematics (SIAM)

Q: *List some benchmarks.*

A:
- Whetstone: Used at the British Central Computer Agency in Algol, Fortran, and PL/1.
- Linpack: Developed in 1983. It compares the execution rate measured in MFLOPS for engineering/scientific application performance.
- Drystone: Developed in 1984. Results are presented in Drystone Instructions Per Second (DIPS) for mostly integer performance.
- Debit-Credit: Developed in 1973 for application level benchmark.
- TPC: Transaction Processing Performance Console, derived from Debit-Credit.
- SPEC: System Performance Evaluation Cooperative, consists of 10+ benchmarks for various engineering and scientific applications.

Q: *What is TPC Benchmark A?*

A: A remote terminal emulation (RTE) benchmark that performs on-line transaction processing (OLTP) operations. It represents the banking application containing teller terminals running only one type of transaction—an account update.

Q: *What is Remote Terminal Emulation (RTE)?*

A: It emulates the terminals, the terminal communication equipment, the operators, and the requests to be submitted to System Under Test (SUT). RTE consists of three phases: preemulation, emulation, and postemulation.

Q: *What is TPC Benchmark B?*

A: A batch-oriented database stress benchmark that performs multithread transaction submit operations. It uses the same convention and scenario as TPC A without the OLTP aspects. The model is a set of tellers at a bank with multiple branches.

Q: *What is TPC Benchmark C?*

A: A remote terminal emulating (RTE) benchmark that performs OLTP operations. It is a representation of an order entry application containing operator terminals. The model is a set of operator terminals at a company that stocks and sells parts, having multiple warehouses.

Q: *What are the limitations of RTES?*

A:
- The conditions for sending successive requests may not be realistic.
- It may not be possible to vary the input in successive repetitions.
- The think-time model may not be realistic.
- It does not have a modern Graphic User Interface.
- It does not support a client/server model.
- Modern communications technology is not emulated.

Q: *What is the bandwidth and throughput of Fast SCSI bus?*
A: Ten Mbytes per second bandwidth with 7.5 Mbytes per second excluding the SCSI protocol overhead.

Q: *What is the correct approach for performance evaluation?*
A: 1. Select the area and environment.
   2. Select the evaluation techniques and performance metrics.
   3. Define the parameters, data volume, interval, and duration.
   4. Conduct the performance measurement.
   5. Analyze the statistics in the metrics.
   6. Design a simulation or experiment to isolate the bottlenecks.
   7. Formal results for presentation.

Q: *What are some of the more common mistakes made in performance measurement?*
A: ▪ No planning, no organized goal, and no objective
   ▪ Biased goals—comparing two systems running different applications
   ▪ Unsystematic approach—using different parameters, factors, and configuration
   ▪ Overlooking of important parameters
   ▪ Assuming no change in the future
   ▪ No history data with which to compare
   ▪ No log of environmental changes

Q: *What are the tasks in a performance measurement project?*
A: ▪ Define system.
   ▪ Define service/process.
   ▪ Select the metrics model.
   ▪ Define parameters.
   ▪ Define factors and permutations.
   ▪ Define input data and volume.
   ▪ Define experiment technique.
   ▪ Design experiment.
   ▪ Analyze and present findings.

Q: *What are the factors in capacity planning?*
A: ▪ Standard terminology
   ▪ Capacity definition
   ▪ Standardization of workload
   ▪ Defining of measured model
   ▪ Defining of client/server data model

Q: *What information do you need when involved in performance simulation modeling?*

A: ■ The type of simulations model

■ How to verify and validate the model

■ How to schedule events

■ How to run the simulation

■ How to generate random events

■ What distributions to use and when

■ The size of the data

Q: *What are the steps in capacity planning and management?*

A: 1. Instrument the environment and system.

2. Monitor the system usage and transaction response time.

3. Categorize the workload.

4. Project the performance under different alternatives.

5. List and select the alternatives.

Q: *What parameters should be in a Queuing Model?*

A: ■ Interarrival time distribution

■ Service time distribution

■ Number of servers

■ Number of buffers

■ Population size

■ Service discipline

Q: *What is a Queuing Network model?*

A: A model in which jobs departing from one queue arrive at another queue.

Q: *What are some of the parameter tests and objectives involved in benchmarking?*

A: ■ Include a complete transaction cycle in the workload, not just the average.

■ Distribute I/O evenly.

■ Multiple load configurations.

■ Test with cache and without cache.

■ Vary the buffer size.

■ Define the quality and quantity of samples.

■ Exclude the overhead of monitoring.

■ Assure the same initial conditions.

21
Networks and Network Administration

John H. Lister

Introduction

Since its inception in the early 1970s, IBM's Systems Network Architecture suite of programs and protocols (SNA) has had an immense impact on computer networking and data communications. SNA introduced the concepts of abstraction and virtualization to networks. Instead of an application program having specialized code to support all the different devices that could connect to it and the links to which they were attached, the program could deal in a standard manner with an abstract representation of the devices. The management of the network connectivity and the physical devices was the responsibility of a specific network management and control program, the Virtual Telecommunications Access Method (VTAM) with management of the links and the remote devices being delegated to the Network Control Program (NCP) running in an outboard communications front-end processor (originally a 3705 Communications Controller, currently a 3745). Enhancements to SNA have permitted the growth of large networks supporting many applications residing on multiple processors with access available from any device connected anywhere in the network. The SNA Network Interconnection (SNI) architecture permits internetwork connectivity while maintaining separate network architectures, conventions, and management responsibilities.

SNA continues to evolve; the recent addition of APPN (Advanced Peer to Peer Networking) and HPR (High Performance Routing) facilities—which are just starting to appear in released products—to the architecture will allow the migration of the "host-centric" SNA network of the past to a flexible, high-performance, peer-oriented network well matched to the communications requirements of the 1990s.

The current software environment that is the basis for the technical questions and answers in this chapter includes: ACF/VTAM Version 4.2 for MVS/ESA, ACF/NCP Version 7.2, ACF/SSP Version 4, NetView Version 3, and NetView Performance Monitor Version 1.6.

Questions and Answers

This section is designed to explore a candidate's knowledge of SNA architecture, message formats, and protocols.

Q: *What is a session?*
A: A session is a logical connection between two SNA entities.

Q: *What means are used by SNA to regulate traffic flow through the network?*
A: SNA uses message *pacing* in order to regulate information flow in the network, to prevent network congestion, and to prevent buffer overflow at a logical unit. SNA supports two independent pacing mechanisms: *session pacing* and *virtual route pacing*.

Q: *How do these two pacing mechanisms differ?*
A: Virtual route pacing regulates the flow of messages, on behalf of all sessions, between the subarea nodes of a network. Session pacing controls the flow of messages between logical units on a specific session to avoid buffer overflows and loss of information on that session.

Q: *How does session pacing control the flow of data?*
A: Session pacing controls the flow of data by dividing the traffic in a given direction on a session into *pacing windows*, a specific number of message units. This number may be predefined for a session, or may vary, depending on the capabilities of the nodes supporting the session endpoints. When one session partner starts to send the message units associated with a pacing window, it turns on the pacing request bit in the request header of the message unit. The session partner may then send up to the pacing window numbers of message units to the other partner before it must wait for a pacing response. The receiving session partner determines when to send a pacing response, which can depend on processing rates and buffer availability.

Q: *How is a session established between two logical units?*
A: The fundamental message flow that establishes an SNA session is the sending of the BIND request from the logical unit that is originating the session to the logical unit that is the target of the session request. The session is activated when the target logical unit responds positively to the bind.

Q: *How are the parameters for a session determined?*
A: The BIND request which is used to establish the session carries the session parameters, such as the message sizes in each direction, the optional SNA

services that will be used and the LU type. Optionally, the BIND request can carry user data.

VTAM

This section focuses on the other aspects of VTAM: customizing and tuning VTAM, defining the network, and VTAM problem-determination tools.

Q: *How is an SNA network defined to VTAM?*

A: Each of the components of an SNA network is defined in a member of a partitioned dataset SYS1.VTAMLIST. For NCPs, VTAM also uses the Resource Resolution Table (RRT), in SYS1.VTAMLIB, to map logical unit names to network addresses.

Q: *Name some of the resources in VTAMLIST.*

A: Some of the VTAMLIST resources include: VTAM start parameters, VTAM configuration lists, route definitions, application major nodes, local non-SNA and local SNA major nodes, cross-domain resource manager major nodes, adjacent SSCP major nodes, cross-domain resource major nodes, and switched physical unit major nodes.

Q: *How can a node in an SNA network be activated automatically at VTAM initialization?*

A: The configuration member ATCCON00 contains a list of members in VTAM-LIST that should be processed by VTAM on start-up. Each member is processed and the major node it represents is added to VTAM's in-storage table of network elements. At this stage the node is *defined* to VTAM. If the node has ISTATUS=ACTIV specified, either explicitly or by inheritance from a higher-level node, VTAM will queue an activation request for the node when higher-level nodes in the path have been activated.

Q: *How does an application interface with VTAM?*

A: An application is defined to VTAM by means of its entry (its ACB name) in VTAMLIST.

Q: *How is the connection made between VTAM and the ACB in storage?*

A: The application program issues the operating system OPEN with the ACB as one of the arguments. This results in a supervisor call machine instruction (SVC 19) which routes control to the operating system. The operating system OPEN routines inspect and validate the control block and determine that it is a VTAM ACB, then pass the request to VTAM. VTAM inspects the control block and makes a correlation between the ACB name and the application name in an active application major node. If it can find a match, VTAM opens the ACB (changes various fields in the ACB to reflect its open status) and inserts the addresses of other control blocks and routines that the application program will need in order to be able to communicate with VTAM.

Q: *How does an application program make requests to VTAM?*

A: An application program issues assembly language macros such as SEND and RECEIVE, with a Request Parameter List (RPL) as an argument, which gives VTAM details of the request to be performed.

Q: *How does VTAM inform an application program of the completion of a request or of an external event?*

A: There are two notification methods that an application program can use. The first is to pass to VTAM in a request the address of an exit routine which will be called when a given request has completed. The second is to pass the address of an Event Control Block (ECB) which will be posted when the event is complete.

Q: *Where does VTAM store messages in transit through the network?*

A: VTAM maintains a set of *buffer pools* (fixed-length areas of storage used to hold control blocks or data in transit through the network). The location of the buffer pools varies according to the operating system and VTAM release level. In MVS/ESA, most of the buffers are in Extended Common Storage (ECSA).

Q: *How can a systems programmer control the sizes of the buffer pools?*

A: The VTAM start options member ATCSTR00 contains the specifications for the VTAM buffer pools. For each of the pools, the systems programmer specifies the size of each buffer, the number of buffers that VTAM is to build at initialization time, and the parameters that VTAM will use to determine when to expand and contract the buffer pools according to changes in the network load.

Q: *What are some of the considerations in choosing the buffer pool parameters?*

A: The goal of choosing the buffer pool sizes is to provide maximum throughput with minimum overhead. Choosing larger buffer pools minimizes the number of times that VTAM has to request virtual storage from the operating system, but costs more in allocated virtual storage. Choosing small values for the expansion and contraction points can result in a considerable overhead because VTAM is constantly acquiring and releasing buffer pool storage from the operating system.

Q: *How would a systems programmer determine VTAM's buffer usage?*

A: The VTAM command D NET,BFRUSE issued from an operator or NetView console displays the current number of buffers from each pool in use, the number of buffers currently in the pool, and the maximum usage of each pool, together with the total storage VTAM has allocated in both its private region and the common area.

Q: *What is the maximum number of sessions that an application program can support?*

A: It depends on the resources available in the system. Each active session consumes a few hundred bytes of control blocks, both in the private area and common storage, to describe the session to both VTAM and the application program. Both the application and VTAM require buffers to support traffic on the session. Processor resources limit the total amount of traffic that an application can support so that, for example, a CICS application could support several thousand sessions, each of which had relatively light traffic (one to two messages per session per minute). Conversely, VM could support only a limited number of highly active users, each of whom consumed a significant amount of processor cycles.

Q: *Which tuning parameters should be considered for an application that is expected to support a large number of sessions?*

A: When an application program LU is defined to VTAM, the EAS parameter on the APPL definition statement specifies an estimate of the number of concurrent sessions the application will have with other logical units—either other programs or devices. VTAM uses this operand to determine how it will allocate storage for the control blocks representing these sessions. Coding a large number causes VTAM to preallocate storage from the common area for a hash table which it uses to store the session representations. This allows fast lookup of session information. If the EAS value is coded significantly smaller than the number of sessions that are established, VTAM will not refuse to establish the additional sessions, but the search time for session information will be increased as VTAM must search a number of separately linked tables. Conversely, if an application will have only a few simultaneous sessions (TSO and NetView applications are specific examples of this application category), then EAS=1 should be coded in order to save system common storage.

Q: *How is the logon string that a user types at a terminal converted into a session initiation request by VTAM?*

A: The user's logon character string, which is usually a keyword naming the application with which the user is requesting a session, is translated to a formal session request by the VTAM component Unformatted Systems Services (USS). Tables, prepared by the network systems programmer, allow an installation to customize logon request strings to its needs.

Q: *How does VTAM determine which session parameters to use in starting a session?*

A: VTAM uses a *Logmode* or Logmode entry in a table to specify the session parameters. The session initiation request (through the Logmode parameter) supplies or defaults a Logmode name which is searched in the table.

Q: *How does VTAM determine which network route to use for a session?*

A: VTAM's resolution of a session request results in the Bind parameters and the Class of Service (COS) information being obtained from the Logmode entry. VTAM uses the COS name from the Logmode to index its Class of Service table (Costab) which lists the virtual routes and traffic priorities that are to be used by this session.

Q: *What entries in the COS table are required?*

A: The entry ISTVTCOS is used by VTAM for SSCP-to-SSCP and SSCP-to-PU sessions and is required. A blank COS entry was required for communications with older versions of SNA networks; however, it is strongly recommended as a "default" for sessions where no explicit COS name is specified in the Logmode entry.

Q: *In a multidomain (or multinetwork) environment, where are the Logmode and COS name entries resolved?*

A: The Logmode entry is resolved from the Modetab associated with the secondary LU. This supplies a COS entry, which is supplied as a name to the SSCP which owns the primary LU. This SSCP then uses its own Costab to resolve the name into a network route. The fact that the COS name is supplied from one domain and resolved to a route in another means that a significant amount of coordination is required between the network systems programmers responsible for the two domains.

Q: *How many Class of Service tables does VTAM support?*

A: Each VTAM supports one COS table per network. In a multinetwork environment, the COS tables to be used in adjacent networks are specified in the NCP.

Q: *How does a systems programmer prepare a Class of Service table for a network?*

A: The source for a Class of Service table is a series of assembly language macros, shown in the following example:

```
ISTSDCOS COSTAB
ISTVTCOS COS  VR=((0,2),(1,2),(2,2),(3,2),(4,2),(5,2),(6,2),(7,2))
BATCH    COS  VR=((0,0),(1,0),(2,0),(3,0),(4,0),(5,0),(6,0),(7,0))
         COS  VR=((0,0),(1,0),(2,0),(3,0),(4,0),(5,0),(6,0),(7,0))
         COSEND
         END  ISTSDCOS
```

The example shows the required COS name ISTVTCOS used by VTAM for SSCP sessions, which allows the use of virtual routes 0 through 7 at transmission priority 2. If virtual route 0 is available, it is used; then virtual route 1, through all the routes in the list. The batch entry BATCH uses the same virtual routes, in the same order, but at transmission priority 0. The third entry is the recommended blank entry, which resolves to the same set of virtual routes as the BATCH entry. The source is assembled using macros supplied with VTAM. The object code is link-edited into a load module which is placed in VTAMLIB. For a single network environment, the COS table has a standard name: ISTSDCOS. In a multinetwork environment, the COS table for VTAM's native network is ISTSDCOS. COS tables for adjacent networks can have any names, which must match the names specified in the network definitions in the NCPs.

Q: *How does a terminal LU establish a session to an application program in the same domain?*

A: An outline of a session start flow is as follows: The user at the terminal LU sends a character-coded request to VTAM requesting the session. VTAM's USS routines translate the character-coded request into an INITSELF RU. The INITSELF is sent to VTAM's SSCP service. VTAM's SSCP service sends a CINIT request to the application's LU. The application inspects the session request and sends a BIND to the terminal LU. The terminal LU responds to the BIND. The application then sends an SESST request to VTAM's SSCP to notify it of the session start.

NCP

IBM's Network Control Program (NCP) is the second most important component in an SNA network and comprises a dedicated operating system as well as specific hardware management routines and a description of the network topology that it supports. This section examines some of the technical issues surrounding NCP and its generation.

Q: *How can definition items be defaulted in an NCP?*

A: It is possible to specify a parameter for a lower-level node (in the hierarchy) in a higher-level node. The parameter is then applied to all lower-level nodes in a "sift-down" effect. For example, the DLOGMOD (default Logmode) parameter applies to an LU. If it is specified on a LINE macro, it will be applied to all LUs on that line that do not have a DLOGMOD parameter specifically supplied for them.

Q: *How can a network administrator arrange for a terminal to be logged-on automatically to an application at network start-up?*

A: If the LOGAPPL parameter is supplied in an LU definition, VTAM will automatically queue a session initiation request to the destination application on behalf of the LU at the time that the LU is activated.

Q: *What mechanisms does NCP use to minimize network disruption in the event of VTAM failure?*

A: Each dependent resource in an NCP is owned by an SSCP, which is responsible for resource activation and session management services. Should the SSCP which owns a resource fail, then the NCP starts Automatic Network Shutdown (ANS) procedures for the resource. The parameter ANS on the NCP PU macro defining the resource determines the NCP action. If ANS= STOP is coded (or inherited), NCP stops all communications with the resource, and any sessions with LUs that the resource supports are terminated. If ANS=CONTINUE or ANS=CONT is coded, NCP continues communications with the resource.

Q: *In the event of ANS, what happens to sessions with dependent LUs?*

A: A session that is already established will continue, and the dependent LU will still be able to communicate with its session partner, provided that the failure that caused the ANS did not disrupt the partner LU or any of the components in the session path.

Q: *How can resources be defined dynamically to an NCP?*

A: NCP Dynamic Reconfiguration supports the addition and deletion of link-attached resources in an active NCP. Network systems programmers prepare Dynamic Reconfiguration source decks, which are filed in VTAMLIST, instructing VTAM which resources are to be changed.

Q: *What definitions in the NCP source must be included to prepare for NCP Dynamic Reconfiguration?*

A: The NCP must be generated with sufficient spare control blocks to accommodate the additional devices. The PUDRPOOL macro specifies the number of spare PU definitions that the NCP will support; the LUDRPOOL macro specifies the number of spare LU definitions that the NCP will support. In addition, each line that may have devices added to it must have the MAXPU parameter specified to allow for the additional devices. If logical units are to be added to an existing PU, the PU must have the MAXLU parameter specified on its definition.

SDLC

Q: *How is an SDLC link activated?*

A: The two link stations on an SDLC link establish communications when one partner sends the Set Normal Response Mode (SNRM) command and receives an acknowledgment. This starts the communications, establishes the frame-numbering scheme, and determines the primary and secondary roles on the link.

Q: *How are the primary and secondary roles determined on an SDLC link?*

A: It depends on the type of node. If one of the link stations is associated with a type 4 node and one with a type 2.X node, the type 4 node is always the primary. If the link stations are both type 4 nodes or both type 2.1 nodes (a type 2.0 node can communicate only with a type 4 or 5 node), then the Exchange Identification (XID) sequence is used to establish primary and secondary roles.

Q: *How many devices can be connected to an SDLC link?*

A: Only one device can attach to an SDLC link in primary mode. There can, however, be up to 253 secondary mode devices using the SDLC multipoint link protocol.

Q: *What is the maximum frame size that can be supported on an SDLC link?*

A: It depends on the link stations at each end of the link and the size of their buffers. Frame sizes of 4096 bytes between type 4 nodes are not uncommon.

Q: *How does an SDLC link station recover from a transmission error?*

A: When a station on an SDLC link receives a frame in error (detected by the lack of a frame checksum or a checksum in error), the frame is discarded. The sequence numbering of the frames and the acknowledgment of frames by number means that link stations can discover that frames have been received out of sequence and request retransmission.

Token-Ring

Q: *What is the maximum number of devices that a single Token-Ring can support?*

A: The theoretical maximum number of devices on a Token-Ring network is 260. However, this maximum is rarely reached in practice because of electrical restrictions on the total length of cable in the ring and the number of concentrators.

Q: *What are the types of addresses used in a Token-Ring network?*

A: 1. Locally and universally addressed individual station addresses

2. Group broadcast and functional group addresses

Q: *What are the differences between the individual and group addresses?*

A: Individual addresses describe a single station on a Token-Ring and may be the source or destination addresses of Token-Ring frames. Group addresses are used to describe functions, rather than individual stations. A group address is used only as a destination address.

Q: *What considerations are there for choosing locally administered addresses versus universally administered addresses?*

A: Universally administered addresses are managed by the IEEE and are guaranteed to be unique worldwide. For those adapters which support universally administered addresses, the adapter's address is in read-only memory on the adapter and cannot be changed. This means that if an adapter fails, its replacement will have a different universally administered address, which may impact network management schemes. Universally administered addresses do not support any structured assignment which allows identification of the location of a Token-Ring station from its address.

Q: *What procedure does a Token-Ring adapter perform in order to start communications on a ring?*

A: The adapter first of all tests its lobe cable by sending a series of lobe test frames from the adapter to the MSAU, without attaching to the ring. The adapter then connects to the ring and monitors the ring traffic to determine whether it is the first station on the ring. The adapter sends a duplicate address test frame onto the ring to verify that another station with the same individual address is not already on the ring. The adapter waits until the active monitor initiates neighbor notification for the ring, identifies its Nearest Active Upstream Neighbor (NAUN), and identifies itself to its downstream neighbor. The adapter then sends a request initialization frame to the ring parameter server functional address, and uses the response to initialize itself. If there is no ring parameter server, the station uses default values.

Q: *What is the normal procedure for information transmission around a Token-Ring?*

A: A station that has information which it wishes to transmit waits until it receives a token. At that point, it converts the token into a frame (by setting a bit in the Access Control field) and transmits the frame, with destination and source addresses, routing information (if necessary), and the frame data. The frame information is repeated by all the stations on the Token-Ring. When it reaches its destination, the Token-Ring adapter in the station recognizes its address, copies the frame information from the ring into its buffers, and sets the Address Recognized and Frame Copied bits in the Frame Status field. The frame is transmitted around the ring until it reaches the originating station, which removes it from the ring and transmits a token, allowing another station to transmit.

Q: *Token-Rings have been described as "fair." Why is this?*

A: Token-Rings are deterministic, that is, each station can transmit at most one frame before relinquishing control of the token. This means that no one station can gain control of the ring at the expense of other stations.

Q: *What is a beaconing condition?*

A: A beaconing condition exists when a ring station discovers a hard failure in the ring which prevents the ring from functioning correctly. When this situation occurs, the station which discovers the error starts to transmit beacon frames continuously until the problem is resolved or the station removes itself from the ring.

Q: *How does a Token-Ring attempt to recover from a beaconing condition?*

A: When a station on a ring enters the beacon transmit mode, other stations repeat the frame. The frame will eventually arrive at the transmitter's NAUN. When the beaconing station's NAUN copies eight beacon frames, it removes itself from the ring. The station then begins to reattach itself, using the standard lobe attachment tests and duplicate address tests. If these succeed, the station remains reattached to the ring and waits for the beacon condition to terminate. If the ring does not recover after a specified period (the architected timer T(beacon_transmit)), the beaconing station assumes that its NAUN has completed its self-test and has reattached, and that the fault lies with the beaconing station itself. This station therefore removes itself from the ring and goes through the reinsertion attachment tests described here.

Q: *How does a Token-Ring node learn the address of its upstream neighbor?*

A: Every 7 seconds, the active monitor initiates the neighbor notification process on a Token-Ring. It broadcasts an Active Monitor Present frame to all ring stations on its ring the next time it receives a token. The first station which receives this frame copies the information in the frame, including the source address, which is the NAUN address for this station, and sets the Address Recognized and Frame Copied bits in the Frame Status field. Other stations on the ring repeat the frame, but do not take action because they do not require the address information in the frame. When a token is next available, the station which received the Active Monitor Present frame transmits a Standby Monitor Present frame, broadcast to all stations on the ring. The downstream neighbor of this station copies the frame, recognizes that this is its NAUN, and sets the Address Recognized and Frame Copied bits in the Frame Status field. Other stations on the ring ignore this frame, as they are not the downstream neighbor of the transmitter. In turn, all the remaining stations on the ring receive a Standby Monitor Present frame without the Address Recognized and Frame Copied bits set, use this information to update their NAUN information, and transmit a further Standby Monitor Present until the Active Monitor receives a Standby Monitor Present frame, which completes the sequence.

Q: *What are the contents of the Routing Information field?*

A: The Routing Information field comprises the Routing Control field, followed by up to eight 2-byte route designators, which define a ring number (12 bits) and a bridge number (4 bits) through which the frame should travel from its source to its destination.

Q: *How is the Routing Information field built?*

A: The Routing Information field is built during route discovery. As bridges forward-broadcast frames that are used by a ring station requesting a connection with another station, they add the ring number and bridge number to the routing information field, so that when a frame reaches its destination, it has a complete route built from its source, which the destination station can use to return a response.

Q: *How does a Token-Ring node determine the location of another node?*

A: A Token-Ring node which wishes to establish a connection with another node first transmits a TEST or XID frame to its destination on the same ring. If the destination station is on the same ring, then the connection can be established. If the destination station is not on the same ring, then the source station transmits a frame to the destination address with a Routing Information field requesting broadcast to all rings. Bridges forward the frame, which eventually is received at the destination.

Q: *How does a Token-Ring station establish a connection with another node?*

A: After a Token-Ring station has established the location of its partner node, it initiates connection by using an XID frame to negotiate primary and secondary station roles. The primary sends a Set Asynchronous Balanced Mode Extended (SABME) frame to activate the logical connection between the two stations. The secondary acknowledges the frame by sending an Unnumbered Acknowledgment (UA) frame. Finally, the primary sends the first data transmission a Receive Ready (RR) frame to confirm the data transfer mode.

Q: *What are the functions of the active monitor?*

A: The active monitor provides monitoring of the transmission of tokens and information around the ring. It is responsible for maintaining the master clock, which times all information transmission on the ring. It is responsible for resolving error conditions on the ring and for initiating neighbor notification periodically on the ring.

Network Routing

SNA routing, with its three-layer structure, is one of the more difficult concepts that a network systems programmer has to face. Judicious choice of network routes and alternatives, however, is crucial in maintaining network performance, reliability, and availability. This section explores routing concepts and the mechanics of route generation.

Q: *How is routing supported in an SNA subarea network?*

A: SNA routing uses the concepts of subareas to provide routing services, providing the abstraction of "link connections" between individual subareas.

Q: *How is a transmission group made up?*

A: A transmission group comprises one or a number of links of various types between two subareas. Links can be channel connections (a transmission group can comprise only a single channel connection), SDLC links (a transmission group can support multiple physical links), and Token-Ring logical connections (a transmission group supports only a single Token-Ring logical connection).

Q: *What is the difference between an explicit route and a virtual route?*

A: Explicit routes are defined between an origin subarea and a destination subarea over the transmission groups and intermediate subareas which connect them. The explicit route is identified by the origin subarea, the destination subarea, the number of the explicit route which connects the two subareas, and the number of the reverse explicit route, not necessarily the same number, which describes the route in the opposite direction.

A virtual route is a logical connection between two SNA subarea nodes, which is defined over a particular explicit route. Virtual route services provide transmission priorities over the underlying explicit route, flow control through virtual-route pacing mechanisms, and data integrity through sequence number checking of individual Path Information Units (PIUs) over the virtual route.

Q: *How are routing tables generated?*

A: Routing tables can be generated by an automated generation tool, such as IBM's Network Design Aid (NetDA), or its successor NetDA/2.

Q: *Where are network routes defined?*

A: VTAM network routes are stored in VTAMLIST. They are activated to describe the network to VTAM at initialization time. NCP network routes are included as part of the NCP source deck and assembled into control blocks as part of the network definition process.

Q: *How many routing tables do VTAM and NCP support?*

A: VTAM supports one set of routing tables since it only participates directly in one network. An NCP has a set of routes defined for each of the networks to which it is connected.

Q: *How is routing accomplished in a multinetwork environment?*

A: Network routes are entirely contained within a single network. The gateway NCPs, which are responsible for the interface between two networks, also provide virtual route termination services. NCP translates the session routing from the virtual routes and subarea numbers used in one network to those in another whenever an information frame crosses the network boundary.

Q: *How does the SNA architecture identify networks?*

A: Each SNA network is assigned a unique eight-character name by its network administrator. The name is defined to all Type 4, 5, and 2.1 nodes within the network. For VTAM, the network name is specified by the NETID parameter in the VTAM start list member ATCSTR00. For NCP, the native network name is specified using the NETID parameter of the BUILD macro. In earlier releases of VTAM and NCP, naming the network was necessary only if the network supported cross-network sessions. In current releases, the network name is required.

Q: *Can two networks share the same name?*

A: Two networks which are connected to each other via SNI must have unique names. Most names are chosen arbitrarily by the network administrators to represent the organization which they support. IBM has defined a standard for naming networks and provides a registration service to minimize the possibility of name conflicts.

Q: *How is connectivity possible between separately managed SNA networks?*

A: The extensions to SNA, known as SNA Network Interconnection (SNI), permit application sessions between logical units in two or more separate networks.

Q: *How are other network connections defined to VTAM?*

A: VTAM defines the names and the networks of other SSCPs with which it will communicate in a cross-domain resource manager major node, which is filed in VTAMLIST and activated to VTAM.

Q: *What is the function of the GWPATH definition?*

A: Following is a typical definition of a foreign-network SSCP which defines ONETVTM in network OTHERNET:

```
          VBUILD   TYPE=CDRM
          NETWORK  NETID=OTHERNET
 ONETVTM  CDRM     CDRSC=OPT,CDRDYN=YES,ISTATUS=ACTIVE
          GWPATH   SUBAREA=2,ELEMENT=19,                    X
                   ADJNET=NULLNET1,                         X
                   ADJNETSA=6,                              X
                   ADJNETEL=2
```

The GWPATH macro following the CDRM macro specifies the representation of ONETVTM in the adjacent network NULLNET1. The SUBAREA parameter defines the gateway NCP which is used to access the CDRM. The ADJNETSA and ADJNETEL parameters define the subarea and element address of this CDRM in the adjacent network. These parameters must correspond to a GWNAU macro in the NCP, which is used to correlate the address transformation information.

Q: *Where are the boundaries between networks?*

A: Network boundaries always reside in NCPs, called *gateway* NCPs.

Q: *How does a network systems programmer define resources in another network?*

A: Resources in other networks are defined using Cross-Domain Resource (CDRSC) major nodes in VTAM. For resources in other networks, the NETID parameter is coded, defining the network in which the resource resides.

Q: *Why would an installation wish to specify the owner of a foreign-network resource?*

A: Primarily for security reasons. Specifying the SSCP which owns a network resource together with the VFYOWNER=YES parameter as in:

```
          VBUILD   TYPE=CDRSC
          NETWORK  NETID=OTHERNET
 OTHCDRS  CDRSC    CDRM=SOMESSCP,VFYOWNER=YES . . .
```

where SOMESSCP owns OTHCDRS in network OTHERNET, means that sessions cannot be established unless this information is correct. This prevents other resources with the same name from attempting to establish cross-network sessions.

Q: *If the SSCP owner of a foreign-network resource changes, how can the network operator correct this problem?*

A: The owner of a CDRSC can be changed by issuing the MODIFY CDRM command. In the foregoing example, to change the owner of CDRSC OTHCDRS to SSCPTWO, the network operator would issue the command MODIFY NET,CDRM=SSCPTWO,ID=OTHCDRS.

Q: *How does VTAM determine where to forward a session request for a logical unit in another network?*

A: VTAM uses the SSCPs which are specified in an adjacent SSCP list when trying to find a destination logical unit for a session request. Adjacent SSCP lists are VTAM major nodes which are filed in VTAMLIST, and activated on network start-up, or by the network operator.

Q: *What order does VTAM use in searching the adjacent SSCP list?*

A: The order depends on the VTAM start option SSCPORD in the VTAM start member ATCSTR00 of VTAMLIST. If SSCPORD=NO is specified, VTAM searches the table in the order in which the entries were defined. If SSCPORD=YES is specified, VTAM searches the table in the following order:

1. The SSCP that owns the resource (if this is known)
2. The SSCP(s) for which the most recent session-initiation attempt succeeded (if any)
3. The SSCPs for which no session-initiation attempt has been made
4. The SSCPs for which the last session initiation attempt failed

Q: *How would a network operator determine the adjacent SSCP list for a foreign network?*

A: A network operator can use the DISPLAY ADJSSCPS command to show the adjacent SSCP list for a specific network.

Q: *What are the limitations on the number of cross-network sessions?*

A: There are no intrinsic limits in the SNA architecture for the number of cross-network sessions. However, each cross-network session requires storage to represent it in the gateway NCP(s).

Network Administration

NetView

NetView is IBM's strategic network management subsystem: a complex monitoring, analysis, and automation facility.

Q: *What are the major components of NetView?*

A: The major components of NetView are the Command Facility; the Hardware Monitor (formerly the Network Problem Determination Aid, or NPDA); the Session Monitor (formerly the Network Logical Data Manager, or NLDM); and the Status Monitor.

Q: *How does NetView interface with VTAM for command processing?*

A: NetView interfaces with VTAM by opening an ACB defined to VTAM as the primary *program operator.* An application with program operator authority can send commands to VTAM and retrieve the output, using the SENDCMD and RCVCMD macros.

Q: *How can a network systems programmer arrange for automatic execution of commands?*

A: The NetView AT and EVERY commands allow scheduling of NetView, VTAM, and other commands or command lists (Clists) at specified intervals and times of the day. By combining the AT, EVERY, and other Clist support commands, it is possible for a network systems programmer to develop a custom schedule for command execution.

Q: *How can NetView be programmed to react to a network event?*

A: Every VTAM and MVS message starts with an identifier which defines the format and content of the message. NetView has a *message table,* which allows a network systems programmer to associate a command list with a message identifier. The command list receives the entire text of the message, and can parse it to determine the resource(s) which are affected by the event which generated the message, and then take the appropriate action.

Q: *What are the functions of the hardware monitor?*

A: The hardware monitor collects and displays statistical information and error reports (alerts) from network-attached and host-attached devices. It also writes records derived from this information to the SMF log.

Q: *How does the hardware monitor receive data from the network?*

A: Each network device which is owned by a VTAM sends error and statistical information on its SSCP-PU session. For example, a 3174 establishment controller can report an error with a coaxial connection to an attached terminal to VTAM.

Q: *A user complains that a printer is printing slowly. How could you determine the cause of the problem?*

A: The exact methodology of problem determination depends on the information found during diagnosis. However, the following are some specific items which can be checked: Resource utilization of the application which is driving the printer—is this a network problem? Is the application not providing the data fast enough to the network? Link utilization of the facilities in the transmission path to the device—is another session consuming a disproportionate amount of the available bandwidth? Is there a large number of temporary errors on the link(s) in the transmission path which impacts throughput and performance?

Q: *How would a network systems programmer determine the number of errors on a line?*

A: NCP maintains traffic and error counters for each of the links which it connects. At intervals, it forwards this information to VTAM on the NCP's SSCP-PU session. VTAM, in turn, forwards the statistics to the NetView hardware monitor (NPDA) where it is filed in the NPDA database. The information may be retrieved with the command NPDA TOT ST N *lname,* which requests a display of all the statistics records associated with the line. The number of frames retransmitted is also available through NPM.

NPM

The NetView Performance Monitor (NPM) provides monitoring, statistical, analytical, and accounting functions for mainframe-based SNA networks, and is an essential tool for network systems programmers in understanding the traffic flow through a network and its performance characteristics.

Q: *What are the functions of the NetView Performance Monitor (NPM)?*
A: Collection, display, and archiving of network performance information, session information, network and session accounting information, response time information, local area network data, and filtering of information recorded on the Systems Management Facilities (SMF) log.

Q: *How does NPM collect data?*
A: NPM uses hardware and software facilities in the 37X5 communications controllers and NCP to collect utilization, link, and accounting statistics.

Q: *How does NPM collect data from an NCP?*
A: NPM uses a virtual line group defined in the NCP, with the parameter NPASRC=YES. This line group has a single line, with a single PU and at least one LU in it. NPM retrieves data from the NCP by means of a session with the NPA LU.

Q: *What are the steps involved in preparing an NCP for data collection?*
A: 1. Add the NPM library to the JCL for the Network Definition Facility (NDF) so that NPM can be included as part of the NCP load module.

2. Add the parameter NPA=YES to the BUILD macro and, optionally, the SESSAC, GWSESAC, PUNAME, and MAXTP parameters, if accounting data collection and transmission priority performance data collection are required.

3. Specify NPACOLL=YES for each of the resources for which NPM data collection is desired.

4. Specify the SPEED parameter on lines, so that NPM can calculate the line utilization.

5. Define the NPALU line group to NCP.

6. File the NCP definition and generate the NCP.

Q: *How does NPM collect response-time data?*
A: NPM collects response-time data by monitoring messages as they pass through VTAM buffers: incoming from a terminal device, outbound to a terminal, and the final acknowledgment from the terminal.

Q: *How does NPM collect Token-Ring data?*
A: NPM collects Token-Ring data by retrieving it from IBM LAN manager. The LAN manager maintains Token-Ring sessions with bridges, and can collect traffic and error statistics from them.

SSP and the Systems Generation Process

This section deals with some of the mechanics of converting network definitions into programs and loading them into communications controllers using IBM's systems support programs.

Q: *What are the services provided by the Systems Support Programs (SSP)?*
A: The Systems Support Programs (SSP) provide services to:

1. Generate a network control program from source definition.
2. Load a network control program into a 37X5 communications controller.
3. Dump a communications controller.
4. Dump the Maintenance and Operator Subsystem (MOSS) and network scanners in a communications controller.
5. Format communications controller, MOSS, and scanner dumps.

Q: *How would a network systems programmer prepare an NCP definition for inclusion in an SNA network?*
A: In order to prepare an NCP definition for an SNA network the following steps must be performed:

1. Generate or modify a set of NCP source definitions using a program editor.
2. Submit the definitions to the Network Definition Facility (NDF) for generation of an NCP load module, an NCP expanded source (NEWDEFN), a Resource Resolution Table (RRT), and an output listing.
3. Verify the output of the NDF.
4. File the resulting NEWDEFN source in VTAMLIST, and the NCP load module and RRT in VTAMLIB.

Q: *What are the processes performed by the Network Definition Facility?*
A: The Network Definition Facility performs the following:

1. It reads the NCP definition source and validates the definition statements and parameters.
2. It builds the NEWDEFN output if the NEWDEFN keyword is coded on the NDF OPTIONS keyword. (This option is required if Token-Ring or X.25 facilities will be used in this NCP.)
3. It generates NCP assembler language source code for the resources coded in the NCP source.
4. It invokes the NCP tables 1 and 2 assemblies, which read the assembly language source code definitions produced earlier, and generate object code for the NCP control blocks.
5. It generates linkage editor control statements.
6. It invokes the linkage editor to combine the object code defining the NCP control blocks with IBM NCP code modules to produce the NCP load module and RRT.
7. It produces an output listing giving details of the results of the individual steps.

Q: *How can an NCP be loaded into a 37X5 communications controller?*

A: If the communications controller is channel-attached to a System/370 processor, two methods are available: (1) VTAM VARY NET,ACT,LOAD=YES command, and (2) use of the SSP independent loader IFLOAD.

Q: *How is an NCP load module transferred to a Token-Ring-attached Communications Controller?*

A: In order to transfer a load module to a Token-Ring-attached Communications Controller, it must first have an active NCP running. To install the initial NCP into a Token-Ring Controller, a small NCP module containing a minimum set of definitions is prepared and generated using the NDF process. This load module is transferred to the hard disk of a local (or SDLC link-attached) 3745 controller using the VTAM MODIFY NET,LOAD command. Using MOSS commands on the 3745 console, the information is copied to the 3745 floppy disk.

The 3745 floppy disk is transported to the remote 3745 location, where MOSS commands are used to transfer it to the hard disk, load it, and activate it. VTAM can then establish communications with an ownership of the NCP in the remote 3745. VTAM MODIFY NET,LOAD commands are then used to transfer a full NCP over the communication path from the host VTAMLIB to the hard disk of the remote 3745, at which point it can be loaded into the 3745's main storage.

22

Object-Oriented Analysis (OOA), Design (OOD), and Programming (OOP)

Rick Stanley and Candice Zarr

Object Technology for Businesses

For many years, object-oriented technology has had a tremendous amount of success in the development of real-time software for scientific and communications applications. Object technology in these areas has already demonstrated potential for higher productivity through the use of reusable components. As a result, object technology is making inroads into commercial business systems. There are outstanding organizations that have successfully made the transition to object technology. They have achieved enviable levels of quality and productivity.

Object-Oriented Analysis, Design, and Programming represent a new approach to traditional/functional approaches. Most business systems developers and managers are familiar with functional, or procedurally oriented, ways of designing and developing systems. CASE, for example, is an adaptation of these procedural approaches. But there are also new activities and techniques for carrying out structured analysis and design. Object technology is one of them and requires an entirely new way of thinking about development. There is no equivalent for existing, structured, functionally or data-oriented system design in the object-oriented paradigm. They are incompatible.

Though the advantages of object-oriented analysis, design, and programming are many, there are distinctly different ways of describing the business problem and the solution that must be mastered. There are entirely new programming languages and development environments. In the first part of this chapter we will be discussing some of these topics briefly. More detailed information will be found in the questions and answers that follow.

Object Methodologies

Like their traditional brethren, object methodologies rarely cover the needs of the entire system's life cycle. Some concentrate on the analysis of the business requirements; others deal more with the infrastructure design strategy. A sign of the youth of this technology is the large number of methodologies which address the analysis and design of new systems. Much less frequently addressed are techniques for analysis and design of enhancements to existing software, or reuse and library management.

While it would be possible to use object analysis and design techniques for developing a traditional, procedurally oriented system, the converse is not true. Methodologies for analysis, design, and development of object systems are very different from traditional approaches. While the goals of the various object methodologies are the same—to produce an efficient, easily extendable system quickly—some are better suited for some projects than others. There are methods which are event-oriented, and those that more closely resemble data-oriented, transaction-driven methods like information engineering. Others are better for first-timers and simpler systems. Each methodology uses its own notation standards. There are many automated CASE tools for drawing these specific notations and for storing analysis and design information. Some methodologies have plastic templates for hand-drawing their notation.

Analysis Methods

Unlike the traditional approaches that involve interviewing and transcribing or interviewing and modeling, object-oriented analysis methods are concerned with identifying candidate objects, object behaviors, and cooperation between objects. Object analysis is often conducted in informal settings with small (one to five people), knowledgeable groups of business and IS professionals discussing and refining their definition of system components at a high level. Object analysis is described as "middle-out" as opposed to "bottom-up" or "top-down" traditional approaches. Using appropriate toolsets, prototypes can be used to provide a very rapid definition of end-user requirements. The following are some popular analysis methods:

- Booch is fast becoming the standard, especially for C++.

- Rumbaugh's OMT is in some ways similar to Booch, and has been combined with Booch and Jacobson to form a unified notation.

- Jacobson uses Objectory (the Object Factory for Software Development) to "design with building blocks."[1]

---

[1] "Object-Oriented Software Engineering, A Use Case Driven Approach" by Ivar Jacobson, Magnus Christerson, Patrik Jonsson, Gunnar Övergaard, Reading, Mass., Addison-Wesley, 1994.

- Shlaer/Mellor is oriented toward information modeling.
- Coad/Yourdon is popular because this approach is very accessible for the novice.
- Rebecca Wirffs-Brock's "Responsibility-Driven Design," while actually a design method, contains components for analysis which proponents feel is straightforward, natural, and promotes the communication of ideas and team interaction.

Design Methods

Design takes the system components, the objects, and their prescribed behaviors and defines the physical implementations these components will take. Designers may identify existing objects for reuse within the new system. Objects and their behaviors may be combined with other objects to form more generic, reusable, abstract classes. Object subsystem designs (for large projects) are integrated. Object system design promotes an iterative, prototyping approach which facilitates changes and refinements, unlike traditional approaches, in which the entire system is developed based on an agreed set of specifications. Iterative prototyping allows for greater flexibility in designing user interfaces, object behavior and collusion, and for early-on performance testing. Through reuse, there are opportunities for higher-level code quality and a reduced need for testing.

One of the most widely accepted design approaches is Booch, with its well-known "cloud" modeling notation. Booch's approach has been described as "design a little, code a little, test a little, and review a little." It is a cyclic, iterative approach which works well when managed well. Rumbaugh's design method is a more data-intensive approach, which will seem more accessible to those familiar with information engineering and data modeling techniques. Again, Wirffs-Brock is also considered a different approach which models objects with their behaviors and their collaborations. Proponents of Wirffs-Brock feel that it facilitates communication with nontechnicians, as it is easy for them to apply these concepts to the business problem.

The techniques that are used for abstracting objects into classes vary. How class definition takes place and how classes are named is subjective, based upon the development team's perception of the business problem at hand. These decisions will have the effect of either facilitating or hampering the potential reuse of the object. Berard's methodology is a comprehensive, cyclic-iterative approach and includes analysis, design, and testing approaches and implementation procedures, along with techniques for tightly controlled project management.

Object Programming

The most popular languages currently are C++ and SmallTalk, although there are several others which are used successfully: ENFIN, Objective C, Actor, and Eiffel are just a few. There are major differences in hybrid versus "pure" languages. C++

is a hybrid—it's an extension of the procedural C language. C can be combined with C++ in a C++ program, thus reusing legacy code and libraries rather than rewriting from scratch. Depending upon the brand of C++ employed, you will have more or fewer application development tools to help you to test and debug your source code. C++ is also much closer to the machine. That level of detail provides for very tight control over your code, but it can also introduce more bugs and make debugging more difficult.

With any hybrid language, programmers can continue to write procedural code. There is no way to ensure that the object features of the language are being completely employed. This sometimes happens when C programmers are retrained in C++. Like any of us, given a task with a time frame, we tend to solve problems in ways we know will work, rather than searching for and trying out new techniques. SmallTalk advocates point out that in their language, it is not possible (or at least extremely difficult) to write procedural code. The pure object orientation of SmallTalk ensures that systems get the full benefit of object technology. SmallTalk development environments also tend to be more robust—integrating libraries, browsers, debuggers, and editors (although the C++ vendors are catching up). SmallTalk may be either dynamically compiled or interpreted, which places some performance restrictions on applications.

Object Databases

Object databases are developed to provide persistent data for object applications. This ability to store information beyond the life of an object session is part of the impetus that is fueling the growth of object orientation in the commercial world. For application developers familiar with relational database technology (or its predecessors—hierarchical and network databases), there are certain features that they've come to expect.

Working within the framework of expected features, database and application design is greatly simplified. Relational databases contain functionality which ensures that the data is always (or nearly always) available. There are recovery facilities that ensure that data is recovered quickly and in a consistent state after a system failure. Transaction management makes it appear as though each user of the database is the only user. Data updates are conducted so that each user is always presented with a consistent view of the data in an environment where there may be numerous updates, against many resources, being performed concurrently.

Relational databases also take over many of the responsibilities for maintaining integrity in the database. Once resource relationships are defined to the database, the programmer does not need to code logic to maintain these pointers; the RDBMS maintains consistency. RDBMS query language is based upon SQL (Structured Query Language), so skills in developing applications for one RDBMS are fairly transportable to other RDBMS. Transaction management, concurrence, integrity, and standard query languages are features which support the tabular-ized-data paradigm of RDBMs. Currently, these are only partially and inconsistently addressed by object database systems.

Object database technology provides functions which are not available in the traditional database paradigms. Object databases support long transactions—the type of processing which may change the state of an entire database over a period of weeks or months. Features which support long transactions allow the transaction to be suspended, stored, and subsequently restarted. Some ODBM products also support work-group development and versioning. ODBM interfaces to OO languages are vendor-specific—closely linked with specific OO program language vendors. Some, like GEMSTONE, offer an entire application development platform.

Questions and Answers

The questions and answers that follow include definitions as well as OOA, OOD, and OOP concepts and usage.

Q: *What is an object?*
A: An object is a computational entity that knows something and knows how to do something with what it knows. What it knows is contained in its encapsulated data. What it knows how to do is represented by its interface.

Q: *What is encapsulated data?*
A: Data that can only be accessed through an interface is said to be encapsulated. (Unencapsulated data can be accessed by direct reference—i.e., by its name.)

Q: *What is an interface?*
A: In the context of the answers to the previous questions, an interface is a collection of names of services that an object can perform along with a specification of the parameters that each of these services allows or requires. These names are bound, at some point, to methods that provide an implementation of the services.

Q: *What is a method?*
A: A method is the implementation of an object service. It contains the detailed computer instructions for providing the service in support of an item in the object's interface.

Q: *What is a class?*
A: A class is the definition of an object. It specifies the data elements and data formats that combine to reflect what an object "knows." A class also specifies the services that each object created from the class can be expected to perform. The collection of all these services is the object's interface, and represents what the object "knows how to do."

Q: *What is the relationship between a class and an object?*

A: A class specifies the data and methods that operate on the data for each object that results from this specification. The class definition also has some methods of its own that know how to create new objects. An object is an instance of a class. It creates memory space for the member data as defined in the class.

Q: *What does it mean to send a message?*

A: Sending a message is the standard way to invoke an object. The message requests a specific service to be performed by the object and is often accompanied by additional information in the form of parameters. An object typically responds to a message by producing a result.

Q: *Summarize the major difference between C++ and SmallTalk.*

A: C++ is a language in which some relationships (bindings) are determined at compile time (Static or early binding) or at run time (Dynamic or late binding). Type checking is done at compile time. In particular, type checking is done at this time. SmallTalk, on the other hand, determines these relationships and checks for type at execution time. Also, in SmallTalk, there are no intrinsic values that are not objects. SmallTalk also is accompanied by a development and run-time environment as well as a standard class library.

Q: *Discuss the difference between single and multiple inheritance. Why would you choose one over the other?*

A: Single inheritance implies that each class has at most one parent in the class hierarchy, while there can be multiple parents in the multiple inheritance class hierarchy. Some feel that the "real world" is more naturally modeled by the multiple inheritance model.

Q: *What is a method? What is the relationship between methods and messages?*

A: Methods represent the "intelligence" of an object. They know how to access data and produce the appropriate results in response to specific messages that are sent to the object. When a message is sent to an object, the run-time system is responsible for choosing which method responds to that message. The method could be one defined by the class as part of the object's interface, or it could be in the interface of one of the object's parents in the class hierarchy.

Q: *How can you tell if an object model is correct?*

A: There is no absolute way of testing for correctness other than determining whether the model accurately reflects its real-world counterpart.

Q: *What is a class library?*

A: The library containing the set of class definitions along with their inheritance relationships is called a class library.

Q: *What is a class hierarchy browser?*

A: A class hierarchy browser is part of the development environment for developing OO applications. Typically, it has the ability to examine existing class definitions for the purpose of subclassing, copying, or modifying these definitions. In most OO systems, the debugging of the OO application can be triggered from the class hierarchy browser.

Q: *What does CRC design mean?*

A: This is an OO design technique that involves assignment of classes, responsibilities, and collaborations in order to model a real-world enterprise. This is not really a methodology by itself, but a technique that can be used in conjunction with a methodology such as Booch.

Q: *Discuss the relationship between the analyst, designer, and programmer on an OO team.*

A: The analyst works with the user/client to develop a systematic understanding of a problem to be solved by automation. The analyst breaks down the "Problem Domain" into a set of objects and defines the relationships between these objects. The designer works from this analysis to lay out the class's responsibilities and collaborations that can be implemented by the programmer to complete the solution.

Q: *Distinguish a class variable from an instance variable.*

A: Class variables are those used within the class definition itself (as opposed to instance variables which are distinct for each instance of the class).

Q: *What does the term abstract base class mean?*

A: In C++ an abstract base class is one that cannot be implemented directly, but is instead implemented by its subclasses (or derived classes). Base classes and abstract base classes are needed to implement polymorphism in C++.

Q: *What is an OO database?*

A: An OO database stores objects whose lifetime spans the run-units which create and/or use them. These objects are typically shared across applications within an enterprise.

Q: *What is the term used for the situation when the result obtained from sending a message depends on the object to which the message was sent?*

A: Polymorphism.

Q: *Why are GUIs commonly programmed using object technology?*

A: GUIs are populated with graphical objects which must respond to user-generated events such as mouse clicks. Object technology is based on events and event-handling as the means by which objects collaborate. It is thus a natural for implementing GUIs.

Q: *List three components of object technology.*

A: There are certainly more than three components in object technology, but here are the ones probably thought of most commonly:

1. An OO programming language
2. A class library that extends the language
3. A development environment that facilitates use of the language

Q: *What does the term* event-driven *mean?*

A: Applications whose components respond to external stimuli ("events") are called event-driven. Most simulations of real-world activity are done with this technique. Also, GUIs are almost entirely driven by events such as keys being pressed or the mouse being clicked.

Q: *List three techniques for reengineering an existing program so that it is object-oriented.*

A: 1. "Wrappering" is a technique that puts a thin shell around an existing program. This shell ("wrapper") receives incoming messages and routes them to the appropriate internal procedure within the application. This technique allows the application to participate with other parts that have engineered with object technology, but is not a permanent solution, since the real benefits of OO design can be realized only when the application has been completely redone using OO design methodology.

   2. Using a reengineering tool, the potential objects within an application are brought to the attention of the "reengineer," and assistance is provided in overcoming some of the routine, detailed work involved in defining the class definitions for the new objects.

   3. A "magic tool" that takes an existing application and produces a corresponding OO application. To date, no such tools have been successfully demonstrated, and the viability of this approach has not been proven.

Q: *Why is object technology suitable for client/server applications?*

A: The object model is based on the ability to send and receive messages in an asynchronous and recursive manner. This is the same model needed to support client/server applications. Thus, object technology is a natural fit for client/server applications.

Q: *How does object technology lead to reusability?*

A: The class hierarchy provided by most OO development environments contains classes whose methods are designed for reuse. These classes typically encapsulate the complex parts of the application. The classes can be either directly reused or can be specialized for a particular use through subclassing.

Q: *What is the theoretical basis for the claim that object technology produces more easily maintained applications?*

A: The objects in the object model are intended to directly reflect the objects in the problem domain. Thus, if one understands the problem domain, the OO application, with proper analysis, design, and abstraction, explains itself and is easier to maintain.

Q: *Discuss briefly the history of Object Technology (OT).*

A: Object technology is rooted in the approach to solving real-world problems by simulating these problems on a computer. Originally, this work was done by mathematicians using mathematic modeling tools such as queueing theory. In 1967, the SIMULA programming language brought the world of simulation to the computer, making it much easier to create these models.

Borrowing on this approach, Alan Kay at Xerox Parc invented the SmallTalk language that was centered completely around objects, and was thus called the first "pure" object-oriented language. Kay also invented the notion of class hierarchies, based on his background in classification theory in the field of biology. This work took on added importance with the introduction of iconic interfaces used first in the Xerox Star computer. These interfaces have since grown to be the rapidly developing and generally accepted graphic user interfaces used on the Apple Macintosh and PC-compatible computers running OS/2, Windows NT, Windows 95, and Unix operating systems, and Windows 3.x under DOS. Those who are expert in object technology believe that much larger application areas (especially those targeted for distributed, client/server, or peer-to-peer environments) are best served by being reengineered to the object-oriented paradigm.

Q: *Distinguish between the interface and implementation of a class.*
A: An interface is the external protocol presented to clients of a class of objects. It is carefully designed so as not to change. The class definition contains not only this interface definition, but also the hidden implementation that supports the interface. This implementation is free to change as long as the interface remains constant. Since the interface is essential to type-checking at time of compilation, it is useful for language supporting strong type-checking to have interface definitions that can be separated from the class definition. In this way, separately compiled clients of a class can be checked to make sure objects are referenced in the proper manner.

Q: *Describe static and dynamic binding.*
A: Static binding takes place at the time of compilation; dynamic binding takes place at run time. It is difficult to support polymorphism with static binding.

Q: *What is a garbage collector?*
A: When an object is no longer referenced by another object, then it is necessary to reclaim the system resource (typically, storage that has been previously acquired) needed to support it. A garbage collector periodically scans the active object space for objects no longer being referenced and releases the system resources for any such objects. This feature is not available in all OO languages.

Q: *What are the advantages and disadvantages of garbage collection?*
A: *Advantages:* This automatic process relieves the application programmer from the duties of freeing objects that are no longer needed. This represents a substantial savings in the amount of detailed, low-level programming that the programmer must do.
   Disadvantages: The garbage collection process is typically not under control of the application. This can lead to unpredictable delays in processing. In SmallTalk this manifests itself in the form of a vacuum cleaner icon appearing on the screen from time to time, indicating that garbage collection is taking place. This is sometimes quite annoying to the end user of the application.

Q: *Discuss the life cycle of an object.*

A: Objects, like their real-world counterparts, have a life cycle in which they are born, mature, grow old, and die. In the case of objects, an object is created, initialized, remains in a "last-used" state, is finalized, and then destroyed. Finalization is the point in the life cycle at which an object has the opportunity to clean up things, knowing that it is about to die. It's like writing its last will and testament. More seriously, it involves closing files, releasing locks, and abandoning any other resource to which it has laid claim during its existence. When the object is destroyed, any references to it are no longer valid. It is important that no such reference remain; otherwise, dangling references might occur, as they sometimes do in C++ when destruction is not done properly.

Q: *What does "genericity" mean?*

A: Genericity deals with the ability to define modules with generic (i.e., non-type-specific) parameters. These parameters can later be specified to generate a family of modules whose main distinguishing feature is their actual parameter types. This is implemented by the template feature in C++. Thus, one has a generic module, 'Display(T)', where T can be replaced with a specific type, such as circle or square, with T being replaced everywhere in the generic module with the actual parameter type.

Q: *What does subclass mean?*

A: To create a subclass (using inheritance) means to specialize an existing class for some specific purpose. What you are really saying when you create a subclass is that the parent class is not exactly what is needed. The subclass need only specify how it is to be treated differently from its parent.

Q: *What is a derived class?*

A: It is synonymous with the term *subclass.* A class derived from another, more abstract, class is called a derived class. For example, a CheckingAccount is derived from the more abstract class, BankAccount, which might be, in turn, derived from the even more abstract class, Account.

Q: *Discuss the difference between a method and a subroutine.*

A: Methods and subroutines are very similar. They both "know a secret" about some specific and sometimes quite complex process. However, methods are designed to be inherited or overridden. If they are inherited, there is zero work on the part of the OO programmer required to exploit the method's functionality. That is, a message that binds to an inherited method requires no new definition by the implementor. If a method is overridden, it is usually the case that some additional functionality is introduced in the overriding method; then the remainder of the functionality is inherited. Subroutines, by contrast, have no such capability. If a subroutine is not quite right, then either the source code must be copied and modified (if it is available) or some means of intercepting calls to it and possibly modifying its results must be introduced. This leads to a Rube Goldberg solution that causes later maintenance problems.

Q: *Can you have global variables in an OO application?*
A: Yes, but the locality of reference should be carefully controlled. This is typically done with class variables. A class variable is accessible by all instances of the class by sending messages to the class definition (or by direct reference, depending on the policy of the OO language). An example would be a class variable containing an interest rate. This rate would be accessed by all instances of a bank account class containing the variable.

Q: *What is the difference between a class and a type?*
A: A type is the specification of an interface; a class is the complete implementation, together with the interface. A type may have many different implementations.

Q: *How can object technology be used to extend a programming language?*
A: The classes defined using object technology are really language extensions. They extend the range of types that the language can reference along with operations ("methods") that give intelligence to the types. For example, a bank account is likely to be imbued with intelligence to display itself and to accept a message to withdraw funds from itself. Every class that is defined enriches the language in some way.

Q: *Distinguish between abstract datatype and intrinsic datatype.*
A: Abstract datatypes permit reference to objects in the problem domain; intrinsic datatypes are all about mapping data items to computer storage. An example of an abstract datatype is a propeller; an example of an intrinsic type is a packed decimal value.

Q: *What is a member function?*
A: This comes from C++; it means the same thing as "method." It comes from the usage: a function that is a member of a class definition.

Q: *How old is OT?*
A: Approximately 25 years old. It started in 1967 with SIMULA.

Q: *What is considered by most to be the first OO programming language?*
A: SIMULA.

Q: *What is a persistent object?*
A: An object whose lifetime exceeds the run-unit in which it was created is called persistent.

Q: *What is an embedded system?*
A: Embedded systems are those which are a part of a tool, like an oscilloscope or an intelligent robot. Object technology has been used quite successfully in this environment.

Q: *Can object technology be used in an embedded system?*
A: It has been . . . most notably by Object Technology International with their proprietary version of SmallTalk that can run in a very space- and processor-constrained environment.

Q: *Describe a compound object.*

A: Most objects contain references to other objects and are, therefore, compound (also called *complex*). This is another way of reuse in an object system. It is done by taking advantage of a preexisting collection of cataloged objects which can be reused as components of a newly defined object. *Example:* a clock is composed of gears and springs and dials and hands. Each of these might be objects whose class has already been defined.

Q: *What does object collaboration mean?*

A: This is how objects work together to produce the automated solution to a business problem (or any of a large variety of problems that have solutions in the real world, but not in a computerized environment). Objects collaborate by sending one another messages. The receiving object may in turn send messages to other objects to fulfill its responsibility but, ultimately, it must produce a result which it returns to the object which sent the original message.

Q: *How does object-oriented design lend itself to distributed application design?*

A: OO design is based on a model of computing in which events are triggered by messages. In this model, an object must always be prepared to respond to a message—even when it is already in the process of responding to the message. This is very similar to the model needed for distributed application design, where components of the application may be deployed across a hierarchy of processors and communicate with one another by sending messages. OO design, therefore, provides a good basis for application distribution. It is like drawing perforated boundaries in the application indicating where the application can be broken apart in order to be distributed.

Q: *What is the Object Management Group (OMG)? What are its main goals?*

A: The OMG is a consortium of hardware manufacturers and software vendors who are committed to promoting the OO model of computing. Its main goals are to provide a framework or infrastructure in which class definitions can be shared across languages and objects can collaborate, even when they are objects that were created in different language environments. The Common Object Request Broker Architecture (CORBA) is a product of OMG and lays the groundwork for this kind of leveraging and sharing. It addresses the issue of distribution across a network of processors.

Q: *Which programming languages best support rapid prototyping and incremental development?*

A: Languages that feature incremental compilation and dynamic binding are best suited for rapid prototyping and incremental development. This is because changes can be introduced without requiring massive recompilation and relink editing. These languages typically defer type-checking until execution, and dynamically load methods as they are required. SmallTalk, Objective-C, and OO COBOL are examples of this type of language.

Q: *What are intrinsic data types in SmallTalk?*

A: Intrinsic data types are those that focus on the mapping of data to computer storage and those that place restrictions on the type of operation that can be done on data elements. These are familiar to those who have programmed in third-generation languages such as COBOL and FORTRAN. Examples are FIXED, FLOAT, PACKED DECIMAL. There are no intrinsic data types in SmallTalk. There are only objects which are, in turn, instances of class definitions that reflect data types typically in the problem domain rather than data types that belong to the solution domain. That is, the data types have to do with the problem to be modeled rather than being concerned about laying out bits in computer memory. An example that is often given to illustrate this is as follows: In SmallTalk, to perform the addition $1 + 1$, the "+" message is sent to the object 1 accompanied by another instance of 1 as a parameter. One pleasant side effect of this is that neat constructs like heterogenous collections of objects can hold anything in SmallTalk. There are no restrictions like saying that collections can hold abstract data types but not intrinsic data types.

Q: *Why would one choose to use an Object-Oriented Database (OODB)?*

A: Let's be clear about what an OODB is and does. An OODB is a place where persistent objects are managed. A persistent object is one whose lifetime spans units of execution. That is, an object may be created by an application and still be required on subsequent executions of that same (or perhaps another) application. The OODB is the place where the object lives between these executions. An OODB performs all the same services that other database management systems perform: sharing, locking, and committing across an enterprise, as well as services such as backup and restore. The main difference is that an OODB is active (the procedures are stored with the data), while other DBMSs are passive (only the data values are stored). Another distinguishing feature of OODBMS is that references to other objects are stored as well as simple data values. Back to the original question, an OODBMS becomes necessary when an enterprise commits to object technology and needs to share its objects across individual departments within the enterprise.

Q: *How can object-oriented database management systems and relational database management systems coexist?*

A: One way is for the OODBMS to have a way to access the RDBMS when necessary to produce simple object instances—instances that do not reference other object instances. This "side-door" approach allows a single model of data to be maintained. This is an advantage to the OO programmer, since it reduces the complexity of the applications he or she develops. Another way is to define classes whose encapsulated data are the rows of a relational table and whose methods are the stored procedures that access the table. The first approach is preferable, since the complexity of accessing relational tables is contained within the OODBMS and does not have to be addressed by the application developer.

Q: *What is ANSI? ISO? Why are they important for object technology?*

A: ANSI is the American National Standards Institute. ISO is the International Standards Organization. Without such organizations the computer industry and object technology would be chaotic, with no control over language development, class libraries, database interfaces, etc. The C++ language is currently in the process of being standardized by the ANSI and ISO organizations.

Q: *What does concurrent object environment mean?*

A: There are two interpretations of the phrase, "concurrent environment," depending on the point of view of the speaker. From the object modelist's point of view it means that an object can send multiple messages to receiving objects without waiting for a response from the first receiver. From an OO database point of view, it means that shared objects in the database can be concurrently accessed by multiple object spaces.

Q: *What does conformance mean in an OO context?*

A: In a typed OO environment, it means that one object can be used in place of another, as long as their types conform. This usually means that the surrogate object has all the services of the one it's being used in place of—plus, perhaps, some additional ones. This is Polymorphism.

Q: *What is SOM? What is its role in IBM's OO strategy?*

A: SOM is System Object Model. It is an IBM implementation of the OMG Common Object Request Broker Architecture. It contains an Interface Definition Language which permits class hierarchies to be defined without being concerned about implementation details. Its role in IBM's OO strategy is to supply a single object model that all of its languages must support. SOM also contains a variety of object engine mechanisms. Object engines are the base-level support for OO. These engines do resolution of names and object identifiers during execution of an object space.

Q: *What does remote procedure call mean? How does it play a role in OT?*

A: A remote procedure call is like any other procedure call, except the called procedure may be located on another processor. In the context of object technology, it could be the underlying mechanism for transmitting messages, even when the receiver is not located in the local object space. This allows for an object space to become distributed across processors or a hierarchy of processors.

Q: *What has been the main use of OT to date?*

A: Graphic User Interface (GUI) development has been the most visible way that object technology has been used to date. In fact, to many, object orientation and GUI development are synonymous.

Q: *Has OT been used successfully in large-scale commercial applications?*

A: Only in a few instances, to date, has object technology been deployed on an enterprisewide basis. The reasons for this are many, but perhaps the most important is that a very high level of commitment within the enterprise must be made before object technology has a chance to succeed. Also of considerable importance is the fact that most enterprises have "legacy" applications whose continued use would be dependent on reengineering them for use in an object-oriented setting.

Q: *Distinguish between deep copy and shallow copy as these terms are used in OT.*

A: A shallow copy is one that produces an exact copy of a given object instance. If that object instance contains references to other objects, a shallow copy reproduces the object references, but not the object instances to which they refer. A deep copy, on the other hand, copies not only a given object instance, but also all the objects (not just the references, but the objects themselves) to which the instance refers, either directly or indirectly.

Q: *Distinguish between object, object instance, and instance.*

A: These terms are used interchangeably in object technology—they mean the same thing.

Q: *Distinguish between class method and instance method.*

A: A class method (sometimes called factory method) is one that is associated with the class, rather than with instances of the class. It usually has to do with producing new instances of the class. By contrast, an instance method is a part of the set of services that every instance of the class is expected to have. For example, every instance of the class OrderClerk might be expected to have a service called placeOrder, while the OrderClerk class might be expected to have a service called createNewClerk. In this example, placeOrder would be an instance method, while createNewClerk would be a class method. This is implemented in C++ as static member functions.

Q: *Discuss the importance of reentrancy in an object environment.*

A: Object environments are, typically, event-driven. This means that objects must be able to respond to external events—even when they are already processing such an event. In order to do this, they must have a reentrant base of support. Reentrancy allows a process to be suspended ("stacked") temporarily in order to process a more recent event. Recursion is also necessary for an object environment, as methods must be shared, and it is entirely possible for a method to send a message to itself either directly or indirectly.

Q: *List five elements of the OT infrastructure.*

A: Language, development environment, class library, training, and OO database management system.

Q: *Describe the mentoring approach to OO training.*

A: To have a mentor means to have someone to whom you can turn for advice and leadership. This technique is often used in OO training. A group of people is chosen who have both the technical and interpersonal skills to become mentors. They are then given special "mentor" training. After this training, they return to their environments to help others in the organization learn the OO approach to design, analysis, and programming.

Q: *Name five OO programming languages. Identify those that support dynamic binding and those that support static binding.*

A: SmallTalk, C++, Eiffel, Objective-C, OO COBOL. Each supports some form of dynamic binding. C++, Objective-C, and OO COBOL also support static binding.

Q: *What are pre- and postconditions in EIFFEL?*

A: These are conditions that must exist before (preconditions) and after (postconditions) the successful execution of a method.

Q: *Does C++ support error handling? How?*

A: Yes, through a new language feature called Exception Handling. C++ allows an object to be "thrown" when an exception needs to be raised. This object is "caught" by a method that has been declared to handle the particular exception. The object that is thrown and caught has encapsulated information regarding the exception.

Q: *What are the principal things that must be changed to introduce OO to an existing 3GL?*

A: The language, the execution environment, and the development environment.

Q: *What work is being done to add OO features to COBOL?*

A: The ANSI X3J4.1 committee is completing a technical report recommending a set of features to be added to the COBOL language to support OO programming. Micro Focus has developed an OO programming capability for its COBOL environment that includes extensions to the OO execution environment as well as a new OO development environment.

Q: *What does legacy code mean?*

A: Legacy code is code that was written some time previously that has typically been used for production work for some time, and which has typically had several programmers assigned to maintain and extend it over its lifetime. These programmers have inherited this code as their "legacy."

Q: *Why is OT important for emerging technologies such as multimedia and virtual reality?*

A: Because of its ability to contain complexity through encapsulation, object technology is ideal for environments like multimedia and virtual reality, as these systems tend to be quite complex.

23

C and C++

Rick Stanley

Introduction

C and C++ are two separate and distinct languages that coexist in the real world. C++ was based on the C language, but adds the Object Oriented paradigm. Applications in C++ are written using both C libraries and C++ class libraries. This chapter is separated into two sections covering specific topics of each. A C programmer applying for a job is not expected to know C++, but a C++ programmer is expected to have a thorough knowledge of the C language and be able to program proficiently in it. The C++ applicant should have a working knowledge of the C++ syntax and semantics to be hired for any position in C++.

An Introduction to C

The C programming language was invented by Dennis Ritchie of AT&T Bell Labs in the early 1970s to write the Unix Operating System. It is a compiled procedural language that is a low-level language closest to the operating system (just above assembler) but is also a high-level language with a good set of constructs. The code is broken down into functions and modules for easier maintenance and code reuse. A function should do one thing, only one thing, and do it well. C's closeness to the operating system results in efficient code that makes the programs quite fast while keeping the size of the executables relatively small. It is still an integral part of most installations of Unix, but is one of the most widely available languages ever. It is available on the most sophisticated supercomputers and the simplest home computers.

Its ability to be ported easily comes from the language's design. The language consists of approximately 35 key words, 45 operators, and the rules that control them. The hardware-specific features, such as I/O, are not part of the language definition, but are placed in a function library provided by the compiler manufacturer for the specific computer and operating system combination it is to be used for. Many other libraries are produced by third parties to provide a rich set of reusable, pretested code.

On the opposite side, it is accused of being a very cryptic language. I find the people making this accusation are nonusers. Once you learn the syntax and semantics, the code becomes as readable as BASIC, Pascal, or COBOL. Perhaps more readable!

C is also a loosely typed language. It allows the programmer incredible freedom, but at the same time requires him or her not to abuse the language. This is true especially in the use of pointers. Knowledge and experience are the C programmer's greatest assets.

C has been used as a general purpose programming language, as a systems language to write operating systems (Unix and OS/2), for applications such as compilers, database management systems, word processors, etc., as well as for creating other languages.

The original classic version of C was documented in the reference manual portion of a book published in 1978 called *The C Programming Language* by Brian Kernighan and Dennis Ritchie, and has been dubbed K&R C. In 1990, the ANSI/ISO organizations adopted a new standard for the C language, commonly referred to as the ANSI Standard. This chapter will assume the use of an ANSI standard compiler, even though many implementations of C still use older K&R compilers (Unix among others).

The following sources are just a few of the standard reference materials used by C programmers.

Kernighan, Brian, and Dennis Ritchie, *The C Programming Language,* 2nd edition, Prentice Hall, 1988. (This is the classic tutorial and reference manual for the C language. This edition was published as the ANSI/ISO standard was being adopted. Every C programmer should own this book!)

Summit, Steve, C FAQ, (A list of Frequently Asked Questions posted at the beginning of each month on the USENET newsgroup, comp.lang.c).

Waite, Mitchell, and Stephen Prata, *New C Primer Plus*, 2nd edition, Sams Publishing, division of Prentice Hall, 1993 (the best tutorial on the C language I have found, other than K&R).

Compilers

Compilers are available for most of the currently used computers and operating systems. The standard C compiler that comes installed as part of the Unix operating system is "cc." It is a command line compiler that compiles K&R style C code. The Free Software Foundation of Cambridge, Massachusetts, distributes an ANSI compiler called "gcc." This compiler is available free via ftp, and can be obtained by tape or disk. A version of this compiler is available for the MS-DOS operating system as well. Other Unix compilers may also be available.

PC-based compilers usually come in the form of an Integrated Development Environment (IDE). This environment provides a built-in compiler, editor, debugger, make (or project), and on-line help. These IDEs run usually under Windows or OS/2 but some provide a DOS environment. They usually also provide the ability to run the compiler from the DOS command line, or from a third-party programmer's editor.

All compilers provide a standard library of reusable functions for such areas as math, string handling, memory management, I/O (several levels), error handling, and many others. Most of the manufacturers provide some functions and other features that are extensions to the language. These extensions should be avoided if your code is to be portable.

Third-Party Libraries and Utilities

There may be more support for the C (and C++) language than any other computer language in history. To name but a few of the types of libraries provided by various manufacturers:

Data entry and windowing libraries

Graphical User Interface (GUI) libraries (including Microsoft Windows SDK)

Database libraries (for virtually any type of data file format)

Financial math libraries

Communication

Graphics

Third-party utilities include

Make (for assistance in handling multiple module programming)

Lint (source code analysis tool for finding potential bugs the compiler can't catch)

Array and Memory Allocation Bounds Checkers

DOS extenders

Version control systems (To handle different versions of the life of a project—a must for any systems development today.)

Many programmer's editors are available that will integrate with the compiler to assist in compiling, error correction, and can also integrate with most major version control systems on the market.

Terminology

Data type: Every data constant and variable must have a data type. Integer types include char, int, short, long, signed, and unsigned versions. The IEEE floating point types include float, double, and the new long double.

Compiler: The software program(s) that convert the text file (source code) into a machine code object module that the linker will use to create the executable.

Preprocessor: The first step in the compile process. It is used to replace #define constants and macros, #include header files (declarations), and do selective inclusion and exclusion of source code for portability to other compilers.

Pointer: The hardest topic to learn, and the most abused thing in C. A pointer is a data variable that holds as its data the address of another data object in memory. It is used extensively to pass and return arrays and addresses of other data to be referenced in the function, or to return them to the calling function. In C, data can be passed by value (a copy of the data) or by address (sometimes improperly referred to as "Pass By Reference"). C++ gives you true references.

Indirection: The act of going to the address contained in a pointer and getting the data (or address at that location).

Dynamic memory allocation: Not all memory is allocated for a program at compile time. The program has a pool of available unused memory (the heap). The functions, malloc(), and calloc() are used to obtain some of the heap and allocate it to the current program or process. Once the memory is no longer needed, it can be returned to the program using free(), to be used again in other areas of the program.

Statement: Any declaration, definition, function call, or expression that ends with a semicolon.

Function: A block of one or more statements that is called from another function or called from within itself (recursive function calls). A function may be defined with optional formal parameters (or data that is passed into the function), and an optional return value. All functions in ANSI C should be declared.

Module: A compilation unit or source code file (a .c file) that is compiled into an object module. A source code module may contain one or more related functions. The linker is responsible for combining several object modules into an executable file.

Scope: Data can be declared as having global, local, or static scope. Global scope means the data is accessible from any function in any module in the program. Local data is defined and is only accessible within a block of code surrounded by braces ({}). Static global data and functions are only accessible from point of declaration to the end of the file, and are not known by the linker. Static local data is initialized only once inside a block of code and thereafter retains the value it had when it last exited the block where it was declared.

Education

Any book that proposes to teach you C (or C++) in a three-week time frame is not recommended. The best way to learn C is to take a good course in the language from a college or university in your area. Most offer continuing education courses in both languages, as well as other important areas of computer use. The interaction with an experienced teacher and other students will put you further ahead than someone trying to learn the language in isolation. The best way to learn the language is by doing, not just by reading. Experience is the best teacher.

However, it is possible to learn on your own. See the list of good C books in the introduction to this chapter for a place to start.

User groups specifically aimed at C and C++ users can be found in many areas of the country. Seek them out. This is a good way to learn more about the languages, and also a good place for networking. Job leads are sometimes announced at these meetings.

The Interview

Other chapters have discussed how to prepare for the job interview. I will only tell you what I would expect from three different levels of interviewees:

Entry level.   Completion of one course in the C programming language. Knowledge of the syntax and semantics of the language. The concept of multiple module programming. High level I/O. The ability to use pointers to two levels of indirection. Would be hired to maintain existing code and to code small parts of a large-scale system.

Intermediate.   The completion of both an introductory level and an advanced level course in C. Previous experience as a C programmer would be required. A thorough knowledge of all levels of I/O, advance use of data and function pointers. The ability to design and code an entire medium-size program and produce system documentation. The ability to be a team leader on part of a large system.

Advanced.   Extensive knowledge of the C language and data structures using C. The ability to lead several teams of a large C system. Teach and advise other leaders and members of teams. Do system analysis and design of large-scale projects.

Questions and Answers

Q: *What is the* main() *function?*

A: The main() function is the first user-defined function called in your program. There must be one main() function, and ONLY one main() function in any program. The startup code added to your program will call the main() function, optionally passing command line arguments. After returning from main(), the startup code will return to the operating system.

Q: *What are the valid data return types for the* main() *function?*

A: There is only one—'int', Period! The only valid ANSI prototypes for main() are:

```
int main(void);                         /* No command line arguments   */
int main(int argc, char *argv[]);  /* With command line arguments */
```

Any other function in your program may return any data type, including void. (No data returned.)

Q: *How would you open a file passed into the program as a command line argument?*

```
progname datafile.dat
```

A: ...

```
FILE *fp = NULL;
if(argc > 1) /* Filename has been passed */
{
        fp = fopen(argv[1], "rb"); /* Open "datafile.dat" for
                                reading in binary mode */
        if(fp == NULL)
                error(); /* File could not be opened */
}
...
```

Q: *List the three main steps of a compile process in C.*

A: 1. Preprocessor

2. Compiler

3. Linker

Q: *What is the difference between the following two lines:*

```
extern int x;
int x = 0;
```

A: The first is a declaration only of an integer x, and the second defines data space for x and initializes x to the value 0; A declaration does not create any data space, and is usually placed in a header file.

Q: *In the following code, what is the value of* a, *and what is the value of* b *after the assignment?*

```
int a = 10, b = 0;
b = a++;
```

A: The value of a is 11, and the value of b is 10. The value of a post-increment (or post-decrement) is the original value of the variable.

Q: *Now what are the values of* a *and* b *in the following code:*

```
a = 10;
b = a++ * ++a;
```

A: *Undefined!* The code may result in different answers on different compilers and/or operating systems. You should *never* increment or decrement a variable *and* use it more than once in an expression.

Q: *What are lvalues and rvalues?*
A: An lvalue is a reference to a non-const memory location where data can be stored. It is used on the left side of an assignment expression. An rvalue is a reference to data that is normally used on the right side of an assignment expression. These are not C keywords, but are commonly used when describing the effects of C & C++ statements, expressions, function calls, etc.

Q: *What is* `size_t`*?*
A: A `size_t` is a type-defined data type of some unsigned integer value, usually an unsigned int. It is the type evaluated by the sizeof keyword, and some standard library functions. It is type-defined in stddef.h.

Q: *What is* `sizeof`*?*
A: It is both a keyword and an operator that evaluates (at compile time) to the number of bytes that a data type, instance of a data type, or array of a data type, take up in memory.

Q: *What does* `sizeof('A')` *evaluate to?*
A: It will evaluate to the number of bytes an int takes up in memory (2 or 4 bytes). A character constant is not the sizeof a char in the C language.

Q: *What is the problem with the following code:*
```
int ary[10], x;
for(x = 0; x <= 10; x++)
{
      printf("%d\n", ary[x]);
}
```
A: The loop will execute 11 times, not 10. This is commonly referred to as an Off-By-One error. The loop should have been written as `for(x = 0; x < 10; x++)`

Q: *Are these two identifiers the same?* `count  Count`
A: *No.* All keywords and identifiers in C are case-sensitive. The same case must be used consistently throughout the program for all uses of the same identifier.

Q: *Which of the following identifiers are illegal?*
```
_count
3D
$val
register
```
A: All but the first. `_count` is legal in C, but the compiler reserves the use of the leading underscore and the use of two underscores in identifiers. `3D` cannot start an identifier with a leading digit. `$val` A '`$`' is illegal for use in identifier names. `register` is reserved as a keyword.

Q: *In the following code, what is the order of evaluation of the operators?*
```
z = x * ++y - i / j;
```
A: It would be interpreted as:
```
z = ((x * (++y)) - (i / j));
```

Q: *How would you determine this?*

A: Examine the Operator Precedence Table for levels of precedence and associatively of operators within the same level. This is published in most tutorial and reference books on the C language.

Q: *For the declarations:*
```
int foo(int value);
int bar(void);
extern int x;
```
are the following function calls legal?
```
foo(sizeof(x));
foo(3 * 5);
foo(bar());
```
A: Yes. `sizeof(x)` is interpreted at compile time and the constant value is passed to `foo()`. `3 * 5` is evaluated to a single value that is then passed to `foo()`. `bar()` is called first and the return value is passed to `foo()`.

Q: *Can function* `foo()` *recursively call itself? Is the following legal?*
```
void foo(void)
{
     /* some code */
     if(/* Some condition test */)
          foo();
     /* Other code */
}
```
A: Yes. As long as the level of recursion is controlled. Uncontrolled recursion can lead to a Stack Overflow error.

Q: *Should the goto keyword be used freely in a program?*

A: The goto keyword should be avoided if possible. The only legitimate use of this keyword would be to escape from a heavily nested loop or if statement.

Q: *Is a pointer and an array name the same thing?*

A: *No.* A pointer is a variable that holds as its data the address of another object in memory. It can be defined as const or non-const. A non-const pointer may be assigned a different address. The name of an array evaluates to the constant address of an area of memory of one or more objects of the type declared. The array's address will never change for the life of the array.

Q: *Given the following definitions:*
```
int ary[10];    /* An array of 10 ints */
int *ptr = ary; /* A pointer to the first element of the array */
```

Are the following four statements equivalent?
```
ary[2] = 5;
*(ary + 2) = 5;
*(ptr + 2) = 5;
ptr[2] = 5;
```
A: Yes! In the above operations, the array name can be used as a pointer, and the pointer can be subscripted as an array.

Q: *In the above examples, what does* `*(ary + 2)` *mean?*
A: Take the address represented by `ary`, add 2 times the sizeof an int to get the address of the 3rd element, and dereference the pointer.

Q: *Is the following code legal in C?*
```
const int dim = 10;
int ary[dim];
```
A: No. A const object may not be used as a dimension when creating an array in C. You must use either of the following:
```
int ary[10];
```
or
```
#define dim 10
int ary[dim];
```

Q: *What is the correct definition of a string in C?*
A: A string is a "Null Terminated Array of Chars" or a series of characters in an array or dynamically allocated area of memory, which is terminated by a null byte (`'\0'`) A string is an array of chars, but not all arrays of chars are strings.

Q: *For the following definition:*
```
char str[100] = "A sample string";
```
What is the difference between the following two statements?
```
sizeof(str)
strlen(str)
```
A: The keyword/operator expression, `sizeof(str)` would evaluate to 100 or the number of bytes the array takes up in memory. The function call `strlen(str)` would return 15 or the number of characters in the string contained within the char array, up to but not including the null byte.

Q: *How would you write a function to properly pass in an array of 10 doubles?*
A:
```
void display(double ary_ptr[], int dim)
{
    int x;
    for(x = 0; x < dim; x++)
        printf("10.2f\n", ary_ptr[x]);
}
```
Always pass the size of the array along with a pointer to the array.

Q: *Write a function to swap two ints.*

A: This is a common question on any C language interview test. The answer is of course:

```
void swap(int *left, int *right)
{
        int temp = *left;
        *left = *right;
        *right = temp;
}
```

Q: *After successfully reading in data from a disk file, if the next* fread() *returns 0, what are the two most likely possibilities that may have occurred?*

A: The End Of File has been flagged (there is no more data to read from the file), or some sort of disk error has occurred. Check for EOF first using feof().

Q: *In the function call:*

```
FILE *fp = fopen("Datafile.dat", "r+");
```

what does the "r+" do?

A: fopen() attempts to open the file for Reading and Writing.

Q: *In the PC environment (DOS / OS/2 / Windows / etc.) what is the difference between a text and a binary file?*

A: In text mode (the default) a newline ('\n') in memory is converted to a '\r''\n' (0x0D0A) (in that order!) on disk. On reading the file, the two-character combination on disk is converted to a single newline character in memory. This conversion does not occur in binary mode. On other operating systems such as Unix, this conversion does not take place.

Q: *How does the* fseek() *function search for data in a file?*

A: It doesn't. fseek() is used only to set the position of the next read or write that will occur. It knows nothing about the data within a file. It takes two arguments, a long offset, and a starting position within the file (Beginning, Current position, or End of file).

Q: *In the following* printf() *statement, how will the format string affect the data output?*

```
printf("%-10.2f", 1234.5678);
```

A: It will create a field of 10 spaces, left justify the numerical output, and limit the decimal places to two.

Q: *Given the following code, what value should retval have after the code is executed?*

```
int x = 5, y = -1, retval = 0;
if(x < 10)
        if(y > 1)
                retval = 1;
else
        retval = 2;
```

A: 2. The else is tied to the inner if, not the outer if! The indentation has no effect on C!

Q: *What is the following statement used for?*
```
assert(x >= 0);
```

A: An assert macro is used to stop the execution of a program if the condition passed to the macro is false. In this case, as long as x is greater than or equal to zero, the program will continue, otherwise, the program will stop and a diagnostic message will appear on the screen. The assert macros may be eliminated with the defining of the constant, 'NDEBUG'.

Q: *What is the difference between* malloc() *and* calloc()*?*

A: malloc() takes only one argument, the size in bytes of the memory to allocate on the heap. The memory is not initialized. calloc() takes two arguments, the number of elements to allocate, and the size of each element. The memory is initialized to null bytes if the allocation was successful.

Q: *How would you call* malloc() *to dynamically allocate memory for an array of 10 ints?*

A: int *p = (int *) malloc(10 * sizeof(int));

p should be checked against NULL to insure that memory was properly allocated.

Q: *What is multiple module programming?*

A: It is the concept of modularizing a C program into multiple source files, compiling them separately, and linking the object modules together to form one executable.

Q: *What is Make?*

A: Make, Nmake, Imake, etc., is a program that is used to control the compilation of many source files. It examines the executable and object files against the source and header files that were used to create them, to see if any source files need to be recompiled to form an updated executable program. In some compilers "make" is referred to as "project".

Q: *Why do you need to know Make and multiple module programming?*

A: You would not be hired as a programmer without knowing these topics. Most programs consist of many source and header files, and the only way to properly handle the compilation process is with Make.

Q: *How can you turn the following code into a while loop?*
```
int x;
for(x = 0; x < 10; x++)
{
        /* Some code */
}
```

A:
```
int x = 0;
while(x < 10)
{
```

```
        /* Some code */
        x++;
}
```

Q: *What would be the purpose of the following statement?*
```
for(;;)
```
A: This is the proper way to create an infinite loop. The programmer must provide some way to break or end the infinite loop.

Q: *The prototype for the standard library function* qsort() *follows:*
```
void qsort(void *base, size_t n, size_t size,
        int (*cmp) (const void *, const void *));
```
What is the fourth parameter?
A: It is a pointer to a function that takes two const void pointers and returns an int. It is used to compare two elements of the array that has been passed to qsort().

Q: *How would you sort an array of ints using* qsort() *(assuming the inclusion of the proper header files)?*
A:
```
int ary[10] = { 23, 38, 94, 23, 12, 3, 99, 47, 36, 83 };
int compare(const void *left, const void *right)
{
        if(*(int *)left > *(int *)right)
            return 1;
        else if(*(int *)left < *(int *)right)
            return -1;
        else
            return 0;
}

int main(void)
{
        qsort(ary, 10, sizeof(int), compare);
        return 0;
}
```

Q: *Are all function pointers the same?*
A: No. Function pointers and the functions to be assigned to them must match in both the signature (parameter list) and data return type.

Q: *What is wrong with the following code?*
```
#include <stdio.h>
char *str;

int main(void)
{
        gets(str);
        printf("%s\n", str);
        return 0;
}
```

A: The pointer is not assigned the address of a legitimate area of memory. This is called an uninitialized pointer. This type of pointer can point to any area of the data segment, possibly overwriting other data.

Q: *After the above program has finished, you get the following message:*

```
null pointer assignment
```

What has caused this?

A: Because the pointer is a global pointer and because it is uninitialized, it points to the address 0, which is called the "Null Data Segment". This area should never be accessed in your program, and the compiler/program will warn you after the program has finished if this area has been written to.

Q: *What is the difference between* gets() *and* fgets()?

A: gets() is considered a dangerous function. It has no control over the size of the char array that is being written to. Memory overwrites can occur. The newline char is read and replaced with a null byte. fgets() takes a second argument that specifies the number of characters to read (count), and a third that specifies the FILE pointer. It reads in up to and including the newline char or up to count − 1 characters, whichever comes first. A null byte is appended after the newline character.

Q: *What does the following statement display to the screen?*

```
printf("%s %f\n", 12.345, "Hello World");
```

A: Garbage! The arguments to the format string have been reversed. The compiler only checks that the first argument is a const char *. It knows nothing about the order of the other arguments. printf() and scanf() are examples of variable argument functions.

Q: *Why does the following function not work correctly?*

```
double foo(int a, int b)
{
    return a / b;
}
```

A: An integer divided by an integer results in an integer value. The data return type is a double.

Q: *How would you correct this?*

A: Cast one of the variables to a double before the division. This will cause the other to be promoted to a double, and floating point division will occur.

```
return (double)a / b;
```

Q: *How many times will the following* printf() *statement execute?*

```
int x;
for(x = 0; x < 10; x++);
    printf("Hello World!\n");
```

A: Once. There is a semicolon after the closing paren of the for loop. The empty for loop will execute 10 times, but the printf() statement will execute only once after the loop has completed.

Q: *Why doesn't the following code work correctly?*
```
int main(void)
{
        printf("%f\n", foo())
        return 0;
}

double foo(void)
{
        /* ... */
}
```

A: `foo` was not declared before it was called. The compiler assumes the return value from `foo()` is an int, not a double. Simple rule: Always properly prototype (declare) your functions.

An Introduction to C++

"C with Classes," the original name for the C++ language in the early development, was started by Bjarne Stroustrup at AT&T Bell Labs around 1979. Many features needed to be added to the language to make it usable. With the addition of some of these features the name was changed to C++. The only standard for C++ that exists at the moment is the ARM (the base document for the proposed C++ standard). In 1990 the ANSI C++ committee was established to define a C++ standard. In late April of 1995, the "Working Paper for Draft Proposed International Standard for Information Systems—Programming Language C++" was released for public review. After the public review period and subsequent analysis of the comments, the proposed standard will be submitted for adoption by ANSI (American National Standards Institute) and ISO (International Standards Organization). Until then, the language and all the compiler implementations that are available are inconsistent. Some of the compilers allow new features of the proposed standard, but not all.

C++ is a hybrid object-oriented programming language (see Chapter 22 for a detailed description of OO). The language allows for both procedural and OO programming. It can be used by a beginner as simply a "better C" without the use of any OO constructs, or by an OO programmer to implement an OO system. This allows the C programmer to make an incremental move from C to C++, adding new concepts as the programmer becomes more fluent in the language. Pure OO languages such as Smalltalk require that all functions and data be part of a class.

C++ is, in the words of Bjarne Stroustrup and Andrew Koenig, "as close to C as possible—but no closer."[1] It is (with very few exceptions) a superset of the ANSI C programming language. ANSI C code can be easily ported to C++ with very few

---

[1] Andrew Koenig and Bjarne Stroustrup: "C++: As close to C as possible—but no closer." *The C++ Report*, July 1989.

exceptions. C++ has advantages over other OO languages in its ability to reuse legacy C code without complete rewrites. The existing tools for C can also be reused with C++. In the long run, C++ (and OO in general) leads to increased productivity, decreased maintenance costs, and less complexity in large-scale systems.

C++ is a more strongly typed language than C, but not as strongly typed as Pascal. This allows for more compile time error checking, and less debugging at run time. It contains all of the operators, keywords, and rules of C, adds additional keywords and operators and adds the concepts of const, inline and overloaded functions, true references, etc., but also adds the OO concepts of classes, inheritance, encapsulation, polymorphism, templates, exception handling, and others. The preprocessor has been virtually eliminated with the correct use of const (constants) and the use of inline functions (macros).

C++, if used correctly, can be as efficient as C, and in the case of larger systems, probably more efficient. It supports low-level code and, at the same time, high levels of abstraction. C programs are said to break down between 50,000 and 100,000 lines of code. Structured programming cannot handle large-scale complex programs. OO languages, by the nature of their design, can and will be used to handle the complex large-scale systems of the future.

C++ and object-oriented programming in general may not be for all programmers. There will still be a demand for procedural-based languages for a long time to come.

The following sources are some of the standard reference materials used by C++ programmers.

Booch, Grady, *Object-Oriented Analysis and Design With Applications,* 2nd edition, Benjamin/Cummings (the first book to read on the concepts of object-oriented programming).

Cline, Marshall, *C++ FAQs,* Addison-Wesley (frequently asked questions). A subset is posted monthly on the USENET newsgroup, comp.lang.c++.

Ellis, Margaret, and Bjarne Stroustrup, *The Annotated C++ Reference Manual,* (ARM), Addison-Wesley (reference book only; ANSI Standard Base Document).

Lippman, Stanley, *C++ Primer,* 2nd edition, Addison-Wesley (another excellent tutorial book on the C++ language).

Stroustrup, Bjarne, *The C++ Programming Language,* 2nd edition, Addison-Wesley (a tutorial book on the C++ language).

Stroustrup, Bjarne, *The Design and Evolution of C++,* Addison-Wesley (how and why the C++ language was created).

Teale, Steve, *C++ IOStreams Handbook,* Addison-Wesley (currently, the only reference book on the iostreams library, prior to the proposed standard).

Advanced books:

Coplien, James, *Advanced C++ Styles and Idioms,* Addison-Wesley.

Meyers, Scott, *Effective C++,* Addison-Wesley.

Compilers

As with C, compilers exist for almost all computers and O/Ss on the market today. The standard compiler for Unix is "CC," which uses the C++ to C translator, cfront to convert C++ code to K&R C code to be run through the "cc" C compiler (cfront can also translate to an ANSI C compiler). The FSF also produces a C++ compiler called g++.

Most PC-based C++ compilers are both a C++ and an ANSI C compiler. The IDE works with both compilers and selects the compiler based on the source file extension (.c for C source, and .cpp for C++ code).

Third-Party Libraries and Utilities

The standard C library is fully usable for both C++ and C. In addition, the compiler provides a class library, and other third-party manufacturers produce C++ class libraries for all areas of programming. (See this section in the C portion of this chapter.) Some are produced in both C and C++ versions. Microsoft produces the MFC class library and Borland produces the OWL library for Windows development.

Terminology

There are a tremendous number of new buzzwords for C++. Many of these are as a result of the OO paradigm. A small selection follows:

Class: A struct with default private access. Both data and member functions can be encapsulated or combined into a single unit. Usually the member functions of the class and "friend functions" are the only functions that have direct access to the data of a class.

Object: An instance of a class. The data space created for the data of a class. Public member functions are called to work with the data hidden within the object.

Constructor: (ctor for short) A function that is automatically called whenever an object is created. It is used to initialize the member data of the object.

Destructor: (dtor for short) A function that is called automatically whenever the object is destroyed. If member data pointers point to allocated data, it is the dtor's responsibility to delete the allocated data, or do any other cleanup necessary.

Encapsulation: The combining of data, and functions that will work on that data, within a class.

Inheritance: Creation of a new "derived" class based on an existing "base" class. A derived object has the same functionality as the base, but usually has additional functionality. This is the main way code-reuse is accomplished in C++. Multilevel class hierarchies are created combining classes with similar functionality. For example: A Rectangle class and Triangle class are both derived from a Shape class.

Polymorphism: Using objects of several different classes within a class hierarchy, interchangeably. The proper function for the class object will not be chosen at compile time (static binding, as in C), but is delayed till run time (late binding, using "virtual" functions). For example:

```
Void Show(const Shape &blob)
{
    blob.display(); // Display the shape properly
}
    . . .
    Rectangle r;
    Triangle t;
    Show(r); // Will call the display() virtual member function of
             // the Rectangle class
    Show(t); // Will call the display() virtual member function of
             // the Triangle class
```

Template: The compiler will use the class or function template to create one or more class or function definitions at compile time, based on the actual data types used by the programmer. The programmer defines and maintains the class or function once, no matter how many actual classes and functions are created by the compiler. If the template is never used, no definitions are created.

Exception handling: A new error handling scheme is needed for C++ to handle problems that can occur, such as incomplete construction, or memory allocation problems using new: These new problems require a different approach than in C. An "Exception" is "Thrown" from a statement in a "Try" block, and caught by a "Catch" handler.

Education

C++ is not an easy language to learn. Not that the syntax and semantics of the language are so difficult to follow, but the programmer coming from C or COBOL or any other procedural language has to learn the new concepts of OO. Breaking the bad habits of structured top-down programming is not easy.

C++ can be learned gradually. The experienced C programmer can use C++ initially as a "better C" and gradually add the concepts of OO as more experience is gained. In this way, the C programmer can become effective almost immediately.

Again, I recommend a good course in C++ to gain both a knowledge of the syntax and semantics of the language and the concepts of OO. If a course on the concepts of OO is available, I would recommend this first before learning the language.

The Interview

A prospective employer will look for the following when interviewing a candidate for a C++ programming job:

Entry level.   Completion of at least one course in C++. Knowledge of the syntax and semantics of the language. Ability to use the standard class libraries such as the iostream library. Would be hired to maintain existing code and as a member of a team of programmers creating an application. Would not be required to design classes, but would be required to use them in creating the application code.

Intermediate.   Completion of at least two courses in C++, and in OO analysis and design. Previous employment as a C++ programmer would be required. Would be hired as a team leader on a large-scale project, and would be required to design and create classes based on specifications provided.

Advanced.   The main analysis and design person, and lead programmer on a large-scale project. Advanced knowledge of OOA, OOD, and OOP, as well as C++. Ability to effectively use an OOA&D tool such as Rational Rose. Thorough knowledge of all areas of C++ including templates and exception handling, and of the other new additions to the language and standard class library provided by the proposed C++ standard.

Questions and Answers

Q: *How do features common to both C++ and C differ?*

A: 1. In C, `int foo();` declares a function that returns an int and takes an unspecified number of arguments. The compiler does no error checking on the arguments passed, if any. In C++, this same function declaration specifies a function that takes no parameters (void) and returns an int. In C++, `int foo();` and `int foo(void)` ; are equivalent.

2. const was adapted by the ANSI C committee from C++ but not implemented the same. In C++, `const int x = 10;` creates a constant that can be used to define an array dimension at compile time. This is not allowed in C (`"#define x 10"` must be used in C).

3. In C, `sizeof('A')` is the size of an int, (2 or 4 bytes, depending on the OS/Computer/Compiler) and `sizeof(char)` is the size of a char, but in C++ `sizeof('A')` and `sizeof(char)` are equivalent.

4. `NULL` was defined to be a `"(void *)0"`, but in C++ the constant 0 is used for this purpose. The constant 0 is safe to be assigned and compared to any built-in data type, or pointer.

5. The keyword `'struct'` was needed to define an object in C. In C++, the tag name is the type.

Q: *Are the following two examples the same?*

1. `#define max(a, b) (((a) > (b)) ? (a) : (b))`
2. `inline int max(int a, int b) { return (a > b) ? a : b; }`

A: *No.* The macro will not work correctly in all cases. The arguments to the macro may be evaluated more than once. This example of an in-line function will accept only ints, but it will evaluate the arguments only once, and do type checking on the data as well.

The following do not work correctly using the #define macro:

```
int x = 10, y = 5, z;
double d = 12.34;
z = max(x++, ++y);  // x incremented twice, y incremented once!
z = max(d, x);  // data type mismatch, and loss of data
                //(truncation and/or modulus)!
```

Q: *How would you write a generic version of the max function, for use with most any data type?*

A:
```
template <class T>
T& max(T &a, T &b) { return (a > b) ? a : b; }
```

Q: *What can I assume about the following line of code?*
```
    foo();
```
A: It is a function call, its name is foo, and no arguments are being passed explicitly. Because of default argument values, and the fact that it is legal to ignore the return type (if data is being returned), you cannot assume anything else about this function call. You would need to check the documentation about this function call, or look at the header file where it is being declared, to obtain more information.

Q: *What are* new *and* delete?

A: They are new C++ keywords that perform dynamic memory allocation. They are replacements for malloc() and free().

Q: *What does* new *do when used to create a user-defined class object on the heap?*

A: It attempts to allocate memory for the object, and if successful calls the appropriate ctor for the class to properly construct it.

Q: *If you use* malloc() *to allocate some memory, is it safe to use* delete *to destroy it?*

A: *No.* If you malloc() memory, then free(). If you new memory, then delete. Don't mix the two.

Q: *What is* _new_handler?

A: In the event of a failure to properly allocate memory, new will call the function pointed to by this function pointer, if a function address has been assigned to the _new_handler pointer.

Q: *How do you set this pointer?*

A: Either by assigning the name of a properly defined function to this pointer, or by using the function,
```
    set_new_handler().
    void handler(void) { /* ... */ }
    void (*old_handler) (void); // Pointer to a _new_handler function
    old_handler = _new_handler;
    _new_handler = handler;
```

or

```
old_handler = set_new_handler(handler);
set_new_handler()
```

may not yet be available on all systems.

Q: *You have* new'*d memory on the heap for a char array:*

```
char *p = new char[129];
```

Which of the following statements should you use to delete the memory?

```
1) delete p;
2) delete [] p;
3) delete [129] p;
```

A: Number 2. The result of number 1 is undefined. It may work correctly on some compilers, but may fail on others, and may only delete the first element. In earlier versions of the C++ language, number 3 was needed, but the parameter was later dropped, and it is not supported by all current compilers.

The simple rule here is: If you use [] in the new statement, use [] in the delete statement for the same block of memory. If you did not use [] in the new, DO NOT use [] in the delete. This goes for *all* built-in and user-defined types.

Q: *What are the* public:, protected:, *and* private: *labels used for?*

A: They control access to the members of a struct or class. The public section(s) allow full access to the public members to any user of the class. This is usually referred to as the *interface* of the class. The private section(s) of the class restrict access to the private members to other members of the same class, or friends of the class. No other user of this class, including derived classes, can access private members. The protected section hides the protected members from outside users, while allowing access to other members of this class, and derived class members. The protected and private sections comprise the *implementation* of the class.

Q: *What are the differences between a struct and a class?*

A: A struct is public by default. All members are accessible by any user of that struct, unless the protected or private labels are used. Any legal ANSI C struct is also a legal C++ struct. A class is private by default. There is no other difference between these two types.

Q: *What other functions should be created for the following string class?*

```
class String
{
   public:
      String();
      String(const char *);
   private:
      size_t length;
      char *str;
};
```

A: Since this class is designed to point to dynamically allocated memory, it would be necessary to create a copy ctor to create new objects based on existing ones, to prevent uncontrolled shared representation, a destructor to properly delete the allocated memory, preventing memory leaks, and an assignment operator for the same reasons as the copy ctor.

Q: *Does the compiler define a default copy of these three functions for you if you do not?*

A: Yes, if you do not declare these functions for a class. You should define these for most of the classes that you will create. In the following example class, these three functions can safely be provided by the compiler. The data is all self-contained. No shared representation will result:

```
class Alpha
{
  public:
    Alpha();
    Alpha(int i, const char *text);
  private:
    int x;
    char ary[256];
};
```

Q: *Would shared representation ever be acceptable in C++?*

A: Yes, the string class could be rewritten to allow for controlled shared representation. This would cut down on the amount of dynamic memory allocation if two objects needed only to read the same char data.

Q: *What is a default constructor?*

A: It is the constructor that takes no arguments or a constructor with default arguments that also serves as the default ctor. For the Alpha class, it would be called to create an object called a:

```
Alpha a; // Default ctor called
```

Q: *What does the following code do?*

```
String s1();
```

A: It declares a function that takes no arguments and returns a string by value. It does not create an object using the default ctor.

Q: *What is* 'this'?

A: In a nonstatic member function of a class, the compiler adds an extra parameter to the function definition, as the first parameter, that is a const pointer to the current object. This pointer is used by the compiler to access the member data of the current object by the member function. It is also used by the programmer to return a pointer (this) or a reference (*this) to the current object.

Q: *In a nonstatic class member function, you see the statement,* delete this;. *What effect does this statement have on the program?*

A: It is an object committing suicide! It is used by some programmers, however, it is considered very dangerous. It assumes the object was instantiated on the heap using new, and that no other references will be made to this object and its member data after the execution of this statement. These are bad assumptions to make. Simple rule, don't do it!

Q: *Are overloaded operator functions really necessary?*

A: They are what some authors refer to as "syntactic sugar." In other words, they are not necessary for the class, but they make operations on the class objects easier. For example:

```
String s1("Hello "), s2("World!"), s3;
s3 = s1 + s2;
```

would concatenate s1 and s2 into a temporary object and then assign it to s3. Overloaded operator functions should be defined descriminately for any class you create. Not all operators are appropriate for a class. What would s1 / s2 mean?

Q: *What is a "hasa" relationship?*

A: It is the C++ slang term for a container, or membership, relationship.

Q: *How is this implemented?*

A: Most commonly it is implemented as in the following:

```
class Alpha
{
    String text;
    // ...
};
```

class Alpha 'hasa' string object as its member data.

Q: *What is an "isa" relationship?*

A: This is the C++ slang term for true inheritance. It is a public inheritance relationship:

```
class Shape { /* ... */ };
class Triangle : public Shape {/* ... */ };
```

An object of class Triangle 'isa' Shape. Where Shape pointers or references are used, you can use a Triangle instead.

Q: *What are* cin *and* cout?

A: They are objects of the iostream class library, a replacement for the stdio I/O functions. cout is an object of class ostream_withassign, and cin is an object of istream_withassign. They are the C++ equivalents of scanf() (cin) and printf() (cout).

Q: *What does the '<<' operator do in the statement:*

```
cout << value;
```

A: The compiler checks the type of "value" at compile time, and uses the appropriate "insertion operator" to insert the data into the stream. If value is an int, it would be comparable to a call to

```
printf():
    printf("%d", value);
```

As opposed to the `printf()` function call, these operators are typesafe. There are a full set of insertion operators (`cout`) and extraction operators (`cin`) for all built-in data types. If an insertion operator is not defined for the string class, then the following code will not compile:

```
String s("Test string");
cout << s;
```

Q: *How would you replicate the following* `printf()` *statement using* `cout`?

```
printf("%-10.2f\n", 1234.5678);
```

A: cout << setiosflags(ios::fixed | ios::left)
       << setprecision(2)
       << setw(10)
       << 1234.5678
       << resetiosflags(ios::fixed | ios::left)
       << setprecision(6)
       << endl;

Q: *Which of the two overloaded functions will be called in the following code:*

```
void bar(int x) { /* Some code */ }
void bar(unsigned char x) { /* Some code */ }
int main(void)
{
        bar('a');
        return 0;
}
```

A: The compiler should flag this function call as an "ambiguous call to over-loaded function." The compiler could convert the char constant to either an int or an unsigned char by implicit conversion. It can't decide which function to use. Be explicit in this case by casting to one of the two types.

Q: *Why is the following code illegal?*

```
class Alpha
{
        public:
                // ...
        private:
                const int size = 100;
};
```

A: It is illegal to initialize a const data member in the class. It must be declared only in the class, and initialized in the ctor.

Q: *Could you replace the line:*

```
const int size = 100;
```

with the line:

```
enum { size = 100 };
```

A: Yes, this is legal.

Q: *For the following partial declaration of the string class:*

```
class String
{
    public:
        String() : length(0), str(0) { }
    // ...
    private:
        size_t length;
        char *str;
};
```

What is the purpose for : `length(0), str(0)`?

A: The code between the ':' and the '{' is the initialization list for the class ctor. `length` will be initialized to the value 0, and the pointer `str` will also be initialized to the address 0; The initialization here is optional, but is mandatory for const and reference member data. It could be replaced with assignments within the ctor body.

Q: *Why should the* `operator+()` *for the string class return a String by value as in the following definition:*

```
String String::operator+(const String &ref) { /* ... */ }
```

A: In a statement such as `s3 = s1 + s2;` the `operator+()` must create a temporary object concatenating the strings in both `s1` and `s2`, to be able to assign to `s3`. Since this temp object *must* be a local stack object, it cannot be returned by reference. Allocating this object on the heap will result in memory leaks. The `operator+()` is not a very efficient function.

Q: *Why in the following code is the if statement needed?*

```
String& String::operator=(const String &ref)
{
    if(&ref != this)
    {
        length = ref.length;
        delete [] str;
        str = new char[length + 1];
        assert(str != 0);
        strcpy(str, ref.str);
    }
    return *this;
}
```

A: To prevent deletion of the data in the event of an assignment to itself:

```
s1 = s1;
```

No action will be performed in the assignment operator. All assignment operators should perform this check.

Q: *Why must the following function be declared as a friend of the string class instead of a member function?*

```
ostream& operator<<(ostream &os, const String &s) { /* ... */ }
```

A: The first argument to the function is not of class string. In order to be consistent in the use of cout, it must be declared as a friend.

Q: *Should data members of a class be made* `public:`, `protected:`, *or* `private:`?
A: `private:` In most classes, only the members and friends of that class should have direct access to the data members.

Q: *Should the const keyword be used with caution?*
A: No, just the opposite. Pass and return class objects, arrays of data, etc., as const if possible, if the function is not designed to alter the data passed. Design const into the class, instead of retrofitting it later.

Q: *Can functions be const?*
A: Yes, member functions of a class may be declared and defined as const if the function is not meant to alter the members of the current object. The constness does not hold true if a member pointer is accessed, and the data pointed to is changed. Also, only const member functions are allowed to be called for const objects!

Q: *Would you create a conversion operator function for the string class such as the following two functions?*

```
String::operator char *();
String::operator const char *();
```

A: *No!* Although currently legal, this is a direct violation of the concepts of data hiding and encapsulation. This can lead to dangling pointers and, in the case of the first function, allow the user to directly alter the data within the class object. This kind of programming can only lead to a disaster.

For the following three questions:

```
class A { };
class B1 : public A { };
class B2 : public A { };
class C : public B1, public B2 { };
```

Q: *How do you prevent the creation of two copies of class* A *in a* C *object?*
A: Declare B1 and B2 to inherit `virtual public A`. This will create one copy that is shared by B1, B2, and C.

```
class A { };
class B1 : virtual public A { };
class B2 : virtual public A { };
class C : public B1, public B2 { };
```

Q: *When creating a* C *object, who calls the base class ctor for the* A *class,* B1 *or* B2*?*

A: Neither. Class C will call A's ctor, B1's ctor, and B2's ctor, in that order. When instantiating a C object, B1's ctor and B2's ctor will not call A's ctor even if defined that way!

Q: *Now say that* B1 *inherits a virtual public* A*, and* B2 *inherits a virtual private* A*! What access rights does* C *have to* A*'s members?*

A: Public. The access rights in this case follow the path of least resistance.

Q: *What is the size of the following Empty class?*

```
class Empty { };
```

A: It is guaranteed to be nonzero. The size will probably be one byte.

Q: *Describe the* bool *data type provided in the proposed C++ standard.*

A: This new boolean data type called bool, will have only two values. true (equal to 1), and false (equal to 0). Any integer value can be assigned to a bool. Any nonzero value will become true, and a zero value will become false. bools can also be assigned to ints. The value of the conditional operations will be of the bool type.

Q: *How could you simulate the* bool *keyword until it is available in your compiler?*

A: Either of two ways:

```
const int false = 0;
const int true = 1;
typedef int bool;
```

or

```
enum bool { false; true };
```

The latter can be used in overloading a function, but may fail in some expressions.

Q: *What is the STL?*

A: It is the Standard Template Library created by Alexander Stepanov and Meng Lee of Hewlett-Packard Laboratories. It is ". . . a set of well-structured generic C++ components that work together in a seamless way." This library will become part of the proposed ANSI/ISO C++ standard.

24
PowerBuilder

Robert Pesner

Introduction

The following topics will be covered in this chapter:

1. PowerBuilder components
   a. PowerBuilder painters
   b. PowerBuilder objects
   c. PowerScript
2. PowerBuilder data management capabilities
   a. DBMS support
   b. DataWindows
   c. Embedding SQL
   d. Pipelines

Overview of PowerBuilder

PowerBuilder 4.0 is the latest release of Powersoft Corporation's object-oriented application development tool. PowerBuilder provides a complete development environment, including "painters" to create the objects that make up a Power-Builder application; a PowerBuilder-specific scripting language to code responses to events involving these objects; a built-in editor; and a debugger. PowerBuilder is particularly oriented to developing applications that manipulate data managed by relational database management systems. To this end, it has objects designed to allow relational data access in a DBMS-independent way and includes a DBMS-independent administrative front-end that can be used to create and manage databases stored on database servers. PowerBuilder supports the following environments: Windows, Windows NT, Macintosh, and Unix (Sun Spar C and HP PA-RISC). This chapter will concentrate on the Windows and Windows NT versions.

PowerBuilder comes in two versions: Desktop and Enterprise. They differ in the relational database management systems they support. The Desktop version supports Watcom SQL (which is included) as well as ODBC-compatible DBMSs, and comes with ODBC drivers for Btrieve, Clipper, dBase, FoxPro, Netware SQL, and Paradox. The Enterprise version adds support for ALLBASE, Sybase SQL Server, Microsoft SQL Server, Oracle, DB2 and DB2/2, INFORMIX, SQLBase, DEC RDB and XBD. (Access to a remote database server requires that the appropriate DBMS client software be installed on the PC running the PowerBuilder application.)

As an object-oriented environment, PowerBuilder creates applications that consist of objects. These objects have properties and methods, and generate events that can trigger developer-written programs called scripts. Most of these objects are user interface objects, designed to display information to or receive information from a user. Developing a PowerBuilder application consists mainly in designing the user interface using the Window and DataWindow painters and writing scripts to respond to events generated when the user runs the application. Each PowerBuilder object has a predefined set of events it can generate; however, for those objects that correspond to Windows control windows (such as entry fields or list boxes) PowerBuilder can pass any Windows message to the object as an event. In addition, the developer can define application-specific events for any object and generate them from a script.

All PowerBuilder applications start out with one Application object, created and managed by the Application painter. This object can be used to write application initialization and termination logic in the object's Open and Close events, respectively. For example, an application object Open event could be used to connect to a remote database.

Most PowerBuilder applications also use the application object Open event to display a Window object to the user. Window objects are created and managed using the Window painter. These objects are essentially Windows standard windows, and can be configured to include a title bar, a System Menu, a minimize and maximize button, and an action bar. Action bars are created using the Menu painter. Windows act mainly as containers for various user interface objects, such as radio buttons, check boxes, entry fields, list boxes, and push buttons. The full collection of Windows control windows is available, as well as some additional controls specific to PowerBuilder.

In addition, PowerBuilder provides a very powerful combination of a DataWindow object and a DataWindow control object, which are designed specifically for relational data access. This terminology is confusing. Essentially, a DataWindow object consists of two things: an SQL Select statement that automatically retrieves data from a relational database; and a definition of how this data should be displayed to the user. A DataWindow control object displays a DataWindow object in a Window.

DataWindow objects are created and managed by the DataWindow painter, which provides several methods for specifying the underlying Select statement, including direct SQL coding (done using the Query painter) and selecting tables, columns, Where clause conditions, etc., from graphical displays. Where clauses can reference program variables at run time. In addition, the DataWindow painter provides several forms skeletons, called Presentation Styles, to start the data display definition, such as one record at a time, several records in a table or grid, labels, etc. These skeletons can be highly customized, with headers, footers, grouped data, summed data, etc. Data from individual columns can be represented as radio buttons, check boxes, lists, etc., as well as the normal entry field. Finally, DataWindow objects can also be used for updating the database. For this purpose, edit masks and validation rules can be defined that do local validation on input data before sending it to the remote database.

A DataWindow object is incorporated into the application's user interface by associating it with a DataWindow control object, which can be placed in a Window object in the same way as any of the normal user interface control objects.

In addition to accessing data using DataWindows, PowerBuilder applications can use standard embedded SQL to directly access data. PowerBuilder also provides a Data Pipeline object, which can facilitate transferring data from one or more tables in one database to one table in the same or different database. This can be used, for example, to replicate data between a centralized enterprise database and local distributed databases. Data Pipelines are created and managed using the Data Pipeline painter.

Event scripts are written using PowerScript, PowerBuilder's scripting language. It is a fairly standard third-generation structured language, which is interpreted at run time. It uses strong datatyping with a lot of standard data conversions and supports local and global variable scoping. It has an extensive list of functions and can also call any function contained in a standard Windows dynamic link library, including Windows functions. It has a large set of variable datatypes and supports structure definitions, which can then be used as user-defined variable types. The Structure painter creates and manages structures.

All PowerBuilder objects are stored in libraries, which are created and managed using the Library painter. When a newly created object is saved, a library to hold it is specified. Each application object is given a list of libraries that contain objects the application can use. This allows the creation of libraries of objects that can be easily shared between applications.

PowerBuilder applications can be run in the development environment, which provides a debugger that can be used to step through event scripts, set breakpoints and examine variable values. PowerBuilder can also generate an "executable" form of the application. This can be distributed with the PowerBuilder Deployment Kit, which provides a run-time environment for the executable.

Terminology

Application object: The top-level object in an application; its Open and Close events provide an opportunity to do application initialization and termination processing.

Attribute: A property of an object, which can take on at least two possible values. Each object in PowerBuilder has a defined set of attributes.

CheckBox control: A user interface object that can be placed in a Window object or used in a DataWindow. It represents an item of information that can be "on" or "off."

Client: In the client/server model, an application that sends a request to a server application. PowerBuilder applications are often clients of database management systems.

CommandButton control: A user interface object that can be placed in a Window object. It provides a way for a user to request an action.

DataWindow control: A user interface object that can be placed in a Window object. It is linked to a DataWindow object; the data retrieved by the DataWindow object is displayed through the DataWindow control.

DataWindow object: An object that contains the equivalent of an SQL SELECT statement and specifications about how the returned data should be displayed in the application's user interface. It can also be used to update database tables with information a user inputs into the DataWindow object.

DropDownListBox control: A user interface object that can be placed in a Window object or used in a DataWindow. It appears as a SingleLineEdit control with an attached ListBox control that only appears when the user clicks on a downward pointing arrow to the right of the SingleLineEdit control. The user can type information into the SingleLineEdit control or select a choice from the list in the attached ListBox.

EditMask control: A user interface object that can be placed in a Window object. It is similar to a MultiLineEdit control but uses a mask to control what data is allowed to be entered.

Enabled: A status of an object that allows a user to interact with it. Disabled user interface objects normally appear grayed; if a user clicks on a disabled control the system will beep.

Event: Part of the definition of an object. Each object in PowerBuilder has a defined set of events that it can generate, and developers can define new events for objects. Events can invoke scripts written by the application developer to respond to the event.

Environment object: An object that is automatically part of every Power-Builder application. It contains information about the application's hardware and software environment. This object must be populated using the GetEnvironment function.

External function: A function implemented in a Windows dynamic link library (DLL); it must be declared in a script before it can be called. The declaration specifies the parameter list for the function and the name of the DLL that contains it.

Function: A subprogram that can be called from a script. There are several kinds of functions: built-in as part of PowerBuilder, coded by a developer in a PowerBuilder library, and external (implemented in a Windows DLL).

Global variable: A variable declared in a script to be available to all scripts in the application. Global variables maintain their existence throughout the application.

Graph control: A user interface object that can be placed in a Window object. It can display data supplied by a script in various formats.

GroupBox control: A user interface object that can be placed in a Window object. It is used to group related user interface controls. It is required to establish the range of mutual exclusivity of a group of RadioButton controls.

HScrollBar control: A user interface object that can be placed in a Window object. It is used to allow a user to initiate a horizontal scrolling action.

Inheritance: The ability of a user-defined object to start off with attributes, events, and methods carried over from an existing object, called the parent. If the parent is a user-defined object and its definition is changed, the change is automatically applied to its children.

Instance variable: A variable declared in a script to be associated with an object. It is available to all scripts for that object and lasts as long as the object lasts. It can also be available to other scripts using the object_name.variable syntax if it is a public variable. Variables are public by default.

Library: A named collection of PowerBuilder objects stored in a separate file with a .PBL extension. All PowerBuilder objects are stored in libraries. Libraries can be shared by applications.

Line control: A user interface object that can be placed in a Window object to display a line. Line controls have no events.

ListBox control: A user interface object that can be placed in a Window object. It can present a list of choices for a user to select from.

Local variable: A variable declared in a script to be available only to that script. Each time the script is invoked, local variables are allocated; values are not maintained from one invocation to the next.

Multi Document Interface (MDI): A way of designing a graphical application with a major window, called the MDI frame, which contains subwindows, called MDI sheets. The PowerBuilder development environment is an example of an MDI application.

MenuItem object: A user interface object used to construct action bar menus and pop-up menus. MenuItem objects generate Click events when a user clicks on a menu choice.

Method: Part of the definition of the object. Each object in PowerBuilder has a defined set of methods that can be applied to the object and that perform some operation on it. In some PowerBuilder documentation, object methods are referred to as object functions.

MultiLineEdit control: A user interface object that can be placed in a Window object. It is typically used to allow a user to enter several lines of free-form text. It can also be used to display free-form text in read-only mode.

Object: The building block of PowerBuilder applications. Objects have attributes and methods and can generate events. Most objects in PowerBuilder are created and managed using object-specific painters.

Object linking and embedding (OLE): A way to create something in one application and use it in another application, allowing changes made in the own-ing application to be reflected in the using application. For example, a spreadsheet managed by EXCEL can be embedded in a PowerBuilder application; whenever changes are made to the spreadsheet in EXCEL, the changes can be reflected immediately in the PowerBuilder application. The owning application is known as the OLE server; the using application is the OLE client.

OLE 2.0 control: An OLE client object that can be used to embed something provided by an OLE server into a PowerBuilder application.

Oval control: A user interface object that can be placed in a Window object to display an oval. Oval controls have no events.

Painter: A PowerBuilder component used to create and manage objects of a cer-tain type. PowerBuilder has painters for Application objects, Window objects, DataWindow objects, etc.

PainterBar: A toolbar with icons showing the various functions relating to the currently active painter.

Picture control: A user interface object that can be placed in a Window object to display a bitmap image.

PictureButton control: A user interface object that can be placed in a Window object. It is essentially a CommandButton control that displays a bitmap image instead of text.

Pipeline: An object that can be used to move data from one or more tables in one database to one table in the same or another database.

Popup menu: A list of choices presented in a free-floating window, usually dis-played by right-clicking with the mouse on an object. Objects in the PowerBuilder development environment have pop-up menus; applications can also include pop-up menus.

PowerBar: A toolbar with icons showing the various painters in PowerBuilder. It shows a configurable subset of the icons in the PowerPanel.

PowerPanel: A window with icons showing the various painters in PowerBuilder. Display it by clicking on File and PowerPanel in the main PowerBuilder menu or typing Ctrl-P.

Private variable: A variable associated with an object that *cannot* be accessed by scripts associated with other objects. Private variables are declared using the PRIVATE option.

Public variable: A variable associated with an object that can be accessed by scripts associated with other objects. Variables are public by default.

RadioButton control: A user interface object that can be placed in a Window object or used in a DataWindow. RadioButtons are used in groups that represent a range of mutually exclusive choices.

Rectangle control: A user interface object that can be placed in a Window object to display a rectangle. Rectangle controls have no events.

RoundRectangle control: A user interface object that can be placed in a Window object to display a rectangle with rounded corners. RoundRectangle controls have no events.

Scope: The extent to which a variable is available in scripts. Variables can have local, instance, or global scope.

Script: A program written in the PowerScript language that is run when an event occurs. Scripts are associated with a specific event for a specific object.

Server: In the client/server model, an application that accepts a request from a client and carries it out. Servers for PowerBuilder applications are most frequently database management systems.

SingleLineEdit control: A user interface object that can be placed in a Window object or used in a DataWindow. It provides a way for a user to enter in a line of text.

Shared variable: A variable declared in a script to be associated with a class of objects, rather than with an individual object. It is available to all scripts for any object of that class and exists beyond the life of any particular object of that class.

StaticText control: A user interface object that can be placed in a Window object. It is used to display read-only text.

Structure: A collection of variables defined in a specific order using the Structure painter. Structures can be used to declare variables and so become user-defined datatypes.

StyleBar: A toolbar that is used to control the attributes of text associated with an object.

Transaction object: An object whose attributes are used to connect to a relational database and return status information about a command issued against the database.

User object: An object designed by the developer, usually made up of a combination of standard PowerBuilder control objects. User objects are displayed by linking them to a User object control, which is placed in a Window object. User objects can have their own events.

User object control: A user interface object that can be placed in a Window object. It is linked to a User object, which is displayed through the User object control.

Visible: An attribute of most objects that determines whether they are visible to the user. This attribute can be changed at run time.

VScrollBar control: A user interface object that can be placed in a Window object. It is used to allow a user to initiate a vertical scrolling action.

Window object: An object that is used to organize the user interface. Applications generally have a main window and several subsidiary windows that display dialogs, provide for data entry and display, etc.

Questions and Answers

Q: *What versions does PowerBuilder come in and what are the differences between them?*

A: PowerBuilder comes in the Desktop and the Enterprise versions. They differ in their support for database management systems. PowerBuilder Desktop supports Watcom SQL and ODBC-compatible DBMSs. PowerBuilder Enterprise adds support for a number of other DBMSs, including ALLBASE, Sybase SQL Server, Microsoft SQL Server, Oracle, DB2 and DB2/2, INFORMIX, SQLBase, DEC RDB, and XBD.

Q: *What are "painters" in PowerBuilder?*

A: Painters are used to create and manage objects. There are 13 painters in PowerBuilder: Application, Database, Data Pipeline, DataWindow, Function, Library, Menu, Project, Query, Report, Structure, User Object, and Window painters.

Q: *What kinds of toolbars does PowerBuilder have?*

A: PowerBuilder has four kinds of toolbars:

PowerBar	Displays icons representing the painters and other general functions like the debugger
PainterBar	Displays icons representing functions associated with the active painter
StyleBar	Displays attributes of a font associated with the active object
ColorBar	Displays color choices for the active object

Q: *What is the basic structure of PowerBuilder applications?*

A: PowerBuilder applications generally consist of an Application object and at least one Window object that is opened in the Application object's Open event.

Q: *What is event-driven programming? How does it differ from traditional programming?*

A: In traditional programming, the application designer determines the order of functions. In particular, the designer controls which routines execute and when. In event-driven programming, an application does initialization processing and then waits for the user to make a choice using the application's user interface. This choice generates an event that invokes an application routine. The order of routines is thus controlled by the user rather than the designer.

Q: *What are the main categories of PowerBuilder objects?*
A: 1. Application
   2. Data Pipeline
   3. DataWindow
   4. MDI Client
   5. MenuItem
   6. Project
   7. Query
   8. Report
   9. User Object
   10. Window

Q: *What are object attributes and how are they managed in PowerBuilder?*
A: Each object in PowerBuilder has properties associated with it, which are called attributes. Some object attributes are initially set when an object is created during development, using the object's Style dialog box. Attributes can also be changed at run time in event scripts, using an object_name.attribute syntax.

Q: *What are object methods and how are they invoked in PowerBuilder?*
A: Each object in PowerBuilder has operations that can be applied to it, which are called methods. Object methods are invoked in event scripts using an object_name.method(parameters) syntax.

Q: *How is the user interface built up in PowerBuilder applications?*
A: The developer designs a main window and other windows using the Window painter. Main windows often have action bar menus created using the Menu painter. A menu is associated with a window using the window's style dialog. The main window is usually displayed in the Application object's open event script. Other windows may be displayed in menu-clicked event scripts or other event scripts.

Q: *What is an application template?*
A: When creating an application object with the Application painter, PowerBuilder can initialize the new application using an application template. This template sets up a Multiple Document Interface (MDI) application structure by creating the following objects in the application:
   a. w_genapp_frame: a frame window
   b. w_genapp_sheet: a sheet window
   c. m_genapp_frame: a frame menu
   d. m_genapp_sheet: a sheet window menu, a descendant of m_genapp_frame
   e. w_genapp_toolbars: a dialog box for controlling whether a toolbar displays
   f. w_genapp_about: an About dialog box
   A set of initial scripts is also created automatically.

Q: *What are the main uses for the Application object open event script?*

A: The Application object open event script can be used for any initialization tasks. Often this will include connecting to a database. The script will also generally open the main application window.

Q: *What are the main uses for the Application object close event script?*

A: The Application object close event script can be used for any termination tasks. Often this will include a final COMMIT and disconnection from a database.

Q: *What are some important attributes of Window objects?*

A: Window object attributes control the size and placement of the window; whether it has a System menu, title bar, action bar, scroll bars, minimize and maximize buttons and a sizing border; whether it is enabled or visible and what type of window it is.

Q: *What are control windows?*

A: Control windows are prebuilt user interface objects such as check boxes, radio buttons, command buttons, list boxes, etc. They can be placed in windows; some can be used in DataWindows. They mostly correspond to standard control windows provided by Windows.

Q: *What controls does PowerBuilder supply beyond the standard set that is part of Windows?*

A: The additional control beyond those provided by Windows include the following: DataWindow, EditMask, Graph, Line, Oval, Picture, PictureButton, Rectangle, and RoundRectangle.

Q: *What are the different kinds of menus and how are they used?*

A: There are two types of menus in PowerBuilder: action bar menus and pop-up menus. Both are defined using the Menu painter. Action bar menus are associated with a window object. Typically this is done at design time; however, action bar menus can be changed at run time. Pop-up menus are typically displayed when a user clicks on an object in the application user interface. A clicked event script uses a menu item's PopMenu method to display that menu item's submenu at a specified location on the screen. If the menu item is not part of the active window's action bar menu, the menu item's menu must be created using the CREATE statement.

Q: *What are some important attributes of MenuItem objects?*

A: MenuItem object attributes control whether the MenuItem appears with a check, appears grayed, has a shortcut key, and is visible. MenuItems that will only be used as pop up menus can be made invisible.

Q: *What is the difference between a DataWindow object and a DataWindow control object? What is the relationship between the two?*

A: A DataWindow object combines an SQL SELECT statement with specifications about how retrieved data should be displayed. It is not directly a user interface object. A DataWindow control object can be placed in a Window object like any other control object, and is therefore a user interface object. DataWindow control objects are linked to DataWindow objects, which are displayed through the DataWindow control object.

Q: *How can the underlying SQL SELECT statement in a DataWindow object be specified?*

A: There are several ways of doing this. When creating a DataWindow object with the DataWindow painter, the painter will provide the following choices:

Quick Select	Allows prompted selection of columns from one table, with sorting and simple selection criteria
SQL Select	Allows prompted selection of columns from one or more joined tables, with ability to use full SQL capabilities
Query	Uses a saved query created with the Query painter
External	Used when the data is provided by the application itself

In addition, if PowerBuilder has been told that a DBMS with stored procedures is available, the DataWindow painter will show "Stored Procedure" as a fifth choice.

Q: *What are the default styles for displaying retrieved data in a DataWindow object?*

A: When creating a DataWindow object with the DataWindow painter, the painter will provide the following style choices:

Composite	Builds the DataWindow from stored reports
Crosstab	Presents the data in a spreadsheet format
Freeform	Presents the data in a highly flexible way, usually one row at a time
Graph	Presents the data in one of several graphical formats
Grid	Presents the data in a row and column tabular format, with rows and column separated by grid lines, allowing column ordering and widths to be changed at run time
Group	A tabular format that automatically guides the designer through the process of identifying columns used to group rows
Label	Presents data in mailing label format
N-Up	Presents data with two or more rows on a single line of output
Tabular	Presents data in a basic row and column format, with optional grouping by columns

Q: *In what ways can a DataWindow display data items retrieved from a database?*

A: Data items in a DataWindow can be displayed as any of:

1. CheckBox
2. DropDownDataWindow

3. DropDownListBox

4. Edit

5. Edit Mask

6. RadioButton

Q: *How is the display specification of a DataWindow object structured?*

A: It consists of a number of bands that can be used to customize the appearance of the DataWindow when it is linked to a DataWindow control or to a Report object. These bands are:

1. Header band—Information in this band appears at the beginning of each screen in a displayed DataWindow and each page in a printed DataWindow.

2. Group Header band—Information in this band appears at the start of each group in a Group style DataWindow.

3. Detail band—Information in this band appears for each row retrieved by the DataWindow's underlying SELECT statement. Depending on the DataWindow style, there may be one or more rows displayed in the Detail band.

4. Group Trailer band—Information in this band appears after the last item in each group in a Group style DataWindow.

5. Summary band—Information in this band appears at the end of the displayed or printed DataWindow.

6. Footer band—Information in this band appears at the end of each screen in a displayed DataWindow and each page in a printed DataWindow.

Q: *How can data in a DataWindow object be used to update a database?*

A: After a user makes changes to the information in a DataWindow object being displayed through a DataWindow control, use the DataWindow *control*'s Update( ) method to send the changes to the database server.

Q: *What is a dynamic DataWindow object?*

A: A dynamic DataWindow is a DataWindow that is controlled or modified at run time under the control of an event script. DataWindows can be created at run time using the Create() method of a DataWindow *control*. (This will detach the DataWindow from the transaction object, so reattach it using the SetTrans or SetTransObject methods.) An existing DataWindow can be modified in three ways using the Modify() method of a DataWindow *control:* its attributes, including the underlying SELECT statement can be changed; control objects can be added and control objects can be removed.

Q: *What is a Data Pipeline?*

A: A Data Pipeline is a definition of a data source and a data target. The data source can be one or more columns from one or more tables, specified as a SELECT statement directly or using the DataWindow-style SQL Select constructor. The data target can be a new or existing table in the same or a different database. The Data Pipeline definition includes what to do if the destination table exists (replace, refresh, append, or update); whether COMMITs should be done after a certain number or records or just at the end of the operation; how many errors must occur before the operation is terminated; and whether PowerBuilder-specific extended data attributes should also be copied to the destination. The Data Pipeline must be linked to a user object you create as a child of the supplied Pipeline System Object. This user object must be defined at development time and created in some application event script using the Create statement. It is linked to the Data Pipeline using its DataObject attribute. The application must also provide some way, such as a Commandbutton, for the user to use to indicate when the operation should begin. Before the operation is started, the application must connect to the source and destination databases, using different transaction objects, even if the source and destination tables are in the same database. Finally, start the operation using the Start() method of the user object.

Q: *What is a Transaction object and what is it used for?*

A: A Transaction object is a special object used to connect to a database and maintain information about the status of operations done to that database. There is one Transaction object automatically created as part of every PowerBuilder application. It is used by default for all database operations. Other Transaction objects can be created if necessary, for example to use a Data Pipeline or to access multiple databases simultaneously.

Q: *What is embedded SQL and how is it used?*

A: Embedded SQL is the technique of coding SQL statements in an event script, as opposed to using a DataWindow to issue the SQL statement. Embedded SQL might be used to issue SQL statements other than SELECT or UPDATE, such as CREATE TABLE. It might also be used to retrieve data that will never be displayed to the user, but used in internal application logic. To issue embedded SQL in an event script, simply code the SQL statement as if it were a PowerScript statement with two exceptions: first, if you need to use a Transaction object other than the default, add a USING trans_object_name clause at the end of the SQL statement; second, end the statement with a semicolon.

Q: *What are the functions of the DataBase painter?*

A: The DataBase painter provides a database-independent way to administer a database and to issue SQL statements against the database. It provides the same prompted methods to construct SELECT statements as the Data-Window painter does. It also allows you to issue any SQL statement supported by the DBMS.

Q: *How does PowerBuilder provide transparent access to a variety of relational and nonrelational database management systems?*

A: PowerBuilder has drivers for the DBMSs it supports, so that it can provide a uniform interface to accessing the databases and internally translate the application or DataBase painter requests into the specific form required for the connected DBMS. PowerBuilder also allows you to directly issue statements with syntax specific to the DBMS.

Q: *What would the requirements be to use, for example, SQL Server from a PowerBuilder application?*
A: The requirements would be:
1. SQL Server installed on a database server
2. Network connectivity to the database server, generally provided by a network operating system such as Novell Netware or IBM LAN Server
3. Windows SQL Server client installed on the PowerBuilder machine
4. PowerBuilder support for SQL Server installed on the PowerBuilder machine

Q: *How do you use a Graph control?*
A: A Graph control is placed in a window during development, like any other control. Attributes usually set at development time determine the type of graph. The data used to construct the graph is provided at run time using various methods of the Graph control object.

Q: *What is PowerScript?*
A: PowerScript is a third-generation language with object-oriented syntax used to program event scripts. It is specific to PowerBuilder.

Q: *How is program logic implemented in PowerBuilder applications?*
A: The developer writes event scripts using the PowerScript language. These scripts are invoked when an object in an application generates the event the script is for. These events usually reflect actions the user takes interacting with the application's user interface.

Q: *How are event scripts created?*
A: Painters that manage objects with events, such as the Application, Window, and Menu painters, have a Script icon in their Painter bars and a Script choice in the Edit menu pull-down. In the Window painter you can also right click on an object and select Script from the pop-up menu.

Q: *How do you put a comment in an event script?*
A: Everything on a line in a script following "//" is considered a comment. Alternatively, surround the comment text with "/*" and "*/".

Q: *What kind of decision constructs are available in PowerScript?*
A: PowerScript supports an IF . . . END construct with optional ELSE and ELSEIF, and a CHOOSE CASE . . . END CHOOSE construct allowing the execution of different code based on the values of an expression.

Q: *What kind of looping constructs are available in PowerScript?*
A: PowerScript supports DO . . . LOOP loops with WHILE or UNTIL clauses on the DO, for top-tested loops, or on the terminating LOOP statement, for bottom-tested loops. It also supports a FOR . . . NEXT construct for iterated

loops. EXIT and CONTINUE can be used to jump out of loops or to jump to the loop test, respectively.

Q: *What are the possible meanings of "+" in PowerScript?*
A: This operator means addition if the operands are numeric and concatenation if the operands are strings.

Q: *What are the choices for variable scope? How is scope determined?*
A: Variables can have local, instance, or global scope. Variables with local scope are accessible only in the script they are declared in. Variables with instance scope are associated with an object and are accessible in any script associated with the object. They may also be accessed in scripts associated with other objects if they are public, which is the default. Variables with global scope can be accessed in any script. Scope is determined by how a variable is declared. Local variables are declared at the beginning of some script. Nonlocal variables are declared using the Declare pull-down menu in the script editor.

Q: *In PowerScript, what is an enumerated datatype and how would you use it?*
A: An enumerated datatype is a set of alternative values that can be used when setting an object attribute or as a parameter to a method. The values are strings ending with "!"

Q: *What is the difference between a string variable and a character array?*
A: A string variable is actually implemented as a pointer to a buffer. The buffer is dynamically allocated when the variable is first assigned a value and real-located as the value (really the length of the value) changes. A character array is an array of one-byte character variables whose length is set when the array is declared, and is thus allocated once.

Q: *What kind of pasting can you do in the PowerScript editor?*
A: You can use standard text paste if there is text in the Windows clipboard. You can also paste from the Paste Object, Paste Global, and Paste Instance drop down list boxes in the script editor. These show a list of the existing declarations of each type. You can paste SQL statements by constructing them using the same prompted methods available in DataWindows, by using the Paste SQL button. You can paste PowerScript statement syntax skeletons by using the Paste Statement button. Finally, you can paste PowerScript function syntax skeletons by using the Paste function menu choice in the Edit pull-down menu.

Q: *What kind of functions can a script call?*
A: Scripts can call built-in PowerScript functions, object methods (which are also built-in), functions written in PowerScript created using the Function painter, or functions in a Windows dynamic link library (DLL).

Q: *How do you create PowerScript functions and why would you want to?*
A: Create PowerScript functions when you have script logic that must be run in several event scripts. Create the function using the Function painter, which

will prompt you for a function name and a parameter list, and then put you in the PowerScript editor.

Q: *What's involved in calling a function in a Windows DLL?*
A: Functions in Windows DLLs must be declared as global or local external functions in the PowerScript editor, using the Declare pull-down menu. Global external functions can be declared once in any script and used in any script. Local external functions can only be used in the script they are declared in. The declaration must specify the function's parameter list and the name of the dynamic link library. Since many external functions take pointers to structures as parameters, you may have to create structure definitions using the Structure painter before declaring the external function.

Q: *How can you tell quickly what event scripts exist for an object?*
A: One way is to edit a script for any event for the object. Look at the Select event drop-down list. Events with scripts will have a script icon to the left of the event name.

Q: *What is a user-defined event? How is it generated?*
A: A user-defined event is an event associated with an object that is not built into PowerBuilder. A developer can create new events for any PowerBuilder object. However, such events will never be generated automatically, in the way say, a Clicked event is generated when a user clicks on a CommandButton. However, a script can generate a user-defined event using either the Trigger-Event or PostEvent methods that each object has. TriggerEvent will call the script associated with the user-defined event immediately, while PostEvent will add the event to the end of the list of events waiting to be processed.

Q: *How can a PowerBuilder application respond to standard Windows messages that don't correspond to an object event?*
A: Most PowerBuilder controls, such as CommandButtons and ListBoxes, correspond directly to an underlying Windows control. However, not all the Windows events associated with the underlying control are defined as PowerBuilder events. A developer can define any Windows message associated with the underlying Windows control as a user-defined event. A script for that event will be run if the underlying Windows event occurs.

Q: *What are the main features of the PowerBuilder debugger?*
A: The debugger can set breakpoints at lines of an event script, single-step through script execution, and display the current values of all variables currently in scope.

Q: *What are the windows in the debugger and what do they show?*
A: The debug window shows script code. You can open a Variables window, which shows the current values of all variables currently in scope. You can also open a Watch window and choose the variables to have their values displayed.

Q: *How do you make a program stop at a certain line in an event script using the debugger?*

A: When you start the debugger, it will ask you to create an initial set of breakpoints. If you are stopped at a breakpoint, you can use the Edit Stop button to add or remove breakpoints.

Q: *How are structures created in PowerBuilder? How are they used?*

A: Structures are created using the Structure painter. The painter prompts you for a series of structure elements. For each element, provide a name and a datatype. The datatype can be a built-in datatype selected from a drop-down list box, or it can be a previously defined structure. Elements can also be declared as arrays by adding square array brackets with the array size to the end of the element *name.* Structures are used by declaring variables using the structure name as the datatype in scripts.

Q: *What are the different kinds of user objects you can create in PowerBuilder?*

A: There are two groups of user objects in Powerbuilder; each has subgroups. The groups are Class user objects and Visual user objects. Class user objects are not user interface objects; they have no visual component. There are two subgroups: Custom and Standard. Custom Class user objects are used when you need to build an object from scratch, specifying all of its attributes and methods. Standard Class user objects are used when you want to modify or add to the characteristics of one of the built-in nonvisual objects, such as the Transaction object. Visual user objects are user interface objects. There are four subgroups: Custom, External, Standard, and VBX. Custom Visual user objects are built up out of standard control windows, which then function as a group and can be added as a unit to windows. External Visual user objects are implemented in a Windows dynamic link library (DLL), which is identified in the definition of the External Visual user object. Standard Visual user objects are based on a single standard control window, adding some application-specific behavior. The Standard Visual object can then be used in windows like a built-in control. Finally, VBX Visual user objects are implemented as Visual Basic control extensions; the user object definition identifies the VBX file implementing the control.

Q: *What is the difference between a user object and a user object control? What is the relationship between the two?*

A: User objects are created with the User Object painter. User Object controls are controls that can be placed in a Window Object. User Object controls are linked to user objects, which are displayed through the User Object control. The relationship is similar to that between a DataWindow and a DataWindow control.

Q: *What is inheritance? Why would you use it?*

A: Inheritance allows a newly created object to be based on an existing object type. The new object starts off with all the attributes, events and methods of the parent object, and can then have additional attributes, events, and methods defined. Also, some of the inherited attributes, events, or methods can be replaced. If the definition of the parent object changes, this change can be propagated to all child objects inheriting from the parent. Design changes can be easily propagated throughout a complex group of applications by changing parent object definitions.

Q: *How do you create an object that inherits behavior from another object?*

A: Whenever you open certain painters, the dialog box has a button labeled "Inherit . . .". Clicking on this will show a list of the existing objects in that category. Selecting an existing object will create a new object with all the attributes, events, and methods of the existing object, including event scripts.

Q: *What is Multiple Document Interface?*

A: Multiple Document Interface is a way of designing graphical applications that consist of a main window, called an MDI frame, and multiple child windows, called MDI sheets. MDI sheets all appear within the MDI frame. There can be more than one instance of a particular MDI sheet in existence at one time. An MDI sheet can have its own action bar; often MDI sheets take over the action bar of the MDI frame, changing it based on which MDI sheet is active. MDI frames can have a microhelp control which can display a short help message about what the user is doing. The PowerBuilder development environment is itself an example of an MDI application. The main Power-Builder window is an MDI frame. Each painter is an MDI sheet.

Q: *What can you do with the Library painter?*

A: You can manage libraries, including create new ones, delete old ones, look at lists of objects in libraries, and copy or move objects from one library to another. You can also go directly to the painter that manages a particular object. Finally, you can export an ASCII definition of an object to a file or create a new object by importing an ASCII definition.

Q: *How can multiple PowerBuilder applications share objects?*

A: Place the objects to be shared in a separate library. In the Application painter for each application that needs to access the shared objects, edit the Library list and add the shared library. To edit the Library list, either select Library List from the Edit pull-down menu, or use the LibList PainterBar button.

Q: *How are objects stored in libraries?*

A: Objects are stored in two forms: source and compiled. Each time you change the definition of the object, the changes are saved in the source version and it is recompiled. If you upgrade the library to a new version of PowerBuilder, the source version is used to create a compiled version compatible with the new release. Source versions can be exported and imported using the Library painter.

Q: *What is a dynamic PowerBuilder library? What are the advantages and disadvantages of using dynamic libraries?*

A: A dynamic PowerBuilder library is a way of sharing objects between applications when the applications are deployed as executables. Normally a

PowerBuilder executable contains the definitions of all objects used in the application, copied out of the libraries listed on the application's Library List. This can result in large executables and also means that all executables have to be regenerated if a minor change needs to be made to a single script. You can also place objects in a dynamic library, where they can be accessed by the PowerBuilder application executable at run time.

Q: *What is a PowerBuilder project and how do you create one?*

A: A project is a definition of a name for the application executable and indicates which application objects should get placed in the executable and which, if any, should get placed in dynamic libraries. Once a project is defined, the executable and any dynamic libraries can be regenerated using the predefined specifications.

Q: *How can you add on-line help to a PowerBuilder application?*

A: MDI applications can use the MDI microhelp control to display short messages. More extensive help must be created following the standard Windows help specifications. PowerBuilder does not supply any tools to help with doing this.

Q: *How are PowerBuilder executables created?*

A: PowerBuilder executables can be created from the Application painter, using the Create executable selection in the File pull-down menu. Or you can create a Project and generate the executable from the Project painter.

Q: *What is required to run a PowerBuilder executable on a user machine?*

A: First, the PowerBuilder Deployment Kit, which provides the run-time environment for the PowerBuilder executable. Second, depending on what data access the application does, DBMS client software might also be required, along with any network software required to connect to a remote database server.

Q: *What can you change about PowerBuilder toolbars?*

A: You can determine what icons appear in the toolbar, and whether or not text appears under the icon.

Q: *What categories of things can you customize in the Preferences painter?*

A: The Preferences painter can customize settings in these categories:

Application
Database
DataWindow
Debug
Library
Menu
PowerBuilder
Window

Q: *What is PB.INI?*

A: PB.INI is a file created in the Windows directory that contains PowerBuilder settings that need to be remembered from one PowerBuilder session to another.

Q: *How are reports created?*

A: Reports can be created using the Report painter. Report objects are actually the same as nonupdateable DataWindow objects, and can also be created in the DataWindow painter.

Q: *What is the difference between creating a composite report and nesting a report in another report?*

A: A composite report (or DataWindow) consists of several previously created reports (or DataWindows). A previously created report (or DataWindow) can also be nested in a report (or DataWindow). Both allow several reports or DataWindows to appear on the same screen or page. However, a composite report does not have its own data source, and therefore cannot link data in the different subreports. If a report is nested in another report, the data in the nested report is linked to the data in the main report. This can be used to retrieve rows in a nested report that logically are detail records for a row in the main report.

25
Delphi

Robert Palomo

Introduction

Delphi 2.0 is Borland International's 32-bit successor for Windows 95 and Windows NT. Developers will be able to leverage their 1.0 experience and applications to get going quickly with the new release. The user interface will be largely the same, with a few additions, and 16-bit applications using standard Delphi VCL components will recompile under Delphi 2.0 with few, or no, modifications. Borland seems to have scored a hit with application developers. Here are a few reasons why:

Performance. Borland drew upon its years of experience with compiler technology to architect Delphi as a Windows application development tool featuring a native code compiler. Executables are small, fast, and fully distributable. There are no run-time DLLs or distribution licenses to worry about.

Scalability. Delphi applications can be easily ported from the local desktop to network file servers and to client-server systems.

Extensibility. Delphi is truly object-oriented. You can develop reusable controls, windows, or even entire modules. Or you can take advantage of ready-made third-party components, many of which you can customize. You can write DLLs that can be called from any Windows application program developed in any programming language.

The main problem for many developers who otherwise might like Delphi's many advantages is the fact that Delphi is based on the Pascal programming language, which has not been considered mainstream in recent years.

Delphi and Delphi Client-Server

Delphi for Windows is focused toward the desktop, although it does include a 16-bit version of Borland's InterBase (a speedy SQL-based back-end database management system) to enable you to develop and test SQL database applications. Delphi Client-Server includes native drivers enabling seamless connection of a Delphi application to Oracle, Sybase, MS-SQL, and Informix servers, or ODBC databases.

Terminology

Alias: A name that represents a location for database tables and, for database servers, server connection parameters. (Use the BDE Configuration utility to define and maintain aliases.)

Ancestor: An object from which another object is derived.

BDE: Borland Database Engine, also called IDAPI (eye-dap-ee).

Class: Also called "object type." (See Object Pascal under Q&A section.)

Class method: A method providing global behaviors for an object class. (See Method.)

Component: Generally, a self-contained object having configurable design-time properties, responding to a defined set of events, and represented by an icon on the Component Palette. Also, any object descending from the class TComponent. Components may be visual or nonvisual.

DBD (Database Desktop): A stand-alone utility that ships with Delphi enabling you to create and maintain Paradox and dBASE tables and set up BDE aliases and other configuration parameters.

Expert: An interactive dialog enabling you to customize a standard form or application template by responding to a series of questions about the desired characteristics. You can develop your own experts as well.

File extensions:
```
.PAS (See Unit.)
.DCU (See Unit.)
.DFM (See Form file.)
.DPR (See Project.)
```

Form: The core component around which Delphi applications are built.

Form file: A binary file with a .DFM extension that contains the graphical image of a form.

Gallery: A set of prebuilt application frameworks and forms that you can reuse and customize in your own Delphi projects. You can add your own applications and forms to the Delphi gallery.

IDE (Integrated Development Environment): Delphi's main development tool set. Includes the menu bar, SpeedBar, Component Palette, Object Inspector, and Code Editor.

Inheritance: The assumption of the properties and behaviors of an existing object by a new object.

MDI (Multiple Document Interface): An application format, like that of the Windows File Manager, that can display multiple windows inside another main window.

Method: A procedure or function that governs a certain aspect of an object's behavior. Objects inherit the methods of their ancestor(s).

Nonvisual components: Components that display on a form at design time and whose properties you can manipulate, but that have no visual representation at run time. Example: components of type TDataSet.

Object Inspector: A component of the IDE that displays design-time property and event sets for a selected component on a form.

Palette: A tabbed multipage control in the Delphi IDE from which you select components to place on forms. You can add pages and components to the default set.

Procedure: A subprogram callable from another program, module, or procedure. Similar to a subroutine in BASIC-derived languages, a procedure returns no value.

Project file (.DPR extension): Object Pascal source code defining the component files of an application project. Normally created and maintained by Delphi.

Standard control: A control visible at run time and with which the application user can interact. Ancestor class is TControl; usually a member of class TwinControl.

TDB: Turbo Debugger.

Template: A set of reusable, modifiable application frameworks (application templates) and forms (form templates). These are contained in Delphi's Gallery.

Type: A description of how data should be accessed and stored (as opposed to a variable, which actually stores data of a given type). Pascal is considered a strongly typed language.

Unit: A code module that can be independently compiled. Every form has an associated unit file. Unit source code files have a .PAS extension and compile to binary object code files having a .DCU extension. (.DCUs are linked into the final .EXE or .DLL file.)

Uses clause: A line in a Pascal unit file beginning with the reserved word **uses** and specifying the identifiers of other units whose code is used by the current unit.

VCL: Visual Component Library.

A Delphi Job Interview

Most employers will try to determine the level of your skills according to this formula:

Beginner: Anyone who has written event-driven programs in a Windows- or other GUI-based development environment can probably adapt quickly to Delphi. Users of Visual Basic, Access, Power Builder, Revelation OpenInsight, and similar Windows-based development tools will catch on right away to building forms and dialog boxes in the Delphi IDE. The biggest stumbling block for most people will be the Object Pascal language. Pascal has not been considered a mainstream language in recent years and thus may be unfamiliar to many programmers. (Previous exposure to Borland Turbo Pascal or another Pascal compiler should be a big plus when beginning with Delphi.) Pascal is a relatively friendly language, however, and some time spent with one of several available tutorial book/disk combos should prepare someone with programming experience or training to handle a beginning Delphi job.

At a minimum you should be able to deal with constants, variables, types, blocks, units, procedures, and functions, and basic constructs such as for and while loops, if/then/else, and case statements.

Intermediate: At this level, in addition to a solid grasp of the Pascal language, you should have a background in object-oriented programming concepts. You should thoroughly understand such ideas as object hierarchy and inheritance, polymorphism, methods, properties, and class libraries. You should have a knowledge of Delphi's component architecture and be able to trace the hierarchical ancestry of a component in source code and determine its key properties and methods. At this level, depending upon the job requirements, you may also need to understand the basic principles of connectivity between Delphi and a local or remote database.

Expert: At this level, you should have considerable expertise in a true object-oriented development environment, and know Object Pascal quite well. You should have Windows development experience and have at least a working understanding of the Windows Application Program Interface (API). You should thoroughly understand Delphi components and be comfortable writing new components. You need enough technical background to understand and deal with the engineering issues involved in performance, memory management, I/O management, and so forth. Depending upon the job, you may need to handle connectivity from a Delphi front end to an Inter-Base or other supported SQL-based database server environment. In such case, you should have a good working knowledge of SQL, relational databases, and server-dependent views, rules, stored procedures, and triggers.

Questions and Answers

Delphi IDE

Q: *Where would you look in the source code of a Delphi application for a summary of the names and locations of the forms used in the project?*

A: In the application's project (.DPR) file. You can open this file in the Code Editor by choosing Project Source from the View menu, or from the Project Manager. (*Note:* manually modifying this file is not recommended for beginners.)

Q: *Demonstrate how to add a screen capture utility residing on the network to the menu bar of the Delphi installation on your workstation.*

A: Delphi enables you to add your favorite Windows utilities to the Tools menu and also delete any of the default selections. To add or delete commands from the Tools menu, Choose Options | Tools and follow the dialog boxes to specify the location of the program's executable file.

Q: *Demonstrate how to set up your workstation's Delphi installation so that when you start Delphi, the project open in the previous work session opens automatically in the IDE.*

A: This functionality is controlled from the Environment Options dialog box. Choose Options | Environment to display this multipage dialog. Choose the Preferences page and check the Desktop checkbox in the Autosave group.

Q: *Demonstrate how you would set up the Delphi installation on your workstation to enable integrated debugging.*

A: Choose Options | Environment to display the Environment Options dialog and display the Preferences page. Check the Integrated Debugging checkbox in the Debugging Group. Display the Library page and check the Compile With Debug Info checkbox.

Q: *You are ready to do a final build of an application. Demonstrate how you set up your Delphi system to provide the smallest, fastest-loading .EXE file.*

A: You need to remove debug information from the compiled .EXE and set the compiler option that provides optimal size and load speed for the compiled executable.

On the Library page of the Environment Options dialog, uncheck the Debug Info box in the Options group. On the Linker page of the Project Options dialog, check the Optimize for Size & Load Time box and uncheck the TDW Debug Info checkbox.

Q: *Set up your Delphi system so that compiled output is stored in a \BIN directory under the main project directory.*

A: Go to the Directories/Conditionals page of the Project Options dialog box. Specify the directory path for the BIN directory in the Output Directory edit field.

Q: *In the Object Inspector, what does a "+" character in front of a property name indicate?*

A: It indicates that the property has an array of individual values that you can set at design time, and that you can expand the cell by double-clicking to display these values. For example, double-clicking Font+ causes the Object Inspector to display font attributes such as font name, style, color, point size, etc.

Q: *What is indicated if a button with a " . . . " character appears in the value column of the Properties page of the Object Inspector when you select a property?*

A: A pop-up Property Editor is available, which you can display by clicking the button. Several types of editor dialog boxes exist and the appropriate type for the selected property displays automatically. Examples of properties having editors include StringList, Font, and Color.

Q: *You have just added a new form to a project that already has multiple forms and you need to test-run this form. Describe your approach.*

A: While it's certainly possible, and maybe even desirable, to display the new form via the application's user interface, this may not always be practical if the application is large. In such a case, you can change the project's main form designation and auto-create specification.

Open the Project Options dialog (Options | Project on the Delphi menu bar). Choose the Forms page. If you don't need any other forms created in memory in order to do your testing, move all forms except the one you are testing to the Available Forms list. Otherwise, move the ones you don't need and leave the ones you do need.

Use the Main Form combo box to specify your new form as the application main form. When you close the dialog and run the application, the new form is the first to display and you can test it as needed. Don't forget to go back and reset the Auto-create Forms and Application Main Form specifications before compiling the final version of the application.

Q: *How do you specify the icon for a window to display when the user minimizes it? Assume the .ICO file exists.*

A: Open the Project Options dialog (Options | Project) and choose the Application page. Use the Browse button to specify the .ICO file containing the icon image.

Q: *The icon file that you are using for your application main window was accidentally wiped out by a junior intern. There is no backup. How does this affect your application?*

A: Not at all. The icon image is compiled into binary format and stored in your application's .RES file. If you want, you could use screen capture and paint programs and an icon editor to re-create the icon file from the image in your application, making yourself look like a true technical wizard.

Q: *A new form has been developed that is to be the main form for all new application projects. Demonstrate how you would set up your Delphi installation to use this form as the default main form.*

A: Open the Gallery dialog box (Options | Gallery). Choose the Add button and specify the location of the form unit file. Choose the Default Main Form button and close the dialog. A copy of the specified form is opened as the default main form in a new project.

Q: *In the Delphi IDE, how would you go about checking out the company's stock of standard forms?*

A: These should be set up in the Delphi Form's Gallery as form templates. You can add to, modify forms in, or delete from the stock Forms Gallery that ships with Delphi. Choose Options | Gallery from the Delphi menu bar, and the Form Templates page of the Gallery Options dialog box to review the current stock of form templates.

Q: *Your interviewer sits you in front of an open Delphi project on a workstation. The Delphi Palette window is the only thing displayed on the screen. Your interviewer asks you to quickly display the design form, the source code, and the Object Inspector Properties page for the form named EmployeeWin.*

A: The first thing to do is to display the Project Manager (View | Project Manager). Type Alt+VP. Then you can quickly display the design form by double-clicking on the form name in the Project Manager window. Typing E in the form column jumps to that section of the alphabetically listed form names.

Double-clicking the unit name will then display the form source code in the Code Editor. If you place the insertion point in the source code and press F11, you'll get the Object Inspector. If the Properties page isn't on top, click its page tab. You should be able to do all these operations in five seconds or less!

Q: *There are six or seven forms, the Object Inspector, the Code Editor, the Project Manager, and who knows what else open in the IDE (it's basically a mess!). Your interviewer asks you to quickly find the design form called EmployeeWin and display it at the front. Impress the interviewer with how fast you can do this.*

A: Press Alt+0 (zero). This gives you a list of all the windows open in the IDE. Double-click on EmployeeWin to display it on top.

Q: *How would you create a new component palette page for custom components?*

A: The Palette page of the Environment Options dialog box (Options | Environment) enables you to fully customize the Delphi Component palette.

Projects and Forms

Q: *Explain the difference between opening a .PAS file in the Code Editor and opening a file as part of a project.*

A: The Code Editor enables you to open and edit any text file directly from the Delphi IDE. Object Pascal source code files have a .PAS extension. .PAS files may reside anywhere and, depending upon how you open them in the Code Editor, may or may not be tracked as belonging to the current project. (Files that comprise the project are tracked in the .DPR file.)

The File | Open File menu command opens a file in the code editor but does not add it to the current project. The File | Add File command opens a file in the editor and adds it to the uses clause of the .DPR file the next time you save the project.

Q: *What are the main sections of a form unit?*

A: Interface and implementation. The interface section determines what is visible and accessible to any program or unit using the current unit. You can declare constants, types, variables, procedures, and functions that other programs or units can use.

The implementation section contains the actual code for the procedures and functions declared in the interface section of the unit.

Q: *What is the purpose of a .DFM file?*

A: This file, created and maintained by Delphi when a form is saved, stores the graphical image of a form in binary format.

Q: *The File | Save Project As menu command will create a backup copy of the entire project currently open in the IDE: True or False?*

A: False. This command copies only the project (.DPR) file. This file tracks the other files used in the project. Because these can reside in any location, and because they may be used by other projects, the Save Project As command on the File menu only copies the .DPR file. If you want to back up the project file and all files used in the project to a separate location, you need to locate all the files (use the Project Manager) and copy them manually (or write a batch file that does the same thing).

Q: *You need to place five Edit components on a form, align their left edges, and space them equidistantly in a vertical orientation. Demonstrate a quick way to do this.*

A: First, display the alignment palette (Alt+V+A). Press and hold the Shift key and choose the Edit component on the Component palette. Release Shift and in the form, click five times to drop five Edit components. Click the Select Pointer on the palette. Drag a "rubber band" around the Edit components to select all of them. Click the Align Left Edges and Space Equally, Vertical buttons on the Alignment palette.

Q: *Describe the technique for displaying a form as a modal dialog box at run time.*

A: Set the form's BorderStyle property to bsDialog to give the form a dialog box style of border at run time. In the component event handler that calls the dialog, call the ShowModal method.

For example:

```
procedure TForm1.Button1Click(Sender: TObject);
begin
MyDialog.ShowModal;
end;
```

Note: Don't forget to properly declare the form units in the uses clauses of each form unit. (See "Circular reference" question in Object Pascal section of this chapter.) Also, the foregoing assumes that the form has been created in memory with a prior call to the CreateForm method of the TApplication object.

Q: *In a dialog box, there is a radio button component with the following options: Up, Down, Left, Right. The new specification call for this component is to be replaced by a more graphical control. Any suggestions?*

A: Replace the RadioGroup component with four TSpeedbutton components. Use bitmaps from the stock Delphi image library (arrow1u.bmp, arrow1r. bmp, etc.) in the Glyph property of each. Set the GroupIndex property of all to the same nonzero integer value (any number not already used by another group of TSpeedbuttons). Set the AllowAllUp property of all the buttons to True to allow a no-selection option, or False to require a selection. In the OnClick event handlers, use the Down property to determine the state of each button and provide the appropriate event handling code. Example: if Speedbutton 1. Down = True then Do This;

Q: *How do you designate a form as a MDI Frame or MDI Child window?*
A: Set the form's FormStyle property to either fsMDIFram or fsMDIChild. Specifying the former for the application's main form creates the form as a MDI Frame at run time. Specifying fsMDIChild in this property creates a MDI Child window and displays the form in the desktop space of the form you specify as the MDI Frame.

Q: *You have created a MDI Frame window and three MDI Child windows. The specification states that the MDI Children are not to be visible to the user when the MDI frame first runs. How would you display the MDI Child windows in this case?*
A: The normal way for non-MDI windows is to set the Visible property of forms to False, specify them as being auto-created in memory in Project Options, and call the Show method in an event handler at run time. However, if you specify fsMDIChild in a form's FormStyle property, Delphi generates an error message "Can't Hide an MDI Child Form" if you try to set the form's Visible property to False at design time. Furthermore, if you leave the MDI Children specified in the Auto-create list in Project | Options | Forms, they will display in the MDI Frame workspace at run time.

If you don't want MDI Child forms to display until called for, then you must remove the form identifier from the Auto-create Forms list in the Project Options dialog, and use the CreateForm method in the event handler that displays the form: Application.CreateForm(TMyMDIKid, MyMDIKid);

Q: *What method would you call to close a MDI Child window?*
A: In the case of a MDI application, calling the Hide method for the MDI Child windows, as you might expect to do, generates an error. There are a couple of ways to approach this task. Probably the best approach is to use the FormClose event of the MDI child form itself, calling the Close method of TForm from the appropriate code. For example:

```
procedure TMainForm:Destroy1; {code in the MDI main form}
begin
   MyMDIKid1.Close;
end;
```

Then, in the FormClose event handler for MyMDIKid1, use the event's variable parameter, Action, with the constant caFree to indicate that the form is to be destroyed.

```
procedure TMyMDIKid1.FormClose(Sender: TObject; var Action: TCloseAction);
begin
   Action := caFree;
end;
```

If you don't specify caFree, the default action of the MDI child form is to Minimize when the form's Close method is called.

Q: *You have come across a custom object on a Delphi installation you inherited from a departed developer. You need to trace its derivation in the object hierarchy. What do you do?*

A: Delphi provides the Object Browser, which enables you to visually step through the object hierarchies, units, and global symbols of a Delphi application. The Object Browser graphically displays object hierarchies in your application. It also lists the units your program uses, and enumerates the symbols declared in the interface or implementation section based on your compiler setup. The Browser also lists all global symbols, their declarations, and the references to them in the application source code.

You access the Object Browser with Search | Browse Symbol. This menu command is disabled unless you have set up the compiler to compile symbol information(Options | Project, Compiler page).

Q: *You are assigned to a project in progress. You want to modify a form, but want to have some idea of the effect on other applications. What would be your approach?*

A: Delphi's first version does not have a change impact analysis feature. However, using the Project Manager can sometimes give you a clue as to whether or not a form may be used by other applications.

If the Path column is empty for a form listed in the Project Manager, it means that the form files reside in the main directory for the current project. This doesn't guarantee that other projects do not use the form, but it does mean that the form was probably created as part of this project. Path information in the Path column indicates that the form files reside in a directory other than the main project directory. This could be your clue that other projects use the form and that you should probably do some checking before making changes.

Q: *In the course of your interview, a question arises about the syntax of a Windows API function. You don't have a reference manual and neither do the people in the meeting. Delphi is running on your laptop. Can you help?*

A: Delphi includes a Windows Help file that contains reference information for the Windows Application Program Interface (API). On a normal Delphi installation, you can bring up Help and choose the API button in the Help window to get the contents of the Windows API Help file. Or, you can simply search Help for the function and Delphi Help will display the information from the correct Help file (again, assuming a standard installation).

Q: *In this job, you need to coordinate with the documentation people who are writing the Help file for the application under development. How do you go about implementing context-sensitive Help in a Delphi application?*

A: Every component that can receive the focus at run time has a HelpContext property, which has an integer value. If the value remains unchanged from its default of zero, the component will not display Help at run time, even if a Help topic exists in the Help file. You need to design a numbering scheme for the HelpContext properties (called Context IDs) of the components of your application that you want to have context-sensitive Help. You'll need to provide a list of the numeric Context IDs and the associated interface component(s) to the Help author so that these can be integrated into the Help project file.

Database Issues

Q: *How would you access a set of Paradox tables stored on a network file server?*

A: One method would be to specify an alias for the location in the BDE Configuration utility and specify that alias in the DatabaseName property of TTable or TQuery components that access the tables at that location.

Another method (and it's the *only* method to use if accessing tables on a SQL server) is to use a TDatabase component. The main advantages to doing database access this way are that you can specify the location of the data "on the fly" from a configuration file or user input, and you don't need to deal with setting up BDE aliases when you install your application on end users' systems.

Place the TDatabase component on the application's main form (or somewhere else that will always exist in memory during the entire run time of the application). Then set these key properties as follows:

DatabaseName: Any unique identifier to designate this database location. For example: dbMyApp. The identifier you specify here appears to TTable and TQuery objects in the project as a BDE alias.

DriverName: Choose STANDARD from the drop-down list when using Paradox tables. Don't leave this blank.

Params: If you want to access data via the TDatabase at design time, pop up the property editor and enter PATH= followed by the path to the database. For example:

```
PATH=G:\PROJ1\DATA
```

(*Note:* you must set Connected to False before doing this, and then set it back to True.)

As you place TDataSet objects (TTable, TQuery) on project forms, you can specify dbMyApp in their DatabaseName property. Making sure dbMyApp. Connected is set to True, you can select any table on the location to which dbMyApp points for the TableName property of these objects. The net effect is like using a valid BDE alias.

Now, at an appropriate spot in your code you can set the data location for all TTable and TQuery objects in the application at run time.

```
procedure TMainForm.Initialize;
var
  DBPath: string;
```

```
begin
  DBPath := GetPathLocation; {Your custom function returning data
    from an INI file}
  dbMyApp.Connected := False; {Disconnect required before setting
    new path}
  dbMyApp.Params[0] := DBPath; {Specify the full path location}
  dbMyApp..Connected := True; {Reconnect so data set objects can
    find the data}
  ...
  ...                {any other stuff you need to do}
  ...
end;
```

Q: *What is the principal difference between a Database component and a Table component?*

A: The Database component is used to establish and maintain a connection with a database in a client/server system. The application can then open and close tables on the server without having to re-establish the connection and go through the user login procedure. The Table component accesses data from a specific table at a specific system location.

Q: *How would you go about retrieving a subset of the data in a local dBASE or Paradox table?*

A: You can filter the data with an appropriate SQL statement in the SQL property of a Query component, or you can use the SetRange method of class TTable with an object of that type.

  Example: Table 1. SetRange ([Key 1], [Key 1]);

Q: *Describe the basic design-time technique for displaying data in a database type component such as a TDBGrid. Assume an alias exists for the data location.*

A: In addition to the visual TDBGrid component, you need two nonvisual components: a TDataSet component and a TTable (or a TQuery) component. After placing all three components from the palette onto a form, you need to do the following:

TTable component: Set the Database property to the alias for the location of the database tables. (This can refer to a TDatabase component.) Set the Table property to the name of the desired database table (if the alias is valid, the names of all tables at the location display in the drop-down list of the Object Inspector's Table field.) Set the Name property to a descriptive value. Set the Active property to True.

TDataSource component: Set the component's DataSet property to the name of the TTable component (the drop-down field in the Object Inspector displays the names of all Table and Query components on the current form).

TDBGrid component: Set the DataSet property of this component to the name of the TDataSet component (the drop-down field in the Object Inspector displays the names of all TDataSet components on the current form).

Q: *In a data entry form, you need to provide the user a means of looking up a column value in a secondary table and writing a different column value to the primary table. How might you do this?*

A: The TDBLookupCombo component enables the user to update a column in the current record with a value looked up from a different table. The component can display a value from one column in the lookup table (CustomerName, for example) and write the corresponding value from a different column of the same lookup table record (CustomerID, for example).

   There are several key properties to focus on when doing this type of operation with this component. The LookupSource property points to a TDataSource component, which in turn is hooked to a TTable, which encapsulates the lookup (secondary) table.

   LookupField is the name of a field in the dataset specified by LookupSource. It links that dataset to the one representing the main table (i.e., the table being updated).

   The LookupDisplay property is optional (in the case described here, you would use it). You can set this property to display a column other than the one specified in LookupField. You could also use this property to specify multiple columns in the TDBLookupCombo (CustomerName and CustCity, for example).

Q: *Modify the alias for the Paradox database located on G:\APPS\DATA\ PDOX\LIVE to point to G:\APPS\DATA\PDOX\TEST.*

A: You need to run the BDE Configuration utility. Normally, this stand-alone utility is available in the Delphi program group. If your installation is different, find the file BDECFG.EXE (normally in the \IDAPI directory). The Aliases page enables you to add a new alias or edit an existing one. Select the existing alias in the Alias Names list and modify the Path in the Parameters list. Aliases provide a quick way of switching between different data locations without having to modify the applications that use the data.

Q: *How would you bring a subset of the data in a table into a data-aware component such as a grid, and enable the user to modify records in that subset?*

A: You need to use a TQuery component to return a live result set. By default, a TQuery returns a read-only result set, so you need to set the RequestLive property to True at design time. Your SQL SELECT statement must conform to the BDE requirements for a live result set as specified in the manual Database Application Developer's Guide.

Q: *In a TQuery, you need to write a SELECT statement. One of the columns specified in the WHERE clause may vary at run time. How do you allow for this?*

A: Delphi and the BDE support the use of dynamic SQL statements (also called "parameterized queries") to handle variable values in SQL statements. This subject is well documented in the manuals and on-line Help. You should become familiar with this technique.

Q: *Write a simple dynamic SQL SELECT statement.*

A:
```
SELECT CustNo, CustName, CustCity, CustState
FROM CUSTOMER.DB
WHERE CustState = :State
```

Q: *In the above SELECT statement, how can you supply a value for :State?*

A: First, you need to define the parameter(s) and its datatype using the parameters Editor (right-click a selected TQuery and choose Parameters Editor from the SpeedMenu). You can supply a default value in the Parameters Editor, including a null value. At run time, your code can supply values to parameters via the following properties of TQuery: Params, ParamByName, or DataSource (see the Delphi database documentation for details).

Q: *Is there any way to query tables of different types in different databases at the same time?*

A: Yes. Delphi, via the BDE, supports heterogeneous queries that join tables of different types on different database servers. A standard BDE alias must exist for each database (see Delphi database manual for details). The following code illustrates a heterogeneous query.

```
SELECT CUSTOMER.CUSTID, ORDERS.ORDERNO
FROM :INTBASE:CUST, :ORACLE:ORDERS
WHERE CUSTOMER.CUSTNO MATCHES ORDERS.CUSTNO
```

Q: *What is required to access an ODBC database from a Delphi database application?*

A: You need the ODBC driver from the ODBC database vendor and the Microsoft ODBC Driver Manager. You need to set up an appropriate ODBC driver connection for the BDE using the BDE Configuration utility.

Object Pascal

Q: *What is a Type?*

A: A Type, in Object Pascal, is essentially a description of how data is to be stored and accessed. This contrasts with a Variable, which is the actual data storage.

Q: *What is the difference between a Class and an Object Type?*

A: In Borland's Pascal documentation the two terms are interchangeable. Borland defines a class as "A list of features representing data and associated code assembled into a single entity."

Q: *Why are Types significant in Pascal?*

A: The language is structured in such a way as to require compatibility between two types in an expression or relational operation. Type compatibility is a precondition of assignment compatibility. Thus, a variable of type String cannot equate to a variable of type Integer:

```
var
StringNo: string;
IntNo: integer;
begin
StringNo := 1;        {In this variable type, the data is
     character, not numeric}
IntNo := StringNo; {These types are incompatible and will
generate an error}
end;
```

Q: *How would you fix the error in the previous code example?*

A: Object Pascal provides type conversion functions for many of the types commonly used in variables. The documentation provides information about the full range of these. In the preceding example, you could use either the IntToStr function, or the StrToInt function:

```
var
StringNo: string;
IntNo: integer;
begin
StringNo := 1;
StrToInt(IntNo) := StringNo; {Data is converted to integer type}
end;

var
StringNo: string;
IntNo: integer;
begin
StringNo := 1;
IntNo := StrToInt(StringNo); {Data is converted to integer type}
end;
```

Q: *How do you think Pascal's strong adherence to typing would impact the way you write custom procedures and functions?*

A: Any data from a calling code block passed to a procedure or function's arguments or parameters must be type-compatible with the arguments or parameters.

In the following example, the datatype being passed to MyFunction is not type-compatible with the parameter of the function. In this case, a compiler error would be generated.

```
procedure Button1click(Sender: TObject);
var
Name1: string;
begin
MyFunction(Name1);
end;

function MyFunction(param: byte): byte;
begin
.... {Function code lines}
```

```
. . . .
. . . .
end;
```

Q: *Create an enumerated type and write a case statement using it.*

A: An enumerated type in Pascal is where you create a simple type and specify or enumerate the possible values the type can take. You can then declare variables of the new type.

```
type OneToFive = (one, two, three, four, five);
var
choice: OneToFive; {Variable declaration of new type}
oddev: string;    {Variable of standard string type}
begin
case choice of
'one', 'three', 'five': oddev := 'odd';
'two', 'four' : oddev := 'even';
end;
```

Q: *Find the error in the following code example:*

```
unit Empdet1;
interface
uses
   SysUtils, WinTypes, WinProcs, Messages, Classes, Graphics,
   Controls, Forms, Dialogs, StdCtrls, DB, DBTables, DBCtrls,
   ExtCtrls;

type
   TForm1 = class(TForm)
      Button1:TButton;
   private
      { Private declarations }
   public
      { Public declarations }
   end;

var
   Form1: TForm1;

implementation

 {$R *.DFM}
procedure TForm1.Button1Click(Sender: TObject);
begin
Form2.Show;
end;
end.
```

A: The unit for Form2 is not declared in the uses clause. Assuming the form is defined in a unit name Unit2, the uses clause should be as follows:

```
uses
SysUtils, WinTypes, WinProcs, Messages, Classes, Graphics,
Controls, Forms, Dialogs, StdCtrls, DB, DBTables, DBCtrls,
ExtCtrls, Unit2;
```

Q: *What is a circular reference error, and would you avoid having one occur?*

A: Circular unit references occur when you have units that are mutually dependent. Mutual dependence occurs when, in either the implementation or interface section, you reference a unit in a uses clause and that unit in turn references the current unit in a uses clause in the same section. This essentially hides the inner details of the unit referenced in the uses clause; the referenced unit is private and not available to the program or unit using the unit it is referenced in.

A frequent problem for new Delphi users is when the code in one form unit displays another form, and the code in that form redisplays the first form. Circular reference errors can be avoided by making the declaration in different sections of the two units. For example, if Form1 declares Form2 in the Interface section, then Form2 should declare Form1 in the Implementation section or vice versa. Study the following example to see how to do this correctly:

First unit source code:

```
unit Unit1;        {Unit identifier}
interface         {Unit1 interface section references Unit2 in uses
clause}
uses
   SysUtils, WinTypes, WinProcs, Messages, Classes, Graphics,
   Controls, Forms, Dialogs, Unit2;
type
  TForm1 = class(TForm)
    BtnShowFrm2: TButton;
    procedure BtnShowFrm2Click(Sender: TObject);
  private
    { Private declarations }
  public
    { Public declarations }
  end;
var
  Form1: TForm1;
implementation
{$R *.DFM}
procedure TForm1.BtnShowFrm2Click(Sender: TObject); {Button
event handler}
begin
Form1.Hide;
Form2.Show;{This line won't work unless Unit2 is declared in a
uses clause}
end;
end.
```

Second unit source code:

```
unit Unit2;
interface
```

```
uses              {Declaring Unit1 here would cause circular
reference error}
  SysUtils, WinTypes, WinProcs, Messages, Classes,
Graphics, Controls,
  Forms, Dialogs;

type
  TForm2 = class(TForm)
    BtnShowFrm1: TButton;
    procedure BtnShowFrm1Click(Sender: TObject);
  private
    { Private declarations }
  public
    { Public declarations }
  end;
var
  Form2: TForm2;
implementation {Unit2 implementation section references Unit1
in uses clause}
{$R *.DFM}
uses
  Unit1;        {Declaring this unit here prevents a circular
reference error}

procedure TForm2.BtnShowFrm1Click(Sender: TObject);
begin
 Form2.Hide;
 Form1.Show;
end;
end.
```

Q: *In a database application, how would you establish a master-detail relation-ship between TTable components on a form and their related data display components?*

A: For many applications, you can use the Database Form Expert to create a master-detail form. To do this the Gallery must be enabled for new forms in the Environment Options dialog box (Options | Environment). Choose File | New Form in an open project, and select Database Form Expert from the Experts. Simply follow the prompts of the Expert to create a master-detail form. You can then modify the form as desired.

The key properties to look at in the TTable component representing the detail table are: IndexFieldNames, MasterFields, and MasterSource. You should study these properties and master-detail form concepts in the *Delphi Database Application Developer's Guide* and Delphi on-line Help.

You can manipulate these properties in code to do different types of lookups with a master-detail relationship between two tables, as shown in the following code:

Example source code:

```
{This procedure dynamically changes the detail table, looks up
a value in a field, and displays it in a DBText component on a
status line. Values of parameters are set in the calling
procedure.}

procedure TMyWindow.ShowStatlineInfo(TblName: string; IdxField:
string;
MstrField: string; DisplField: string);
begin
LookupTable.Close;        {Close the detail table via its TTable
                    component}
LookupTable.TableName := TblName; {Specify name of detail table
                        in current database}
LookupTable.IndexFieldNames := IdxField; {Set property based on
parameter value}
LookupTable.MasterFields := MstrField;  { ditto }
LookupTable.MasterSource := DSrcMaster; { Specify master table's
                    Datasource}
If LookupTable.Active = False then        {Open the detail table}
LookupTable.Open;
DBTextStatline1.DataSource := DSrcDetail; {Set DataSource
                        property for data display
                        component}
DBTextStatline.DataField := DisplField;   {Set field to display
in data display component}
end;
```

Q: *How would you configure the system so that passthrough SQL and Delphi method calls through the BDE to the server will not interfere with each other?*

A: The setting of SQLPASSTHRUMODE in the BDE Configuration Utility (BDECFG.EXE) determines whether passthrough SQL and BDE calls share the same database connection. This mode has three possible settings: The SHARED AUTOCOMMIT (the default) and SHARED NOAUTOCOMMIT settings enable use of a single database connection, while the NOT SHARED setting requires separate connections for passthrough SQL and Delphi method calls. You should use the NOT SHARED setting and separate database connections to ensure that passthrough SQL and calls generated by Delphi methods do not bump into each other.

Q: *A subset of the rows of a table have been brought into the application through a TQuery component. How would you create a new table mirroring the structure of the original table and write this subset to it?*

A: Delphi provides TBatchMove, a nonvisual component that will handle this requirement. It can create tables on the destination that correspond to source tables, automatically mapping the column names and datatypes. If you move data between different types of tables, Delphi maps the datatypes according to a fixed scheme.

The Mode property of TBatchMove enables various types of batch operations. The batCopy setting copies records from a TDataset object to a table. It creates the destination table based on the structure of the source table. Therefore, the destination table should not pre-exist unless it's OK for it to be overwritten. Other settings of this property enable other batch operations. Lookup "BatchMove" in Delphi's on-line Help system for further information.

Component Writing

Q: *Write a basic unit source code file for a custom edit component that derives from a TEdit component.*

A:
```
unit Unit1;
interface
uses
   SysUtils, WinTypes, WinProcs, Messages, Classes, Graphics,
   Controls, Forms, Dialogs, StdCtrls;

type
  NewEdit = class(TEdit)
  private
   { Private declarations }
  protected
   { Protected declarations }
  public
   { Public declarations }
  published
   { Published declarations }
  end;

procedure Register;

implementation

procedure Register;
begin
  RegisterComponents('Samples', [NewEdit]);
end;
end.
```

The Component Expert (File | New Component) will generate this code based on your responses to the Expert's dialog box.

Q: *Sketch the VCL object hierarchy showing the main inheritance path of interest to a component writer.*

A: (Editor: See bitmap file) Don't forget about the Object Browser (View | Browser) if you want to study the VCL component hierarchy.

Q: *What is the base ancestor class for nonvisual components?*

A: TComponent. It contains all the properties and methods needed to visually represent the component on a form at design time.

Q: *What base ancestor class would you most likely use to create an original control (i.e., one not related to an existing control)?*

A: TWinControl. This class has a property "Handle" that encapsulates the window handle of a standard Windows control. "Handle" enables the control to receive the focus and receive a handle to be passed to Windows API functions.

Q: *What if the original control you want to create doesn't need to receive the input focus?*

A: Use TGraphicControl as the base ancestor class. An abstract class descended from TControl, this class provides a canvas for painting, and handles WM_PAINT messages from the Windows API.

Q: *In a component unit, what is the purpose of a private declaration?*

A: Private parts of object types are typically used to hide the implementation details of the object from the users of the object. This declaration represents one of the four levels of access control for components. An object declared private is invisible to code outside the component unit. Within the unit, code can access the private section as if it were public.

Q: *What is the difference between an object part declared protected and one declared private?*

A: Object parts declared protected are also invisible to all code outside the object unit except units containing object types derived from the object having the protected declaration.

Q: *What is the difference between object parts declared public and those declared published?*

A: Public object parts are available to any code having access to the object as a whole. They define the object's run-time interface (for example, read-only properties are run-time-dependent properties).

Object parts declared published are also public, but this declaration causes Delphi to generate run-time type information for the published object part. This enables the Object Inspector to access object properties and events at design time.

Q: *Outline the basic steps involved in creating a new Delphi component.*

A: 1. In a new project, create a new unit (File | New Unit).

2. Derive a new type from an existing type.

3. Declare and write code for properties, events, and methods of the object.

4. Register the component with Delphi.

5. Create a Windows Help file for the component documenting its properties, events, and methods.

Consult the printed manual *Delphi Component Writer's Guide,* and the Windows Help file CWG.HLP (both provided with all versions of Delphi) to learn about the component writing process.

Q: *What object methods should always be declared private?*

A: Methods that implement object properties. This prevents the component user from calling methods that manipulate data for properties.

Programming

Q: *What are "Watches" and how are they used?*

A: Delphi enables you to set up "Watch expressions," which allow you to observe changes in the values of program variables and expressions as you step through your code with the Integrated Debugger. The Watch List is displayed in the Watch window (View | Watches). You can add, delete, or edit Watch expressions in the Add Watch dialog (Run | Add Watch). This feature is quite useful in cases where code compiles and the program runs fine, but you are getting wrong data values.

Q: *Your interviewer has asked you to step through a piece of code displayed in the Code Editor using the Integrated Debugger. How do you activate it?*

A: First make sure that the Integrated Debugging option is enabled in the Environment (Options | Environment, Preferences page) and that the compiler is compiling debut information (Options | Environment, Library page). If these options are not enabled, set them and recompile the code.

To activate the debugger, set a Breakpoint at the line of the source code where you want the Debugger to kick in. Click the mouse just to the right of the Code Editor border next to the code line on which you want to set the Breakpoint. The line highlights and a Breakpoint symbol displays in the left margin of the code. (You can also set break points with the Code Editor SpeedMenu . . . right-click on the Editor window to display this menu.) Now run the program. The code will run up to the Breakpoint and stop, displaying the Code Editor at the front. You can now step through the code line by line using the Speedbar buttons or the F-keys.

Q: *With your interviewer, you are confidently stepping through code in the Debugger when you accidentally trace into a lengthy function that you actually meant to step over. Recover gracefully and don't waste the interviewer's time.*

A: Use the Call Stack window (View | Call Stack) to return to the point where the function was called and then resume debugging.

Q: *Use a single TSpeedButton event handler to globally toggle the display of "fly-by" hints in the application.*

A: First, make sure that the ParentShowHint properties of all controls are set to True and that the ShowHint property of each form is also set to True. (We're assuming that some text appears in the Hint property of the appropriate forms and controls.)

Set the GroupIndex property of the TSpeedbutton to a unique integer value. Set the AllowAllUp property to True. Now, some simple code in the TSpeedbutton's OnClick event globally toggles the display of Hints.

```
procedure TMainForm.Speedbutton1Click(Sender: TObject);
TMainForm.mnuOptionsHintsClick(Sender: TObject);
begin
  Case Speedbutton1.Down of
    False: Application.ShowHint := False;  {or vice versa,
depending on what you want the}
    True: Application.ShowHint := True;  {Down state of the
component to represent.}
  End;
end;
```

The TApplication object has a number of properties and methods that affect the application as a whole. In this case, it eliminates the need to do complex looping through all the forms and controls to take care of this small housekeeping chore.

Q: *Your prospective employer wants to port a Visual Basic application to Delphi. They have a number of custom VBX controls which they've heard you can use in a Delphi application. They want to know some specifics.*

A: As long as the VBX controls conform to Microsoft VB 1.0 specifications, you can add them to the Delphi VCL. The installation procedure is fundamentally the same as that for installing native Delphi custom components. In the Install Components dialog, you specify VBX to open a special dialog for specifying the VBX component to install. Delphi generates a "wrapper" unit for the VBX so that Delphi recognizes it as an object type. You can specify a name for the new control and the Component Palette page in which it is to appear in the Delphi IDE.

Q: *After the VBX has been added as a Delphi component, a decision is made to modify it. How would you do this?*

A: Modifications to the VBX control should be done in Visual Basic and the control reinstalled as a Delphi component.

Q: *In a MDI application, how would you add the standard Window menu functionality with Window arrangement options and a list of open Windows?*

A: Delphi provides a menu property and methods that neatly encapsulate this task. First create the Window command on the application menu bar, and then the Cascade, Tile, and Arrange Icons commands on the Window menu. Next, create an event handler for each of the Window menu commands. Place the appropriate method call in each, as shown in the following code:

```
procedure TMDIFrame.MnuWindowTileClick(Sender: TObject);
begin
Tile;
end;

procedure TMDIFrame.MnuWindowCascadeClick(Sender: TObject);
begin
Cascade;
end;

procedure TMDIFrame.MnuWindowArrangeClick(Sender: TObject);
begin
ArrangeIcons;
end;
```

To create a list of open windows on the Window menu at run time, specify the name of the Window menu component in the WindowMenu property of the MDI Frame form. For example, if the component name is Window1, specify this name in the WindowMenu property of the MDI Frame form.

26

Visual Basic

Mike Conners

Introduction

Visual Basic 4.0 is the latest GUI development system by Microsoft. There are three different editions of VB: Standard, Professional, and Enterprise. All three editions come with 16-bit and 32-bit versions that give the user the capability to develop applications not only for Windows 3.1, but for Windows 95 and Windows NT as well. Below are some of the new features of VB 4.0.

- The ability to create Classes and Collections. This new and very powerful feature gives the user the ability to create reusable objects.

- New Data-Bound Controls. Three new bound controls are included: DBList, DBCombo, and DBGrid.

- The new Jet Engine—version 2.5 for 16-bit applications and version 3.0 for 32-bit applications. New Jet Engine features include: cascaded updates and deletes, the ability to maintain referential integrity, the new Data Access Objects (DAO), and overall improved speed. Jet Engine 3.0 also supports database replication.

- The new Object Browser. This new tool allows you to view and select all of your classes, properties, and methods in your application in a hierarchical display.

- Enhanced OLE Automation.

- A new development environment. The new system gives you more options to customize your development environment, such as loading or compiling your application in the background, changing the way you view your code, and automatic version incrementing implemented upon creating an executable file. Another new and very powerful feature is the ability to create Add-ins that can then be added to the VB development menu. A sample Add-in that comes with VB 4.0 allows you to resize all of your command buttons at the same time.

- Windows 95 Custom Controls. These include: a status bar, tool bars, list views, tree views, a tab control, a slider control, and a RichTextBox control. These new controls give the user the ability to create applications that have the look and feel of the Windows 95 interface.

- Remote Data Objects (RDO) and the RemoteData Control (RDC). (Enterprise Edition only). These give the user the ability to create client/server applications that can access ODBC data remotely without using a local query processor.

Proficiency Levels

The proficiency levels listed below are the author's opinion of a candidate's qualifications at the entry, intermediate, and advanced levels.

Entry level: Knowledge of the basic controls and property settings. Capable of creating simple entry screens. Usually this individual has less than one year of Visual Basic programming experience.

Intermediate level: Ability to manipulate data, perform simple queries, create menus, and perform debugging functions. Basic knowledge of ODBC, DDE, OLE, and MDIs. Usually this individual has one to two years of Visual Basic programming experience.

Advanced level: Extensive knowledge of DDE, ODBC, OLE, and Windows APIs. Advanced data manipulation through ODBC databases. Usually this individual has more than two years of Visual Basic programming experience.

Questions and Answers

Q: *Describe the fundamental variable datatypes.*

A:

Integer	A 2-byte positive or negative whole number; declaration character: %; Range: −32,768 to 32,767.
Long	A 4-byte positive or negative whole number; declaration character: &; Range: −2,147,483,648 to 2,147,483,647.
Single	A 4-byte floating-point number; declaration character: .; Range: −3.402823E38 to −1.401298E−45 and 1.401298E−45 to 3.402823E38.
Double	An 8-byte floating-point number; declaration character: #; Range: −1.79769313486232E308 to −4.94065645841247E−324 and 1.79769313486232E308 to 4.94065645841247E−324.
Currency	An 8-byte number with fixed decimal point; declaration character: @; Range: −922337203685477.5808 to 922337203685477.5807.
String	A string of characters declared using the "$" character. Range: 0 to approximately 65,500 characters.
Variant	The default datatype. Capable of storing floating point numbers, text strings, dates, and times. No declaration character. Range: Date values: January 1, 0000 to December 31, 9999; Numeric values: same as Double; String values: same as String.

Q: *How do you display the Menu Design window?*
A: The Menu Design window is displayed by selecting Menu Design from the Window menu or by selecting the Menu Design button on the tool bar.

Q: *What is a separator bar and how is it created?*
A: A separator bar is a bar that divides menu items into logical groups that can contain one or more menu items. It is created during menu design by designating a hyphen (-) as its Caption property setting.

Q: *In Visual Basic code, what does the ampersand character (&) in front of a letter do?*
A: When the code is run, the letter is displayed underlined. When the Alt key is depressed immediately prior to the letter being depressed, it causes an event to occur. For example, when you press Alt and F in a windows program, it causes the File menu to be displayed.

Q: *When creating a menu using Visual Basic's Menu Design window, which items will appear on the menu bar as a menu title?*
A: Items that are left justified (or first-level entries) in the list box of the menu dialog control will appear on the menu bar as a menu title.

Q: *When the program is run, what occurs when the Checked property was selected during menu creation using the Menu Design window?*
A: A checkmark will be displayed next to a selected menu item.

Q: *What is an Input Box and how is it created?*
A: An Input Box is a dialog box that displays a prompt and allows the user to enter a response using keyboard characters. It returns the text entered by the user. It is created using the InputBox or InputBox$ function. The syntax is:

```
InputBox[$](prompt [,[title] [,[default][,xpos,ypos]]]
```

where `prompt` is the message with a maximum length of 255 characters that is displayed in the dialog box, `title` is the message that is displayed in the title bar of the dialog box, `default` is the default response if no other input is provided, and `xpos` and `ypos` designate the x and y coordinates of the upper left corner of the Input Box.

Q: *What are the four options concerning projects?*
A: New Project, Open Project, Save Project, and Save Project As.

Q: *What are properties?*
A: Properties are option settings that affect the way an object looks or acts. Most properties can be set either at run time or at design time, although some properties can only be set at design time.

Q: *What is a form?*
A: A form is a window that is the interface of your application. You customize it by adding controls, graphics, and pictures.

Q: *How do you close a database?*

A: A database is closed using the `Close` method. The syntax is:

```
objectname.Close
```

where `objectname` is the property of a database or recordset data control or a variable that identifies a Database, Recordset, or QueryDef.

Q: *What are Events?*

A: Events are actions recognized by a form or control.

Q: *How do you quit an application?*

A: By using the End statement. (*Note:* You can also use the Stop statement, but this is generally used for debugging purposes.)

Q: *What is the Visual Basic default datatype?*

A: The Variant datatype is the Visual Basic default. It can store numeric, date/time, or string data.

Q: *What is the difference between a toolbar and a menu?*

A: A toolbar provides quick access to commonly used commands. A menu lists all commands used to build or run an application.

Q: *What function is used to connect to a database using ODBC?*

A: The OpenDatabase function, which is only available in the Professional Edition, allows you to connect to a database using ODBC.

Q: *What is the HotKey for running an application?*

A: The HotKey (a keyboard key or combination of keys that will trigger action) that is used for running an application is F5.

Q: *What is the main difference between a Snapshot and a Dynaset?*

A: Records that result from a Dynaset object can be edited; records in a Snapshot cannot.

Q: *How are the environment colors set?*

A: Environment colors are set by selecting Options from the menu bar, then selecting the Environment option. This opens a window that lists items whose colors can be set. Select the desired items and their desired settings.

Q: *How do you specify a fixed-length string?*

A: A fixed-length string is specified with a declaration such as:

```
Dim stringname as String # 20.
```

Q: *What is the difference between Trim($) and RTrim($)' ?*

A: Trim and Trim$ remove leading and trailing spaces whereas RTrim and RTrim$ remove only trailing spaces.

Q: *How do you set a breakpoint?*

A: A breakpoint is set either from the menu bar, toolbar, or by pressing F9. In all cases, make sure you are at the point in the code where you want to insert the breakpoint. Then choose Toggle Breakpoint from the Debug menu, or click the Breakpoint button on the toolbar, or Press F9.

Q: *What HotKey do you use for stepping through code.*
A: The F8 key allows you to single-step through code.

Q: *How do you bring up the Debug window?*
A: The Debug window appears only when the application is in break mode. It is opened by pressing Ctrl-B or through the menu.

Q: *How do you create a Dynaset?*
A: A Dynaset, which is a results set from (for example) an SQL statement that can be edited, is created from a specified table, QueryDef, or SQL string using the CreateDynaset method. The syntax is:

```
Set dynaset = database.CreateDynaset(source[,options])
```

or

```
Set dynaset = (recordset|querydef).CreateDynaset([options])
```

where dynaset is an object variable of type Dynaset; database is an object variable identifying an open database or database property of a data control; recordset is an object variable identifying an existing recordset object or Recordset property of a data control; querydef is an object variable identifying an existing QueryDef object; source is the name of an existing recordset, QueryDef, or SQL statement; and options is a numeric expression indicating one or more allowable option settings.

Q: *How do you create a Snapshot?*
A: A Snapshot, which cannot be edited, is created from a specified table, QueryDef, or SQL string using the CreateSnapshot method. The syntax is:

```
Set snapshot = database.CreateSnapshot( source[,options])
```

or

```
Set snapshot = (recordset|querydef).CreateSnapshot([options])
```

where snapshot is an object variable of type Snapshot; database is an object variable identifying an open database or Database property of a data control; recordset is an object variable identifying an existing recordset object or Recordset property of a data control; querydef is an object variable identifying an existing QueryDef object; source is the name of an existing recordset, QueryDef, or SQL statement; and options is a numeric expression indicating one or more allowable option settings.

Q: *Define the four ways the scope and lifetime of a variable can be declared.*
A: The scope and lifetime are declared in four ways: Local, Module, Global, and Static. A Local variable is only recognized within the procedure it is declared. It can be declared using Dim. A Module-level variable shares information with all procedures in a code or form module for the lifetime of the application. It is also declared using Dim. The value of a Global variable is available in every form and code module in an application for the lifetime of the application. It can be declared in any module using the declaration Global. A Static declaration will preserve the value of a Local variable.

Q: *What is the Shell function and what parameters can be passed?*

A: The Shell function runs an executable program and returns the task ID of the executed program. The syntax is:

```
shell (commandstring [,windowstyle])
```

where `commandstring` is the name of the program to execute along with any required arguments and `windowstyle` is the number corresponding to the style of the window in which the program is to be executed.

Q: *How is text highlighted in a text box?*

A: Text is highlighted in a text box using the SelLength, SelStart, and/or SelText properties. SelLength determines the number of characters selected. SelStart determines the starting point of selected text. SelText determines the string containing the currently selected text.

Q: *What is a control array?*

A: A group of controls that share the same name, type, and event procedures. Common uses for control arrays are menu controls and option button groupings.

Q: *What is the difference between a list box and a combo box?*

A: Items may be added to a combo box list by typing in the desired entry. A list box cannot be added to unless code is included to allow additions. A combo box will drop down, while a list box is a fixed size.

Q: *When an array is resized, how is data kept in the array?*

A: Data is kept in an array that is being resized using the Preserve keyword. For example:

```
ReDim Preserve namearr (UBound(namearr)+5)
```

Q: *What is a VBX?*

A: A VBX is a custom control such as a list box, a Combo Box, or a text box.

Q: *What types of files make up a project and what are their extensions?*

A: The types of files that make up a project are forms (.FRM), modules (.BAS), controls (.VBX), and text (.TXT) files.

Q: *How can you determine the number of items in a list box?*

A: By using the statement `ListCount -1`.

Q: *What is the Frame control used for?*

A: The Frame control is used for grouping controls or for dividing a form into sections.

Q: *How is the data control used?*

A: A data control is used by placing the control on a form. You must select the database and record source to be used. For example:

The database would be Biblio.

The records source would be the Authors table.

The application can use all records in the Authors table.

Q: *How is a menu created?*
A: Using the Menu Design window.

Q: *How is a toolbar created?*
A: To create a toolbar, you first place a picture box on the form. Place any controls you want displayed inside the picture box. Then, set the design-time properties. And finally, write the code.

Q: *How can the color of the comments be changed?*
A: The color of the comments can be changed by selecting Options from the menu system and selecting a new color.

Q: *What is the Shape control?*
A: The Shape control allows you to create squares, rectangles, ovals, or circles on a form. These shapes can be transparent or filled in with a color.

Q: *How are items added to a list box?*
A: Items are added to a list box using the AddItem method. The syntax is:

```
listbox .AddItem item [, index]
```

where `listbox` is the name of the list or combo box, `item` is the string expression to add to the list, and `index` specifies where the new item is to be inserted. An index of "0" represents the first position. If `index` is not specified the item will be added to the bottom of the list or, if the list is sorted, in the proper sorted order.

Q: *How are the upper and lower bounds of an array determined?*
A: The upper and lower bounds of an array are determined by using the "LBound" and "UBound" functions.

Q: *Using Visual Basic defaults, how many elements are in the array declared in the statement "Dim Sums(20) as integer"?*
A: There are 21 elements in the array.

Q: *How do you clear the contents of an array?*
A: The contents of an array are cleared using the ReDim command.

Q: *How are items removed from a list box?*
A: Items are removed from a list box using the Clear and RemoveItem methods. Clear removes all entries in a list. RemoveItem is used to remove individual items. The syntax for these methods are respectively:

```
listbox .Clear
```

and

```
listbox .RemoveItem index
```

where `listbox` is the name of the list or combo box and `index` specifies the location of the item to be removed. An index of "0" represents the first position.

Q: *What Visual Basic statement is used to delete a file?*
A: A file is deleted from a disk using the Kill (filename) statement.

Q: *Name the four "move" methods.*
A: Move first, Move last, Move next, and Move previous.

Q: *Name the four "find" methods.*
A: Find first, Find last, Find next, Find previous.

Q: *What are the two ways of displaying the Properties dialog box?*
A: The Properties dialog box is displayed using the F4 hot key or by selecting "Windows" from the menu bar and then selecting the "Properties" option.

Q: *What are the two ways of displaying the Procedures dialog box?*
A: The Procedures dialog box is displayed by using the F2 HotKey or by selecting Windows from the menu bar and then selecting the Procedures option.

Q: *How do you disable a control?*
A: A control is disabled by setting the enabled property to False within the program code or through the Properties box.

Q: *How do you make a control visible or invisible?*
A: A control is made visible by setting the visible property to True and invisible by setting the visible property to False within the program code or through the Properties box.

Q: *What is a picture clip (PicClip) control and how is it used?*
A: A picture clip control allows you to select an area in a source bitmap and display that area on a form or in a picture box. One such use for a picture clip is the ability to store all the images required for an application in one bitmap and allowing you to select only the necessary images for each point in an application.

Q: *Which record sets support Bookmarks?*
A: Tables, dynasets, and snapshots support Bookmarks.

Q: *What is the limit of the Tag property?*
A: The Tag property is limited to 32 kbytes

Q: *What is the maximum number of objects allowed in a project?*
A: You are limited to 256 distinct objects in a project.

Q: *What is the maximum number of forms allowed in a project?*
A: Approximately 230 forms are allowed in a project.

Q: *What is the maximum number of forms allowed to be loaded at one time?*
A: A maximum of 80 forms is allowed to be loaded at one time.

Q: *What is the maximum number of procedures allowed in an application?*
A: There can be a total of 5200 modules, forms, and/or DLL declarations.

Q: *What is the hWnd property.*
A: The hWnd property is the handle to a form or control.

Q: *What are the three options of a project?*

A: The three options of a project are the command line argument, the start-up form, and the help file.

Q: *What is the Options Compare statement?*

A: The Options Compare statement declares the default comparison mode to use when string data is compared. The default text comparison mode is binary. To change to text mode, include the statement Options Compare Text. To return to binary mode use the statement Options Compare Binary.

Q: *What are Huge arrays?*

A: Huge arrays are those whose total size exceeds 64 kbytes. The maximum size for a Huge array is 64 Mbytes in the enhanced mode and 1 Mbyte in the standard mode.

Q: *What does ME refer to?*

A: ME refers to the instance from which your code is executing.

Q: *What does the Calls dialog box display?*

A: The Calls dialog box displays a list of all procedures that have been started, but not completed.

Q: *What is Dynamic Data Exchange (DDE) and what must be specified to begin a conversation?*

A: DDE is a mechanism supported by the Microsoft Windows operating system that enables two applications to "talk" to each other by a continuous automatic mode of data exchange. The name of the source application it wants to *talk* to and the conversation topic must be specified by the destination (client) application to initiate the exchange with the source (server). If either the destination or the source changes the application or the topic, the conversation is terminated.

Q: *Name and explain the three main parts of a DDE conversation.*

A: Applications   The names of the source and destination applications

Topics   The subject of the DDE conversation, usually some unit of data

Item   Identifies the piece of data actually being passed during a DDE conversation

Q: *What is Object Linking and Embedding (OLE)?*

A: OLE allows Visual Basic to display and manipulate data from other Windows-based applications. An OLE application is created by placing the MSOLE2.VBX control in your application, sizing it, and selecting the object type from the Object dialog box.

Q: *What is an OLE object?*

A: An OLE object is a discrete unit of data that has been supplied by an OLE application. Visual Basic allows access to three types of OLE objects: linked, embedded, and those manipulated by OLE automation. Linked and embedded objects display an object in a Visual Basic form and allow the user to access the object's data. However, linked objects can be accessed by other users and applications, while embedded objects can be accessed only by the Visual Basic application in which their data is maintained. OLE automation manipulates objects from other applications from within a Visual Basic application.

Q: *What is an object class?*

A: An object class determines the application that provides the object's data and the type of data the object contains.

Q: *What is a container application?*

A: A container application is an application that allows you to display objects from other applications.

Q: *What is an invisible object?*

A: An invisible object is an object that has a function but works behind the scenes. For example, once a spell checker is activated, you do not see the actual spell checking taking place until an error is found and then an error function is activated. The spell checking function is an invisible object.

Q: *What is an Multiple-Document Interface (MDI) application?*

A: An MDI application is one that has multiple forms within a single container form.

Q: *Explain drag-and-drop.*

A: Drag-and-drop is a capability that allows you to place the mouse cursor on a control, hold the button down while dragging the control to another location, and releasing the mouse button, thereby dropping the control at the new location. In multiple-form operations, a control can be dragged and dropped to another form.

Q: *How would you search a list box or combo box using the Windows API?*

A: You would use the Window API, SendMessage, with the constant LB_FIND-STRING (for a list box) or CB_FINDSTRING (for a combo box). For example:

```
entrynum = SendMessage(List1.hWnd, LB_FINDSTRING, 0, "Mi")
```

Q: *How do you sort a list box or a combo box?*

A: By setting the sort property to True through either the Properties box or a statement in the Visual Basic code.

Q: *What is one way to use a custom cursor from a DLL in Visual Basic using the Windows API?*

A: You must first have a resource DLL that contains all the cursors you may want to use. Use the LoadLibrary API to load the Cursor.DLL into memory and the LoadCursor API to load the cursor handle into memory. Then use the SetClassWord API using the constant GCW_HCURSOR and the handle from the LoadCursor library. *Note:* Make sure you unload the cursor since the loaded cursor will be used throughout Windows.

Q: *How do you use an icon from a DLL?*

A: You must first have a resource DLL with the icons you want to use. Use the LoadLibrary API to load the Icon .DLL into memory. Then use the LoadIconByNum API if you know the icon number or LoadIconByString API if you know the name of the icon along with the handle from the LoadLibrary. Finally, use the DrawIcon API to display the icon in the picture box.

Q: *What is another way of writing the following code?*

```
If   i = 100   then
    MsgBox "The value is" + STR$(1)
Endif
```

A: If i = 100 then MsgBox "String".

Q: *Can a horizontal scroll bar be added to a single column list box and if so, how?*

A: Yes. A horizontal scroll bar is added by using the SendMessage API and including the constant LB_SETHORIZONTALEXTENT.

Q: *What is a "Hot Spot" and how is it created?*

A: A "Hot Spot" is an icon that can be clicked on to bring up help.

Q: *Explain what Optimistic Locking is.*

A: When Optimistic Locking is selected by setting the LockEdits property to False, the page is locked only when an edited record is updated with the Update method. This property causes a page to be locked only for the brief time the record is actually being updated rather than the entire time the record is being edited. If conflicting updates or deletions are expected to occur, Optimistic Locking should not be selected as the update may not succeed.

Q: *What is Pessimistic Locking?*

A: Pessimistic Locking is the Visual Basic default. It locks the page as soon as the Edit method is invoked and does not unlock the page until the record is updated using the Update method. Using Pessimistic Locking guarantees that the record updates will be successful. However, it could cause the page to be locked out for an unacceptable amount of time. To change to Pessimistic Locking from Optimistic Locking, the LockEdits property should be set to True.

Q: *Explain page locking.*

A: Page locking is an automatic function of Visual Basic that is activated if you do not lock the entire database, Table, of Dynaset. Visual Basic stores as many records as possible in each 2 kbyte page. When a page containing the record you are editing is locked, all other records on that page are also locked.

Q: *Name and explain the seven Option Arguments.*

A: DB_APPENDONLY   Determines if the application can write to but not read from the recordset

DB_CONSISTENT   Determines how multiple table updates are made

DB_DENYREAD	Determines if other users can read the recordsheet
DB_DENYWRITE	Determines if other users can write to the record-set
DB_INCONSISTENT	Determines how multiple table updates are made.
DB_READONLY	Determines if the application can write to the recordset
DB_SQLPASSTHROUGH	Determines if the query is to be processed by an external database server

Q: *What is the difference between a picture box and an image control?*

A: An image control uses less resources and repaints faster than a picture box. It can also be stretched, while a picture box cannot. An image control can be placed in a container but cannot be used as a container.

Q: *What is the advantage and the disadvantage of a Variant datatype?*

A: The advantage of a Variant is that a variable takes on the properties of that variable, thus allowing it to take any form without specifying a particular format. The disadvantage is that it uses up a lot of resources.

Q: *How do you read or write a string from an .INI file you created?*

A: You read and write to an .INI file by using the Windows APIs, GetPrivate-PrefileString or WritePrivateProfileString.

Q: *What are the five common dialog boxes?*

A: The five common dialog boxes are Open, Save As, Print, Color, and Font.

Q: *What is the limit of the Text property?*

A: The Text property is limited to 32 kbytes per test box.

Q: *Explain the Seek method including what happens if a Seek is unsuccessful.*

A: The Seek method is a fast way of locating a record in an indexed table. It is available only with the Professional edition. The syntax is:

```
table.Seek comparison, key1, key2....
```

where `table` is the name of an open table; `comparison` is either $<$, $<=$, $=$, $>=$, $>$, or $<$ $>$; and `key1`, `key2`, etc. are each a single value for each field in the table's current index. If the Seek method is successful, the first record that satisfies the specified criteria will become the current record. If the Seek method is unsuccessful, the value of the NoMatch property of the recordset will be True and the current record will remain unchanged.

Q: *What is the FieldSize method?*

A: The FieldSize method returns the total length of the data in a text or binary field. The syntax is:

```
sizevar = fieldobject.FieldSize( )
```

where `sizevar` is the variable of Long or Variant type and `fieldobject` is a field of Memo or Long Binary field datatype.

Q: *What is the limit of the Caption property?*

A: The Caption property is limited to 1 kbyte. The Caption property of command buttons, option buttons, check boxes, and frames is limited to 255 characters. Any caption over these limits is truncated.

Q: *Which databases do QueryDefs support?*

A: QueryDefs support Visual Basic and Microsoft Access databases.

Q: *How do you assign an object variable?*

A: An object variable is assigned by using the Set statement. For example:

```
Global anyform As Form
Set anyform As ME
```

Q: *What is the Option Explicit statement and where is it placed?*

A: An Option Explicit statement is a line of code that stipulates that Visual Basic always generate an error message whenever it encounters a name not previously declared explicitly as a variable. It is placed in the Declarations section of a form or module.

Q: *How do you remove a forms title bar?*

A: A forms title bar can be removed by setting the form's ControlBox, MinButton, and "MaxButton" properties to False; its Border Style to a nonsizable border; and its caption equal to an empty string.

Q: *What are two formats in which forms and modules can be saved?*

A: Forms and modules can be saved in either binary or text formats.

Q: *What is an event-driven application?*

A: An event-driven application is an application in which a user action or system event executes an event procedure.

Q: *What is the Sub Main'?*

A: Main is a Sub procedure that is called first by the application on start-up. It is contained in a code module and is usually used to load some code, such as for opening a database, or for checking to see if a file exists before a form is displayed.

Q: *What is the IsEmpty function?*

A: The IsEmpty function returns a value indicating whether or not a Variant variable has been initialized. The syntax is:

```
IsEmpty(variant).
```

Q: *How do you pass objects to procedures?*

A: Objects are passed to procedures by declaring the parameter of a Sub or Function with an As Control type. For example:

```
Sub MakeEnabled (C As Control)
    C.Enabled = True
End Sub
```

Q: *How do you determine the type of an object variable?*

A: The object variable type is determined by using the If TypeOf statement. For example:

```
If TypeOf source is TextBox then ...
```

Q: *How do you set a value to nothing?*

A: A value can be set to nothing by assigning Nothing using the Set statement. For example:

```
Set anyform = Nothing
```

Q: *Name three classes of errors.*

A: Three classes of errors are compiler errors, run-time errors, and logic errors.

Q: *What are the debugging tools available on the toolbar?*

A: The debugging tools available on the toolbar are Breakpoint, Instant Watch, Calls, Single Step, and Procedure Steps.

Q: *What is an alternative to setting a breakpoint?*

A: The alternative to setting a breakpoint is to place a Stop statement in a procedure.

Q: *What is the difference between a breakpoint and a stop statement?*

A: A Breakpoint is a temporarily designated stop point. When you leave an application all breakpoints are cleared. A Stop statement remains embedded in the code until it is manually removed by the developer. If it is left in an executable file, it acts the same as an End statement.

Q: *What is a Watch expression?*

A: A Watch expression is an expression that you define and that Visual Basic monitors as your application runs.

Q: *Explain an On Error statement.*

A: An On Error statement allows you to trap an error and direct the application to a predefined label. For example:

```
Sub PrintStatement (MyText As String)
    On Error goto ckerror
    Printer.Print Trim(String)
Exit Sub
```

where `ckerror` is an error handling Sub.

Q: *What is a timer control?*

A: A timer control allows the user to activate a timed event after a predetermined interval has elapsed. Common uses for the timer control are digital or analog clock displays and alarm clocks.

Q: *What is an Idle Loop?*

A: An Idle Loop is a loop that executes statements only when nothing else in the environment requires immediate attention. You create Idle Loops using the DoEvents( ) function.

Q: *Explain how the SendKeys statement works.*

A: The SendKeys statement issues the proper commands to the active window as if they had been entered at the keyboard.

Q: *What is the Show method and what are the style option settings?*

A: The Show method is used for displaying a form. The style option is either "0" for modeless or "1" for modal.

Q: *What is an SQL Passthrough?*

A: An SQL Passthrough is an SQL statement that is passed to an ODBC database for processing.

Q: *What is the difference between the Execute and ExecuteSQL methods?*

A: Execute and ExecuteSQL differ in three ways. First, ExecuteSQL returns the number of rows affected by the SQL statement and Execute does not return a value. Next, ExecuteSQL operates only on a remote ODBC database such as SQL Server or Oracle. And finally, Execute allows setting of options that affect how the SQL statement is executed.

Q: *Other than the obvious visual effect, what are the main differences between a command button and a 3-D command button?*

A: A command button has a "default" property; a 3-D command button does not. A 3-D command button can have a bitmap added to it.

Q: *What is the difference between the MsgBox statement and the MsgBox ( ) function?*

A: The MsgBox statement will display a message, but will not return a value. MsgBox( ) is a function that is used when a user is to make a selection; it returns a value indicating which button the user selected. The syntax for the statement is:

```
MsgBox message [,[type][,title]
```

and the syntax for the function is:

```
MsgBox( message [,[type][,title]]
```

where `message` is the message to be displayed, `type` is an optional numeric value that specifies the number and types of buttons to display, and `title` is the string expression that is displayed in the title bar of the dialog box. The default `type` is "64," which is the information icon and the default `title` is "Microsoft Visual Basic" for Visual Basic Applications in the development environment or the application name for executable files created by Visual Basic.

Q: *What is the maximum number of items that can be added to a list box or combo box?*

A: The maximum number of items is limited to 5440. However, each item is limited to 1 kbyte and the total data segment is limited to 64 kbytes.

Q: *How is a DLL function called?*

A: A DLL is called using the declare statement. For example:

```
Declare Function SendMessage Lib "User" (ByVal hDC As Integer,
ByVal Msg as Integer as LONG
```

Q: *How do you trap when the user closes your application using the control box?*

A: You can trap when the user closes your application using the control box by placing code in the QueryUnload event of a form.

Q: *What is the Control collection?*

A: The Control collection is a collection of loaded controls on any loaded form.

Q: *What is the Forms collection?*

A: The Forms collection is an array that holds all loaded forms and forms instances. This is a Global array that is automatically created by Visual Basic.

Q: *How do you create user-defined types?*

A: User-defined types are created using the Type statement. For example:

```
Type Client Profile
    Name as String
    Address as String
    Zip as Integer
    Phone as Long
    Credit_Limit as Currency
End Type
```

Type statements must be placed in the declaration section of a module.

Q: *What is the maximum number of dimensions you can declare in an array?*

A: You can declare up to 60 dimensions.

Q: *What are DLLs and what are the advantages of using them?*

A: DLLs are libraries of procedures that applications can link to and use at run time rather than link to statically at compile time. DLLs can be updated independently of an application and many applications can share the same DLL.

Q: *How are resources used by snapshots freed up assuming that the snapshot was declared as MySnap?*

A: Resources used by snapshots can be freed up with the statement Set MySnap = Nothing.

Q: *How is a form or control passed to a Sub or Function?*

A: A form or control is passed to a Sub or Function by the As type parameter in the Declare statement. The type is declared as As Form or As Control. For example:

```
Declare Sub mysub (anyform As Form,anycontrol As Control).
```

Q: *What are the different types of combo boxes? Describe them.*

A: *Drop-down combo box*—the default setting. Only one item is displayed until the detached arrow at the right of the combo box is clicked with the mouse.

At that time, the list drops down, an item is selected, and the list returns to one line with the selected item displayed. The list can also be opened by pressing ALT+DOWN ARROW.

Simple combo box—the list is displayed at all times. If the size of the List Box is not large enough to accommodate the entire list, a vertical scroll bar is automatically inserted.

Drop-down list box—Like the drop-down combo box, only one item is displayed until the detached arrow at the right of the combo box is clicked on with the mouse. At that time, the list drops down, an item is selected, and the list returns to one line with the selected item displayed. The list can also be opened by pressing ALT+DOWN ARROW.

Q: *What is the difference between a Sub and a Function?*
A: Sub procedures do not return a value; Function procedures do.

Q: *What is the Outline Control used for?*
A: The Outline Control is used for displaying items in a hierarchical format.

Q: *Without using third-party controls, how are 3-D Frames created?*
A: 3-D Frames can be created by using the line or shape controls to draw the 3-D effect on the form.

Q: *Without using third-party controls, how is 3-D Text created?*
A: 3-D Text can be created by using two print statements. The first print statement would be in one color and the second print statement would be offset and in a different color.

Q: *What is a pop-up menu and how is it created?*
A: A pop-up menu is a menu that it not accessible from the menu bar. It appears (pops up) when a predesignated event occurs. For example, clicking the right mouse button can activate a pop-up menu. It is created using the Popup-Menu method. The syntax is:

```
[form .]PopupMenu menuname [,flags [,xpos [,ypos]]]
```

where `menuname` is the name of the pop-up menu to be displayed, `flags` defines the location and behavior of a pop-up menu, `xpos` specifies the location of the x coordinate of the upper left corner of the pop-up menu, and `ypos` specifies the location of the y coordinate of the upper left corner of the pop-up menu.

Q: *How do you make a form stay on top?*
A: You can make a form stay on top by using the SetWindowPos API using the constant HWND_TOPMOST.

Q: *What is the New keyword?*
A: The New keyword is used to declare a variable of a specific form type. Using this declaration specifies that Visual Basic should always ensure that an instance of the form exists when you use the form variable.

Q: *How is the BiVal keyword used?*

A: When an argument is declared with BiVal it not only enables other datatypes to be passed to an argument of a particular datatype, it also specifies that values are passed to that argument "by value" rather than "by reference."

Q: *How is the first element of an array set to "1" instead of "0", the default?*

A: The first element of an array can be set to "1" with the statement "Option Base 1" or with the statement "Dim Sums(1 to 20) as integer."

Q: *What is a bookmark and how is it used?*

A: A bookmark is a property of a recordset that allows you to mark your place so that you can return to it later. Both Snapshots and Dynasets support bookmarks.

Q: *What is a QueryDef?*

A: A QueryDef is an object variable that contains an SQL statement that describes a query.

Q: *Explain how BeginTrans and CommitTrans work.*

A: BeginTrans allows for temporary input of data. The data input is made permanent when CommitTrans is activated.

Q: *What is AppendChunk?*

A: AppendChunk is a method that allows you to add text to a Memo or Long Binary field using a specified Table or Dynaset. Using AppendChunk with fields larger than 64 kbytes conserves memory. The syntax is:

```
fieldobject.AppendChunk(source)
```

where `fieldobject` is a field of Memo or Long Binary field type data and `source` is the string expression containing the data you want to append to `fieldobject`.

Q: *What is the FieldSize method?*

A: The FieldSize method returns the total length of the data in a Text or Long Binary field. The syntax is:

```
sizevar = fieldobject.FieldSize()
```

where `sizevar` is a variable of Long or Variant type data and `fieldobject` is the field name of the Memo or Long Binary field datatype.

Q: *What is the GetChunk method?*

A: The GetChunk method allows you to extract all or part of a Memo or Long Binary field based upon a starting byte and the number of bytes requested. The syntax is:

```
stringvar = fieldobject.GetChunk(offset, numbytes)
```

where `stringvar` is a variable of String or Variant type, `fieldobject` is the field name of the Memo or Long Binary field datatype, `offset` is the numeric expression for the number of bytes to skip before copying begins, and `numbytes` is the numeric expression for the number of bytes to copy. It conserves memory when working with fields larger than 64 kbytes.

Q: *Name the controls that can be used as bound controls.*

A: The controls that can be used as bound controls are CheckBox, Image, Label, PictureBox, and TextBox (in the Standard version). The Professional Edition also includes the 3DCheckBox, 3D Panel, and MaskEdit.

Q: *Explain the LOGINTIMEOUT parameter of OpenDataBase.*

A: The LOGINTIMEOUT sets the number of seconds that Visual Basic waits for an external ODBC server to respond. It is set as part of the `connect argument`. An example of how a `connect argument` would be coded is:

```
ConnectArg$ = "ODBC;LOGINTIMEOUT=10;UID=HOLLY;PWD=RAGS;"
```

Q: *Explain the QUERYTIMEOUT.*

A: The QUERYTIMEOUT sets the number of seconds that Visual Basic waits for an external ODBC server to complete a query. If the query times out, the external server is told to stop processing it and a trappable error message is sent to your application. By setting the QUERYTIMEOUT to "0", you allow the server an infinite amount of time to respond.

Q: *How do you add to a Control Array at run time?*

A: Controls can be added to the Control Array at run time using the Load statement with the control name and the new index value. The syntax is:

```
Load control(index%)
```

Q: *How do you define a QueryDef?*

A: A QueryDef is defined using the statement:

```
"Dim MyQuery As QueryDef."
```

Q: *What is the difference between a Modeless Form and a Modal Form.*

A: When a form is loaded using the Show method and the style is set to Modeless "0", Visual Basic code is executed that occurs after the show. When loaded Modal, no other code on any other form is executed until the form is hidden or unloaded.

27

COBOL II, PC COBOL, and OO (Object-Oriented) COBOL

Peter Guglielmino

Introduction:
COBOL Yesterday and Today

In the current data processing environment a strong emphasis is being placed on client/server applications, and the rehosting of mainframe applications onto lower-cost platforms. This trend is being fueled by the continued influx of high-performance, low-cost workstations and servers. However, recent disclosures in trade publications suggest that this trend may have hidden costs. The cost of maintaining distributed applications may be as much as three times that of maintaining the same functionality centrally. In addition, many organizations face the enormous task of migrating years of tested and established code to new platforms and programming languages. Many legacy systems are not well documented, nor is their internal logic fully understood. Many applications contain large batch components that have extremely complex data flows both into and out of the application. There is a tremendous legacy of COBOL application code and expertise that needs to be integrated into the evolving world of information technology. Currently there are new releases of COBOL for all hardware platforms. There are new versions of COBOL that include object-oriented features that help to reduce the time and cost of developing new applications and integration of these new systems with legacy systems. This chapter will explore IBM COBOL II and IBM COBOL/370, Object-Oriented COBOL, and the new IBM COBOL family. The use of COBOL in both batch and on-line environments will be covered as well.

IBM vs. COBOL II

The VS COBOL II licensed program contains three components:

1. VS COBOL II library—Supplies routines requested by the object program. These routines perform functions such as input and output requests.

2. VS COBOL II Compiler—Translates COBOL source programs into object programs.

3. COBTEST—This tool allows you to examine, monitor, and debug VS COBOL II programs.

Migration of older OS/VS COBOL and DOS/VS COBOL programs to VS COBOL II is not always required. An OS/VS COBOL program running below the 16-Mbyte line can call a VS COBOL II program running above the 16-Mbyte line. Various compiler flags have been included in the product to aid in the migration of older COBOL source programs to VS COBOL II.

A VS COBOL II program must be reentrant to use the full benefits of the extended architecture environments. A CICS application program that is always compiled to be reentrant and makes use of the COBOL Library Management Facility can be placed in the extended link pack area, allowing transactions from separate CICS regions to share it. IMS programs can also run above 16 Mbytes. By specifying the DAT(31) compiler option flag, data areas that an IMS application programs uses to communicate with IMS/VS can reside above the 16 Mbyte line.

VS COBOL II also provides several performance improvements over older versions of COBOL.

The COBOL Optimizer

If the OPTIMIZE compiler option is set during compilation, the COBOL II compiler performs the following:

Eliminates unnecessary transfers of control.

Where possible places procedure code in-line, thus eliminating linkage code.

Removes constant computations and replaces them with results computed when the program is compiled.

Uses results of initial computations for later repetitions of the same computations.

Consolidates the moves of contiguous, equal-sized items into a single move.

Flags lines of code that will never be executed with a warning message and deletes the code from the object module.

FASTSRT

The FASTSRT compiler option will call the SORT/MERGE product, which will read the input files, sort/merge the files and write the output files. This will eliminate the need for VS COBOL II to process the input and output files and thus reduce the number of times the data has to be moved.

VS COBOL II programs that are compiled as RESIDENT and use the Library Management Facility can specify that the library routines be preloaded, thereby increasing the performance of the application. VS COBOL II provides a full-screen interactive debugging tool called COBTEST. COBTEST will allow you to monitor the execution of your program, examine the contents of data items, and alter the flow of execution. COBTEST will display the source listing and highlight the currently executing line of code allowing the programmer to "watch" the program execute. Breakpoints can be set to temporarily halt program execution, and allow the contents of data items to be displayed and changed. Since COBTEST runs under ISPF you can use all the features of ISPF, such as assigning COBTEST commands to PF keys, and split screen to browse or edit files. COBTEST also provides a batch mode for debugging under CICS. In batch mode the COBTEST requests are all entered into a CICS temporary storage queue. During the execution of the program the results of the debugging requests are written to another CICS temporary storage queue and can be inspected after the transaction completes. In addition to COBTEST, VS COBOL II provides a formatted dump, procedure cross-reference listing, data division map, nested program map and diagnostic message listing.

IBM COBOL/370

COBOL/370 is one of the tools that "snap" into the AD/Cycle framework. This framework provides a comprehensive set of tools and services for developing and maintaining applications. COBOL/370 is part of the languages tool set. Language Environment/370, which is a prerequisite product for COBOL/370, provides a common run time environment for any language compiler that conforms to its architecture. Both COBOL/370 and C/370 adhere to the LE/370 architecture. LE/370 provides storage management, condition handling, run-time message handling, and interlanguage communication. Unlike VS COBOL II, which is composed of three components—compiler, run-time library, and debugger—COBOL/370 contains only the compiler. However, the compiler has built-in support for LE/370 and CODE/370. CODE/370 is an optional product that provides debugging functions that may be used from a host or host-attached workstation. On a host-attached workstation CODE/370 provides a graphical user interface.

LE/370 greatly facilitates interlanguage communications and reuse of program code. Programs can share code that is written in different languages. This will enable the programmer to code a routine in the language best suited for a particular programming problem. Once the routine is coded, it can be called easily from a like or different language program. LE/370 provides "one" environment and therefore all LE/370 compliant compilers use the same standard for parameter passing and return code processing. This in essence brings us one step closer to the object-oriented programming model. The LE/370 term for a collection of programs is an *Enclave*. An Enclave is an independent collection of routines that comprise an application. One of the routines is considered the "main" program and this may or may not be a COBOL program. The LE/370 run-time environment provides more than 80 services that can be accessed from the COBOL call statement. These services include:

Condition handling

Dynamic storage management

Date and time calculations

Math calculations

Message handling

National language support

General LE/370 services

LE/370 also allows concurrent application execution under multiple MVS tasks. In previous versions of COBOL, applications were limited to one task per MVS address space. With LE/370, COBOL applications can use ISPF services such as CALL ISPLINK or ATTACH to create multiple MVS tasks within a single address space. The improved interlanguage communications of LE/370 also allows both COBOL and C subprograms to be reentrant. The LE/370 library routines are reentrant so storage utilization is reduced by sharing both library routines and subprograms.

IBM SAA AD/Cycle CoOperative Development Environment/370 (AD/Cycle CODE/370) is an optional product that fits into the AD/Cycle framework. This product provides cooperative processing between an OS/2 workstation and a VM or MVS host system, language-sensitive editor, invocation of COBOL/370 compiler and Debug tool, Graphical User Interface, and online hypertext information. The language-sensitive editor includes the ability to highlight various COBOL language constructs such as:

Sequence numbers

Indicator area

Compiler directives

Comments

Separator (i.e., period or parenthesis)

User-defined word

Pseudo text

Numeric literals

Non-numeric literals

Picture strings

Preprocessor string (i.e., EXEC, END EXEC)

Reserved words

These constructs can be highlighted by both color and typestyle. Syntax errors are flagged and highlighted when the Enter key is pressed, allowing the programmer to correct the problems immediately. The editor also tries to place the cursor at the correct level of indentation to eliminate unnecessary keystrokes and maintain a more readable piece of code. From an OS/2 window the programmer can invoke the COBOL/370 compiler. The program is compiled on the host, but the compiler error messages will be displayed in an OS/2 window. There are visual aids (i.e., check marks and colors) that help the programmer keep track of the errors that have been fixed and those that still remain. Once the compile time errors have been fixed the program can be interactively debugged from the OS/2 workstation. Interactive debugging is also available for CICS applications. The CODE/370 advanced debugger allows mixed language debugging. If an application contains COBOL/370 and C/370 programs the Debug tool automatically determines the language of the program being executed. Changes to variables, program flow and animated execution can be specified for either or both program languages. Animated execution provides a slower execution of the program and allows the programmer to see each line of code highlighted as it is executed. The programmer can set breakpoints at various spots in the program. If the program execution encounters a breakpoint the program execution is interrupted to allow the programmer to inspect data areas or change the program flow of execution. Dynamic breakpoints can also be set in response to exceptions and conditions during program executions. Single-step execution will allow the programmer to focus on a particular routine.

COBOL/370 builds on the functions of OS/VS COBOL and VS COBOL II by adding intrinsic functions, language extensions, support for LE/370 and CODE/370. COBOL/370 also provides upward source program compatibility with VS COBOL II Release 3, Release 3.1, and Release 3.2. In addition, LE/370 supports either load modules or object modules compiled with Release 2 of OS/VS COBOL and all releases of VS COBOL II. It is possible to have applications that have a mixture of programs from all three compilers. There is also a COBOL and CICS/VS Command Level Conversion Aid that will help in the conversion of pre-Release 3 VS/COBOL II and OS/VS COBOL source programs to COBOL/370.

Object-Oriented COBOL

Object-oriented software development promises to redefine how future applications are developed and maintained. Code reuse and the ability to use objects across heterogenous platforms and networks will greatly improve the speed with which applications can be developed and deployed. C++ is by far the language of choice for object-oriented development. However, recently the ANSI Object COBOL Task Group has announced the W731 Object COBOL specification. This specification was put into place to allow COBOL to integrate more effectively into the object-oriented software development environment. Object COBOL is much like C++ in that Object COBOL is COBOL with object extensions. Object COBOL extensions include the INVOKE verb, the "Object reference" and object-oriented sections for class and instance data.

Object COBOL uses interleaved identification divisions with paragraph identifiers to define classes, objects, object methods, and object data. The CLASS-Id paragraph is used to define classes that consist of class object definitions and object definitions. The class object definition may include its own data and procedure divisions. The data defined in the class object is global to all instances of that class. The object definition includes data and methods. Object methods are defined under the object procedure division, and the object data is defined in the file or working storage sections of the data division. A method is instantiated or "called" with the use of the INVOKE verb followed by the object identifier and the method name. An example follows:

```
IDENTIFICATION DIVISION.
CLASS-OBJECT.
PROCEDURE DIVISION.
METHOD-ID. method-name-1.
LINKAGE SECTION.
01 data-name-1 USAGE IS OBJECT REFERENCE SELF.
PROCEDURE DIVISION RETURNING object-item-1
    INVOKE SUPER 'CBL-NEW' RETURNING object-item-1
    EXIT-METHOD.
END CLASS-OBJECT.
```

Here the method CBL-NEW is invoked to create an instance of a class object. Once the object has been created the object's handle is placed in the field object-item-1. Invocation of a method creates a local copy of any data contained in the working storage section of the method. This data is created each time the method is invoked and is destroyed when the method completes.

Micro Focus has been an early adopter of the ANSI Object specification. Their Object COBOL Tool runs on the OS/2, Windows 3.1, Windows NT, and NCR Unix platforms. The tools consists of a SmallTalk like browser and support classes. IBM's newest release of COBOL, IBM COBOL Family also contains the object-oriented extensions to COBOL.

IBM COBOL Family

The IBM COBOL family is a series of products that allows programmers to develop high-performance applications running on host systems and workstations. Workstation COBOL will initially be delivered for the OS/2 and AIX environments. Future workstation platforms will include the 32-bit, windows environment Workplace Operating System and other Unix environments. Object-oriented capabilities are supported in both IBM COBOL for OS/2 and the new release of the host COBOL, IBM COBOL for MVS & VM (formerly IBM COBOL/370). Programmers will be able to develop applications that can define and access objects enabled to System Object Model (SOM), which is IBM's strategic object-oriented technology. The language neutrality offered by SOM will allow SOM-based classes to be accessed from various languages. The new IBM COBOL compilers offer direct-to-SOM (DTS) support. This eliminates the need for programmers to learn the SOM Interface Definition Language (IDL) and the SOM structure APIs. Procedural and object-oriented COBOL can be combined, allowing a smooth transition to pure object-oriented COBOL.

The IBM workstation and host COBOL environments are built on a common compiler strategy and code base. Functions are implemented in a consistent manner across all platforms. This will enable the programmer to develop, compile, and test applications on either the OS/2 or AIX workstations and finally move all of the application, or pieces of the application, to the host environment for final system test. The following is a description of the various IBM COBOL Family members.

IBM COBOL for MVS & VM Release 2

IBM COBOL for MVS & VM is the IBM COBOL compiler component for MVS and VM. The supporting run-time environment is Language Environment for MVS & VM (formerly LE/370). IBM COBOL for MVS & VM is compatible with VS COBOL II and IBM COBOL/370 Release 1. IBM COBOL for MVS & VM provides the following features:

Object-oriented language extensions based on the ANSI OO COBOL standard

Support for direct creation of SOM objects on the host using COBOL language syntax

Optional SOM Interface Definition Language (IDL) generations

Access to existing SOM-based class libraries

Improved interoperability with C and C++

Source-level compatibility with IBM COBOL for OS/2 and IBM COBOL for AIX

Intrinsic functions

Programmer access to all of the elements in a table at once

Improved dynamic calls

Support for year 2000

IBM COBOL for OS/2

IBM COBOL for OS/2 provides an application development environment using visual programming and construction from components technology. A visual GUI builder provides a WYSIWYG (what you see is what you get) interface. Applications are created by selecting controls from the control palette and dragging them to the design editor. Developers then code and test the application logic for these controls using COBOL language-sensitive editors and debug tools. IBM COBOL for OS/2 also can be integrated into Workframe/2. Workframe/2 is a project-oriented application development environment that groups files into logical units or projects. IBM COBOL for OS/2 also can be integrated with IBM TeamConnection for OS/2. TeamConnection for OS/2 provides the LAN-based library for configuration management and version control, which provides the support a team of developers requires for large and complex applications. IBM COBOL for OS/2 includes the following:

GUI builder

Source-level GUI debugger

Data assistant for building SQL queries and data structures

Transaction assistant for utilizing existing CICS External Call Interface (ECI) transactions

Execution trace analysis and performance tuning

COBOL language-sensitive editor

WorkFrame/2 Integration

Host communications for MVS file access

32-bit SOM-based, object-oriented support

Support for

DB2/2

CICS OS/2

IMS Client Server/2

Local record-oriented file access

Novell Btrieve file systems

TeamConnection for OS/2

IBM COBOL for AIX

IBM COBOL for AIX integrates the COBOL for AIX tools into the Common Desktop Environment (CDE). The CDE uses a database to associate filetypes with applications. What this means is developers can double-click on a file and CDE will automatically launch the tool that understands that file's data. IBM COBOL for AIX also provides a program builder that contains a GUI for setting compiler and linker options, creates a makefile that is used by the AIX make command to construct and maintain programs and libraries, and lists errors in a window that allows the COBOL-sensitive editor to position the programmer at the error in the source listing. IBM COBOL for AIX provides the following:

LPEX—A COBOL language sensitive editor

Program builder

Program debugger

Source-level compatibility with IBM COBOL for OS/2 and IBM COBOL for MVS & VM

COBOL on-line documentation

Support for:

DB2/6000

CICS/6000

ENCINA Structure File SYSTEM (SFS)

Configuration Management Version Control (CMVC) LAN Library

The COBOL Job Interview

The following questions are divided into beginner, intermediate, and advanced job candidate levels.

A *beginner* should be able to describe the structure of a COBOL program, be able to code basic routines given the proper program specifications, and use basic debugging techniques to solve a coding problem.

An *intermediate* COBOL programmer should be able to develop an application consisting of several COBOL modules and be able to pass and receive data between the programs. In addition, the intermediate programmer should be able to develop programs for both the TSO and CICS environments and be able to use the debugging facilities in both environments.

The *advanced* COBOL programmer should be able to develop application program specifications for both batch and on-line applications. The advanced programmer should be able to develop and code multilanguage applications and be able to implement procedures to set up the various COBOL debugging environments for the less skilled programmers in the department. The advanced programmers should also be familiar with the various releases and platforms that COBOL supports, and be able to develop and implement migration plans to different platforms and newer releases of the COBOL products.

Questions and Answers

Questions for the Beginner

Q: *Name the different divisions in a COBOL program.*
A: A COBOL source program contains the following four divisions:

Identification Division

Environment Division

Data Division

Procedure Division

Q: *What is defined in the Data Division?*
A: The Data Division is divided into three sections:

File Section

Working-Storage Section

Linkage Section

Q: *What is defined in the File Section?*
A: The File Section defines the structure of data files (including sort-merge files).

Q: *What is defined in the Working-Storage Section?*
A: The Working-Storage Section describes records and data items that are not part of data files but are required by the program.

Q: *What is defined in the Linkage Section?*
A: The Linkage Section describes data items that are referred to by the calling and the called programs. Storage for the data items in the Linkage Section is not reserved within the program because the data area exists elsewhere.

Q: *What is the maximum length allowed for a COBOL label?*
A: Thirty characters—but for readability, they shouldn't be too long.

Q: *What datatypes are represented by the following:*

COMPUTATIONAL-1 or COMP-1

COMPUTATIONAL-2 or COMP-2

COMPUTATIONAL-3 or COMP-3

COMPUTATIONAL-4 or COMP-4

A:

COMPUTATIONAL-1 or COMP-1	Specified for internal floating-point items (single precision). COMP-1 items are 4 bytes long.
COMPUTATIONAL-2 or COMP-2	Specified for internal floating-point items (double precision). COMP-2 items are 8 bytes long.
COMPUTATIONAL-3 or COMP-3	(internal decimal) For COBOL/370, this is the equivalent of PACKED-DECIMAL.
COMPUTATIONAL-4 or COMP-4	For COBOL/370 this is the equivalent of BINARY.

Q: *What is an External Decimal item?*

A: External Decimal items, also referred to as zoned decimal items, represent numeric fields defined as follows:

> Each digit of a number is represented by a single byte. The 4 low-order bits of each byte contain the value of the digit. The 4 high-order bits of each byte are zone bits; the 4 high-order bits of the low-order byte represent the sign of the item.

```
                          Value         Internal Representation
    PIC S9999 DISPLAY  + 1234           F1   F2   F3   C4
                       - 1234           F1   F2   F3   D4
```

Q: *What is the range of values that can be defined by the following:*
```
    PIC 9999.
    PIC S99.
```

A: For PIC 9999 the valid range is 0 through 9999. For PIC S99 the valid range is −99 through +99.

Q: *Can I initialize a pointer data item with an address using a VALUE clause?*

A: A VALUE clause for a pointer data item can contain only NULL or NULLS.

Q: *What is the result of the following:*
```
    01 INVREC-OUT.
        05 INVCODE              PIC X.
        05 ITEM-NUMBER          PIC 9(6).
        05 INVOICE-QUANTITY     PIC 9(5).
        05 ITEM-INFO.
            10 UNIT-PRICE       PIC 9(5)V9(2).
            10 DISCOUNT         PIC V9(2).
            10 SALES-PRICE      PIC 9(5)V9(2).
    INITIALIZE INVREC-OUT
```

A:
INVCODE	1 byte blank
ITEM-NUMBER	6 bytes of zeros
INVOICE-QUANTITY	5 bytes of zeros
UNIT-PRICE	7 bytes of zeros
DISCOUNT	2 bytes of zeros
SALES-PRICE	7 bytes of zeros

Q: *How can I convert a three-character month abbreviation to the number of the month:*

A: Code the following:
```
    EVALUATE TRUE
        WHEN MONTH(1:3)='JAN'
        COMPUTE MONTH-NUM=1
            .
            .
            .
```

```
WHEN MONTH(1:3)='DEC'
   COMPUTE MONTH-NUM=12
              .
END-EVALUATE
```

Q: *What is the advantage of using level 88 Condition names?*

A: If the conditional values must be changed, the Procedure Division coding for conditional tests does not need to be changed.

Q: *Set up a definition that would let me determine what category a particular record belongs to based on the following ranges:*

Category1	0–1
Category2	2–5
Category3	6–8
Category4	9–10

A: 01 WS-CATAGORY   PIC 99.

    88 CATEGORY1   VALUE 0, 1.

    88 CATEGORY2   VALUE 2 THRU 5.

    88 CATEGORY3   VALUE 6 THRU 8.

    88 CATEGORY4   VALUE 9, 10.

WS-CATEGORY is the conditional variable; CATEGORY1, CATEGORY2, CATAGORY3, and CATAGORY4 are condition-names. Individual records in the file can have only one of the values specified in the condition-name entries.

The following IF statements can be added to the above example to determine the CATEGORY of a specific record:

IF CATEGORY1 . . .	(Tests for values 0, 1)
IF CATEGORY2 . . .	(Tests for values 2 through 5)
IF CATEGORY3 . . .	(Tests for values 6 through 8)
IF CATEGORY4 . . .	(Tests for values 9,10)

Q: *What COBOL statement could be coded to perform this calculation?*

$$(A+B)/(C+D)=E$$

A: COMPUTE E=(A+B)/(C+D)

Q: *What are some of the types of file organization supported by COBOL/370?*

A: QSAM	Physical Sequential
VSAM	Sequential (Entry Sequenced Data Set ESDS)
VSAM	Indexed (Keyed Sequenced Data Set KSDS)
VSAM	Relative (Relative Record Data Set RRDS)

Q: *Why would I use a QSAM file?*

A: If a large percentage file will be referenced or updated, sequential processing will be faster than indexed processing.

Q: *Why would I use an VSAM KSDS file?*

A: If the application program processes only a few records on the file during a run, an indexed file structure will allow you to access the records with a key field, which will more efficient than processing the entire file.

Q: *How do I code an open for an input file in a COBOL program?*

A: To open a file for input, the open statement should read

```
OPEN INPUT input01.
```

where `OPEN` and `INPUT` are COBOL-reserved words and `input01` is a name defined by you in an FD entry.

Q: *How do I indicate that I will be processing variable-length records?*

A: Use the RECORD IS VARYING clause on the FD (File Definition).

Q: *What MVS JCL statement needs to be coded to support this COBOL file definition?*

```
ENVIRONMENT DIVISION.
INPUT-OUTPUT SECTION.
FILE-CONTROL.
    SELECT GOVREPT
       ASSIGN TO OUTFILE
       ORGANIZATION IS SEQUENTIAL.
        .
        .
        .
DATA DIVISION.
    FILE SECTION.

       FD GOVREPT
          LABEL RECORD STANDARD
          BLOCK 0 RECORDS
          RECORD 80 CHARACTERS
```

A: `//OUTFILE DD DSNAME=GOV211.SDD001 ...`

The `//OUTFILE` relates the COBOL ASSIGN TO name to MVS. The `DSNAME =` supplies the name of the MVS sequential dataset that will be created.

Q: *What is wrong with the following code segment?*

```
READ FILE1
   AT END
     MOVE A TO B
     READ FILE2
END-READ
```

A: The END-READ scope terminator will be paired with the second read. It should be recoded as follows:

```
READ FILE1
   AT END
     PERFORM
        MOVE A TO B
```

```
        READ FILE2
      END PERFORM
  END-READ
```

Questions for the Intermediate COBOL Programmer

Q: *I am having a problem reading the EOF. I keep getting the Error "Read part Record Error: EOF before EOR or File opened in Wrong Mode (error 18)". I created the input file using the OS/2 E editor. I opened the file for sequential read.*

A: A file with CR/LF delimited records should be accessed as 'line sequential' instead of 'sequential'.

Q: *I would like to be able to scan for particular text strings. My plan was to define a field called SEARCH-STRING that would be a PIC X(10) field that would be ACCEPTed at run time. I would then compare that field against my file using INSPECT . . . TALLYING . . . FOR ALL SEARCH-STRING. This works when I ACCEPT a full 10-character string, but anything less, of course, is automatically padded with spaces by COBOL and doesn't match the file text. For example, if the input file contains ABCDEFGHIJKLMN and SEARCH-STRING is ABCDEFGHIJ I get a match, but if the SEARCH-STRING is ABC I don't. Is there any way around this problem?*

A: Assuming your search-string does not contain imbedded spaces, the following will work:

```
Inspect search-string tallying a for characters before space
Inspect ...          tallying b for all search-string (1:a)
```

Q: *I compiled the sample program DEMO.CBL using the statement COBOL DEMO <Enter>. It asked me for .LST files .OBJ files and I entered DEMO.LST and DEMO.OBJ respectively. Then I linked it using link demo . . . \cobol\lcobol.lib. I got the .EXE file, which ran properly. But I could not use the animate feature. When I said animate demo, it just gave me the output and did not go into the animate screen. What do I have to do to animate the DEMO program?*

A: You need to compile with the /ANIM directive COBOL DEMO /ANIM. This produces *.IDY and *.INT files used by the animator; the link edit step is not required. Then issue ANIMATE DEMO.

Q: *I'm looking for some way to enable the user to specify at execution time what the program should do.*

A: ACCEPT is also used to receive certain data from the operating system, such as date, time, and for you, the command line parms. If you define a string variable XXXX then execute the statement ACCEPT XXXX FROM COMMAND-LINE you will find any parms from the command line are now in XXXX.

Q: *Is it possible to have your EXEC CICS statements in copybooks?*

A: You will need to translate your copybooks prior to compiling and include the translated copybook into your program. The easiest way would be to have two libraries (in MVS terms) one containing the untranslated source that you would modify, the other containing the translated output that is included into your program.

Q: *How do I generate a RANDOM number in COBOL?*

A: COBOL/370 provides the Intrinsic Function RANDOM.

Q: *What facilities are provided by COBOL/370 to facilitate structured programming?*

A: COBOL/370 offers several language elements that facilitate structured programming. They are:

EVALUATE statement	Permits "case" constructions
In-line PERFORM statement	Permits "do" constructions
TEST BEFORE and TEST AFTER in the PERFORM statements	Function as "do-while" and "do-until" constructions
Scope terminators	Permit nesting of structured programming constructs

Q: *What needs to be changed to migrate the following code segment from OS/VS COBOL to COBOL/370?*

```
77 TIME-IN-MYPROG PICTURE X(6).
        .
        .
        .
    MOVE TIME-OF-DAY TO TIME-IN-MYPROG.
```

A: In COBOL/370 you must use the TIME special register in an ACCEPT statement. Also TIME is now an 8-byte external decimal field with the following format:

```
    HHMMSSCC
Where HH is Hour
      MM is Minutes
      SS is Seconds
      CC is hundredths-of-seconds
```

Therefore the code segment must be changed as follows:

```
77 TIME-IN-MYPROG PICTURE X(8).
        .
        .
        .
    ACCEPT TIME-IN-MYPROG FROM TIME
```

Q: *What needs to be changed to migrate this code segment from OS/VS COBOL to COBOL/370?*

```
77 DATE-IN-MYPROG PICTURE X(8)
        .
        .
    MOVE CURRENT-DATE TO DATE-IN-MYPROG.
```

A: In COBOL/370 you must use the DATE special register in an ACCEPT statement. Also DATE is now a 6-byte alphanumeric field with the following format:

```
      YYMMDD (year, month, day)
Where YY is Year
      MM is Month
      DD is Day
```

Therefore the code segment must be changed as follows:

```
77 DATE-IN-MYPROG PICTURE X(6)
        .
        .
        .
      ACCEPT DATE-IN-MYPROG FROM DATE
```

Q: *How can I query the current date and time during program execution?*

A: Use the intrinsic function CURRENT-DATE. This function returns a 21-character string. We are interested in characters 1–14, starting from the leftmost character and reading to the right.

The returned field contains the following:

1–4	Four numeric digits of the year in the Gregorian calendar
5–6	Two numeric digits of the month of the year, in the range 01 through 12
7–8	Two numeric digits of the day of the month, in the range 01 through 31
9–10	Two numeric digits of the hours past midnight, in the range 00 through 23
11–12	Two numeric digits of the minutes past the hour, in the range 00 through 59
13–14	Two numeric digits of the seconds past the minute, in the range 00 through 59

Q: *What must be changed in the following to migrate the following to COBOL/370?*

```
77  WS-DATA    PICTURE X(9) VALUE "ABCDEFGHI"
        .
        .
        .
      TRANSFORM WS-DATA FROM "ABC" to "XYZ"
```

A: COBOL/370 does not support the TRANSFORM statement; it must be replaced with the INSPECT CONVERTING statement. The TRANSFORM statement needs to be changed as follows:

```
77  WS-DATA    PICTURE X(9) VALUE "ABCDEFGHI"
        .
        .
        .
      INSPECT WS-DATA
        CONVERTING "ABC" to "XYZ"
```

Q: *How must the following be coded to be accepted by the COBOL/370 compiler:*

```
      EXAMINE DATA-LENGTH TALLYING UNTIL FIRST " ".
```

A:
```
MOVE 0 TO TALLY.
INSPECT DATA-LENGTH TALLYING TALLY FOR CHARACTERS BEFORE " ".
```

Q: *How does this statement need to be changed to be supported in COBOL/370?*

```
MOVE CORRESPONDING GROUP-ITEM-A TO GROUP-ITEM-B GROUP-ITEM-C
```

A: In COBOL/370 the MOVE CORRESPONDING statement cannot have more than one receiving field. The statement needs to be changed as follows:

```
MOVE CORRESPONDING GROUP-ITEM-A TO GROUP-ITEM-B
MOVE CORRESPONDING GROUP-ITEM-A TO GROUP-ITEM-C
```

Q: *How could I move a piece of a character field to another field?*

A: You could use a reference modifier as follows:

```
MOVE INVOICE-RECORD(1:20) TO CUSTOMER-NAME
```

The substring is specified in parentheses immediately following the data item. The first number represents the position (starting at the left of the data item) of the character you want the substring to start with. A colon follows and the last number within the parentheses is the length of the substring. If the length is omitted, the substring will automatically extend to the end of the data item.

Q: *How would you calculate a date 30 days from the current date with COBOL/370?*

A:
```
01  YYYYMMDD        Pic 9(8).
01  Integer-Form    Pic S9(9).

       .
       .
       .

Move Function Current-Date(1:8) to YYYYMMDD
Compute Integer-Form = Function Integer-of-Date(YYYYMMDD)
Add 30 to Integer-Form
Compute YYYYMMDD = Function Date-of-Integer(Integer-Form)
Display 'Due Date: ' YYYYMMDD
```

Q: *What do I have to do to find an entry in a table defined in the working storage of my COBOL program?*

A:
```
01 MYTABLE.
   05 MYTABLE-ENTRY OCCURS 100 TIMES
       ASCENDING PART-KEY
       INDEXED BY INDX-1.
       10  PARTNO                PIC 99.
       10  PART-KEY              PIC 9(5).
          .
          .
          .

       SEARCH ALL MYTABLE-ENTRY
         AT END
           PERFORM NOTTFND
             WHEN PART-KEY (INDX-1) = VALUE-1
               PERFORM FOUNDIT
       END-SEARCH
```

Q: *How would you code the following? I would like to perform a different routine for an input record depending on a value in the first field of the record.*

A:
```
01  Filea-Input
    05  Request-Type              Pic X.
            88  Add-Request           Value "A".
            88  Change-Request        Value "C".
            88  Delete-Request        Value "D".
    05  .
        .
        .
        .
Evaluate True
  When Add-Request
    Perform Add-Record
  When Change-Request
    Perform Change-Record
  When Delete-Request
    Perform Delete-Record
End-Evaluate
```

Q: *What is the difference between a static call and a dynamic call?*

A: The static call statement results in the called subprogram being link-edited with the main program into one load module. The dynamic call results in the dynamic invocation of a separate load module.

Q: *How would you code a Dynamic call statement to a subprogram called PROGRAM2?*

A:
```
DATA DIVISION.
WORKING-STORAGE SECTION.
    77  PGM-NAME               PICTURE X(8).
    01  RECORD-1.
        05  FIRSTNAME          PICTURE X(15).
        05  LASTNAME           PICTURE X(25).
        05  LOCATION           PICTURE X(30).
PROCEDURE DIVISION.
    MOVE "PROGRAM2" TO PGM-NAME.
    CALL PGM-NAME USING RECORD-1.
    STOP RUN.
```

Q: *How can I select and/or modify the output of a COBOL sort or merge?*

A: On a SORT/MERGE statement an OUTPUT PROCEDURE can be specified. The SORT/MERGE will pass control to the output procedure once the files have been sequenced by the SORT/MERGE statement. In the output procedure the records will be made available one at a time. The RETURN statement in the output procedure is the request for the next record. The compiler inserts a return mechanism at the end of the last statement in the output procedure and when control passes the last statement in the output procedure, the return mechanism passes control to the next executable statement after the SORT/MERGE statement.

Q: *How do I debug a VS COBOL II program under CICS?*

A: ▪ Translate your program.

▪ Compile with the TEST option specified and link-edit your program.

▪ Define your programs and transaction to the CICS system.

Q: *Where do I place the debugging commands to debug a VS COBOL II program that runs under CICS?*

A: For CICS/VS, store the debug tool commands in a temporary storage queue with the following 8-character name CSCOxxxx (where xxxx is the identifier of the test terminal).

Q: *Where can I find the results of a COBTEST debug session for a CICS COBOL application?*

A: You look at the contents of a CICS temporary storage queue called CEBRxxxx (where xxxx is the terminal identifier).

Questions for the Advanced COBOL Programmer

Q: *How do I issue a wait for a period of time in a Microfocus COBOL program under both OS/2 and DOS?*

A: In OS/2 you can issue the following API call:

```
        Call OS2API '_DosSleep'
using by value SnoozeTime, where SnoozeTime is defined in
working storage as ...
        01 SnoozeTime          Pic 9(9)  Comp-5 Value 0.
```

SnoozeTime is specified in milliseconds. This API is documented in the OS/2 Control Program Programming Reference. Another way that will work in both OS/2 and DOS is to simply ACCEPT START-TIME from TIME then add the amount of time you want to wait to START-TIME then perform an ACCEPT END-TIME from TIME until END-TIME > START-TIME.

To loop for 1 second do the following: . . .

```
ACCEPT START-TIME FROM TIME.
ADD 100 TO START-TIME.
PERFORM UNTIL END-TIME > START-TIME
    ACCEPT END-TIME FROM TIME
END-PERFORM.
```

where START-TIME and END-TIME are defined as . . .

```
01 START-TIME        Pic 9(08) Value Zero.
01 END-TIME          Pic 9(08) Value Zero.
```

Q: *There are two programs, PROGRAMA and PROGRAMB. PROGRAMA issues a CALL to PROGRAMB. What will happen to PROGRAMA if PROGRAMB issues a STOP RUN when it has finished its processing?*

A: If PROGRAMB issues a STOP RUN statement, the effect is that all COBOL programs in the run unit are terminated, and control returns to the caller of the main program, typically the operating system.

Q: *What should the PROGRAMB issue when its processing is completed so that control is returned to PROGRAMA?*

A: PROGRAMB could issue either an EXIT PROGRAM or a GOBACK.

Q: *If PROGRAMA repeatedly calls PROGRAMB, what will happen to data items in PROGRAMB?*

A: The internal values in PROGRAMB will be as they were left, except that return values for PERFORM statements will be reset to their initial values.

Q: *What is required to force data items in PROGRAMB to be in its initial state each time it is called from PROGRAMA?*

A: If PROGRAMB is dynamically called and then cancelled it will be in the initial state the next time it is called. If PROGRAMB has the INITIAL attribute it will be in the initial state each time it is called wether the call is dynamic or static.

Q: *Is it possible to mix (ILC) VS COBOL II and AD Cycle C/370 in the same program?*

A: A single program cannot be written in two languages, but you can mix a VS COBOL II program with an AD/Cycle program in an ILC application. The AD/Cycle C program will require LE/370, so the VS COBOL II program must also be running under LE/370 for this application to run. (You would have to do a run-time migration for the COBOL.)

   Since this application could not be running prior to LE/370, it already will have been linked with LE/370. If you had a VS COBOL II and C/370 application running under VS COBOL II and C/370 run time then it would have to be linked with LE/370 to run under LE/370. Under CICS, you cannot do native-language CALLs between VS COBOL II and AD/Cycle C. You would use EXEC CICS LINK or EXEC CICS XCTL. If you compile the COBOL with COBOL/370, you can then use native COBOL or C language for interprogram communication. (Native-language ILC under CICS was never allowed before LE/370, so this is an advantage of using LE/370.)

Q: *I want to get the line number where an error occurred. The debugging guide says you won't get the line number if you also use OPTIMIZE. Is there anything I can do to get the line number when using OPTIMIZE?*

A: For programs compiled with OPTIMIZE, the line number is useless for debugging, since you may have many copies of that line! The only way to determine where you are in the program is to use an offset, and that is what you get with VS COBOL II compiled with OPT and FDUMP, or COBOL/370 compiled with OPT and TEST(NONE,SYM). You will still get symbolic information for the data items (variables), but line numbers are meaningless in COBOL with OPTIMIZE option.

Q: *How can I use CODE/370 to debug assembler code that calls COBOL routines?*

A: You can debug mixed applications that contains assembler and COBOL or C. However, only debugging of high-level language program routines is allowed. For example:

COBOL program A calls Assembler program B, which in turn calls COBOL program C. You can step under control of the debugger thru A, then the debugger will lose control thru the assembler routine B, and regain control when C starts executing, and give control back to the user. If your Assembler routine is the main, then you'll need to use the CEETEST function in your COBOL program so the debugger gets control in the second routine. For example, Assembler program A calls COBOL program B with call CEETEST. It is not until the Call CEETEST is called that the debugger is initialized.

Q: *I am trying to compile a VS COBOL II program with Micro Focus COBOL Toolbox and I am getting an error on a COPY command stating that the copybook cannot be found. What can I do to solve the problem?.*

A: Set the COBCPY environment variable. The COBCPY environment variable directs the COBOL compiler to look in additional directories for simple COPY filenames if they cannot be located in the given or default library. For example:

```
COBCPY="/usr/group/sharedcopy:.:/usr/mydir/mcpy"
export COBCPY
```

Q: *What is the difference between intermediate code and native code compilation when using the Micro Focus COBOL Compiler?*

A: Intermediate code (.int code) is code produced when the source program is syntax-checked. The gnt code is produced when the generator component converts intermediate code to native code. Native code is also called generated code (.gnt code). Native code is the code that the microprocessor understands directly without the need for an interpreter. Both .int code and .gnt code must be run using the Micro Focus run-time environment. The Micro Focus run-time system contains support modules needed by a COBOL program to enable it to run. The run-time system provides an interface between the program and the operating system. It is based on the shared run-time system, and runs .int and .gnt files. You can also tell the Micro Focus COBOL compiler to produce an AIX executable with the following command:

```
cob -x program.cbl
```

This will produce an AIX executable called program which you can run with the following command:

```
./program
```

Q: *I found a core file created when I executed my program. What do I use to analyze the core file?*

A: Invoke dbx on the executable that produced the core. For instance, if cobrun produced the core, type the following command:

```
dbx 'whence cobrun'
```

At the (dbx) prompt, type the where command as follows:

```
(dbx) where
```

This will give you a stack trace. Use this information along with the source to the program that produced the core.

Q: *What is required to migrate older OS/VS COBOL applications to IBM COBOL/370?*

A: IBM COBOL/370 does not support the following OS/VS COBOL language elements:

- Report Writer
- ISAM file handling
- BDAM file handling
- Communication Feature
- Segmentation

OS/VS COBOL Report Writer applications can be run using LE/370 without recompiling. If you want to recompile the OS/VS applications with Report Writer statements, you must continue to use the OS/VS COBOL compiler. The OS/VS COBOL Report Writer programs will not run above the 16-Mbyte line. As an alternative the Report Writer Precompiler can be used to migrate to COBOL/370. The COBOL Report Writer Precompiler will recompile existing Report Writer applications, and the Report Writer applications can run above the 16-Mbyte line. To migrate OS/VS COBOL programs that contain ISAM files you will need to convert any ISAM files to VSAM KSDS files. The IDCAMS REPRO facility will perform this conversion unless the file has a hardware dependency. Next you must convert the ISAM COBOL language to VSAM/KSDS COBOL language. The COBOL and CICS/VS Conversion Aid (CCCA) program offering can be used to help modify the file definitions in your COBOL programs. Another alternative is to move the ISAM statements into an I/O program that can be compiled by the OS/VS COBOL compiler, then you can put the rest of the application logic into programs that can be migrated to COBOL/370. The application can then be run in a mixed environment using LE/370.

BDAM files that are used by programs that you wish to migrate to COBOL/370 will need to be converted to VSAM RRDS files. At this point the same steps required to modify OS/VS COBOL programs that use ISAM files need to be completed. TCAM applications that use the OS/VS COBOL SEND and RECEIVE statements run with the LE/370 library in compatibility mode. However, the QUEUE run-time option of OS/VS COBOL is not supported. OS/VS COBOL programs that use segment priority numbers on section names or the SEGMENT-LIMIT clause coded in the OBJECT-COMPUTER do not require any programming changes. COBOL/370 accepts the segmentation language but does not perform any overlay.

Q: *With OS/VS COBOL, if you call an assembler program it is possible to pass the addresses of paragraph names defined in the calling COBOL program that the assembler program could return to instead of returning to the next instruction after the call. This practice violates the principle of structured programming. How would you change the following COBOL code to maintain a structured programming style?*

```
CALL "MYASSM" USING PARM-1,
                     PARAGRAPH-1
                     PARAGRAPH-2,
NEXT STATEMENT.
      .
      .
PARAGRAPH-1.
      .
      .
PARAGRAPH-2.
```

A: The COBOL code needs to be changed as follows:

```
CALL "MYASSM" USING PARM-1,
                    PARM-2.

IF PARM-2 NOT = 0
   GOTO PARAGRAPH-1,
        PARAGRAPH-2,
        DEPENDING ON PARM-2.
```

The assembler program needs to be changed to pass back a return code of zero in PARM-2 if there were no errors and if there were errors than a nonzero return code must be passed back in PARM-2. After the call to the assembler program the COBOL program would use PARM-2 to determine which paragraph to go to in an error condition.

Q: *How must an assembler program be set up to call a COBOL/370 subprogram?*

A: The assembler program must set up the following:

- R13 must point to the assembler program's register saver area (18 words), and the first word of the save area must be zero.
- R1 contains the address of a parameter list made up of one or more contiguous fullwords. Each fullword contains the address of a data item to be passed to the COBOL program. The last fullword should have the high-order bit set to 1 to flag the end of the list.
- R1 must be set to zero if no parameter list is passed.
- R14 must contain the return address in the assembler program.
- R15 must contain the address of the entry point of the COBOL program.

Q: *How do I locate the working storage of a COBOL program using a CICS transaction dump?*

A: CICS makes a copy of working storage for each invocation of the COBOL program. Using a CICS transaction dump you need to locate the System TCA

(Task Control Area). At offset X'48' for CICS/ESA Version 3.3 is the field TCAPCHS, which is the pointer to the COBOL TGT. For CICS Version 4.1 TCAPCHS is at System TCA +X'40'. CICS uses the term HLLRSA (High Level Language Register Save Area) when referring to the COBOL TGT. The COBOL program's register save area begins at offset x'0c' from the beginning of the COBOL TGT. The registers are saved in the following order:

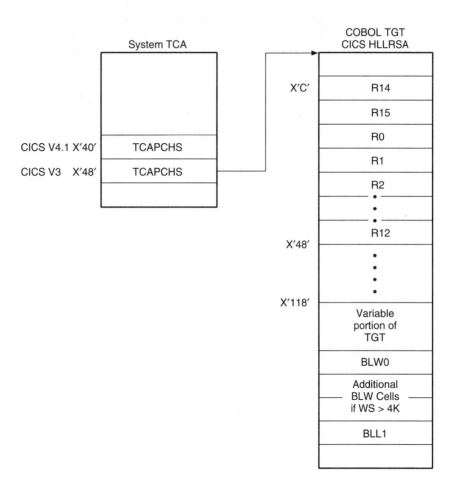

The COBOL TGT memory map gives the offset from the beginning of the TGT to the location of the Base Locators for Working Storage. You then add this offset to the starting address of the TGT to find value of the first BLW. Each BLW occupies one word (4 bytes). Each BLW can address 4K of data. If Working Storage is greater than 4K, additional BLW cells will follow the first BLW. The first BLW cell will contain the beginning address of the copy of working storage for this CICS task.

Q: *How do I locate the data in the Linkage section of a COBOL program using a CICS transaction dump?*

A: The Linkage section data items are addressed using BLL cells. The BLL cells follow the BLW cells in the COBOL TGT.

Q: *How do I find the failing COBOL instruction using a formatted dump?*

A: The second word of the PSW printed in the dump points to the next instruction to be executed. The next word of the PSW contains the instruction length in the left four bytes and the interrupt code in the last four bytes. Using the Module Index, locate the module that has a load point equal to or less than the address of the next instruction (from word 2 of PSW). Subtract the entry point of the COBOL program from the address of the next instruction. This will give the offset of the next instruction to be executed in the COBOL program. Use the procedure map of the COBOL program to locate this offset into the COBOL program. Then back up to the previous instruction to locate the failing COBOL instruction.

28

SAS

Sheryl Hert Harawitz

Introduction

Statistical Analysis System (SAS) is a leased product of the SAS Institute of Cary, N.C. SAS is utilized on mainframes running under MVS, CMS, and VSE; mini-computers using VMS, AOS/VS, PRIMOS, and Unix workstations; and personal computers using DOS, OS/2, and Windows. SAS can access a variety of file types, including VSAM (sequential and direct access), BDAM, ISAM, and partitioned datasets.

The latest SAS release has a new engine which uses MultiVendor Architecture (MVA). MVA is platform-independent in that a SAS program written for the personal computer will also work on a mainframe computer. Since SAS is platform-independent, it is an ideal tool for environments with a multitude of computer systems. The SAS programming language and procedures remain constant across systems.

SAS Products

The core product of SAS is BASE/SAS software. BASE/SAS enables you to access a variety of data sources, manipulate the data, write reports, build simple graphs, analyze data, and perform simple statistical analysis. Over the years SAS has not only expanded the range of hardware and operating systems on which it will run, but has also expanded the number of products. Bear in mind that SAS is a leased product and each of the following components is leased separately from BASE/SAS described here.

1. SAS/STAT software used to be included with the BASE/SAS, but with the new release it became a separate package. This component product offers ANOVA

(Analysis of Variance), regression analysis, categorical analysis, multivariate analysis, psychometric analysis, cluster analysis, and nonparametric analysis.

2. SAS/FSP is the software package used for full-screen data entry, letters, and spreadsheets.

3. SAS/AF software module is used for creating menus and screens.

4. SAS/GRAPH software is a complete graphics package, including mapping capabilities. It is compatible with a wide range of graphic interfaces and plotters.

5. SAS/ACCESS is the interface product for linking SAS to DB2, Oracle, Adabas, and other databases.

6. SAS/CPE is an interactive system used to monitor computer performance.

7. SAS/ETS software package is for economic and time-series analysis.

8. MXG is a related package which can be leased from Merill Consultants in Texas. With this package data can be extracted from MVS, VM, VSE, etc., operating systems. The software consists of data input and formats statements for these data types and the procedures necessary to convert these data types into SAS data sets.

Terminology

SUGI: SAS Users Group International. Every year SAS holds a conference in which SAS users are invited to submit papers on application development, computer performance, database management, econometric and operation research, graphics, and other topics.

Observation: Refers to a line of data or a record.

Variable: A field or data element.

SAS Log: SAS Log is where SAS puts information about the processing of the data step. Items typically included are the number of observations, error messages, warning messages, the name of the data sets accessed, and number of variables on the data sets.

SAS output file: This is where SAS puts the output from SAS procedures.

Options: Options sets the options such as page size, line size, block size, and some 100 other options.

SAS data sets: SAS data sets are created by Data Step and/or Procedures. These files differ from ordinary data sets in that they contain both the data and information about the data. They store the following information: the variable names (field or column names), data types (alpha or numeric), length, informat names, format names, and associated labels.

A SAS Job Interview

When a job calls for:

A beginner. Almost anyone who has written programs in COBOL or any other computer language and has the basic programming skills can program in SAS. It should be remembered that SAS programs are often written by noncomputer professionals.

An intermediate. The interviewer would expect you to be familiar with (1) formatting data and (2) some macro language.

An expert. You would be expected to be able to (1) use the macro language and (2) create an intricate production program system.

Some of the following sections will demonstrate how to write a small program. When asked to do this, keep the programs as simple as possible. Other questions in an interview may require you to find out what is wrong with the program. Still other questions will ask you to solve typical programming problems using basic logic skills.

The Structure of a SAS Dataset

SAS, because its roots are in the statistical world, uses the word *variable* as a synonym for *field,* and the term *observation* in place of *record.* Every sentence in SAS ends in a semicolon.

The following conventions are used: Keywords are *capitalized* and must be written as is. Variables (fields) are written in *lowercase.* Variables can be any 8-byte word that begins with an alpha.

A "Basic" SAS Program

```
//sas        EXEC PGM=SASAI
//SASLOG     DD DSN=                      SAS log information
//SASLIST    DD DSN=                      SAS output
//ddname1    DD DSN=file1.data,DISP=SHR   input data set
//ddname2    DD DSN=file2.data,DISP=OLD   output data set

  DATA anyname;
   INFILE ddname1;
   INPUT  name1 name2 name3 number1 number2;
   IF name1  > name2;

   total1 =number1+number2;
   ...etc..;
   /*  comments ....... */
   PROC PRINT;
   PROC FREQ;
     TABLE name1;
```

A SAS program consists of two divisions: the DATA STEP and the PROC STEP. The data step begins with the word "DATA" while the proc starts with the word "PROC."

Components of a SAS Program

SAS programs begin with a DATA STEP. The data step begins with the word "DATA." The data step is where SAS is given instructions about the location of the dataset and the description of the data elements. As SAS executes the data step, the data is evaluated and brought into SAS's working storage.

The data step contains the basic data retrieval, programming, and data manipulation language. It is the section of the program where you can create new variables and select specific records for processing (if statement, do loops, etc.). The end product of a SAS data step is the creation of a SAS dataset for use in the SAS Proc or as an output file.

Keywords Used in a Data Step

DATA: The first word used in a SAS program. For example:

```
DATA anyname;
```

says start a data step and call the dataset anyname. (Please note that SAS statements start with a key word and end with a semicolon.)

INFILE statement: Used for locating the external source of a data file. For example:

```
//file1   DD DSN=what.ever.it.is.called
DATA anyname; INFILE file1;
```

Here INFILE file1 says refer back to the line of JCL with the ddname file1. This is where the data is located.

INPUT statement: Tells SAS what the data elements are to be called and where in the data set they are located. The two most common input statements are column input and formatted input. An example of a column input statement is the following:

```
INPUT   dept $1-10
      salary 25-30;
```

This statement says the data in columns 1–10 is alphanumeric (the $ indicates alphanumeric data) and the data in bytes 25–30 is numeric. The first variable (field) will be called dept and the second variable will be called salary.

A formatted input statement is as follows:

```
INPUT @1 dept $10.
      @25 salary 5.;
```

This statement says that the variable dept starts in byte 1 and continues for 10 bytes, while salary starts in byte 25 and continues for 5 bytes. (Please note that the period after 10 and 5 indicates to SAS that this is formatted data. A common error is to leave out the period.)

PUT: The opposite of an INPUT statement. It tells SAS how to write the variable. For example, the following statement:

```
PUT @25 name $20.
    @89 dept $10.;
```

says to write the variable name at byte 25 as a character 20 bytes.

FILE: The opposite of an INFILE statement. The following statement tells SAS that the data should be put into an external data file with the ddname of new.

```
FILE new;
```

SET: Locates a SAS data set, that is, a data set that had been previously inputted into SAS and outputted as a SAS data set. When you use the SET statement, you do not have to supply an INPUT statement, since SAS stores format, labels, and attributes with the data set.

```
SET dept1;
```

LABEL: The keyword that associates a SAS variable with a longer name. Since SAS variables can be only 8 bytes, it is often necessary to associate a longer name with the variable for use in procedures such as Report.

```
LABEL dept='Department';
```

MERGE: Brings together multiple data sets by matching on a variable.

```
MERGE file1 file2; BY name1;
```

where file1 and file2 are SAS data sets and name1 is the variable (field) that you want to match on.

FORMAT statements: Inform SAS about outputting the variable.

```
FORMAT date1  mmddyy8.;
FORMAT date2  yymmdd8.;
```

will result in the data looking like 08/08/92, while FORMAT yymmdd8. will result in the data looking like 92/08/08. SAS has an extensive list of formats. (Please note that formats end with a period.)

PROCs

The word "PROC" is used to invoke SAS procedure. A SAS Proc is basically a prewritten program that produces statistical analysis, creates reports, and/or outputs datasets. The following are some of the Procedures available in BASE/SAS:

PROC PRINT: Produces basic columnar reports. For example:

```
PROC PRINT; VAR date1 name;
```

will produce a report with two columns of data: date1 and name.

PROC FREQ: Produces cross-tabulation tables, mainly for categorical data.

```
PROC FREQ; TABLE dept*sex;
```

will produce a table such as the following:

```
          TABLE OF DEPARTMENT BY YEAR

DEPT         SEX
                 | FEMALE | MALE  | TOTAL
           _____|_____|_____|
SALES      |      200    |  100   |  300
PERSONNEL  |      100    |  200   |  300
TOTAL             300       300      600
```

PROC SORT: Sorts the data set.

```
PROC SORT; BY name1;
```

will produce a data set sorted by name field.

PROC MEANS: Produces descriptive statistics such as mean, standard deviation, minimum and maximum values.

PROC PLOT: Produces simple plots. For example:

```
PROC PLOT; PLOT total*shares;
```

PROC CALENDAR: Produces a calendar or a schedule. For example:

```
PROC CALENDAR; ID date1; VAR item1 item2;
```

PROC CHART: Produces bar charts, block graphs, and pie charts. (Bear in mind that this proc is different from SAS/GRAPH, which is another component with many more graphic capabilities.

```
PROC CHART; VBAR sex;
```

(VBAR is a keyword indicating vertical bars.)

PROC COMPARE: Compares two datasets and lists the differences between them.

```
PROC COMPARE DATE=file1 COMPARE=file2;
VAR phone address;
ID name;
```

This program will compare the two files (file1 and file2) by matching on the variable name, and will list the differences found on the variable's phone number and addresses.

PROC FORMS: Most commonly used for producing labels.

PROC SUMMARY: Produces summary statistics on numeric fields.

```
PROC SUMMARY; CLASS dept; VAR salary; OUTPUT OUT=anyname
MEAN=;
```

This program says create a data set called anyname and for each dept calculate the mean salary. To print this data set, use the following:

```
PROC PRINT DATA=anyname;
```

Questions and Answers

Q: *Why would a staff person alter a SAS program from*

```
DATA group1; INFILE file1; INPUT name $20. salary pd6.2;
```

to

```
DATA group1;
INFILE file1;
INPUT name $20. salary pd6.2;
```

A: Technically, the two programs are identical; therefore, the staff person changed the program for readability or personal preference.

Q: *Describe the data extracted with the following SAS statement:*

```
INPUT @1 test $10. @25 test2 PD6. @40 test3 MMDDYY6.;
```

A: Test would be an alphanumeric variable which was 10 bytes. Test2 would be a 6-byte packed decimal with no decimal places which started at byte 25. Test3 would be a date field (i.e., 010646) starting at byte 40.

Q: *Write an INPUT statement for a data set with department in bytes 35 through 45 and salary starting in byte 62, ending in byte 69, with two implied decimal places.*

A: INPUT dept $35–45 @62 salary 8.2;

Q: *Write a SAS INPUT statement for the following COBOL record:*

```
01  name-file-record.
    02  social-security-num    pic x(9).
    02  last-name              pic x(15).
    02  first-name             pic x(10).
    02  data-of-birth.
        03 month-of-birth      pic 9(2).
        03 day-of-birth        pic 9(2).
        03 year-of-birth       pic 9(2).
```

A: INPUT ssn $9. lname $15. fname $10. dob mmddyy6.;

Q: *Our company would like to put SAS programs into production. Is there a SAS equivalent to a COBOL copybook?*

A: Yes. By using SAS macro's language, you can store the INPUT statements in a library that can be called by multiple programs.

Q: *Write a SAS statement for a file which has five salaries, each 6 bytes wide.*

A: The statement INPUT (salary1-salary6) (6.); declares five variables: salary1, salary2, etc., each 6 bytes long.

Q: *Write a SAS statement for a data file that contains two different record types. The record type is located in byte 6 of the file. Record type 1 has the client's name in bytes 35–55 and Record type 2 has the client's name in bytes 20–40.*

A: Input @6 type 1. @;

```
IF type=1 THEN INPUT name $35-55;
IF type=2 THEN INPUT name $20-40;
```

(Note the @ sign at the end of input statement holds the pointer for further processing with the next input.)

Q: *We want to reformat a file. Write a program that reads a dataset with the variable name in bytes 24–34 and salary in byte 85–95 and writes the data to a file with name in byte 1–10 followed by salary.*

A:
```
//filein      DD  DSN=....
//fileout     DD  DSN=....

DATA rewrite; INFILE filein;
              INPUT salary 10-15 name $24-34;

              FILE fileout;
              PUT name $1-10     salary 11-16;
```

Q: *How would you alter the foregoing program to include a calculated variable called salary2, which is calculated by multiplying salary by 1.10?*

A:
```
DATA rewrite; INFILE filein;
              INPUT salary 10-15 name $24-34;
              salary2=salary*1.10;

              FILE fileout;
              PUT name $1-10 salary 11-16 @17 salary2 8.2;
```

(Note you can mix columnar and formatted data.)

Q: *The personnel department requested a report that lists the names of all employees and their social security numbers. After receiving the report, they requested that the social security number 123456789 be changed to 123-45-6789. How long would you expect it to take to recode the program?*

A: It should take about 5 minutes since the only line of code needed to be changed is the following:

```
FORMAT socnum SSN.;
```

Q: *An employee that you supervised gave you the following program. How would you rate his work?*

```
DATA test1; INPUT name 1-30 date_of_birth 31-35;
```

A: This employee has little experience with SAS programming. First, SAS variables can be only 8 bytes. The data step has no INFILE or SET statement; thus, no data.

Q: *How do you differentiate macro variables from regular SAS variables?*

A: Macro variables begin with the % sign.

Q: *What is the difference between the following two SAS statements?*

```
DATA dept1; INFILE file1; INPUT dept $1-4 name $20-40;
```

and

```
DATA dept1;
INFILE file1;
INPUT dept $1-4
      name $20-40;
```

A: There is no difference. The SAS programming language is not space-sensitive. Each statement begins with a keyword and ends with a semicolon.

Q: *What is wrong with the following statement?*
```
INPUT dept $1-10 filler $11-20 name $21-40 filler $41-60;
```
A: The variable name "FILLER" is used twice. Unlike COBOL, SAS does not use filler. If you do not need the data in a field, just skip over it, or else you have to use a unique name such as filler2.

Q: *What is wrong with the following statement?*
```
DATA dept1; SET dept; INPUT name $1-20;
```
A: There is no need for an INPUT statement when SET is used. SET indicates an existing SAS dataset.

Q: *How would you print a list of department salaries with dollar signs, commas, and two decimal places?*
A: First format the data with the following statement:
```
Format salary DOLLAR12.2;
```
Then use PROC PRINT.

Q: *Write a program to calculate the age of our clients.*
A:
```
DATA age;
INPUT name birth MMDDYY6.;
age=(DATE()-birth)/365.25;
```

Q: *Write a program that would process records 5000 through 6000.*
A:
```
INFILE dept5 OBS=1000 FIRSTOBS=5000;
```
This statement limits SAS to 1000 observations, with the first observation starting at record number 5000.

Q: *Write a program to merge two data sets.*
A:
```
MERGE file1 file2;
```

Q: *Write a program to match two data sets on id number and include only those records that were on the first data set.*
A:
```
MERGE file1 (IN=data1) file2 (IN=data2); BY id;
   IF data1;
```

Q: *Our company has two files. File 1 has the names of our departments and the manager's names. The second file has the salespersons' names, amount of their annual sales, and their department. Write a program to list the salesperson, his or her annual sales, and manager's name.*
A:
```
DATA file1; INFILE mgmt; INPUT dept $ manager $ ;
        LABEL manager='Manager's Name';
DATA file2; INFILE sales; INPUT sales $ amount dept $;
        LABEL sales='Salesperson's Name'
                 amount='Total Sales';
PROC SORT DATA=file1; BY dept;
PROC SORT DATA=file2; BY dept;
DATA file3; MERGE file2 file1; BY dept;
PROC PRINT LABEL; VAR sales amount manager ;
```

Q: *Write a second program that prints a summary of the number of salespersons, and the total amount of sales per manager.*

A: Add the following to the preceding program:

```
PROC SUMMARY DATA=file3 NWAY; CLASS manager;
        VAR amount;
        OUTPUT OUT=summary1 SUM=;
PROC PRINT;
```

Q: *Change the preceding program to find the average amount of sales per manager.*

A: The only line of code that has to change is:

```
OUTPUT OUT=summary1 MEAN=;
```

Q: *What procedure could you use to calculate the standard deviation?*

A: The standard deviation can be calculated with PROC SUMMARY, PROC UNIVARIATE, PROC TABULATE, PROC CORR, and PROC MEANS.

Q: *Our company has been collecting data on the age of our customers and the amount of their purchases. We would like to know if there is a relationship between the customer's age and the amount of money spent per year. How would you proceed?*

A: First, check the accuracy of the dataset by looking for outlying data elements. That is, find the youngest and oldest customers and see if these ages are correct. The following program would do that.

```
PROC FREQ; TABLE age amount;
```

Next, prepare a graphic and analytic presentation of the data by using PROC CORR and PROC PLOT.

```
PROC PLOT; age*purchases;
PROC CORR; VAR age purchases;
```

Q: *What procedure would you use to perform a T test?*

A: PROC UNIVARIATE

Q: *Our company would like to know the percent of males and females in each department. How would you go about answering this user inquiry?*

A: Obtain or create a file with the employees, their departments, and their gender. The following program would produce a table with each department, the percent of females and males in each department, the number of males and females in each department, and the overall count and percent of males and females.

```
PROC FREQ; TABLE dept * sex;
```

Q: *The personnel department would like to know the average salary for each job title. What procedure would you use to find the average salary for each job title?*

A: Proc summary is an efficient way to provide means for variables. A typical program would be the following:

```
PROC SUMMARY;
CLASS title;
```

```
VAR salary;
OUTPUT OUT=file1 MEAN=;
PROC PRINT;
```

Q: *Are there any other procedures which could be used to find the average salary for each job title?*

A: A combination of PROC SORT and PROC MEANS, as in the following program, will work.

```
PROC SORT; BY title;
PROC MEANS; BY title;
VAR salary;
```

Q: *Our company has a very large database, with over 1 million records. We would like to find out the distribution of our customers by zip code, but each time we try to run the program we run out of space. How would you handle this problem?*

A: One way to handle this is to take a random sample of the records by using the following:

```
If ranuni(0) LE .25;
```

would produce a sample with approximately 250,000 customers.

Q: *Our company placed addresses in a free-form field; that is, the street name can be anywhere in a 30-byte field. We need to locate the customers who live on Wilson Street. How would you go about solving this situation?*

A: First, define the 30-byte field, then use index feature to locate the words "Wilson" and "Street," as in the following program:

```
INPUT address $30.;
IF INDEX(address,'wilson') AND INDEX(address, 'st');
```

Q: *The following program produced no output. Why?*

```
PROC SUMMARY; CLASS sex; VAR salary; OUTPUT OUT =test MEAN=;
```

A: Proc summary does not produce printed output, but outputs the data to a SAS data set that could be printed with Proc Print or used as input to another procedure or data step. To see the output of Proc Summary, it needs to be followed with a Proc Print.

Q: *How would you output the data to disk rather than paper?*

A: If using SAS5, then change the //FT12 ... line to indicate the location for the output data set. If using SAS6, then change the //SASLIST line to indicate an output data.

Q: *What procedure would you use to print a quick report?*

A: Proc Print will produce a reasonable report with the following statement:

```
PROC PRINT;
```

Q: *What is the difference between the following two statements?*

```
total=salary1+salary2+salary3;
total=sum(salary1,salary2,salary3);
```

A: The difference is the way SAS handles missing values. In the first statement, if any of the variables have a missing value, then the total will have a missing value. In the second, SAS will add the variables even if one of the variables is missing.

Q: *Our company has decided to install Version 6 of SAS. How would you go about converting programs from Version 5 to Version 6?*

A: You should analyze the programs and check to see if any program modification is necessary for the conversion. Most programs will run without modification under the new SAS.

Q: *What version of SAS have you worked with?*

A: Try the truth. Version 5 is the old version; the current version is 6.07. If you have used Version 5 you will have no problem with Version 6.

Q: *What is the major difference between Version 5 and Version 6 of SAS?*

A: The major difference between SAS 5 and SAS 6 is the storage of SAS datasets. With SAS 6, you can now compress the SAS datasets, thus saving disk space.

Q: *Our company is experiencing a shortage of DASD space. How would you address this problem among the SAS users?*

A: First, I would expect the SAS users to eliminate duplicate files, and then I would compress the data sets.

Q: *How would you alter the following program to use less work space?*

```
DATA dept1; SET dept;
PROC PRINT; WHERE age LE 18;
```

A: Put the select statement in the DATA step.

Q: *What is the difference between an informat and a format statement?*

A: An informat is used to read data into a SAS dataset, while a format is used for printing and/or writing the data.

Q: *What kind of graphics can SAS produce?*

A: This is dependent upon which components of the SAS system your company has. BASE/SAS has very limited graphing capabilities. It can produce bar and block charts, time lines, and two variable plots. On the other hand, SAS/GRAPH can produce basic graphs, three-dimensional color charts, and maps.

Q: *What is the difference between a Data Step and a Proc Step?*

A: Basically SAS Proc Step operates on SAS Data Sets.

Q: *Where in a SAS program would you find the following statement?*

```
IF age GE 55;
```

A: This would be found in a Data Step. This statement says select only those records where age is greater than or equal to 55.

Q: *Where would you put the following statement in a SAS program?*

```
TITLE "This is the title of my report";
```

A: This statement can be placed anywhere in a SAS program.

Q: *Have you ever installed SAS?*

A: Yes or no, depending upon your experience. If you have never installed SAS on the mainframe, don't worry. SAS technical support will walk you through, if needed. Installing SAS on a personal computer is as simple as installing any other software.

Q: *What would you recommend as minimum requirement for SAS on the personal computer?*

A: As a minimum, you would recommend 4 megs and a math coprocessor.

Q: *How do you handle lease expiration?*

A: Each year you must use PROC SETINIT to inform the software that you have paid your yearly fee. After paying your bill, SAS will send you the information necessary to use the procedure Setinit.

Q: *What is wrong with the following SAS program?*

```
DATA department; INFILE mydata; INPUT dept $3. date MMDDYY6.;
```

A: SAS variables can be only 8 bytes long; department is 10 bytes.

Q: *What is the difference between the following two SAS statements?*

```
DATA dept; SET dept1;
DATA dept; INFILE dept1;
```

A: The first statement says that the data being brought in is already a SAS dataset. The second statement requires an input statement because it is a regular dataset.

Q: *We need to make labels from a SAS dataset. How would you go about doing this?*

A: First you should find out the size of the labels in stock (on hand). The information needed is the size of the labels and the number of spaces between the labels.

Q: *SAS is using a lot of computer resources. What would you do to lessen the impact?*

A: First, you would ascertain which type of computer resource SAS was using a lot: CPU, I/O, or Disk Space. To save I/O, I would use SAS datasets. To save disk space, I would write out only those variables that I needed for the current analysis. To save CPU, I would put the select statements as early as possible in the program.

Q: *What problems have you experienced in working with SAS?*

A: One problem is that SAS uses a lot of computer resources.

Q: *What are some limitations of SAS?*

A: The three limitations of SAS are (1) Proc Print produces a very limited range of reports, (2) the SAS manual is not only unwieldy, but the index is incomplete, and (3) the variable names are limited to 8 bytes.

Q: *How did you overcome these limitations?*

A: To overcome the problem of customized reports, I would use the SAS programming language. As for the variable name, use SAS label statements to attach a more meaningful name to the variable.

Q: *How would you go about setting up a training class for our staff?*

A: First, determine if the class is for computer professionals who need to add SAS as another tool or for noncomputer professionals. Based upon that information, contact SAS for their training kit.

Q: *What would you do to decrease SAS consumption of CPU time?*

A: Assign as many variables as possible with one statement. Write conditional statements in order of their probability of occurrence.

Q: *What would you do to decrease SAS usage of disk space?*

A: An easy way to decrease disk space usage is to store numeric data as characters.

Q: *The output dataset contained no observations. What could have caused this?*

A: Unless otherwise specified, all datasets are temporary and are deleted at the end of the SAS session. To create a permanent dataset requires a two-level name (i.e., mydata,setone), where mydata tells the location of the dataset, and setone is the member name.

Q: *What is wrong with this program?*

```
DATA mydata; INFILE dept; INPUT ssn $9. name $20.
PROC PRINT;
IF SUBSTR(name, 1,1)='A';
```

A: The "IF" statement belongs in the Data Step, not in the Proc.

Q: *What do the initials SAS mean?*

A: SAS stands for Statistical Analysis System, which is a product of SAS Institute of Cary, North Carolina.

Q: *Our company is trying to decide between SAS and SPSS. How would you compare the two products?*

A: Both products are similar in that both can handle basic statistical analysis. However, SAS is a business-oriented product capable of handling more data types and file structures, while SPSS is more research-oriented, with more sophisticated statistical analysis.

Q: *How would you correct this error?*

```
  127    DATA STOCK1; SET STOCK;
NOTE: The data set WORK.STOCK has 40 observations and 10 variables.
  128            set stock;
  129            total=price*shares
  130
  131    DATA stock2; SET stock;
DATA stock1; SET stock;
```

```
- - - -
ERROR: Syntax error detected.
NOTE: Expecting one of the following:( [ {
```
A: The error is in line 129. There is a semicolon missing after the word "shares."

Q: *What does the following NOTE message mean?*
```
139      DATA stock3; SET stock;
140           FORMAT bought DOLLAR8;
141           FORMAT shares COMMA4;
```
NOTE: Variable COMMA4 is uninitialized.

A: Variable COMMA4 is uninitialized, meaning that SAS is looking for a variable called COMMA4, but the program is calling for a format call COMMA4. (with a period at the end). The period is missing after the COMMA4.

Q: *Why does COMMA4 have a ".", while NAME is blank?*

OBS	YEAR92	TEMP	YEAR	COMMA4	NAME
1	227.63	−0.0067	1992	.	
2	195.74	−0.0046	1992	.	
3	140.73	0.0777	1992	.	
4	152.88	0.0033	1992	.	

A: "COMMA4" is numeric; thus, missing values are indicated by ".", while NAME is alphanumeric. Data and missing values are spaces.

Q: *What is meant by the following SAS NOTE?*
```
142           FORMAT name $25.;
```
NOTE: Variable NAME is uninitialized.

A: Variable NAME being uninitialized probably means that there is no such variable on the data set. This is probably due to a spelling error on the variable list.

Q: *What is the problem with the following program?*
```
132           total=shares*price;
133
134           IF total GE 5000
135
136   PROC PRINT;
PROC PRINT;
- - - -
ERROR: Syntax error detected.
```
*NOTE: Expecting one of the following:** < > >< MAX MIN.*

A: The problem with the program is a missing semicolon on line 134. Without the semicolon, SAS continued reading.

Q: *Why was the error message in the preceding question different from the error message on p. 356, even though the error was the same in both questions?*

A: The error message in the preceding question is related to the IF statement, while the error message on p. 356 is related to an assignment statement. Neither error message indicates that it is a missing semicolon.

Q: *What is the difference between these two SAS sentences?*

```
PROC SORT; BY id;
```

```
PROC SORT;
BY id;
```

A: There is no difference between the two sentences. SAS language is not space-sensitive. Each sentence begins with a keyword and ends with a semicolon. The layout of the program has more to do with easy reading and personal preference.

Q: *What is the difference between the Data Step and the Proc Step?*

A: Basically, SAS operates by either creating SAS datasets or analyzing SAS datasets. Datasets are created in the data step and used by the procs.

Q: *Can SAS use COBOL copybooks as input?*

A: No, SAS has its own input statement language.

Q: *We have SAS on our personal computers, and your experience is with mainframe SAS. Is your experience transferrable?*

A: Yes, the SAS programming language and procedure are independent of the computer hardware and operating system. Thus, all experience on the mainframe will be transferable to the personal computer version of SAS.

Q: *When would you use SAS over COBOL?*

A: I would use SAS when the programs need to be written quickly and the user request matches one of SAS's built-in procedures.

Q: *When would you use COBOL over SAS?*

A: I would use COBOL when computer resources were at a premium.

Q: *How would you access COBOL com3?*

A: COBOL comm3 translates to a SAS PDx.n, where x indicates the number of bytes occupied and *n* indicates the number of decimal places.

Q: *What does the following SAS statement mean?*

```
INPUT @1 salary PD4.2;
```

A: This statement says the salary is a 4-byte packed decimal field with two implied decimal places.

Q: *What is the difference between these two statements?*

```
A.  name EQ 'gat';
B.  name = 'gat';
```

A: Line A is a logical statement indicating that name should equal "gat," while B is an assignment statement where the "gat" should be placed into the variable called name.

Q: *What does the following SAS "note" mean?*
Note: The data set WORK.STOCK has 40 observations and 10 variables.
A: This is a message found on the SAS log and indicates that the data set had 10 variables (fields) and there were 40 records in the data set.

Q: *What is the difference between a SAS "note" and a SAS "warning"?*
A: An SAS warning contains information about input statements that could seriously compromise the results of the data analysis. An SAS note contains information about the data sets.

How well can you read SAS output? The next series of questions is based upon the following output from a SAS program, where Stock is the number of purchase orders and Year is the year in which the purchase took place. (*Hint:* There is no need for a calculator to answer any of the following questions. Every answer is in the table.)

```
TABLE OF COMPANY BY YEAR

STOCK                  YEAR

Frequency
Percent
Row Pct
Col Pct          1991    |    1992    |    Total
APPLE               0    |       8    |       8
                 0.00    |   20.00    |   20.00
                 0.00    |  100.00    |
                 0.00    |   25.00    |
IBM                 3    |      11    |      14
                 7.50    |   27.50    |   35.00
                21.43    |   78.57    |
                37.50    |   34.38    |
Vanguard            5    |      13    |      18
                12.50    |   32.50    |   45.00
                27.78    |   72.22    |
                62.50    |   40.63    |
Total               8    |      32    |      40
                20.00    |   80.00    |  100.00
```

Q: *What procedure created this output?*
A: This was created by Proc Freq; Table company * year;

Q: *How many orders were placed in 1992 for Vanguard?*
A: Thirteen.

Q: *Of the total number of orders, what percent went to Vanguard?*
A: 45 percent.

Q: *Of the total number of orders, what percent went to IBM in 1992?*
A: 27.5 percent.

Q: *Of the 1991 orders, what percent went to IBM?*
A: 37.5 percent.

Q: *Of the Vanguard orders, what percent took place in 1992?*
A: 72.22 percent.

The following questions are based upon hypothetical dataset listed.

File 1 layout	From	To
Last name (alphanumeric)	1	15
First name alphanumeric	16	25
Social security number	26	34
Sex (m or f)	35	35
Blank	36	36
Date of birth (mmddyy)	37	42
File 2 layout		
Social security number	1	9
Salary (2 decimal places)	10	17
Commission (no decimal)	18	25

Q: *Given the preceding file layout, write a SAS program to input these files:*
```
DATA file1;
INFILE ddname1;
INPUT  lname $1-15      fname $16-26
       ssn   $26-34     sex   $35
       blank $35        @37  dob mmddyy6.;
```
A:
```
DATA file2;
   INFILE ddname2;
   INPUT ssn $1-9    @10 salary 8.2    @18  comm 8.;
```

Q: *Produce a list of all the personnel and a sum of the salary and commissions.*
A:
```
PROC SORT DATA=file1; BY ssn;
   PROC SORT DATA=file1; BY ssn;
   DATA both; MERGE file1 file2; BY ssn;
   PROC PRINT; VAR lname fname ; Sum salary comm;
```

Q: *Write a report showing the relationship between age and salary.*
A: `PROC CORR; VAR age*salary;`

Q: *Write a SAS to produce a report giving the average salary for males and females.*
A:
```
PROC SORT; BY sex;
   PROC MEANS; BY sex; VAR salary;
```

Q: *Write a program to list those persons who received no commissions.*
A: `PROC PRINT; WHERE comm LE 0; VAR lname fname;`

Q: *Write a program to create a calendar of our employees' birthdays.*
A: Add a statement in the Data Step to create a variable which contains the date of employee's birthday and a duration variable (which is needed for Proc Calendar) containing the constant 1 (the number of days the birthday will last).

```
long=1;
birth=COMPRESS(MONTH(dob) || DAY(dob) || '1993';
birth2= INPUT(birth,mmddyy8.)

PROC CALENDAR;
    START birth2 ; VAR name; DUR long;
```

Q: *What is the SAS Display Manager?*
A: That is the interactive component of SAS.

Q: *What kinds of information will you find on the output log?*
A: The output log contains the results of SAS procedures.

Q: *In which language is SAS written?*
A: SAS is written in C.

Q: *What denotes a SAS system variable?*
A: A system variable is denoted by two underscores. For example, _FREQ_, _NULL_, _N_ are variables created by SAS.

Q: *What is wrong with the following statement?*
```
If age EQ 45 OR 49 OR 52;
```
A: The statement should read:
```
IF age EQ 45 OR age EQ 49 OR age EQ 52;
```

Q: *How do you code for a variable-length file?*
A: First, create a variable for the counter. Then input the variables with a do loop using the counter to position the pointer.

Q: *What information is available with Proc Content?*
A: Proc Content provides a list of the variables in the dataset, along with the length, type of variable, and any labels associated with them.

Q: *How do you define your own formats?*
A: Formats are defined with Proc Format. These can then be used in the data step or in the procedures.

Q: *How do you create a running total?*
A: Use Retain to prevent SAS from reinitializing a variable each time a new record is read into the data step. For example, the following will create a running total of sales:
```
RETAIN sales
sales=sales+sales
```

Q: *How do you create two datasets from one?*

A:
```
DATA good bad; SET total;
       IF status='good' THEN OUTPUT good;
       IF status='bad' THEN OUTPUT bad;
```

will create two datasets: one dataset named good and one named bad.

Q: *What does First.byvariable Last.byvariable mean?*

A: After sorting a dataset and using the by statement, SAS creates a variable last.xxx which marks the end of the group.

Q: *How would you write a statement to calculate the age of a person as of January 1, 1993?*

A:
```
Age=('01jan93'd -dob)/365.25;
```

where dob is a variable with the person's date of birth.

Q: *Are these two statements always identical?*
```
IF gender EQ 'f' ;
IF gender EQ 'm' THEN DELETE;
```

A: The two statements produce different results if gender contains missing values.

Q: *A Proc Freq on salary produced reams of paper. Why?*

A: Proc Freq will produce a count for each different value of salary, even if the value varies by one cent.

Q: *What are some system options that can be set?*

A: Some options that are available for setting are CENTER/NOCENTER, OBS=xx (where xx is a number), DATE/NODATE, LINESIZE=xx, and PAGESIZE=xx.

Bibliography

Aronson, Monte, and Alvera L. Aronson, *SAS System: A Programmer's Guide,* McGraw-Hill, Inc., New York, 1990.

SAS User's Guide: Basics, SAS Institute, Cary, N.C.

29

WWW, HTML, and Java

Ichi Murase

Introduction

The Internet has had, and will continue to have, a profound impact on the computer industry—customer and developer alike. It is allowing users to implement systems quickly at lower costs. It is providing "built-in" cross-platform compatibility, and it is providing a worldwide market for products and services. Companies have low-cost access to customers—worldwide.

Web page and program developers have a wide range of development tools, utilities, macros and facilities from which to choose. Much of it is free. Shareware costs to the user are nominal. In addition, most program development tools have built-in object-oriented structures and implementation techniques. With all these benefits it is little wonder that demand for analysts and programmers is continuing to exceed the available supply of trained developers.

Developers can be trained in their own homes. The tools, browsers, compilers, and utilities are available to a majority of PCs having a 14.4- or 28.8-kbyte modem. The typical PC is more than equipped to support programmer training. To become proficient all one has to do is study, practice, develop web pages and programs and then program and develop increasingly complicated applications.

What You Have to Be Able to Do

To get a job as an Internet developer you have to be able to:

- Browse the web, extracting and downloading what you need
- Build web pages
- Build applications using what has become the industry standard—Java and Hot Java

To pass a technical interview you should be able to answer correctly a majority of the WWW, HTML, and Java questions listed below. The rewards are there—the competition is there—you can also be there.

Questions and Answers

Q: *Why did Mosaic make the Web so popular?*

A: Developed by the National Center for Supercomputing Applications (NCSA), Mosaic was the first to introduce color and graphic browsers. Mosaic made the browser appear seamless and caught the attention of the public.

Q: *Name some other Browsers.*

A: Netscape, Spry, Hot Java, Lynx, Viola, Perl, Midas.

Q: *What are some Netscape features?*

A: On the Netscape you can access HTTP, Gopher, FTP, WAIS, NNTP, ARCHIE, SMTP, and so on. Netscape is HotJava and JavaScript enabled, which allows you to embed and use Java Applets in your HTML document. Netscape uses an extended version of HTML standard, which allows greater control of displayed text and images.

Q: *What is URL?*

A: Universal Resource Locator locates scripts and programs, locally and throughout the Internet.

Q: *How do you set up E-mail tag?*

A: To set up an E-mail form you enter the following tag in an HTML document:

```
<A HREF="MAILTO: im@internet.com">send e-mail</A>
```

Q: *How is CGI used?*

A: The basic pattern of Common Gateway Interface is straightforward. You enter data in the browser, the data is passed to the CGI program on the host and processed, and the cgi program responds. The CGI program on the host site, written in Windows, DOS or Unix platform, does all the processing. The form and its parameters permit the user to enter data in a field, select from a checklist or radio button or other options. For example, to obtain a magazine subscription, the user inputs name and address, checks off one or more magazines from the drop-down menu list, and submits the data for processing.

Q: *Describe how the Form tag is used to access a CGI program.*

A: `<FORM ACTION="/cgi-win/yourprog.exe" METHOD="POST'></FORM>`

The first attribute ACTION points to the program executed when the form is completed and transmitted to the host site. Your program is preceded by `/cgi-win/`. This indicates an executable Windows program. The final attribute METHOD specifies the method used to transfer data to your program.

Q: *The INPUT tag has a parameter called TYPE. Name some of the Input types.*

A: Input Type =`"Text"`   The input field type is text.

Input Type =`"Password"`   The input field type is password.

Input Type =`"Checkbox"`   The input field contains a checkbox to check on or off.

Input Type =`"Radio"`   The input field contains a radio button to toggle on or off.

Input Type =`"Submit"`   The input field will have a submit button; when pressed, it sends data to the URL.

Input Type =`"Image"`   Displays an image; when pressed sends data to target URL. The image can be in GIF or JPEG format.

Input Type =`"Reset"`   Resets all the fields to their default values.

Input HiddenType =`"Hidden"`   Allows you to send a hidden data to the CGI program.

Q: *What CGI tag is used to create a Multi-Line Text area for client comment?*

A: The TEXTAREA tag is used. The following creates a scrollable 3 × 50-byte area.

```
<TEXTAREA NAME="Your Comment" ROW=3 COLS=50></TEXTAREA>
```

Q: *What is an anchor and how is it used?*

A: Anchor has two formats:

HypterText Anchor   `<A HREF="url">anchor-name</A>`

Named Anchor   `<A NAME="anchor-name">Text. . .</A>`

In your document you may want to display something that illustrates a point you want to make. If you want to bring a photo from hyperspace you use the hypertext anchor: HREF. To do this you give the place holder an anchor name and fill in the Uniform Resource Locator with the hyptertext address of the file. For example, if the anchor name is Johnny O'Shay the URL should refer to his photo.

If you have a large document you may want to go from one location to another, skipping paragraphs, pages, or chapters. To navigate from one location to another you need a pair of anchors. To illustrate:

From anchor: `<A HREF="#SierraMadre"> Madre</A>`

To anchor: `<A NAME="SierraMadre">Sierra Madre: History</A>`

Note the # sign when HREF refers to a local anchor.

Q: *What does HTTP stand for?*

A: HyperText Transfer Protocol. HTTP is part of the suite of protocols in the TCP/IP.

Q: *What is the HTML Table?*

A: The HTML Table is part of the latest HTML version 3 incorporated into Mosaic and Netscape. The vertical and horizontal grid lines with borders enhance the appearance of displayed data. It may be used with `<PRE` tag when the data uses monospace fonts like Courier.

Tags used with Table are Caption, TR (table row), TH (table heading), and TD (table data cell), assisted by attributes like Border, Align, Valign (vertical alignment), Rowspan, and Colspan (spanning of rows and columns).

Q: *When Align is used with `<IMG>` tag, what are some of the values?*
A: Top, bottom, and center.

Q: *Why would you use the 'alt' attribute in setting up the `<IMG>` tag?*
A: Some browses display only text, like the Unix-based Lynx. The 'alt' allows insertion of a substitute text in place of the missing graphic.

Q: *How do you draw a line across the page using HTML?*
A: You can use the `<HR>` tag that creates a horizontal line across the page. A multicolored image line using the `<IMG>` tag improves the look of the page.

Q: *Netscape has made extensions to the HTML Standard. Can you name some of these extensions?*
A: Some of the Netscape's extensions are:
- The ability to center text on a page using `<CENTER>` tag
- The `<HR>` width attribute, which enables a thicker line
- Change of font size as a percentage of the basic `<BASEFONT>`
- Allows a choice of bullet symbols
- The `<BLINK>` tag allows text blinking

Q: *If you want to emphasize a text in HTML what tags might you use?*
A: `<EM>`   tag for emphasis
`<BLINK>`   tag if you use Netscape browser
`<B>`   for bold
`<I>`   for italics

Q: *In HTML tags are usually paired (`<` ... `/>`). Cite examples of tags that are not paired.*
A: `<IMG>`   Images
`<HR>`   Horizontal line
`<BR>`   Line break
`<LI>`   List item
`<DT>`   Definition term
`<ISINDEX>`   Indicates the document as a gateway sript allowing searches

Q: *What is MIME?*
A: MIME is short for Multimedia Internet Mail Extensions. Multimedia means different types of files. When Hot Java receives a document, it also gets information on its content-type. This information, called the MIME, is used by the server to interpret the document. MIME content-type has two parts. The first part of the combination is type, such as image, audio, video, text, or application. The second part is the subtype, for example: image/gif or image/jpeg,

text/plain, application/octet-stream. When the server receives the type/ subtype information it calls on a helper application to translate the particular MIME combination. In Java this helper is called the content handler. Hot Java looks initially for the content handler locally but, if it is not found, looks to the host that sent the document and downloads the handler.

Q: *What is the difference between Hot Java and other browsers?*
A: Hot Java does not need to "hard wire" content handlers or protocol handlers on the client system. When MIME is analyzed for content-type, Hot Java initially looks for handlers locally but, if they are missing, looks to the host or other network sources for the handlers and downloads them into the system. This flexibility in calling helpers makes Hot Java dynamic and extensible. The local unit, represented by a PC or handheld device, need not maintain a large inventory of handlers—Internet can become a just-in-time browser. In addition, the Hot Java displays interactive content. A graph on the current stock price movement, for example, may move as the browsing takes place.

Q: *What is meant by inline images?*
A: Inline images are displayed within the client's browser window. Inline images, usually in GIF format, are displayed using `<IMG>` tag. The `<img>` tag has no end tag, and is always followed by the SRC attribute that points to the image file. These GIF files can be located in the local directory or on any server on the Web.

Q: *What are external images?*
A: External images are not displayed as part of the document, but displayed in a separate window on request. A hotspot on the browser may ask if you want to see a picture of the President's dog. When requested, the image is called from a local directory or from a remote site on the Web.

Q: *What is GIF?*
A: GIF (Graphic Interchange Format) is the most widely used Internet graphic format. Icons, logos, and graphic images used on the Web are in GIF format.

Q: *How is a GIF file inserted in HTML text?*
A: In-line GIF images are inserted with one of three alignment values—TOP, BOTTOM, and CENTER:

```
<IMG ALIGN=Alignment_Value SRC="filename.GIF">
```

External GIF image insertion takes this format:

```
<A HREF="file-name.gif">anchor-text</A>
```

Q: *TCP/IP is the generic name for a suite of protocols used on the Internet. Name some of these protocols.*
A: SMTP   (Simple Mail Transfer Protocol)
   TELNET
   FTP   (File Transport Protocol)
   Domain Name Service   (Maps names to addresses)

Q: *In HTML the* <PRE ... /PRE> *tags are used in what situation?*

A: Usually to enclose a preformatted text using monospaced T1 fonts.

Q: *What is Common Gateway Interface?*

A: CGI allows the server to input data from the client. The data received are processed at the server site and, if required, return output or respond to the query. CGI script on the server site is accessed through the browser's URL. The browser also tells the server the type of document sent. This type, called content type, informs the server how to handle the document. In CGI programming activity occurs on the server side. In the Java applet, programming activity is on the client side.

Q: *Name other image (or graphic) files used on the Web.*

A: JPEG   Joint Photographic Experts Group files; Netscape and Hot Java can display JPEG

XBM   X Window System Bitmaps

PICT   Graphic format used in Macintosh

GIF   Can be used both for in-line and external display

Q: *In HTML, WYSIWYG is not always true. Why not?*

A: What you see on the Net depends on the browser used. Browsers use different graphic default functions and tag sets. For example, Netscape has an extended tag set that is different from HTML's version 3. An HTML document with a Java applet tag will not display the applet unless the browser is Java enabled.

Q: *What is image mapping?*

A: You may want to display a weather map of the United States and invite the user to click various locations for weather conditions. You do this by placing "hotspots" at each of these sites, and map the image coordinates. When the hotspot is clicked, the server takes the coordinates and checks to see if a URL can be activated for these values. The URL for the location is returned and displayed.

Q: *FTP is one of the applications on the TCP/IP stacker. What does it do?*

A: FTP (File Transport Protocol) divides information into packets, each with a destination address. FTP sends it to its destination. At the destination server the packets arrive from different routes and are assembled.

Q: *What is contained in a Java tag on the HTML?*

A: The minimal applet tag, called standard attributes, includes the image name, height, and width. The applet tag should also have an alternate content parameter for browsers that are not Java-enabled and therefore cannot display applets. The code attribute in the sample below contains the applet with class suffix. Width and height are in pixel value.

```
<APPLET CODE="MOONDOG.CLASS" WIDTH=200 HEIGHT=50></APPLET>
```

Q: *What does the Codebase attribute do in the applet tag?*

A: The applet format sample in the previous example assumes that you have placed the applet class file (e.g., Moondog.class) in the same directory as the HTML document. If the applet class file is located in a subdirectory of the document file, the applet format has to include a path to this directory. Codebase attribute points to the directory that contains the applet class. In the following example, the applet class (Moondog.class) applet program in bytecode is located in a subdirectory of the document directory Moondog.

```
<APPLET CODEBASE=MOONDOG
CODE="MOONDOG.CLASS"
WIDTH=200 HEIGHT=50></APPLET>
```

Q: *What do Java class files contain?*

A: Java class files contain Java bytecodes for the applet. Java class files are created when source code files (ending in java) are compiled with the javac command.

Q: *What is the function of align, vspace, and hspace attributes?*

A: The align attribute controls the placement of the applet on the page. Alignment can be one of the following: left, right, top, bottom, texttop, middle, absmiddle, absbottom, and baseline. Together with align, vspace and hspace control the vertical and horizontal space around the applet.

Q: *How does Hot Java browser differ from other browsers?*

A: The Hot Java browser, together with the Interpreter, is designed to download, security check, interpret, compile, and display the Java applet. During the life of the applet the browser waits for resource requests from the applet that may call for files from the host server or servers located on the Net. The function of the Java browser is virtually without limit.

Q: *Java is called the "interactive Web language." Why is it interactive?*

A: Java Applet on the Web page can be executed in place by self-execution or activated by the user. Additional resources can be downloaded over the Net using IP packet and activated.

Q: *What is the main difference between a Java application and a Java applet?*

A: Java applications are stand-alone programs that execute all the class objects on their own. Applets, by contrast, require the Hot Java browser for interpretation and execution.

Q: *Can C be linked to the Java application?*

A: Yes. C may be linked to the Java application but not to Java applets. However, the dynamic linking of C modules to Java poses security and portability problems. One of the arguments put forward for linking is the relative slowness of Java compared to C. This problem may be resolved by better Java code generators in the future.

Q: *What is a bytecode?*

A: Bytecode is an intermediary, interpretable code returned as a result of compiling Java source code. This code can be ported across the network and executed as an applet by using a browser designed for a particular platform.

Q: *Is binary bytecode unique to Java?*

A: No. bytecode is also used by TCL. Many of the techniques used in Java exist elsewhere in languages like Smalltalk, Pascal, and Lisp.

Q: *What is JVM?*

A: JVM stands for Java Virtual Machine, a hypothetical computer specification. This machine has a central processing unit with stack frames, registers, instruction set, garbage collection heap, primitive data types, and control pool. Java source code program written to this specification compiles an output, in bytecode, which is portable. An interpreter tailored to the target machine interprets, binds, and executes the Java program.

Q: *What are some of the method modifiers?*

A: Public methods   May be accessed by any method

Private methods   May be accessed by methods in this class only

Protected method   Accessible only by methods is this class and its subclasses

Friendly method   May be accessed by methods that belong to the same package

Other method modifiers are static and final.

Q: *How does Java handle memory management?*

A: In Java memory management, the management of the garbage collection heap is handled by a background process called automatic garbage collection. During periods of low usage, objects not in use are placed on the garbage collection stack and removed using multithreading.

Q: *How does Java handle multiple inheritance?*

A: Multiple class inheritance is not supported in Java. In multiple inheritance an object is derived from two or more separate objects, and contains all the variables and methods of the parent objects.

Q: *What is the highest class in Java?*

A: Object is the highest class. The template for the Java object class is found in the Java Language Package (a.k.a. Java.lang).

Q: *What is the Runnable Interface?*

A: As the name suggests, Runnable Interface implements the run( ) method. Printable Interface implements the print( ) method. Interfaces are abstract classes that declare a set of methods. These interfaces are implemented by other (noninterface) classes using the keyword implements. Java uses Interface to bypass limitations placed on multiple inheritance.

Q: *How is threading used in the Java?*

A: Java handles memory management in the background. It can also be used to run one or more applets.

Q: *Briefly describe the Package concept.*

A: You can think of Package as a toolbox, a convenient way to group classes and interfaces related to each other in some way. Following are some of the Java Packages: Java Language, Java I/O, Java Utility, Java Networking, Abstract Windows Toolkit, Java Browser, and Java Applet.

Q: *What is AWT?*

A: AWT stands for Abstract Windows Toolkit Package. This library provides you with graphical user interface components such as buttons, menus, scrollbars, and so on.

Q: *What does the Layout Manager do?*

A: Unlike other GUI applications such as Visual Basic or Borland Delphi, Java GUI containers do not have the luxury of precise information on the placement of components. The location and size of the various components placed on the container, for example, may differ according to the browser and platform used. Layout Manager carries out this task according to a guideline policy. The user has a choice of layout options: BorderLayout, GridLayout, CardLayout, and so on.

Q: *How does Java's class architecture simplify writing multithread programs?*

A: Java encapsulates multithread in the thread class. By writing applets and applications that extend the thread class, the task is simplified.

Q: *How are pointers used in Java?*

A: Java does not use pointers. A pointer has been defined as a variable that contains the address of a variable.

Q: *What does the javap disassembler command do?*

A: The javap disassembles the bytecode file and returns information about member variables and methods. The use of bytecode architecture simplifies reverse engineering, especially into similar languages like Smalltalk.

Q: *What is casting?*

A: Casting occurs when one data type is changed to another. For example, you convert an integer type into a float type. Java has two integer and character types: primitives and object. Primitives and object types can cast directly among themselves except that boolean cannot convert to integer type. To cast between primitives and object you have to use Wrappers.

Q: *What is the Interpreter?*

A: Interpreter interprets, links, and executes Java's bytecode into the target machine language. The interpreter does not compile. Bytecodes are the machine language equivalent of the Java Virtual Machine. They are intermediary because they are not specific to any machine. This lack of specificity enables Java's portability. When compiled, bytecodes are placed in class files (files with class suffix). In the class file state, references to methods and variables are still made by name and not by physical location. The interpreter resolves the name references into physical addresses for each specific platform using the interpreter.

Q: *Describe the Javac compile options for debugging.*

A: -g

This option turns on the debugger. When this option is on, debugging tables become part of the code generated used in debugging the generated bytecodes.

-ng

This option turns off the inclusion of debugging tables in compilation. Without the requirement to carry debugging information, the bytecode binary's size is reduced.

Q: *HOTJAVA can display URL from the command line. What is the syntax?*

A: `C:\ hotjava URL <ENTER>`

Q: *What is the Java compile command line format?*

A: `C:\> javac options filename.java.`

Q: *Why did Java eliminate the use of pointers?*

A: The architectects of Java considered pointers as one of the primary problem sources in a system that ported bytecode over the network. To provide system stability and portability the pointers were eliminated.

Q: *What is an instance variable?*

A: Data associated with a class are called variables. For example, an instance of a circle class contains data required to draw an actual circle. For the variable to become an instance variable, the class in which it is encapsulated must be instantiated.

Q: *Describe Java's do-while syntax loop.*

A: The do-while loop first executes a statement, and then interrogate the while expression to see if the statement is true. If true, the process continues until false. In do-while loop, a statement executes at least once even if the statement is false.

Q: *Explain the role of handlers in Hot Java.*

A: When the Hot Java browser receives an unknown MIME type (e.g., image/gif, text/plain) it loads protocol or content handler as a helper. Each protocol or content handler is programmed to translate a specific MIME type into a form that can be used by Hot Java.

Q: *Java uses the Unicode format. What is it?*

A: Unicode is a 16-bit character set that allows Java to support more world languages on the Web. Unicode Consortium, which you may join on the Internet, supplies the mapping standard that identifies the code. Other organizations such as Microsoft, Adobe, Bitstream, etc., offer Latin and non-Latin character sets. Windows NT supports a Unicode TrueType font by the name of "Lucida Sans Unicode" for the Latin set.

Q: *Java is said to be similar to C++. What are some differences?*
A: From the developer's standpoint the automatic garbage collection simplifies coding.

The following data types, found in C++, are not supported: struct, union, and pointer.

Java strings are objects that are checked for array logic both at compile and run time.

Q: *How does Hot Java activate the applet?*
A: Hot Java turns the binary applet over to the Java Interpreter. When the Interpreter completes checking the bytecode for security, it is loaded into memory. The program cycle of the applet starts with loading.

1. When loaded, the init() method initializes the applet variables and resizes the component.
2. Hot Java displays the HTML document on the window and calls the start ( ) method. Threads are started if the applets use multithread.
3. Later, when the page changes, Hot Java invokes the stop( ) method to cease the applet threading.
4. Finally the applets call the destroy( ) method to reclaim resource.

Q: *What is the scope of a local variable?*
A: The scope of a variable is from the point it is declared in block of code to the end of the same code block.

Q: *What is the difference between method overriding and overloading?*
A: When a descendant class has a method with the same name and argument as the ancestor (parent) class, the method in the descendant (subclass) will be used. Overriding allows the programmer to introduce variation in the behavior of the public method by inserting new variable or class instances.

In overloading, methods can have the same name as long as at least one of the parameters is different. The methods are considered "overloaded" because they perform different functions using the same name.

Q: *What are hidden variables?*
A: Hidden variables fall within the scoping rules that resolve references to variables declared within a method. You may declare identical names for variables if they are in different coding blocks. However, to prevent reference error, variables in different blocks are hidden from each other.

Q: *How are the try and catch keywords used?*
A: These keywords are typically used to handle Java exceptions. When an error occurs during run time a Java object throws an exception. You can monitor the exceptions by placing the try keyword in front of the block of codes where an error might occur. The generated error can be caught by placing the

catch keyword with its matching exception type name just after the try block of code. In the absence of monitoring exception, run-time system will terminate threading and display an error message.

Q: *How is the throw keyword used to handle exceptions?*
A: Throw can be used when you have an object that requires monitoring. To monitor an object you throw an exception. You do this by creating a new exception handler and placing the throw keyword in front of the new exception handler.

Q: *How would you code: shift right and zero fill?*
A: >>>

Q: *What operator will you use for variable assignment in Java?*
A: =

Q: *In multithreading do the applets run simultaneously?*
A: No. In multithreading each applet receives a share of the single CPU time. The time share allocated may be adjusted by establishing priorities.

Q: *How does Java control priorities and conflicts in multithreading?*
A: Java has a number of methods that assign different priority and time share to the applets. To avoid conflict between threads Java uses the synchronized keyword. Only one of the synchronized threads can be active; others wait until the active thread runs its course.

Q: *Can you assign an integer 1 to a boolean variable?*
A: No. A boolean variable in Java can be only true or false. It cannot have an integer value.

Q: *What is propagated when the right shift (>>) operator is invoked?*
A: The sign is propagated. All Java integers are signed.

Q: *What is the Internet Firewall?*
A: Information travels between Internet client and host in the form of Internet Protocol packets; Firewall, the gatekeeper, checks the content of the packets for unauthorized entry. The effectiveness of the Firewall depends on the policy options you select; the more restrictive options carry fewer risks but also fewer rewards.

   Firewall as applied to Java applets supports several options. The most restrictive option prohibits the applet from accessing Internet resources including its own host. In the other extreme, access is unrestricted and an applet may connect to any host on the net. Finally, the default option allows the applet to access data only from its host.

Q: *Is Java fast?*
A: No. Currently Java is about twenty times slower than C, which is again slower than machine language. Plans are under way to bring the speed up to the level of the C language.

Q: *What is Java Appletviewer. What does it do?*

A: Appletviewer, found in the Java Development Kit, allows you to view applets without the HotJava browser. It is a useful tool for testing.

Q: *How do you declare a Package?*

A: `package package_name;`

Q: *Name the priorities used by the Thread class for multithreading.*

A: ■ Max_Priority

  ■ Min_Priority

  ■ Norm_Priority

Q: *How is the new operator used?*

A: You use the new operator to create an instance of a Class. "New" allocates resource to the created class.

Q: *How is the extend keyword used?*

A: The extend keyword is used to inherit from an existing class.

Q: *What is a disassembler?*

A: Java can disassemble Java bytecode files using the Javap command. Javap command prints out all the encapsulated variables and methods.

Q: *Which command would you use to run the Java application's class file?*

A: You use the Java command to run the class file. The class file contains byte-codes. The java command interprets the class file.

Q: *Would one use a different command to compile a java application and applet?*

A: No. You use the same command—javac.

Michael Rothstein, the author/coauthor of four books on various aspects of systems analysis, programming, and information technology, has more than thirty years of data processing experience. He began his career working for Univac Corp. Mr. Rothstein has also worked for IBM Corp., as a Systems Engineer and Industry Specialist, for Motorola Corp., and for Bankers Trust Co. Mr. Rothstein is currently an independent consultant. Some of his clients have been: Metropolitan Life Ins. Co., Paine Webber, Teachers Ins. Co., Citibank, Blue Cross/Blue Shield, and the N.Y.C. Housing Authority.

Mr. Rothstein received his B.A. from Queens College and his M.B.A. from City University. He has taught at UCLA (summer short courses), at New York University's Management Institute, and at the Productivity Institute of the State of Israel.